SKIING SUN VALLEY

Skiing Sun Valley

A HISTORY FROM UNION PACIFIC TO THE HOLDINGS

JOHN W. LUNDIN

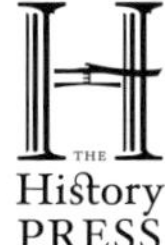

Published by The History Press
Charleston, SC
www.historypress.com

First published 2020

Manufactured in the United States

ISBN 9781467143936

Library of Congress Control Number: 2020941946

This book is dedicated to filmmaker and philosopher Warren Miller (1924–2018). Warren will always be associated with Sun Valley through his ski movies and his early days living in a freezing cold trailer in a parking lot at the resort with the approval of Sun Valley's manager Pat Rogers, who felt Warren offered "local color." He inspired my generation to seek freedom through skiing. When I was growing up, the ski season in Seattle did not start until Warren showed his new movie. He asked people to ski their favorite run when they heard of his death. His was Christmas Ridge at Sun Valley. Thanks for the memories.

CONTENTS

PART THREE. SUN VALLEY OPENS DECEMBER 1936, CHANGING SKIING IN THIS COUNTRY

PART FOUR. BALD MOUNTAIN OPENS FOR SKIING AS WORLD WAR II LOOMS ON THE HORIZON

PART FIVE. SUN VALLEY DURING WORLD WAR II

Part Six. Sun Valley after World War II

Part Seven. Sun Valley after Union Pacific

ACKNOWLEDGEMENTS

This book was written in conjunction with the Center for Regional History of the Community Library in Ketchum, Idaho. The center obtained a number of Union Pacific's Sun Valley materials after the resort was sold in 1964, including internal company documents (cited as "Snoddy papers from U.P. Museum, MS 0694") and 4,000 historic photographs. The center also has the collection of Dorice Taylor, Sun Valley's long-time publicist; photographs taken by Lloyd Arnold, Sun Valley's long-time photographer; over 500 oral histories, including a number from people involved at the resort from its beginning that provide unique personal insights into its history (cited as "OH"); and other valuable resources.

Special thanks go to railroad historian Maury Klein, professor emeritus of history at the University of Rhode Island, who gave the author access to Union Pacific's Sun Valley documents he collected for his multi-volume history of the Union Pacific Railroad, which are stored at the John W. Barriger III National Railroad Library at the University of Missouri–St. Lewis. They are cited as "Klein Collection."

Thanks also go to a number of people for their help with the book, including Jenny Emery Davidson, The Community Library's executive director; Mary Tyson, director of the Center for Regional History; and Ryan Gelskey for preparing the photographs for this book. Others who provided materials include Peggy Proctor Dean, Charles Proctor's daughter (cited as Proctor Family Collection); Tim Silva, president and general manager of the Sun Valley Resort; Karen Bossick of *Eye on Sun Valley*; the family of Mary Jane Griffith Conger; the Union Pacific Museum; Alan Engen and the J. Willard Marriott Library Special Collections Division of the University of Utah; the family of Matt J. Broze; and the Idaho Department of Parks and Recreation. Thanks to my wife, Jane, who contributed editorial advice and proofreading. Artie Crisp, my editor at The History Press, provided valuable guidance and help throughout the publication process.

Most of the pictures in this book are from the Community Library and are not further identified. Where pictures come from other sources, the sources are identified. The spelling of various terms has changed over the years, but I used the spelling found in the original sources: Elk Horn–Elkhorn, Steilhang–steilhang, Riverside Run–River Run, Baker's Creek–Baker Creek, Saw Tooth Mountains–Sawtooth Mountains, and others.

INTRODUCTION

This book explores the early days of Sun Valley under Union Pacific Railroad (U.P.) ownership, primarily the period from 1936 to 1964, when the resort was sold to the Janss Company, although it traces major developments up to the present. Sun Valley was the concept and pet project of board chairman Averell Harriman, who created the resort as a central part of a plan to increase passenger traffic during the Great Depression of the 1930s. It cost $1.5 million to build in the Wood River Valley in Idaho in 1936 (about $27 million in today's dollars). Sun Valley brought modern skiing to this country, and for several decades, it occupied a unique place as America's first and only high-end destination ski resort designed to replicate the romance of European ski areas.

Issues that are not central parts of existing books about Sun Valley are examined here. First, there is a primary focus on Sun Valley's relationship with Union Pacific, and discussion of how railroad economics determined the resort's role and future. Second is an examination of how Harriman used ski racing as an important part of his plan to make Sun Valley an international ski destination and the country's center of skiing. The locations of Sun Valley's races, the main participants, the winners, and the excitement they generated are described. Sun Valley subsidized and trained the country's best ski racers and was the major force in the U.S. Olympic ski teams through 1952. The book traces the development of Sun Valley's ski lifts, lodges, and new ski runs. It explores how important what we now call backcountry skiing was in the resort's early days and describes the numerous areas around Sun Valley where it took place. Much of the information comes from Union Pacific documents and oral histories of people who were involved with the resort from its beginning.

The Union Pacific Railroad has been a critical part of the Wood River Valley's economy from the time a branch line was built to Hailey in 1883, linking its silver mines to outside markets, attracting outside capital and causing an economic boom. When the international silver depression of the 1890s caused the Valley's mines to close, the railroad was key to the next economic era, sheep grazing and agricultural development. Sun Valley was built in the Wood River Valley because Harriman wanted a remote site served by Union Pacific.

Sun Valley Was Averell Harriman's Daring Creation

Sun Valley was the vision and creation of one man: Averell Harriman, son of wealthy railroad tycoon E.H. Harriman, who restored the Union Pacific Railroad after a group he led brought it out of bankruptcy in 1897. Averell became chairman of the board of the Union Pacific in 1932 and had to face challenges caused by the Great Depression, which decimated railroad passenger travel. According to his biographer, Rudy Abramson,

> *Union Pacific . . . was a billion-dollar corporation facing the hardest times it had seen since his father salvaged it from bankruptcy. It was sapped by the Depression and challenged by trucks, buses, automobiles, and airplanes. Its chief consolation was that the condition of just about every other railroad in the land was worse.*

Harriman faced the challenges head on and convinced a dubious board to modernize its rolling stock by investing in a new fleet of diesel-powered streamliner trains and building a ski resort to create a new destination for passengers.

Sun Valley was never intended to make a profit. It was part of Union Pacific's long-term plan to recapture passenger traffic and a source of publicity designed to add luster to railroad travel in the winter. Harriman said Sun Valley operated with a deficit but "we didn't run it to make money; we ran it to be a perfect place . . . and the publicity

I thought was worth very much more than the deficit." Harriman's gamble worked. U.P.'s streamliners soon were filled to capacity, operating throughout the country, and by 1939, Sun Valley increased the railroad's passenger traffic by 250,000 people, resulting in $250,000 a year in additional revenue.[1]

SKIING WAS A FLEDGLING SPORT IN 1936

In the late 1920s and early 1930s, alpine skiing began to appear in several areas of the country, particularly the Northeast and Northwest. There were no lifts, so skiers had to be fit enough to hike, herringbone, or use skins to climb up hills before skiing down. Equipment was rudimentary, there were few formal lessons available, and the sport involved more backcountry mountaineering than downhill skiing, limiting its appeal. A number of small ski areas opened. Peckett's–on–Sugar Hill near Franconia, New Hampshire, opened the country's first ski school in 1929 using Austrian ski instructors. This is where Averell Harriman, Nelson Rockefeller, Lowell Thomas, and others learned to ski.

Ski technology advanced in the 1930s. In 1932, North America's first rope tow was installed at Shawbridge, Quebec. In 1933, patents were obtained for a laminated ski by Anderson & Thompson in Seattle and Splitkein in Norway. In 1934, the first rope tow in the United States began operating at Woodstock, Vermont. In 1935, the Kandahar cable binding was introduced, which held a skier's heel to the ski, and the first overhead cable lift in the United States (a J-bar) was installed in Hanover, New Hampshire, by the Dartmouth Outing Club. However, most ski areas operated without lifts through the 1930s; where lifts were installed, they were typically rope tows.

Franklin Delano Roosevelt's New Deal contributed to the growth of the ski industry in the 1930s by building roads and shelters and clearing hills and trails for skiing. Roosevelt was a booster of winter recreation. The Civilian Conservation Corps (CCC), Works Progress Administration (WPA), and U.S. Forest Service carried on a multitude of tasks. Among the most notable were projects associated with the new ski industry, according to Douglas Brinkley in *Rightful Heritage, Franklin D. Roosevelt and the Land of America*.

Interest in skiing was stimulated by the 1932 Olympics in Lake Placid, New York, which offered nordic ski events (jumping and cross-country). Alpine skiing's popularity grew after the National Downhill and Slalom Championships were held on Mount Rainier, Washington, in 1935, which were the tryouts for the 1936 Olympics in Garmisch-Partenkirchen, Germany. The 1936 Olympics were the first to offer alpine skiing, and a tram was constructed for the competitors.

Skiing grew in popularity in the 1930s in spite of the Great Depression. In 1933, there were from 2,000 to 4,000 Seattle-area skiers, and a Seattle store sold 2,000 pairs of skis in one month. By 1934, there was a growing interest in winter sports around Seattle, as 2,500 skiers were in local ski clubs, 3,000 to 5,000 spectators attended ski jumping events, and 10,000 persons participated in winter sports every weekend. In 1936, the federal government reported there were 100,000 skiers in the country, including 25,000 to 30,000 in the Pacific Northwest. A report prepared for Averell Harriman in April 1936 noted "the rapid growth of skiing and winter sports in the country," saying the ski industry was booming in Seattle, where there were around 20 ski clubs. By 1938, there were 65,000 skiers in Washington, the manufacture and sale of ski equipment was a $3 million industry, and every weekend, 20,000 people went to local ski areas.

Sun Valley opened in December 1936, offering a modern, high-class resort experience in the remote mountains of Idaho. It was the country's first destination ski resort that attracted "the carriage trade," Wall Street barons, the Chicago social set, Hollywood stars and producers, and serious skiers from all over the world. The new resort, accessible primarily by train, offered a lavish lifestyle, a luxurious lodge with high-end shops, and a ski school with Austrian instructors who made skiing sexy.

Chairlifts were invented by Union Pacific engineers for Sun Valley based on a system used to load bananas onto ships, so skiers could ride up mountains quickly and in comfort. They were installed on Proctor and Dollar Mountains but not on Bald Mountain until the 1940 season because Baldy was too challenging for most skiers at the time. The *Seattle Times* of June 6, 1937, said, "Skiers are not made by climbing hills. Skiers develop proficiency by coming downhill. Skiers at Mount Rainier can get in around 4,000 feet of skiing a day. At Sun Valley, with its chairlifts, a skier can get in 37,000 feet a day." Filmmaker Warren Miller said, "Now you could finally ski downhill all day long and never have to climb back up. Just sit down in a moving chair and be hauled back up for as many rides as your strength, skill, and money allowed. All . . . for only a couple of dollars a day."

Sun Valley was called the "St. Moritz of America." Harriman's biographer said, "Sun Valley became the San Simeon of the affluent sportsman; the harassed city dweller's outer suburbia . . . the most 'in' place to get a suntan this side of Waikiki, and stars came to ski." Dartmouth College's famous ski racer Dick Durrance said Sun Valley was "the most important influence in the development of American skiing. . . . Its concentrated and highly successful glamorization of the sport got people to want to ski in the first place." The resort had a monopoly on skiing grandeur for several decades, and it influenced areas that developed later.

Steve Hannagan, Sun Valley's brilliant publicist, believed the key to establishing a "chic" image was to use celebrities, attractive women, Olympic stars, and monied families. "It is my opinion . . . Sun Valley can be made into an exclusive winter sports resort which will capture the interest of all America, and become the trademark of everything that is winter sports just as Florida has become synonymous with a summer vacation in winter." Hannagan convinced *Life* magazine to publish an eight-page spread on Sun Valley in March 1937, giving the resort millions of dollars of free publicity. Articles about the resort appeared throughout the country in many different magazines and newspapers.

Harriman used ski racing to make his new resort an international destination and the country's center of skiing. He paid the expenses for some of the best skiers to come to Sun Valley, making its tournaments first-class international competitions. From the late 1930s until the 1950s, Sun Valley played a major role in supporting American ski racing by offering young, talented skiers room and board, jobs, and coaching, allowing them to see a life they never experienced before.

The Sun Valley Ski Club formed in fall 1936 to sponsor sanctioned ski races. Beginning in 1937, Sun Valley hosted major ski tournaments every year. Some of Europe's best skiers worked for the Sun Valley Ski School. Ski instructors were considered superior to the average American amateur and were not permitted to race against true amateurs, so Harriman held "open" tournaments where instructors could compete. The resort's annual races included intercollegiate races over the Christmas holidays, interstate races at the end of January (the Western States Team Championships), the Ski Club's own annual tournaments, and Harriman Cup/Sun Valley Open races.

Harriman Cup tournaments were the country's most prestigious and competitive events, attracting the best skiers in the world. The *American Ski Annual 1943* said, "Just as it is the dream of every tennis player to compete once at Wimbledon, it is every skier's hope to participate in the famous Harriman Cup Races at Sun Valley." The *Sun Valley Ski Club 1956 Annual Report* agreed.

> *Every American sport has its moment of supreme glory: that particular event in which the entire panorama seems to be compressed into one sharply defined focal point. Baseball has its World Series, golf its National Open, and horse racing its Kentucky Derby. For skiing, it is the Harriman Cup.*

Sun Valley hosted a number of the country's most important tournaments in the early years: 1937, the Sun Valley International Open Downhill and Slalom Championships, the country's first truly international ski tournament; 1938, the National Downhill and Slalom Championships; 1939, the National Four-Way Championships; 1940, the National Downhill Championships; 1941, the third annual National Four-Way Championships; and 1942, the sixth annual Harriman Cup Races and Official International Downhill and Slalom Tournament. Sun Valley also played a crucial role with the U.S. Olympic ski teams. Skiers intending to try out for the 1940 and 1948 teams trained at Sun Valley under the resort's ski instructors. Sun Valley hosted tryouts for the U.S. alpine teams for the 1948 Olympics at St. Moritz, Switzerland, and the1952 Games at Oslo, Norway. These teams trained at Sun Valley after they were selected. Sun Valley's Gretchen Fraser won gold and silver medals in the 1948 Olympics, becoming the first American to win an Olympic medal in skiing. She became a spokesperson for Sun Valley afterwards. In 1952, Fraser and Cortlandt Hill, members of the Sun Valley Ski Club board of governors, were managers of the U.S. Olympic ski teams.

Locations for Harriman Cup races reflect Sun Valley's development. When the resort opened, neither Proctor nor Dollar Mountain had enough vertical for a downhill race. In 1937 and 1938, the downhill was held on a mountain north of Sun Valley near where the Sawtooth National Recreation Area headquarters is now. Harriman named it for Dick Durrance, who won the first race there. It took racers three hours to hike up the mountain to the start of the three-and-a-half mile course, which they finished in five minutes. In 1939 and 1940, downhill races were held on the Warm Springs side of Mount Baldy on a narrow course through the trees designed by Durrance. Racers had to hike to the top of Baldy to reach the start until chairlifts were installed for winter 1940. In 1941, the downhill was changed to the River Run side of Baldy.

Because Harriman wanted an improved area for slalom racing and a ski jump so Sun Valley could host four-way tournaments, Ruud Mountain was developed in summer 1937 with a 40-meter ski jump and a chairlift, giving competitors the rare luxury of riding to the top of the course. It was named after Sigmund Ruud, a famous Norwegian jumper who, along with Alf Engen, designed the hill and jump. The Ruud lift is still there, the only remaining example of the original single chairlifts at Sun Valley, and is listed in the National Register of Historic Places.[2]

RAILROAD ECONOMICS DETERMINED SUN VALLEY'S FUTURE

Averell Harriman became involved in the war effort in 1941, spending the war years in England and Russia. In 1947, Harriman became President Harry Truman's secretary of commerce and was forced to sever ties with Union Pacific. Harriman said "that broke my relationship with the management of Sun Valley,"and he never again had a major role in the resort. With Harriman gone, Sun Valley's relationship with Union Pacific changed.

During World War II, demand for rail traffic overwhelmed railroads, wearing out rolling stock and physical plants. In 1946, Union Pacific was in worse shape than when E.H. Harriman overhauled it in the early 1900s, according to railroad historian Maury Klein. New management took over Union Pacific, and passenger traffic became less important than freight because of competition from airlines, bus service, and automobiles. Since Sun Valley was built to promote passenger service, its postwar role diminished and the subsidy necessary to keep the resort running became harder to justify.

Union Pacific had to decide whether to reopen Sun Valley after World War II, as it needed substantial work after it was used as a Navy rehabilitation center. Publicist Steve Hannagan said the cost of operating the resort was the price for bringing "attention to the Union Pacific at a cost cheaper than any other known means." If seen as a money-making project, he said, "it would fail miserably." Unless Union Pacific was willing to subsidize the resort "as an advertising, good will and business projecting endeavor, to the extent of $350,000 to $500,000 annually," it should be abandoned.

Sun Valley reopened in December 1947, but conditions were different. Union Pacific management changed, adding more uncertainty. In February 1946, George

Ashby replaced William Jeffers as president. Arthur Stoddard replaced Ashby in 1949. Harriman said Stoddard "was never very keen on Sun Valley. He didn't understand this, your basically goodwill value throughout the West, particularly Idaho."

The year 1952 is often seen as the end to Sun Valley's glory years. Pat Rogers, Sun Valley's long-time manager responsible for much of its ambiance, left because of Stoddard's austerity program designed to cut its $500,000 yearly loss. "Elegance began to go," according to Dorice Taylor, the resort's publicity director. Sun Valley was still a major destination resort, but Union Pacific did not invest the money necessary to keep it at the same level that made it famous before the war. Its facilities declined, it lost much of the atmosphere for which it was known, and its place in the ski world changed as other resorts grew and competed for the ski market.

In 1964, a report prepared for Union Pacific by the Janss Company, a real estate development firm from Los Angeles, said it would take $5 million to bring the resort back to a competitive condition. Unwilling to make that investment, Union Pacific sold Sun Valley to the Janss Company in 1964. Stoddard said, "The operation of Sun Valley has been rather remote from our business of running a railroad. I am glad that it can now pass into hands which will continue to provide the development it deserves." Taylor's chapter on the sale is called "We Are Dumped." Harriman disagreed with the decision.

> *I never would have approved that sale if I had stayed on the Board. . . . From the standpoint of the railroad financially, it might have been wise. But I thought it was very important for the goodwill of Union Pacific to keep Sun Valley, that it would always stay there.*

Sun Valley has had three owners since it opened in December 1936. Union Pacific spared no expense to make the resort one of the best in the world but let it decline after World War II. The Janss Company purchased the resort in 1964, and Bill Janss took it over from his family's company in 1968. Janss brought the resort back but lacked the money to take it to the next level. In 1977, Janss sold Sun Valley to the Holding family, owners of Sinclair Oil Company, who made Sun Valley one of the premier year-round resorts in the country and restored its international status. However, unlike the 1930s and 1940s, when Sun Valley was the only high-end ski destination resort, it now shares its position in a highly competitive business with other resorts started after World War II.[3]

Resources Used for the Book

Sun Valley's story has been told in several books: *Sun Valley, A Biography*, by Doug Oppenheimer and Jim Poore, local journalists, 1976; *Sun Valley*, by Dorice Taylor, Sun Valley's long-time publicist, 1980; *Sun Valley, An Extraordinary History*, local historian Wendolyn Spence Holland's seminal book, 1998; and *The Sun Valley Story*, by Van Gordon Sauter, 2011.

More information about the resort can be found in *Dick Durrance, the Man on the Medal*, by Dick Durrance; *Nice Goin': My Life on Skis*, by Friedl Pfeifer; *A Bird of Passage, The Story of My Life*, by Otto Lang; *Gretchen's Gold, The Story of Gretchen Fraser, America's First Gold Medalist in Olympic Skiing*, by Luanne Pfeifer; *Sun Valley Guide*, by Andy Hennig; and a Union Pacific manuscript, "History of Sun Valley," by Ken Longe. Railroad history can be found in Maury Klein's splendid multi-volume series *Union Pacific*; two biographies about E.H. Harriman, *The Life and Legend of E.H. Harriman* by Maury Klein and *Railroad Tycoon* by George Kennan; and Averell Harriman's biography, *Spanning the Century*, by Rudy Abramson. Other key resources include Sun Valley Ski Club annual reports, which provide detailed coverage of the resort's ski races and other major events; *The Valley Sun*, Sun Valley's newspaper; archives of the *Hailey Times*, *New York Times*, and the *Seattle Times*; and the *American Ski Annual*, the official yearbook of the National Ski Association, begun in 1934.

Union Pacific presidents include Carl R. Gray (1920–October 1937); William W. Jeffers (October 1937–February 1946); George Ashby (February 1946–March 1949); and Arthur Stoddard (March 1949–January 1965). Sun Valley managers include Ray Stevens (1936–1937); Ken Singer (1938); Pat Rogers (July 1938–1952); and Winston McCrea (1952–1965).

Howard C. (Alan) Mann, chief engineer, was Union Pacific's vice president in charge of operations. G.T. (Glen) Trout was chief bridge engineer and chief engineer for the local line. B.H. Prater was general supervisor for engineering for the Challenger Inn & Village. Lloyd Castagneto, bridge and building supervisor, directed the construction of the chairlifts, Challenger Inn and Sun Valley Village. Ed Seagle was project engineer and liaison between Union Pacific and the Sun Valley Lodge contractor, and chief engineer of Sun Valley operations after it opened, staying until 1965, observing the full span of Union Pacific's ownership. W.T. Wellman was the Union Pacific architect who worked on the plans for the lodge and Inn. James Curran was the Union Pacific bridge engineer who designed the chairlifts that became used all over the world.

A number of people played critical roles in Sun Valley's development. Steve Hannagan was its brilliant publicist. Charles Proctor and John E.P. Morgan assisted in the design and layout of the ski hills and lifts. Los Angeles architect Gilbert Stanley Underwood designed the Sun Valley Lodge and Challenger Inn. J.V. McNeil Co. of Los Angeles was the general contractor for the lodge, Village, and Inn. Sun Valley's chairlifts were invented and designed by two Union Pacific engineers, James M. Curran and Glen H. Trout, along with Gordon Bannerman of American Steel and Wire Company of Worcester, Mass. American Steel and Wire Company manufactured the system's components, and Union Pacific employees installed the chairlifts at the resort.

Part One

UNION PACIFIC AND AVERELL HARRIMAN STRUGGLE WITH THE GREAT DEPRESSION

1

HARRIMAN FORTUNE WAS BASED ON THE UNION PACIFIC RAILROAD

W. Averell Harriman was born in 1891, the son of Edward H. Harriman, who became one of the country's wealthiest men from his control of the Union Pacific Railroad. E.H. Harriman may be best known for hiring Pinkerton detectives to capture Butch Cassidy and the Sundance Kid, which resulted in their flight to Bolivia. Harriman's idea of using mobile posses on trains to pursue criminal gangs worked so well that "train robberies ceased on the Union Pacific, even though they continued to plague other western roads," according to railroad historian Maury Klein.

E.H. Harriman was one of the most important empire builders of the early 20th century, a "cold-blooded businessman imposing his own brand of order on an industry desperately in need of fresh thinking," in Klein's words. His name was as familiar at the time as other titans associated with the industries they controlled: J.P. Morgan, banking; John D. Rockefeller, oil; and Andrew Carnegie, iron and steel. According to Klein, "Harriman burst onto the railroad scene like a comet at the age of fifty and worked his magic on the industry in a single decade," transforming railroads into "well-built, efficient operations. He modernized and reorganized the old systems into new, often larger, and always more profitable ones . . . that ensured the survival of railroads in an era that would produce new forms of competition in transportation."

In the 1890s, Union Pacific, and virtually all of the country's railroads except the Great Northern, went into bankruptcy because of the international silver depression

(1888–1898), which was ended by the Klondike gold rush of 1898. Silver prices dropped in 1888, followed in 1892 by a crash. Weakness in the economy and the failure of railroads and manufacturing companies touched off a national depression. In 1893, a Wall Street panic, "Industrial Black Friday," sent over 15,000 commercial houses, 600 banks and other fiscal institutions, and over 190 of the nation's railroads into bankruptcy including Union Pacific and its subsidiary the Oregon Short Line. Twenty percent of American workers (between two and three million) were unemployed.

In 1897, E.H. Harriman was a 50-year-old Wall Street banker who had been president of the Illinois Central Railroad since 1889. The Illinois Central was a well-run organization that, unlike most railroads, ran north–south (generally from Chicago to New Orleans), not east–west. Harriman toured the West in 1896, becoming convinced the region had the potential for enormous growth.

Harriman was part of a group of investors who bought Union Pacific out of bankruptcy in 1897 for $81.5 million, which was "a financial gamble as daring as the one embarked on by the original promoters of 1862," Klein wrote. This was nearly double the cost to replace the system, but it got the federal government out of Union Pacific affairs and they obtained the railroad's facilities and adjacent lands from its original 1862 Congressional charter. Harriman believed the West was "the sleeping giant of this country with its natural resources and rapidly increasing population . . . and the Union Pacific ran a long, straight route through its prosperous underbelly," according to Klein.

Harriman became chairman of Union Pacific's executive committee, giving him effective control of the railroad. Shortly thereafter, he inspected the entire Union Pacific system, concluding that "traffic was there in huge quantities and could be handled only by transforming a tolerable nineteenth-century road into an efficient twentieth-century one." In late 1898, the post of chairman of U.P.'s board was abolished, leaving Harriman in complete control.

Over the next two years, Harriman's group regained control of Union Pacific's branch lines that were separated in bankruptcy, including the Oregon Short Line (going through Idaho to Oregon with a branch into the Wood River Valley) and the Oregon Railway and Navigation Company (from Huntington, Oregon, to Portland). By 1900, his group controlled the entire Union Pacific system, a total of 2,855 miles, and he turned the railroad around in five years. Over the next decade, according to Klein, Harriman spent $160 million bringing Union Pacific into a condition to compete in the new economy, "replacing not only old equipment but old ways of doing business." Harriman understood that to make money, a railroad had to "haul greater loads at lower rates as cheaply as possible." He introduced "new styles of management, organization, physical operation, financial structure, labor relations, and safety programs," transforming Union Pacific from "a faded, mediocre carrier to the most efficient railroad west of the Mississippi River."

E.H. Harriman was involved in the reorganization of three other railroads: the Baltimore & Ohio, the Kansas City, Pittsburgh & Gulf, and the Chicago & Alton, modernizing them using the formula he used for Union Pacific. He prospered greatly as the American West recovered from the depression of the 1890s and its economy grew during the first two decades of the 20th century, stimulated by federal investments in agricultural infrastructure under the Reclamation Act of 1902. According to Klein, banker Henry Morgenthau said

> *the decade from 1896 to 1906 . . . was the period of the most gigantic expansion of business in all American history. In that decade the slowly fertilized economic resources of the United States suddenly yielded a bewildering crop of industries. . . . The cry everywhere was for money—more money—and yet more money.*

Harriman was at the forefront of this movement, acquiring control over railroads and related transportation companies, dominating much of the rail transportation in the West. Key to his success was the purchase of the Southern Pacific Railroad in 1900 for $40 million. Southern Pacific was the largest transportation system in the world, with 9,441 miles of rail from New York to New Orleans and San Francisco and 16,186 miles of shipping lines from San Francisco to the Far East. Harriman said, "We have bought not only a railroad, but an empire," according to Klein.

The Southern Pacific owned the Central Pacific, the Sunset route to New Orleans, the Morgan line of steamers operating from New Orleans to New York, a road into Mexico, another one from San Francisco to Portland, and a steamship company working in the Pacific trade. This transportation network gave the Southern Pacific a stranglehold on California business and transcontinental traffic.

To understand Harriman's success, one must understand the role railroads played in the country's economy at the time, as described by railroad historian Larry Haeg:

> *Railroads didn't "own" America in 1901, but over the previous half century they had revolutionized its commerce and culture. . . . At the time . . . railroads were America's manifest destiny, prime agent of the Industrial Revolution, first modern business enterprise, first big business, greatest centralizing technology in history, mobilizers of the "greatest era of civilized progress the world had ever known," primary tool for settling the unpopulated West, and the creator of global markets for isolated towns. . . .*
>
> *Railroads represented the largest investment of capital in any enterprise in human history, equaling about one-eighth of the total wealth of the United States. Their annual revenue was about three times that of the federal government. Deemed to be "public functions" . . . they were the largest private landholders in America. They comprised two-thirds of the listings on the New York Stock Exchange. . . . They employed more people than any other American enterprise. About one of every ten Americans depended on railroads for a living.*

According to Klein in his Harriman biography, "Harriman sat atop the largest transportation network empire in the world and presided over so many systems and companies that his associates had trouble remembering which one he served on at any given time." He was one of a small number of industrialists in the early 1900s who controlled commerce through a system of interlocking directorates. Fifty-seven men held 1,460 seats on the boards of major corporations. Harriman sat on the boards of 59 companies, including 30 railroads, five traction companies, half a dozen steamship lines, some banks, trust companies, insurance, and telegraph companies. By 1906, Harriman controlled 23,000 miles of railroads with a capitalization of $1.5 billion and net earnings of nearly $70 million, with income from other sources of $18.5 million, for total receipts of more than $88 million. Union Pacific had a surplus of $100 million, providing Harriman with financing for any enterprise he wished to undertake, according to biographer George Kennan.

In the early 1900s, Harriman and his rival James J. Hill, who built the Great Northern Railroad and controlled the Northern Pacific, entered into an agreement to form a holding company, the Northern Securities Company, , organized by financier J. Pierpont Morgan. Their plan was to establish uniform methods of management and accounting for the three rail giants, plus the Southern Pacific and Burlington Railroads, "to impose order on the chaotic rail industry." In 1904, the U.S. Supreme Court ordered the dissolution of Northern Securities because it violated the Sherman Antitrust Law. The agreement between the rail giants caused a public backlash; Harriman became regarded as a proponent of combination and consolidation and was vilified as a classic robber baron, known as "the Octopus." But even in this losing fight, Harriman made money. Union Pacific invested $89.4 million in Northern Securities and received back $144.4 million, a profit of $55 million, or a 62 percent return. Harriman and Union Pacific spent the next decade battling the Hill railroads in Washington and Oregon, fighting to maintain their rail system's dominance of the West.

When E.H. Harriman died in 1909, he controlled the Union Pacific, Southern Pacific, St. Joseph and Grand Island, Illinois Central, Central of Georgia, Pacific Mail Steamship Co., and Wells Fargo Co. He extended the railroad map and joined two giant companies, Union Pacific and Southern Pacific, which remains one of the largest and strongest systems in a country where railroads went out of fashion a half century ago. Kennan said he made "a great fortune by serving both railway shareholders and the public better than they had ever been served before. . . . Harriman did more than create the new Union Pacific Railroad after 1898. He also gave it the leadership and principles to ensure continuity through rapidly changing times." Klein said, "By sheer force of example, Harriman dragged the railroad industry into the new era of high-volume traffic carried at low rates," calling him "the man who saved railroads."

RAILROAD RANCH: HARRIMAN FAMILY'S FIRST CONNECTION TO IDAHO

Klein said E.H. Harriman was "determined to imprint [his children] with a sense of values and responsibility." He was a domineering father, and his attitudes placed a heavy burden on his children to measure up to the high standards expected of them. Harriman prodded the children into reaching beyond what they thought themselves capable of doing. He expected of them the same perfectionist standards he demanded of himself and would not tolerate lack of effort or dishonesty.

The Harriman family's connections to Idaho began in 1908, when E.H. bought a share of Railroad Ranch on the Snake River, 37 miles from West Yellowstone, sight unseen, on the recommendation of former U.P. executive Silas Eccles, who owned another share. E.H. died in 1909 before visiting the ranch. It began in the late 1890s, when several U.P. executives bought land and formed the Island Park Land and Cattle

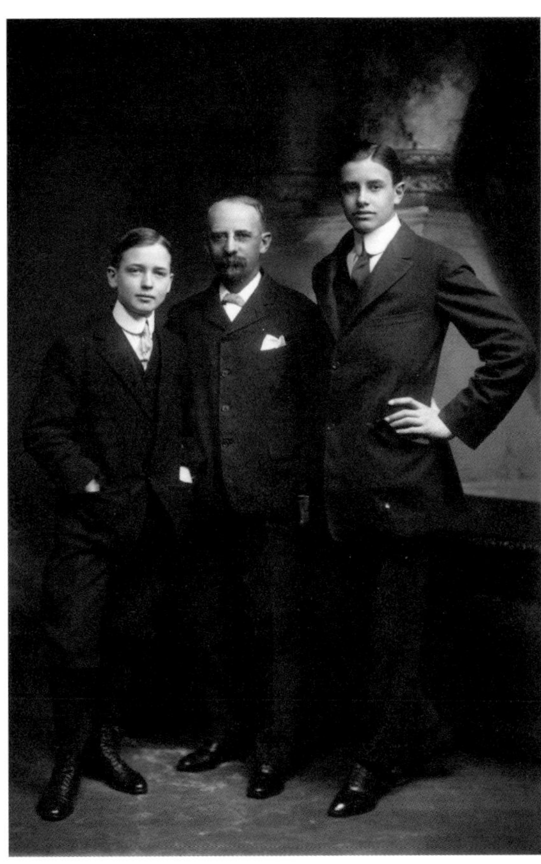

Roland, E.H. and Averell Harriman. *Courtesy of Idaho Parks and Recreation Department.*

Company, becoming known as Railroad Ranch. Eccles went to work for the Guggenheims, who controlled American Smelting and Refining Company, and in 1906, three Guggenheim brothers bought into the ranch. Members of the Jones family, who controlled Atlantic Richfield Company, bought into the ranch in 1949.

Averell Harriman first visited Railroad Ranch in 1909 while working on a Union Pacific survey crew near Idaho's Teton Mountains. His mother, Mary, brought the family there in 1910, and they fell in love with the ranch. Railroad Ranch was expanded by purchasing nearby property, and it became the owners' private retreat and hunting and fishing preserve, surrounded by a working ranch. Each family had a private house built in hunting lodge style. Averell and Roland were frequent visitors through the 1930s. The concept of wealthy families sharing a private recreation facility was Averell's original idea for Sun Valley.

In 1977, Averell and Roland gave the ranch to Idaho for a state park and wildlife refuge, becoming Harriman State Park, containing eight miles of Henry's Fork of the Snake River. The ranch has an active cattle operation and is a prime destination for hunting and fishing. It is part of a 16,000-acre wildlife refuge in the greater Yellowstone ecosystem, home to moose, elk, the largest flock of trumpeter swans in the world, sandhill cranes, and other animals. The April 1999 issue of *Sports Afield* rated Henry's Fork as one of the top ten fishing rivers in the country, and in 2012, readers of *Trout* picked Idaho's Henry's Fork as the best trout stream in America.[4]

2

1932

Averell Harriman Becomes Union Pacific's Board Chair, Looks for Ways to Increase Passenger Revenue

E.H. Harriman died in 1909 when Averell was 18 years old and entering Yale. E.H.'s wife, Mary, was the sole beneficiary and executor of his estate, valued at nearly $70 million, according to biographer Abramson (between $12 billion and $42 billion in 2019 dollars). In 1918, *Forbes* listed Mary Harriman as the 11th richest person in America, with a net worth of $80 million. In 1998, *American Heritage* said E.H. Harriman was the 24th richest American in history. John D. Rockefeller led both lists. Mary Harriman became one of the wealthiest women in the world and managed the estate admirably until her death in 1932, delegating business management to trusted associates and her sons when they were old enough.

Averell worked for Union Pacific to learn the business, beginning at the bottom, initially working summers on a survey crew. In 1912, he joined the boards of Union Pacific and Illinois Central Railroad. After graduating from Yale in 1913 (where he rowed and played polo), Averell moved to Omaha, Nebraska, to learn Union Pacific business. "He learned locomotive operations, traffic control, maintenance and purchasing," according to Abramson. "He spent several weeks traveling the territory, some of it with gangs working on the tracks." He was put in charge of a project to ferret out waste in the railroad, spending nearly a year traveling around the system as he inspected "foundries, car shops, and rolling mills, called on freight agents, and covered long stretches of the road with repair crews." He became a vice president in 1914 at age 22, in charge of $50 million of yearly purchases, and in 1918 joined the board's executive committee. Aware he could not escape his father's enormous shadow, he branched out in other directions.

During World War I, Averell gained control over a number of shipyards, taking advantage of the wartime demand. After the war, he opened the first shipping link to Germany, the Hamburg-American Line, and by the age of 29, he was one of the most powerful figures in American shipping. He also was active on Wall Street, forming an investment firm with his brother in 1919, Harriman Brothers and Company, and his own investment firm, W.A. Harriman and Company, investing in mining, aviation, and other fields. Harriman's firm invested heavily in Germany after World War I, which along with other U.S. investors, provided financing that enabled Germany to make its war reparation payments. Harriman has been criticized for dealing with German industrialists who later assisted Hitler's Nazi Party. In 1924, his investment firm obtained a concession from the Russian government to mine manganese in the country of Georgia. The Harriman fortune was diminished by the Depression but withstood the crash of 1929 because "it was so massive and too securely rooted in the productive machinery of the country to be pulled down by the collapse by inflated stock prices," according to Abramson. Harriman Brothers merged with Brown Brothers, Harriman's chief competitor, in 1930 to become Brown Brothers Harriman and Company, the largest private bank in America. The Harriman brothers contributed more than $8 million to the new firm.

Averell Harriman had been a member of the Union Pacific board's executive committee since 1918, but until the early 1930s, his primary focus had been on other ventures. The Depression hit the railroad industry hard, and it "collapsed like a rotten trestle," as rail traffic fell 50 percent, according to Abramson. In 1930, Harriman became chairman of the executive committee of the Illinois Central Railroad, which was losing $3.5 million a year and saw its stock drop from $136.75 a share to $4.75. Like his father before him, Averell toured the West to size up the problems of the company, returning determined to take the offensive and aggressively moving to restore its profitability.

In 1932, Harriman became chairman of the board of directors of Union Pacific. In 1927, U.P. was one of five railroads that were among the 10 U.S. corporations with assets over $1 billion, but many saw it as a giant in a declining industry. During the 1920s, Union Pacific passenger revenue declined by half, and in the three years following the crash they declined by half again. According to Abramson, in 1932, the railroad was facing the hardest times it had seen since his father salvaged it from bankruptcy. It was sapped by the Depression and challenged by trucks, buses, automobiles, and airplanes. Its chief consolation was that the condition of just about every other railroad in the land was worse.

Railroad passenger ridership declined from its peak in 1920, when passengers took 1.27 million trips and traveled one billion miles. By 1930, there were 707,987 passenger trips accounting for 26.9 million miles. Automobiles, trucks, and buses had taken away railroads' short-haul business and were threatening their long-haul business. The number of cars and trucks in the country increased from 1 million in 1920 to 3.4 million in 1929. In 1933, *Railway Age*, a trade publication, reported that "the condition of passenger service of the railroads is nothing short of appalling. Since 1920, there had been a reduction of more than 70 percent in their passenger revenues, and the decline is continuing." Things were so bad that Robert S. Lovett, Averell's predecessor as chairman of U.P.'s board, believed the best days of American railroads had passed, and he advised Roland Harriman to take up another career.

Klein said Harriman "took it personally because he had more or less grown up on trains," and explored every way to improve passenger service. Even before the Depression began, he recommended that Union Pacific install phones and show movies on its long-distance trains, but he got a gentlemanly rebuff from Carl Gray, U.P.'s president. Harriman would not wait out the Depression and "was not content to renew the company's strength," Klein wrote. "He decided to counterattack the forces of depression at the road's weakest point: its passenger traffic." He made a commitment to modernizing passenger service "to save the credibility of the railroad."

Harriman wanted to do something creative. His first major project was to utilize a new type of passenger train "to turn the disaster of passenger traffic around," according to Klein. He purchased diesel-powered locomotives and passenger cars, the Pullman M-10000, which used new two-cycle diesel engines produced by General Motors. They were made of aluminum alloy and were air-conditioned, faster, cheaper to operate, and more efficient and comfortable than conventional steam trains. "Nothing like it had ever been seen before," Klein wrote. This was a gamble, since Union Pacific invested $50 million on the new passenger trains, and passenger travel accounted for less than 10 percent of its income in 1932. Abramson said,

> *With trains running half empty and passenger cars standing idle, they ordered revolutionary new high-speed trains, betting that passengers would reappear if they found*

> *comfortable and economical service once again. . . . It was a move of stirring audacity, considering economic circumstances and the outlook for the passenger business. . . . Harriman took the risk because he was certain that passenger service would otherwise continue to deteriorate, dragging the entire railroad industry down with them.*

Union Pacific was one of the first railroads to introduce these new trains, ushering in the age of streamliners with great fanfare, "the train of tomorrow," according to Klein. "It was more than a new train, a bold display of modernism; it was an *event*—something wholly unfamiliar and bewildering to traditional railroaders who had not yet grasped the curious ways in which the world was moving." Its inaugural run went from Los Angeles to New York in 57 hours, 14½ hours less than E.H. Harriman's record trip in 1906, and 23 hours less than regular transcontinental trains, giving Union Pacific a huge amount of free publicity. The *City of Portland* began its regular run on June 6, 1935, from Chicago to Portland, Oregon. Union Pacific also introduced a cheaper alternative, the *Challenger*, an all-coach service, to show economy train travel could be modern and profitable. The new train was as luxurious as it was fast, and it was, Klein wrote, "sleek, glamorous, and thoroughly modern, offering amenities once reserved only for the rich." Union Pacific's new trains served new clientele who had money and "wanted to get places in a faster, more luxurious way than ever before." The new trains increased passenger service revenue by 21.4 percent in 1935, and 34.7 percent in 1935.

Harriman took steps to bring more vision to Union Pacific's management. He replaced the company's long-serving president, 64-year-old Carl Gray, with William Jeffers, U.P. executive vice president, who was more attuned to his ideas and better equipped to meet the challenges of the changing economy. In April 1937, Union Pacific announced Jeffers would replace Gray in October 1937. Gray had been president since 1920 and was in charge when Sun Valley was planned and built. Jeffers was an "energetic, feet-on-the-ground clear thinker," and had the breadth and vision for the railroad as part of the West, according to Klein. Jeffers had worked for Union Pacific since he was 16.

Harriman also modernized Union Pacific's freight service with renovated boxcars and powerful locomotives to handle longer trains at higher speeds. In 1936, Union Pacific budgeted $8 million for new equipment and, in 1937, ordered 4,088 new freight cars and 2,000 more in 1939. As he did in all of his business operations, according to Abramson, Harriman was obsessively attracted to the details of both the

Challenger service and the new streamliners. Recovery of the passenger service became a consuming personal mission, Abramson wrote. The man who had kept an eye on his Soviet mining enterprise between polo matches fussed over the *Challenger* like a professional housekeeper, installing electrical outlets and telephones and equipping streamliners with windows that polarized light and eliminated glare.

Harriman's gamble on passenger service worked in the short term. By the end of 1936, U.P.'s streamliners were filled to capacity, running between Chicago and Los Angeles, San Francisco, and Denver. However, Averell learned from his father that a railroad only prospered when its territory prospered. His new trains needed a destination for passengers, somewhere new and exciting to go.

In summer 1935, Harriman came up with a revolutionary idea for generating new passenger traffic, according to Klein—a ski resort in the remote mountains of the West, a destination that might enhance the railroad's lagging passenger revenues. Just as Union Pacific streamliners were at the forefront of a new development in transportation, Sun Valley launched a new form of tourism. The resort was a progenitor of other winter sports facilities in the West.[5]

Part Two

AVERELL HARRIMAN AND UNION PACIFIC BUILD AN AMERICAN ST. MORITZ

3

1935

Harriman Decides to Build a Ski Resort and Sends Count Schaffgotsch to Find a Site

In 1935, Averell Harriman was looking for a way to attract more passengers to ride Union Pacific's new fleet of streamliner trains. The railroad went along the northern tier of the United States, and in the winter, passengers preferred southern routes because of the weather. The 1932 Winter Olympics at Lake Placid, New York, created an interest in winter sports that, according to Maury Klein, Harriman

> *believed would grow rapidly if the right facilities could be provided. And what better place for those facilities than on the line of the Union Pacific? Ski trains already ran out of several cities for local enthusiasts, but no mountain resort existed where people may spend a week or two skiing.*

Harriman had skied, but by his own admission was not a good skier. However, he felt the slopes of the western United States could rival those of Europe and attract an increasing number of American winter sports enthusiasts. Harriman wanted to attract wealthy skiers who had gone to European ski resorts and make skiing attractive and accessible to a new generation, using the excitement of a world-class ski resort.

Harriman explained his thinking when he became U.P. board chairman, inspired by his banking associates in Europe, whom he often found were on ski vacations, according to Luanne Pfeiffer in *Sun Valley's Salad Days*:

> *People were looking to the railroad not for their efficiency in handling freight but in the way they handled passengers. . . . The Santa Fe had about twice the number of passenger business at that time as the Union Pacific. Their advertising campaign read "Go to the sun through the sun" and they booked people going west through the southern states. The U.P. went through the mountains and that meant snow. . . .*
>
> *So I thought we should do something to make snow profitable to the railroad. . . . I do not mean to imply that I started skiing in the U.S. because I did not. . . . We simply made it easier for the people to take up the sport. My idea was to create a new industry for us, not just make one place popular, but by popularizing one place make way for more along the lines of the U.P.*

Railroads had long been involved in tourism and operating resort hotels to promote passenger business. Yellowstone National Park was formed in 1872, after lobbying by the Northern Pacific Railroad, which built a line to the park in 1883 and promoted tourism there. In 1903, Union Pacific created a Bureau of Service National Parks and Resorts to promote tours to scenic spots, offered tours to Yellowstone and Rocky Mountain National Parks, and built a branch line to West Yellowstone in 1909. Union Pacific began operating resorts, building two hotels on the Grand Canyon's southern rim and operating hotels in the Utah national parks. However, a ski resort was something else. The railroad's two top executives, Carl Gray and Bill Jeffers, reflecting the attitude of most railroad men, sought to convince Harriman "to forget his resort and stick to railroading," according to Abramson. Jeffers reputedly said, "I've been with the railroad umpty-ump years and in that time the railroad has spent millions getting rid of snow; now we're spending millions to play in the goddamned stuff." However, Jeffers grew to love Sun Valley, learned to ski in his 40s, and contributed the Jeffers Cup for one of the resort's annual races.

Harriman discussed the possibility of a ski resort with Carl Gray in fall 1935; Gray reacted negatively, "after having discussions with our people about the possibilities of skiing." On September 25, 1935, Gray wrote to Harriman,

> *Our difficulty seems to be that with the exception of the Yellowstone Park territory . . . and the Denver Mountain park, we do not have any considerable amount of dependable snow. . . . Recently the Rocky Mountain Park Transportation Company employed a Swiss who was very familiar with skiing as it is followed in Europe, and tried very hard to build up an interest, without any success.*

On October 2, 1935, Harriman told Gray that he had seen

> *tremendous interest in skiing in all parts of the country. Ski trains are being run out of New York, Boston, and other Eastern cities; also Chicago, San Francisco and other points in the West. In Salt Lake City and Seattle, it has been become very popular locally. . . . It has occurred to me that some day there will be established a ski center in the mountains here of the same character as in the Swiss or Austrian Alps. . . . I believe it is worthwhile for us to investigate the present centers of sport in our territory, having in mind that we might assist through our advertising and otherwise in promoting these places. . . .*
>
> *My thought was that we invite the young Austrian I mentioned to you* [Count Felix Schaffgotsch] *to make a trip over our territory and advise us whether any of the existing places are susceptible of development. We should know whether we have an asset which would be worthwhile our following up. . . . It is conceivable that it is possible to build up long haul travel to a popular center.*

In his oral history, Harriman said he had not thought of Union Pacific building a ski resort. "I thought originally we could get a group together and have a sort of club arrangement," in the same way Railroad Ranch was acquired by a group of wealthy industrialists for their own use. William Paley, president of Columbia Broadcasting System, said, "Sun Valley started with a group of avid skiers wanting a private club for 8-10. Every time they talked about it, the scheme got bigger." Abramson agreed:

> *At first, he had thought about organizing a club made up of his friends and building a lodge somewhere out West near the Union Pacific line. He and CBS president William Paley kicked the idea around at Arden, and he later mentioned it to Herbert Swope* [a neighbor on Long Island], *Dorothy Schiff* [owner of the *New York Post*] *and a few other possible investors and members, but there was no great enthusiasm. The obvious alternative was to make it a railroad project.*

According to Klein, Harriman said Steve Hannagan, the publicist he hired for Sun Valley,

> *persuaded me that this was something good for the Union Pacific Railroad. We'd get a lot of publicity, and of course, a lot of goodwill in Idaho. . . . There will be no publicity in starting a lodge, a fifty-room lodge in the mountains. It's something everybody does.*

> *But you build a million-dollar hotel and I'll guarantee you a lot of publicity. So I took it up with the Board of Directors and they finally agreed that we should go ahead with it. Although it was a lot of money, and the directors were not skiers.*

There are several stories about how Harriman met Austrian count Felix Schaffgotsch, but Harriman settled the issue in his oral history:

> *I thought it was a good idea to start some place in the West, so I employed Count Felix Schaffgotsch, who was an Austrian, not so expert in skiing, but he'd had a lot to do with development of resorts in Austria. He had rented me the place I took in Austria to shoot chamois, and I knew him that way and I liked him.*

Harriman asked Schaffgotsch to tour the entire West to find the best place for a ski resort in a location served by Union Pacific, and to report only to him. The count's expenses were paid by U.P., and railroad personnel escorted him through six states in six weeks. Harriman wanted a place far enough from a city so it would not be overrun with weekend skiers.

On November 27, 1935, Harriman told Carl Gray "our skiing expert" was arriving in Omaha the following Saturday:

> *He believes it will be best for him to go directly to Seattle and see the skiing on Mount Rainier, which he is told is the best skiing in the country, and then after visiting Lake Tahoe and the mountains near Los Angeles, work back through Salt Lake, spending most of his time from there east.*

He needed a guide who knew how to ski, and "should not be allowed to go on mountain trips alone as there is always danger of an accident, sprained ankle, or something of the kind." Union Pacific's E.A. Klippel Jr. traveled with Schaffgotsch from Omaha to Seattle and Portland, and other railroad personnel met him at other locations. While Schaffgotsch left on his search, Harriman enrolled in skiing lessons at Saks Department Store in New York.[6]

When the count arrived in the Northwest, he did not reveal the real reason he was there. The *Seattle Times* on December 6, 1935, said "Austrian Count Bored at Home, Here for Skiing." Schaffgotsch said that he got bored always skiing in Austria, but "this is different." In 1935, a friend, Hannes Schroll, won the country's first national downhill and slalom championships held on Mount Rainier, and he told the count it was a wonderful skiing resort.

Ken Syverson, a skier from Tacoma, took Schaffgotsch to Mount Rainier, where they climbed from Paradise Lodge at 5,000 feet up the glacier on skis to Camp Muir at 10,000 feet and skied down. They left Paradise at 1:30, and at 5:00 he was having dinner in Seattle. The count liked Rainier: "I had a very nice run today down on to Paradise Glacier. Powder snow. At Camp Muir, though, it was wind-blown." He was amazed there was so much skiing around Seattle and Tacoma "so close in." Schaffgotsch found many of the qualities he sought at Mount Rainier but rejected it because it was too close to a population center. He wanted a remote location to provide "alpine seclusion."

The count next visited Mount Hood in Oregon, giving the same cover story. He found slush instead of snow, then headed to Yosemite National Park in California. Shortly before Christmas, Schaffgotsch was in Los Angeles and gave Harriman his first report:

> *I have done practically all the developed resorts from Mount Baker (Seattle) to Mount Baldy (Cal.). All these places are weekend resorts, and no competition of any sort. Besides, most of them are four to seven hours drive from the towns, which makes it too near for a longer stay and again too far for every weekend. The hotels and inns are built as summer resorts and now only adapted for winter sports, which is jumping and tobogganing.*

Schaffgotsch then moved on to Colorado, Utah and Idaho. He visited most of the areas that later became successful ski resorts, including Yosemite, the San Bernardino Mountains, Lake Tahoe, Steamboat Springs, Aspen, and others. When he was in Salt Lake City, Schaffgotsch met Alf Engen, one of the country's top ski jumpers who later worked at Sun Valley, visiting local areas including Brighton and Alta. Engen said the count "wore his title well." He rejected all the locations he saw for different reasons—either the snow conditions or locations were unacceptable. The count rejected Aspen because it had too many trees and was at too high an altitude.

Even while the count was on his tour, Union Pacific began promoting skiing at destinations served by its trains. The *Union Pacific Bulletin* of January 1936 published several articles about skiing: "Western Sportslands Thrill Austrian Count," "Ski Stuff You Should Know," and "Mount Hood's Sport Carnival."

According to Dorice Taylor, the count reached Idaho in January and met Bill Hynes, who was in charge of U.P.'s freight and passenger service in Boise. Hynes had no idea what a ski area was and thought it was a waste of time and money. They met in Pocatello, and Hynes showed him eastern Idaho near the Montana border, which lacked high mountains. They hired an airplane that flew them over the Teton Mountains for a look at Wyoming. The count liked what he saw, so in Victor, Idaho (the terminus of a branch of U.P.'s Yellowstone line), they hired a horse-drawn sleigh that took them over Teton Pass for a closer view. They saw open slopes, sunlight, powder snow, and the beauty of high mountains. Holland wrote that the count told Harriman he saw "a perfect place" on the road to Teton Pass, with the best snow conditions he had seen in his life. However, the state of Wyoming would not agree to keep Teton Pass open in the winter, making the area impossible to develop. A discouraged Schaffgotsch left for Denver, convinced he could not find the perfect spot for Harriman's ski resort.

If the Wyoming Highway Department had been more cooperative, Harriman's ski resort might have been located in Jackson Hole, with access by train through Victor. That would have required a more circuitous route, however. Passengers would have had to transfer from the main line at Pocatello to the Yellowstone branch, then transfer again to get to Victor.

The prospects of finding a place for Harriman's ski area looked bleak when a chance meeting occurred. On January 12, 1936, Schaffgotsch left Idaho on his way to Denver, ready to give up his search. Bill Hynes returned to Boise, where he met a friend, Joe Stemmer, director of Idaho highways. Over drinks, Hynes said he had been all over eastern Idaho "with a crazy Austrian and six pairs of skis," according to Klein. Stemmer asked Hynes if he had taken the count to Ketchum. Hynes said, "By God no, I forgot."

Sun Valley came that close to never being built. History would have changed if Hynes had not met Stemmer that night. Holland wrote, "Bill Hynes now likes to tell how three scotch and sodas were really behind the founding of Sun Valley."

Hynes sent Schaffgotsch a telegram in Denver, telling him about a snowy location at Ketchum, in the Wood River Valley in the remote mountains of central Idaho. Ketchum was an old mining town on a Union Pacific spur line built in the 1880s to haul ore from its silver mines. The Wood River Branch cost more money to keep clear of snow than any other Union Pacific branch except its Yellowstone line.

Schaffgotsch met Hynes at Shoshone to take the Wood River Branch to Ketchum, but the line was blocked by snow and the district engineer had to plow the route to get through. The party reached Ketchum on January 16, 1936. The count initially thought he was wasting his time. The Wood River Valley was too wide to provide the shelter a resort needed. However, as the train approached Ketchum, the valley narrowed, providing the shelter he wanted.

Word got to Ketchum in advance of his arrival that an Austrian count was looking for a place to build a million-dollar hotel. The thought that anyone would invest a large amount of money around Ketchum seemed absurd. Jack Lane, a local sheepman and owner of the town's mercantile store, warned, "Don't take any of his checks." Lane continued his skepticism about Sun Valley. When he saw the lodge and swimming pool, he said that in five years they would be using the pool as a sheep dip.[7]

THE WOOD RIVER VALLEY WHEN SCHAFFGOTSCH ARRIVED

Idaho's economy has long been a roller coaster ride of boom-bust cycles. When Schaffgotsch arrived in the Wood River Valley in 1936, it had been in a down cycle since the end of World War I. Ketchum was just a shadow of the thriving mining town it was during the heady days of the 1880s silver rush. It had been established in the early 1880s, along with Bellevue and Hailey, after silver was discovered in the Wood River Valley, resulting in a boom that attracted many thousands of fortune seekers.

Ever since Union Pacific completed its transcontinental line in 1869, it desired a direct route to the Pacific Northwest. In 1881, spurred on by competition from Northern Pacific, which was building its line to Puget Sound, U.P. incorporated a subsidiary to build a new rail line to Portland by the shortest route, "the short line." Between 1882 and 1884, the Oregon Short Line built a connection from U.P.'s main line at Granger, Wyoming, through Idaho to Oregon.

Robert Strahorn, a U.P. publicist, played a role in getting a branch built into the Wood River Valley. In 1877, U.P. financier Jay Gould hired Strahorn to tour the territory that would be served by his planned Northwest connection, publicize its economic potential, and help select routes. Strahorn and his wife, Carrie Adell, fell in love with the Wood River Valley and its economic potential. In 1882, with other U.P. insiders, Strahorn formed the Idaho and Oregon Land Improvement Company to develop towns where they knew the Oregon Short Line would go. They acquired land in advance of the arrival of the tracks; laid out townsites; installed irrigation systems, bridges, roads, and other infrastructure; and promoted the sale of land. They made substantial profits trading on inside information, developing a series of railroad towns along the Oregon Short Line tracks in Idaho and Oregon, including Hailey, Shoshone, Mountain Home, Caldwell, Weiser, and Ontario, Oregon.

In 1882, Strahorn's company owned the Shoshone townsite and bought the townsite of Hailey and surrounding land for $100,000, including the 2,500-acre Croy ranch and 8,000-acre Quigley ranch. The *Wood River Journal* of June 24, 1882, said Hailey would be the terminus for the Wood River Branch being built from Shoshone, and become the smelting and commercial center of the territory, the "Denver of Idaho." Historian Clark Spence, in *For Wood River or Bust*, said Union Pacific and its publicist were so involved with boosting the merits of the Wood River Valley and its mining potential that the *Denver Republican* called it "the much-lauded Wood River Country . . . the biggest mining fraud of the age . . . a mining boom inaugurated by a railroad corporation."

At Strahorn's urging, beginning in 1882, the nearly 70-mile-long Wood River Branch of the Oregon Short Line (OSL) was built from Shoshone to Hailey to access the area's silver mines. OSL tracks reached Hailey in May 1883, its planned terminus, where Strahorn and his associates expected to make huge profits from their land investments. Against their wishes, the tracks were extended north to Ketchum in 1884 to reach the Philadelphia Smelter. The railroad expedited the flow of capital into the valley, brought an era of industrialization to its mining industry, and caused an economic boom.

If the Oregon Short Line had not extended its tracks to Ketchum in 1884, Count Schaffgotsch would not have selected the Wood River Valley as the site for Harriman's ski area in 1936.

Hailey was the intended terminus of the Wood River Branch when it was built in 1883, and there were no plans to continue to Ketchum because of investments made by Strahorn and his associates. However, the Philadelphia Smelter was north of Ketchum, 14 miles from the Hailey depot. Wealthy Philadelphia businessmen invested over $500,000 in the smelter and wanted a direct connection to the railroad. In 1883, the Philadelphia Smelter was the largest enterprise in Idaho Territory and "the most complete smelting works in the West," according to Spence. It received ore from 52 mines and produced 40 tons of bullion a day, enough to fill three railcars, providing much of the business of the

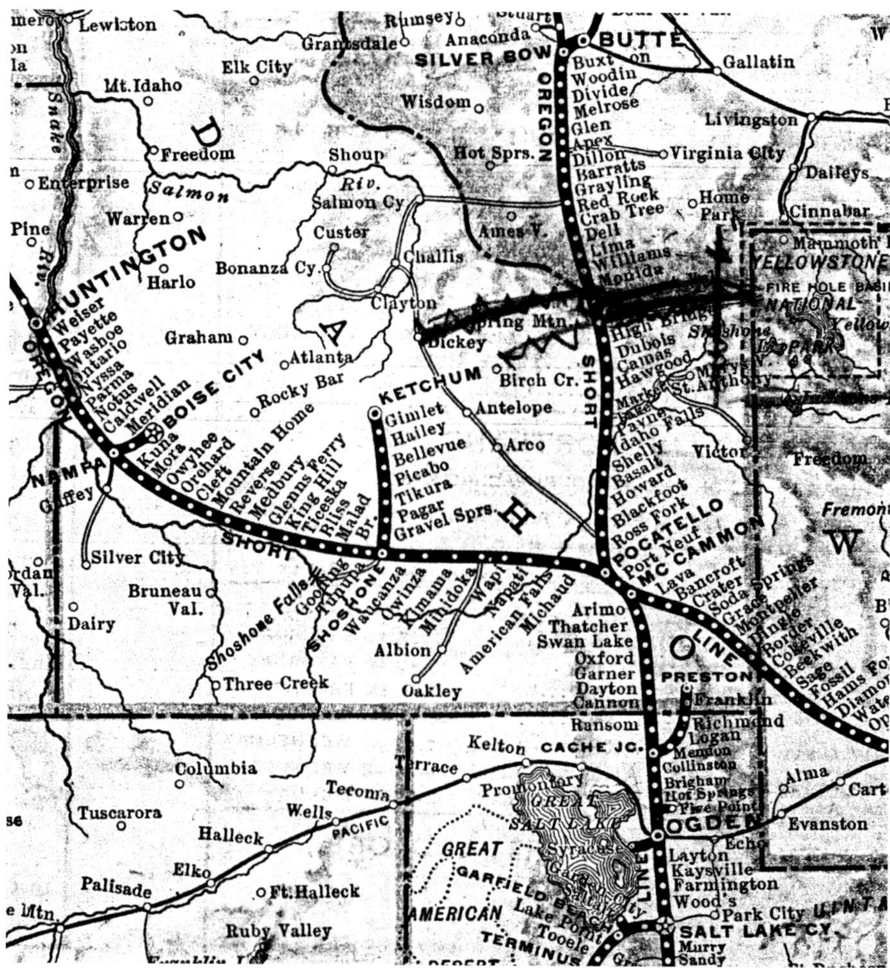

Partial Map of the Oregon Short Line Railroad showing the Wood River Branch from Shoshone to Ketchum, late 1800s.

railroad. Processed ore had to be taken by wagon to the Hailey depot, an expensive procedure. The smelter's desire to have the tracks brought to Ketchum was opposed by those who stood to make a fortune from Hailey being the OSL terminus.

The *Wood River Times* of April 2, 1884, reported that at a meeting of the directors of Union Pacific, the "subject of extending the road to Ketchum was not even mentioned." The manager for Union Pacific's Idaho Division said the Ketchum extension would not be built. Nonetheless, in summer 1884, the tracks were extended from Hailey directly to the Philadelphia Smelter, half a mile north of Ketchum's town limits.

The hills around Hailey were not suitable for a destination ski resort, and Schaffgotsch was disappointed in that part of the valley. If Strahorn and his associates had prevailed, and the Wood River Branch ended at Hailey, it is unlikely that Count Schaffgotsch would have been taken to inspect the area, and certainly would not have selected it. Only because the tracks were extended to Ketchum, which was surrounded by mountains suitable for a ski area, did the count select the Wood River Valley as the place to build the Sun Valley Resort in 1936.

In 1884, Ketchum annexed the area around the Philadelphia Smelter, known as the Rhodes Addition, since the Oregon Short Line depot was outside of downtown in what is now the Warm Springs area. In 1934, Union Pacific's separate subsidiaries were eliminated, the Oregon Short Line was integrated into its corporate structure, and OSL routes were thereafter known as Union Pacific routes, including the line from Shoshone to Ketchum.

The Wood River Valley thrived until the international silver depression of 1888. The depression hit the Wood River Valley hard since its economy was based on silver. By 1888, according to Carlos A. Schwantes, "many of the important Wood River mines ceased operations. Bust had replaced boom and many inhabitants left in the spring and winter." "The Wood River Mining Region is deader than a lime fossil," reported the *Ketchum Keystone* on October 12, 1893. The hard times lasted until 1898, when the Klondike gold rush ended the depression.

Agriculture became a major part of Idaho's economy in the 1890s and early 1900s, boosted by the National Reclamation Act of 1902, which provided federal funding of dams and water projects to promote agriculture in the arid West. OSL's Wood River Branch opened the valley for summer grazing of sheep, and its economic base changed from mining to sheep ranching. In the 1920s, it was said that Ketchum and Hill City on Camas Prairie shipped more sheep than any other rail depot in the country.

Idaho's economy was strong in the first two decades of the 1900s, due to the Reclamation Act and demand for its wool and metals during World War I. Idaho was hit by an agricultural depression in the 1920s as demand for its products plummeted after the war ended. "The Roaring Twenties hit Idaho with a dull thud," read the *Idaho Statesman Centennial Edition*. Idaho's economy was further devastated by the Great Depression in 1929.[8]

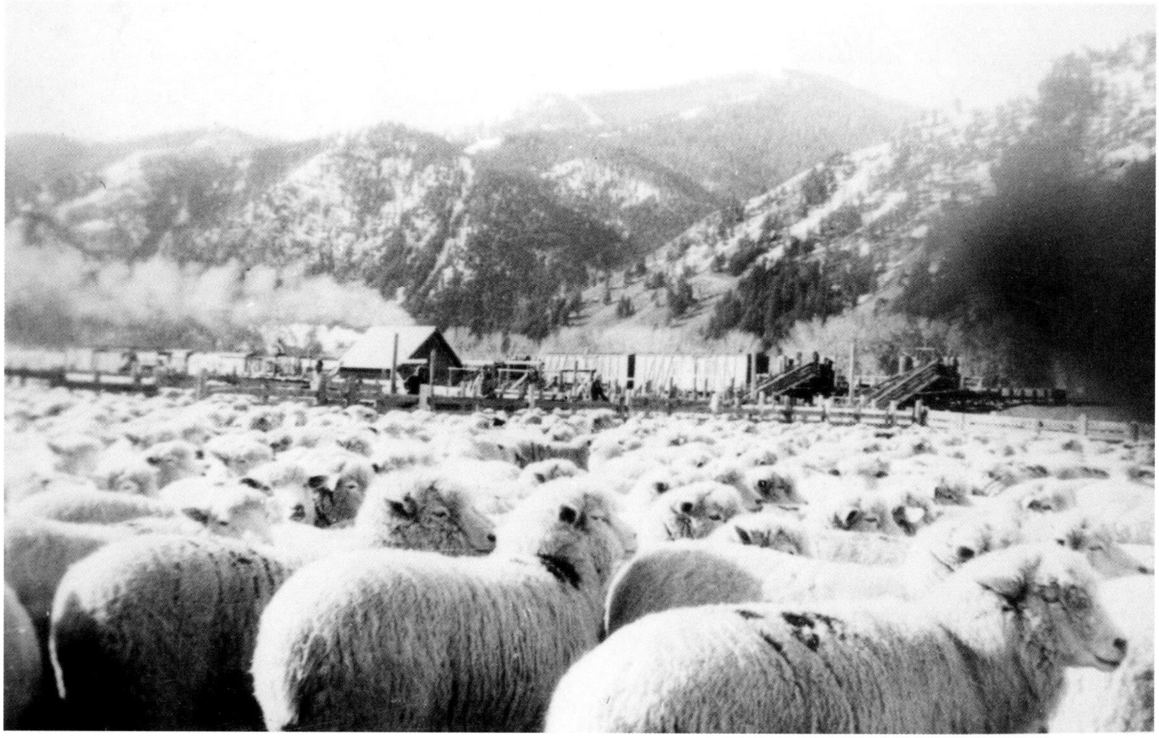

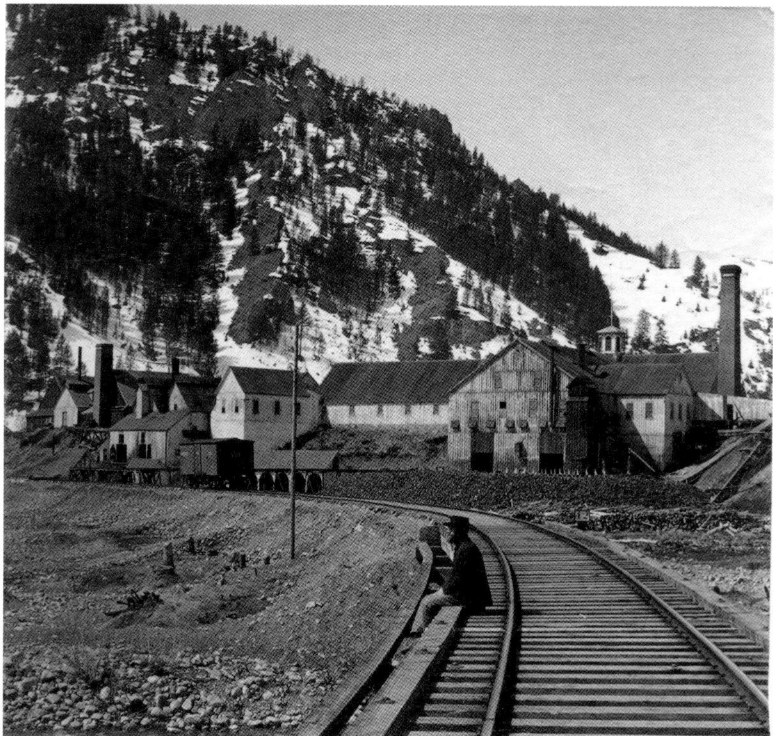

ABOVE Oregon Short Line depot in Ketchum near the present Y.M.C.A., showing the stockyards filled with sheep awaiting shipment out of the Valley, around 1938.

LEFT Oregon Short Line tracks leading to the Philadelphia Smelter at the intersection of Big Wood River and Warm Springs Creek. *Photograph by Eugene Antz.*

Count Schaffgotstch Finds the Site for a Ski Resort, Harriman Inspects the Area

When Count Schaffgotsch arrived in February 1936, Ketchum was a small mountain village, snowbound as it often was in the winter with only half of its 270 residents staying in town. Trains from Shoshone, the area's connection to the outside world, ran a few times a week and only when they could get through the deep snow that often shut down the tracks. The sheep industry that thrived in the summer was nonexistent, as the sheep were in their winter homes in the desert. The Griffith grocery store was open two hours a day. Bald Mountain Hot Springs Lodge offered the town's only lodging. The count stayed there after the hotel was dug out for him and had to get meals from a local woman, since the town's restaurants were closed for the season. The Ketchum Kamp was the town's largest saloon. Lane Mercantile was the town's general store, a place where the "elite of the sheep growers and buyers met to talk over prices," according to Holland.

The valley's residents used skis to get around for many years before Sun Valley was built. This was not the skiing wealthy Americans did in Europe but was a means to travel in the winter. Long homemade skis with leather pouches for bindings were standard equipment. A single pole was used as a brake to slow down or a rudder to assist in turning.

The skis used by Roberta Brass Garrettson, whose family owned the ranch U.P. bought for its resort, were made at the Board Sawmill in Warm Springs. They had a canvas housing into which her shoes were inserted, with a leather strap going around the housing to hold her foot in. She used very long skis, like miners did, because they gave better traction in deep snow. She used a handle from a broken pitchfork to push her along on the level and dragged it between her legs to slow down, riding it downhill to keep from going too fast.

When Schaffgotsch arrived in Ketchum, he met Marvin Obenchain, a descendant of a Ketchum pioneer family who knew the local territory and could get around on his long, handmade skis. He described their exploration of the surrounding hills and the count's location of the place where the lodge would be built:

> *I was his companion in all the places where he skied. We spent several hours at the top of Dollar Mountain from before sunup, to see where the first ray of sun hit the valley*

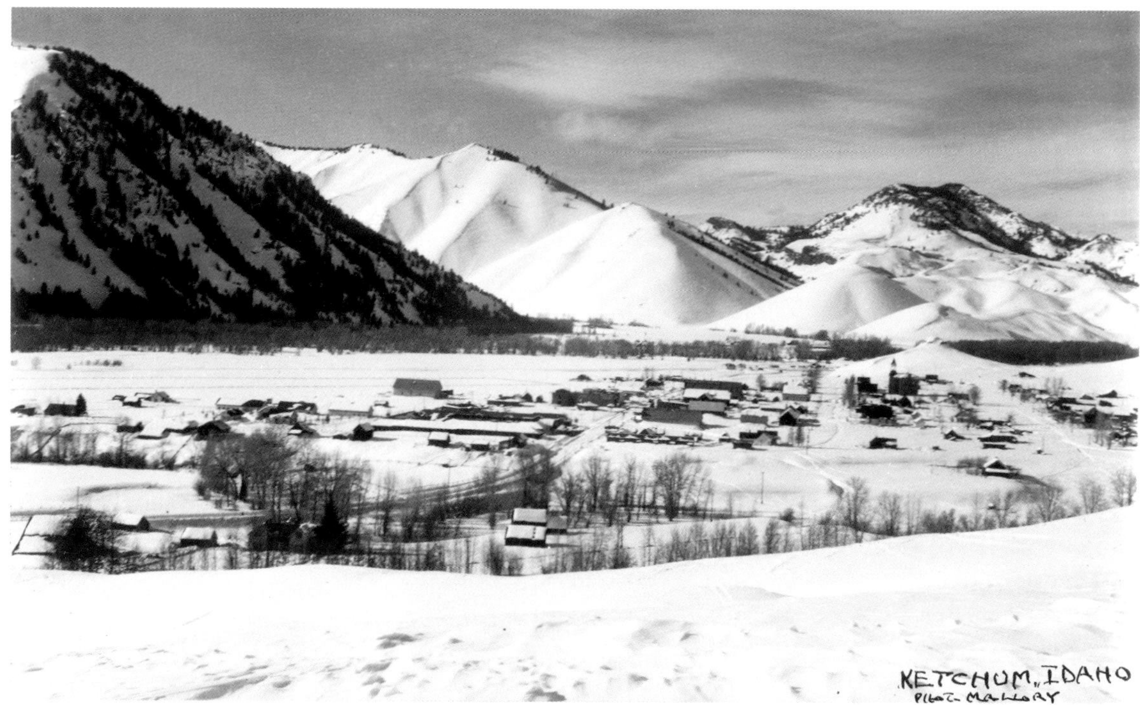

Aerial view of Ketchum, 1936, looking northwest toward Bald Mountain, Warm Springs Canyon, and Griffin Butte. *Photograph by Martyn Mallory.*

> *floor. Then, we'd ski down and mark that spot, and do that each morning until we had the correct spot marked. For all of my work with Felix, I was awarded free lift rides on all the mountains for several years afterward.*

The count admired how Marvin Obenchain could ski, using his own body to "drop anchor" to control his speed downhill, and Obenchain was amazed at the count's beautiful turns using his modern equipment.

After touring the mountains around Ketchum, Schaffgotsch felt the area offered the combination of snow, weather, and accessible hills he was seeking, as he told the *Idaho Statesman* on March 22, 1936:

> *I have traveled all over most of the western part of the country and nowhere have I seen such a place. . . . When I stepped off the train and saw it, I said, this is the place. It*

> *didn't take me long to see the possibilities ahead. The climate is perfect—just like we have in Austria—the mountains are perfect, everything is perfect. As a matter of fact, it is more perfect even than our favorite spot in Austria.*

The count skied to the Brass ranch one day and told Roberta, "This is the most beautiful valley I've been in, and I've been to Canada. I've been to Colorado. This is it. This is where Union Pacific is going to put in a ski resort. Next year, there will be a thousand people here." The count showed her where he planned to locate the lodge. She said it was where the cattle and horses go when the weather is cold. She did not believe him when he said a thousand people would be there next winter.

Schaffgotsch sent Harriman a series of telegrams. The first read, "am expecting you here in Ketchum. Perfect place, any number excursions, ideal snow and weather conditions. Accommodations primitive, log cabins, own cooking. Bring skins to climb hill." The second read, "it's ski heaven. When are you coming out?" A third read, "this without doubt is the perfect place."

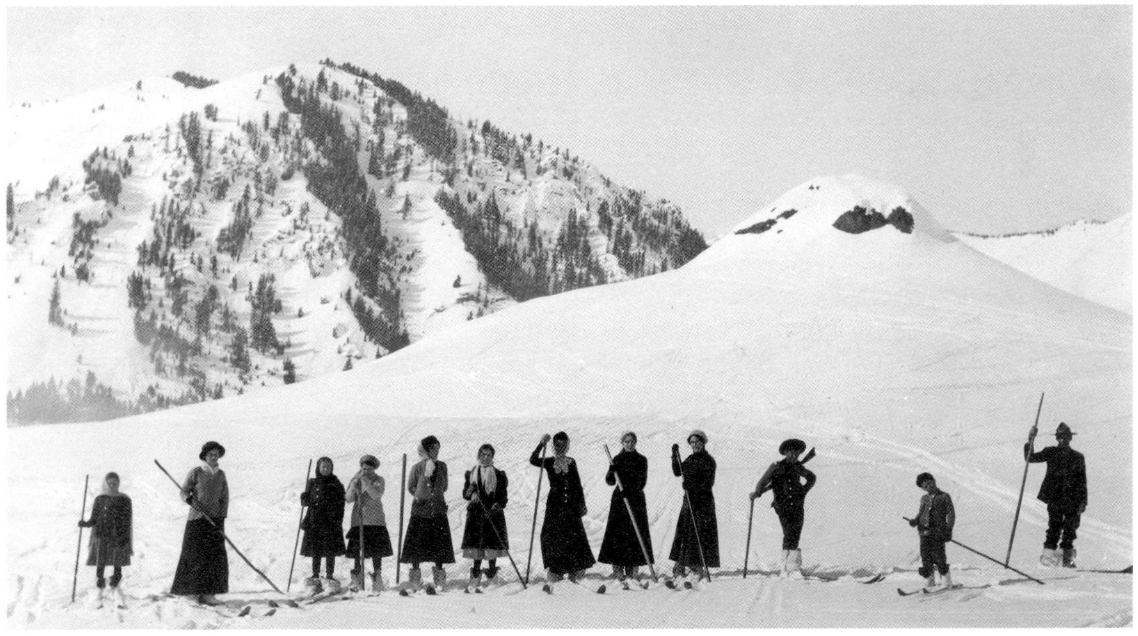

Ketchum residents on skis using a single pole with Bald Mountain in background, around 1880s.

Schaffgotsch said the "Sawtooth Mountain Range" protected the valley, and Sun Valley's advertising thereafter said the resort was located in the Sawtooth Mountains. The Sawtooth Mountains are located about 40 miles north of Sun Valley, beyond Galena Summit. Bald Mountain is in the Smoky Mountains, and Sun Valley faces the Pioneer Mountains to the east. Sun Valley is almost surrounded by Sawtooth National Forest, which was created by President Theodore Roosevelt in 1905–1906. Either the proximity of the Sawtooth National Forest caused confusion or Sawtooth Mountains sounded better in advertising.

After receiving the count's telegrams, Averell and his second wife, Marie Harriman, their daughter Mary, and friends William and Dorothy Paley traveled by Harriman's private railroad car, the "Overland," to Shoshone, pulled by a Union Pacific train. Getting farther was a problem.

In the winter of 1936, Val McAtee worked for Union Pacific in Shoshone, reporting to the roadmaster for the Ketchum and Hill City branches. He later worked for the contractor who built Sun Valley Lodge and for Lloyd Castagneto, building the resort's ski lifts.

One day in February 1936, McAtee's boss told him to help open the line to Ketchum, which was blocked by snow. A 40-man crew had to open the line using a rotary snowplow because a special trainload of dudes from New York were coming to Shoshone to go on to Ketchum, for reasons unknown to him. It took McAtee's party from 4:00 am to 3:00 p.m. to get from Shoshone to Ketchum, where five feet of snow blocked the tracks. They plowed the switchyards, turned around, plowed the railroad yards at Hailey, and went back toward Shoshone. When they reached Richfield, north of Shoshone, they spent two days clearing the Hill City line through Camas Prairie. When they got back to Shoshone, they were sent to clear the main line from Minidoka to Bliss.

When they finished, they were sent back to Ketchum to clear the line for the Harriman special. The tracks were drifted in again, and they were stopped by a freight train carrying ice that was stuck east of Picabo. McAtee's train had to back up to Ticura, unhitch the rotary snowplow, and take two engines to pull the ice train back to Richfield, where it was put on a siding. They returned and plowed the line to Ketchum in a blinding storm, allowing the Harriman train to reach Shoshone, where it headed east on the main line. The crew went home for sleep after seven days of continuous plowing.

The Harriman party arrived in the Wood River Valley on Washington's birthday, February 18, 1936. Schaffgotsch met them with an enclosed wagon heated by a

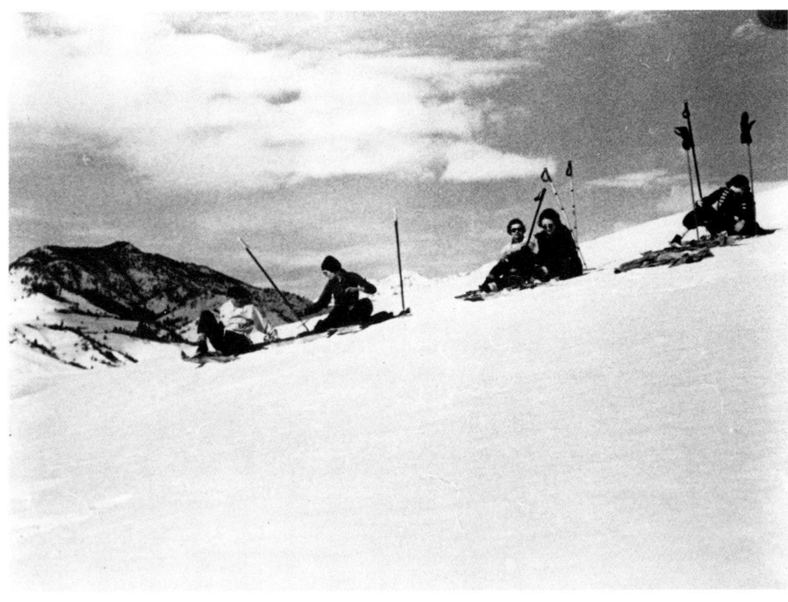

"Count Schaffgotsch's location trip, 1936." Averell and Marie Harriman and daughter Mary, and William and Dorothy Paley, February 1936, first look at Ketchum.

woodstove, surrounded by much of Ketchum's population, to see if he could live up to his promise to bring Harriman to their town. The count gave the party a tour around the valley, pointing out the terrain on Dollar Mountain, the quality and quantity of the snow, and the mountains that protected the valley. Harriman later described his reaction:

> *I remember very vividly getting out of the car and putting on my skis, skiing into Sun Valley on this powder snow. . . . The most beautiful view of Sun Valley! Can you imagine? There wasn't . . . a ranch house in the middle of it, which you could see. And there were all the mountains and Baldy in the background and the hills covered with snow. And I fell in love with the place then and there.*

Harriman returned to New York after a few days, anxious to start the process to build his resort so it could open by next ski season.[9]

The Community Library has several pictures labeled "Count Schaffgotsch's location trip, 1936," with no more information. One shows two men and women skiing, another shows the party resting. These could be Averell Harriman and his daughter Mary and Bill Paley and his wife when they visited the site.

4

HARRIMAN BEGINS A FAST-TRACK PROCESS TO ACQUIRE PROPERTY, PLAN A SKI RESORT, AND CONVINCE THE UNION PACIFIC BOARD TO APPROVE HIS PROJECT

Showing the control Harriman had over Union Pacific's board, he immediately began the process of building his ski resort when he returned from Idaho, not waiting for the board's approval, which came on May 5, 1936, according to Abramson:

> *Without even waiting for their formal endorsement, he sent in land agents to start negotiations for property. He also hired Steve Hannagan, the public relations man who would make the valley outside Ketchum famous. . . . Union Pacific executives, having said all they prudently could to temper the chairman's excitement, loyally fell into step, with Harriman and Hannagan setting a fast pace.*

Beginning in late February, Harriman moved at lightning speed, committing Union Pacific money to the project. "From then on the preliminaries of the building of Sun Valley moved with a swiftness unbelievable to the easy-going residents of the region," according to Dorice Taylor. The resort was planned, land acquired, and the lodge and ski lifts constructed in the wilderness of Idaho between March and December 1935, a tribute to Harriman's leadership and the capabilities of Union Pacific engineers.

Harriman decided to purchase the Brass Ranch during his visit. On February 20, 1935, he directed E.M. Sawyer, a U.P. lawyer in Salt Lake City, to obtain clear title to the Brass Ranch in Idaho,

> *for my personal account but in name of nominee on basis indicated. Purchase to be inclusive of all real estate, water and range rights. Satisfactory to make contract with present owners permitting them to continue operations for two years reserving unrestricted right to us to build one or more hotels and in addition residences and business buildings, or sell or lease all or any portion of land to others for similar purposes, subject of course, to their right to farm unused area.*

Harriman did his due diligence for the prospective ski resort, investigating the economics of the sport of skiing and seeking advice from people involved in the ski industry.

According to Holland, Harriman wrote the assistant secretary of commerce in February 1936 seeking information about the importation and manufacture of ski equipment the prior five years. "I want to learn how rapid the growth of the sport has been . . . and in what parts of the country it has become most popular," he wrote. In 1931, the production of skis and snowshoes totaled $163,032. Harriman realized only a small group of people skied, which in the East was done on narrow and icy slopes, with no ski resorts in the West. Ski trains were started in parts of the country in the mid-1930s to stimulate passenger traffic.

Harriman initially consulted with Roland Palmedo, a polo-playing friend and successful investment banker who was the founder of the Amateur Ski Club of New York, helped organize the first women's international ski team in 1934, and was the prime organizer of the 1936 Women's Olympic team. Harriman sought his advice about the possibility of a ski resort in Idaho:

> *Roland thought skiers would never travel to such a remote area and advised against the idea. Roland believed in rustic, nature-based ski areas, while Harriman believed in luxury and glitz, as well as business for his company.*

Harriman was not dissuaded and sought the advice of others with long experience in the ski industry who ended up playing critical roles at Sun Valley: Charles N. Proctor and John E.P. Morgan.

Charles N. Proctor's father, Charles A. Proctor, was a professor at Dartmouth College and advisor to the school's Outing Club. He helped organize the country's first downhill championships in 1933 and the first national downhill and slalom championships on Mount Rainier in 1935. Charles N. was captain of the Dartmouth ski team in 1927 and a member of the 1928 U.S. Olympic team, competing in cross-country and jumping. He coached Harvard's ski team, was in charge of ski trail design for the Forest Service, working at Cannon Mountain and Pinkham Notch, and ran a ski store in Boston. Proctor had been a judge for the championships on Mount Rainier in 1935. Harriman asked Proctor to gather information about skiing in the United States and later hired him to help lay out the ski runs and lifts at Sun Valley, paying him $300 per month plus expenses. After working at Sun Valley, Proctor became manager of the Badger Pass Ski Area at Yosemite in 1938, retiring in the 1960s. Charles N. Proctor was inducted into the U.S. Ski and Snowboard Hall of Fame in 1959 and Charles A. in 1966.

John E.P. Morgan was an avid skier and hockey player after World War I and an administrator of the 1932 Lake Placid Olympics. Klein described Morgan as a "fellow banker" of Harriman's. Morgan later helped form the National Ski Patrol and worked with the National Ski Association, and along with Charles "Minnie" Dole, helped convince the U.S. Army to start training mountain troops in 1940, which led to the formation of the 10th Mountain Division. Morgan was inducted into the U.S. Ski and Snowboard Hall of Fame in 1972.

On March 2, 1936, Harriman wrote Charles N. Proctor at his Boston store, Ski Sports Inc., saying, "I am anxious to have you see our new ski country," and he would arrange a time for him to visit in the next few weeks. He was making "a quantity and quality analysis of our market," and asked if Proctor knew the number of ski clubs in the country and the number of members in the clubs. He also wanted an indication of the "comparative popularity of the sport in various parts of the country and the income groups from which its followers come." Proctor contacted his associates at the 1935 Rainier tournament, asking for information about skiing in the Northwest.

John E.P. Morgan's report to Harriman of April 3, 1936, said the success or failure of a destination ski resort in the West was "completely unknown and unpredictable," since there was nothing in this country to compare it with, according to Holland. "The two factors greatly in its favor are the rapid growth of skiing and winter sports in the country, plus the reported perfection of the location. The existence and cooperation of a large railroad organization should be most helpful." The ski industry was booming in the Seattle area, where there were around 15,000 pairs of skis and 20 ski clubs.

Harriman made sure that work proceeded in several arenas at once.

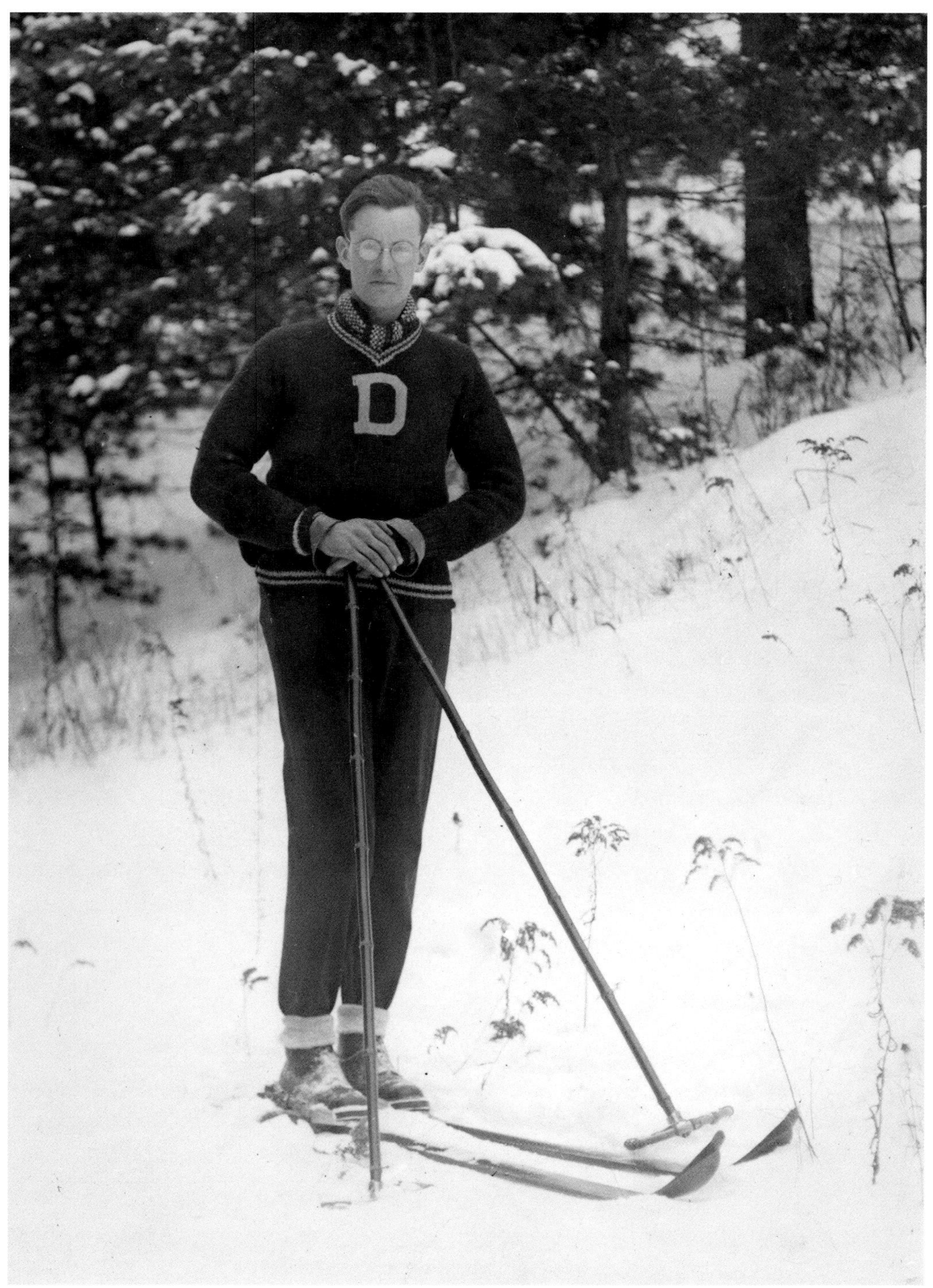

Charles Proctor at Dartmouth, 1927. *Courtesy of Peggy Proctor Dean.*

First, in New York, he played the role of commander in chief. He hired Morgan and Proctor to work with U.P. engineers on logistical planning for the new resort and used U.P. lawyers to buy property. He hired a core team for his project: Steve Hannagan, a successful New York publicist known for turning a sandbar into Miami Beach; architect Gilbert Stanley Underwood to design the Sun Valley Lodge; and J.V. McNeil Company of Los Angeles to be general contractor. He worked with Union Pacific staff in Omaha and pushed the Union Pacific board to accept his plan for a ski resort.

Second, Harriman sent his team to Ketchum, where Morgan, Proctor, Count Schaffgotsch, and U.P engineers examined the land, laid out plans for the lodge, surveyed areas for skiing, and determined ski lift locations.

Third, in Omaha, Harriman had U.P. engineers analyze alternatives for ski lifts, eventually inventing the chairlift.[10]

Land Is Purchased for Sun Valley Resort

On March 25, 1936, the Union Pacific Land Company obtained title to the Brass Ranch, paying $39,000, or just under $10 an acre.

The *Hailey Times* of March 26, 1936, said Union Pacific purchased the 3,888-acre Brass Ranch. "Among those interested are a number of Union Pacific officials, but it is generally understood that the company, as a corporation, is not financially interested."

The Union Pacific Land Company, the railroad's Nebraska subsidiary, was the purchaser, although the land was subsequently transferred to Union Pacific. Three deeds were involved. Appendix A contains a description of all the land acquisitions for Sun Valley.

The first deed, dated April 23, 1936, included 908.41 acres in sections 5, 7, 8, and 18, together with 1,250 inches of water rights from Trail Creek with a priority date of April 25, 1881, and 325 inches of Trail Creek water rights with a priority date of October 5, 1883. These water rights were originally obtained by I.I. Lewis, an early pioneer, for his farm on Trail Creek. This parcel abutted the town of Ketchum and was where the Sun Valley Lodge and Dollar Mountain were located.

A second deed, dated May 1, 1936, included 2,480 acres in Sections 5, 8, 9, 17, and 20, "subject to the Aerial Tramway of the Hailey Triumph mines." Brass had

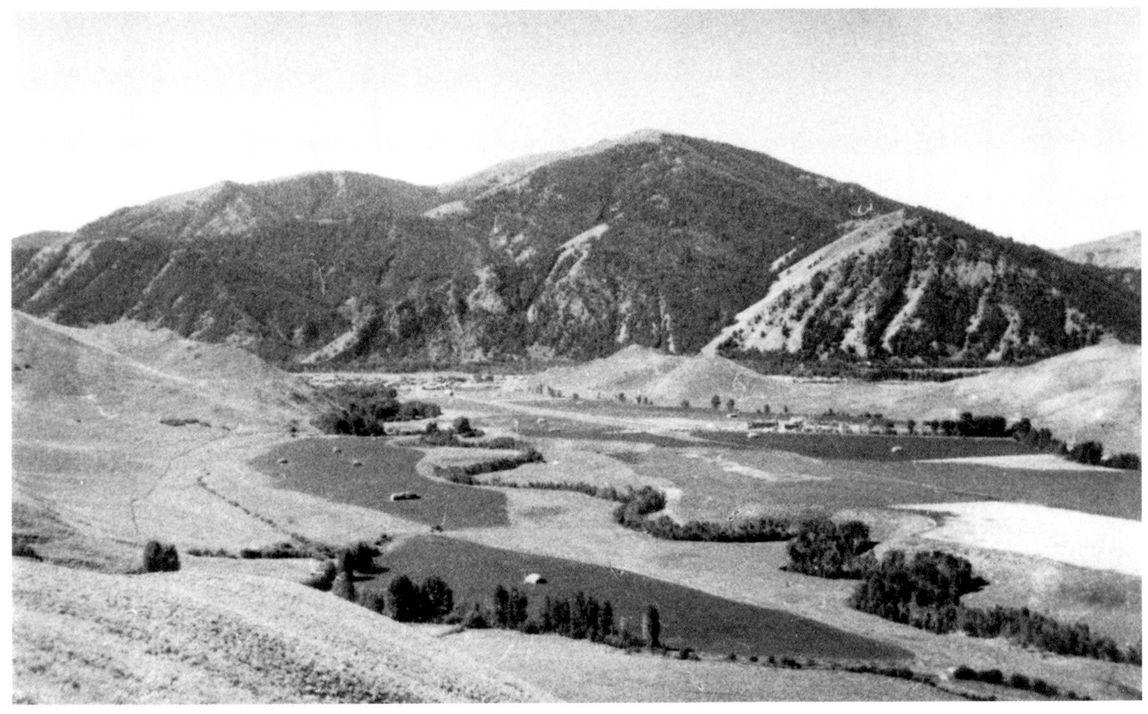

Brass Ranch with Ketchum and Bald Mountain in the background, mid-1930s.

use of the land for two years, which was "not to interfere with the buildings and other improvements contemplated by the purchasers."

A third deed dated April 23, 1936, included platted lots in Ketchum: lots 1, 2, 3, and 4 on Block 100; lots 1, 2, 3, and 4 on Block 101; lots 1, 2, 3, and 4 on Block 102; and lots 5, 6, 7, and 8 on Block 87. On July 16, 1936, the Union Land Company bought lots 5 and 6 in Block 44 in Ketchum from the estate of Fred Howe for $435. It is not clear how the railroad planned to use these lots.

Two problems soon arose. First, as Dorice Taylor described, when "the stakes for the lodge were driven, the builders found half of the building was off the 3,881 acres purchased for the resort. The Ketchum Livestock Association obligingly sold an additional 40 acres, and Count Felix had the lodge where he wanted it." In addition to the 40 acres, Union Pacific purchased two rights of way from the association, one for a water line to the lodge site, and the second for a "balloon track" at the depot to permit trains to turn around. The second problem was that the planned route of the ski lift on Dollar Mountain went over land being homesteaded by James A. Grimm. After investigating other routes, it was determined the location selected by U.P. chief engineer Glen Trout and Proctor was "excellent and much superior to anything else available." U.P. obtained an easement over

Grimm's land to permit operation of the Dollar chairlift, so long as it did not interfere with the cultivation of his land. In exchange, the railroad built a rustic 24-foot-by-25-foot cabin for Grimm, with a kitchen, bath, dressing room, and living room, costing $600–700. Grimm agreed to remove "existing unsightly facilities" from his land. Union Pacific subsequently purchased 96.74 acres from Grimm in July 1940 and 260 acres from Eleanor E. Grimm on January 28, 1948, for $22,000.

The 1938 map in the color insert following page 256 shows land owned by Union Pacific or "the Union Land Company" in sections 5, 7, 8, 9, 17, and 18, Township 4N, Range 18 E, and in section 21. Land owned by James Grimm on Dollar Mountain is shown in sections 7, 18, 19, and 20. The map shows Union Pacific–owned sections 5, 8, 9, and 17, where Dollar Mountain is located, part of section 7, where the lodge is located, and portions of sections 20 and 21, through which the road leading into Elkhorn ran. A section of land contains 640 acres.

The map on the facing page is the original Ketchum plat map from the 1880s, which shows the lots purchased by Union Pacific in 1936, highlighted on the right side.

As part of the purchase of the Brass Ranch, Union Pacific acquired Brass's sheep and Forest Service grazing permit. Harriman directed Howard C. Mann, U.P.'s vice president in charge of operations, to obtain a new permit to keep out small sheep owners who might obtain the grazing rights, and make arrangements with "some reliable sheep man" for the sheep operation. Harriman discussed the issue with John P. "Jack" Lane, owner of Lane Mercantile in Ketchum, who had a sheep ranch between Shoshone and Jerome known as Box L, with grazing rights adjacent to Brass on Corral Creek, east of Ketchum. Lane agreed to care for the railroad's sheep until they were taken to market. John Peavey, who owns Flat Top Ranch in the Little Wood River drainage, later obtained the Lane Ranch grazing rights on Corral Creek.[11]

Steve Hannagan is Hired as Publicity Agent

Hiring Steve Hannagan as Sun Valley's publicist was a stroke of genius by Averell Harriman.

By 1936, Hannagan was a successful pioneer of public relations who created innovative publicity campaigns for a number of institutions and individuals. Beginning in 1917, he promoted events such as the Indianapolis 500 race and worked with Eddie Rickenbacker, Henry Ford, Jack Dempsey, and Walter Winchell. He was best

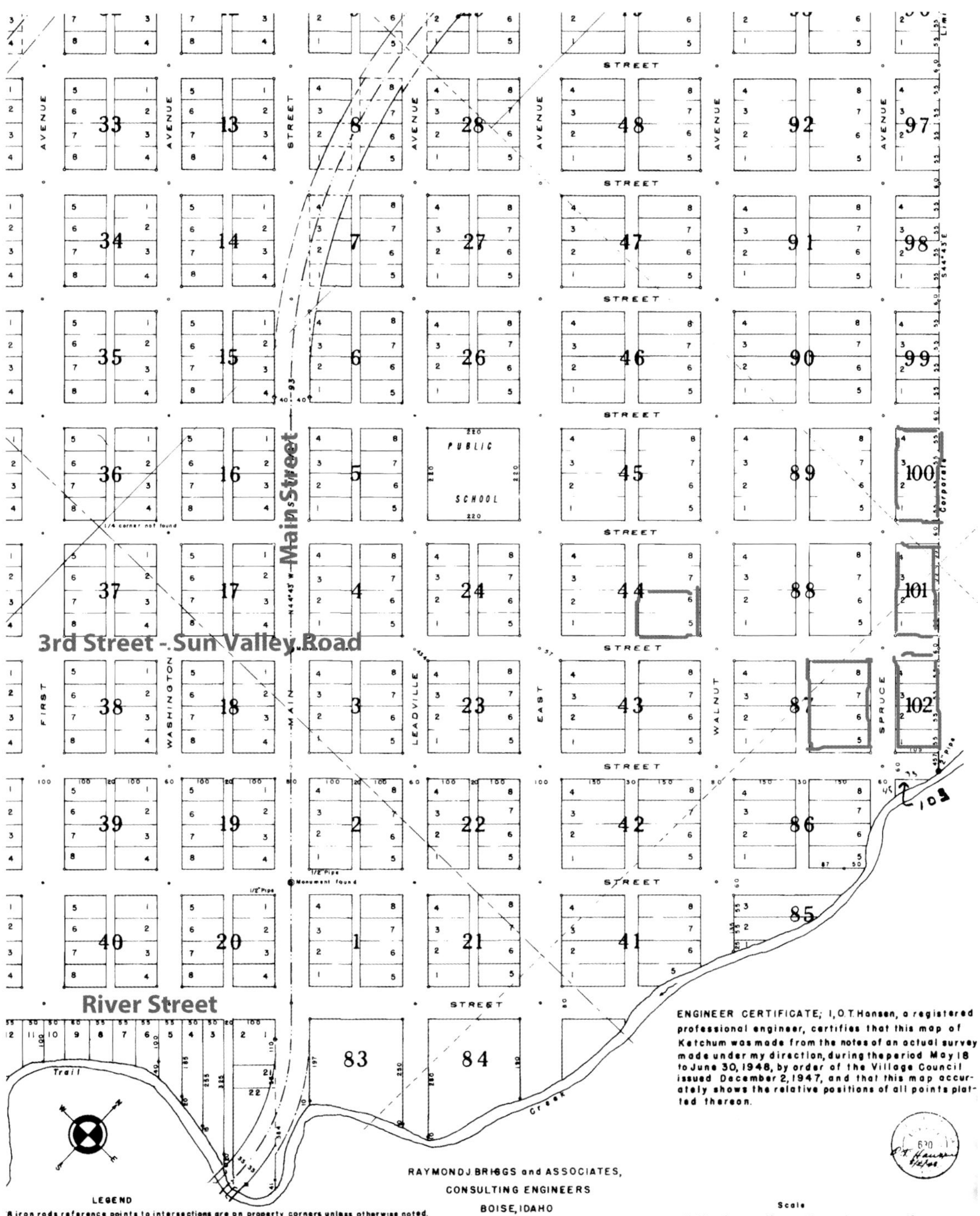

Main Street
3rd Street - Sun Valley Road
River Street
PUBLIC SCHOOL
FIRST
WASHINGTON
MAIN
LEADVILLE
EAST
WALNUT
SPRUCE
AVENUE
STREET
Trail
Creek
1/4 corner not found
Monument found
ENGINEER CERTIFICATE; I, O.T. Hansen, a registered professional engineer, certifies that this map of Ketchum was made from the notes of an actual survey made under my direction, during the period May 18 to June 30, 1948, by order of the Village Council issued December 2, 1947, and that this map accurately shows the relative positions of all points plotted thereon.
RAYMOND J. BRIGGS and ASSOCIATES,
CONSULTING ENGINEERS
BOISE, IDAHO
LEGEND
8 iron rods reference points to intersections are on property corners unless otherwise noted.
Scale

known for changing Miami Beach from a mosquito-infested swamp into an exclusive playground for the rich. Part of his work involved trying to get Al Capone to move out of Miami Beach, fearing the gangster's presence would compromise residents' safety and depress property values.

In 1947, *Collier's* called Hannagan the "Prince of Press Agents," according to biographer Michael K. Townsley. Hannagan knew and worked with the rich and famous of the time, and he pioneered many modern publicity techniques.

In March 1936, Harriman sent Hannagan, Morgan, and Proctor to Idaho to work on his project, along with key Union Pacific personnel including vice president Bill Jeffers, U.P. chief engineer H.C. Mann, and local chief engineer Glen Trout.

Jeffers and Hannagan traveled by train to Ketchum and toured the area in a sleigh equipped with a wood-burning stove. According to Dorice Taylor, Hannagan was used to sunny Miami, hated the cold, and said, "We looked around . . . and all I could see was just a godforsaken field of snow. . . . This is ridiculous." However, as they walked around, the sun came out and it warmed up. Hannagan took off his vest when he began to sweat and realized that when the temperature warmed, the snow didn't melt. He had his idea for a publicity theme and named the new resort "Sun Valley" to downplay the snowy weather and emphasize warmth. He came up with the idea of using a picture of a skier stripped to the waist, with the slogan, "Winter Sports under a Summer Sun." (See image in color insert.)

Hannagan's memorandum to Harriman of March 28, 1936, laid out his vision to make the resort a successful venture for the railroad and "a memorable experience for guests," and became the blueprint for the resort:

> *Frankly, I was disappointed by my first impressions. But it is a location that grows on one. The climate is ideal. The geographical surroundings are entrancing. When it came time to leave I wanted to remain longer. Following discussions with winter sports minded people in various parts of the country, I find that there is a need for such a sports center. . . . From the standpoint of availability, Ketchum is not the most ideal spot. On the other hand, it may be just as well . . . to have the resort isolated. Certainly it makes it controllable.*
>
> *The resort must not be just another ski mountain like those in the East. It has to have European cachet, smart people, vivacious celebrities, and an elegant ease that would motivate people to travel by train across the country in mid-winter to an isolated town where flat land vanished and all roads went uphill.*

> *This is one city in which roughing it must be a luxury. It may seem isolated, rustic, Continental. But it must have every modern convenience. It is not enough to build a hotel and then mark with flags and signs the things you propose to do in time to come. You must do these things and have them in operation when the hotel opens.*

Hannagan had specific recommendations for the resort's amenities:

> *There should be an ice skating rink. There should be a glass walled but open hot water pool. . . .*
>
> *People like to leave the hotel. Nearby there might be a billiard parlor. And a bowling alley. And certainly a motion picture show. Mechanical devices must be installed to take people to the top of the mountain. It will be necessary to make it nationally known quickly. This needs to be done with unusual pictures showing the unusual climate of Idaho . . . skiing in shirts skinned to the waist, bathing . . . in the open. If society people or celebrities are attractive enough and elastic enough to be models in these pictures—well good.*

Hannagan convinced Harriman that he had to think big. "If you build a luxury resort in the wilderness, that will be news." Union Pacific, he said, should build a million-dollar resort for 250 guests, in a facility that looked traditional but had the conveniences and sophistication of the best hotels. Starting a $1 million luxury hotel where the glamorous and famous would go and become part of the attraction, exuding robust health and vigorous exercise in the sun and snow, would create much more publicity for the railroad.

> *If it is not done on this scale it should not be done at all. . . . It would be my hope to make every newspaper and magazine reader, every theater goer, every radio listener conscious that there is a great winter sports resort in America—a resort more colorful, modern, more exclusive than any other in all the world.*

Hannagan believed the key to establishing a chic image for Sun Valley was to use celebrities, attractive women, Olympic stars, and monied families from all over. They should be invited to Sun Valley and photographed utilizing the resort's facilities, which would appear in local newspapers all over the country.

> *Imagine, swimming pictures—with snow-capped mountains in the background. . . . It is my opinion Sun Valley can be made into an exclusive winter sports resort which will capture the interest of all of everything that is winter sports just as Florida has become synonymous with a summer vacation in winter.*[12]

Architect Gilbert Stanley Underwood Is Hired

Harriman did not hesitate when selecting a person to design his new ski lodge, hiring architect Gilbert Stanley Underwood, who had a long association with Union Pacific.

After graduating from college, Underwood opened an office in Los Angeles in 1923, where he became associated with Daniel Hull of the National Park Service. Hull recommended Underwood to the Utah Parks Company, a subsidiary of Union Pacific formed in 1923, to develop facilities in national parks served by its trains. Utah Parks was a concessionaire for the National Park Service and owned and operated tourist facilities, restaurants, lodging, and bus tours in parks and national monuments, many designed by Underwood. These included the exquisitely designed Escalante Hotel in Cedar City, Utah, where its "circle loop tour" of Utah parks began. Underwood designed lodge complexes for Utah Parks at Cedar Breaks National Monument, Zion National Park, Bryce Canyon National Park, the North Rim of Grand Canyon National Park, and the Ahwahnee Hotel at Yosemite National Park (1925–1927), his best known. Underwood's buildings were done in the Rustic style of architecture, and his national park hotels are listed in the National Register of Historic Places.

Underwood also designed Union Pacific railroad depots in the late 1920s and early 1930s, in Topeka, Kansas, (Great Overland Station, 1927); Lund, Utah, 1927 (demolished 1970); Abilene, Kansas, 1929; Marysville, Kansas, 1929; Gering, Nebraska, 1929; Shoshone, Idaho, 1929; Greeley, Colorado, 1930; and the Art Deco Union Pacific home office and railroad complex (Union Station) in Omaha, Nebraska.

In 1932, the Depression caused Underwood to close his office and go to work for the Federal Architect's Project, where he was prohibited from doing work not related to his government office. However, Harriman's offer to design a magnificent lodge for a new ski resort was too good to pass up. Underwood accepted the commission without telling his boss, Engleburt Reynolds, and assembled a crew to work secretly at his home in the

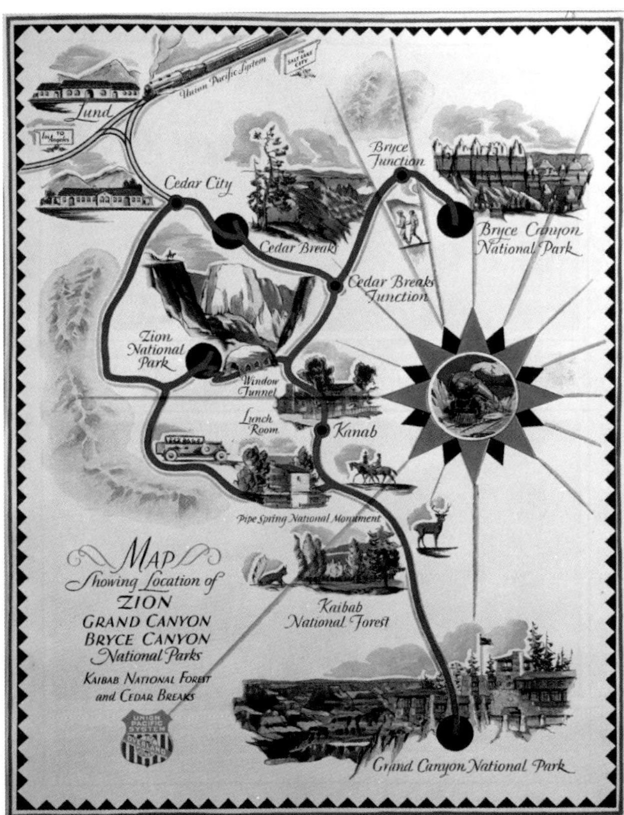

Map of Union Pacific's Utah Parks Division, formed in 1923 to operate bus tours from Lund, Utah, and hotels in Zion, Bryce, and Grand Canyon.

basement. Underwood had to plead illness so he could stay away from his government job to supervise his crew, making his superior concerned about his health. According to Underwood biographer Joyce Zaitlin, "What Reynolds said when the completed lodge and its architect received a great deal of publicity at a later date has not been recorded."

The Sun Valley Lodge had little in common with Underwood's Rustic-style national park hotels. It was to offer the latest in modern luxury to

> *appeal to wealthy and glamorous patrons, especially personalities from the theatrical and film world. . . . The lodge was organized along the lines of Harriman's instructions, which were to provide visitors with a vast and spectacular view of the skating rink . . . and the gentle slopes beyond.*

Underwood also designed Sun Valley's Challenger Inn and Village in 1937. After his work at Sun Valley, he was hired by John D. Rockefeller to reconstruct Colonial Williamsburg in Virginia and design the lodge at Jackson Lake, Wyoming. The Sun Valley Lodge resembled the Timberline Lodge at Mount Hood, Oregon, for which Underwood had done the preliminary design, with a central core for public spaces with guest rooms angularly attached to it. Timberline opened in February 1938 and cost over $1 million, representing the high point of federal assistance to the ski industry.

Underwood coordinated the design for the Sun Valley Lodge with Harriman and prepared plans working with U.P. architect Bill Wellman. On March 19, 1936, Underwood wrote Howard Mann, saying he had an "intensive conference" with Harriman and his associates and was working on a plan that expressed their ideas. He warned, "their ideas, by the way, are not cheap," in a masterpiece of understatement. He was preparing a 1/16th scale model for Harriman. The hotel would be based on a wing plan, set to get the most sun possible, with the ability to build extensions if needed and have 100 percent baths and large, sunny rooms.

Work proceeded at full speed. By early April, Underwood had sent Harriman his preliminary plans. On April 13, Harriman asked H.C. Mann to prepare cost estimates based on Underwood's plans, since Harriman decided to have Union Pacific handle the contracts and inspect the work. American Radiator Co. was asked to submit layouts and cost estimates for the plumbing and heating work. Harriman requested budgets for the kitchen, restaurants, furniture, furnishings, and fixtures for the lodge and estimated costs for water, roads, sewage disposal, light, and power. He also wanted to know "the time it would take to construct, equip and complete it ready for operation in accordance with Underwood's plans."

J.V. McNeil Company Is Hired as General Contractor

J.V. McNeil Construction Co. of Los Angeles was hired to build the Sun Valley Lodge. The company was established in 1886 and had experience with many types of commercial construction.

On May 19, 1936, J.V. McNeil Company sent a proposal to U.P. chief engineer Howard Mann, agreeing to build the Ketchum lodge in accordance with plans and specifications furnished by the company. They would receive a fixed fee of $25,000, payable in seven equal monthly installments, with the first due on July 1, 1936. Union Pacific would provide free transportation for men, equipment, and materials. Completion and opening of the lodge would be on or before December 15, 1936. Subcontractors had to be approved by Union Pacific and paid directly by them. The lodge was to be a fire resistant, reinforced concrete structure with an exterior appearance of timber achieved by pouring concrete on rough pine boards. A service garage and swimming pool would be built along with the hotel.[13]

5

HARRIMAN AND FRIENDS PLAN THE SUN VALLEY RESORT

Not long after Averell Harriman returned to New York in late February 1936, he sent his team of Count Schaffgotsch, Charles Proctor, John E.P. Morgan, and Union Pacific personnel to Ketchum to work on the details of developing his ski area. Roberta Brass took them around on her homemade skis, while they used their modern ones. Local newspapers reported on their activities with great interest. Harriman's team determined the location for the lodge and the locations and layouts for the chairlifts. They explored the area surrounding Ketchum for suitable hills for backcountry skiing, going over Galena Summit to the north, east into the Boulder and Pioneer Mountains, and as far south as the East Fork of the Big Wood River. This was done as Union Pacific engineers were working with the architect and contractor to stage the huge construction project that would begin as soon as the snow melted.

When Count Felix Schaffgotsch and his friend Count Hans Erwein Graf Wilczek arrived in Idaho in March, Schaffgotsch was interviewed by local papers. Articles appeared in the *Idaho Statesman* on March 22, 1936, "Austrian Count to Build Winter Resort in Idaho," and in the *Hailey Times* of March 26, "Ketchum Hills Selected for Ideal Winter Playground Site, Brass Farm Taken Over for Sports." This was, according to the articles, "a decision that had been anxiously awaited" since the count first visited, "reconnoitering for a location for a winter playground."

The *Hailey Times* said Schaffgotsch and "about 10 others" purchased the Brass Ranch to make "the spot and surrounding territory comparable to anything in Austria." The

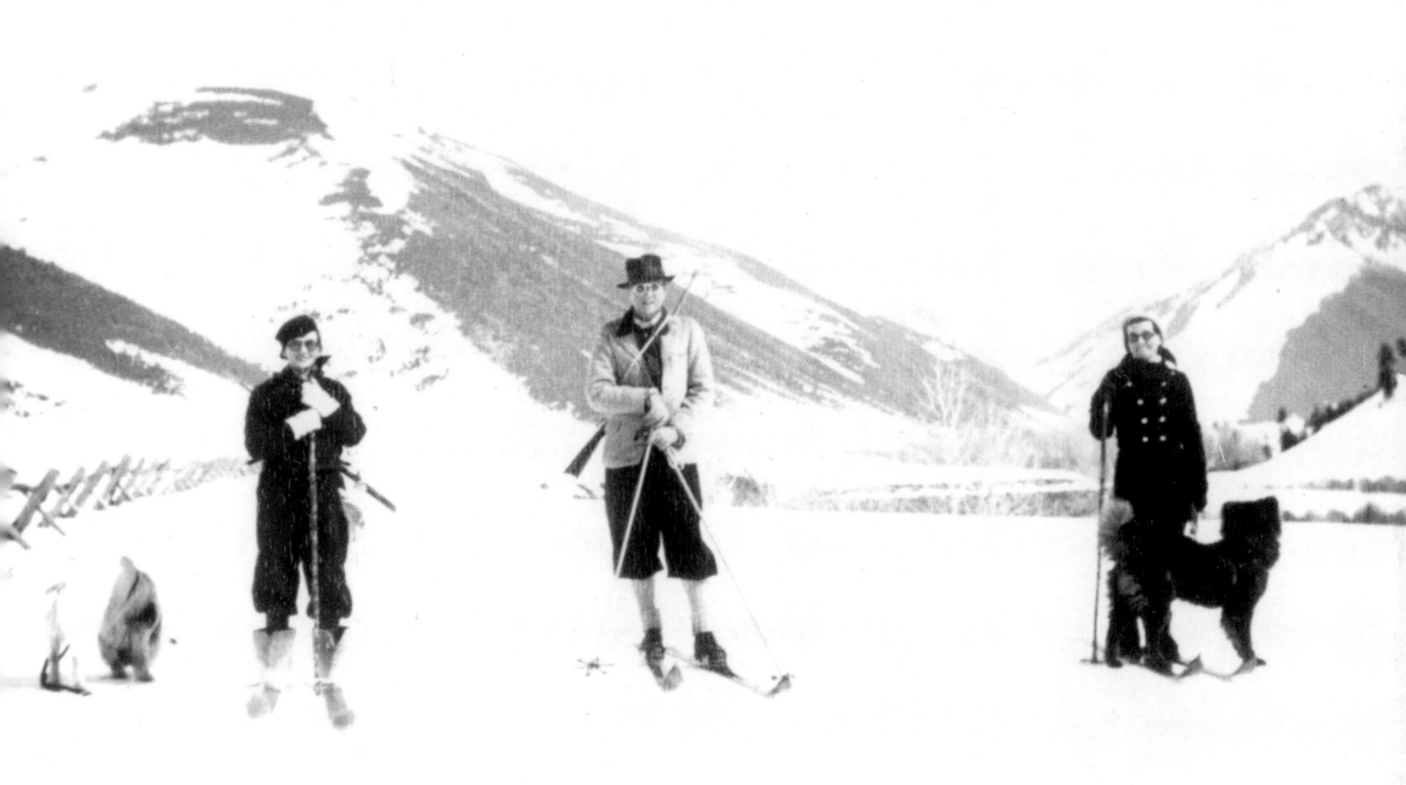

Count Schaffgotsch's March 1936 survey of Ketchum, with his friend Count Wilczek and the Brass sisters on Brass Ranch.

hotel, it reported, would be rustic in design on the outside and deluxe on the inside. Plans called for a 120-room hotel that could be enlarged to be "one of the most beautiful winter playgrounds in the United States" and one of national prominence.

Harriman directed Charles Proctor "to transform locals into ski instructors—as they did in Europe—rather than bringing in outsiders." Proctor arrived in Ketchum on March 25, staying at the Bald Mountain Hot Springs Lodge.

On March 26, the *Hailey Times* said Proctor was teaching Ketchum and Hailey boys to ski. He took them on daily hikes "up the mountains overlooking the ranch and puts them through their paces," so when the resort opened, they could work as instructors and guides. Modern ski equipment (skis, metal bindings, leather boots, and double poles) were shipped to Ketchum so the locals could learn new skiing techniques. Nine young men between 16 and 21 quit school and skied for 33 consecutive days, from 7:00 to 11 a.m. (except Easter Sunday). They included Donald Wilson, Junior Read, Fred Board, and Jimmy Glenn from Hailey and Jack Majors, Bill Price, Marvin Obenchain, Tom Reid, and David Brandt of Ketchum.

Proctor's students skied the back side of Dollar Mountain facing Ketchum, so people could see them. The *Hailey Times* said that on weekends, spectators came from Hailey and Twin Falls to watch:

> *It is surprising how quickly information of Ketchum's good fortune spread and how spontaneous the response. Sunday, a veritable cascade of lower country motorists, laden with skiis, passed through Hailey on their way to Idaho's future winter playground. . . . It's an inspiring sight to watch these young athletes come streaking down the snow-covered hills above the town, swerving and turning in graceful arcs on the precipitous descent. . . . Practically everyone has skiis strapped to his shoes and the continual ascent and descent of the sport lovers is remindful of a sugar loaf bespeckled with busy ants.*

As Proctor's students improved, they "ventured into more difficult terrain, climbing up Cold Springs Canyon on Bald Mountain, past the future site of the Roundhouse," according to the paper. Proctor took one class to Elkhorn Gulch to make movies demonstrating proper skiing techniques. They went up Baldy several times, once with Proctor's wife, Mary, who was in Ketchum during her spring vacation, "to the horror of the local people." She become "the first woman to ski down Baldy." As snow around Ketchum receded, "Charley and his boys explored the higher elevations at Galena," where Proctor recorded "valuable information on snow conditions, vertical drop, weather and terrain."

On April 27, Proctor sent Harriman a "Report on the Boys' Skiing." He wrote: "Generally speaking, the boys did very well as a group. They all worked very hard with one exception, and kept at it with enthusiasm till the end." The last 10 days, they skied between 6:45 and 11:00 a.m., and drove up the valley for 17 miles. There were three top skiers, with the others described as "stiff and awkward," "too young," lacking "serious interest in learning," "not coordinated well," and "very poor and awkward." Harriman approved selling the ski equipment to the boys at cost. Proctor arranged with

Count Schaffgotsch to have his ski films shown to New England ski clubs and inserted captions advertising Sun Valley.

Proctor's work with the local kids paid off. When Sun Valley opened in December 1936, its publicity said,

> *Young men who have grown up with the Sawtooth Mountains as their back yard and are thoroughly familiar with the mountain country have been trained by Charles N. Proctor, noted New England skier, as guides for ski parties making extended ski tours to the sportiest slopes of the Sawtooth range.*

In late March, John E.P. Morgan, Schaffgotsch, Proctor, and Glen Trout, chief engineer of the local Union Pacific line, scouted the area around Ketchum to determine the best locations for the lodge, ski runs, and ski lifts.

Roberta Brass took Proctor on horseback around the ranch, going to what the locals called Back Pay Mountain. Proctor liked the mountain and decided to make it one of the resort's ski hills. Proctor, Morgan, and Trout agreed that the mountains closest to the lodge (Dollar and Back Pay) were the best to develop for skiing since they were not too steep. Morgan asked Proctor if they could name Back Pay Mountain after him, and he reluctantly agreed. They examined Bald Mountain but rejected it as a ski site. At 9,200 feet, it was considered too high, and there were few skiers in the country who could handle its steep slopes, terrain, and elevation. They discussed different kinds of ski lifts, including trams, rope tows, and the Upski sled used at Yosemite.

On March 30, Proctor told Harriman, "Sun Valley seems to me to offer about all any skier could desire in the way of weather, snow & terrain," and provided weather information he got from the locals:

> *There are only occasional severe storms with wind. . . . From what the local boys tell me, the snow is excellent during the winter. . . The terrain looks ideal for touring. . . . In fact I have never seen anything that looked any better even at this late season. There are more runs and more variety than any place I have ever seen.*

He provided information from the U.S. Geodetic Survey about the height of local mountains. "Judging from my very brief acquaintance with the Sun Valley country, I should say it provides as excellent a combination of weather, snow & terrain as could be found anywhere." There was a need, he said, "for a rail funicular to some high country nearby." The boys he was teaching to ski "are a fine bunch & should make good guides & teachers."

Steve Hannagan sent his first memo to Harriman naming the resort on March 28, 1936, yet on March 30, as seen here, Proctor was already calling the resort "Sun Valley," and talking about building a "rail funicular."

U.P. vice president W.A. Jeffers went to Ketchum in April to review plans for the new resort. On April 11, he told Harriman he toured the area by car with chief engineer H.C. Mann, Sawyer and Smith, John E.P. Morgan, and Steve Hannagan. There was still 20–24 inches of fine snow at Ketchum. They were considering using hot spring water for a swimming pool, and Sawyer was negotiating with Carl Brant, owner of Bald Mountain Hot Springs Lodge, about "getting control of the Hot Springs." Morgan and Mann inspected the proposed hotel location. Idaho had restrictive liquor laws that prohibited the sale of liquor by the drink. However, they met with Idaho's governor and local senator Rockwell and reported, "With respect to the liquor question. . . . There will in my opinion be no difficulty of any kind or character . . . if [we] refrain from opening bar which I understand is not contemplated." Jeffers said a winter and summer resort could be developed with the right publicity: "There seems to be no doubt as to the success of the undertaking." Jeffers approved a plan to be released "so construction work may be undertaken."

On April 15, 1936, Harriman asked Proctor to provide U.P. engineers with his description of a "proposed location for hoist on Proctor Mountain and best location for ski tow practice hill . . . to give company engineers idea of desired objective in surveying possibilities." Proctor spent four days with U.P. engineers "working over the tramway sites," and he and Trout secured "a suitable profile for an aerial tramway up Proctor Mountain," just east of Trail Creek. When they surveyed the practice hill (Dollar), they found that the upper tower for the first location on Trout's map was not on Brass Ranch property. However, it was the best route because it opened the country on the low range over to Elkhorn Creek, offering more skiing territory. Trout proposed a second route if there was any trouble over property.

Count Schaffgotsch had identified sites around Ketchum for backcountry skiing. On April 15, Harriman asked Proctor to investigate those sites thoroughly, including skiing on the pass above Galena and at an area up the East Fork Road past the Triumph Mine.

On April 26 and 27, Proctor wrote Morgan, who had returned to New York, summarizing his explorations: Galena "had short runs and lots of trees," and the area above Galena was not particularly practical for skiing and was inferior to that near Ketchum. He identified interesting country near Baker Creek for practice runs. He explored an area in the Boulder Mountains, 12 miles north of Ketchum, and found a course five and a half miles from the road with a steep, hazardous descent of 4,200 feet that would attract national champions. The area had "a real possibility of getting fairly high by road," and was "very well suited for later development. . . . Most people will prefer to try the hills near the hotel but champions want a course that challenges their ability. Well, the one on Boulder will have everything."

An area east of North Fork had three runs, each with a descent of 4,200 feet. Areas up Lake Creek and Eagle Creek had not been thoroughly explored. The mountains east of Ketchum were "too steep and avalanche prone." An area Schaffgotsch favored above Elkhorn Creek was "too far from the lodge on a bad road." The area beyond the Triumph Mine on the East Fork of the Big Wood was "fine territory," but was not superior to the area around Proctor Mountain. Mount Baldy offered a tremendous variety of terrain, dropping off into the valley at every direction, but it was too advanced for the average skier. Proctor also explored areas east up Trail Creek and Corral Creek, north to Stanley Basin, Sun Beam Dam, and a number of lakes at the foot of the "Saw Tooth Mountains."

In late April, Morgan sent Harriman a memo analyzing the costs to operate a ski lodge in Idaho. Ketchum offered "unusual opportunities for the development of a ski and winter sport lodge not as yet in existence in this country." It was not a weekend resort but a vacation place where facilities needed to be available to entertain guests over a continued period. He had confidence in the location, as skiing conditions had been checked by a number of people. Hot springs, fishing, shooting, and beautiful country were attractions for visitors. It needed a modern hotel "with every facility for fine service and entertainment, along with ski tows, ski lifts or hoists to higher altitudes, swimming pool, skating rink, and a ski jump." It would cost $650,000 to construct the hotel, and all necessary developments could "probably be carried out at a capital investment not to exceed $1,000,000."

Morgan provided a projection of revenues and expenses, which were reasonable expectations of operations "if the hotel is operated for a four-month winter season," based on 60 percent average capacity. Better than 80 percent average use could be attained if the group he discussed later in the memo "secured the patronage which the hotel is designed to serve." Summer operations warranted further consideration. Morgan included operational costs for a staff of 89 and a hotel with 100 double and 20 single rooms, along with administrators, credit manager, five-piece orchestra, doctor and nurses, and other staff.

Morgan proposed that as an alternative to having Union Pacific operate the ski resort, a wealthy group of sportsmen be organized to provide capital for the project and operate it. It appears Morgan had a specific group of sportsmen in mind, as he offered to negotiate with them immediately:

> *Another method of operation has been suggested to which you might wish to give some consideration. A group of sportsmen might be organized who would be primarily interested in assisting to develop Ketchum as a winter sports resort. If a satisfactory contract could be secured from the Railroad for a group to rent and operate the properties and participate in the profits, the necessary working capital could probably be secured. Such a group would lend a sporting atmosphere to the situation and if properly organized, could secure the cooperation of their friends in bringing about a successful venture.*

Harriman was urged to make a decision quickly so the resort could be opened for the 1936–1937 season. "Negotiations may be entered into with the group referred to immediately. The efforts of such a group together with those of your own organization and full cooperation of both should make possible a most attractive development."

On April 30, Proctor sent Harriman topographic maps of the area around Sun Valley with runs marked, saying he was on his way to Omaha to meet with U.P. engineers to discuss ski lift options.

Harriman recognized the contributions made by his associates to Sun Valley by naming areas for them, although some were never formally adopted.

The Community Library has a picture of "Schaffgotsch Mountain" next to Bald Mountain, although no other reference to it has been found and it does not appear on early Sun Valley maps. Proctor Mountain was named for Charles Proctor, and Morgan Ridge on Proctor Mountain was named for John E.P. Morgan. Durrance Mountain, 10 miles north of Sun Valley, behind the present Sawtooth National Recreation Area headquarters, was named for Dick Durrance, Dartmouth's famous ski racer, after he won the first Harriman Cup in 1937. Bright Mountain, just south of Durrance

Mountain, was named for Alex Bright, a member of the Sun Valley Ski Club board of directors. It was the site of the downhill race for the first intercollegiate tournament between Dartmouth and the University of Washington in December 1937. Hauser Mountain, named after Hans Hauser, Sun Valley's first Ski School director, is just north of Eagle Creek, several miles north of Ketchum. Several other peaks were named by Florian Haemmerle, who was in charge of the resort's backcountry program. He named Salzberger Spitzl after friends from Salzburg and Florian Nudl for himself.

Ketchum native Mary Jane Griffith Conger is a descendant of Albert Griffin, who formed Ketchum with Isaac Lewis in 1880. Beginning in 1925, her father, Albert R. Griffin, and his brother Oscar operated Griffith Market on Ketchum's Main Street. Averell Harriman approached her father and said Union Pacific would build boardwalks and upgrade the entire town into an Austrian-style mountain village if Ketchum would change its name to Sun Valley. Albert R. Griffith politely declined, saying they liked Ketchum.[14]

Union Pacific Board Finally Approves the Sun Valley Resort in May 1936

On May 5, 1936, a skeptical Union Pacific board of directors, which had no real interest in skiing, adopted a resolution approving Harriman's plan to develop a ski resort in the remote mountains of Idaho. The approval came well after Harriman had begun implementing his plan using railroad money, even though there were many uncertainties.

The chairman of the board referred to previous informal discussions of the committee concerning the possibility of developing a winter sports resort at Ketchum and stated that

> *after thorough investigation by a number of competent outside persons, as well as by Union Pacific officials, there was general agreement that the natural advantages of Ketchum, such as climate, altitude, snow conditions, winter sunshine, protection from heavy winds, abundance of good ski terrain, the existence of sulphur hot springs, etc., provide an unusual opportunity for the development of a type of ski and winter resort not as yet existent in this country.*

The resolution acknowledged the influence of Averell Harriman, although it had no idea about the annual subsidy that would be needed to operate the resort:

> *The Chairman further stated that having himself visited Ketchum, given considerable thought to the project, and studied carefully the plans and estimates for its construction, development and operation, he was now prepared to recommend the project, believing (1) that it could be made at least to carry itself financially; (2) that it would be an important traffic adjunct to the Union Pacific; and (3) that it would be a demonstration to the people of Idaho of the friendly interest the Union Pacific has in the welfare and prosperity of their state.*

The board received various cost estimates for the resort. H.C. Mann provided an estimate of $488,000 to construct the lodge, $25,000 for increasing the size and making changes, $17,000 for a refrigerating plant, and $120,000 for furnishings and equipment. The total came to $650,000, not including construction of the garage, swimming pool, ski tows, or tramway.[15]

6

SUN VALLEY LODGE IS BUILT, CHAIRLIFTS ARE DESIGNED AND INSTALLED ON DOLLAR AND RUUD MOUNTAINS

In spring 1936, Union Pacific engineers had to coordinate several major projects being done at the same time in the remote mountains of Idaho at the end of a branch line near a small town that had few amenities. A lodge and a mechanism to transport skiers up the hills had to be designed and constructed. These jobs rushed forward at full speed before the Union Pacific board approved the project.

Materials, equipment, and labor had to be obtained and imported by rail to Ketchum, and lodging and meals had to be provided for the workforce brought in to do the work. The sleepy town of Ketchum was overwhelmed by the invasion of men, equipment, and materials brought there to build something called a ski resort in a very short time. "By summer, Ketchum was taking on the atmosphere of a gold-rush town," wrote Abramson. Additional rail sidings were put in at the Ketchum depot and boxcars were sent in outfitted with bunks, showers, office equipment, and a commissary, creating a large construction camp where the workers lived and ate. Married workers lived in family cars. Workers walked from the camp to the construction site each morning and evening.

Chief engineer Howard Mann made Sun Valley Union Pacific's highest priority, and Glenn Trout expedited the acquisition and transportation of materials to the site. Bridge and building supervisor Lloyd Castagneto oversaw the installation of the chairlifts using Union Pacific employees. Averell Harriman was involved in virtually every decision, large and small. Staging for construction of the lodge began while Harriman's associates continued evaluating the surrounding hills for skiing sites and ski lifts, investigating amenities for the lodge and negotiating with local businessmen and politicians.

BUILDING THE SUN VALLEY LODGE

Oral histories of two Union Pacific employees who were involved in Sun Valley from its beginning provide insight into how the resort was built. Ed Seagle worked for Union Pacific at the Grand Canyon and was transferred to Sun Valley in September 1936 to be the liaison with the contractor building the lodge. Seagle became chief engineer for Sun Valley Operations once the resort opened, staying until after it was sold to the Janss Company in 1964. Val McAtee worked for Union Pacific at Shoshone and went to work in Sun Valley in June 1936. McAtee helped build the lodge and worked as a mechanic on the ski lifts in the winters and on construction crews in the summers, retiring in 1964.

Seagle said work on the lodge began as soon as the snow melted. The resort was Harriman's project, and he told Union Pacific what he wanted done. Initial plans called for a three-story hotel with a center section, but Harriman kept extending it, saying they didn't have enough room. There were so many revisions to the plans it was hard to keep track, and costs rapidly escalated. The contractor was working on a cost-plus basis—his fee was based on a percentage of the overall cost. A bunkhouse and construction building were set up near the lodge, where a railroad architect and three draftsmen worked.

Seagle said the contractor used his own crew, supplemented by local labor and workers from outside. Since this was the Depression, the project attracted workers from all over. Ultimately, there were over 400 carpenters working on the lodge who received 65¢ or 70¢ per hour. The wood used as forms for the lodge and the rough-cut wood used to give the concrete a wood-like appearance came from Flowers Mill near Adams Gulch north of Ketchum.

There were limited facilities where people could stay. Seagle and other U.P. employees stayed at Bald Mountain Hot Springs. Workers lived in "outfit cars," railroad cars with steel bunks for eight men—U.P. provided the bedding. There were "commissary cars" where they ate, shower cars, and kitchen cars. Workers were issued "pie books," scrip used to pay for food. Local restaurants accepted the scrip, which the railroad redeemed. Workers were paid weekly by check, cashing them at Lane Mercantile. They went to Hailey, where there was a red light district, gambling, and saloons. Soon, there were new saloons built in Ketchum to accommodate the workers.

Jack Lane's son Pete ran Lane Mercantile in Ketchum, at the corner of what became Sun Valley Road and Main Street. Lane Mercantile was the meeting place for the sheepmen, and Lane saw Sun Valley as a way to keep the store open during the winter when the sheep business dried up. Dorice Taylor said the store was the unofficial headquarters for the builders and railroad officials: "Lane's apartment above the store became the hangout for all the higher up railroad and construction men. It you weren't invited upstairs to the Lane kitchen for a drink you didn't rate—period."

Jack Lane said, "Sun Valley was practically built in the store. It had to be—there was nowhere else in town to sit down." Lane Mercantile served as a "phone booth and impromptu resort office until Sun Valley's construction crews ran their own phone line out to the site." Romances bloomed during all this activity, and two families important to Sun Valley were united. Pete Lane married Jeanne McNeil, daughter of Larry McNeil, who managed McNeil Construction Company, and Larry's son Bruce McNeil married Bobbie Lane, Jack's daughter.

The *Idaho Statesman* of May 25, 1936, reported that Union Pacific officials arrived in Ketchum to start preliminary work on a $500,000 hotel outside Ketchum: Howard C. Mann from Omaha, chief engineer of Union Pacific; W.T. Wellman from Omaha, Union Pacific architect; H.S. Severin, engineer in charge of construction; and Lawrence McNeil of the J.V. McNeil Construction Company. The paper predicted that the hotel would provide jobs for more than 200 men and that work would start immediately. Local labor and materials would be used "as far as possible."

On June 11, 1936, Union Pacific announced that work was underway on a $500,000 sports project, including a 120-room hotel in central Idaho where 60 men were employed. The *Hailey Times* of June 11 said, "Big Men Are Interested At Ketchum," as U.P. president Gray arrived. Excavation for the hotel was progressing rapidly, with dirt being removed "by a giant scoop-shovel and then carted away in trucks." Local sawmills contracted to furnish between 400,000 and 500,000 feet of lumber, both rough and finished, included Board Bros., Cutler Bros., Frank Young, Flowers Bros., and the Self-Help Co-op Mill.

On June 13, 1936, John E.P. Morgan sent H.C. Mann a memo recommending the ice rink be 165 feet by 60 feet and the swimming pool have a 70 foot diameter and providing his thoughts about ski lifts.

On June 16, 1936, Gray told Harriman, "This whole project is now well underway. . . . The contractor is employing a good force and excavations are well under way. Form lumber is being delivered on the site, with cement and reinforcing bars, and . . . matters are well lined up to make good progress."

U.P. reached an understanding with the Ketchum Livestock Association on the purchase of 40 acres necessary to put the lodge in its desired location and for rights-of-ways for a water line for the lodge and a balloon track at the depot to allow trains to turn around, which was reported by Gray to be "much easier to clear with a snow plow than the ends of a wye." (A wye is a triangular joining of three rail lines with a switch at each corner connecting to each incoming line, allowing a train to turn around.) No Forest Service land was available for filing or entry, so no one could obtain land that would interfere with the resort. There was a large CCC camp on Warm Springs Creek, and Gray was exploring whether CCC or WPA labor could be used to build cabins and ski trails. There would be no difficulty securing permits from the Forest Service for the funiculars or tow lines. Gray was concerned about getting guests to the tow lines or funiculars from the lodge, but Mann and Trout were working on several plans.

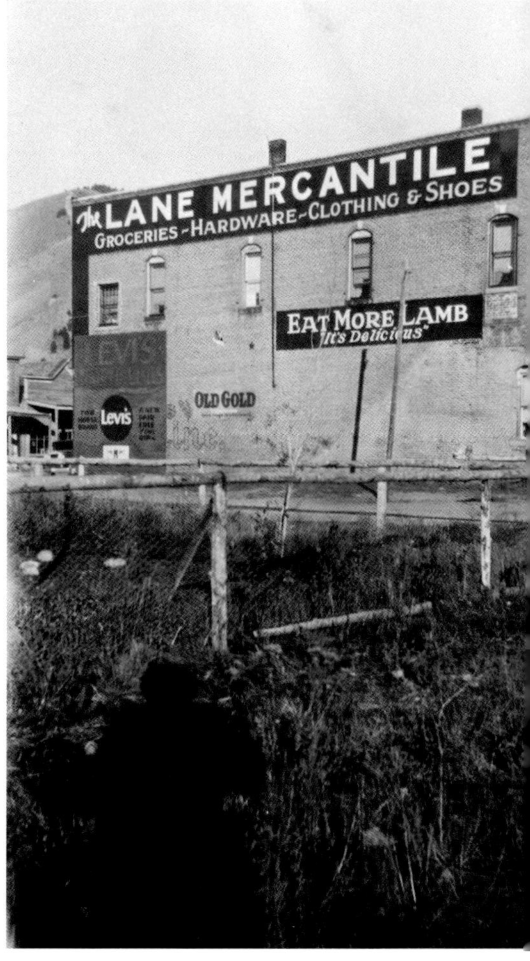

Lane Mercantile, where Sun Valley was planned and romances flourished, at the corner of Main Street and what is now Sun Valley Road.

They were exploring building a new road from the Ketchum depot to the lodge along the "low saddle which lies between our depot and hotel site. It looks like we can lead a new road out of the highway to Stanley opposite the depot, over this saddle, and directly to the west of the hotel," reducing the distance by 2,800 feet. The state would build the road and possibly close the road from the northern town limits to the public. This road was called Penny Mountain Cutoff and later became Saddle Road, going from the lodge over a hill to reach the depot in Warm Springs. Gray met with "leading citizens here, such as Lane, Sanger, Price, Griffith and Brandt," and reached an agreement about "barring of undesirables." He believed the sheriff in Hailey would cooperate fully.

Workers were brought from all over the West. Bruce McNeil, Larry McNeil's son, came with several fraternity brothers from the University of Southern California. They worked six days a week, 10 hours a day for 40¢ or 50¢ an hour, plus room and board, which they considered to be good wages. They lived in the outfit cars at the Ketchum Depot, heated by pot-bellied stoves. Mattresses were provided, but they brought their own sleeping bags. Workers used trench toilets. Meals were provided in a dining car, although they also ate at the Ketchum Kamp that served food family style.

When they arrived in late June, the lodge's foundation had been dug, the foundation laid, and cement was being poured on the second floor. Labor unions were attempting to organize some of the skilled workers, but the company had its own "goon squad" that handled the union organizers. The sheriff and Joe McNeil, who played football in college, could handle any trouble. On their days off, they played water polo in the Bald Mountain Hot Springs pool, watched movies in Hailey, traveled to Craters of the Moon, the ice caves outside of Shoshone, Redfish Lake, and other sites, and hung out in the "apartment" above Lane Mercantile.

A July 8, 1936 report prepared for W.A. Harriman said the author and Glenn Trout explored whether the No. 1 tow on Dollar could be placed in a location "that would not be on the Grimm property," but the locations selected by Trout and Proctor for both Dollar and Proctor Mountains were superior to anything else. They decided not to extend the Proctor tow to the top of the mountain, as it was a narrow rocky point, steep on all sides and dangerous. The tow would stop on a bench 200 feet below the peak. They would build a "good sized cabin protected from prevailing winds," with a stove, chairs, and views. Initial estimates indicated that electrical motors for the tows were superior to gasoline engines. Three operators were needed, "older, experienced capable men" who were "familiar with electrical installations to handle matters in case of emergency, breakdown, etc.," to be paid $90 a month. Buses owned by U.P.'s subsidiary Utah Parks could provide transportation from the train station to the lodge and from the lodge to the ski hills, which would take about 15 minutes. A new road was necessary since the present one was on Grimm's property.

Harriman and Schaffgotsch were impressed with the outdoor swimming pool at Bald Mountain Hot Springs Lodge, filled with natural spring water from Guyer Hot Springs, which they wanted to replicate at the lodge. Union Pacific was negotiating with Carl Brant, the owner of Bald Mountain Hot Springs Lodge and Guyer Hot Springs, for natural mineral water to be brought to the lodge, and a hydraulic engineer was exploring several hot springs on Warm Springs Creek. Guyer Hot Springs on Warm Springs Creek, beyond the present Warm Springs lifts, had attracted tourists and locals to its waters since the 1880s. In 1929, Brant closed the hotel and spent $50,000 bringing hot spring water into Ketchum via an underground pipeline to supply water to his new operation, Bald Mountain Hot Springs Lodge.

Union Pacific and Brant were unable to reach an agreement for spring water for the lodge. Since early publicity mentioned the resort would have pools filled with hot mineral spring water, vats were installed in the lodge's basement where minerals were mixed into water for the swimming pool. When Sun Valley was sold to the Janss Company in 1964, the vats were still there, but almost no one could remember their original purpose, according to Dorice Taylor. A Utah Oil representative would submit a proposal to build a service station, garage, and restaurant opposite Bald Mountain Hot Springs Lodge. Union Pacific received an offer from a Twin Falls businessman to build a laundry facility in Ketchum.

By 1936, Union Pacific's train between Shoshone and Ketchum "was never fast or frequent," as reported by Gray to Harriman, operating just a few days a week. The northbound train leaving Shoshone in the morning took two hours and 45 minutes, and the southbound train leaving Ketchum in the afternoon took three hours and 15 minutes. By 1929, motor car or bus service shuttled passengers from Shoshone to Ketchum, and U.P. concluded it was more efficient to do the same. "The bus trip up the highway is far superior to the train, as the view is very good," Gray wrote. A local man with the bus franchise was said to be reliable, and U.P. could lend him buses to meet trains at Shoshone. Summer operations were being considered, and a local man was doing a report on hunting and fishing. Roberta Brass wanted to organize sleigh rides for guests. They explored whether the Odd Fellows Hall could be used as a movie theater but decided a new facility should be built.

The *Hailey Times* of July 9, 1936, said work on the $750,000 hotel was proceeding, with 150 men and a weekly payroll of $5,000, which would increase as more plumbers and electricians were added. Footings were in and concrete for the northeast wings would be

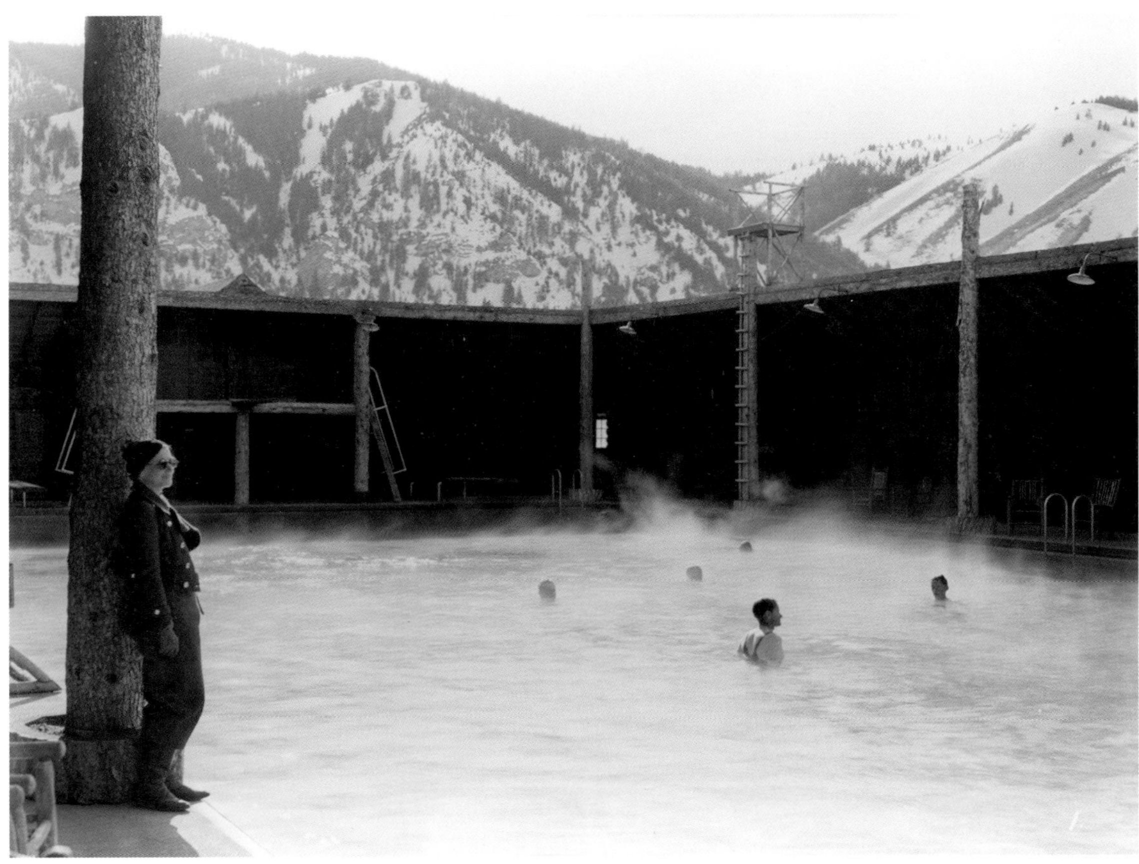

Bald Mountain Hot Springs Lodge pool, using water from Guyer Hot Springs. *Courtesy of Peggy Proctor Dean.*

poured in the next 10 days. Construction started on tramways on nearby hills. By late July, the first floor had been framed. Three coal-burning boilers were installed in the basement to provide steam heat using coal brought from Wyoming by rail. Large heaters were installed in the basement to heat water for the lodge and its swimming pool.

The final design of the lodge took shape by late July. It had been expanded to a three-story facility with four wings in the shape of a double Y. Rough, unfinished timbers were placed on the wet cement on the lodge walls, which left impressions that made the walls appear to be built from wood. Planks were installed horizontally on the first two floors and diagonally on the third floor. An acid-etching stain developed in Los Angeles that penetrated pores in the concrete was applied to provide a wood color to the concrete. Idaho stone was quarried near Magic Reservoir, and redwood was used in the interior.

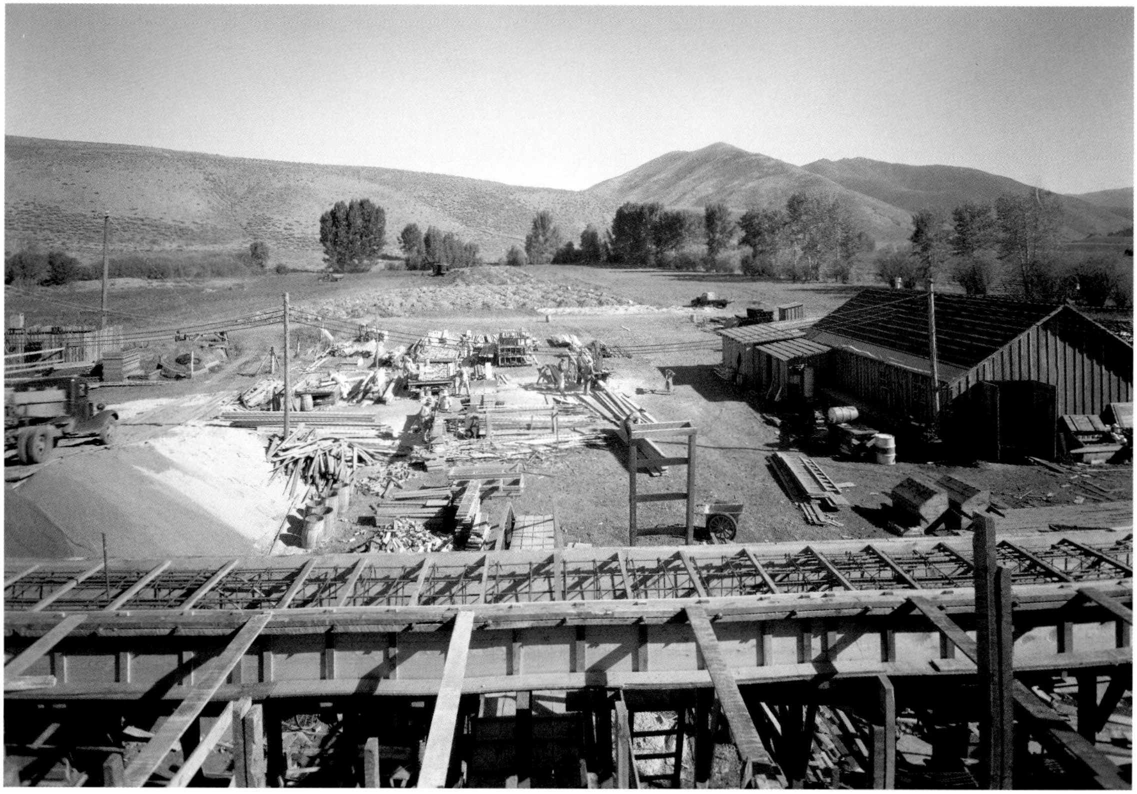

ABOVE Sun Valley Lodge under construction, summer 1936.

RIGHT U.P. board chair Averell Harriman and publicist Steve Hannagan inspecting the lodge being built, summer 1936.

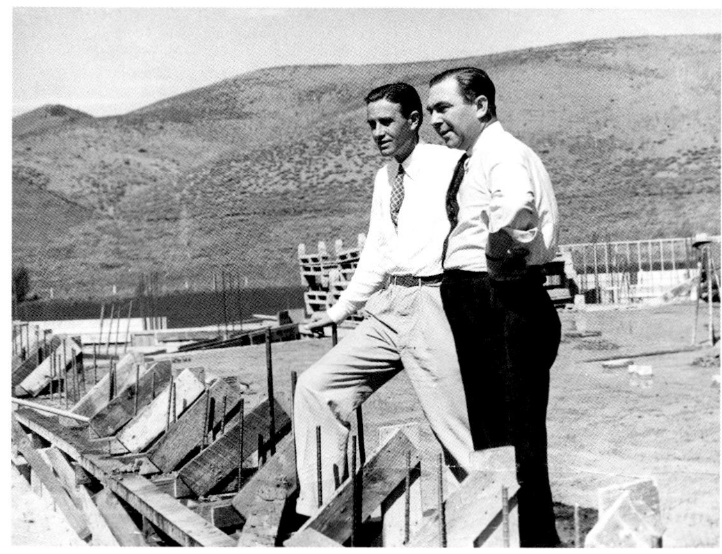

By early August, 28,000 cubic yards of cement had been poured and the lodge's second floor completed. Crews graded the site and placed soil from the excavation of the basement around the lodge to assist in drainage. The roof was framed in September after the concrete work was done, and plans were made to enclose the building and work on the interior. The workforce had grown to 400, and more railroad cars were brought in for living quarters. A 150,000-gallon water storage tank was placed on a hillside near the lodge. By October, the payroll increased to $12,000 a week. Half the men were local, with others from California.

Not everything went smoothly, as the contractor experienced labor difficulties. Telegrams dated October 26 and 27, 1936, said the labor situation was "very tense." Cement finishers, brick layers, and tile setters were leaving the job to unionize the work. The issue involved getting the men to work over eight hours. The contractor said union members wanted to drag the job along since there was a shortage of skilled labor. McNeil gathered the men together, "explained the situation, and gave them three or four hours to talk it over," according to the telegrams. After meeting, the men said they would not work more than eight hours, causing McNeil to take drastic action—"shipping these men to Shoshone under guard of the Sheriff." Some of the brick layers made threats against certain people and "were talking to other crafts on the job, and it was thought best to take these men to Shoshone before they could stir up more trouble."

By the end of November 1936, over 500 men were working, generating a $32,000 weekly payroll. All outside work had been done, interior partitions were in, and painting would be finished in 10 days. Fir trees were brought in from Galena and planted around the hotel. Kitchen equipment and electrical fixtures were being installed and carpets laid. The lodge's picture windows were oriented toward the setting sun. The interior was first class. The draperies, rugs, furniture, and accessories were designed by Marjorie Oelrichs and made by Mandel Brothers of New York City. "Nothing is spared in making it an ideal place of the kind," said the *Hailey Times*. Oelrichs was married to Eddy Duchin, a famous band leader for whom the Duchin Room in the Sun Valley Lodge would be named. Kathleen Harriman said Marjorie Duchin was one of her mother Mary's best friends.

Harriman understood that people staying for several weeks had to be entertained with more than skiing, so a range of amenities was provided. The lodge had an elegant dining room, a dance floor, billiard tables, a beauty parlor, a barbershop, and a branch of Sax Fifth Avenue, which included a ski shop. South of the lodge, there was a natural ice skating and curling rink and a paddle tennis court. The resort offered outdoor swimming pools with heated water, sunbathing in roofless igloos, tobogganing, skating, horseback riding, and dog sledging.

The lodge had special apartments for its high-end employees, since no housing was available in Ketchum. Ed Seagle, the chief engineer for Sun Valley, lived in one of the apartments, as did the lodge manager, Don and Gretchen Fraser, when he was the resort's sports director, and others. They ate in the lodge's dining facilities as part of their compensation package. Separate employee housing was built for the lower-level employees, and cottages were built in later years for a few special employees.

A 220-room hotel and two chairlifts were built in just seven months so the resort could open on December 21, 1936, with Harriman overseeing every detail. The lodge and surroundings cost $1.5 million, although press accounts gave various figures. Harriman acknowledged his role developing Sun Valley in his modest way: "I think I stimulated most of everything that happened here."

Gilbert Stanley Underwood wrote an article about the Sun Valley Lodge for *Architectural Record* in 1938. He included detailed floor plans and listed the equipment and materials used for the construction, along with the suppliers and subcontractors. The lodge's location and site influenced its design, since it was "comparatively isolated" in a "little sheltered valley" surrounded by mountains. The lodge was oriented for maximum winter sunlight, and it was necessary to include unusually large areas for storage and employee lodgings. "The strenuous and somewhat hazardous character of some sports makes the inclusion of a complete medical and surgical element a necessity in a hotel group so isolated," Underwood wrote. Towlines were 200 yards southwest of the lodge. The resort had a skating rink, a glass-enclosed swimming pool with steam-heated water, and tennis courts for summer.

On May 24, 1961, Lawrence McNeil, who oversaw work done by J.V. McNeil Co., responded to Sun Valley publicist Dorice Taylor's questions about issues that arose when he built the lodge in 1936. "It was a tough job to handle to bring in or manufacture on the site, all of the items needed for construction in such a remote area and accomplish the work in the very short allotted time; it called for all the ingenuity and drive of everyone concerned," he said. The original plans called for the lodge to be as fireproof as possible. Whose idea was it to pour concrete in log molds? McNeil said that his company used two small lumber mills to produce most of the form lumber,

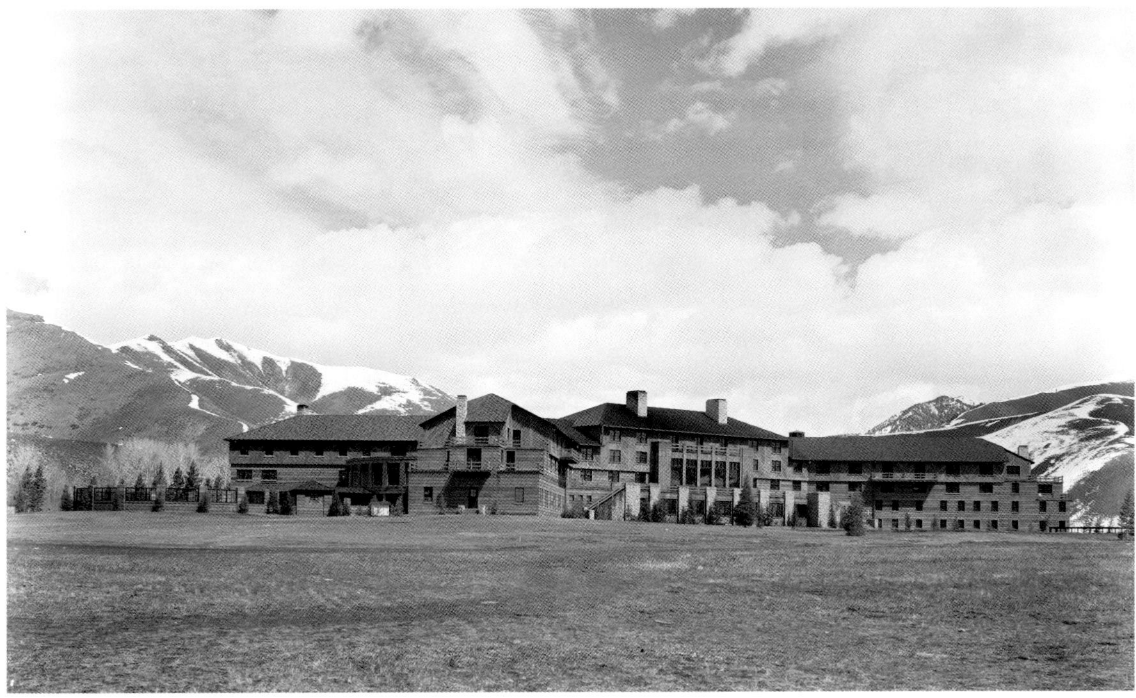

Sun Valley Lodge completed.

rough sawing local "Bull Pine." It occurred to "several of us, including [U.P. architect] Bill Wellman, that permitting the grain of this particular wood to rise would produce an exterior concrete surface the exact reverse of the rough cut timber," and its effect could be enhanced by applying a chemical stain to reproduce the original color of the timber. No single individual could take credit.

Union Pacific Engineers Invent Chairlifts for Sun Valley

U.P.'s publicist Steve Hannagan said that mechanical devices had to be installed to carry people to the top of the slopes as a critical ingredient for the new resort.

This was a time when skiing was done by hiking or "herringboning" up hills before skiing down, limiting the sport to the most athletic. The first rope tow in the United

States was installed at Woodstock, Vermont, in 1934, and they soon began to appear elsewhere, making skiing accessible to people who lacked the physical prowess to hike up steep slopes, but they presented challenges of their own. Otto Lang, the famous Austrian ski instructor, said rope tows were "ghastly—as if designed to pull one's arms out of their shoulder sockets. . . . Still, anything was preferable to climbing back to the top of the hill after every run, which was time-consuming and exhausting." Filmmaker Warren Miller said, "You could build a ski resort for the cost of the rope, an old automobile engine, and about a dozen automobile wheels for the rope to run on. Estimated cost was less than five hundred dollars and a lot of sweat."

There were a few more-sophisticated ski lifts available. In December 1934, Swiss engineer Ernest Constam built the world's first J-bar or single overhead cable lift at Davos, Switzerland. In 1935, the first overhead cable lift in the United States (a J-bar) was installed in Hanover, New Hampshire, by the Dartmouth Outing Club. Otto Lang called them "Rube Goldberg–type contraptions in various experimental stages, but none was satisfactory in terms of comfort."

Members of the 1936 U.S. Olympic ski team were impressed by the tram built in Garmisch-Partenkirchen, Germany, for the Games, allowing them to get in far more training runs than ever before. Harriman's estate in New York was reached by a funicular. Early correspondence shows that tramways were considered for Sun Valley. Proctor's memo to Harriman of March 30 said there was a need "for a rail funicular to some high country nearby." When Glenn Trout came to Ketchum in April, he planned to survey for tramways.

On April 15, Harriman sent a telegram to chief engineer H.C. Mann, asking him to develop recommendations and cost estimates for

> *a method of lifting skiers two thousand feet above the valley floor to mountains east of trail creek. Proctor knows the point which is desired to reach. There have been a number of ways this problem has been approached in other places from hoists pulling up, to sleds to aerial tramways. Suggest you have one of your engineers discuss the problem with Proctor and examine terrain with a view of making a recommendation how the problem can be solved in the most economic manner. Our approach should be to develop as inexpensive a method as possible with a capacity of say one hundred people an hour. After your investigation, will want a rough estimate of cost of construction and operation.*

On April 17, Harriman asked Charles Proctor to give his best thought "to the problem of the proper location for the funicular." On April 26, Proctor told John E.P. Morgan he spent four days with the Union Pacific engineers "working over the tramway sites," and he and Trout secured "a suitable profile for an aerial tramway up Proctor Mountain." By having "the tramway on Proctor Mountain and the small tow at the first location more skiing territory is opened up."

In an interview in 1966, Proctor said, "Alan Mann, chief engineer for the U.P. got me together with Glen Trout, then chief U.P. bridge engineer, and told us to get going. The U.P. people were not concerned about costs in this project and I was given full rein to develop a functional solution to the problem of transporting skiers up the mountains of Sun Valley."

Proctor concluded that rope tows were not suitable for Sun Valley, based on experiences at Gunstock Mountain Resort at Gilford, New Hampshire. A long rope tow, the Gunstock Ski Hoist, was installed there for winter 1935, one of the first in New England. The towlines necessary to have such a lift on Dollar Mountain would be longer. Proctor did not feel it would be reasonable to expect people to hold onto a rope for as long as would be necessary to get up these slopes. The experience at Gilford showed that for the average person, it is almost impossible to hold onto a rope tow for more than 1,500 feet.

Proctor asked Glen Trout to obtain plans and costs for the overhead cable lift (a J-bar) in Hanover, New Hampshire, and discussed his idea for a new style of ski lift that sounded like a rudimentary chairlift:

> *I suggested to Mr. Trout that he try to devise some sort of arrangement enabling a person to sit down in some sort of basket or at least lean against a bar or other support while being pulled up. Mr. Trout seemed to have many good ideas along this line and I feel sure that he will be able to produce something which will be more satisfactory than anything we have seen in this country.*

On April 30, Proctor told Harriman he was stopping in Omaha on his way home to meet with Union Pacific engineers and "look over different schemes for ski lifts."

In Omaha, Union Pacific engineers evaluated all available systems for ski lifts, including rope tows, a J-bar, an up-ski toboggan similar to that at Yosemite, cable cars, and a cog railway. Jim Curran, a young U.P. bridge engineer, previously worked for Paxton-Vierling

Ironworks, where he designed a conveyor with hooks to load bananas onto boats using a continuous single cable in a loop. He came up with an innovative idea—a chairlift that carried a single skier per chair, based on his mono-cable system for bananas. Curran believed carrying skiers involved the same issues as handling bananas, chairs could be substituted for hooks, his system would have a greater capacity than other systems, and it would be more comfortable than a rope tow or J-bar. Mining operations had used aerial trams for years, but they were bi-cable units. Curran's use of a mono cable was unique.

Other U.P. engineers thought Curran's design was too dangerous and rejected it. However, when Charles Proctor came to Omaha, Curran slipped his design back in with the other plans. Proctor liked Curran's idea, and he showed it to Harriman, who ordered Union Pacific engineers to develop chairlifts. U.P. engineers developed a model at their facilities at Omaha using an old pickup truck and a chair hung on a cable to experiment with moving parts. John E.P. Morgan helped determine the appropriate speed for the system, experimenting with skis sliding on straw and roller skates.

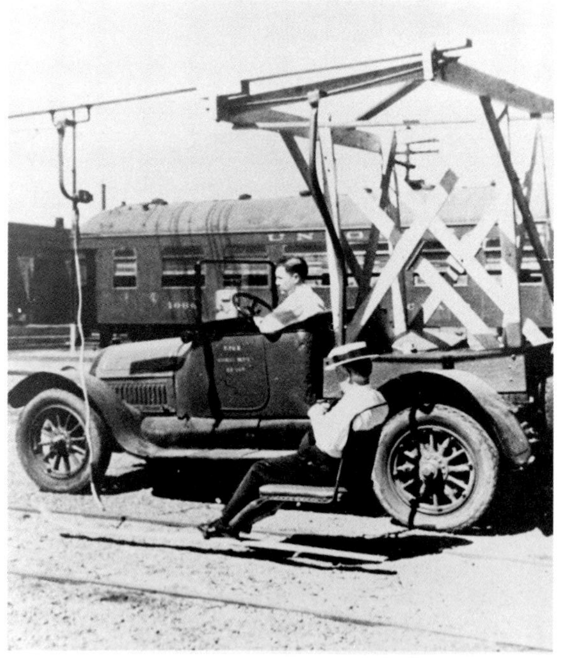

Union Pacific engineers in Omaha, Nebraska, experimenting with a chairlift invented for Sun Valley by James Curran using a system to load bananas onto boats.

Union Pacific engineers were assisted in developing the chairlift by Gordon H. Bannerman, assistant tramway engineer at the American Steel and Wire Company in Worcester, Massachusetts, the company that helped the Dartmouth Outing Club design and build the country's first J-bar. American Steel built the bull wheels, cables, sheaves, and other components for the Sun Valley lifts. Bannerman was listed as one of the inventors of the Sun Valley Aerial Ski Tramway when it was patented in 1937, and he assisted in the design and building of the three chairlifts installed on Bald Mountain for winter 1940.

In his 1966 interview, Morgan said he sent copies of the chairlift plans to "friends he knew who loved to ski and were judged imaginative enough to aid the project." Morgan wrote chief engineer H.C. Mann on June 13, 1936, with suggestions for improving the design of the chairlifts:

> *For the small chair* [on Dollar], *an adjustable chain or bar should be attached to the upright and the back of the seat to prevent the seat (and the rider) from going over backwards. For the long chair* [on Proctor], *a blanket should be attached since the ride was long enough for the rider to get cold. The depth of the seat might be increased to 16 inches to provide greater confidence and lessen the problem of the leg and foot rest. The best suggestion for a foot rest was to make it on a wide flat padded part to support the back of the leg, and make it adjustable where it was attached to the seat to accommodate both male and female guests. A practice chair might be installed at the bottom of the big lift where strangers could practice. Sun Valley needed a telephone connection on all tows from the top to the bottom, and to the hotel in case of first aid, accidents, etc.*

Components for Sun Valley's chairlifts built by American Steel were shipped to Ketchum by train. Chairlifts on Dollar and Proctor Mountains were installed by Union Pacific crews, led by Lloyd Castagneto, bridge and building supervisor, who reported to Glen Trout, chief bridge engineer. In his 1966 interview, Proctor said U.P. engineers "elicited the aid of America Steel and Wire, plus others, in determining the chair spacing, angles of climb and locations on Dollar and Proctor Mountain."

In July 1936, Union Pacific crews began installing the lifts on Dollar and Proctor Mountains. U.P. engineers were experienced in building virtually everything and were used to improvising and being creative. Since chairlifts were invented for Sun Valley, no one had experience installing them, so U.P.'s engineers had to figure out how they should be put together and work. Castagneto had no plans, so he and his initial crew of 100 had to "build what they sent me," he said. The lift towers were creosoted wood, unlike later ones made from steel. By October 1936, concrete bases were poured and the lift poles were set. The big drive wheels (bull wheels) and the wooden lift towers were man-handled up the mountains to their proper locations, dragged by tractors using a special trailer built for them. Crews installed the chairlifts "the hard way, by manual labor, we didn't have all of the fancy machines that we have now," said Val McAtee, who worked for Castagneto.

On Dollar, the lift towers were in the valley, not on the ridge, which turned out to be too cold and the snow was not good. They were later relocated to the ridge.

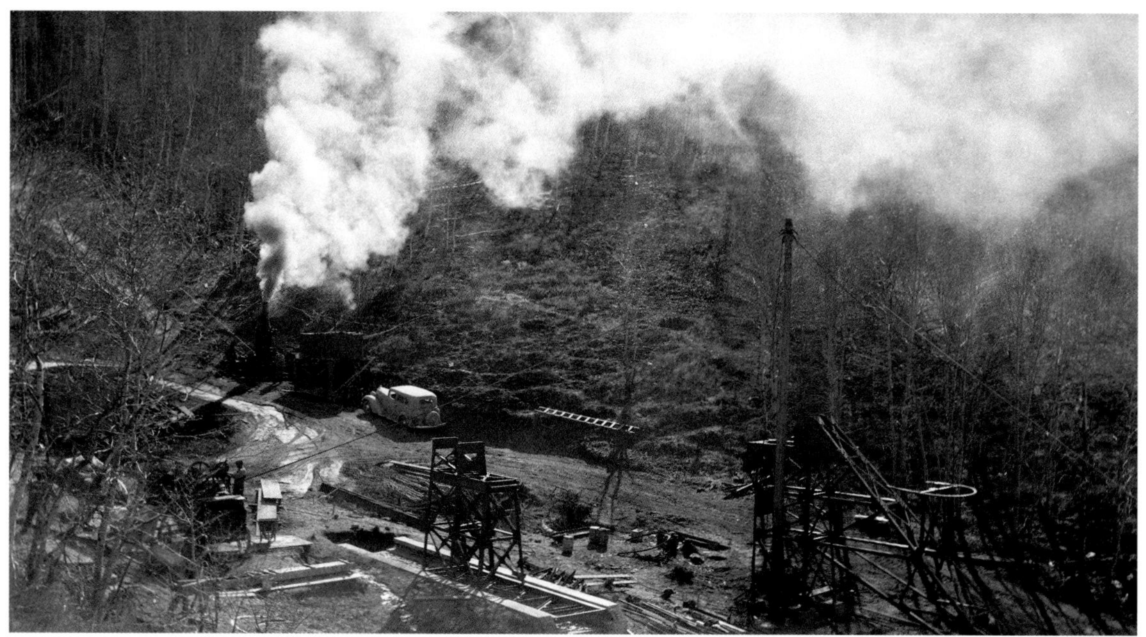

Union Pacific crews building the Proctor chairlift, fall 1936. *Photograph by Sheldon Zadoc Thayer.*

A rope was attached to the chairs for skiers to grab to be pulled up to the speed of the chair before sitting down. According to Ed Seagle, the ropes would catch in the snow after the skier sat down, twirl around, and end up twisted around the cable. The chairlift would have to be stopped to remove the rope, so ropes were discarded after about a month. Proctor Mountain faced north and was cold, making for an unpleasant trip in the chair. Seagle decided blankets should be given to those riding the chairs to keep them warm, a system used for years.

On July 22, the *Hailey Times* said work began on a new road up the hill to reach the base of a tram about a mile up Trail Creek. By the end of November 1936, the Proctor Mountain chairlift was finished and ready to be tested, although problems emerged, as described by the *Hailey Times* of November 26, 1936, when 20 female volunteers were loaded on the lift:

> *Some of the ladies waved to the crowd of onlookers, while others gripped the bars attaching the chairs to the moving cable until their knuckles blanched. Suddenly the lift motor stalled, leaving the women suspended like so many bunches of bananas.*

The nervous women were lowered down with ropes, as Curren frantically searched for the cause of the stoppage, which was a blown fuse. Once it was replaced, none of the women were willing to try the lift again. The resort manager ordered his secretary, Florence Law, onto the lift. "This time everything worked perfectly, making Ms. Law the world's first official chairlift passenger," the *Hailey Times* reported.

Lift controls were located at the top of the chairlifts, with auxiliary controls at the bottom, and a telephone connected the top and bottom operators with each other and with the lodge.

Glen Trout wrote Gordon Bannerman at American Steel and Wire Company on December 3, 1936, saying "the operation of the chair line is very satisfactory, the chairs being much easier to get on or off than we anticipated. . . . The general opinion of people who have ridden up the tram is that they will prove quite an attractive facility for the purpose intended." In winter 1937, Trout told Bannerman, "The chair lines operate very satisfactorily, having had practically no trouble with them." Minor problems had emerged. The four intermediate towers on Dollar did not have back legs, so back legs were installed to prevent them from wobbling. Ed Seagle, who was in charge of the chairlifts, called them "real work horses . . . practically the only lift failures he has to contend with are those caused by power failures in the electric lines running to the resort."

Union Pacific and American Steel and Wire Company decided to patent the chairlift system they developed, as Bannerman told Trout: "We don't want home made chair tows build around the country, which if not designed and constructed properly, will give trouble, and thus reflect on the bona fide installations such as yours." But only the application of the ski tows to transporting passengers could be patented—the mono-cable tramway could not.

A patent was applied for the Sun Valley Aerial Ski Tramway in summer 1937 and issued on March 28, 1939, serial No. 2152235A, with a priority date of November 11, 1937. The inventors were Gordon H. Bannerman and two Union Pacific engineers, James M. Curran and Glen H. Trout. The patent was assigned to the American Steel and Wire Company, and a non-exclusive, royalty-free licensing agreement was signed in favor of Union Pacific. A second patent was submitted for "other Rope Fittings."

Sun Valley's chairlifts revolutionized skiing, influencing what was done elsewhere in the country, according to Otto Lang:

> *Credit must be given to the engineering department of the Union Pacific . . . for coming up with a solution. Thanks to the ingenuity of one staff engineer, James Curran, the*

> *problem was solved. Skiers around the world should be eternally grateful to him for his invention of the chairlift—perhaps the most popular, efficient, and universally accepted mode of uphill transportation for skiers and summer sightseers.*

An article in *Ski Area Management* magazine in May 1999 said James Curran, who created the chairlift system used all over the world, believed it was one of the minor things he designed and was not in the "mainstream of his work." Their benefits were limited to the rich, whom he disdained: "They were about as useful as a carnival ride." Curran was proudest of his bridge designs that benefitted more of the population by helping them get places or transport supplies. He is credited with many unique railroad bridge designs, including bridges over the Snake River at American Falls, Idaho, and the Willamette River in Portland, Oregon. He was also known for devising strategies to replace old bridges without significantly disrupting rail traffic, according to the article.

RAIL LINE AND ROAD BETWEEN SHOSHONE AND KETCHUM ARE IMPROVED

Beginning in July 1936, Union Pacific upgraded the roadbed for its Shoshone to Ketchum branch. The railroad acquired 70,000 tons of egg gravel and sand from the Dill gravel pit in Shoshone for roadbed and lodge construction, requiring 2,000 railcars to ship it to Ketchum, using four cars a day. One crew started at Shoshone and another at Ketchum, laying 300,000 new ties and gravel to make the roadbed smoother and more durable. The road between Shoshone and Ketchum was paved. *Railway Age* said, "Trains were met at Shoshone by buses that carried passengers to the lodge 'over a newly constructed paved highway.'" West Coast Power Co. rebuilt its power lines to Ketchum to provide additional power for the new development.

Louis Holliday described the trip he and a companion had to Sun Valley in fall 1936. He was working at the Union Pacific station in Omaha and was asked if he wanted to go to a new ski area somewhere in Idaho. He and a friend were soon on the train headed for Ketchum, where he worked as a busboy in the Sun Valley Lodge at its opening in December 1936. After a year, he went to work in the Ram until 1940, then worked in the Sun Valley photography department. Holliday and his friend arrived in Ketchum on November 5, 1936:

> *We left Shoshone at 5:30 in the morning on the train, and pulled into Ketchum at 3:30 in the afternoon. The engineer and brakeman stopped the train to talk to farmers along the way. They would get out their guns and shoot a couple of ducks and pheasants on Silver Creek. Very interesting. Half of the windows in the car we were in were broken out. By the time we got there, there were two guys ready to go back to Omaha.*

Final arrangements were being made for the resort's guests in late fall 1936. Union Pacific Stages Inc. contracted with Union Pacific to provide transportation between Shoshone and the Sun Valley Lodge and between the lodge and other points of recreation; to operate trucks to transport materials and supplies at the resort and recreational equipment of guests; and operate repair shops and garage operations. Union Pacific rented three buses and established "daily turn-around service between Shoshone and Ketchum" to improve handling of mail and passengers. A parlor car at Denver was put into service. The Union Pacific Board authorized a salary of $1,000 a year to K.M. Singer as general manager of Sun Valley Lodge and "related activities at Ketchum."

Part Three

SUN VALLEY OPENS DECEMBER 1936, CHANGING SKIING IN THIS COUNTRY

7

DECEMBER 1936

Sun Valley Resort Opens to Great Acclaim

Union Pacific began to publicize Sun Valley in fall 1936. On September 21, Harriman wrote U.P. president C.R. Gray saying Hannagan recommended spending $15,000 "for three insertions in class magazines advertising Sun Valley, plus $3,000 for special winter editions of large city newspapers." This would be charged to railroad advertising expense, and the circular advertising expenses borne by the hotel.

On September 5–12, 1936, *Railway Age*, a trade publication, ran articles informing railroad executives about the innovative steps taken by Union Pacific, although it got the idea of the chairlift wrong:

> *The Union Pacific is creating a new winter sports mecca near Ketchum, Idaho, in the Sun Valley in the Sawtooth Mountains northeast of Boise. Sun Valley Lodge, as it will be known, will be opened at Christmas time with accommodations for 200 guests. . . .*
>
> *The Union Pacific's new winter sports resort . . . is planned to attract the thousands of Americans who make pilgrimages to famous European sports centers for winter activities. The lodge, designed in western American style, will be air conditioned and includes private sun porches in igloo style for winter sun-bathing, bachelor apartments, and game and club rooms where regular dancing parties with Eddy Duchin's band are planned. Other features to be offered will be a glass-enclosed swimming pool fed by warm spring water, and a flood-lighted ice skating rink. A skiing course is being laid*

> *along a two-mile mountain side with a cable-mounted basket to hoist the skiers back up the mountain. Daily sleeping service will be operated to Ketchum, which is located on the Shoshone-Ketchum branch, 69 miles from the main line. At the opening of the lodge at Christmas time, it is planned to have on hand Count Felix Schaffgotsch as master of winter sports, and Hans Hauser, Austrian ski champion, with assistants, who will conduct a skiing school on Dollar Mountain, opposite the lodge.*

American skiers got their first idea of what Harriman had built in fall 1936 in an article by Charles N. Proctor in *American Ski Annual, 1936*. Proctor described Harriman's vision of building a ski resort "comparable to the well known resorts in Austria, Germany and Switzerland."

> *Sun Valley Lodge will provide the most luxurious modern hotel accommodations for some 350 guests. Skiers with small budgets will find reasonably priced accommodations in Ketchum. Snow conditions for skiing last from early December to April. The weather is cold at night and moderate during the day.*
>
> *The hills and mountains rising directly from Sun Valley at 6000 feet plus the higher mountains nearby offer every conceivable kind of skiing terrain. The nearby hills rise to heights of 8500 feet providing slopes almost entirely free from timber. There is everything here from the easiest practice slopes to a wide variety of runs with 2500 foot descents.*

Sun Valley offered two ski lifts making surrounding terrain easily accessible, one on Dollar Mountain with short, easy runs, and the second on Proctor Mountain giving access to a large area with a variety of terrain. Sun Valley also offered a wide variety of backcountry skiing:

> *The skier wanting harder and longer runs can catch the foot of Bald Mountain in ten minutes by car from Sun Valley Lodge. Bald Mountain rises to 9200 feet and provides several runs with over 3200 foot descents. Some of these are almost entirely in the open while others offer variety with wood running through widely scattered trees. Some routes offer very steep fast running while others give opportunity to follow gradual slopes the entire distance.*

Skiing in nearby mountains was part of Sun Valley's allure, along with cross-country skiing/ski touring and cabins for spending the night or for lunch:

> *To the north the Boulder Peaks rise to nearly 11,000 feet. From one of the lower ridges near these peaks at least five different runs radiate from a point 4000 feet above the valley. These runs vary in length from approximately two and a half miles to five . . . and offer a great variety of downhill skiing. The hardest runs are very steep with open wood running as well as open slopes. The easier routes follow more gradual slopes with very little wood running. All these runs can be reached by a short drive from Sun Valley Lodge. If this region proves popular it will probably be possible to keep an old mine road open part way up Boulder Mountain. This will enable a skier to reach the start of all the runs by a short 2000 foot climb. . . .*
>
> *There are any number of short easy half day or day cross-country tours taking the skier through beautiful country and giving a fine variety of running. For the experienced ski mountaineer there are plenty of rugged mountains for long hard trips which will provide winter climbing at the end of the skiing. . . . Cabins and shelters have been located at convenient places so the ski tourer will find comfortable camps for spending the night or for lunch. . . . The mountains extend in all directions from Sun Valley with practically no timber thick enough to spoil the slopes for skiing. It is all perfect ski terrain but hardly any of it has ever been skied over!*

On October 30, Harriman set December 21 as the opening date for Sun Valley Lodge, directing U.P. president Gray to notify agents so guests could be booked for Christmas vacation. This generated publicity all over the country. The *Seattle Times* of November 18, 1936, described the exciting new resort to its readers, many of whom would flock to Sun Valley:

> *Sun Valley was born—a fashionable ski resort costing Harriman and the Union Pacific something more than $1,000,000; offering a luxurious, ultra-modern hotel with accommodations for some 200 guests; sun-bathing in roofless ice igloos; mid-winter swimming in outdoor swimming pools fed by natural hot springs; ski-tows to raise skiers 1,470 feet in elevation on a 6,500 foot-long hoist; the other which gives the skier 650 feet of elevation above the valley level.*

Hans Hauser, twice downhill and slalom champion of Austria, will head a staff of five Austrian expert ski instructors. . . . A number of Seattle skiers plan to invade Ketchum this winter for several days of skiing to look over the area. It is high in the Sawtooth Range, 5,900 feet in elevation. . . .

This is the ultra ultra in winter resorts and is super deluxe in every thing from sports offered, to smart ski togs. Skiing, skating, sun bathing, dog sledding and tobogganing are assured at Sun Valley, which was built by and will be operated by the Union Pacific. Eddie Duchin and his orchestra have been engaged for the Sun Valley season. They tell me that you must take your fanciest lodge clothes to Sun Valley.

The *New York Times* of December 13, 1936, announced the opening of Sun Valley: "Interest in Winter sports has been heightened this year by the erection of the largest snow resort in the West. This is the Sun Valley Lodge in the Sawtooth Mountains near Ketchum, Idaho . . . Sun Valley will primarily be a Mecca for skiers."

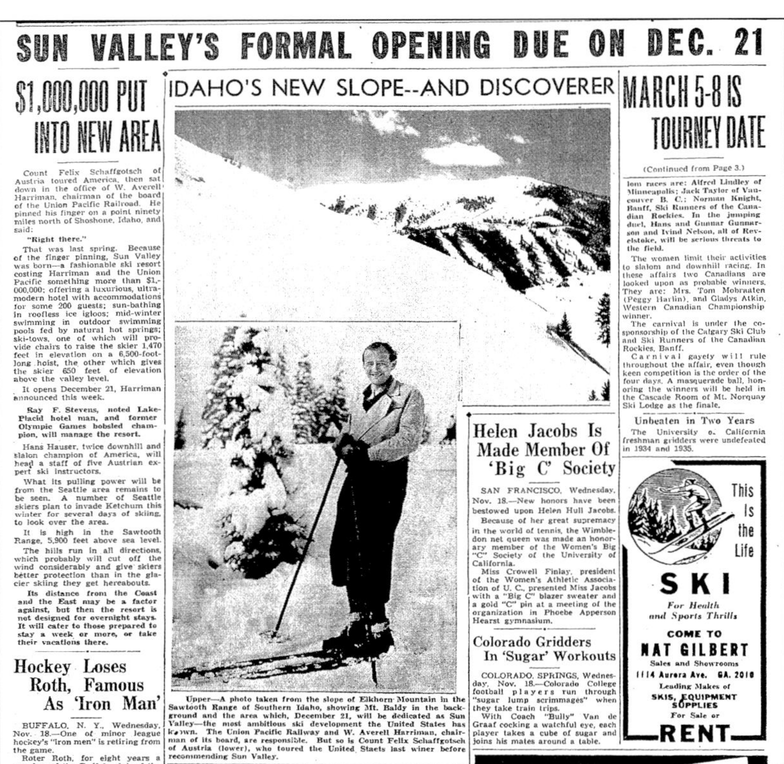

SUN VALLEY'S FORMAL OPENING DUE ON DEC. 21

$1,000,000 PUT INTO NEW AREA

Count Felix Schaffgotsch of Austria toured America, then sat down in the office of W. Averell Harriman, chairman of the board of the Union Pacific Railroad. He pinned his finger on a point ninety miles north of Shoshone, Idaho, and said:

"Right there."

That was last spring. Because of the finger pinning, Sun Valley was born—a fashionable ski resort costing Harriman and the Union Pacific something more than $1,000,000; offering a luxurious, ultra-modern hotel with accommodations for some 200 guests; sun-bathing in roofless ice igloos; mid-winter swimming in outdoor swimming pools fed by natural hot springs; ski-tows, one of which will provide chairs to raise the skier 1,470 feet in elevation on a 6,500-foot-long hoist, the other which gives the skier 650 feet of elevation above the valley level.

It opens December 21, Harriman announced this week.

Ray F. Stevens, noted Lake-Placid hotel man, and former Olympic Games bobsled champion, will manage the resort.

Hans Hauser, twice downhill and slalon champion of America, will head a staff of five Austrian expert ski instructors.

What its pulling power will be from the Seattle area remains to be seen. A number of Seattle skiers plan to invade Ketchum this winter for several days of skiing, to look over the area.

It is high in the Sawtooth Range, 5,900 feet above sea level.

The hills run in all directions, which probably will cut off the wind considerably and give skiers better protection than in the glacier skiing they get hereabouts.

Its distance from the Coast and the East may be a factor against, but then the resort is not designed for overnight stays. It will cater to those prepared to stay a week or more, or take their vacations there.

Hockey Loses Roth, Famous As 'Iron Man'

BUFFALO, N. Y., Wednesday, Nov. 18.—One of minor league hockey's "Iron men" is retiring from the game.

Roter Roth, for eight years a member of the Buffalo club of the

IDAHO'S NEW SLOPE--AND DISCOVERER

Upper—A photo taken from the slope of Elkhorn Mountain in the Sawtooth Range of Southern Idaho, showing Mt. Baldy in the background and the area which, December 21, will be dedicated as Sun Valley—the most ambitious ski development the United States has known. The Union Pacific Railway and W. Averell Harriman, chairman of its board, are responsible. But so is Count Felix Schaffgotsch of Austria (lower), who toured the United Staets last winer before recommending Sun Valley.

Helen Jacobs Is Made Member Of 'Big C' Society

SAN FRANCISCO, Wednesday, Nov. 18.—New honors have been bestowed upon Helen Hull Jacobs.

Because of her great supremacy in the world of tennis, the Wimbledon net queen was made an honorary member of the Women's Big "C" Society of the University of California.

Miss Crowell Finlay, president of the Women's Athletic Association of U. C., presented Miss Jacobs with a "Big C" blazer sweater and a gold "C" pin at a meeting of the organization in Phoebe Apperson Hearst gymnasium.

Colorado Gridders In 'Sugar' Workouts

COLORADO, SPRINGS, Wednesday, Nov. 18.—Colorado College football players run through "sugar lump scrimmages" when they take train trips.

With Coach "Bully" Van de Graaf cocking a watchful eye, each player takes a cube of sugar and joins his mates around a table.

MARCH 5-8 IS TOURNEY DATE

(Continued from Page 3.)

lom races are: Alfred Lindley of Minneapolis; Jack Taylor of Vancouver B. C.; Norman Knight, Banff, Ski Runners of the Canadian Rockies. In the jumping duel, Hans and Gunnar Gunnarson and Ivind Nelson, all of Revelstoke, will be serious threats to the field.

The women limit their activities to slalom and downhill racing. In these affairs two Canadians are looked upon as probable winners. They are: Mrs. Tom Mobraaten (Peggy Harlin), and Gladys Atkin, Western Canadian Championship winner.

The carnival is under the co-sponsorship of the Calgary Ski Club and Ski Runners of the Canadian Rockies, Banff.

Carnival gayety will rule throughout the affair, even though keen competition is the order of the four days. A masquerade ball, honoring the winners will be held in the Cascade Room of Mt. Norquay Ski Lodge as the finale.

Unbeaten in Two Years

The University o. California freshman gridders were undefeated in 1934 and 1935.

Seattle is told of Sun Valley's opening. *Seattle Times*, November 18, 1936.

On December 19, 1936, the *Boise Capital News* said Sun Valley was "THE winter sports paradise, the skiing resort which will surpass the famed skiing centers of Europe, and a Mecca for winter sports enthusiasts from all parts of the world. . . . From the combined standpoints of modern transportation, ski lifts and runs and luxury hotel accommodations, Sun Valley is designed to be America's outstanding skiing and winter sports center."

Hannagan worked to ensure the resort's opening was filled with beautiful people, saying "the key was not merely to get people there but to get the *right* people there for the opening. . . . Society is like a band of sheep. . . . Get a few bellwethers . . . headed in the right direction and the rest will surely clamber after." To make sure Hollywood sent the right people, Schaffgotsch worked with producer David O. Selznick to bring members of the movie set to Sun Valley for its opening. Harriman reserved excellent suites for a party of 20 and sent a special train from Hollywood direct to Sun Valley, taking 30 hours. Selznick said the trip would offer a time to take "casual photographs of stars en route and at American St. Moritz," and turned his publicity department loose.

Averell Harriman was not at the lodge's opening—he was in New York at his daughter Mary's debutante party and joined the festivities later. William Jeffers, executive vice president of the railroad, presided at the ceremonies. The Sun Valley Lodge dedication was broadcast live over a radio station in Salt Lake City, which could be heard by Omaha listeners, where U.P.'s headquarters were located. Harriman was still involved in the smallest details for the opening, communicating by telegram. He suggested using dog teams to carry mail "for atmosphere," was concerned about blankets for the Proctor Mountain chairlift, suggested changes in the bachelors' lounge to make it a game room, and numerous other ideas. On December 29, Schaffgotsch and Morgan told Harriman that long mirrors should be installed due to complaints from the female guests. The dog and horse sleighs were being well used, and almost all guests were taking ski instructions with weekly tickets.

The guest list for the opening of Sun Valley Lodge shows the success of Hannagan's efforts. It included David O. Selznick, Claudette Colbert, Gloria Baker, Wesley Ruggles, Joan Bennett, Madeline Carroll, and others from Hollywood. Other well-known guests included Mr. and Mrs. Nelson Rockefeller, Sterling Rockefeller, Mr. and Mrs. Robert Lehman, Fred Pabst, members of the Du Pont family, Mr. and Mrs. Corland Hill, and others.

The story of Sun Valley's challenging opening is well known. The resort's ski slopes were bare, and there was no evidence of snow anywhere. Disgruntled guests renamed Sun Valley the "Ketchum Con," according to Abramson. *Life* magazine sent photographers to the opening, "but all they did was sit by the fireplaces and drink highballs and take pictures of the skiers with wheelchairs and crutches. Too many rocks and not enough snow," wrote Val McAtee. Harriman allowed guests to stay for free, their charges paid by Union Pacific until snow came. He had Sun Valley publish ads telling people to come and stay for free, saying it would be worth their gamble. Other stories of the resort's opening are not as well known.

Bill Castegnato said John E.P. Morgan, the New York financier who was instrumental in laying out Sun Valley's ski hills and lifts, was standing outside the lodge's entrance next to a Sun Valley vehicle. A guest, believing Morgan was part of the staff, asked if he could take her to Ketchum. Morgan drove her to where she wanted to go and she gave him a dime tip, which he accepted, thanking her graciously. Ed Seagle said the opening banquet was so successful the guests called for a parade of the chefs, who came out to be greeted by great applause. One guest was so pleased he sent five cases of champagne to the kitchen for the chefs and their staff.

The New Year's Eve party gave rise to another iconic story. A Chicago socialite tried to join David Selznick's table where Joan Bennett and Claudette Colbert were sitting, and asked the women to dance. According to Dorice Taylor, "Selznick took exception and inflicted a black eye on the Chicagoan with one punch." Those in charge thought the event was ruined and Sun Valley's image undermined. Steve Hannagan disagreed, saying, "This is wonderful. It will make headlines in every paper in the country." Hannagan's headline for the story was "Sun Valley Opens With a Bang."

SEASONS GREETING

Reveillon de Fin d'Annee

MENU

Les Huitres Blue-Point

Le Beeftea aux Paillettes d'Or

Celery Olives Amandes

La Barquette d'Hommard Sun Valley

Le Faisan en Voliere Saint-Hubert

La Pomme de Terre Gaufrette

Les Haricots Verts au Gratin

La Salade Millionaire

La Peche aux Liqueurs Sarah Bernhardt

Frivolites

Cafe Royal

SUN VALLEY LODGE
December 31, 1937

"HAPPY NEW YEAR"

Menu for New Year's Eve dinner at Sun Valley Lodge, December 31, 1937.

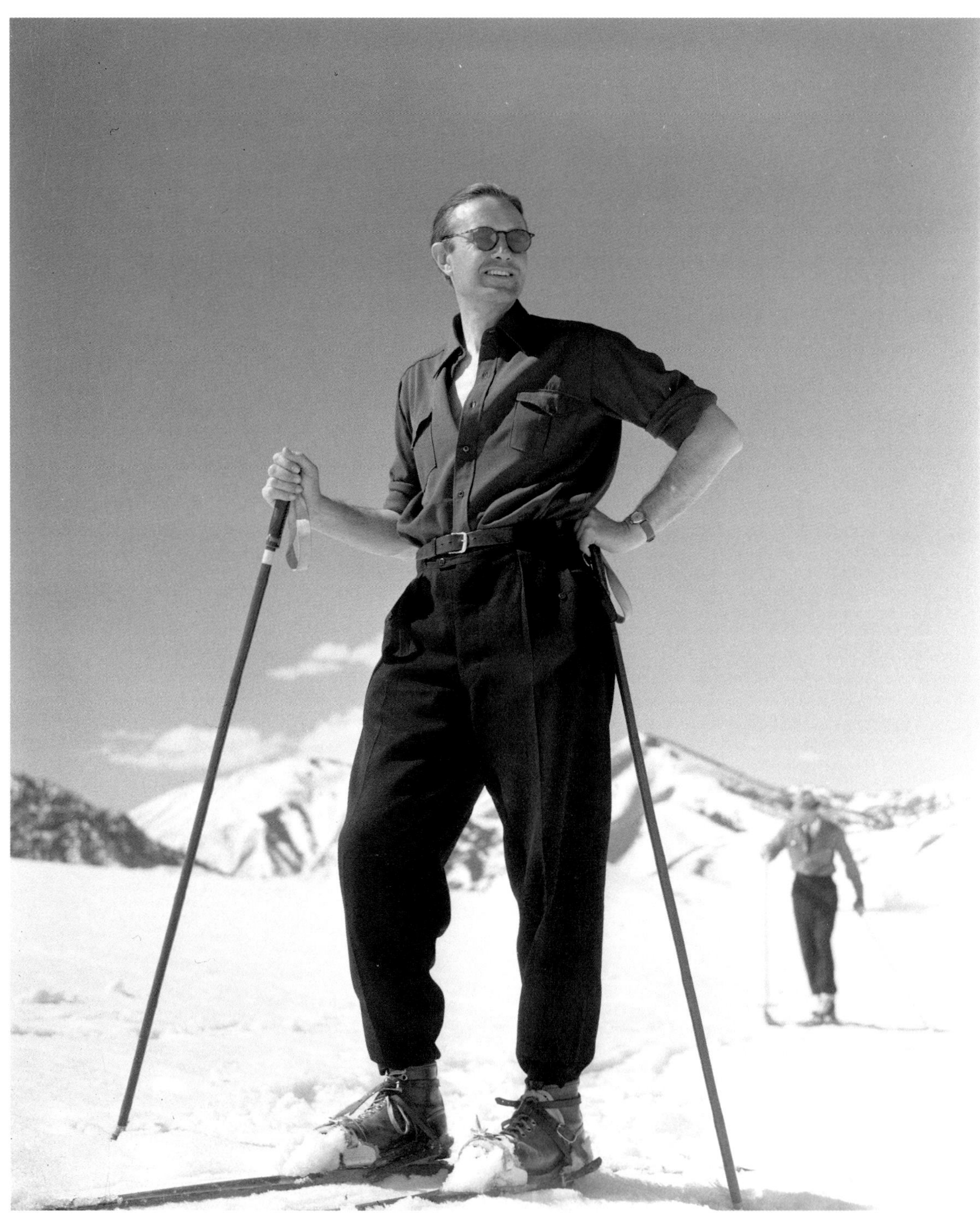

Averell Harriman on skis, 1937.

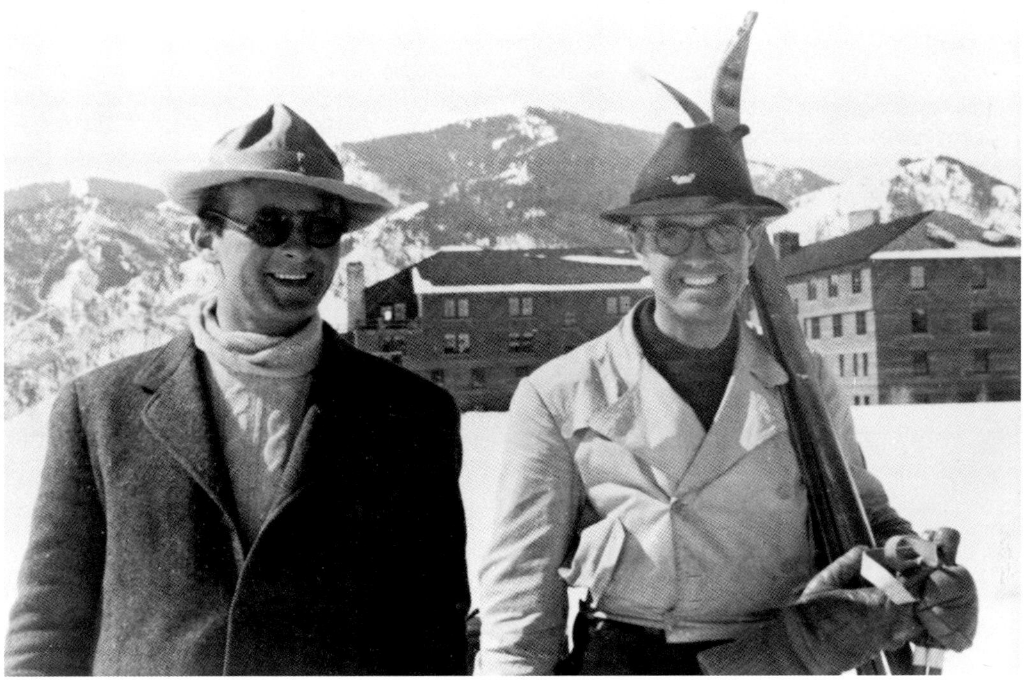

Count Felix Schaffgotsch and Averrell Harriman with Sun Valley Lodge in background, 1937.

Once Sun Valley opened, its operation was turned over to the Union Pacific operations department under vice president of operations Howard Mann. Ed Seagle became chief engineer of Sun Valley operations, in charge of all mechanical equipment, including the boilers, ski lifts, snowplow equipment, and virtually everything else. Seagle was on call twenty-four hours a day, seven days a week, and supervised 100 employees, including painters, carpenters, plumbers, and cabinet makers. Ironically, Union Pacific would not let Seagle ski, saying it was too dangerous and they were worried he would break his leg, taking him out of work. Seagle was primarily responsible for Sun Valley operations until 1964, when the Janss Company bought the resort.

For Sun Valley's first winter, guests were taken between the lodge and the ski lifts by Pierce Arrow open touring cars from U.P.'s Utah Parks Division, with side curtains that snapped on, no heaters, and ski racks bolted to their sides. They were parked outside since there was no garage. The first bus to start pulled the others to jump start them. The following year, a garage was built and Sun Valley obtained six Ford busses.

"Sun Valley was off and running in a great way and has never slowed down or missed a beat," wrote Val McAtee.[16]

SUN VALLEY MADE SKIING EXCITING, SEXY AND ATTRACTIVE

When Sun Valley opened, skiing was a new sport. There were few ski lifts, and skiers had to hike to the top of the hills before sliding down. Skiing was typically done in private clubs or on local mountains, ski gear was rudimentary, and there were limited lessons available. As described by Joy Lucas in *Ancient Skiers of the Northwest*, "Little was known about downhill skiing and skiers learned the hard way—on their own . . . reading 'How to Ski' books was the only way to learn the sport." This limited the number of people interested in skiing, but Sun Valley changed this. Sun Valley made skiing sexy and attractive, accessible to more people, with ski lessons that were an important part of the resort.

Harriman said he "heard from Europeans that the ski school was very important to a resort. Of course, it was very important here for Sun Valley to have a good ski school." He asked Schaffgotsch to establish a ski school based on Hannes Schneider's Arlberg technique taught in Austria. Schneider, known as the father of modern skiing, is credited with founding the first modern ski school at St. Anton, and the style of skiing he developed is considered to be the basis of modern skiing. He developed the stem Christie turn, a "supplementary means of negotiating corners." The count traveled to his native Austria and hired five ski instructors. Hans Hauser, who won the Austrian combined championships in 1932, 1934, and 1936, became the first ski school director.

The roster, salaries, and schedules of Sun Valley's ski school were set in the fall. Count Schaffgotsch would receive $3,000 for the season for promoting Sun Valley, plus expenses between New York and Ketchum and free room and board. Hans Hauser, the head ski instructor, received $1,000. Five assistant instructors, Joseph Benedikter, Franz Epp, Alfred Dingl, Joseph Schwaighofer, and Roland Cossman, received $500 plus expenses from Austria to Ketchum and free room and board. They taught from 10:00 a.m. to noon and 2:00 p.m. to 4:00 p.m. daily. They could give private lessons at other times and on Sunday, at prices set by hotel management. Graham Hobbs of Ontario was the skating instructor, receiving $1,000 for the season, and paid his own transportation and living expenses. The first season, instructors conducted ski lessons on Penny Slope, across the highway from the lodge. As skiers' techniques improved, lessons were shifted to Dollar and later to Proctor.

Sun Valley's ski instructors did more than teach skiing—they had a role in entertaining clients. They were expected to join their clients after lessons in the lodge, and later in the Ram, and were often invited to dine with them and attend the many parties. A number of instructors became romantically involved with their clients.

Beatrice Haemmerle, who married ski instructor Florian Haemmerle, said instructors had to take out any single girl Pat Rogers thought should have an escort. Hans Hauser was a notorious ladies' man and was Florian's roommate one year. Hauser came home late one night, drunk, from one of his romantic escapades. Florian put Hauser's head out the window to sober him up and closed the window on him so he wouldn't fall out. When Florian woke up the next morning, Hauser was still there, pinned under the window.

Ed Seagle said the Austrian ski instructors, who didn't speak English well, got a lot of attention from the Eastern socialites. They learned enough English to be able to look their female clients in the eye and say, "you are so beautiful," and the old gals would "pant like a dog." They had a ball and were "great con artists." Ski instructors had special privileges, including signing chits to pay for drinks marked "ent" for entertainment, that were paid by the resort.

Dorice Taylor first came to Sun Valley in December 1937 and was the resort's publicist after World War II. She said many instructors had limited English skills, so their main command to their students was "bend ze ankles." Hans Hauser was being helped with his English by Hal Smith, whose orchestra played in the Duchin Room. One evening, Hal told Hans what to say to a woman he was interested in, and then told Dorice "watch this." Hauser and the woman were dancing when he whispered something to her. The woman backed up, slapped Hans, and stormed off the dance floor. Hauser later married Virginia Hill, the girlfriend of a notorious gangster.[17]

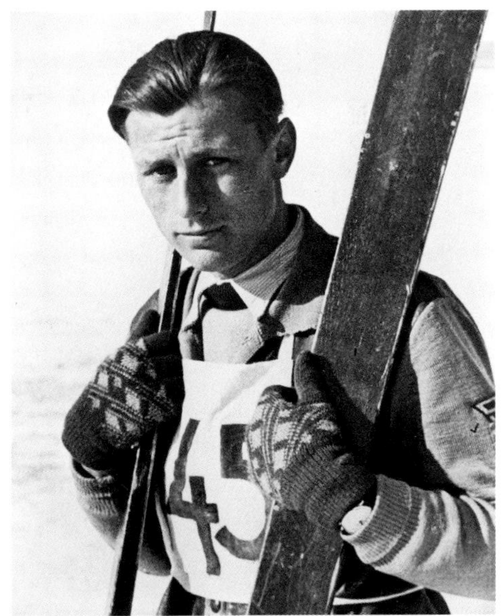

Austrian Hans Hauser, first director of Sun Valley Ski School, 1937.

Sun Valley was the country's first destination ski resort. It attracted visitors from all over the world, including members of the New York social

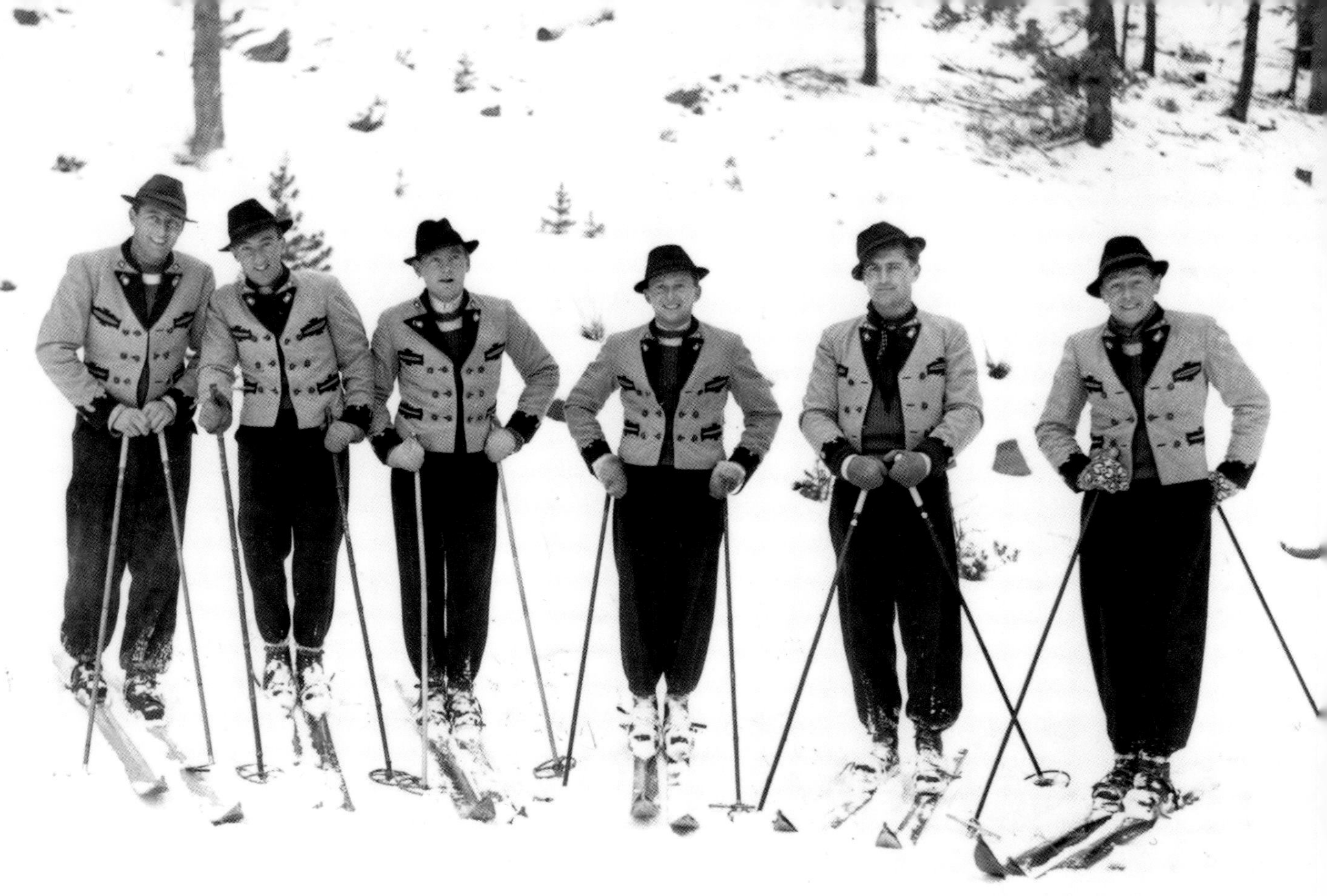

Sun Valley Ski School dressed in Austrian outfits, 1937. Hans Hauser, Roland Cossman, Sepp Benedikter, Franz Epp, Joe Schwaighofer, Al Dingl.

register, people from Chicago's North Shore suburbs, Hollywood movie stars, Eastern businessmen, and Seattle-area residents. The *New York Herald Tribune* said, "Doubtless Idaho will soon be included on Society's annual circuit, and the woods will be full of Vanderbilts, Astors, Belmonts, Goulds and What-nots." The best ski racers in the world came to Sun Valley for tournaments, an important part of Harriman's plan to make the resort well known. Skiers and want-to-be-skiers came for pleasure skiing on its large mountains served by chairlifts, to learn how to ski from a staff of European experts, which gave it a colorful, international flavor, and to socialize with like-minded people.

Otto Lang, in his autobiography, described the impact Sun Valley had on the country:

> *Sun Valley! The name had singular ring to it. When Sun Valley opened its doors to skiers in December 1936, the event created a sensation. The press coverage was extensive, thanks to the astute and imaginative Steve Hannagan . . . Life magazine gave it a front cover and featured a lengthy story, extolling its offerings in luxury, ideal terrain, snow, and sunshine in abundance. Overnight, Sun Valley had joined the ranks of the world-class resorts. There were a dozen or so comparable resorts in Europe, but none in the United States could match its scope and vision at that time. Sun Valley was a magnet for the "beautiful people," a meeting place for movie stars and moguls, chairmen and captains of industry, Greek shipping tycoons, and peripatetic playboys—and playgirls—of the international social set. All flocked to this wintery Shangri-la.*

Friedl Pfeifer, in his autobiography, described the romance of Sun Valley:

> *It is hard to recapture the fascination Sun Valley had back then as a romantic oasis. The social whirl that centered around the Duchin Room in the Sun Valley Lodge, where an orchestra played every night, made Sun Valley a never-never land where everyone was rich and young and all invited to the dance.*

Sun Valley became a grand vision of a paradise for Seattleites, which could be reached in comfort and safety on Union Pacific trains. The *Seattle Times* said, "Sun Valley was 26 hours from Seattle by train, and 20 hours by car, but it might as well be in Seattle's back yard." Seattle newspapers regularly reported on ski races in Sun Valley and local skiers and socialites who traveled there to enjoy the year-round attractions, in both their Sports and Society sections. Sun Valley was mentioned in the *Seattle Times* 227 times in 1937 and 234 times in 1938.

Sun Valley was big news throughout the country, and Hannagan made sure articles about the resort appeared in many publications. On January 23, 1937, *Railway Age* ran a lengthy article, "Significance of Sun Valley Lodge," describing how Union Pacific was leading the railroad industry in a new direction by promoting rail traffic with its winter sports lodge. Railroads, it said, could create new demand for rail travel "by stimulating interest in those pursuits which require travel." Its lodge, with advantages found at winter sports center in the European Alps, presented a reason for Americans to spend their funds at home, not at foreign resorts. Union Pacific operated sleeping cars every Friday from Chicago and Los Angeles direct to Ketchum. Other trains were met at Shoshone by buses that carried passengers to the lodge.

Railway Age said the Union Pacific created an "Elaborate Winter Sports Center" with "all the recreational, scenic, climatic and other advantages heretofore considered to be possessed only by European resorts." The lodge could accommodate 250 guests in 96 large double rooms, 20 medium sized rooms, and 28 small double rooms. The first floor had a dance floor, a game room, a house physician's office, a beauty shop, and a ski room with facilities for waxing and repair of skis operated by Saks Fifth Avenue. The dining room held 230. The second floor had guest rooms, a two-story lounge, bridge and sitting rooms, and sun rooms on the ends of the floor.

An article in *The Power Specialist*, another trade publication, "Swim when It Snows and Ski when the Sun Shines," described the technical aspects of Sun Valley's "very special kind of pool." Although Union Pacific considered using hot water from Guyer Hot Springs, it decided to use conventional water and heat and mineralize it. Its pool contained water heated to 99 degrees in processing tanks in the lodge's basement, "where all of the health minerals—minus the disagreeable sulphur salts—are introduced." After being put in the outdoor insulated concrete pool, the water temperature dropped to 90 degrees. One of the popular times to swim was between 11:00 p.m. and midnight, when it often is around 15 degrees below zero. Swimmers were kept warm by a glass fence surrounding the pool that kept the wind out and enclosed the air warmed by the 90-degree water.

Steve Hannagan convinced *Life* magazine to write an article about Sun Valley, resulting in an eight-page spread on March 8, 1937, "East Goes West to Idaho's Sun Valley, Society's Newest Winter Playground." *Life* had a circulation of one million in 1937, so the resort got millions of dollars of free national publicity that Van Gordon Sauter called "a remarkable publicity coup . . . an incredible piece of publicity placement . . . eight pages of text and pictures featuring high-society guests who were early adopters of the resort."

The cover had a picture of a skier riding a chairlift up the mountain (which cost 25¢ a ride and carried passengers down as well as up). The story read, "since Christmas it has been packed, at from eight dollars to twenty-four dollars a day, with as fancy a crew of rich socialites as have ever been assembled under one roof in the

U.S." Pictures taken by famous photographer Alfred Eisenstaedt showed the resort, the surrounding mountains, skiing, and life at the lodge and around the pool that "functioned as a cocktail bar on sunny days." There were pictures of celebrities, in keeping with Hannagan's vision for the resort, including Mrs. Margaret Vanderbilt, the widow of Alfred Gywnne Vanderbilt Sr., smoking a cigarette and Gloria Baker, an heiress worth $10 million, shown with her head on ski instructor Hans Hauser's lap. Baker's father was so upset when he saw the picture, he ordered her home, according to Dorice Taylor. *Life* showed a number of guests with sports injuries, adding a touch of chilling realism, although most came from ice skating.

Sun Valley's early years were a special time for guests and workers. During its first year, the kitchen was manned with French chefs. Louis Holliday worked in the kitchen and was paid $60 a month, with free room and board and use of Sun Valley's amenities, including skiing, golf, ice skating, and the pool. Waiters finished breakfast duty around 9:30 a.m., going back to work at 4:30 p.m., giving them time to ski. A lot of guests came for the season. "The people who got here were wealthy, and they got good service," Holliday said. "And they showed their appreciation with the green stuff." Waiters often got a $20 tip for a $10 bill. Such tips were normal, and waiters seldom received less. One Hollywood guest would tip $20 when he was brought a 5¢ newspaper. Holliday said it was a "bad night" when an acquaintance working at the Christiania made only $175 in tips. "They'd spend money like it was going out of style." The first few years Sun Valley was open, guests were on the American plan, with one charge for room and board. Employees and guests were close. "We were virtually on a first name basis after about two days," Holliday said. "In the winter time you'd hear all over the mountain, I'll meet you in the Ram about four thirty, and that was the meeting place in Sun Valley." Rank and position didn't matter.

Although Sun Valley was a haven of opulence in Idaho's mountains, Ketchum was a small town. When Holliday arrived in November 1936, Ketchum had 185 people, many of whom left for the winter. There was one drugstore, where Slavey's bar was in 1985, when he was interviewed. The Casino on Main Street had "cubby hole" rooms to rent upstairs, and the Golden Rule store was in the Griffith Building (most recently the Cornerstone Restaurant on Main Street). Bald Mountain Hot Springs was the place to stay. Ketchum later had a number of gambling establishments. The Alpine was owned by Lou Hill and the Sawtooth by Owen Simpson. The Idaho Club was where the Pioneer Restaurant is now, and the Wooden Spur was where Sturtevants Sports Shop is. Club Rio was on Leadville Avenue where the parking lot for Louie's Restaurant was in 1985, in an old church (now part of the Picket Fence). Holiday said a person could go to town with $5 in his pocket, have all he could drink and a steak dinner at the Alpine, Lou would take you home, and you would still have $3.

The *Hailey Times* of December 30, 1936, said it cost Union Pacific $40,727 to operate Sun Valley Lodge that month. After the lodge opened on December 22, it collected $14,467 in revenue and had operating expenses of $55,194. This was a pattern that continued throughout Union Pacific's ownership of the resort.[18]

8

SKIING ON PROCTOR AND DOLLAR MOUNTAINS AND IN THE BACKCOUNTRY AROUND SUN VALLEY

When Sun Valley opened in December 1936, there were chairlifts on Proctor and Dollar Mountains. Proctor offered expert skiing with more terrain and longer runs, and Dollar had easier skiing. Small cabins were built on top of Dollar and below the summit of Proctor where skiers could escape the elements, have lunch, or relax. Sun Valley buses left the lodge every 10 minutes. Lift tickets cost $15 a week, and ski lessons were $3.50 for a half day and $5 for all day.

There were no lifts on Bald Mountain since it was beyond the skills of most skiers in 1936. Hardy skiers used skins to climb Baldy, and Sno-Cats took them up beginning in 1938, but the mountain was not opened for general skiing until chairlifts were installed for the winter of 1940.

Chairlifts were new inventions in 1936, and skiers needed to learn how they worked. According to the *Idaho Statesman* of December 19, 1936, Sun Valley's "chair ski lifts" offered "the utmost in comfort and practicability":

> *The skier will not be required to remove his skis but will be carried up in a chair suspended from a cable with his skis on and his legs resting on a padded leg rest. A rope is suspended from the cable six feet in advance of the chair so that the skier may grab the rope as it comes by, giving himself sufficient speed on his skis to let himself down easily into the chair at its traveling speed. This speed is approximately four hundred feet per minute, and chairs will be suspended at convenient intervals. In the*

> *same way, at the unloading platform the skier will use the rope suspended from the cable to give himself a pull away from the chair.*

An Australian skier, an early visitor to Sun Valley, described the chairlift for his countrymen: "You sit on a small seat with your skis clear of the snow. The chairs hardly ever stop and you stand at the bottom trying to line up your seat with the approaching chair. You speculate about what will happen if you sit down at the wrong time."

Engineers had to estimate how high the chairs should be above the ground. They talked to locals about the average snow depth in the winter, and decided to have the chairs six feet above the ground, a height that proved to be insufficient. Tunnels had to be dug to provide clearance for the chairs. There is a story that Steve Hannagan insisted the chairlifts not be more than six feet above the snow to keep riders from getting vertigo.

Early photographs show the ropes that were attached to the chairlift for skiers to grab and the canvas and flannel robes to keep them warm. Dorice Taylor said that in later years the capes read "Sun Valley" on the back and were kept in a pile at the bottom of the mountain. People began to take them, and they became "the thing to wear" at Eastern football games. Sun Valley began making capes without the name on back, but they were still taken until Bill Janss said no more capes in the 1960s.

The first year, skiers reached Proctor by riding a bus from the lodge to a turnaround, where they took a J-bar (also called a drag line) to the base of the Proctor chair, described by the *Boise Capital News* on December 19, 1936: "A bus will run from the east wing of the hotel to the foot of Proctor Mountain where the skier will find a ski-tow or drag line which will pull him 3,050 feet up a narrow valley to the base of the chairlift which is 320 feet above the valley." The drag line was in constant motion and had a padded bar against which the skier rested while being dragged on his skis at four hundred feet per minute. According to the *Railway Age* of January 23, 1937,

> *The ski tow line* [J-bar] *is similar in all essential respect to the chair lines except that padded bars are provided in place of the chairs. On this line the skier, wearing his skis, simply grasps a rope and maneuvers into position in front of one of the bars so that he is conveyed up the incline in an upright position.*

At the end of the J-bar, skiers loaded onto a chairlift taking them up the mountain to a small plateau below the peak of Proctor Mountain, an elevation gain of 1,500 feet. From

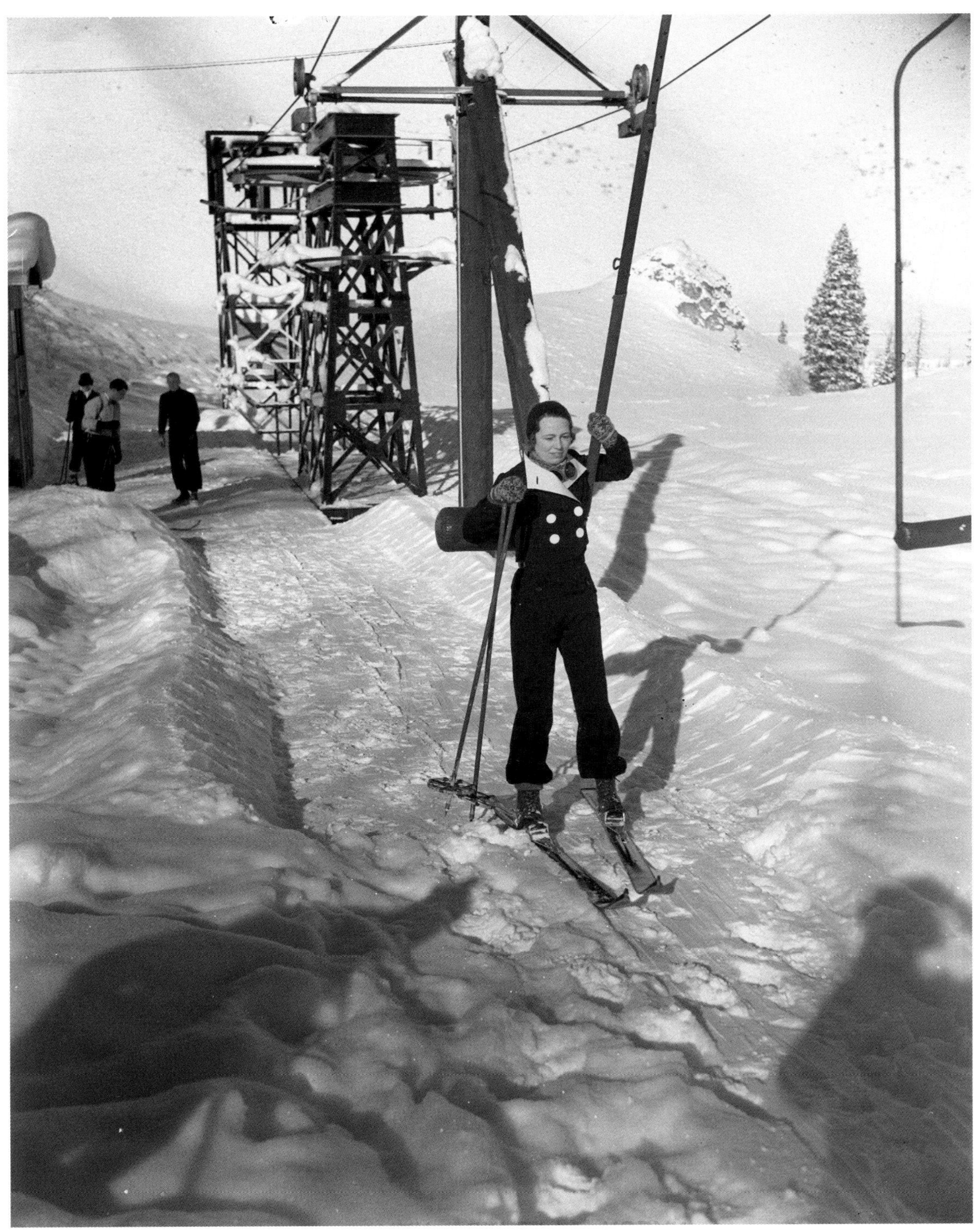

Woman loading onto J-bar leading to the base of the Proctor Mountain chairlift.

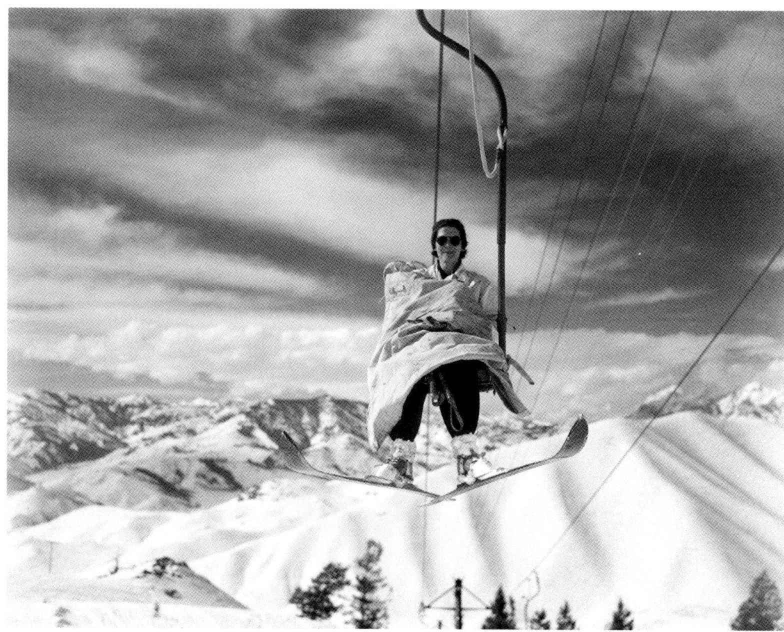

Woman riding on Proctor chair wrapped in blanket to keep warm.

the top of the chairlift, there was skiing in all directions, both steep and gentle, to the valley floor. Climbing from the top station to the top of Proctor gave access to longer runs of one or two miles on open slopes and ridges, or through valleys and ravines.

The J-bar cable was manufactured by American Steel and Wire, and attachments hung from a circulating overhead cable in a similar manner as its chairlifts. However, the J-bar "wasn't a very good lift," according to Val McAtee. It "swung so bad that the cable kept coming off the wheels." Ed Seagle said the J-bar hung from cables but would sag between the poles going up the hill. People would compensate by leaning back, sitting on the padded seat support, and fall off. As a result, it was used for just one season.

In summer 1937, the J-bar was removed, converted to a crude chairlift (without backs or leg supports), and installed on Ruud Mountain, the resort's new ski jumping site. In 1938, skiers were taken all the way to the base of the Proctor chair by bus. The Proctor lift was used regularly until Bald Mountain opened for skiing in winter 1940, and thereafter it was just used occasionally. The Proctor lift was moved to Baldy in fall 1951, where it was installed at the Roundhouse close to the Christmas chair to provide two single chairlifts to the summit, doubling the uphill capacity on that popular part of the mountain.

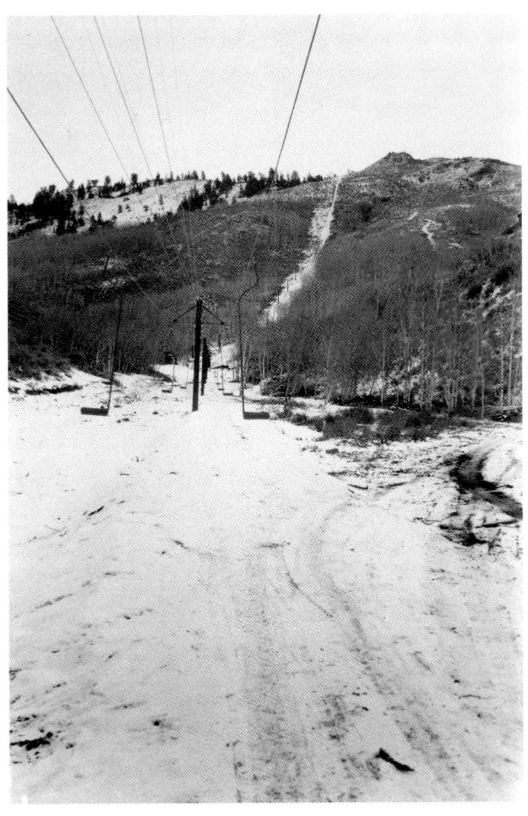

J-bar looking uphill to Proctor chairlift.

A book published by Union Pacific in 1948, *Sun Valley Ski Guide*, by Sun Valley ski instructor Andy Hennig, described ski runs on the lift-served mountains at the resort. He also described backcountry skiing around Sun Valley, where buses would pick up skiers in a variety of locations. "The Skiing," a document in the Proctor family collection, has no identified author but was likely written by John E.P. Morgan in either late 1936 (after the chairlifts were built) or early 1937 (before the Harriman Cup downhill was held on a mountain north of town). It provides details about the extensive backcountry skiing available all around Sun Valley. Backcountry routes were marked for skiers to follow.

The Proctor cabin was near the top lift station, below the crest of the hill. It was a 20-foot-by-30-foot building with a waxing table, work bench, lunch counter, benches, and restrooms. "Here the expert skiers may rest, repair their skis and make ready for the hazardous rides that the vicinity of Proctor mountain affords," Hennig wrote. The cabin had a restaurant, the Hot Potato Hut. Sun Valley ski instructor Florian Haemmerle cooked at the Hot Potato Hut after 1938. It was later moved to make the Sun Valley Gun Club house.

Proctor Mountain was the principal lift-served mountain from 1936 to 1939, "an ideal ski mountain, offering every type of terrain and every grade of ski slope," according to Hennig. "The snow conditions most of the time are excellent." It was at 7,500 feet elevation, with a vertical drop of 1,150 feet, and its ski tow was 3,540 feet long. In early winter, the hill had powder snow and offered wonderful spring snow. The top lift station and the nearby Proctor cabin were sheltered by peaks and ridges. Hennig showed 25 runs on Proctor, plus variations for several of them, some requiring climbing to the top of the mountain from the top lift station. Some runs led to areas for backcountry skiing.

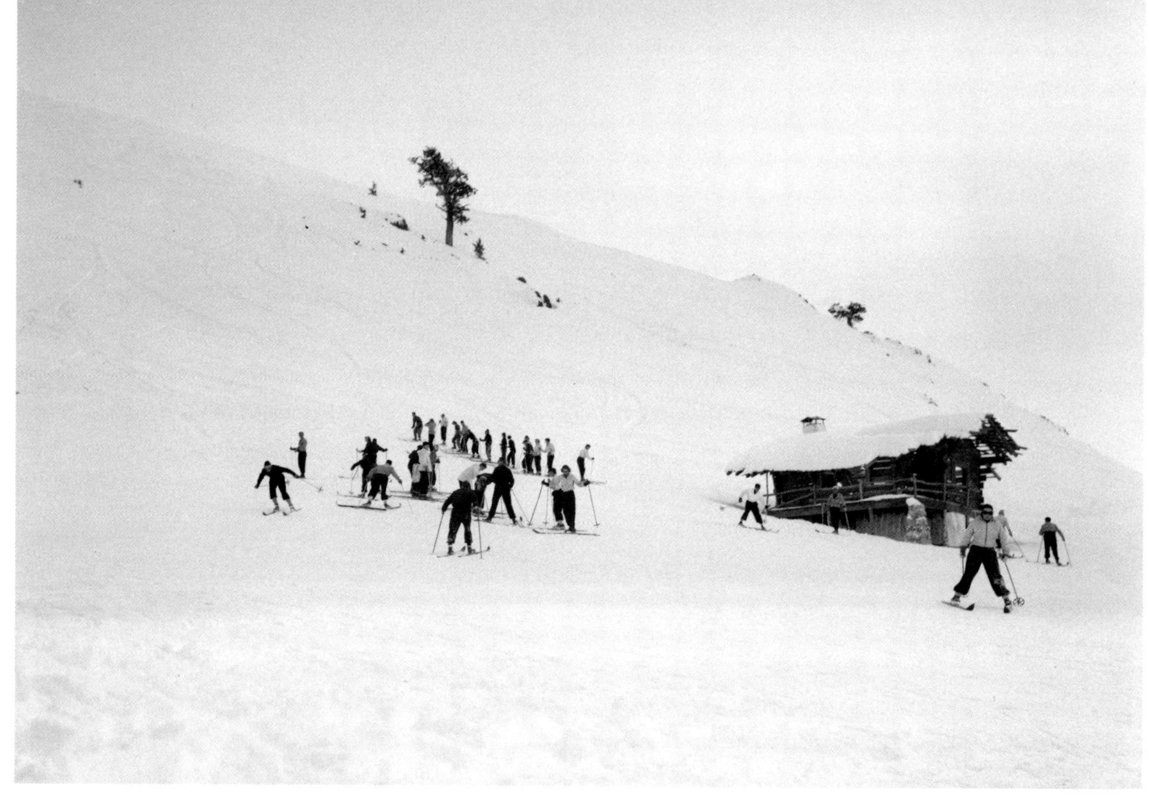

ABOVE Skiers near Hot Potato Hut on Proctor Mountain. Several runs could be reached by hiking up to the top of Proctor.

OPPOSITE A skier enjoys the powder on Morgan Ridge on Proctor Mountain.

From the top of the Proctor lift, skiers could climb a ridge and gain 500 feet of elevation "with longer runs providing still greater variety," Hennig wrote. "Skiing down the spectacular north face slope of this peak into the tremendous, wide bowl, is in itself an exciting thrill for the expert skier." From the base of the bowl, several runs continued down the hill to the bottom of Proctor Mountain.

The Face Run took advanced skiers from the top station, down along the chairlift to its base, and had several variations.

Beutter Ridge, to the right of the chair going uphill, was reached by skiing down from the top lift station into a wide bowl, followed by a 15-minute climb to the next ridge's summit (later named Ruud Mountain), to a slope that dropped 1,000 feet into the valley, providing a one-and-a-half-mile run with 1,150 feet of vertical.

Back Pay Gulch run was the easiest run. From the top station, skiers went right, crossed the upper part of the bowl, then skied down a timber-free slope to Back Pay Gulch, which widened as it descended to a bus pickup point. The run was two and a half miles long with 1,550 feet of vertical.

Several of Proctor's runs led away from Proctor Mountain. To reach Dry Creek Run, skiers climbed for 10 minutes from Proctor Cabin to a saddle, traversed to the next ridge, then went down a long, partially timbered ridge to Trail Creek Cabin, where bus transportation could be arranged.

Victor Run, for intermediates, was a gentle combination of a downhill run and a cross-country trip. It began by going left from the top station, climbing for 30 minutes up White Face, then skiing through, as Hennig put it, a "thrillingly long and wonderful ski bowl," ending between Proctor Mountain and Prospect Hill, where skiers could go to the Dollar lift station.

Morgan Ridge Run was for advanced skiers and provided excellent skiing from February until late May. The run was four miles long, had 2,100 feet of vertical, and involved a climb of about two hours. From Proctor cabin, skiers climbed 10 minutes to a saddle, then followed several ridges until the last long one led to the top of Morgan Ridge. From there, two long and steep timber-free ridges led east, down into Corral Creek Valley. The left ridge ended near the junction of Trail Creek Road and Corral Creek Road. The right ridge ended further back on Corral Creek, near Uncle John's Cabin. It was important to start before 11:00 am, and it was advised not to undertake the trip except in good weather. Skiers could arrange for a dog team to meet them at Uncle John's Cabin.

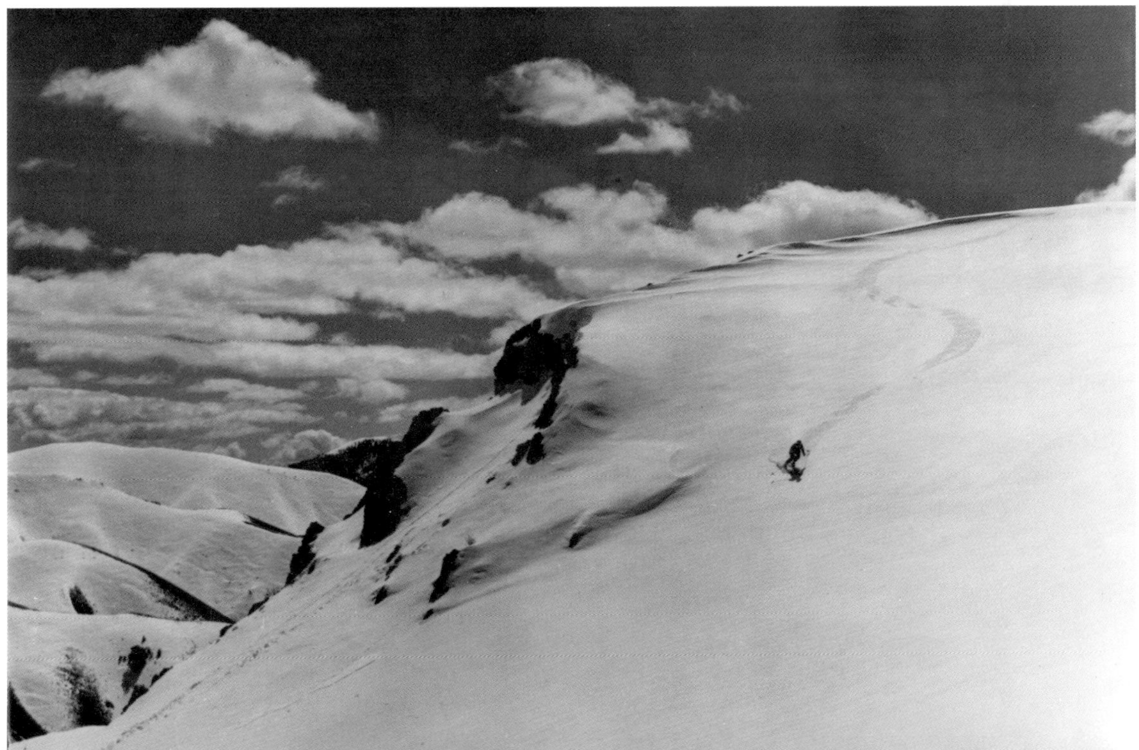

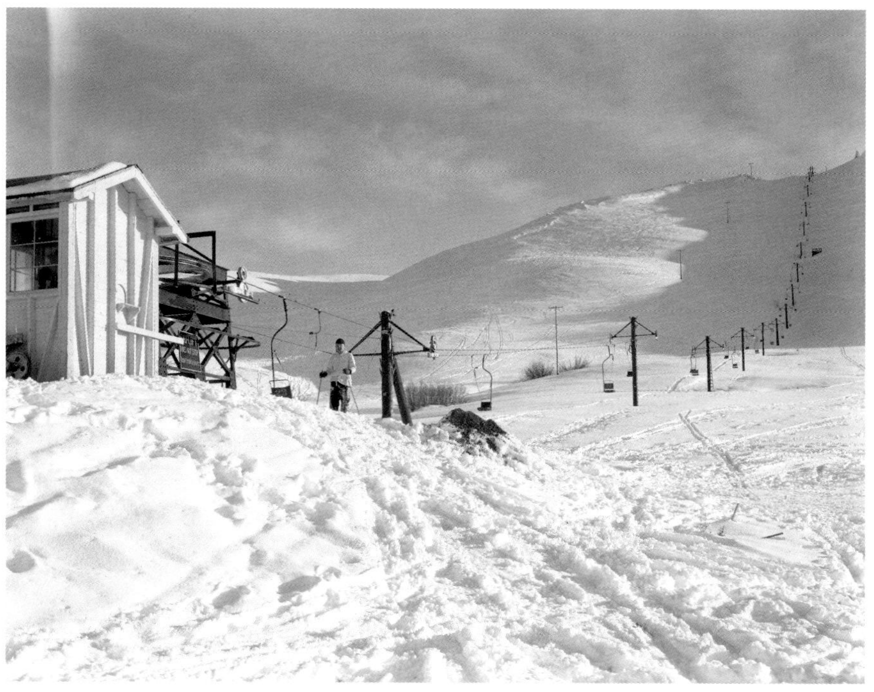

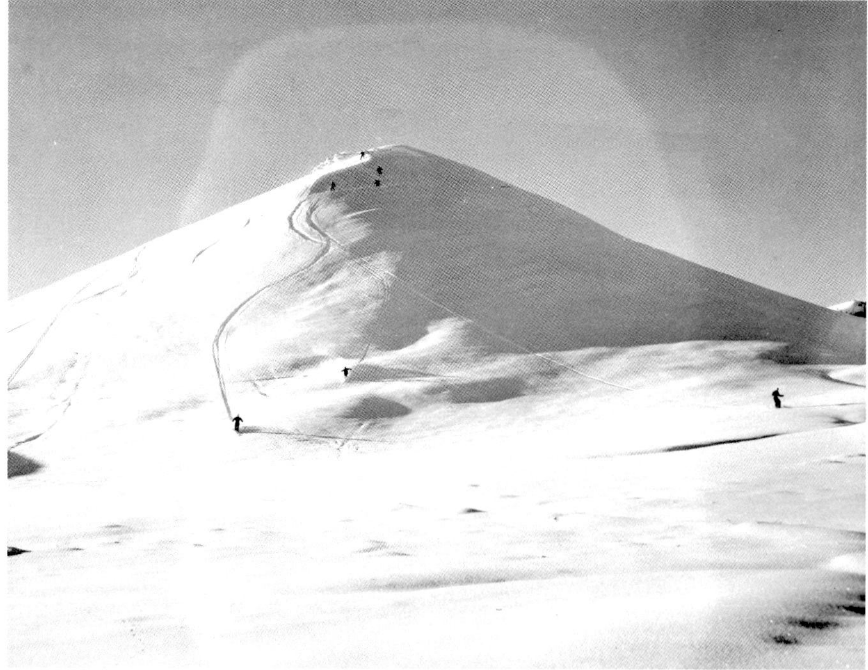

TOP Dollar Mountain chairlift built with wooden poles for lift towers.

BOTTOM Penny Mountain on Saddle Road, northwest of Sun Valley Lodge, where beginners took their first ski lessons, now used as a sledding hill.

Dollar Mountain was closest to the lodge and the easier of the two mountains served by lifts. Hennig said Dollar was "the Biggest Little Ski Mountain in America," offering "unexcelled ski and practice slopes. . . . Being timber-free this mountain provides a great number and variety of wide-open ski runs . . . usually in packed snow conditions." There was a warming hut on the top of the mountain.

Hennig shows six runs on Dollar, two involving some off-piste skiing. Run five went west from the top of Dollar, down into Ketchum, and was skiable when there was enough snow. It was easy and interesting but required a time-consuming bus ride from Ketchum back to the lift. Run 6 was for the skier "who doesn't mind a little hiking," according to Hennig. It went along the south ridge toward what is now Elkhorn, where one could choose a number of ways to ski through untracked snow to the bottom of the mountain.

Beginner and novice ski lessons were taught at Dollar every day except Sunday, although initially, beginning skiers were taken to Penny Mountain west of the lodge. Classes assembled at the Ski School meeting place near the lodge, where skiers were assigned to their proper class levels. Beginner and novice classes learned fundamentals, such as walking, climbing, straight running, and straight snowplows, leading up to making snowplow turns linked by traverses on hard-packed and moderately pitched slopes. Intermediate skiers were capable of making stem turns in deep snow and stem Christies on hard-packed terrain. Advanced skiers were mastering stem Christies in favorable snow conditions (fresh powder and hard-packed snow) on reasonably steep slopes. Expert skiers mastered stem Christies at high speed in any type of snow on extremely steep slopes.[19]

Backcountry Skiing

It would be a mistake to think of Sun Valley skiing when the resort opened as being similar to what we know now, consisting primarily of areas served by lifts. In the 1930s, most skiers engaged in what would today be called backcountry skiing or alpine touring, where the "ski area" was just a place where skiers left to climb surrounding hills before they skied down. Ernest Hemingway described skiing in Europe, where he spent several winters during the 1920s: "Skiing was not the way it is now. . . .

There were no ski patrols. Anything you ran down from, you had to climb up. That gave you legs that were fit to run down with."

The installation of the first rope tow in the United States—at Suicide Six, Vermont, in 1934—marked the beginning of the split between resort skiing and backcountry skiing. Betty Woolsey, a member of the 1936 women's Olympic ski team, passed the Austrian ski teachers examination in 1937. It was, she said, "a useful course that emphasized safety in the mountains, route-finding and avalanche avoidance as well as ski technique," necessary skills in the 1930s.

Ski touring or backcountry skiing in the mountains around Sun Valley was an important part of its winter activities. Charles Proctor's initial article about Sun Valley in fall 1936 discussed skiing on Baldy and in the Boulder Mountains and cross-country skiing in the mountains surrounding the resort. Proctor, Count Schaffgotsch, and John E.P. Morgan explored all around Sun Valley on skis before the resort was built.

Substantial work was done between 1937 and 1940 to provide backcountry skiing options for Sun Valley's guests. Initially, backcountry skiing involved climbing hills using skins, but in 1938, Sun Valley acquired snow tractors to transport skiers to backcountry locations, and later, two backcountry huts were built to offer a true European-style experience.

Before chairlifts were installed on Bald Mountain for the winter of 1940, skiing there was enjoyed by "the hardier brand of winter enthusiasts—the strong and rugged individual to whom walking and climbing is secondary to finding new powder snow," according to *The Valley Sun*. In winter 1937, rather than being satisfied on Proctor and Dollar Mountains, Sun Valley skiers went into the backcountry and "hardy souls ventured up Wood River canyon to the north, and Warm Springs canyon to the west, and realized that miles and miles of perfect skiing lie as a vast Promised Land to be opened to snow sportsmen of the future." Other runs were available in many peaks surrounding Sun Valley.

I Met Him in Paris Is Filmed at Sun Valley

Sun Valley attracted the attention of Paramount Pictures for the making of the film *I Met Him in Paris*, produced by Adolph Zukor, directed by Wesley Ruggles, and starring

Claudette Colbert, Melvyn Douglas, and Robert Young. Half the film was supposed to take place in Paris and half at St. Moritz. Paramount was looking for a U.S. location to film the ski resort scenes. They decided to film at Sun Valley in February 1937, a venture fraught with problems that were described in a letter from Ernst Fegte, the film's art director, to Bill Janss dated March 25, 1974.

In early December 1936, the director and his crew went to Sun Valley to scout the location, arriving at a chaotic scene as construction crews raced to get the lodge ready for its December 21 opening. A location 11 miles north of the lodge at Baker Creek was selected as a filming site. Sun Valley gave permission for props to be erected at the Ketchum depot to make it look like a Swiss railroad station.

Fegte and a crew of 20 arrived in Sun Valley in January 1937 and built a Swiss hotel with an ice rink and church and village surrounding it at Baker Creek. It was cold (38 to 40 degrees below zero), but no snow had fallen. After one month, they could not get the skating rink to fully freeze, so a bar was built to cover the holes. Then they got 18 inches of snow, but it was so cold the actors' breath showed on the film, looking like steam coming from their mouths. Portable heaters known as "salamanders" were used to warm the set but the microphones picked up the sound of water dripping as snow melted. Pails caught the water, but sawdust was needed to mask the noise. The warm interiors melted snow on the roofs, spoiling the outdoor scenes. Luck intervened and more snow fell, preserving the look of the Swiss village and hotel, allowing the film to be completed.

"The picture, when released, proved a box-office hit," said Fegte. "As the saying goes, all's well that ends well." Sun Valley got an abundance of free publicity. Claudette Colbert, the movie's star, became a regular at Sun Valley and one of the best skiers of the Hollywood set there. On May 3, 1937, *Life* published an article about the filming of the movie at Sun Valley. This was the first of a number of movies filmed there.[20]

9

1937

Sun Valley Sponsors the Country's First Major International Alpine Ski Competition and Is a Success in Its First Year

Averell Harriman set out to make Sun Valley an international destination and the country's center of ski racing. He sponsored ski tournaments that attracted the best skiers in the world, and Steve Hannagan made sure newspapers provided extensive coverage. Harriman supported U.S. ski teams and prospective racers by paying their expenses when they trained at the resort under the tutelage of Sun Valley ski instructors and provided jobs for them.

Dick Durrance, the top U.S. ski racer of the 1930s, said Harriman "was determined that Sun Valley would match anything Europe had to offer," and he set out to attract the biggest names in the sport. Harriman, he said, knew one way to "bring Sun Valley into the public consciousness was to get it onto the sports pages. . . . No expense was spared when it came to promotion." Friedl Pfeifer, head of the Sun Valley Ski School beginning in 1938, said Sun Valley played a major role in supporting American ski racing by offering free room and board to talented racers, which allowed many to see a life they had never experienced before. Harriman said competition "was quite important in the development of Sun Valley. It attracted people and, of course, some of the best skiers in the world came here for those competitions." Sun Valley paid the expenses of the top skiers since "we wanted to have an internationally recognized, first class competition."

Sun Valley had ski tows and long, tree-free slopes, making it ideal for race training. Its chairlifts provided fast transportation to the top of the mountains at a time when few other ski areas even had rope tows. This enabled racers to get in far more training than elsewhere to develop skills necessary to compete internationally. A tram was built for the 1936 Olympics in Garmisch-Partenkirchen, Germany, and the U.S. team learned the benefit lifts gave training. Arnold Lunn, a British skiing authority, blamed the disappointing results of the American skiers at the 1936 Olympics on the lack of the country's ski lifts:

> *In the United States you are handicapped by a lack of mountain railways and funiculars. To achieve the standard of a FIS or Alrberg-Kandahar winner, a skier needs weeks of practice during which he can have his 10-15,000 feet of downhill skiing in the day. A skier who has to climb every foot is lucky if he can average 4-5,000 feet a day. Indeed, with your variable weather I doubt if your American racers can average 3,000 feet a day throughout the season.*

Sun Valley sponsored major ski tournaments every year: intercollegiate races over the Christmas holidays, interstate races at the end of January, Sun Valley Ski Club tournaments, and Harriman Cup/Sun Valley Open races. Sun Valley ski instructors helped train college racers during the intercollegiate races.

Harriman hired a number of U.S. skiers to work at Sun Valley during the summers when they were in college and as instructors or on the ski patrol afterwards including a number of members of the 1936 U.S. Olympic team: Dick Durrance and John Litchfield from Dartmouth College, Don Fraser and Darroch Crookes from Washington, and Betty Woolsey from Connecticut. Durrance became a photographer at Sun Valley. In 1939, Don Fraser was the resort's special representative for the Midwest territory, headquartered in Omaha. In December, he became sports director of Sun Valley and was Union Pacific's Sun Valley representative in Denver in the early 1940s. Woolsey was the editor of *The Valley Sun* in 1940. Sun Valley also supported the U.S. Olympic teams over the years, providing them with a place to train and coaching from its ski instructors.

Dick Durrance described Sun Valley's plans to prepare U.S. Olympic teams for the 1940 Games to the *Seattle Times* on August 30, 1939:

> *Sun Valley . . . wants to employ the eighteen first-string American skiers next winter—legitimate employment too—and at the same time give them training under Friedl Pfeiffer and Peter Radacher, two great European racers, for the more strenuous skiing they'll get in the F.I.S. meet.*

When the U.S. team went to the 1936 Olympics in Germany, they learned

> *a hastily-recruited ski team had no chance against the Europeans. . . . They were training for a year. We had only a few weeks. If the team can go to Sun Valley, however, and work on the Bald Mountain downhill course . . . it can get in condition before the first big snow . . . and then we can . . . really learn some skiing before going to Norway.*

The Sun Valley Ski Club was organized in fall 1936. Harriman's biographer wrote, "He began with a ski club for his New York social and financial friends, including Tommy Hitchcock, Nelson Rockefeller, and William Paley." According to John E.P. Morgan's entry in the U.S. Ski and Snowboard Hall of Fame,

> *John organized the Sun Valley Ski Club in a hurry persuading Al Lindley to be its first president and very quickly gathered enough members together to make the club "legit." John secured the nationals there in March of 1937 and helped organize them with the Pacific Northwest Ski Association.*

The Ski Club was organized to promote both serious skiing and entertainment, as described by its constitution:

> *To encourage proficiency and enjoyment of skiing and other winter sports with their attendant relaxations; to promote good fellowship; to encourage the construction and maintenance of ski tows, ski lifts, and all such labor saving devices; to appreciate comfortable accommodation, good food and drink and by all other means to take advantage of the beauty of the mountains in winter or at any other time.*

The club's by laws said it would encourage skiing proficiency and enjoyment, and "encourage, foster and sponsor participation in local, national, and international ski races with a view towards enhancing the United States racing image." A board of governors was established along with an executive committee.

The ski club was a prestigious organization on which a number of well-known professionals and friends of Harriman served. Averell Harriman was chairman of the board of governors, which included people such as Nelson Rockefeller, Robert Pabst, Roland Palmedo, and Charles N. Proctor. A number of Seattle skiers served on the board over the years. Well-known skiers such as Dick Durrance, Don Fraser, Gretchen Fraser, and Darroch Crookes were added later. Al Lindley was the first president, Felix Schaffgotsch was the secretary, and John E.P. Morgan was treasurer.

Al Lindley, a wealthy attorney from Minneapolis, was the club's president its first 14 years. The Ski Club published annual reports each fall containing detailed descriptions of that season's ski races and other key events affecting the resort. In his first president's report, Lindley said the club was "an organization of people who ski for pleasure and satisfaction, who try to ski as well and as fast as they can, but who are not deadly serious about it, and who appreciate the fact that for the best downhill skiing in America, in the most congenial company, one must go to Sun Valley."

The Sun Valley Ski Club was admitted into the Pacific Northwestern Ski Association (PNSA) on February 6, 1937, the regional affiliate of the National Ski Association (NSA), the organization that granted official sanction to ski races. PNSA's territory included Washington, Oregon, Idaho, and Montana, and its "activities greatly increased the interest in skiing in the northwest." As a PNSA member, the Sun Valley Ski Club could sponsor NSA-sanctioned ski races, and it hosted some of the most important ski races in the country for years. As a member of the PNSA, Sun Valley's ski tournaments were an important part of the Northwest's calendar for decades. The top Northwest skiers competed at Sun Valley, and Sun Valley's instructors competed in other Northwest tournaments.[21]

Sun Valley International Open Tournament—The Country's First International Race

The Sun Valley Ski Club got PNSA sanction to sponsor the resort's first ski tournament in winter 1937, the Sun Valley International Open, to include downhill, slalom, and combined competitions. For the first time, the tournament would be "an open competition, with ski instructors meeting amateurs. Ski instructors are generally considered superior to the average American amateur." Harriman had some of Europe's best skiers working as instructors, and he wanted a tournament to showcase them.

Shortly after the event was set, Harriman received a telegram from the Dartmouth Outing Club, asking if the United States National Amateur championships in downhill, slalom, and combined could be included in the tournament. That event had been set for Mount Washington on April 4, 1937, but lack of snow in the East necessitated a change. "We haven't enough snow. . . . You boys had better take it. Since you've got such an outstanding field at Sun Valley, that ought to be the National championships." PNSA approved the expansion of the tournament and took charge of organizing the event under its president, Peter Hostmark from Seattle.

Harriman wanted to give the United States a ski race that would match the big races in Europe, such as the Kandahar in Austria. The snow gods gave Harriman the opening he wanted, and he took full advantage of the opportunity.

The race was called the Sun Valley International Open Downhill and Slalom Competition and was the first major international alpine ski competition in the United States. The tournament was expanded "to make it the No. 1 tournament of the year, because it numbered all the skiing greats in its entry list," according to the *Seattle Times* of March 12, 1937. Sun Valley attracted the "greatest collection of downhill ski racers ever assembled in North America." Two champions would be crowned—the open and amateur. "Ski instructors will be eligible only for the open title. Amateurs will be eligible for both. . . . The presence of the country's great ski teachers will add immeasurably to the quality of the competition."

Union Pacific advertised special trains from Seattle to the tournament, featuring "America's most thrilling ski races . . . the most sensational skiing event ever held in America."

Sun Valley invited a number of Northwest racers, including Don Fraser and Darroch Crookes (members of the 1936 U.S. Olympic ski team) and

Ad for train trip to first Harriman Cup tournament, *Seattle Times*, February 28, 1937.

Don Amick, who was on the 1948 Olympic ski team. "For several years, the three rented a rustic cabin at Paradise Valley on Mount Rainier for $30 a season," according to Joy Lucas in *Ancient Skiers of the Northwest*:

> *Don* [Fraser] *visited Sun Valley for the first time in 1937 with Don Amick to race in the Harriman Cup. As guests of the Union Pacific and Sun Valley, they were given first-class tickets aboard the Portland Rose. When they stepped off the train, a warm bus took them to the Sun Valley Lodge, where all the movie stars were standing around waiting to see the great skiers—and they walked in dressed like bums. They felt like kings to stay in the Lodge, since they were used to the old Guide's shack at Mount Rainier.*

A picture of Crookes and Fraser appeared in the *New York Times* on March 12, 1937, captioned "Olympians to Compete in National Title Meet. . . . The event has attracted the entries of the leading European and American ski instructors, who will oppose this nation's and Canada's foremost amateur runners."

Forty-four of the best European and American skiers entered the tournament—eight ski instructors who were eligible for the open championships and 36 amateurs. Europeans included Sigmund Ruud of Norway; Austrian Hannes Schroll, an instructor at Yosemite who won the 1935 national championship at Mount Rainier; Hans Hauser, Austrian downhill champion and Sun Valley ski school director; Siegfried "Sigi" Engl from Kitzbuhel, then Schroll's assistant at Yosemite; Austrian Otto Lang, ski instructor at Mount Rainier and Mount Baker; five other Austrian Sun Valley ski instructors; and the five-man Swiss ski team.

Top American skiers included Walter Prager, Dartmouth's Swiss ski coach and three-time Federation Internationale de Ski (FIS) downhill and combined champion; Dick Durrance, Dartmouth College, known at the time as "the greatest American amateur skier"; Charles Proctor, Boston; Ken Syverson, Otto Lang's assistant at Mount Rainier; and five winners of the Canadian championships at Banff. Given the talent and experience of the European competitors, Americans were given little chance to win.

Durrance came into national prominence in 1935 when he competed at the national downhill and slalom championships and Olympic tryouts at Mount Rainier. This was the country's first such event, and it made Mount Rainier and Washington skiing well known. Durrance had developed the "high speed turn, especially adapted for downhill and slalom racing, because with it there is less sidewise sliding or braking effect than in other turns, and less tiring to the legs," reported the *Seattle Times* on December 23, 1934. Hannes Schroll, an Austrian teaching at Yosemite, swept the 1935 championships using a European skiing technique that "beats American methods all to pieces." Durrance finished second and led the U.S. Olympic ski team at the 1936 Games. Showing how strong Northwest skiing was, five Washington skiers went to Europe for the 1936 Olympics.

Sun Valley guests created an "informal and entirely unofficial sweepstakes," reported the *Seattle Times*, where chances on 44 racers were sold at a minimum of $10 a man, which "quickly swelled so the pot reached $1,780." Hans Hauser, winner of the Austrian championship two years before, was the "solid choice" to win the championship, going for $605 in late bidding. Norway's Sigmund Ruud, "prime favorite among the experts," went for $275. Switzerland's Pierre Francoli went for $165. "Northwest candidates were bid in for considerably less," led by Hjalmar Hvam from Portland for $50, who said, "I wish I had that much confidence." Durrance was less seriously considered.

The downhill course, set by Seattle's Ben Thomson, was on an unnamed peak in the Boulder Mountains eight miles north of Ketchum near the present Sawtooth National Recreation Area headquarters. Neither Proctor nor Dollar Mountain had the vertical needed to run a Europe-style downhill race, and Bald Mountain had not been developed. According to Ketchum ski racer Mary Jane Griffith,

> *A credentialed squad of top flight skiers spent the week prior to the race preparing the course by digging out rocks and roots, setting course stakes, and positioning rescue toboggans and first aid. Dog teams hauled rescue sleds and first aid supplies up the hill on toboggans which were stationed at advantageous points, and ropes were put up to keep spectators off the course at the finish.*

Alex Bright, a 1936 Olympian and member of the Ski Club's board of governors, described the race in an article in the *Sun Valley Ski Club Season 1936–1937*. Competitors had to hike for nearly three hours to reach the start. The "exacting" downhill course had 3,900 vertical feet of descent. The day before the race, competitors inspected the course, going over "every inch of the race course figuring their lines and trying them out. The race committee supervised a final grooming of the course. Partly covered stumps were trimmed out on the most likely lines."

The racers' day started at 5:00 a.m. with breakfast at the lodge, followed by a half-hour bus ride to the course, then a three-hour climb up the mountain, breaking trail through

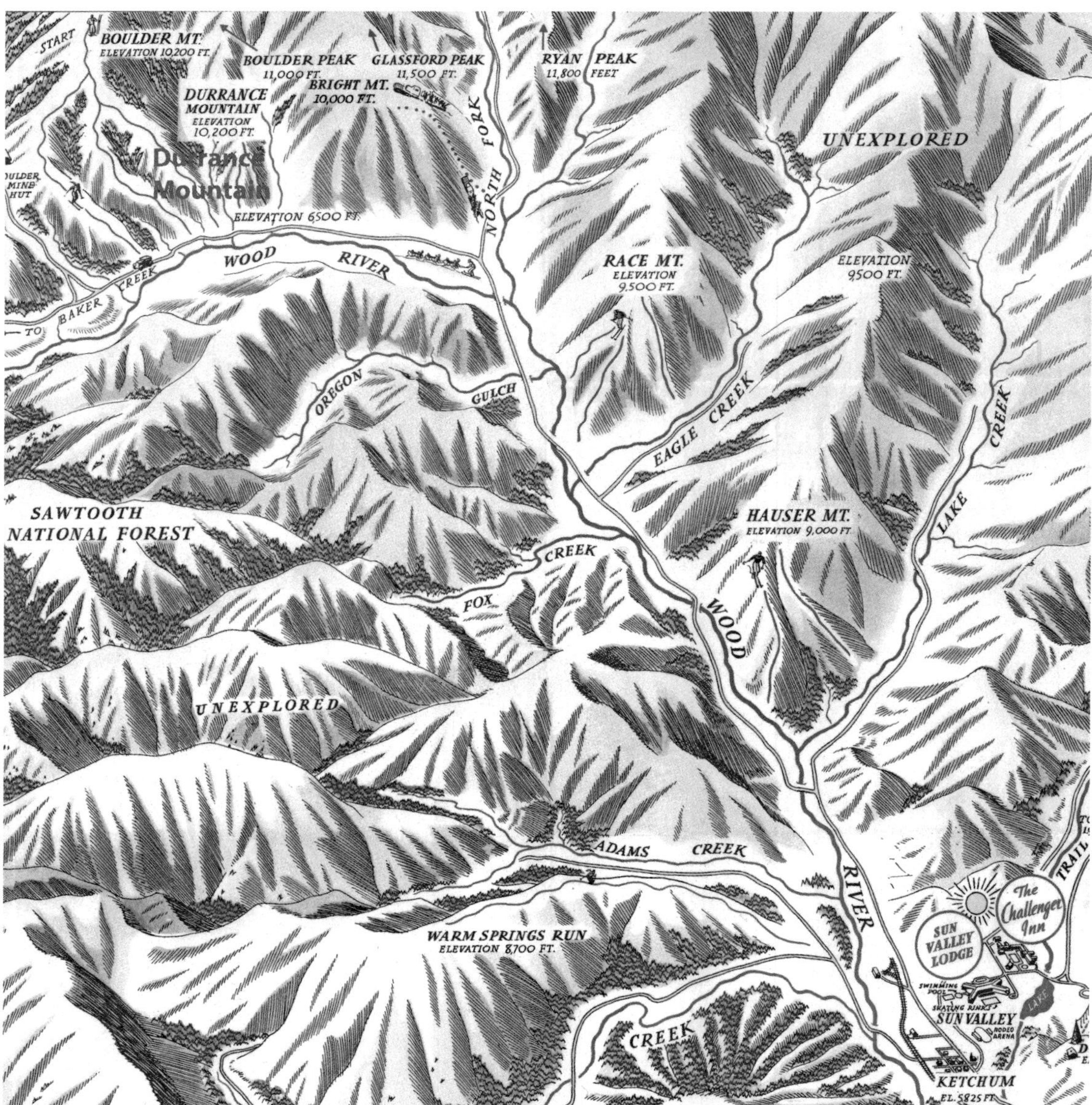

Durrance Mountain, site of the Harriman Cup downhill races in 1937 and 1938, is shown here at upper left, near the headquarters of the Sawtooth National Recreational Area.

newly fallen snow along the route they would likely take. This gave racers a chance to study the course, although "the choice of line was limited," Bright wrote. By 11:00, the racers "clustered in the shelter of a low pine near the top of a shoulder" of the mountain in "light spits of snow. . . . Sandwiches and particularly the pineapple juice provided by the Race Committee made the waiting preliminary to the start as nearly bearable as it ever could be." Even though the race was miles from nowhere, 3,000 to 4,000 spectators "watched the race from points in the lower part of the course from where up to 3/4 of a mile of the race could be seen." Bright's description continued:

> *In the thirty-nine hundred feet of descent every type of skiing from wood running to deep diving schusses was called for. Certainly no other course yet used for a National Championship or major race in this country had provided such an excellent test of skiing. Many European championships are held on courses less exacting and less interesting from a competitive standpoint. The wide differences in times of the competitors are ample testimony to how exacting a real downhill course can prove itself to be.*

Ken Binns, a sportswriter for the *Seattle Times*, described the course in the *American Ski Annual, 1937–1938*. The first third was "a straight schuss through trees, into a long bottle-neck that narrowed into a rock-bound funnel, flanked by rocks. The funnel couldn't have been five feet wide." Only Sverre Kolterud took that section straight—the rest "checked judiciously, or fell in the attempt to make it." The middle third went across a long traverse taken at high speed, made precarious by tightly spaced trees. This led to another bumpy traverse, a little less steep than the initial traverse, which led the racers into view of the crowd half a mile from the finish. From there, the course came down the bottom of a canyon, over a slight roll, and "finished on a 25 degree straight run to the finish."

Durrance described the first Harriman Cup downhill in his book *Man on the Medal*:

> *They set the course on a ridge there that comes from a major range. . . . Just a start and a finish, no control gates, no course preparation. Nothing had been cleared, no trails—it was a wide open mountain. There were some patches of trees here and there, but they were insignificant. They didn't interfere with your skiing or your line.*

Eight inches of snow fell on the course the night before the race, and it began snowing again as the racers prepared. "So we raced on fresh, unpacked snow, kind of wet,"

Durrance said. "I picked pretty much a straight line, the way I wanted to ski it. . . . I hate to turn. I don't like to turn if I don't have to, and in that race, you didn't need to very much."

Everyone expected a European victory, and most believed Walter Prager won. Durrance thought he raced too carefully, "having taken two turns and one fall on the Big Bowl above the Rock Garden." To the surprise of even himself, Durrance won the downhill, beating the impressive group of European ski stars. Bright said, "It took three days for the first racers to reach Sun Valley from the east coast, three hours to walk up the downhill course, and five minutes for Dick Durrance to win it." Prager finished second, Sverre Kolterud from Norway third, and Hans Hauser fourth.

Ben Thomson's 1,600-foot slalom course on Dollar Mountain ran beside its 800-foot chairlift, and 5,000 spectators "lined the slalom course from the base to the ski tow at the 6,000 foot level," according to *Seattle Times* sportswriter Ken Binns. The course, with its 700 feet of vertical drop,

> *proved a thorough test of slalom technique. Its problems were so acute that the Swiss all university team, the Norwegian delegation of Sigmund Ruud and Sverre Kolterud, and the Austrian contingent, led by Hans Hauser of Sun Valley, insisted it was the best course on which they had ever fallen.*

Durrance won the slalom as well, "with marvelous control under high speed," Binns wrote. Switzerland's Pierre Francioli was second and Walter Prager was third.

Dick Durrance swept the tournament, winning both the open and amateur downhill, as well as the slalom and the combined national championship titles. Hans Hauser, the Sun Valley favorite, finished sixth in the combined. Northwest skiers were "taught a lesson in ski development," according to the *Seattle Times*, and did not have a chance against "the ski-quality they encountered."

Praise for Durrance came from many quarters. The *New York Times* of March 15 said he beat "a fast field of international stars, including professional instructors, open champions and the best amateur skiers of the United States, Canada, Norway and Switzerland." The *Seattle Times* wrote,

> *Dick Durrance of Dartmouth, the rocketing, tempo-turning young bullet from the land of no snow, Florida, poured on the heat against the greatest field of foreign and*

> *resident skiers ever assembled in North America. . . . The Durrance victory definitely proved him one of the greatest skiers in the world.*

The *Hailey Times* of March 18 said Durrance won the day

> *in the greatest ski contest ever staged in America. By amazing skill and dash and courage he won the world championship in competition with the best professional and amateur ski experts, not only of this country but of Austria, Switzerland, Norway and other countries where great stress is placed on this form of winter sport. . . . By his undisputed victories both days he was crowned king of all ski racers.*

In his article, Alex Bright described Durrance's unique ski style, saying that Durrance

> *emerged not only as one of the world's foremost skiers but as an exponent of what must on close analysis be admitted a thoroughly distinctive technique. While it is difficult to draw fine lines of distinction between such terms of interlocking styles as are being described indiscriminately by parallel swing, tempo turn, and so forth, the fact remains that Durrance presents a distinctive style. . . . When you watch Dick, all you can see is his head and shoulders coming down the mountain. In essence his stance is with feet well separated, with his vorlage crouched down onto and between his skis.*

Harriman presided at the post-race banquet that ended "two days of companionship with the greatest collection of downhill ski racers to be assembled in North America," announcing that the Sun Valley International Open would be an annual affair, according to Bright. Durrance said, "Harriman was so surprised that an American had done it that he said, 'I think we should name the mountain for you.'" Harriman named the mountain on which the downhill race was run Durrance Mountain. Al Lindley said in his speech, "We live in a golden age of skiing."

Harriman commissioned a giant silver bowl for the winner of the combined event, inscribed with the name of each year's winner, which would be retired when one racer won the competition three times. Thereafter, the Sun Valley International Open became known as the Harriman Cup. Officials invited the finest skiers in the world. "The Harriman Cup became a prize the great prima donnas of the European race circuits coveted," Dorice Taylor wrote, "and the event itself was the glittering

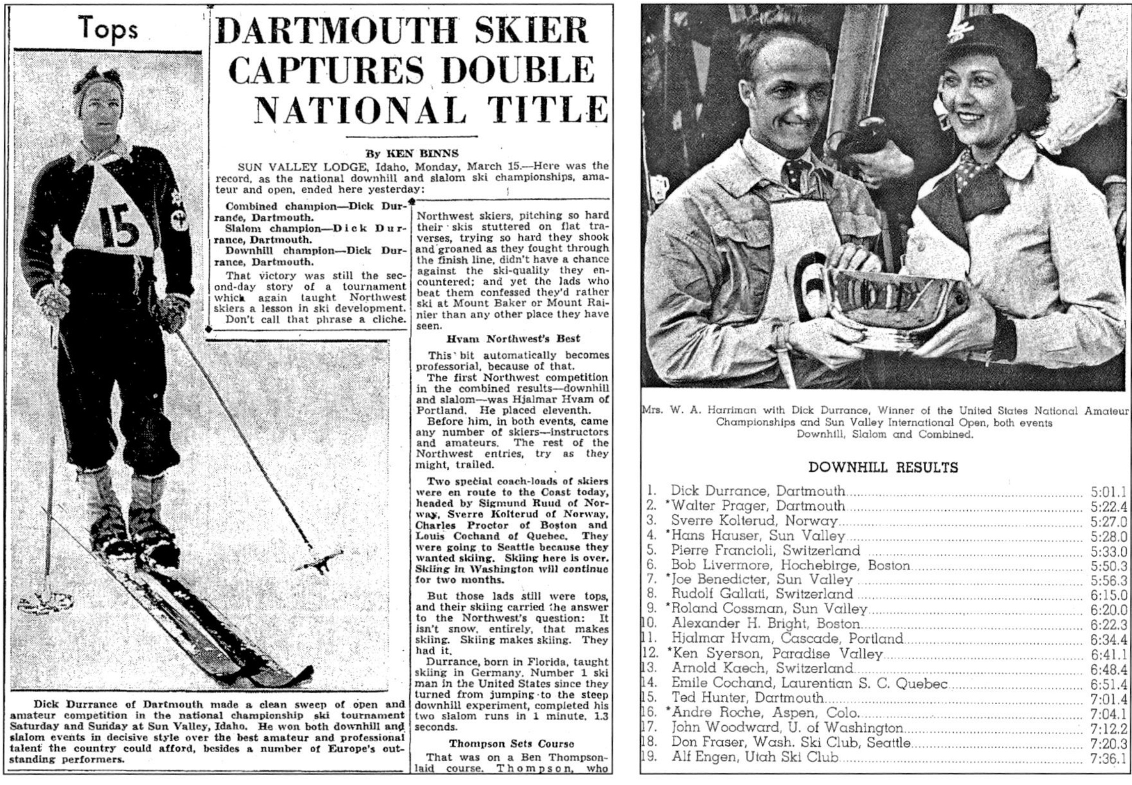

Tops

DARTMOUTH SKIER CAPTURES DOUBLE NATIONAL TITLE

By KEN BINNS

SUN VALLEY LODGE, Idaho, Monday, March 15.—Here was the record, as the national downhill and slalom ski championships, amateur and open, ended here yesterday:

Combined champion—Dick Durrance, Dartmouth.

Slalom champion—Dick Durrance, Dartmouth.

Downhill champion—Dick Durrance, Dartmouth.

That victory was still the second-day story of a tournament which again taught Northwest skiers a lesson in ski development.

Don't call that phrase a cliche. Northwest skiers, pitching so hard their skis stuttered on flat traverses, trying so hard they shook and groaned as they fought through the finish line, didn't have a chance against the ski-quality they encountered; and yet the lads who beat them confessed they'd rather ski at Mount Baker or Mount Rainier than any other place they have seen.

Hvam Northwest's Best

This bit automatically becomes professorial, because of that.

The first Northwest competition in the combined results—downhill and slalom—was Hjalmar Hvam of Portland. He placed eleventh.

Before him, in both events, came any number of skiers—instructors and amateurs. The rest of the Northwest entries, try as they might, trailed.

Two special coach-loads of skiers were en route to the Coast today, headed by Sigmund Ruud of Norway, Sverre Kolterud of Norway, Charles Proctor of Boston and Louis Cochand of Quebec. They were going to Seattle because they wanted skiing. Skiing here is over. Skiing in Washington will continue for two months.

But those lads still were tops, and their skiing carried the answer to the Northwest's question: It isn't snow, entirely, that makes skiing. Skiing makes skiing. They had it.

Durrance, born in Florida, taught skiing in Germany. Number 1 ski man in the United States since they turned from jumping to the steep downhill experiment, completed his two slalom runs in 1 minute, 1.3 seconds.

Thompson Sets Course

That was on a Ben Thompson-laid course. Thompson, who

Dick Durrance of Dartmouth made a clean sweep of open and amateur competition in the national championship ski tournament Saturday and Sunday at Sun Valley, Idaho. He won both downhill and slalom events in decisive style over the best amateur and professional talent the country could afford, besides a number of Europe's outstanding performers.

Mrs. W. A. Harriman with Dick Durrance, Winner of the United States National Amateur Championships and Sun Valley International Open, both events Downhill, Slalom and Combined.

DOWNHILL RESULTS

1.	Dick Durrance, Dartmouth	5:01.1
2.	*Walter Prager, Dartmouth	5:22.4
3.	Sverre Kolterud, Norway	5:27.0
4.	*Hans Hauser, Sun Valley	5:28.0
5.	Pierre Francioli, Switzerland	5:33.0
6.	Bob Livermore, Hochebirge, Boston	5:50.3
7.	*Joe Benedicter, Sun Valley	5:56.3
8.	Rudolf Gallati, Switzerland	6:15.0
9.	*Roland Cossman, Sun Valley	6:20.0
10.	Alexander H. Bright, Boston	6:22.3
11.	Hjalmar Hvam, Cascade, Portland	6:34.4
12.	*Ken Syerson, Paradise Valley	6:41.1
13.	Arnold Kaech, Switzerland	6:48.4
14.	Emile Cochand, Laurentian S. C. Quebec	6:51.4
15.	Ted Hunter, Dartmouth	7:01.4
16.	*Andre Roche, Aspen, Colo.	7:04.1
17.	John Woodward, U. of Washington	7:12.2
18.	Don Fraser, Wash. Ski Club, Seattle	7:20.3
19.	Alf Engen, Utah Ski Club	7:36.1

LEFT Dick Durrance wins Harriman Cup and double title. *Seattle Times*, March 15, 1937.

RIGHT Dick Durrance and Mrs. Averell Harriman holding Harriman Cup and results of the first downhill race on Durrance Mountain. 1936–1937 season.

climax of the Sun Valley Season." Durrance won the cup two more times, in 1938 and 1940, and was given the original silver Harriman Cup, the first racer to retire it. Christian Pravda is the only other skier to win the Harriman Cup three times, racing in the 1950s.

In his oral history, Dick Durrance described the racing conditions of that era. Racers bought their own skis, boots, and clothes and paid their expenses. They raced for fame, not money. "It was a game," he said. Rules required the same skis be used in downhill and slalom events, and they were marked to prevent racers from using different length skis. The goal was to win the combined title. Ski racers then were generalists,

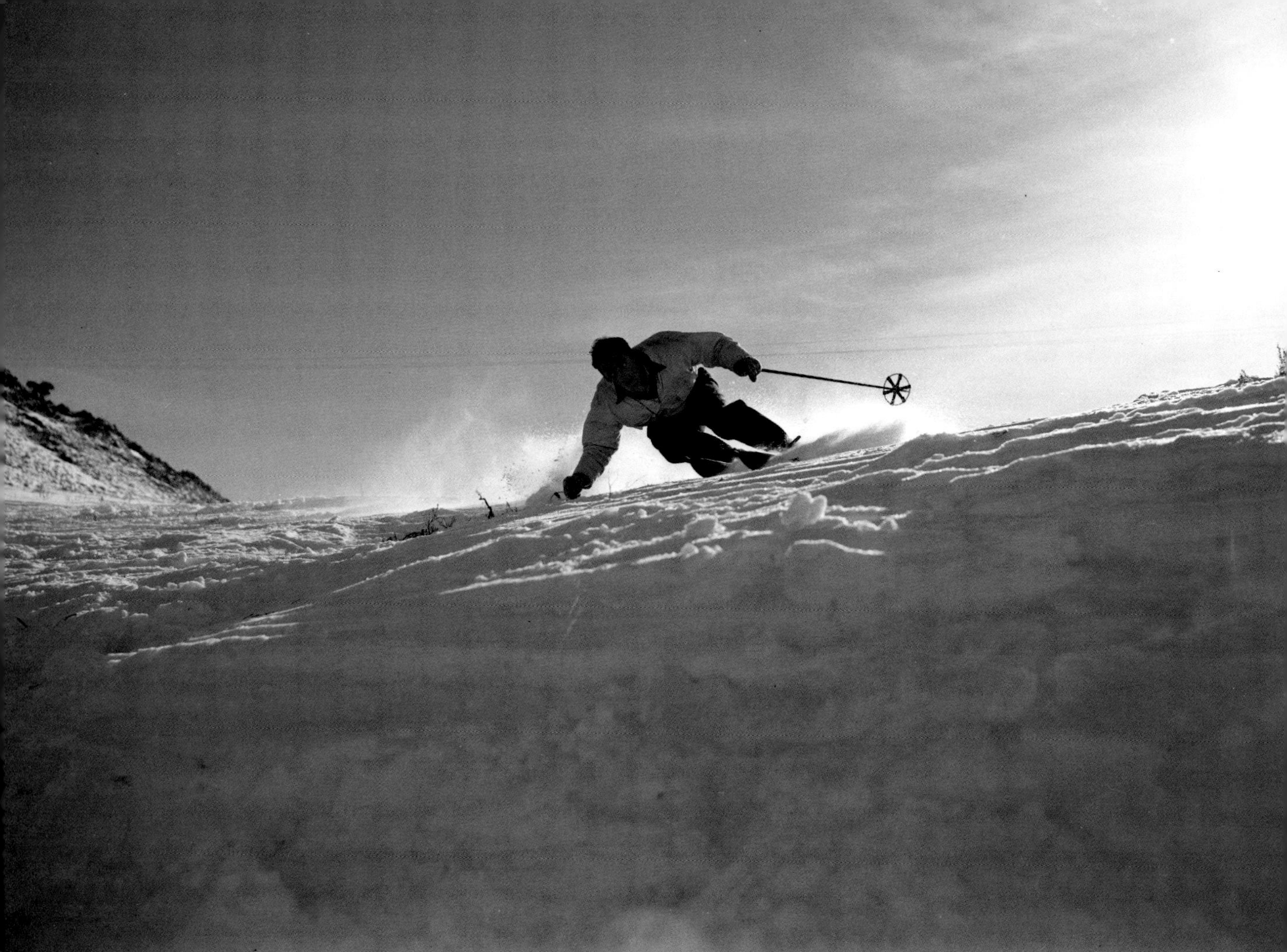

Dick Durrance showing his distinctive ski technique—"his feet well separated, with his vorlage crouched down onto and between his skis."

not specialists as they are today. Most top skiers were four-way racers, competing in downhill, slalom, jumping, and cross-country.

Racers had to climb to starting gates since there were no lifts, which often took several hours. There was limited course preparation, and racers skied on whatever snow was there. There were few or no control gates in downhill races, only start and finish gates. Racers could pick their own line and be innovative. When a trail curved, Durrance would look for a shortcut through the woods. Their biggest challenge was to not get lost. Durrance's strategy was to go straight as long as he could and not fall down. Slalom courses too were different from modern ones, which generally run straight down the fall line. In Durrance's day, slalom courses were designed to use irregularities in the terrain and included traverses and hairpin turns.

In April 1937, a marriage took place that had a lasting effect on Sun Valley. Grace Carter from Seattle married Alfred D. Lindley of Minneapolis, president of the Sun Valley Ski Club. The *Seattle Times* of April 28, 1937, said their marriage caused "ski spills from St. Anton, Austria, to the summit of Mount Rainier—they form a new ski team." Carter was considered by international experts as America's No. 1 junior skier. Lindley, a wealthy Minneapolis attorney, was a "member of the Sam Hill family of railroad note," member of the 1924 Yale crew that represented the United States in the Olympics, and

> *a veteran of American ski teams who represented the United States abroad nearly every year for six years. . . . The couple, who first met at the national ski championships at Mount Rainier in 1935, continued their romance at the Olympic Games* [of 1936].

They lived in Minneapolis, but Grace continued her racing career. She was admitted into the U.S. Ski and Snowboard Hall of Fame in 1966.

In November 1937, an up-and-coming Northwest skier, Gretchen Kunigk from Tacoma, began to be recognized at the national level. For several years in Northwest races, she had battled Seattle's Grace Carter Lindley and Tacoma's Smith sisters, Ethelynne "Skit" (1935 national slalom champion) and Ellis-Ayr (1935 national downhill champion), members of the 1936 U.S. Olympic team, and received instructions from Otto Lang, the famous Austrian ski coach. Kunigk, wrote the *Seattle Times*, "Northwest slalom champion and improving rapidly, has been invited to join the American F.I.S. ski team" at St. Anton am Arlberg, Austria, for winter training. "And it was the opinion of Roger Langley, president of the National Ski Association, that she should be permitted to compete in the [National] championships" the coming year.

Also in April, Hans Hauser and Joseph Schwaighofer represented the Sun Valley Ski School in the Silver Skis Race on Mount Rainier, when went from Camp Muir at 10,000 feet to near Paradise Lodge at 5,500 feet.[22]

SUN VALLEY OPENS FOR THE SUMMER

Sun Valley closed on April 1, 1937. On April 4, *Railway Age* announced "Sun Valley Lodge to Reopen for Summer Season" for summer vacationists desiring mountain trails, fishing, swimming, tennis, and horseback riding.

The *New York Times* of May 30, 1940, said Sun Valley was developing a "year-round center with tennis courts and outdoor swimming pools, horseback treks through mountains, fishing in lakes and streams rarely visited by the sportsman." Fishing would take place in "unmapped and untamed mountain lakes and streams," and hunters would find ruffed grouse, elk, and mountain goats. The Sun Valley Lodge would open on July 1 for the summer season.

Sun Valley's advertisements emphasized the area's access to surrounding wilderness while staying in comfort at the lodge enjoying superb cuisine. The resort could be reached by fast, air-conditioned trains at low cost: "It is the gateway to America's last wilderness," ads read, adding,

> *In this great expanse of virgin territory, high in the Sawtooth Mountain Range near Ketchum, Idaho, roam Rocky Mountain goat, bighorn sheep, mountain lion, antelope and elk. In the limitless mountain lakes and streams lurk the wily rainbow and steelhead trout. At the distinctly modern Sun Valley Lodge, where no item for fine living has been overlooked, is an interesting variety of summer sports—swimming, tennis, dancing and horseback riding. Pack trips of two days or longer take you into the more remote and adventurous regions.*

By the end of the first season, Steve Hannagan's publicity campaign had proved successful, according to Harriman's biographer Abramson. Sun Valley was called an American St. Moritz. Skiers from both coasts found it exciting to cross the country in Union Pacific luxury and ski in the remote Western mountains, and Hollywood adopted it with more enthusiasm than Harriman and Hannagan had dreamed. Film stars loved it for its informality. When they learned from Hannagan that being photographed allowed them to write their Sun Valley trips off as a business expense, they even more gladly allowed themselves to be used as the centerpieces of Sun Valley—and Union Pacific—promotions.

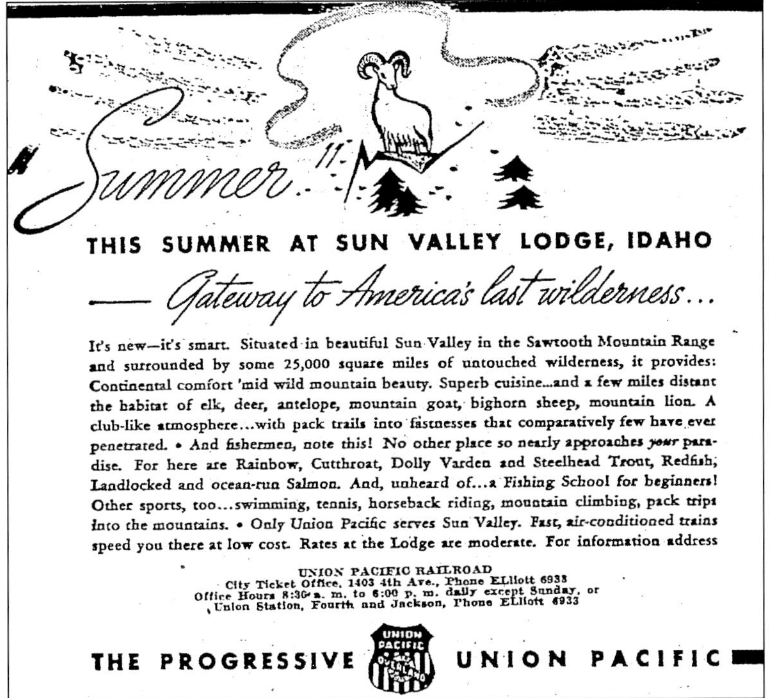

Ad for Sun Valley's first summer season. *Seattle Times*, June 9, 1937.

Railroad Age said Sun Valley attracted 3,900 guests its first year and created a model for the industry: "The railroads as a whole, as the Union Pacific has done individually through its winter sports development, can create new demands for rail transportation by stimulating interest in those pursuits which require travel."[23]

10

SUMMER AND FALL 1937

The Village and Challenger Inn Are Built: A Ski Jump and Lift Are Built on Ruud Mountain

In spring 1937, construction began on the Challenger Inn, designed for the budget-minded traveler, and an alpine village surrounding it. The inn was named after the less costly Challenger passenger train put into service that year. Sun Valley was a major construction area for the rest of the year. As before, Harriman was involved in all phases of planning and implementation. Gilbert Stanley Underwood designed the inn and village, and J.V. McNeil Construction Company was the contractor.

On March 22, 1937, Harriman wrote H.C. Mann, U.P.'s chief engineer and vice president in charge of operations, about his meeting in Sun Valley with contractor McNeil and U.P. architect Wellman regarding plans for the Challenger Inn. Harriman discussed other summer projects and asked for cost estimates.

The projects included building a ski jump and developing a slalom course on a hill near Proctor Mountain, removing the J-bar that ran to the base of the Proctor chairlift and moving it to the new ski hill, extending and widening the road to the Proctor chair so buses could take skiers there from the lodge, and providing amenities for the new hill (parking, spectator seats, a small hut, and a toboggan run). Harriman wanted an expert on ski jump construction to be consulted, such as Alf Engen, since, he wrote, "the exact location and tilt of the takeoff is a highly technical and perhaps controversial question." From 1935 to 1942, Engen, an accomplished ski jumper, advised the U.S. Forest Service on planning and developing winter sports areas throughout the West.

Harriman selected a location for a dam on Trail Creek to create a lake. Cost estimates were prepared, and necessary government approval was explored. The lake would flood Dollar Road, so the road and bridge would have to be raised. Harriman wanted to find a pass through the hills west of Sun Valley to divert the public highway from Ketchum north of the lodge to Trail Creek, to "control motorists and keep them from overrunning our development." Dollar and Proctor Roads, he said, should be widened and improved.

On March 27, 1937, Harriman responded to a friend who inquired about getting his female cousin hired as a ski instructor: "I am told experience has shown that people do not like women skiing instructresses. Both men and women prefer men. We have therefore made it a matter of policy to have only men."

On April 6, 1938, the Union Pacific board approved $1 million for the next phase of the development of Sun Valley to expand its appeal to the large class of moderate-income guests and provide accommodations for winter and summer seasons. The board believed

> *such expenditure will work out financially over a period of time and the completion of the project . . . will set the foundation for a well-rounded recreational center, having great possibilities of growing into a large industry from which the Company will get important direct transportation revenue and many indirect advantages.*

On May 25, 1937, the board approved another $65,000 to construct "barns and corrals and grandstands and other rodeo facilities at Sun Valley." Harriman said the idea for the rodeo grounds came from William Jeffers, who became the railroad's new president in October 1937. Jeffers didn't know about skiing but thought rodeo would attract people. The Challenger Inn and Village were built in summer and fall 1937, and were ready for winter 1938.

The inn was a mountain-style building with 230 guest rooms and 100 rooms for staff, with a number of retail shops. A swimming pool adjoining the inn and a central heating plant for all the resort's buildings were built as well. The Bavarian Village surrounding the inn provided shopping and recreational opportunities for guests. It had a center square surrounded by structures of different appearances, giving the impression of a European resort. Two-story buildings were built of stucco and wood "painted in gay colors having artistically designed balconies and other exterior adornments which will give the whole a most pleasing appearance," wrote the *Hailey Times*. The Aspen and

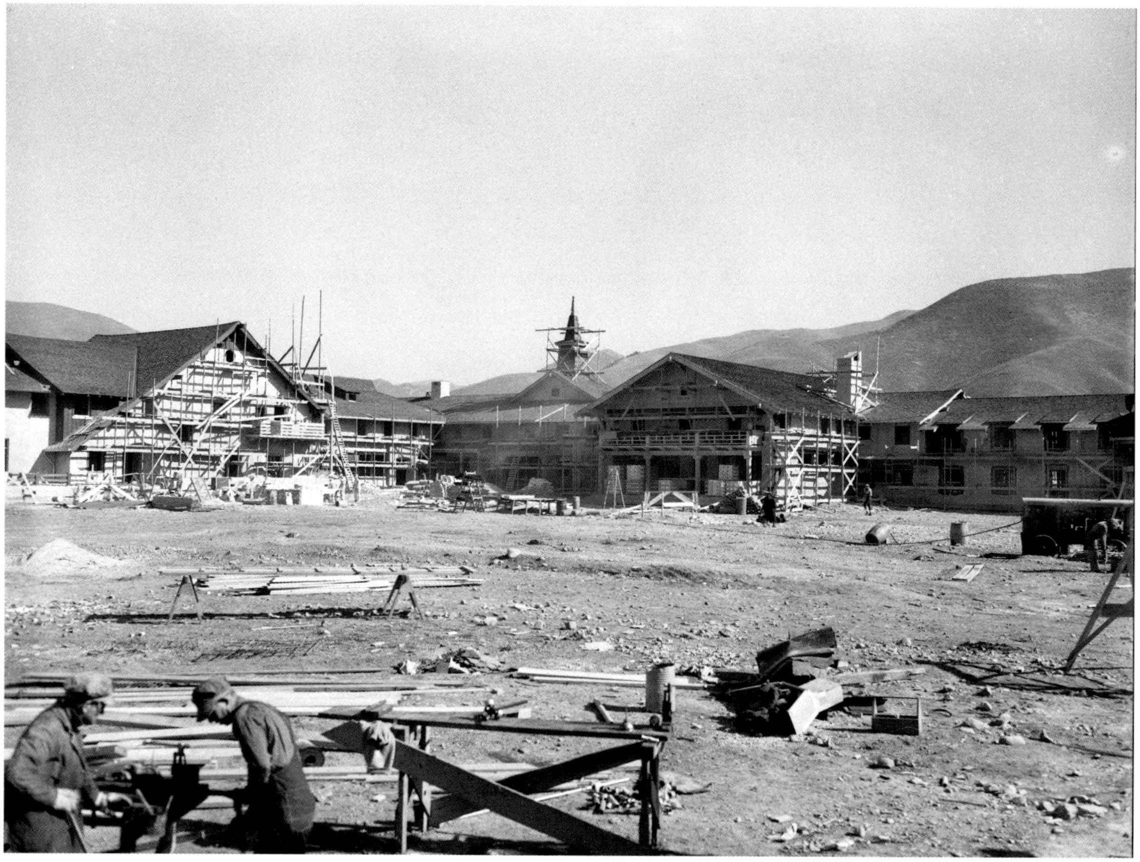

ABOVE Sun Valley Village and Challenger Inn under construction, summer 1937, built to provide more reasonably priced accommodations than the Sun Valley Lodge.

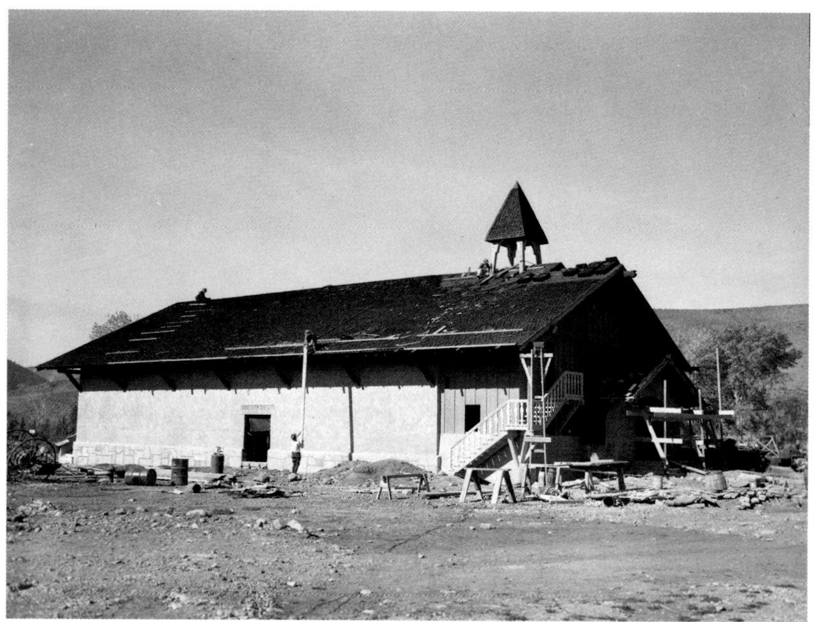

LEFT Opera house under construction, fall 1937.

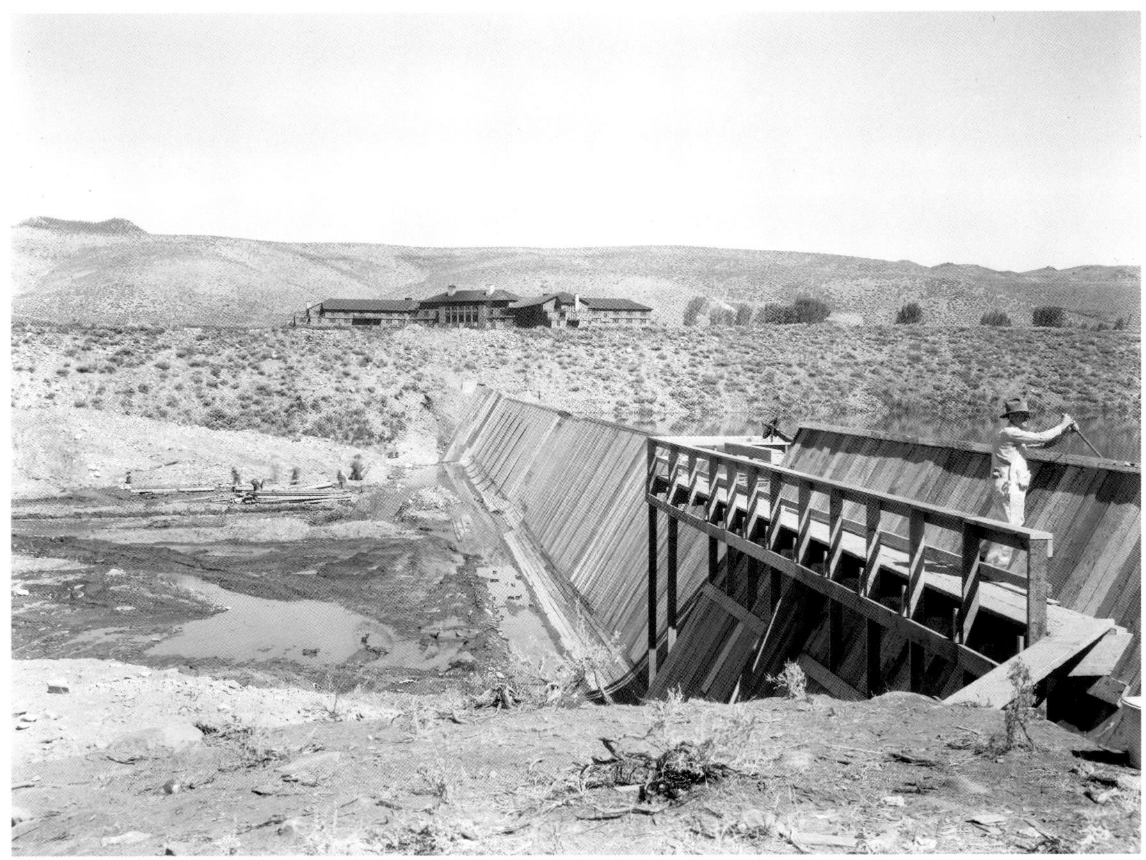

Construction of dam to create Sun Valley Lake, summer 1937.

Willow Cottages and the 500-seat opera house were built. The new development would "provide comfortable and desirably appointed quarters catering to sports lovers at a minimum cost, and make Sun Valley the most sought after sports center in the state of Idaho as well as in the entire country," according to the paper.

Although Harriman originally talked about having the village resemble a Western town, an article in *Architectural Record* by Gordon Stanley Underwood said, "Harriman wanted Sun Valley Village to resemble 'a Tyrolean village' so visitors had the impression Union Pacific 'had transported them to a charming European ski resort.'"

A two-year, resort-wide landscaping plan was begun in 1937 under the direction of Boise landscape architect Charles Davidson. Trail Creek, Sun Valley's main watershed, was diverted into an elaborate system to water its gardens, golf course, and adjoining fields and lagoons in Challenger Inn Square. Trail Creek cabin was built on the creek east of Sun Valley, becoming a popular dining and party site. Trail Creek was

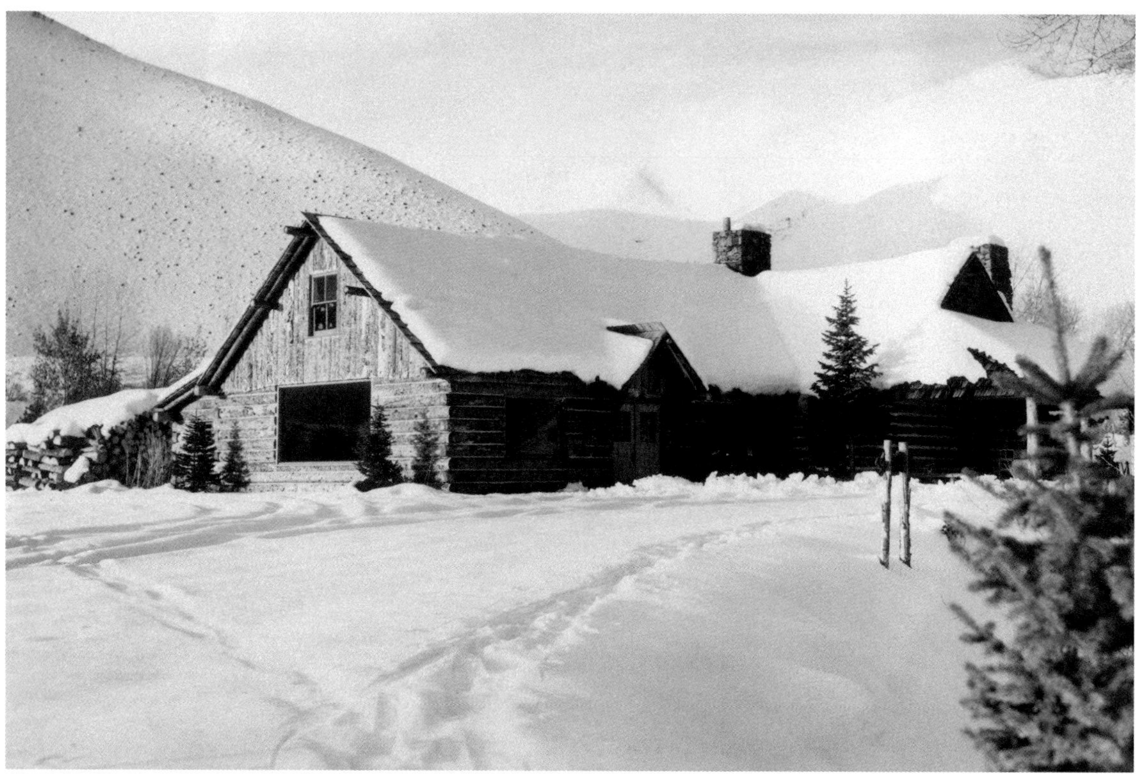

Trail Creek Cabin east of Sun Valley Lodge on Trail Creek, fall 1937.

dammed to create Sun Valley Lake, which was stocked with trout. Harriman provided recommendations, and the final plan needed to be reviewed by him.

An 11,000-seat rodeo stadium and stands, barn, and horse track were built, costing $65,000, for the first Sun Valley Rodeo, held on August 14–15, 1937. It had a covered grandstand on the northwest side, an open grandstand on the south, and a track running around the facility. Dog kennels were built near the stadium. Sun Valley's skeet shooting arena was ready for use in August, with a skeet and trap field and four electrically operated traps. It was in Elkhorn Gulch, "convenient to the lodge, but far enough away that the blasts of the guns do not disturb the guests," wrote the *Idaho Statesman*. "It promises soon to become one of the most popular sports here. In fact, it's rapidly becoming one of the nation's top amusements." Harriman spent a month at Sun Valley that summer.

U.P. architect W.T. Wellman wrote Harriman on September 23, 1937, after meeting with J.V. McNeil contractors and Gilbert Underwood. Wellman asked for Harriman's input on drawings of windows and shutters to be installed on the Challenger Inn and weinstube. Wellman also sent drawings of the ladies' and men's toilets for the new

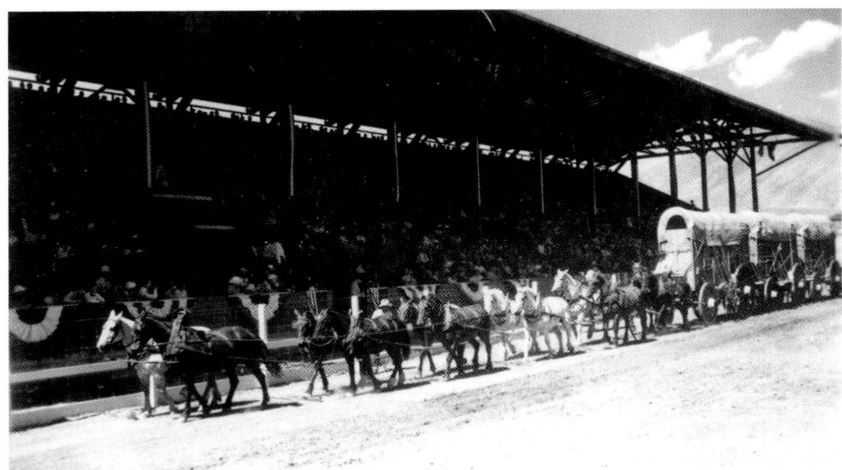

Sun Valley rodeo stadium with parade featuring ore wagons, summer 1937.

theater for Harriman's input, illustrating his attention to detail—here was the chairman of the board of a major corporation, with business interests all over the world, deciding which toilets to use in the opera house.

Lawrence McNeil said Harriman Cottage was built on the resort grounds as a family retreat in 60 days in October and November 1937, under a circus tent heated by salamanders. It was ready for Harriman and his friends when they arrived for Christmas. The telephone switchboard was flown in from Chicago, which was quite a feat since air cargo was unknown at that time. Cottages were also built for William Jeffers, U.P.'s president; Dr. John Moritz, Sun Valley's resident doctor; and the head of the Sun Valley Ski School.[24]

Ski Jump and Lift Built on Ruud Mountain

From the 1910s through the 1940s, ski jumping was the most popular form of winter sport due to the influence of Norwegian immigrants who learned to jump in Norway, and who "organized ski competitions to strengthen their ethnic ties, showcase their abilities, and generate a new sense of belonging to their new country," according to Harold Anson in *Jumping Through Time*. Serious interest in alpine skiing did not appear until the mid- to late 1930s. Alpine skiing (downhill and slalom racing) first appeared in the Olympics in 1936. The public was fascinated by the quest for the longest jump. Newspapers provided extensive coverage of ski jumping events, and the best jumpers were celebrities, much like professional football quarterbacks are today.

Averell Harriman used international ski meets to publicize Sun Valley. One thing was missing its first year—a ski jump. Harriman also wanted a slalom course better than the one on Dollar Mountain used for the 1937 Harriman Cup. Following the Sun Valley Open in March 1937, Harriman asked two Norwegian skiers who participated in the tournament to locate a site for a jumping hill and design a ski jump, according to the *Sun Valley Ski Guide*:

> *In March of 1937 two world-famous ski jumpers, Sigmund Ruud and Alf Engen, selected a choice site on which to build a regulation jumping hill. Alf and Sig recommended the smooth and steeply graded mountain between Dollar and Proctor mountains, and after the jumping hill was completed, this mountain was named for the famous Ruud brother from Kongsberg, Norway.*

The hill selected was not huge. It had an elevation of 6,600 feet and a 600-foot vertical drop. A 40-meter jump was built to take advantage of the natural slope, "making it as near perfect as humanly possible. The profile is shaped to exact international specifications," as reported in the *Sun Valley Ski Club 1937–1938*. A bigger hill would be suitable for class A competitions, but this smaller one offered "splendid competition for all classes of competitors," particularly as part of a four-way competition. It was designed for 140-foot jumps, but a number of jumpers exceeded the design limit.

On August 31, 1937, Harriman approved building a 40-meter ski jump and ski tow costing $12,000 to $14,000, after considering various locations and lengths of jumps. An 80-meter jump could be built later if desired. In fall 1937, U.P. crews built a 40-meter ski jump, and some reports say a smaller 20-meter jump was built for training and junior meets. Val McAtee, manager of the crew that built the jump and the tow, said, "Sigmund Ruud walked along side . . . he knew just about how high that jumper would go out in the air after coming off the jump, and we graded it that way."

McAtee's crew disassembled the J-bar leading to the Proctor chairlift, converted it to a rudimentary chairlift, and installed it on Ruud Mountain. Its padding was taken off and a small seat installed, but it had no back or leg supports. The lift held 50 chairs on each side, for a total of 100. When the electric lift carried a big load, it often blew a fuse.

According to Andy Hennig, although the mountain was chosen primarily as a site for a ski jumping area, its wide open, timber free, long and steep north-facing slopes were "so naturally suited for slalom races" that Ruud Mountain became the permanent center for both competitive events. The lift benefitted both racers and jumpers. Jumpers could get off at a ramp at its midpoint to get to the top of the jump, and skiers could ride to the top. Hennig said,

> *tiring and time-consuming climbing has been eliminated for the racers, thereby allowing much more time for practice purposes and constructive training. This contribution cannot be underestimated in the development of some of our nation's topnotch competitors.*

The *Hailey Times* of September 16, 1937, said the "spectacular circus-act of skiing-jumping" would be done on a mountain between Proctor and Dollar Mountains, which had been equipped with a ski lift up a steep, timberless slope. From the top of Ruud Mountain, two fast downhill runs were available, as well as a slalom course meeting FIS specifications:

> *Skiing authorities who laid it out claim for it the ultimate in slalom courses, including the famed twisters in the French, Swiss and Austrian Alps. It is as perfect for spectators as it is for participants for the entire face of this mountain is visible from a large flat meadow at its foot, which provides a natural audience stand capable of holding thousands.*

Ruud Mountain made Sun Valley the only ski area in the country with official courses for four-way competitions—downhill, cross-country, slalom, and jumping—making it eligible for official FIS tournaments, which had never before been held outside of Europe.

Ruud Mountain was divided into two sections for general skiing, according to Hennig's *Sun Valley Ski Guide*. Left of the lift was the jumping hill, and both sides of the lift had steep and long slopes for slalom and downhill runs. Hennig showed three runs, one on either side of the lift, with the third coming over the ridge from Proctor Mountain into a bowl on Ruud.

The chairlift on Ruud Mountain still exists and is listed in the National Register of Historic Places. Its plaque says it is

> *the only ski lift which stands today as a historical reminder of skiing's beginnings. The same basic design for this lift was used for the first two chairlifts in the world invented for*

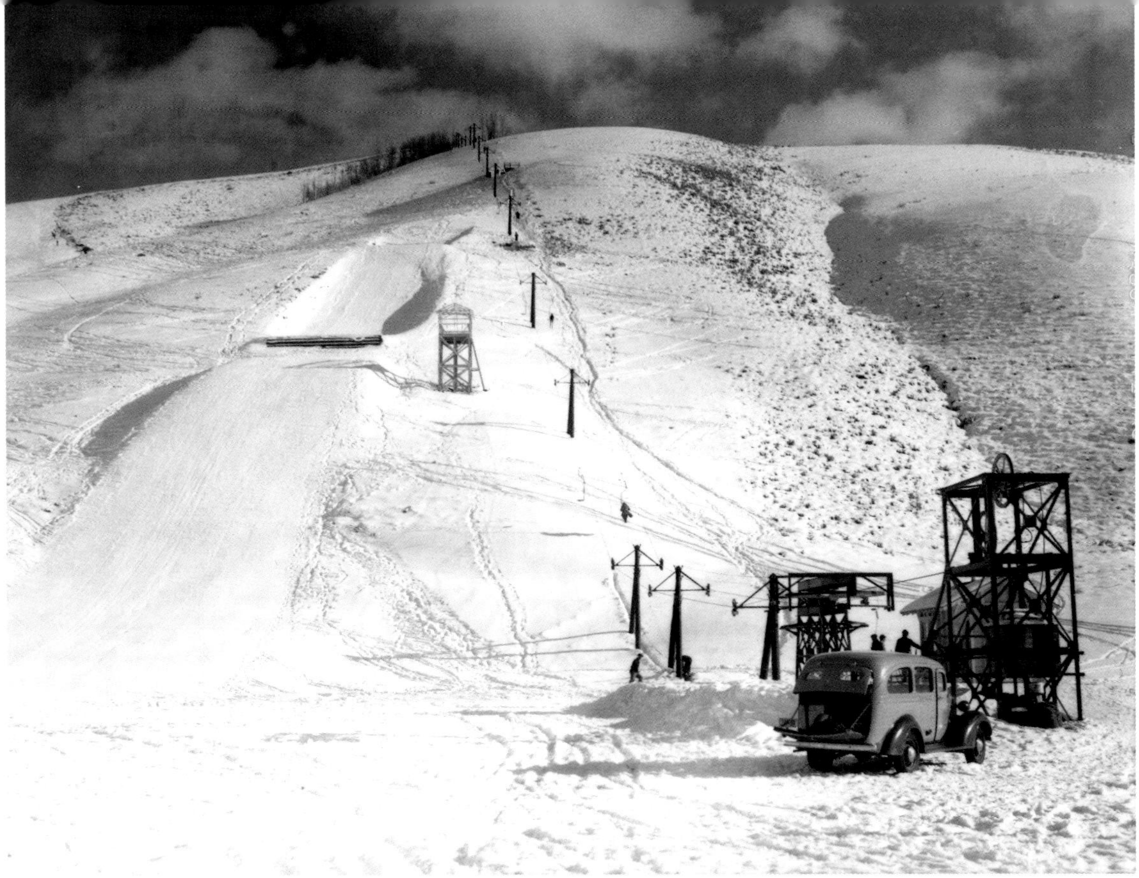

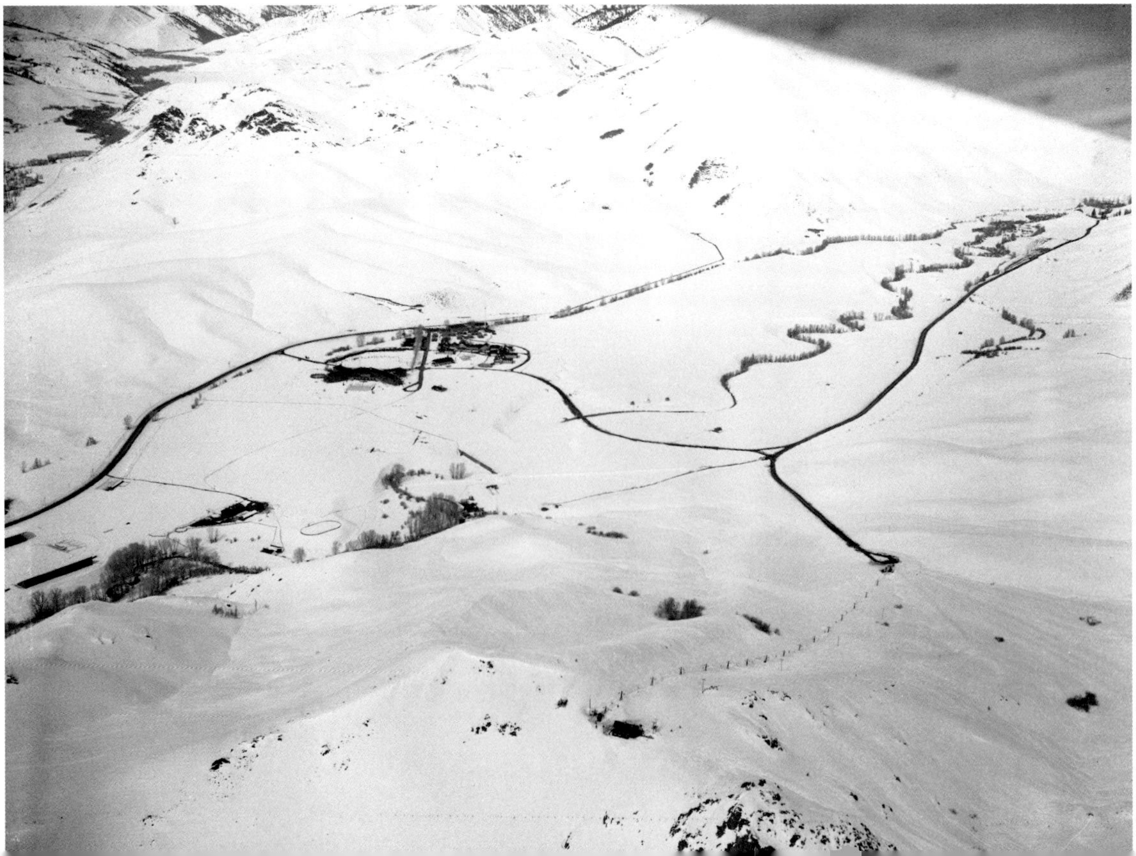

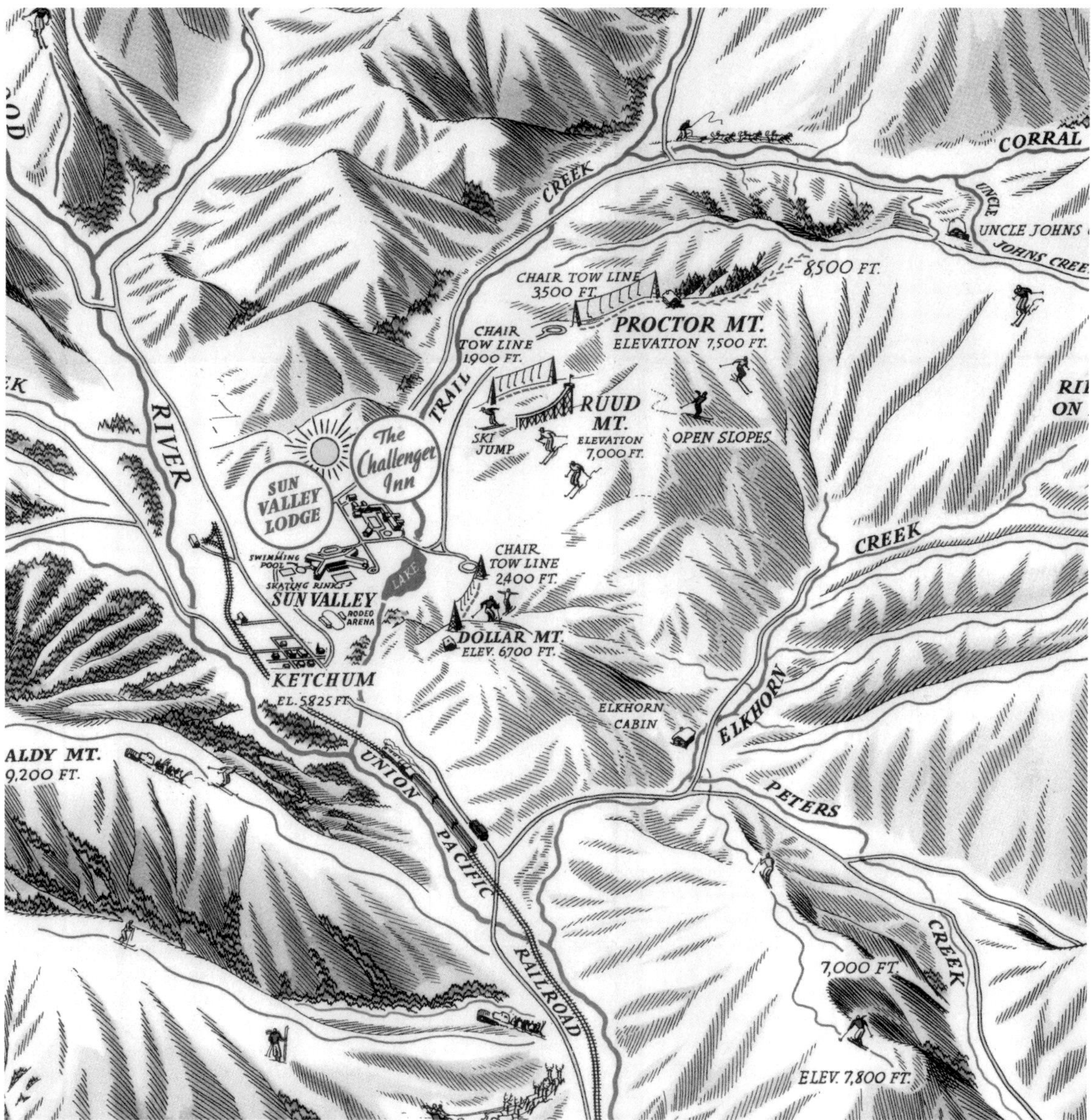

OPPOSITE, TOP Ruud Mountain, Sun Valley's center for jumping tournaments and slalom races.

OPPOSITE, BOTTOM Aerial view of Sun Valley, 1938, showing the road leading to the Proctor Mountain chairlift.

ABOVE Map showing Sun Valley, Dollar Mountain, Proctor Mountain, and Ruud Mountain.

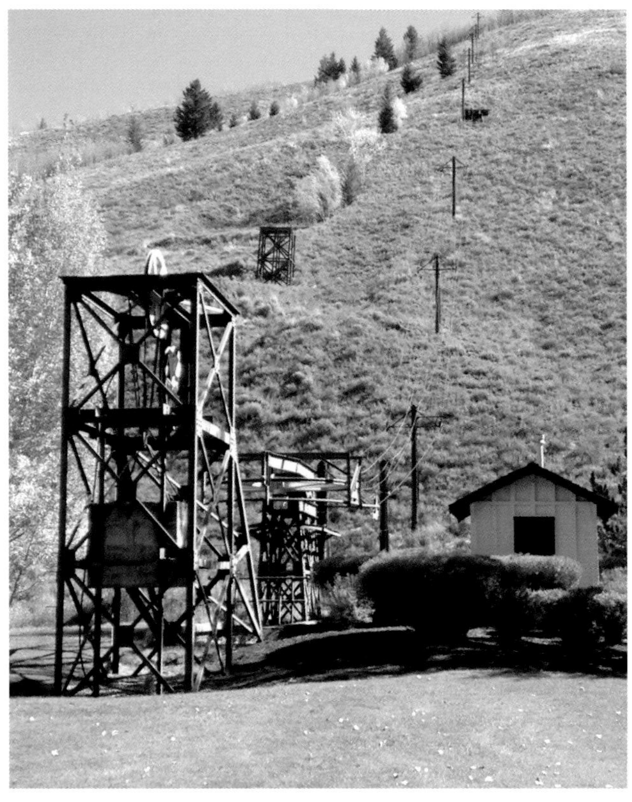

Present view of Ruud chairlift and judges' tower. The chairlift is listed in the National Register of Historic Places. The small wooden structure at top next to a lift tower is where jumpers would disembark the lift to reach the jump. *Author photograph.*

> *Sun Valley by Union Pacific Railroad Engineer James M. Curran. . . . The mountain and chairlift hill was named after Champion Ski Jumper Sigmund Ruud who helped design the ski jump.*

Warren Miller, who skied on Ruud after World War II, was not a fan of the mountain, which had no bathrooms (and no trees to use as a substitute), or of the chairlift with no chairs:

> *there was a small piece of wood about 16 inches long and six or eight inches wide. . . . The loading platform . . . was located a magic distance from the first tower so that if you sank into the seat too vigorously it would set up some sort a sympathetic vibration in the cable that would magnify in scope until it just plain threw the rider out of the lift.*[25]

Other Significant Events

In spring 1937, a new 14-by-14-foot fire lookout was built on top of Bald Mountain with sides that were almost all glass, with a "gorgeous sight of the broad expanse of country from Minidoka to Mount Hyndman," according to Ken Longe. The latest equipment, a "fire finder," was installed, an instrument attached to a map allowing a lookout to accurately report fire locations. When Baldy was opened for skiing in winter 1940, the lookout was used as a warming hut for skiers.

As a special attraction, Harriman arranged for 13 reindeer to be brought to Sun Valley from Alaska. They arrived in fall 1937 and were featured in holiday festivities and also used to carry guests around the resort. The reindeer were introduced to their new food, alfalfa, fitted with special harnesses and trained to pull sleighs, and housed in a barn built near the main road where "every Sun Valley visitor may see them," wrote the *Idaho Staesman*. "Sun Valley officials hope that they may be the nucleus of a permanent stand of reindeer in the Sawtooths."

Problems soon arose. The reindeer refused to eat local alfalfa, and native food had to be imported from Alaska at great expense. They bit children, chased Santa Claus, and were eventually sent home rather than ending their days in the Sawtooths. Actress Janet Leigh said one reindeer, rejecting Christmas cheer, "lowered its antlers and charged at Santa's baggy rear end, chasing him round and round the tree. Everyone shrieked with laughter, and then with fright when it suddenly looked as though Santa Claus might be hurt," according to Holland.[26]

In the 1930s, indoor ski meets were held in several cities to promote skiing. Averell Harriman used these events to publicize Sun Valley and had Sun Valley Ski School's director participate in them. In December 1937, the North American Winter Sports and International Ski Meet was held at Madison Square Garden in New York. Ski jumping and slalom competitions were held during the five-day event. A 152-foot indoor "slide that will reach the top of the arena" was erected, according to the *New York Times*, where Norwegian jumpers would compete. A number of famous ski instructors were there to "impart advice on what not to do and what to do," including Hans Hauser, head of the Sun Valley Ski School. More than 90,000 people attended, and such events "were catching like wildfire in the Middle West and Pacific Northwest where some ten similar carnivals were listed."

In late 1937, the FIS, the highest-ranking body in competitive skiing, gave its sanction to the Sun Valley International Ski Races scheduled for March 12–13, 1938, the first competitive meet to receive such sanction outside of Europe. This elevated Sun Valley races to the "same plane as the European Arlberg-Kandahar, permitting the participation of amateurs and ski-teachers alike, determining the best skier regardless of classification," wrote the *Hailey Times*. A thousand guests were expected to celebrate New Years Eve at Sun Valley.

Ketchum merchants moved quickly to take advantage of the new business that Sun Valley brought to town. Gambling was tolerated by the authorities, although not actually legal, and a number of clubs opened offering a wide variety of games.

On June 19, 1937, the St. Georg Hotel was opened on Main Street by Carl Brandt, owner of Guyer Hot Springs Resort on Warm Springs Creek and Bald Mountain Hot Springs Lodge. In April 1937, Brandt had dismantled the Guyer Hot Springs Hotel, which was "reconstructed board for board on Main Street in Ketchum," according to the *Hailey Times*, to build the St. Georg. It had 28 rooms, each with a shower bath or tub, and many had sun porches. It was a prominent Ketchum landmark until it burned down in 1939 in a $50,000 fire.

In December 1937, a new gambling establishment opened on Sun Valley Road, the Christiania, managed by Dutch Weinbrenner, allegedly a member of Detroit's

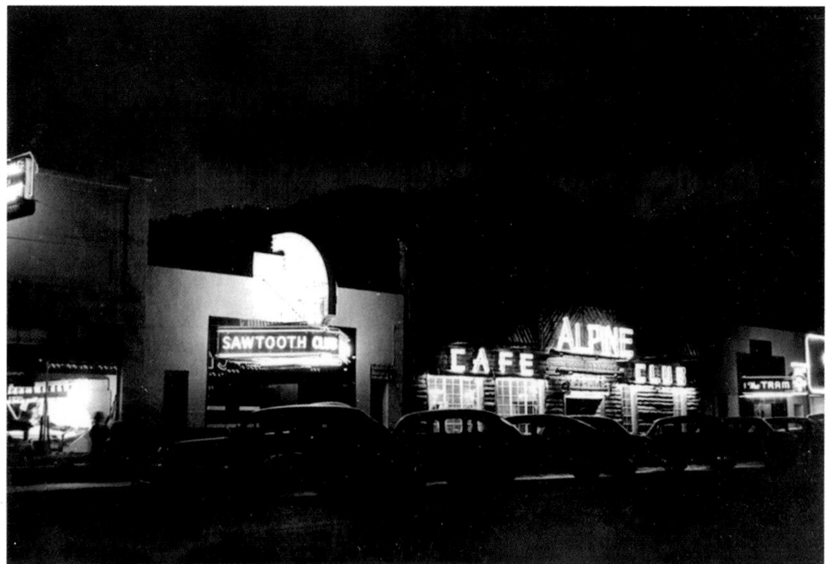

Night view of gambling establishments on Ketchum's Main Street.

Purple Gang, giving rise to rumors that mob money was financing the "very uptown dinner club that brought a touch of class to gambling in Ketchum," according to Oppenheimer and Poore. The Christiania offered a game called chem la fair, which was similar to blackjack, and catered primarily to the resort's wealthier guests. Other Ketchum gambling facilities had limits, but the Christiania offered high-stakes gambling to those who could afford it. It attracted Hollywood high rollers who would go there and sometimes gamble $60,000 or $100,000.

Ed Seagle said Sun Valley cooperated with Ketchum government and businesses to make sure things worked smoothly. Sun Valley buses took guests to Ketchum for its bars, restaurants, and gambling facilities. The Christiania was closely tied to the resort. Weinbrenner lived in an apartment on the fourth floor of the lodge. Invitations to the club were left in mailboxes at the lodge and inn for arriving guests. When guests wrote IOUs to cover their losses, they were charged to their Sun Valley accounts. Weinbrenner was public spirited, giving free milk to the Ketchum grade school and delivering coal to poor residents.

Sun Valley employees went to the Christiania as well. Val McAtee said, "If you didn't gamble, there wasn't much to do." The Christiania was in a different class from other Ketchum establishments, such as the Alpine Club run by Lou Hill, Sawtooth, Slavey's, the Casino, and the Ketchum Club. It had quarters on its second floor for cooks and boarders, served fantastic food, and drinks were free. One night, ski instructor Florian Haemmerle went there with a Hollywood star who was one of his students and lost $450. Weinbrenner told Florian he could return but he didn't want him to gamble his money since he worked too hard for it. He was welcome to bring his students since that would make money for the house. Ski instructor Leon Goodman said the Christiania was "better than anything in Nevada."

Dorice Taylor said the Christiania was a high-stakes gambling house that attracted high rollers, including Darryl Zanuck:

> *A favorite gathering spot for the Hollywood crowd in 1939 was the Christiania Club, a gambling casino built by George Weinbrenner, whispered to have been a member of the Purple Gang of Detroit. The club was "Dutch" Weinbrenner's retirement project and everything was done in perfect taste. Off the entrance hall, cocktails were served around a massive stone fireplace in a lounge with deep, soft carpets, and antique furniture. The dining room was quietly elegant and the gaming*

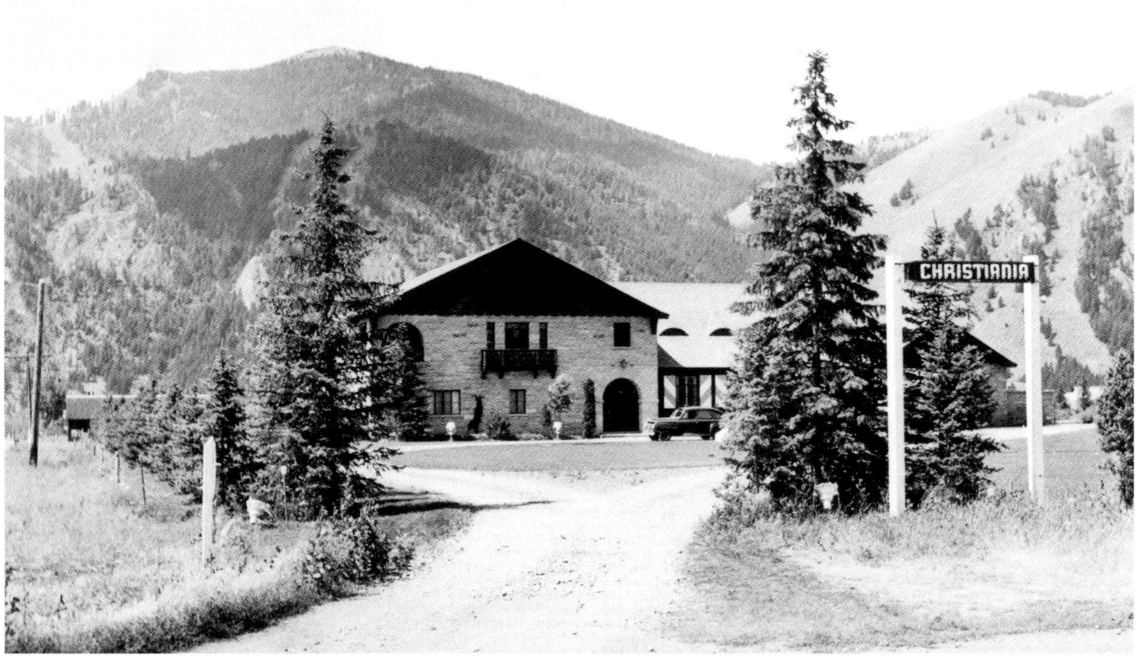

The Christiania Club owned by Dutch Weinbruner, allegedly a member of Detroit's Purple Gang, was a high-class gambling establishment in Ketchum that catered to high rollers.

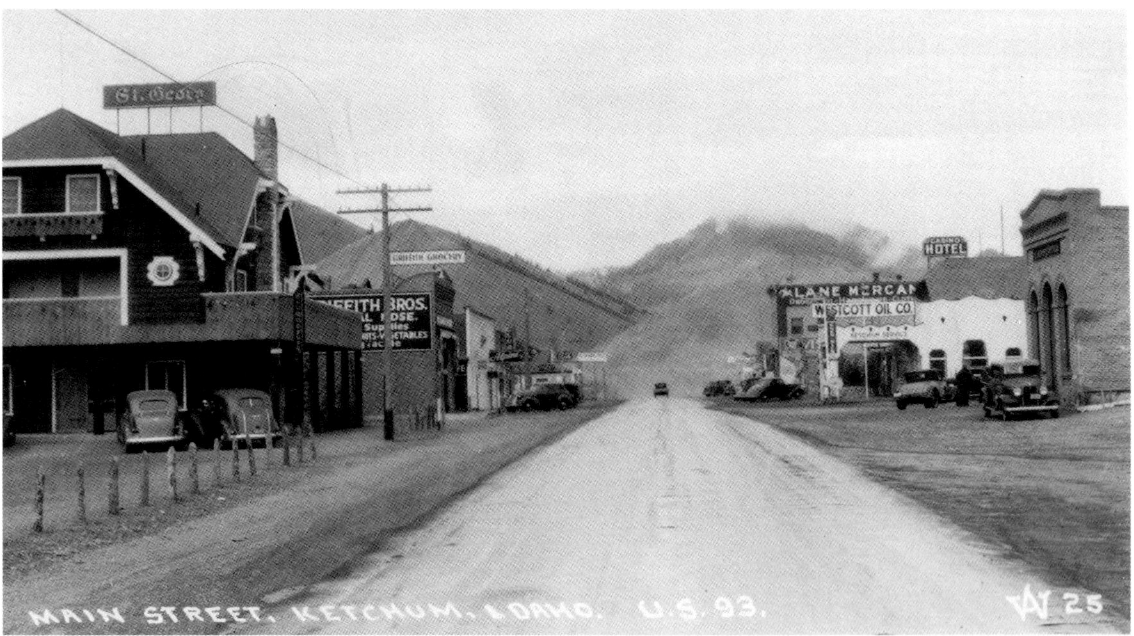

Ketchum's Main Street with St. Georg Hotel on the left, built in 1937, reconstructed from the Guyer Hot Springs Hotel. It burned down in 1939.

> *room had a circular bar over which hung a crystal chandelier. . . . I am a skeptic about the honesty of all gamblers but at least Weinbrenner, as everyone there at the time will agree, gave the local people an even break. The big play at the tables was from the film colony.*

Showing how important the Christiania Club and Weinbrenner were to Sun Valley, in 1949, Steve Hannagan told U.P. president Arthur Stoddard,

> *Dutch Weinbrenner, who owned the Christiania Club, is very ill—may not recover. I am reliably informed that his wife—who is unstable—is heir to the place. We have a real interest in the Christiania and how it is operated, and should keep an eye on it and its developments in case anything happens to Weinbrenner, or if he remains ill.*[27]

11

1938

Challenger Inn and Village Open; Women Race in Harriman Cup; Dick Durrance Locates Race Course on Warm Springs

Sun Valley was big news in winter 1938. The resort was promoted through "colored motion picture films," according to the *Seattle Times*, including 400 feet of movies and 40 natural-colored slides showing "recreational skiing and portions of the national championships held there last March." In Seattle, a promotional movie was shown at Fredrick & Nelson department store and on the University of Washington campus.

On January 22, 1938, *Railway Age* published an article titled "Union Pacific Completes New Hotel in Sun Valley":

> *Union Pacific has undertaken to develop a winter sports center in Sun Valley embodying all the recreational, scenic, climatic and topographical advantages theretofore considered to be possessed only by European resorts. . . . The railroad is now engaged in publicizing the valley as a resort for the summer vacationist and has installed facilities and services designed to augment its appeal in this respect.*

In September 1938, over 180 manufacturers of railway equipment and supplies attended a meeting in Sun Valley. They took a special train from Chicago on which Averell Harriman and U.P. officers served as hosts.

An article about Sun Valley, "Wintersport Parade," in *Ski Illustrated* said, "There will be no other winter sports center in the United States of like accommodations,

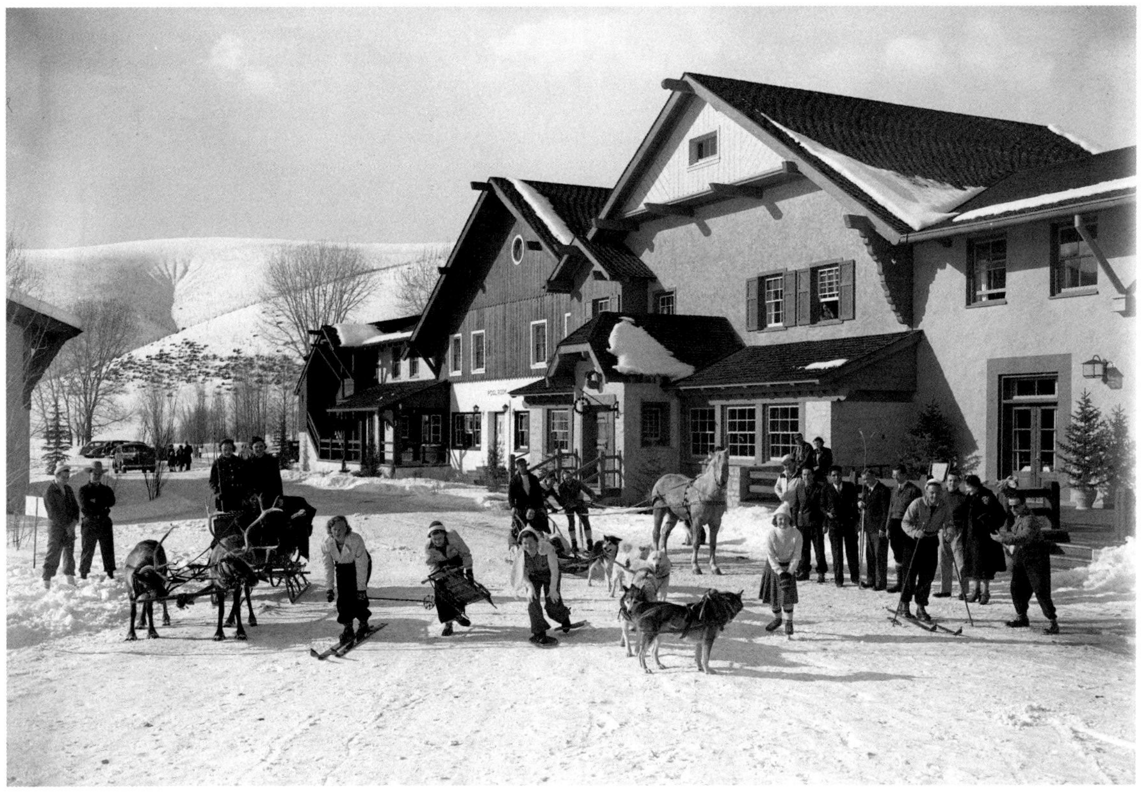

Sun Valley Village showing winter activities from sleigh rides drawn by reindeer, skiing, ice skating, dog sleds, cross-country skiing, and ski-joring.

variety and quality of skiing, snow and sunshine." A village of "Austrian-Swiss type of atmosphere" surrounded the inn. "The Challenger Inn and the Sun Valley Lodge will operate together as one great, bustling self-contained village known to the world as Sun Valley."

The inn had a weinstube (the Ram), a dining room, a store handling general and sports clothing and a ski department, a drugstore, a theater for 500, and tennis courts, which were flooded in winter to become skating rinks. Its swimming pool had 90-degree water and was surrounded by a glass windbreak so guests could swim in the open air all winter. The lodge had a winter sports store operated by Saks Fifth Avenue, and a "beauty specialist of national reputation will afford feminine visitors at the lodge metropolitan luxury in a Rocky Mountain setting," according to *Ski Illustrated*. Summer attractions included an artificial lake, golf course, polo field, baseball diamond, and horseback riding. The rodeo grounds had a quarter-mile oval track, covered grandstand, pens, and chutes for stock.

For the opening of Sun Valley's second season, Harriman orchestrated a splash of publicity combining his two pet projects. He had Union Pacific send one of its new streamliner trains, the *City of Los Angeles*, on its maiden trip from New York to Sun Valley for Christmas.

On December 21, 1937, the first edition of *The Valley Sun* was published, a newsletter designed "to chronicle Sun Valley activities" and whose motto was "Covers the Valley Like the Snow." Its lead article was titled "Packed Houses Greet New Season!—New Streamliner Makes Record Dash from New York." The 17-car train was "the last word in refinement of appointments, powered by the largest Diesel engines ever placed in service in American railroading," the newsletter reported. Chalet Harriman was completed where the Harriman family, including daughters Kathleen and Mary, stayed with friends from New York.

Dorice and Everett "Phez" Taylor traveled to Sun Valley in December 1937 on the *City of Los Angeles*. Phez was a lawyer for the National Bank of New York, and Dorice later went to work in Sun Valley's publicity department. The streamliner was on exhibit in Grand Central Station before it left to show thousands of people the new technology. Dorice said riding the train was "a gala affair," with

> *all the excitement and thrill of a luxury cruise. A trio was on board, wine and champagne were served with dinner, and celebrities and photographers were everywhere. . . . The observation car at the rear of the train was the most comfortable and luxurious I'd ever seen. The "Little Nugget" was a bar car fitted up like the parlor of a Gay Nineties madam.*

After stopping at Chicago and Omaha, the *City of Los Angeles* completed its first cross-country run in record time, arriving on December 21, 1937. It was met by 1,000 to 2,000 people, a couple of bands, dogs, reindeer, and "other instruments of publicity," according to *The Valley Sun*. Ads for Sun Valley and Union Pacific's train service were published in newspapers all over the country. The Taylors were the first to register in the newly opened Challenger Inn.

The Valley Sun described Sun Valley's many attractions. Dorice Taylor said Steve Hannagan organized so many activities because he didn't believe anyone would want to ski. The Challenger Inn and Village offered amenities to satisfy the most demanding guest. There was a lending library, shopping at Saks Fifth Avenue, a Swiss mart (Sutters) where one could buy "fresh orchids for madame" and alpine novelties, a beauty salon and barbershop, and a general store. Guests used to being taken care of by servants would feel welcome. The resort provided a valet who would perform "every known service—valeting, cleaning, pressing, and packing the luggage of women as well as men." He dry-cleaned clothes "in the streamlined period of six hours! And what's more, he has a lady's maid-in-waiting to meet the every feminine demand." There was a post office, Western Union office, and U.P. ticket office, and stock market reports were posted daily. Dr. Oliver W. Everett of Lincoln, Nebraska, was medical director of Sun Valley after 25 years of attending athletes and football players.

For the sports minded, there was "a fresh new idea in snow transportation, the snow tank," serving as a portable ski lift on Baldy and Bright Mountains and on the Hyndman Range at the head of Corral Creek, where a loop of three miles dropping 2,800 feet awaited skiers. Other activities included ski-joring, dog and reindeer sleigh rides, rabbit hunting in the lava fields 30 miles south of the resort (using one ski pole and a .22 caliber rifle), skeet shooting, and trout fishing in the Snake River. Count Schaffgotsch ran slalom races on Dollar every Sunday for guests. In the first race, Kathleen Harriman placed second and Mary Harriman fourth. Ski lifts on Dollar, Ruud, and Proctor Mountains operated from 9:00 a.m. to 4:30 p.m. daily, and buses took skiers between the village and lifts every 15 minutes. Single ride tickets were available at each lift, and daily or weekly passes could be obtained at the sports desks.

U.P. president W.M. Jeffers donated a trophy for the winner of the tri-state meet scheduled during the Sun Valley Mid-Winter Sports Carnival on January 15–16, 1938. A special 14-car train brought spectators and ski teams for the carnival from Butte, Ogden, Salt Lake City, Pocatello, and Boise to see ski-joring, ski-jumping, dog races for a $500 purse, and Idaho's first championship jumping competition between Anaconda Ski Club, Utah Ski Club, Salt Lake Ski Club, and Idaho Ski Club.

Ketchum offered many places of entertainment: the St. Georg Hotel (with a fusion of Swiss and rustic Western architecture), the Casino (featuring a pleasant atmosphere of genuine hospitality), and the Stockmen's Club (a haven for sheepmen, cattlemen, and miners with sawdust on the floor). The Christiania, a "swank new club in Sun Valley," in the words of Dorice Taylor, opened on December 23, 1937, and was

> *a strictly private organization of more than 600 celebrated members already on the roster . . . that represent top selection from the worlds of letters, arts and society. . . . The new stone club house, attractively terraced and landscaped, is distinctly after the manner of Long Island, Saratoga or Miami Beach in appearance and furnishings. . . . Somewhat English in style, it reminds one more of a manor house one would expect to find on a private estate.*

Dorice and Everett Taylor moved to Sun Valley in 1940, when Phez decided to become a country lawyer. He was attracted by a new Idaho law permitting divorces to be granted after a six-week residence, which attracted many clients from the East who preferred Sun Valley over Nevada. He passed the Idaho bar in 1941 and opened a law practice in Hailey, where there were five attorneys. There were none in

Ladies enjoying the sun in their mink coats outside the Sun Valley Lodge.

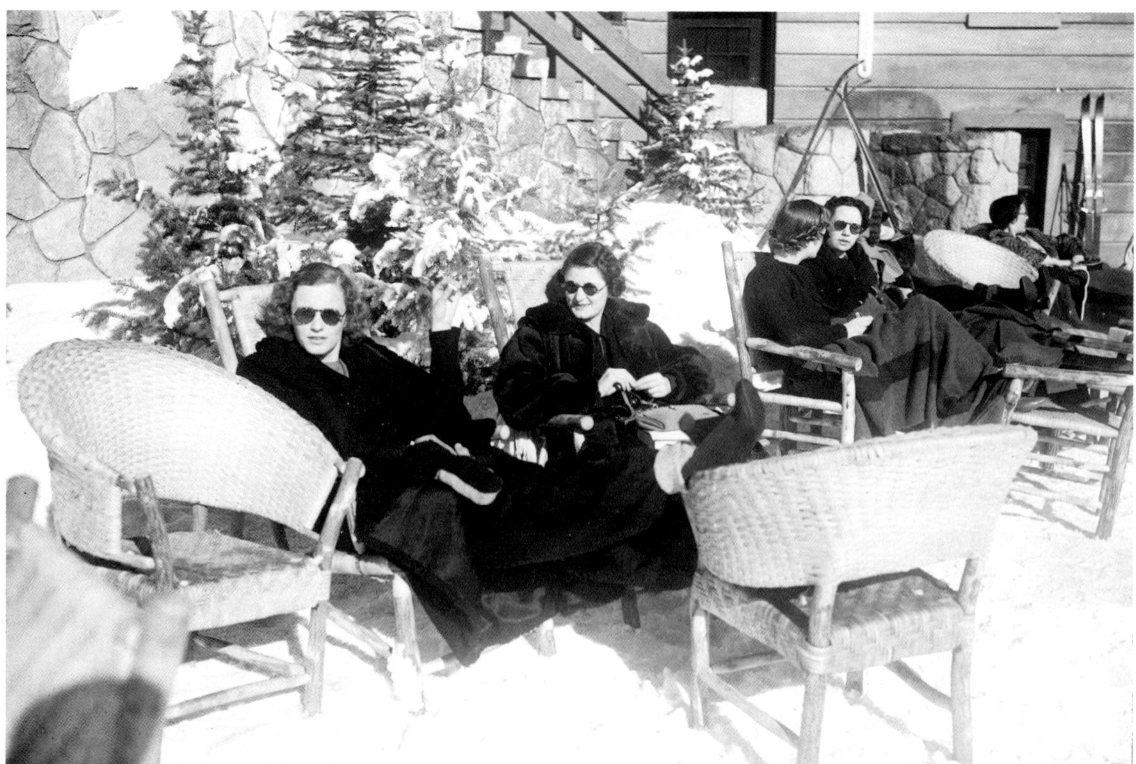

Ketchum. Taylor ended up representing a number of clients from the East, as well as the Sun Valley resort until it was sold in 1964. Dorice was a graduate of Smith College, studied at Oxford and Columbia, and was known as "smart and discreet, whether attending to an ill-mannered celebrity or fishing," according to Holland. She went to work for the Sun Valley publicity department in 1946, writing a column for *The Valley Sun* for free, working there as an employee after 1949, and was the Sun Valley publicity director from 1955 to 1971, staying after the resort was sold to the Janss Company in 1964. Her book, *Sun Valley*, describes their life in Sun Valley and her memories of the people and events that made the resort famous.[28]

Harriman and his family took the *City of Los Angeles* for Sun Valley's second opening in December 1937, getting a lot of publicity, although after the holidays he quietly went home by air on a United Airlines sleeper plane via Cheyenne, according to biographer Klein.

In 1938, Sun Valley was connected by commercial air service to some East and West Coast cities. Harriman was an early investor in the aviation industry, as was Robert Lovett, a fellow investment banker and member of the Union Pacific board, giving the railroad "an open mind toward aviation," according to Klein. In 1929, Harriman's Yale classmate Robert Lehman convinced him to become one of the original investors in the Aviation Corporation of America, begun by Lehman Brothers to buy shares of fledgling airlines and create new organizations for research and development, investment, manufacturing, and sales to develop commercial airlines. Harriman became its board chairman, and the company invested in 90 aviation-related companies, some of which later became famous, including Pan American Airways, Continental Airlines, and American Airlines. According to Klein, Harriman had a "straddle on three major transportation arenas: railroads, shipping, and aviation." The breadth of his activities is illustrated by the fact that in 1932, Harriman sat on the boards of 54 corporations.

In 1929, Harriman urged U.P. president Carl Gray to consider implementing joint transcontinental schedules with United Airlines, which flew routes parallel to those of Union Pacific between Seattle and Omaha. In 1932, a banker suggested U.P. buy United Airlines since its share of passenger service was growing. Union Pacific was "a major transportation company," owning Union Pacific Stages and 71 percent of interstate transit lines that offered long-distance bus transportation. The railroad bought shares in United later in the 1930s and looked into acquiring control of the company, according to Abramson.

In fall 1936, Harriman told Carl Gray the railroad should welcome advertising by United Airlines and

> *encourage the best possible air travel facilities. More people will come to Sun Valley by rail if they can feel sure of being able to return home rapidly in case of emergency. Some will come to the hotel by air where they would not otherwise come at all. Furthermore, I think that a long term point of view calls for development of the resort first, and development of traffic later. The hotel alone will hardly bring the railroad enough business to justify its construction but a large winter resort will. Therefore I think we will do well if we do everything to make the place accessible and popular at the outset.*

Harriman asked Ed Seagle to do a survey of Friedman Airport in Hailey, as he was interested in having United Airlines serve the resort. There were a few flights that came into Gooding, but there was no airport at Twin Falls.

On December 16, 1937, the *Hailey Times* announced a company had formed to provide airline service to Sun Valley from Pocatello and Hailey, connecting with national airlines through Western Express. *The Valley Sun* of January 11, 1938, said, "Flying up to Idaho—the Main Line airway [United] now serves Sun Valley in a breath-taking manner. One can leave New York after business and reach our Village shortly after noon the next day!" The *Hailey Times* of December 23, 1937, announced that the "landing field" at Ketchum was being improved with forest service equipment in preparation for charter air service between Boise and Ketchum, catering to "parties wishing to hunt big game over the primitive area." The Ketchum airfield was in what is now the Big Wood area north of town.

In November 1938, United Airlines' vice president for traffic sent U.P.'s B.H. Prater a copy of a United advertising letter promoting

> *the joint United Air Lines–Union Pacific air-rail service—3 mile-a-minute Mainliner sleeper, and Club type planes to Cheyenne or Salt Lake, where connections are made with Union Pacific trains directly to Ketchum, Idaho. . . . By traveling in Mainliners across the country you can leave later, arrive earlier, and stay longer at Sun Valley. . . . This year you will find the plane-rail fare to Sun Valley surprisingly economical as the plane fare includes all expenses, even meals. . . . The baggage allowance has been increased to forty pounds, and the Mainliner cargo compartments will accommodate skis.*

Announcing — United Air Lines — Union Pacific

1938-1939 Air-Rail Service to Sun Valley

FROM THE EAST

Via Cheyenne	
Lv Boston	8 30 PM
Lv New York	11 25 PM
Lv Philadelphia	10 24 PM
Lv Washington	10 59 PM
Lv Detroit	1 20 AM
Lv Chicago	4 05 AM
Ar Cheyenne	10 01 AM
Via Union Pacific RR.	
Lv Cheyenne	11 35 AM
Ar Sun Valley	7 00 AM

Via Salt Lake City		
Lv Boston	8 30 PM	
Lv New York	x11 45 PM	8 30 AM
Lv Philadelphia	10 24 PM	7 25 AM
Lv Washington	10 59 PM	8 40 AM
Lv Detroit	1 20 AM	12 00 AM
Lv Chicago	x4 25 AM	1 05 PM
Ar Salt Lake City	x1 33 PM	10 13 PM
Via Union Pacific RR.		
Lv Salt Lake City	8 00 PM	11 20 PM
Ar Sun Valley	7 00 AM	2 45 PM

FROM CALIFORNIA

Via Salt Lake City	
Lv Los Angeles	1 00 PM
Lv San Francisco	12 30 PM
Ar Salt Lake City	5 55 PM
Via Union Pacific RR.	
Lv Salt Lake City	8 00 PM
Ar Sun Valley	7 00 AM

Schedules Effective Nov. 1, 1938 — Subject to Change Without Notice

x—Sleeper Plane.

Equally fast and convenient return schedules

UNITED AIR LINES

Printed in U. S. A. DR 6035

Integrated United Airlines/Union Pacific schedule for travel to Sun Valley, 1938. Harriman wanted Sun Valley to be accessible by airplane.

Trips were advertised to Sun Valley from various East Coast cities, connecting with U.P. trains at Cheyenne and Salt Lake City, and from California connecting with U.P. trains in Salt Lake.[29]

Harriman spent nearly two months in Sun Valley in winter 1938. This gave him the opportunity to get deeply involved in the resort's operations and the chance to pursue another dream, learning to be a competent skier, according to Abramson:

> *For Averell, the ski resort was the most satisfying venture of his business career. Union Pacific did not make big profits on Sun Valley traffic, but the notion of rail travel was romanticized and the company's image was polished. . . . To some extent the sport replaced Polo in his life.*

For five years, Harriman fussed over Sun Valley as he had none of his other business enterprises. Whenever there was repainting, samples had to be kept to prove to him that the original colors were unchanged. He dictated the precise location of the furniture in the lodge's famous Duchin Room, ordering it moved if he arrived and found chairs and tables had drifted from their original places.

Union Pacific documents show how deeply involved Harriman was with all aspects of Sun Valley operations. On January 17, 1938, he wrote a four-page letter to K.M. Singer, the resort's new general manager, discussing changes to bus schedules to the

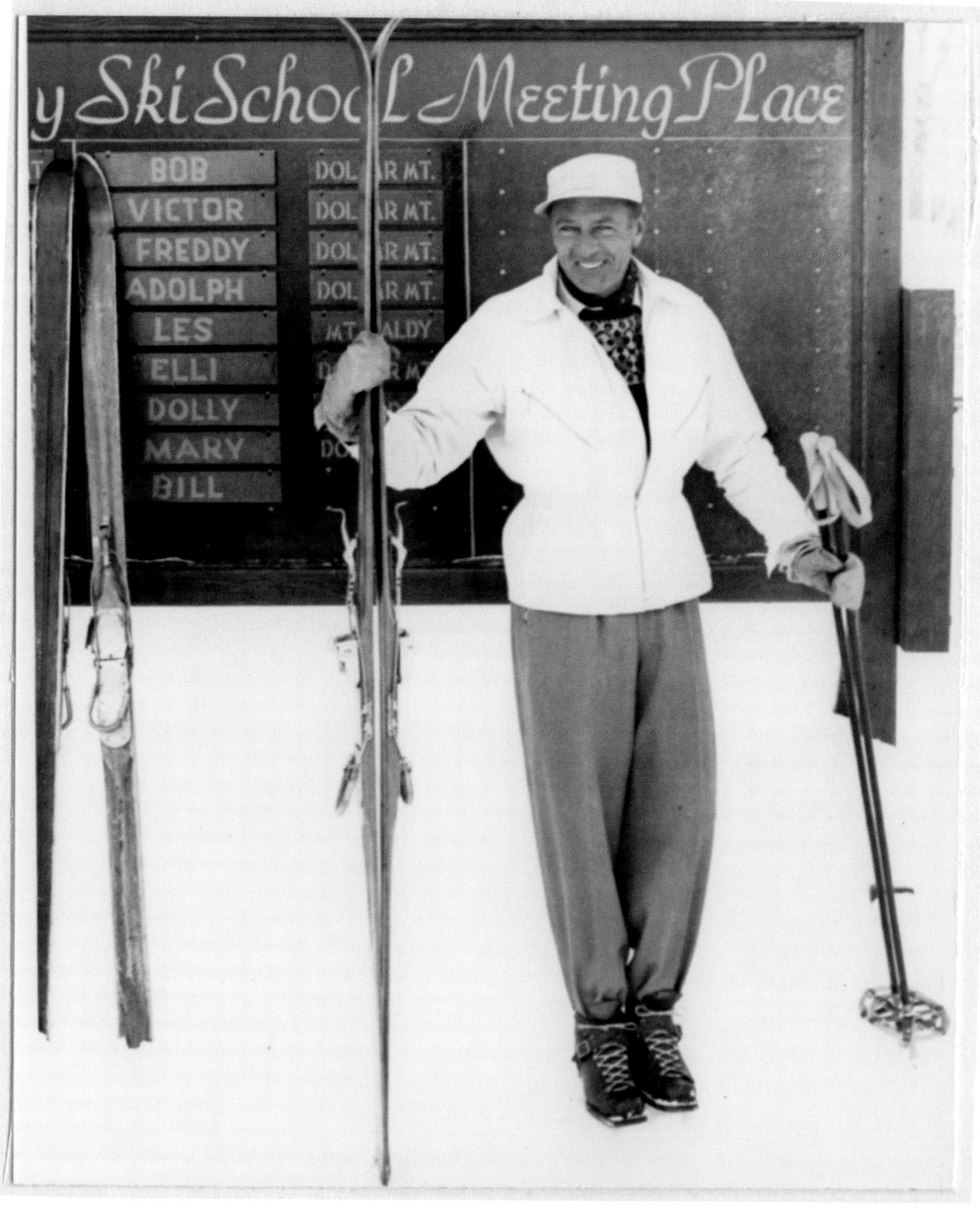
y Ski School Meeting Place
BOB
VICTOR
FREDDY
ADOLPH
LES
ELLI
DOLLY
MARY
BILL
MT. BALDY

lifts, preference for ski classes on the mountains for beginners, pay for part-time ski instructors, promotion of backcountry skiing, deficiencies of the resort's sports desks, and other issues.

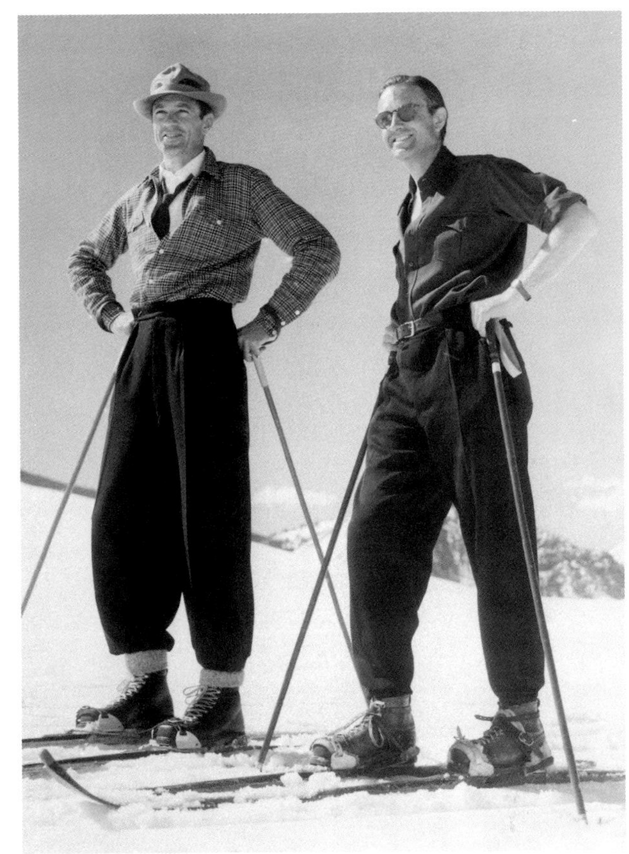

OPPOSITE Gary Cooper at ski school meeting place. Gary and Rocky Cooper were Sun Valley regulars, along with many other Hollywood stars.

ABOVE Gary Cooper and Averell Harriman, skiing companions.

In March, Harriman asked Steve Hannagan to make a film of the Sun Valley Ski School, featuring three men and three women who had never skied. It would show them selecting equipment, entering group lessons, and learning the steps to master skiing techniques, "including of course amusing incidents throughout." He even suggested possible filmmakers. In June, Harriman told Hannigan he was disappointed in the film's dialogue and wanted it rewritten. It was released on December 16, 1938, by Paramount Pictures.

Harriman was able to keep in constant communication at all times by using the U.P. telegraph system that connected his New York office directly to Sun Valley. He could also send and receive telegrams on U.P. trains. His father used the same method of communication. In 1901, E.H. Harriman had leased a private wire from Western Union between New York and Chicago and built an extension to Omaha. "By using the Union Pacific's wires west of Omaha, Harriman had a communication link that enabled him to talk to people in the West by telegraph as a later generation would by telephone," according to Klein in his biography of E.H. Harriman. That winter, Harriman had a chance to work on his skiing techniques and met with the Hollywood stars who came to Sun Valley.[30]

Ski Tournaments

During Christmas 1937, Sun Valley held the first of what became an important tradition, an intersectional ski meet for top college teams. The University of Washington, West Coast champions, met Dartmouth College, East Coast champions. The *New York Times* of December 27, 1937, said, "The eyes of American skiers will be focused on Sun Valley . . . when two of the strongest units in the sport, Dartmouth College and the University of Washington . . . settle the intercollegiate supremacy of this country in skiing."

Dartmouth was the favorite, coached by European champion Walter Prager and headed by Dick Durrance, who won the national championships in Sun Valley the prior spring, "over the most brilliant field of down-hill slalom men ever to compete in North America." Washington won the first annual Pacific Conference title in 1937, by "making a clean sweep of the downhill, slalom and cross-country races." Famous ski instructor Otto Lang coached Washington. Six-person teams competed in downhill, slalom, and jumping.

The downhill course descended 2,000 feet from the summit of Bright Mountain, just south of Durrance Mountain and north of Ketchum. It was named for Alex Bright, a member of the 1936 U.S. Olympic team who was on the board of governors of the Sun Valley Ski Club. The new ski jump and slalom course on Ruud Mountain were used for the first time in competition. Grandstand seats were constructed on the flat in Trail Creek Valley from the foot of Ruud Mountain to the Creek for 2,500 spectators, providing perfect views of the jumps and slalom races. Skiers used the chairlift for both events.

"Dartmouth Ski Team Sweeps Meet with U.W.," reported the *Seattle Times* on January 2, 1938, in spite of Durrance being unable to compete after spraining his ankle. Dartmouth took four of five places in the downhill, nine out of ten in the slalom, and scored the best marks in jumping, winning "hands down." Otto Lang said Washington felt very good about the meet, and learned a great deal, but they were not used to that level of competition.

"The spirit of such an intersectional meet was excellent and attracted favorable comment from the skiing fraternity everywhere," the *Times* said. The Sun Valley Ski Club said it would sponsor a four-event collegiate meet the next year, and it would be an annual event thereafter.

Alf Engen and his new wife, Evelyn, had spent their honeymoon at Sun Valley during Christmas 1937 at Harriman's invitation, and Engen inaugurated the jump he helped

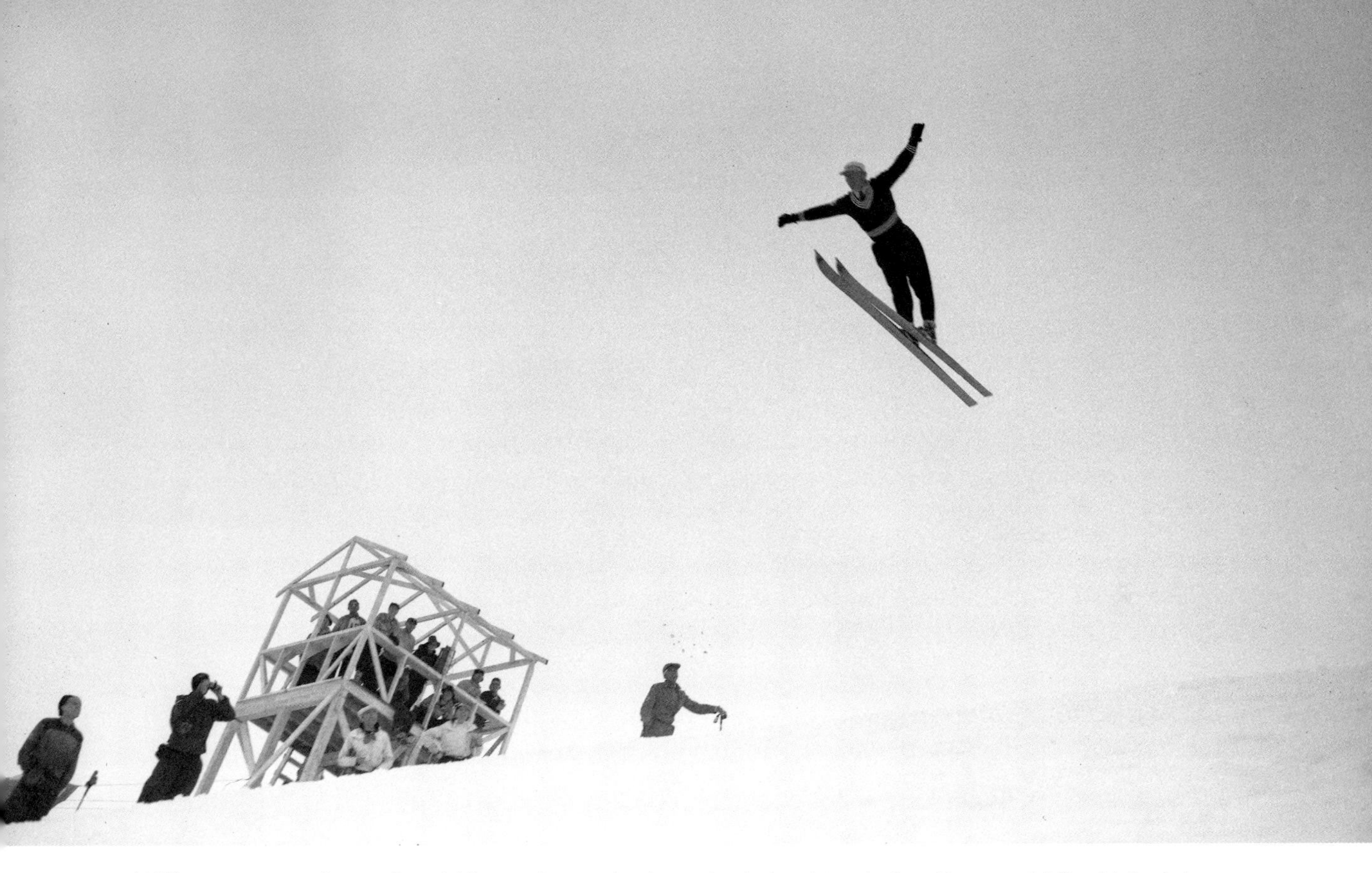

Alf Engen competing at Ruud Mountain on the jump he helped to design. Engen said Sun Valley's jump "for its size comes nearer to perfection than any yet developed."

build the previous summer. After the college meet, a jumping exhibition took place on Ruud Mountain where Walter Prager, Alf Engen, and Otto Lang all jumped over 40 meters, exceeding the design limit of the hill. Single, double, and triple takeoffs were done by Engen, Prager, Lang, Max Hauser, and Whit Miller. Prager said the slalom course was "one of the finest and toughest slalom courses he had ever seen." Engen said Sun Valley's jump, "for its size comes nearer to perfection than any yet developed."

Alf Engen spent the next 10 years off and on living at and representing Sun Valley during the winter months and working for the U.S. Forest Service the rest of the year, overseeing development of new ski areas. Harriman hired him as a sports consultant and superintendent of recreational facilities, and Evelyn did publicity for the resort. They lived in the lodge, as did other employees. Engen later helped to construct new runs on Bald Mountain in 1938 and 1939 when it was being prepared for general skiing, and both he and his wife performed skiing scenes for film stars in movies, including *Northern Pursuit* and *My Reputation*. The Engens left Sun Valley in 1942 so Alf could help develop Snowbasin, but returned after World War II.

The national downhill and slalom championships were held at Stowe, Vermont, one week before the Harriman Cup in March 1938. Ulrich Beutter of the Bavarian all-university team won the national combined championship. Dick Durrance was second, and Walter Prager third. Three Seattle-area skiers placed high in the national championships: Peter Garrett, a Yale student from Seattle, finished sixth in the combined. Don Amick and Don Fraser finished eighth and tenth. In his oral history, Don Fraser said the tournament was a real test for Western skiers who were used to wide-open slopes. It was freezing cold, and the courses were very narrow and went through trees. Racers struggled to stay on the trails, although Dick Durrance proved a master at it. There was no grooming except what the racers did on the way up. Fraser broke two pairs of skis in three days hitting trees.

On March 12–13, the second annual Sun Valley International Open/Harriman Cup tournament was held, a combination downhill and slalom event, said to be the "greatest tournament of all . . . a 'Who's Who' in downhill skiing of the world," according to the Sun Valley Ski Club. The 1938 race was best known for having been run in foul weather and allowing women to race for the first time. The Challenger Inn charged $8 per night and the lodge cost $24 a night.

Seattle played a significant role in the tournament. Seattleite Peter Hostmark, president of the Pacific Northwestern Ski Association, was referee; while Ben Thompson, of Anderson and Thompson Ski Company, was course setter. Otto Sanford was chief timer.

There were 54 entrants from all over the world, including Dick Durrance from Dartmouth; Walter Prager of Switzerland, Dartmouth coach, former FIS downhill and Kandahar winner; Austrian Hannes Schroll, instructor at Yosemite, 1935 U.S. national downhill and slalom champion; Hans Hauser, three-time Austrian champion and FIS winner in 1935; Sigi Engl from Austria, instructor at Yosemite; Birger Ruud, twice Olympic jumping champion; and Sigmund Ruud from Norway, a ski jumper who was one of the best downhillers in Europe. Students included Norwegian Nils Eie, 1937 four-way champion at the World Academic Championships; Ulli Beutter of Germany, 1938 national downhill champion; and Fritz Dehmel of Germany, 1938 Eastern downhill champion. The Pacific Northwestern Ski Association sent Don Fraser, 1938 Northwest combined champion and 1936 U.S. Olympic team member; Don Amick, Northwest slalom champion; John Woodward, University of Washington star; Lon Robinson; Hjalmar Hvam, four-way competitor from Portland; and Ken Syverson, head of the Snoqualmie Ski Bowl ski school.

The women's field was dominated by Seattle-area racers Grace Carter Lindley, then living in Minneapolis; Mrs. Jim (Skit Smith) Babson of Portland, formerly from Tacoma; and Ellis-Ayr Smith of Tacoma, all members of the 1936 U.S. Olympic ski team. Also included were a young Gretchen Kunigk from Tacoma, who married Don Fraser the following year, and Virginia Bowden from the University of Washington.

For the second year, the downhill was held north of Ketchum on Durrance Mountain. Ben Thompson set the downhill and slalom courses but had to shorten them because of icy conditions. The downhill course was three and a half miles long, dropping from 10,500 feet to 6,000 feet, and was held in wet, miserable conditions. As before, racers faced a three-hour uphill climb to the start.

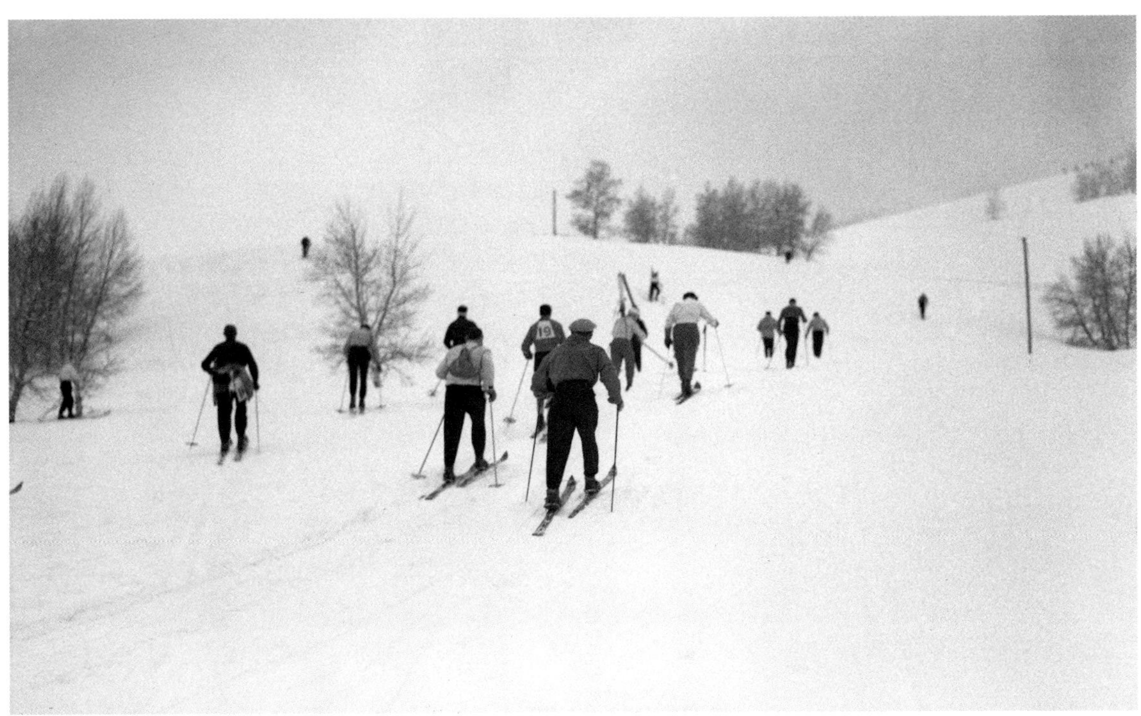

Skiers beginning the three-mile climb up Durrance Mountain for the 1938 Harriman Cup downhill.

Ulrich Beutter of Germany won the downhill, finishing with a tremendous margin of 13 seconds over Dick Durrance, followed by Walter Prager. A number of photographs of the 1938 downhill race on Durrance Mountain were taken, but the snow interfered with their clarity.

"The fireworks of the day occurred in the women's downhill race, over a shorter course," wrote the *Seattle Times*. Grace Lindley won the women's downhill, followed by Virginia Bowden and Gretchen Kunigk. Tacoma's Ellis-Ayr Smith was sixth. In the slalom, Grace Lindley was first, Mrs. Tom Mitchell of Australia was second, Skit Smith Babson was third, Gretchen Kunigk was fourth, and Virginia Bowden was seventh. Grace Lindley, "former Pacific Northwest downhill and slalom champion, skiing for Sun Valley," won the downhill, slalom, and combined titles. Gretchen Kunigk finished second in the combined, followed by Mrs. Tom Mitchell and Virginia Bowden. Kunigk's second-place finish showed she was ready for the national racing scene.

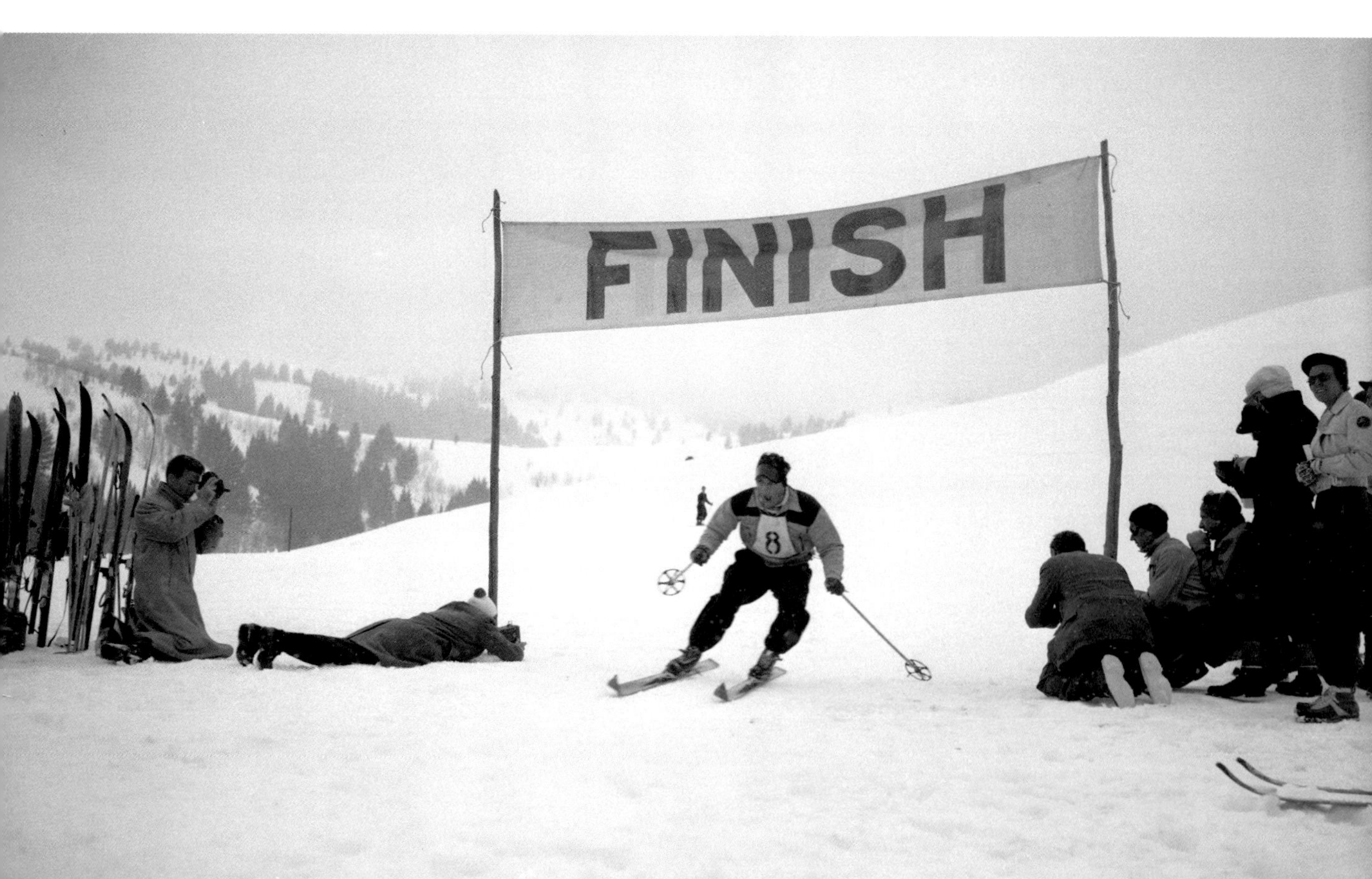

In her article "Women's Events," Grace Lindley wrote, "The first Sun Valley Open races for women have set a precedent and a high standard for future ladies' competitions in this country. For the first time, the heretofore 'Short Subjects' on the big racing programs have now attained equal significance and attention." The downhill on Durrance Mountain was "started at a logical place just below the 'rock garden,' where there was good footing and shelter behind the rocks." The women watched the men race "fighting for balance and vorlage" in bad light and heavy snow, a difficult course the men cut up considerably.

Gretchen Kunigk said Durrance Mountain was "a miserable mountain to ski on." Competitors had to get up at dawn to ride buses north to where the downhill was held, then climb for several hours to reach the race start. The only shelter from the heavy, wet snow at the start was behind some rocks. The women had to wait until the men finished their race before starting, while they crouched on the mountain, wet and miserable. The course was badly cut up when the women got to race: "We were all drowned rats. Everyone appreciated the prompt warm transportation back to the Inn."

The slalom on Ruud Mountain was a deceptively fast course watched by 5,000 spectators in stands across the road from the finish. Walter Prager had two magnificent runs to win the slalom, followed by Dick Durrance and Niles Eie. Beutter paid the price of caution in the slalom, skiing too slowly and finishing 15th. Grace Lindley said Ruud Mountain

> *is the perfect slalom hill. Having the tow available for unlimited rides, one can become thoroughly familiar with the contours of the hill, the general layout of the slalom, and most important, one can gauge the conservative speed one can hold without tiring. . . . The weather was just plain foul—wet, cold slushy. . . . As it was, we were all not only warm, dry and fed, but from our perfect position in the Inn station wagons, we could watch the whole of the men's races and get the time immediately on the loudspeaker.*

OPPOSITE Dick Durrance finishing the 1938 Harriman Cup downhill, where he placed second behind Ullrich Beutter.

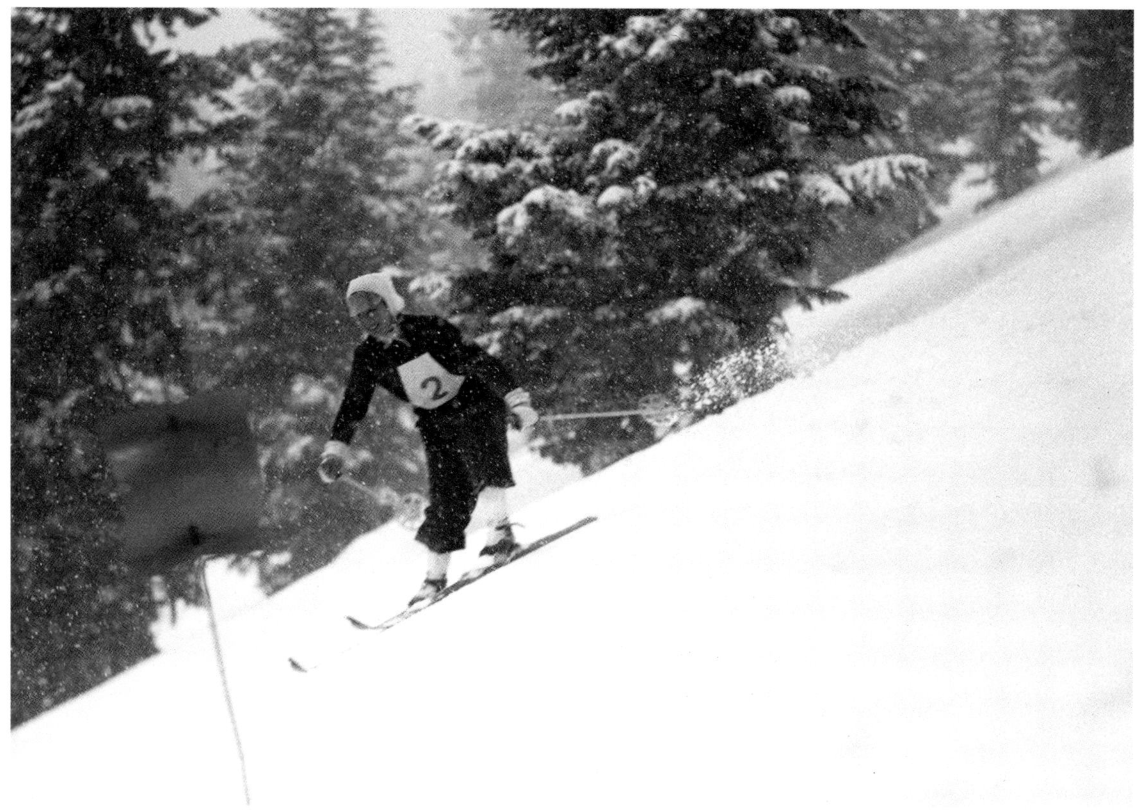

Sun Valley International

SLALOM RACE

AND

SKI JUMP

SUNDAY, MARCH 13, 1938

Champion Skiers of 8 Nations

IN MENS AND WOMENS RACES

including

Birger Ruud of Norway	Dick Durrance of U. S.
Alf Engen of U.S.	Hans Hauser of Sun Valley
Walter Prager of Switzerland	Tom Mitchell of Australia
Ulli Beutter of Germany	W. T. Earle of England
Grace Carter Lindley of U. S.	Gretchen Kunigk of U. S.

and Many Others

Morning Race 10:30 - Afternoon 2:00

JUMPS FOLLOW AFTERNOON RACE

ADMISSION 40c

GRANDSTAND $1.00 Including Tax

PARKING SPACE NEARBY

DOWNHILL RACE SATURDAY MORNING MARCH 12th - 10 MILES NORTH OF SUN VALLEY

ABOVE Up-and-coming racer from Tacoma, Gretchen Kunigk, in the 1938 Harriman Cup downhill on Durrance Mountain, where she placed third.

LEFT Ad for Sun Valley International Slalom Race and Ski Jump, 1938. Admission 40¢.

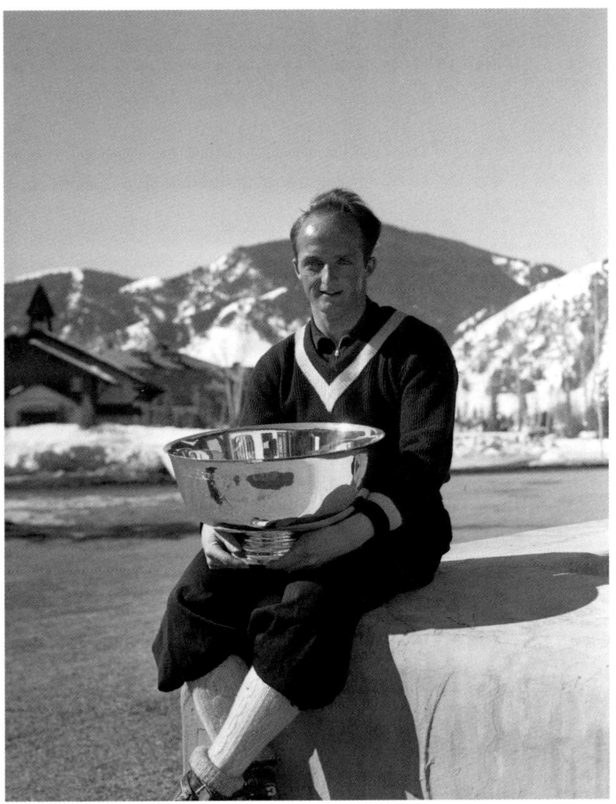

Sun Valley International Open Tournament

Results of Downhill Races

Saturday, March 12, 1938

MEN'S

Place	Name	Club	Time
1.	Ulli Beutter	Bavaria	4:15.0
2.	Richard Durrance	Dartmouth	4:27.4
3.	Walter Prager	Switzerland	4:37.4
4.	Paul Deschman	Sun Valley S. C.	4:51.2
5.	Hans Hauser	Sun Valley S. C.	4:52.6
6.	Hannes Schroll	Yosemite	4:53.4
7.	Roland Cossman	Sun Valley S. C.	5:04.6
8.	Fritz Dehmel	Bavaria	5:10.4
9.	Don Fraser	Wash. Ski Club.	5:15.2
10.	Hjalmar Hvam	Cascade Ski Club	5:16.6
11.	Max Hauser	Sun Valley S. C.	5:16.8
12.	Don Amick	Wash. Ski Club.	5:21.8
13.	Joe Benedicter	Sun Valley S. C.	5:36.2
14.	Scott Osborn	Penguin Ski Club	6:01.6
15.	Martin Arrouge	Reno Ski Club	6:03.8
16.	Barney McLean	Hot Sulphur Springs	6:05.0
17.	Ted Hunter	Dartmouth	6:15.2
18.	Ken Syverson	Seattle	6:18.6
19.	Robert S. Balch	Colo. Arlberg	6:21.4
20.	Earl Edmunds	Reno Ski Club.	6:32.0
21.	Richard Mitchell	Calif. Ski Assn.	6:40.2
22.	Alfred D. Lindley	Sun Valley S. C.	6:46.0
23.	William Klein	Stockton Ski Club	6:47.6
24.	Karl Hostetter	Sun Valley S. C.	6:50.4
25.	Hans Teichner	Colo. Ski Runners	6:50.8
26.	Bud Clark	Norland S. C., Ottawa	7:07.4
27.	Tom Mitchell	Australia S. C.	7:25.0
28.	Tom Souvelewski	Yosemite W. S. C.	7:38.8
29.	Hans Nunnemacher	Heilige Huegel S. C.	8:38.2
30.	Carl Bechdolt, Jr.	Lake Tahoe	9:07.8
31	Kaare Engen	Idaho	9:30.4
32.	Bud Brady	Univ. of Washington	9:39.2
33.	Si Brand	Mt. Lassen S. C.	9:54.0
34.	David Quinney	Utah Ski Club	10:16.4
35.	Joe Bradley	Wisconsin Hoofers	10:21.6
36.	Wayne Poulsen	Reno Ski Club	11:43.0
37.	Frank Howard	Auburn Ski Club	12:19.2
*	Nils Eie	Norway	
*	W. H. Earle	Ski Club of Gt. Britain	

*Did not finish.

Results of Slalom Races

Sunday, March 13, 1938

MEN'S

Place	Name	Club	1st Run	2nd Run	Total Time
1.	Walter Prager	Switzerland	1:22.6	1:27.6	2:50.2
2.	Richard Durrance	Dartmouth	1:25.0	1:26.8	2:51.8
3.	Nils Eie	Norway	1:29.3	1:31.8	3:01.1
4.	Hans Hauser	Sun Valley S. C.	1:29.1	1:32.8	3:01.9
5.	Paul Deschman	Sun Valley S. C.	1:30.0	1:34.5	3:04.5
6.	Don Fraser	Wash. Ski C.	1:34.0	1:36.0	3:10.0
7.	Roland Cossman	Sun Valley S. C.	1:29.0	1:41.5	3:10.6
8.	Fritz Dehmel	Bavaria	1:42.3*	1:44.1	3:26.4
9.	Robert S. Balch	Colo. Arlberg	1:45.0	1:41.7	3:20.7
10.	Bud Clark	Norland S. C.	1:40.3	1:47.3	3:27.6
11.	Hjalmar Hvam	Cascade S. C.	1:37.9	1:50.3	3:28.2
12.	Barney McLean	Hot Sul. Spgs.	1:43.4	1:49.9	3:33.3
13.	Martin Arrouge	Reno Ski C.	1:42.7	1:52.1	3:34.0
14.	Tom Mitchell	Australia S. C.	1:46.9	1:49.1	3:36.0
15.	Ulli Beutter	Bavaria	1:34.0	2:07.6*	3:41.6
16.	Scott Osborn	Penguin S. C.	1:41.5	2:01.8	3:43.3
17.	Alfred Lindley	S. V. S. C.	1:49.7	1:56.5	3:46.2
18.	Richard Mitchell	Calif. Ski A.	1:49.2	2:08.3	3:57.5

*Single penalty 6 seconds

Results of Combined Events

MEN'S

Place	Name	Points
1.	Richard Durrance	422.0
2.	Walter Prager	430.6
3.	Ulli Beutter	454.4
4.	Hans Hauser	456.3
5.	Paul Deschman	457.3
6.	Roland Cossman	476.1
7.	Don Fraser	486.2
8.	Fritz Dehmel	496.2
9.	Hjalmar Hvam	504.0
10.	Barney McLean	557.0
11.	Martin Arrouge	557.1
12.	Scott Osborn	567.1
13.	Robert S. Balch	567.4
14.	Alfred Lindley	609.6
15.	Richard Mitchell	614.0
16.	Bud Clark	614.2
17.	Tom Mitchell	639.4

Page 11

LEFT Dick Durrance holding Harriman Cup, 1938. He was second in the downhill and second in the slalom, but won the combined title.

RIGHT 1938 Harriman Cup results.

Durrance lost to Ulli Beutter in the downhill and to Walter Prager in the slalom, but won his second consecutive combined title and the Harriman Cup, followed by Prager, Beutter, and Hans Hauser.

An informal open jumping tournament was held on Ruud Mountain, which had a lift, to the delight of the competitors, "who had been climbing for their skiing all season, or jumping off rickety scaffolds on artificial snow," according to a report in the *Sun Valley Ski Club Annual 1937–1938*. The meet attracted many of the best jumpers in the world, including the famous Ruud brothers, Birger and Sigmund, from Kongsberg, Norway.

The Ruud brothers toured the United States in 1938, participating in jumping tournaments in a number of areas. At Fox River Grove, Illinois, the Ruuds jumped in front of 30,000 spectators, and 10,000 attended the event at Chicago's Soldier Field. In Los Angeles, 20,000 spectators paid to see the California Open Ski Meet at Memorial

Stadium, where a ski jump was built that soared 60 feet above the Coliseum's rim, designed for 170-foot jumps.. The Ruud brothers were so successful the *Salt Lake City Tribune* said they were "mighty little men . . . who had the precision of machines,"and if they became any better, they would no longer be classified as "genus homo." *The American Ski Annual of 1938–39* said that the brothers "deserve credit for having done more toward developing, promoting, and stimulating the American people to be ski minded than any other skiers in the world." They were inducted into the U.S. Ski and Snowboard Hall of Fame in 1970.

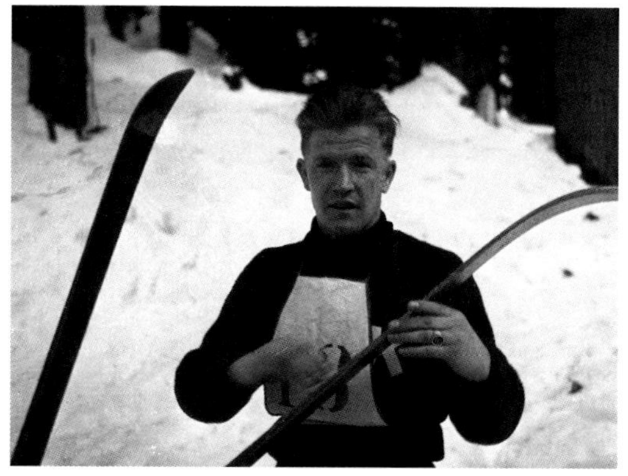

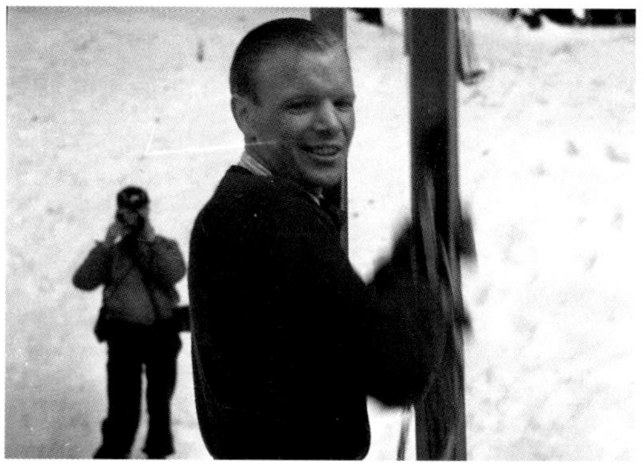

Norway's Birger Ruud (top) and Sigmund Ruud (bottom) at Snoqualmie Pass, 1938. *Courtesy of Matt V. Broze family.*

Birger Ruud won the jumping event in front of a crowd of more than 3,000, despite having torn chest muscles that kept him from completing the Harriman Cup. He leaped 48 meters, a new record for the hill during competition, "jumping in agony which makes him clap hands to his chest after he has landed," the Sun Valley Ski Club reported. Seven other jumpers exceeded 40 meters. Nils Eie placed second "in beautiful form," Sigurd Ulland was third, and Dick Durrance fourth. "But it remained for the great Engen to crown the year's jumping on Ruud Mountain." The spectators

> *cheer tremendously when Alf Engen of Salt Lake and Sun Valley jumps 50.5 meters, which is more than the law can allow on Ruud Mountain, and a new record. They do not learn until later that the judges hadn't realized that Alf thought the competition was underway, which is regrettable, though it takes nothing away from the brilliance of a truly great jumping performance.*

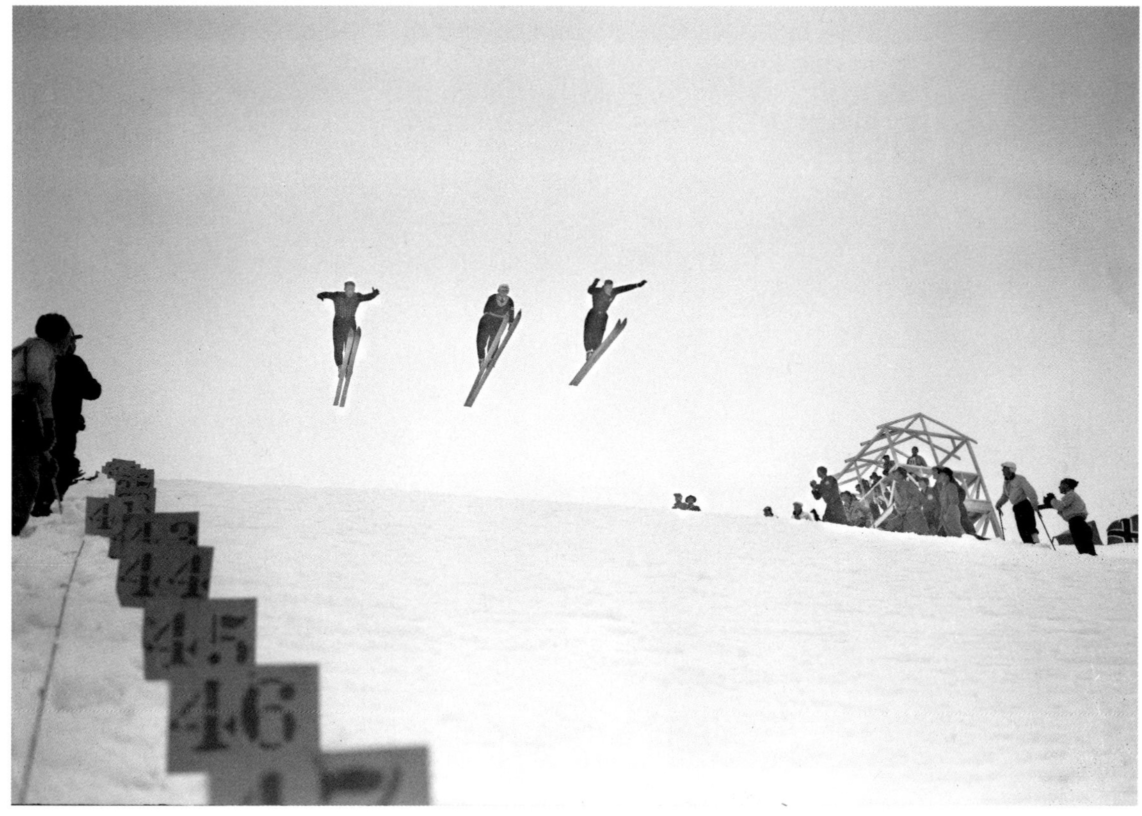

Alf Engen, Nils Eie, and Birger Ruud jumping at Ruud Mountain, 1938.

Engen's jump was counted as the new official record for Ruud Mountain nonetheless. "And without a doubt it will stand as Ruud's all time record," wrote the Sun Valley Ski Club.

Seattle Times writer Ken Binns, in his article "Ecker Hill and Sun Valley" in *American Ski Annual, 1937–1938*, described how much Harriman was a significant part of Sun Valley's racing scene:

> *Let's talk about the Sun Valley Open tournament. . . . And while talking about it we might as well talk about Averell Harriman, because it's his baby as much as ours, or perhaps more; because he sees it every day that he thinks of something new to do, and we see it only in recollection. He's as much a part of Sun Valley, in fact, as Sun Valley is an integral part of American skiing.*

Sun Valley Ski Club members had great success at other races in 1938. At the Women's National Championships in Stowe, Vermont, Grace Carter Lindley was first in slalom and second in downhill and slalom. She was third in the Women's Eastern Downhill Championships. Max Hauser won the downhill in the Pacific Coast Open Championships in Yosemite. Alf Engen placed fourth in the National Jumping Championships, first in the Norfolk Association Jumps, and first in the Spokane and Bozeman Jumping Meets. Roland Cossman was first in slalom, downhill, and combined at the Utah Open Meet. Jarvis Schauffler was first in the downhill and combined at the Rocky Mountain Championships at Aspen.

Gretchen Kunigk, racing's rising star, got hurt in the last race of the season, the Golden Rose race at Mount Hood in June 1938, at Timberline Lodge. The finish gate

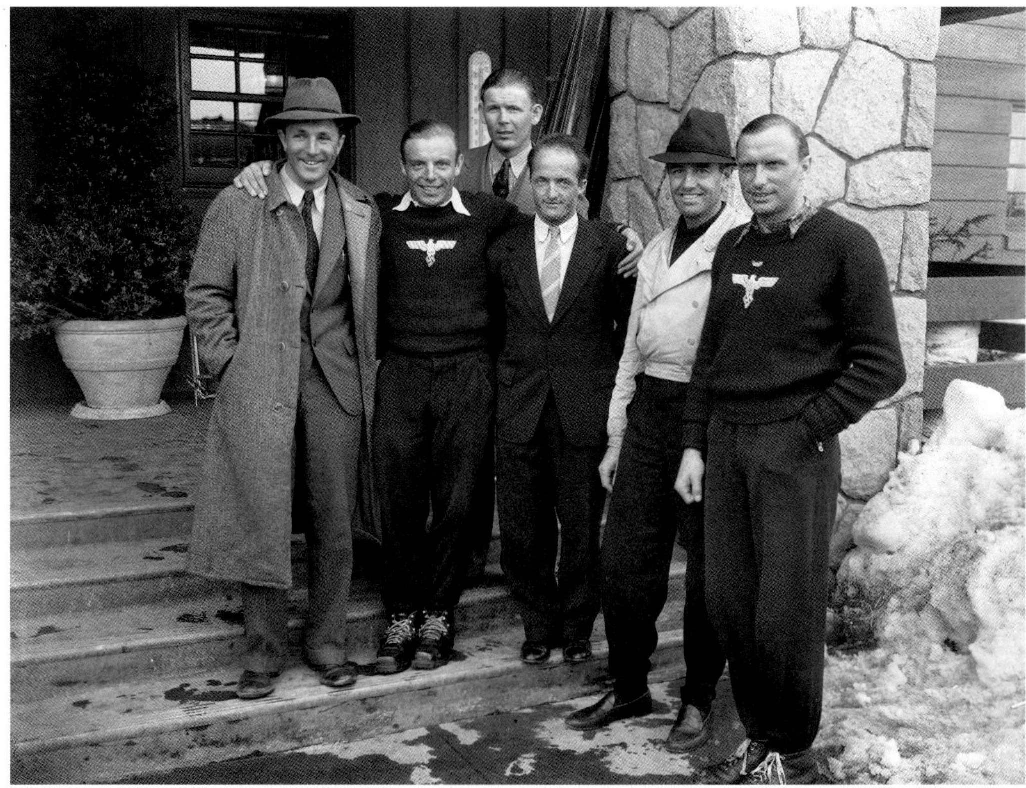

Walter Prager, Elli Beutter, Alf Engen, Dick Durrance, Averell Harriman, and Fritz Hehmel in front of Sun Valley Lodge at end of 1938 Harriman Cup tournament.

was just east of the lodge, and there was some controversy over whether it was too narrow or sufficiently marked. Kunigk "came down at a terrifying clip, [and] crashed into the gate," according to her biographer Luanne Pfeifer. She won the race but could only walk a few feet before collapsing. She had torn ligaments in her knee and torn cartilages in her leg, injuries that kept her out of competition for most of the next season. She returned to competition in April 1939 at the Northwest Ski Championships, where she finished a respectable tenth, but she missed the women's national alpine tournament at Stowe and the 1939 Harriman Cup. However, based on her prior record, she was selected for the 1940 FIS and Olympic teams.[31]

Sun Valley Expands Its Summer Activities

Sun Valley followed Steve Hannagan's recommendations, putting in a swimming pool and a popular bar, and publishing many pictures of pretty women and celebrities. They circulated the pictures back to the hometown newspapers of the guests and got free publicity portraying Sun Valley as a sunshine mecca.

Sun Valley's activities were expanded for summer 1938. The country's second full-size all-year outdoor ice rink was built. The Sun Valley Figure Skating Club was formed and had "a most successful season of unusual skating under a brilliant summer sun or cloudless starlit sky," according to the *Sun Valley Ski Club Annual, 1939*. During dinner, skaters and dancers enjoyed the lodge terrace orchestra. Members of the New York Skating Club and Philadelphia Skating Club visited, with one member training for the 1940 Olympics. For the second summer, a group of Dartmouth skiers took up rock climbing and toured the Sawtooth Mountains to find interesting climbs, recommending it as the ideal summer sport for skiers. Summer activities included fishing, hiking, polo, horseback riding, tennis, swimming, shooting, rodeo, and many others.

On June 12, 1938, the *New York Times* reported on "Summer Plans at Sun Valley," describing the wide array of activities available:

> *There will be horseback riding, swimming, fishing, skeet shooting, and golf on the new course laid out in Trail Creek Canyon, as well as excursions into the hinterlands. Later in the season a five-day trip by saddle and pack horse will take fishermen into the*

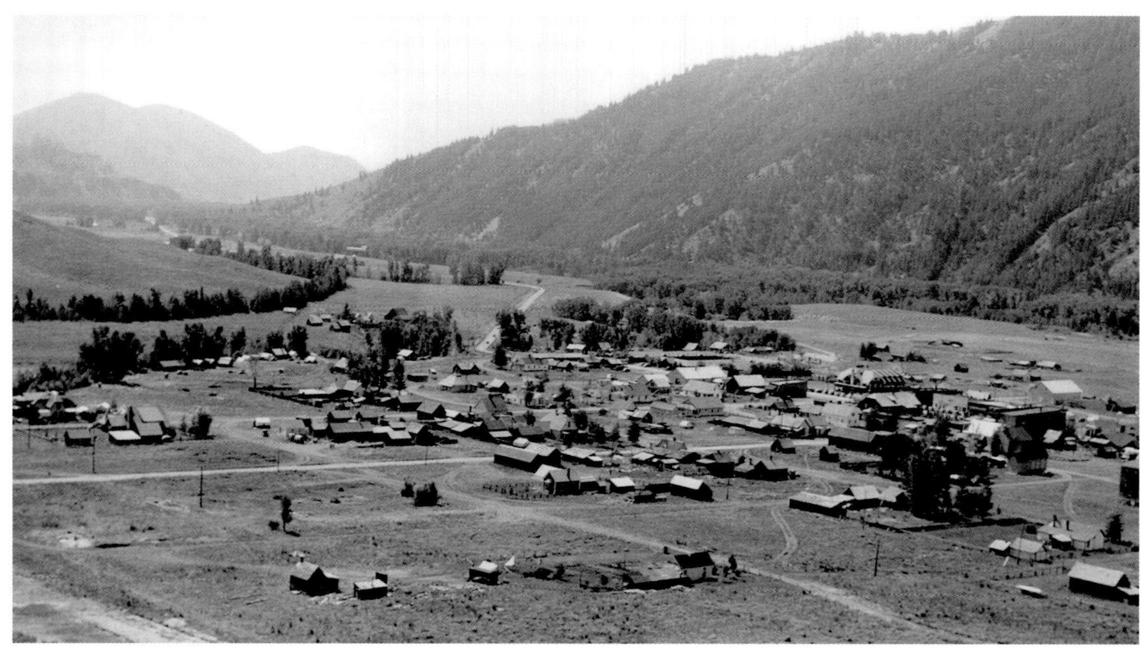

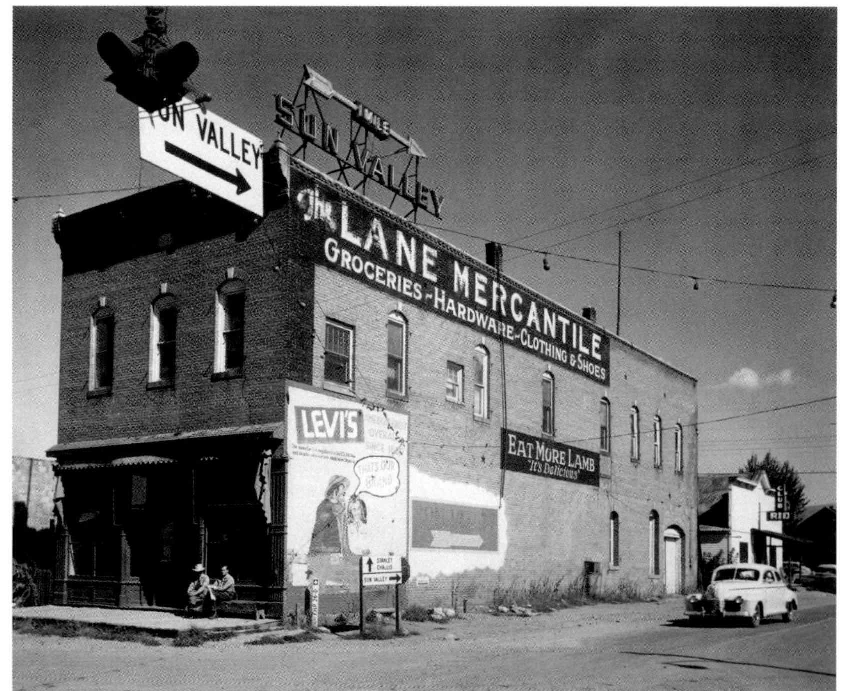

ABOVE Ketchum, 1938, looking southwest. *Courtesy of B&B Blueprints.*

LEFT Lane Mercantile with sign pointing to Sun Valley, around 1938.

OPPOSITE Sun Valley pool and bathing beauties—Steve Hannagan's vision for the resort.

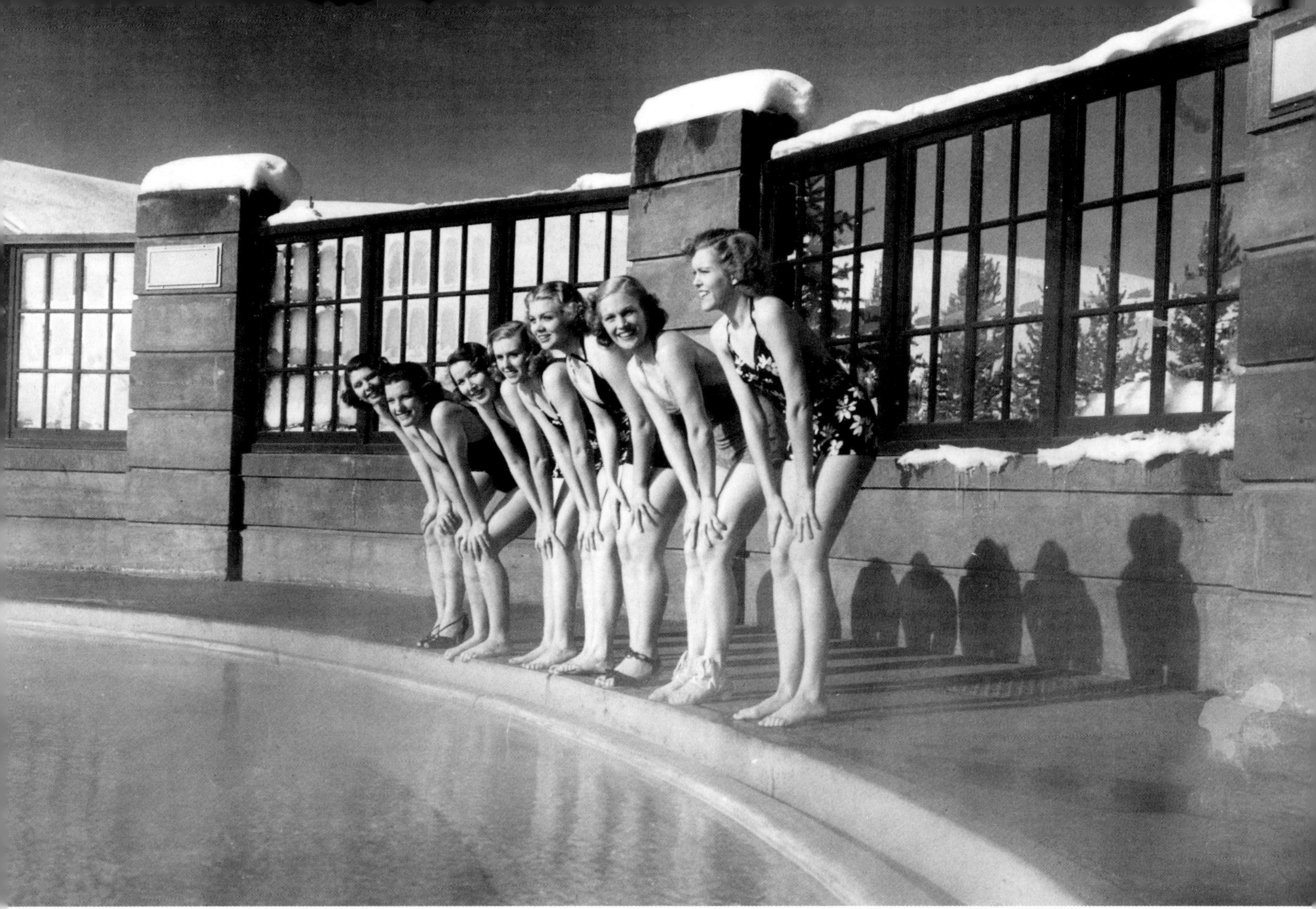

unmapped White Cloud and Salmon River areas, scarcely ever before fished by white men. . . . Just below Sun Valley is spring-fed Silver Creek, where rainbow trout are large and plentiful. The less adventurous fisherman can stick close to home and fish by twilight in the clear waters of Sun Valley Lake.

Mid-June will see the inauguration of mountain climbing expeditions. Members of these parties will tackle such challenging pinnacles as the Finger of Fate in the vicinity of remote Hell Roaring Lake and sharp-rising Hepburn Peak overlooking the blue expanse of Redfish Lake, 5,000 feet below. Provision is made for the less experienced sportsman, who will find plenty of thrill on 12,000-foot Hyndman Peak, almost in Sun Valley's back yard. An even easier climb is the walk up Baldy, 9,200 feet high.

A nine-hole, 18-tee golf course opened on August 6, 1938, designed by William P. Bell, a golf architect from Pasadena, California, who built many of the West's best courses, according to *The Valley Sun*. It was "irrigated by water from Trail Creek through a series of underground pipes that pumped water stored in a tank filled by gravity," and laid out so it was functionally an 18-hole course. The 18-hole, par 72 course of 6,506 yards cost $1 for nine holes and $2 for 18 holes.

In the summer of 1938, Sun Valley's roads were paved, a physiotherapy department was added to the lodge's medical department, a greenhouse was built, and the Skier's Chalet was built, a two-story cottage adjoining the inn with 20 rooms to provide economy accommodations.

Dick Durrance was one of Averell Harriman's favorites and returned to Sun Valley during his summer vacations. When he told Harriman he was interested in photography, Averell got him a 4x5 Speed Graphic, the camera favored by press photographers at the time. Durrance worked as one of Sun Valley's publicity photographers. He took the camera back to Dartmouth, where he became the editor of the *Dartmouth Pictorial*:

> *I'll never forget the first time I saw Sun Valley in the summertime . . . coming up by bus from Shoshone. It had just rained, and that was the first time I smelled sage after a rainfall. It was exhilarating, the nicest, freshest smell I could imagine. Just the atmosphere itself was fabulous. I loved Sun Valley. The summers were totally unlike anything I'd ever experienced. . . . I guess I was totally hooked. . . .*
>
> *I was only doing photography . . . working with Gene Van Gilder, who was head of publicity. . . . Our job was to shoot pictures of anyone who came to Sun Valley and send them to their hometown papers. . . . I'd shoot rodeos, tennis, fishing, horseback riding, rock climbing, anything that was going on.*

In summer 1938, Durrance helped evaluate the skiing potential of Bald Mountain, saying, "Everybody knew that was coming, that Baldy would eventually be the great ski mountain. The first year Sun Valley was open they would run snowcats up there." Durrance, Harriman, and Union Pacific staff traveled up Baldy by truck via Cold Springs. They picked out the location for the future Roundhouse restaurant on "Little Baldy," and looked at the north side of the mountain. "What they saw was a great deal of good skiing on a north face; all the potential for becoming the future of Sun Valley skiing, at least for the better skiers," Durrance said. He suggested a race trail be cut for the Harriman Cup down Warm Springs, which would have more snow in the spring:

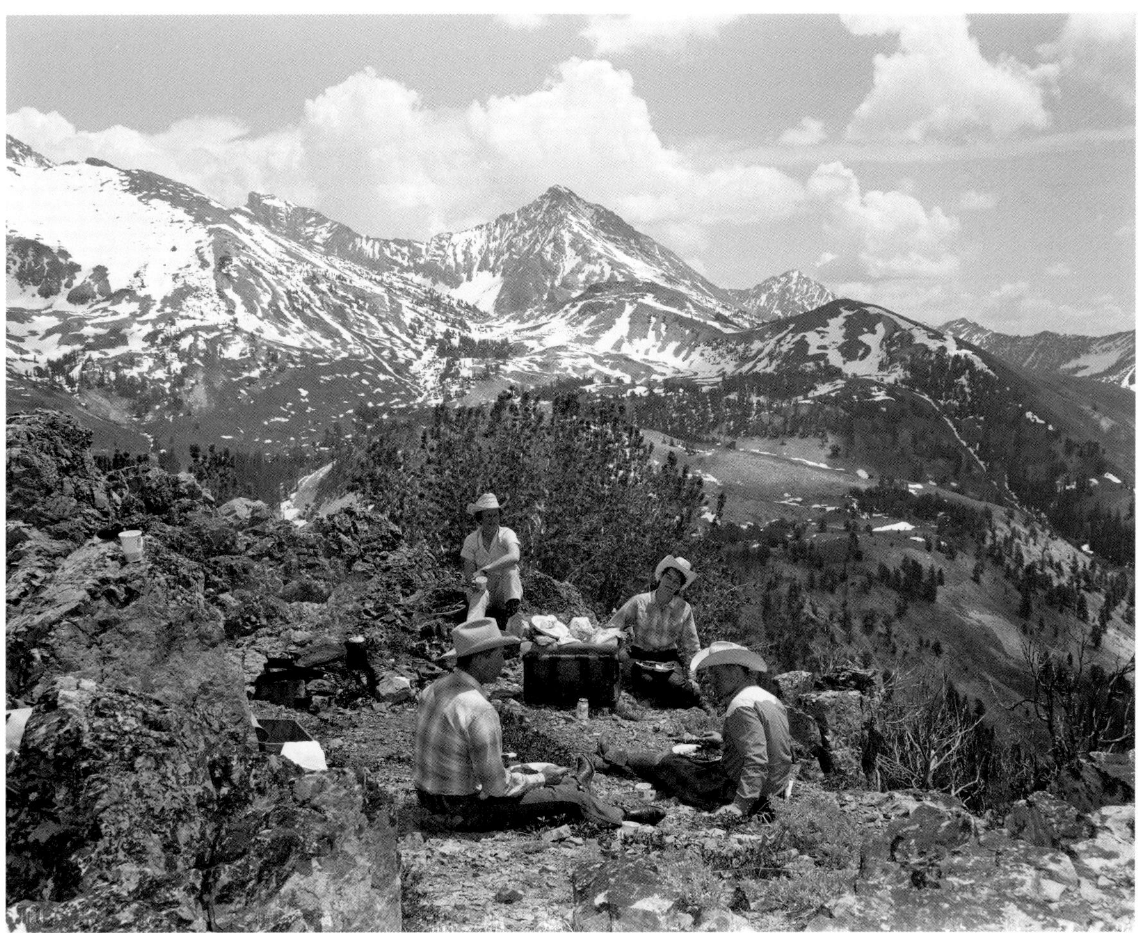

Summer in the Pioneer Mountains.

> *I'd already done a lot of the surveying by myself. I'd climbed the hills across from Mount Baldy, sagebrush hills two or three thousand feet high, and had taken photographs of the whole Warm Springs side from there. Then I'd walked over the terrain to find out where there were gullies and cliffs and where you might put a race trail.*

Durrance designed a "tough race course," starting at the top of the mountain, going down a ridge (now International), and diving into a steep area named the steilhang (German for "steep pitch"). "It was about as steep as a ski jumping hill and two hundred yards long," Durrance said. "I incorporated it into the racecourse, with a very steep ridge that ran down to it." The steilhang went into Warm Springs Canyon; then the course meandered through the woods to finish at Warm Springs

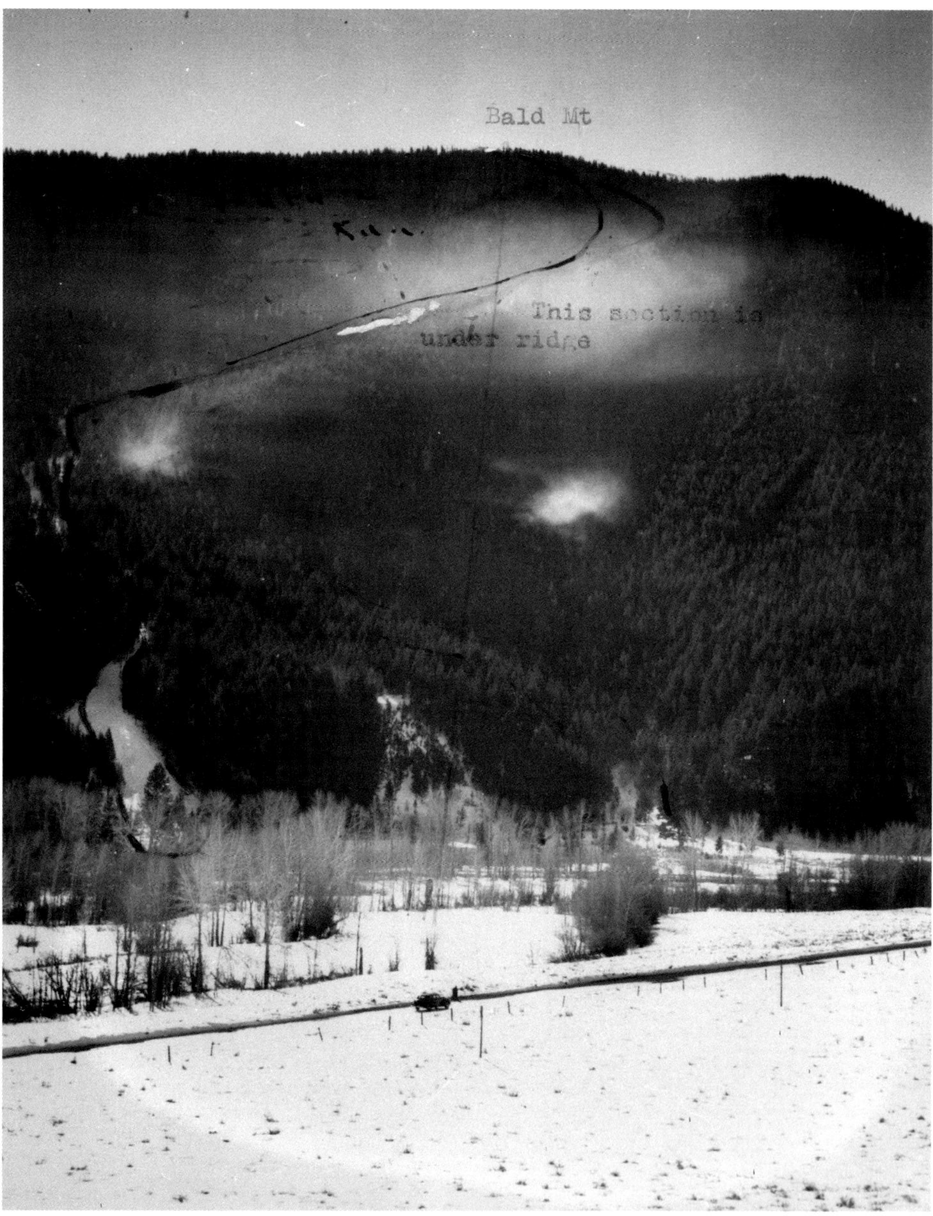

Dick Durrance designed a narrow race course down Warm Springs in summer 1938 that was used for Harriman Cup downhill races.

Creek. The drop was around 3,000 feet in a little over two miles. Skiers had some options and could be inventive about the exact course they took. The only control gates were on the top of the steilhang to make sure racers could not bypass it.

Harriman arranged for the U.S. Forest Service and the CCC to assist in cutting trees on Baldy, to promote skiing as they had done elsewhere. In January 1939, the Forest Service released Alf Engen for three months so he could work at Sun Valley. Pat Rogers reported to Harriman that Count Schaffgotsch, Engen, Durrance, and Pfeifer

> *spent* [an] *entire day on Baldy marking a considerable number of trees to be removed. We have eleven men working there now and figure it will take about ten days to remove the marked trees. We will rush this work through and these men stated that after its completion, it will be the finest ski course in the world and that the down hill races can be held there this year.*

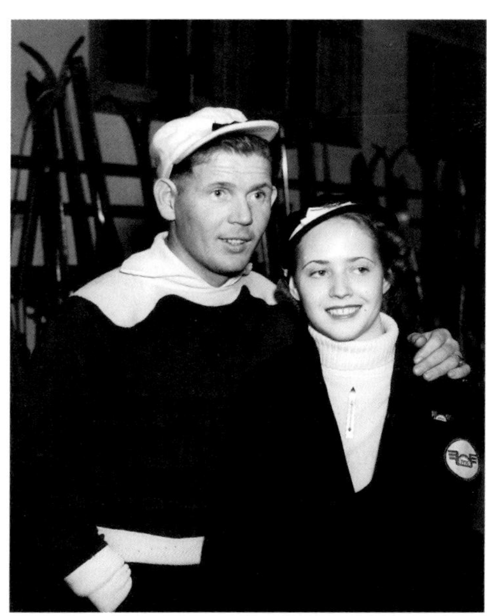

Alf and Evelyn Engen. The Engens lived at Sun Valley off and on for 10 years beginning in 1938.

The Warm Springs course was improved the following summer of 1939 by CCC crews, "by making it wider in places and cutting out the scattered trees in the middle of the trail," Durrance said.

In 1938, Alf Engen was in charge of the Forest Service and CCC crews that cut the race course down Warm Springs, and in 1939, when other runs were cut on Baldy as chairlifts were installed. The CCC had a camp of 250 men at Warm Springs. In his oral history, Engen said they used two-man hand saws—no power tools—and the course was cut from the bottom to the top. The crews left stumps on the run—"it was hard to get the CCC boys to cut down low." Friedl Pfeifer helped to mark the trees to remove—he had a "good eye for a downhill course." Fred Joswig worked for Engen on Baldy in 1938 and 1939, when Engen was laying out the ski trails there, designing the proper twists and turns. In his oral history, he said they cleared a trail "maybe 90 feet wide." Engen contributed "more than any one person to Bald Mountain's development than anyone I know."

Durrance's new course down the Warm Springs side of Baldy was used for the Harriman Cup downhills in 1939 and 1940. It was not the fast, open course it later became, but "was more like a Giant Slalom with 24-inch fir trees as control gates," according to Durrance. The Warm Springs run was open for skiing the winter of 1939, with sno-tanks transporting skiers to the top of Baldy.[32]

12

SUN VALLEY EXPANDS ITS BACKCOUNTRY SKIING WITH SNO-CATS AND HUTS

Substantial work was done between 1937 and 1940 to provide backcountry skiing for Sun Valley's guests. Initially, backcountry skiing involved climbing surrounding mountains using skins. For 1938, Sun Valley acquired snow tractors to transport skiers up hills and built the Pioneer Cabin hut to offer a true European-style experience.

In August 1937, Averell Harriman and William Jeffers went to Portland to view new equipment built by the Forest Service for Timberline Lodge on Mount Hood, a major CCC project. It was a seven-foot-long tractor with one 55-inch-wide track, which operated on snow or on the ground. The cam was located at the rear, and it pulled a sled that could carry 25 or 30 people and negotiate grades up to 30 or 40 percent, at uphill speeds from four to eight miles per hour, and 20 miles per hour downhill. "Snow depth is no obstacle to the tractor, whose wide base prevents it from sinking and stalling even in the softest covering," the *Seattle Times* reported. "The tractor will eliminate arduous uphill climbs." The machine cost about $4,000, and U.P. engineer Trout obtained plans from the Forest Service.

In September 1937, Sun Valley had several machines built by the Monarch Forge of Portland for use at Sun Valley, where they were known as Sno-Cats, snow tractors, or snow tanks. Harriman arranged for them to take skiers to various locations around the resort beginning in winter 1938.

In summer 1937, Harriman wanted a road built into the Boulder Mountains from the North Fork Road, going up through the Punch Bowl to reach the top of the racing hill from the north side. This would eliminate the road taking off from Stanley Basin Road. The Forest Service cooperated with the relocation. John E.P. Morgan explored this area for off-site skiing in 1936. In fall 1937, an area 50 miles northwest of Ketchum was designated as the Sawtooth Primitive Area, containing 201,000 acres of virtually untouched wilderness.

On January 17, 1938, Harriman wrote K.M. Singer, the resort's general manager, encouraging the development of backcountry skiing, which was to be be promoted by the sports desk:

> *I am particularly anxious that the development of excursions into the higher mountains by the guests be encouraged, particularly the use of the snow tank, and wish you would discuss this with Felix and Jarvis with a view to attempting, when we have a good crowd, to have at least one party a day go out.*

Harriman wanted a guide to lead guests in European-type ski touring. Dick Durrance recommended Florian Haemmerle, who coached at Dartmouth in 1935. Haemmerle, from Bavaria, was hired as a ski instructor for winter 1938. However, he had conflicts with the ski school's Austrian instructors over what was happening in Europe, and Harriman split his ski school into two entities. He kept the existing alpine school directed by Hans Hauser and created a new touring school with Haemmerle in charge to take advantage of the limitless terrain around Sun Valley. Andy Hennig was hired to work with him in 1939.

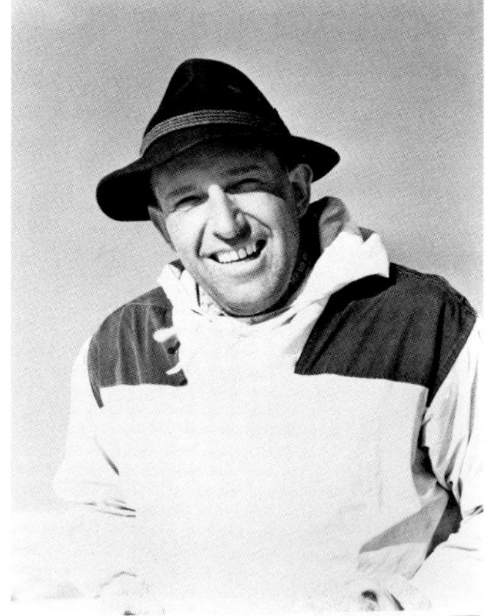

Florian Haemmerle directed Sun Valley's alpine touring school, taking guests into the extensive terrain around Sun Valley for backcountry skiing.

For winter 1938, the Boulder downhill run on Durrance Mountain was available to ski, said by Charles Proctor to be "the longest and toughest downhill race course in the world." Other backcountry areas included Baker Creek, with open slopes both

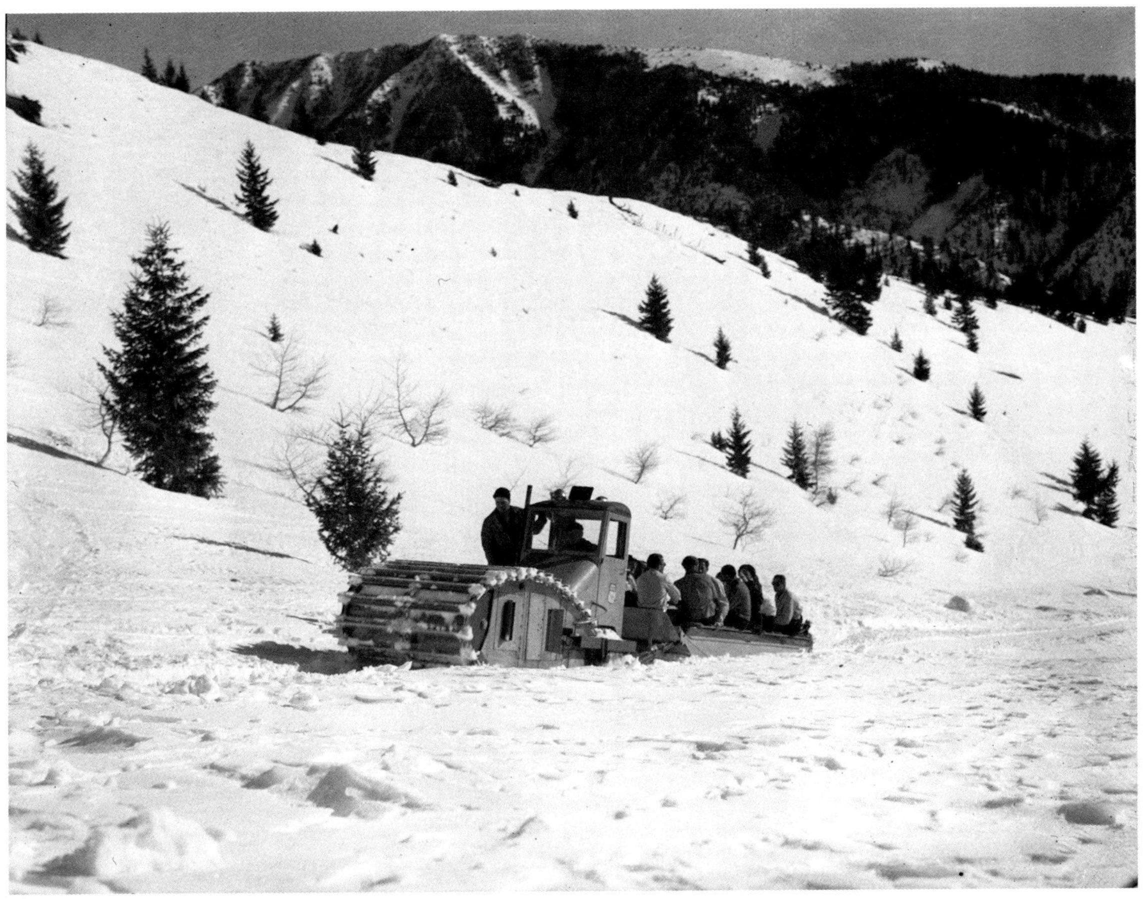

Sno-Cat designed by U.S. Forest Service for Mount Hood's Timberline Lodge, used at Sun Valley to take skiers to backcountry skiing locations beginning in winter 1938.

gentle and sharp; North Fork, with "untold mileage in open and timbered cross-country and downhill skiing"; and Warm Springs Canyon, "with its Old Baldy Mountain elevation of almost 10,000 nerve-tingling courses thru its steep, spruce-timbered shanks." The Wood River Valley had 25 miles of ski runs, "a complete gamut of ski facilities . . . from mild, timberless beginning slopes to the fast-dropping, wooded rock-ribbed high country trails for master skiers." New auto buses, mechanized snow tractors, and ski lifts provided access to Sun Valley's backyard. Up to 25 persons could ride the tractors, and sleds and toboggans could be towed behind. Sawtooth National Forest workers spent August and September clearing trails for the tractors. According to *Ski Illustrated*, *1937–1938*,

> *This monster, which probably will be as revolutionizing in cross-country skiing as the Sun Valley chair-lifts were in fixed up-hill accommodations last year, can move through any cleared way, no matter how deep or drifted the snow, and climb straight up a 40% hill! This, then, is the answer to reaching the ridge tops on Boulder, North Fork and Old Baldy.*

Maps produced by Sun Valley in 1938 show the extensive backcountry skiing around the area, using icons for skiers, Sno-Cats, and dog sleds. "The Skiing," written in late 1936, provides details of the areas shown on the map, using the word "race" to mean ski run.

The first map (which appears on page 188) shows the area north and west of Sun Valley. Farthest north, it indicates that Baker Creek is off the map. Baker Creek is where skiing took place during several Christmas holidays when there was not enough snow in Sun Valley. The Baker Creek practice slopes were five miles beyond the Boulder runs. They were comparatively open in an area that is heavily timbered.

Next is skiing on Boulder Mountain, with three routes leading to the highway. "The Skiing" says these runs are 12 miles north of Ketchum and three miles beyond North Fork. The mountains are too abrupt for skiing, but one group of three ridge top runs provided good skiing, each about three miles long with a drop of 3,900 feet. They were all marked. Charles N. Proctor said the middle run was "the perfect run for expert skiers," consisting of every type of skiing and every type of obstacle one could expect in ski races. "Take an instructor or ski guide with you," he wrote.

The North Fork area had not been explored for skiing in 1936 but offered promise. Skiers wanting to explore for new ski runs could work with the sports office to organize the trip, and a dog sled could transport sleeping bags, utensils, and provisions to stay overnight. The 1938 map shows skiing on Durrance Mountain (site of Harriman Cup downhills in 1937 and 1938) and Bright Peak (site of the downhill for the first intercollegiate tournament in December 1937). These were north of the North Fork of the Big Wood River, where the Sawtooth National Recreation Area headquarters is presently located and were accessed by hiking or Sno-Cat.

The map shows skiing on Race Mountain south of North Fork, six and a half miles north of Ketchum, with two marked runs. "The Skiing" said one was a fast run suitable for skiers of medium skill, three miles long and dropping 3,300 feet. The second was suitable for a skilled skier and was six and a half miles long.

Hauser Mountain is three and a half miles north of Ketchum at the mouth of Lake Creek. "The Skiing" says the run, down a finger ridge, had "open slopes, some steep, some moderate, with a maximum rise of about 1000 feet." Hauser Mountain could also be reached from Lake Creek to the south.

A skier figure is shown on top of the north ridge of Warm Springs Canyon. "The Skiing" discusses the "Warm Springs Race" on the north ridge of Warm Springs Canyon. Skiers cross the Big Wood River, drive a half mile to ranch buildings adjacent to the road, turn right, cross a field, and follow markers up a gulch, now called Heidelberg Gulch. Two runs were available, one two miles long with a drop of 2,200 feet "suitable for the finished skier and a thrilling run for them."

Skier figures are shown in several places on "Old Baldy Mountain," made accessible by Sno-Cats in 1938. One is on top of the mountain, one shows skiing down River Run Canyon, and another one is in Cold Springs Canyon. The route up Baldy began at the base of Cold Springs Canyon where the Big Wood River is on the east side of the road, one mile south of Elk Horn Road. Going up Baldy farther north would require crossing the river. "The Skiing" said there was only one marked run on Baldy, which went down Cold Springs, three and three-quarter miles from the highway with 3,400 feet of vertical. "Aside from this run Old Baldy is considered much too hazardous, abrupt, rough, timbered, to be of interest to skiers." This view of skiing on Baldy changed with the introduction of Sno-Cats to carry skiers to the top in 1938.

"The Skiing" also describes skiing on North Ridge, the prominent ridge to the left when looking up Trail Creek, which had three marked runs. Slaughter House Gulch Run led along Lake Creek Valley, then to the head of Slaughter House Gulch. These runs are not marked on the 1938 map.

Charles N. Proctor's article about Sun Valley in *American Ski Annual, 1936*, said, "Cabins and shelters have been located at convenient places so the ski tourer will find comfortable camps for spending the night or for lunch." This map shows several such cabins. Boulder Mine Hut is at upper right. Elkhorn Cabin in Elkhorn Valley is at lower right. Uncle Tom's Cabin is just east of the Elkhorn Ridge south of Proctor Mountain, and Saw Mill Cabin is farther east on Corral Creek. Some of these may have been existing cabins that Sun Valley fixed up as warming huts, although the cabin

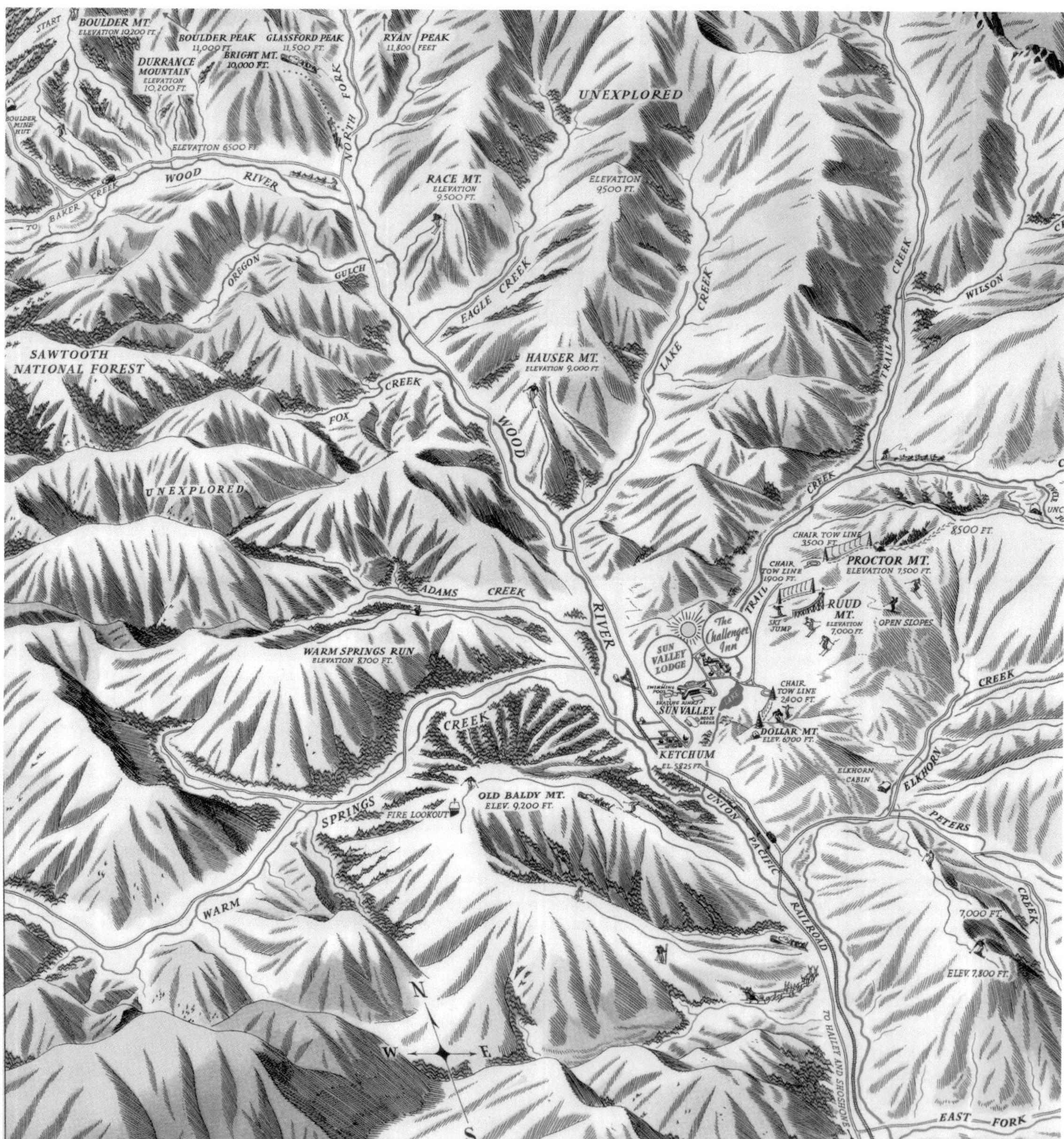

Map showing backcountry northwest of Sun Valley.

on Corral Creek was called "the new shelter cabin" in 1938. "The Skiing" said bus transportation was available at Elkhorn Cabin.

The map on page 190 shows Sun Valley and the lifts on Dollar, Ruud, and Proctor Mountains, along with the ski jump on Ruud. Ski routes are shown from the top of the Proctor Lift into Elkhorn Basin, both on its north and south slopes. Not shown are the runs from the top of Proctor going east toward Uncle John's Cabin and Corral Creek Road. Sno-Cat skiing is shown up Corral Creek Run to the northeast of Sun Valley. Pioneer Cabin is shown, reached by skis from Corral Creek, offering extensive backcountry skiing in the surrounding basin and hills.

"The Skiing" describes trails to Corral Creek Cabin and the Devil's Bedstead Area. Corral Creek is four miles from the lodge, and the Corral Creek Cabin or Sawmill Cabin was at the forks of Corral Creek. One fork of Corral Creek led four miles farther into the Devil's Bedstead section of the Pioneer Range, to an elevation of 12,000 feet. Corral Creek Cabin could be reached by skis or dog sled carrying provisions. The Devil's Bedstead run went along a ridge down to the cabin. It was suitable for skiers of medium ability, but some skiing in the spring was for the expert only: "Do not undertake an outlying section, such as this one, without a guide."

The Ridge Trail on Elkhorn Ridge is shown going from the top of Proctor to the Elkhorn Horseshoe and has several runs into Elkhorn Basin. "The Skiing" provides details of those runs. From the top of Proctor Mountain, skiers could go on top of Elk Horn Ridge above "Elk Horn Gulch." The ridge could be reached from Proctor or from the Triumph Mine up East Fork on the south side of the ridge. There were three runs into the gulch. Skiers could continue on the ridge to Elk Horn Loop, which took them to the Elkhorn Cabin. It consisted of five miles of skiing on the high Elkhorn Ridge from the Proctor lift south, a two-and-a-half-mile downhill run with a mile and a half of flat skiing: "It is a beautiful tour for the skilled skier with necessary endurance."

On the map's bottom right, skiing is shown on the ridge between Elkhorn and East Fork. "The Skiing" says Elk Horn Mountain is the peak south of the Elk Horn shelter. "The skiing slopes are excellent on the side toward the Elk Horn Shelter and Elk Horn Gulch," but there was only one marked run. Skiers climbed the mountain on a marked slope, being careful to avoid three mine openings, going two and a quarter miles to the top, gaining 2,000 feet, then skiing down the same route.

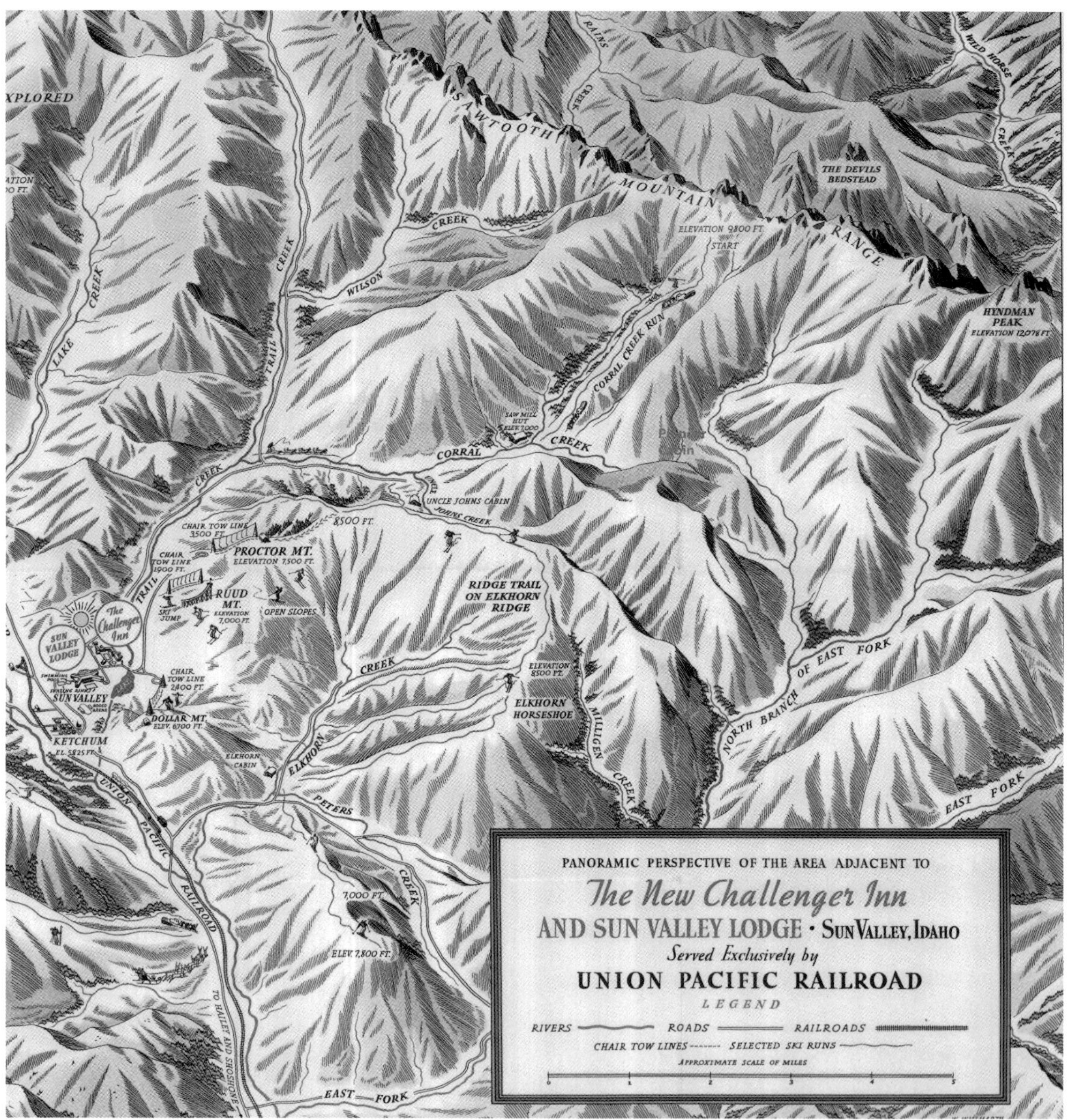

Map showing backcountry skiing east of Sun Valley. Pioneer Cabin is at center, to the right of Corral Creek.

Richard Gale, a Sun Valley guest, described backcountry skiing in "Touring at Sun Valley," in *Sun Valley Ski Club, 1937–1938*:

> *As for the facilities for touring in and about Sun Valley, the field is limitless. There are mountains laying around all over the place some of which are good in cold snow, some during warm spells and some in corn snow. There is such a variety that there is always some slope, somewhere, in any weather or snow condition ready to be scaled. One of the finest touring lands is certain to be the Pioneer Range in the rugged and almost unlimited Devil's Bedstead country, east of Sun Valley, reached by establishing a base camp at the new shelter cabin at the head of Corral Creek. Morgan Ridge is fine for powder snow. Durrance Ridge faces south and is best for corn snow.*
>
> *From the top of Baldy there are seven different descents averaging three thousand feet or more. Baker Creek is long but easy, through scattered timber. There are hundreds of other unnamed mountains accessible to motor roads. In short, there is no spot as yet in this country which offers the variety of mountains to ski on that Sun Valley does.*

On August 3, 1938, Harriman wrote K.M. Singer saying there had been a demand for overnight huts for ski tourers, and Dick Durrance and Konrad Schauffler were going to select one or two possible locations where they could be built for next winter. This began the second phase of Sun Valley's backcountry program, where cabins were built in remote locations for guests to spend the night.

On September 14, 1938, a special use permit was issued by the Forest Service to the Union Pacific for a backcountry ski cabin, the Pioneer Cabin. It covered approximately a quarter acre at the head of Corral Creek between the left fork of Hyndman Creek and the right fork of Corral Creek, "for use of ski parties as overnight shelter and stopping place." The fee was $1.25 until December 31, 1938, and $5 annually thereafter. Garbage pits with fly-tight covers and a fly-proof outhouse had to be constructed, debris and refuse had to be buried or burned, and the area had to be maintained in a clean and sanitary condition. If the permit was abandoned, terminated, or revoked, the permittee could remove all structures, but it would become the property of the Forest Service if not removed.

In fall 1938, Sun Valley built Pioneer Cabin in the Pioneer Mountains, eight miles northeast of Sun Valley at 9,500 feet elevation, facing Mount Hyndman. The comfortable cabin had a room with bunk beds that could sleep six and another room for guides and Sun Valley personnel. It was enlarged in 1939 to accommodate eight guests. There were Pullman mattresses and Pullman curtains for privacy. Sleeping bags were provided, and guides brought fresh liners each trip. The main part of the cabin had a cook stove and a table on both sides. Sun Valley sent one of its chefs on trips to cook gourmet meals with wine, with ski patrolmen transporting food and equipment. After the hard work to get to the cabin, guests were pampered, skiing in the morning and napping in the afternoon.

Ski instructors guided parties into the cabin, arranging transportation and supplies. Motor cars or Sno-Cats took skiers toward Trail Creek Summit, turned off at Corral Creek Valley, and dropped them off at the Sawmill Cabin at the end of the valley where the climb started. The five mile hike into Pioneer Cabin gained 2,400 feet of vertical in a two-and-a-half- to four-hour trip. Dorice Taylor wrote:

> *The first six miles of the trip are made in the little Sno-cat up the winter-bound road from Sun Valley to the Sawmill Cabin. From the Sawmill Cabin to the Pioneer range is a climb of about five miles. . . . The first part of the climb is on the zigzag switchbacks of a horse trail that leads across a roaring mountain stream, up through the quiet forest, and out into the brilliant sunshine above the tree line. The way now lies across the vast unbroken snowfields toward the crest of a ridge high above.*

There were a number of routes from the cabin for intermediate skiers and seasoned ski mountaineers, including up Duncan Peak, over to Hyndman Basin, up Salzburger Spitzl, Handwerk Peak, Goat Mountain, and others.

Dorice and Phez Taylor made their first trip to Pioneer Cabin in winter 1939, with Mary Harriman and two Princeton students, led by Florian Haemmerle. Averell Harriman told Dorice, "Don't let anyone hurry you. Set your own pace and you'll get there easily." They had bear trap bindings on their skis with cables that released, and they used sealskins for climbing. A bottle of rum made the trip more accommodating. They ate bacon and eggs Haemmerle carried and cooked and dehydrated soup stored at the cabin. The logbook showed they were the first party to make the climb into the cabin. When Dorice and Phez went into the cabin in 1940, it had been enlarged to two rooms and "very comfortably outfitted" with a cook provided by Sun Valley.

Florian Haemmerle led a led a group from Saw-Mill Hut to Pioneer Cabin in 1939 and wrote,

> *By mid-afternoon we had crossed the divide and skied down to the little brown Pioneer Cabin. Its icy threshold opens into a cozy two-room hut, with bunks and sleeping bags for eight, and a kitchen lay-out that seemed to expect all visitors to be Paul Bunyans . . . the threshold opens out upon a great glaciated amphitheater, deeply gouged barren, dusted over with snow, and dominated by Goat Mountain and the spectacular battlements of Mount Hyndman.*

When it got too dark to ski, they returned to the cabin where Florian greeted them with mugs of hot tea and cooked a dinner of steak and onions. At night, they skied under a full moon and "white clouds were running pell-mell over the Hyndman range." After a "fine morning of skiing, we reluctantly hit the trail back to the valley."

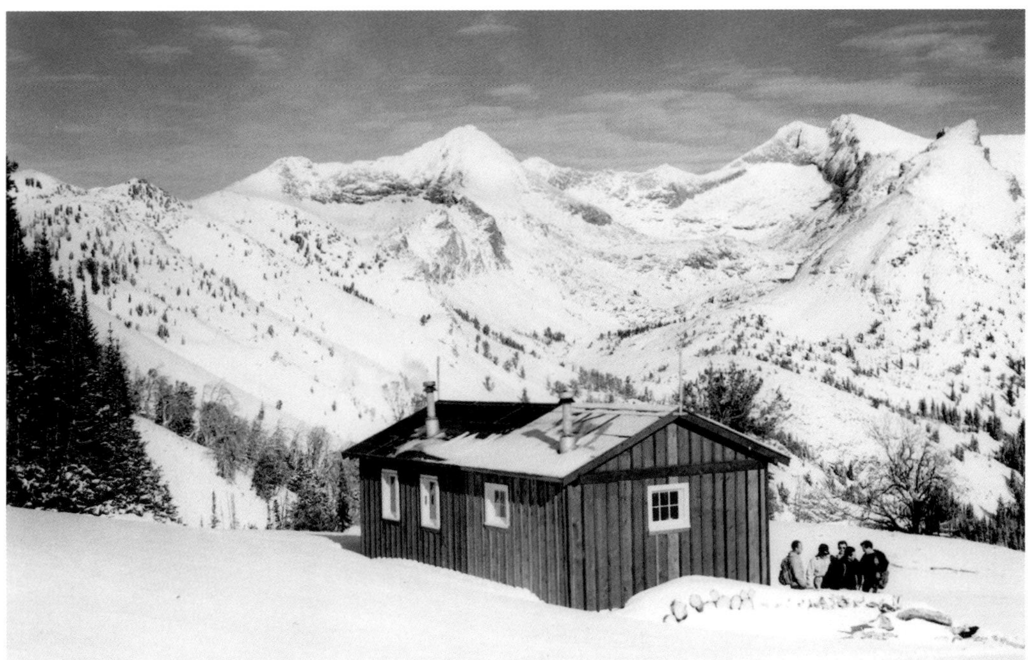

Pioneer Cabin in the Pioneer Mountains east of Sun Valley, reached by a five-mile hike, gaining 2,400 feet of elevation, taking three to four hours.

At the end of April 1940, Andy Hennig, Florian Haemmerle, and Ali Mauracher hiked to Pioneer Cabin, where they scouted new ski runs, explored previously unskied peaks around the cabin, and climbed Galena Peak. There was plenty of snow left after the resort closed in the spring and great skiing in the surrounding mountains.[33]

In 1940, Sun Valley built its second backcountry facility, Owl Creek Cabin, north of Sun Valley, three miles south of Galena Lodge and four miles west of the highway below Silver Peak, the highest in the Smokey Mountains, at the head of Owl Creek Canyon.

Val McAtee described building Owl Creek Cabin in his oral history. Ed Seagle obtained permission from the Forest Service to build a new overnight facility. At a canyon north of Ketchum where they crossed Owl Creek, McAtee and Hank Reid used a caterpillar tractor with a dozer blade to build a five-mile road into the cabin site. They leveled a building site 60 feet wide and 100 feet long and dug a basement. Seagle had drawn plans for a 40-by-60-foot log cabin. Logs were cut and delivered to the site. A crew of two carpenters and six laborers notched the logs at the corners with hand saws, framed the rafters, and hand-split shakes for the roof. They fastened narrow strips of metal mesh lathe in the grooves between the logs and mixed a mortar of sand, cement, and lime, which they used to chink the grooves. The ceiling was left open so the beams and rafters could be seen. Wires were strung at one end and sliding curtains were hung for privacy. Double bunks were installed. There was a large kitchen and dining room at one end with a large window facing Silver Peak. A pipeline was run from a spring 100 feet above the cabin. No environmental impact statement was necessary for the work.

The "new cozy woodland cabin," as described by the *Sun Valley Sun Winter Pictorial Issue* of 1940 was similar to Pioneer Cabin but more accessible. The ski school arranged excursions there. The stone and log cabin slept 16 and was located "in the heart of the primitive Galena Summit region . . . on the fork of picturesque Owl Creek in the heart of some of the wildest and most scenic mountain country in America. . . . At 8,000 feet, it had good skiing from October to June." The cabin was reached by automobile 18 miles north of Sun Valley, then on skis four miles northwest of the highway on Owl Creek,

> *below the spiraling dominance of Silver Peak, Smoky Mountain's highest. . . . Ski experts say that there is nothing more exhilarating than a day's fun in the deep powder snow of the Galena region, topped off with a home-cooked dinner of sizzling steak and trimmings.*

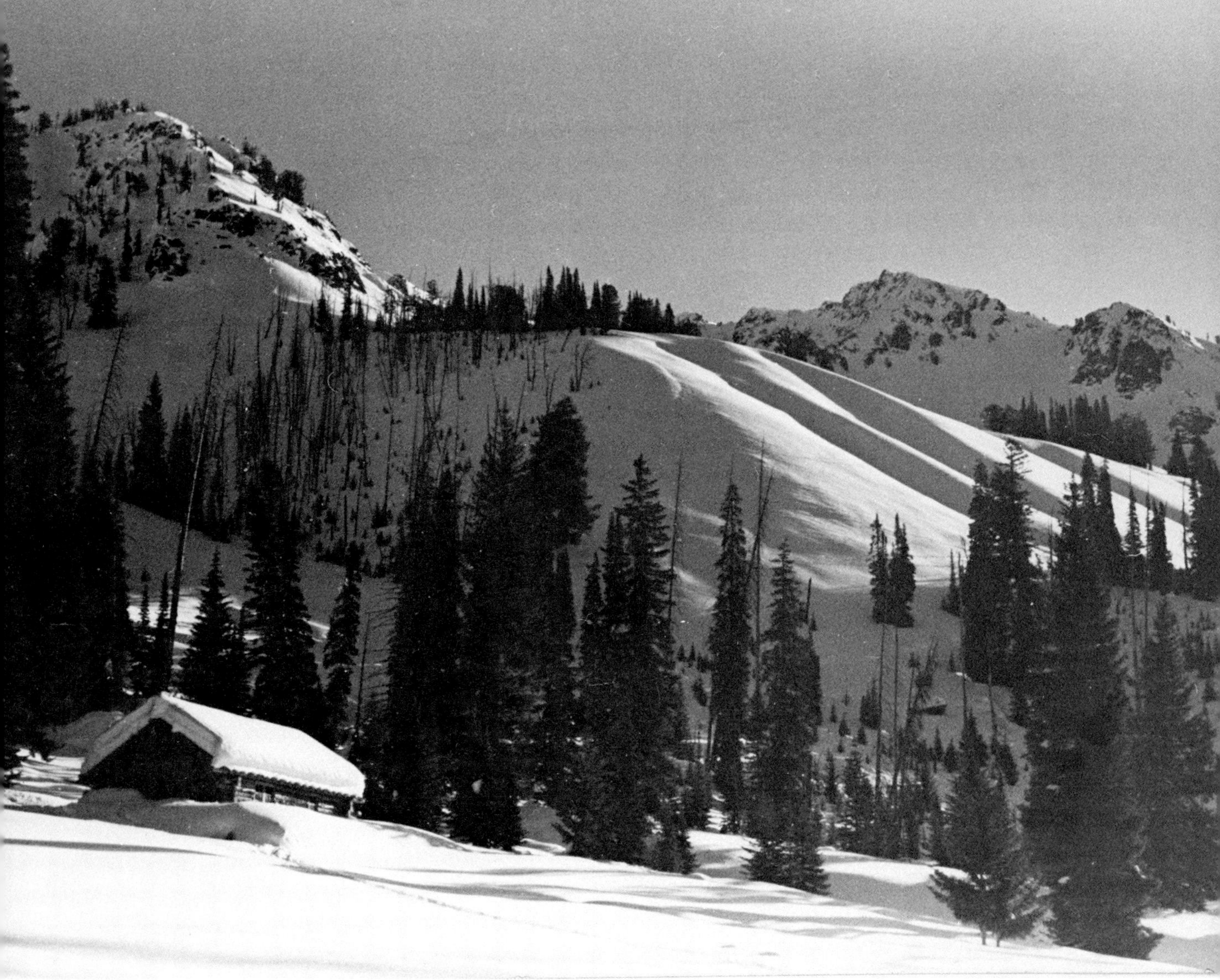

Owl Creek Cabin three miles south of Galena Lodge, four miles west of the highway below Silver Peak, at the head of Owl Creek Canyon.

When the guests were done, they skied down to the highway, where Sun Valley buses brought them back to the resort.

Sun Valley guests Mr. and Mrs. William G. Brumder described a trip to Owl Creek Cabin by a second route, over the mountains from Galena Pass. They left Challenger Inn in the dark with Andy Hennig as their guide, driving to Galena Summit. From there, on skis, they traveled the ridges that led west from the summit, a route that had not been tried before, ignoring Forest Service warnings against the trip. The sun rose an hour into their climb, and the trip was surprisingly uneventful, although avalanche threats led them to travel well apart, holding to the high ridges. They toured up and down ridges, across saddles, and along the rugged, rocky-topped Boulder Range to the west, with Silver Peak dominating the view. Before noon, they arrived at an overhanging drift on top of the narrow north ridge above Owl Creek Cabin, which could not be seen. They dropped off the cornice and descended to the cabin. After inspecting the cabin, they skied out to the Ketchum-Galena Road but had to carry their skis about halfway through the journey. The trip was about 10 miles, the climbing was gradual, and the descents not too steep. The Brumders made three trips into Pioneer Cabin before and after the war. They wanted Sun Valley to build a chain of five or six cabins joining the Pioneer Range to Galena through the Boulder Range for winter skiing and summer horseback trips.

The Valley Sun of February 6, 1942, published an article titled "Get Away From It All at Owl Creek." The author, who had been to a great many ski huts in Europe, said,

> *If there is any one in a more lovely setting than Owl Creek, I haven't heard of it. . . . You find yourself in a lovely peaceful glade beside a running brook, with giant fir trees, old, old trees, hovering protectively over you, giving the whole place a kind of warmth and spring-in-winter bloom.*

There were wonderful runs in every direction, and returning to the cabin, "you get good rough food cooked by a guide whose stories are as good as his steaks." After dinner, there was accordion playing, cards, singing, and sporadic conversation. "Yes, Sun Valley service has penetrated even to Owl Creek, and you won't have to worry about being cold, wet or hungry."[34]

13

HARRIMAN FINDS HIS MAN

Pat Rogers Is Hired as Sun Valley's Manager

Averell Harriman struggled to find the right person to manage Sun Valley after problems the first two years of operation, according to Ed Seagle.

On December 19, 1936, the *Boise Capital News* announced Raymond F. Stevens had been named the resort's first manager. Stevens was an "Olympic bobsled champion, winter sports enthusiast and builder of ski resorts." He was captain of the "great American bobsled that defeated the fastest in the world at Lake Placid during the 1932 Olympics," and worked for the Stevens hotel enterprise, started by his father. "Lake Placid was built into a winter sports capital with world recognition under the wise guidance of the Stevens family," the paper said.

Seagle said Stevens was Harriman's friend but didn't know much about management or running a hotel. He took over a big, challenging operation, with French cooks, German and Austrian waiters, Austrian ski instructors, demanding guests, and railroad bosses who were not happy with his operations. Dorice Taylor said shortly after Bill Jeffers became president in October 1937, he came to Sun Valley, looked through the ice boxes in the kitchen, didn't like what he saw, "and had a new all-American kitchen crew sent in on a Pullman car, fired the others, and put them on the vacated car to go back to New York." The resort was too much for Stevens to run, and he suffered a nervous breakdown. Ken Singer, who represented a kitchen company doing business with Sun Valley and knew hotel operations, replaced Stevens, but he too was replaced fairly quickly.

When Singer left, E.C. Webster, Union Pacific's head of dining car and hotel department, came to Sun Valley to reorganize things. New policies were implemented—things became more liberal and not so formal. This coincided with the opening of the Challenger Inn and the ski chalets in the village, which brought in a more moderate-income crowd in contrast with the predominantly wealthy guests who stayed in the lodge. Sun Valley changed from the European plan, where a set price was paid for room and board, to the American plan, where rooms and food were billed separately.

Dick Durrance said during its first years of operation, there was a conflict of objectives between Averell Harriman and Union Pacific:

> *Eventually, business pressure began to force Sun Valley to broaden its base. Omaha—local base for the railroad people, who paid attention to things like cost accounting—began pushing Sun Valley to cater more to the middle class. The Challenger Inn went up, offering less luxurious surroundings at less luxurious prices. Eventually the Challenger would become the destination of snow trains coming up from Los Angeles and San Francisco. Averell was more involved with the skiing, the railroad more concerned with what went on in the summer. They hired Pat Rogers . . . to manage the lodges.*

Pat Rogers had worked for Union Pacific since 1920, as vice president of the dining car and hotel department. He managed U.P. resorts throughout its system, including hotels at Bryce, Zion, and on the north rim of the Grand Canyon. In 1936, he was made general manager of U.P.'s Utah Park Company. On August 26, 1938, he was appointed general manager of Utah Parks Company and Sun Valley operations by U.P. president Jeffers. He became loved by employees and guests alike, although he had high standards for employee behavior. Winston McCrea, who worked at the lodge's front desk in 1937, was made manager of the lodge and inn, reporting to Rogers. McCrea replaced Rogers in 1952 when Rogers left Sun Valley after years of disputes with Union Pacific over how to manage the resort.

Maury Klein described Rogers's management approach in *Union Pacific*:

> *Nothing proved more revealing in this respect than the appointment in 1938 of W.P. "Pat" Rogers as manager of Sun Valley. Rogers was exactly the kind of man Harriman wanted at Sun Valley. Genial, big-hearted, less a manager than a host. Rogers was an*

> *old-time hotelman who stopped at nothing to ensure his guests a good time. . . . He didn't care about profit-and-loss statements or money. . . . He would just give away the whole place, and of course he was loved by everyone, guests and employees.*

As long as Harriman controlled things, Rogers was the perfect manager to implement his philosophy for the resort. "Under his rule Sun Valley enjoyed its golden years as a resort between 1938 and 1941, and Harriman's involvement remained as deep as ever." Harriman praised Rogers:

> *Rogers was a Godsend; he developed the management of the hotel which was excellent. . . . Pat Rogers was enormously valuable to the development. And when I went abroad, he was in charge and he knew just what we had agreed to do, and he carried it out in a masterful way. I think that Sun Valley owes a great deal to Pat Rogers on the matter of success. He was the manager of the whole area, the lodge, the Challenger, the skiing on the mountains, ski school, everything, both construction and operation.*

Rogers began the practice of hiring good-looking college students to work at the lodge, many of whom were sons and daughters of prominent guests, changing the atmosphere at Sun Valley, and "gave the true meaning to the word 'guest,'" according to Dorice Taylor.

> *He got up early in the morning to say goodby to departing guests, and he was on hand late at night when buses brought in newcomers. When his popularity became so great it overwhelmed physical limits, he devised an ingenious method of greeting his friends. He memorized the daily arrival list, then rode the lift up to the Roundhouse and served the soup. With the names already in his mind, he could spot the guests as they came along the line and greet them warmly. But since the next person was waiting for soup, no one could take up too much of his time.*

The Rogers era got off to a rocky start, however, according to Ed Seagle. Rogers liked to drink, something he fought to hide. Not long after Rogers arrived, he went into Ketchum, had a lot to drink, danced with some of his employees, and was reported to Jeffers. Winston McCrea had a more exciting version. He said after a dinner at the Bald Mountain Hot Springs Lodge, where some of the women employees were staying, the party went to Slavey's. Rogers was "drunk as a lord," got in a fight with Slavey, and the sheriff was called.

Sun Valley was not incorporated and had no police force. Union Pacific stationed two special railroad agents there who reported to the chief special agent in Omaha. They acted as a police force and kept track of everything. They usually chased guests who wrote bad checks or skipped out on their bills, but they also kept track of employees and their actions. They reported Rogers to U.P. president Bill Jeffers, who reacted immediately.

Jeffers sent a telegram on November 11, 1938, to all officers and employees of Sun Valley: "The use of intoxicants by employees while on duty is prohibited. Their use, or the frequenting of places where they are sold is sufficient cause for dismissal." Jeffers said, without naming anyone, that it had been reported that on a number of occasions various officers had been under the influence of alcohol at Sun Valley. "This business of officers or representatives of any department carousing around at Ketchum, as well as Sun Valley, is a thing of the past. Any infraction of the liquor rule will be met with telegraphic dismissal from the service." Jeffers fired Rogers and told Ed Seagle, "You're in charge." This lasted one day before Jeffers reinstated Rogers, but he made him call a meeting for all Sun Valley employees and apologize to them. Rogers never went into the Ketchum bars again.

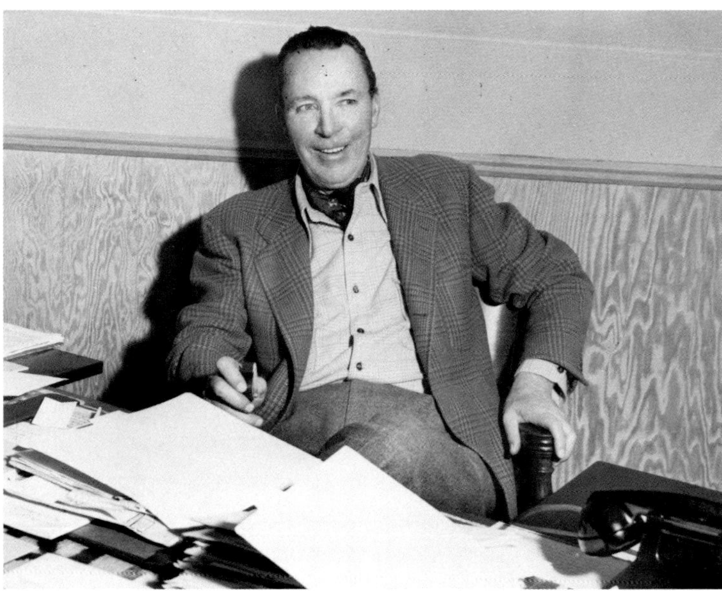

Pat "Pappy" Rogers, who became general manager of Utah Parks Company and Sun Valley operations on August 26, 1938, serving until 1952.

According to Abramson, Harriman was involved in virtually every decision, large and small, with Rogers's help. "When he was away, general manager Pat Rogers wired him daily reports in snowfall, skiing conditions, sales of lift passes, and news of notable guests arriving for the first time."

In 1938, Sun Valley attracted 4,120 guests, a new record. Celebrities and movie stars made the resort a regular stop, creating lots of free publicity, and ordinary vacationers began to come to Sun Valley. Harriman had realized his dream, according to Abramson:

> *Clearly Sun Valley had become something to Harriman that transcended the bottom line of company profits or even his own triumph in making it work. It was his mark on the railroad, like the streamliners, and his own playground as well. The resort was where he sent his friends as well as himself to have a good time, and he insisted that it be all he had promised regardless of cost. Some of the improvements or details made no sense from an economic standpoint, but Averell wanted everything just right because any shortcomings would reflect on himself. What could be more perfect: a resort that made money and at the same time satisfied his craving for a vacation paradise for himself and his crowd.*

Saks Fifth Avenue operated a ski shop in the lodge during Sun Valley's first years of operations. When Saks decided not to continue, Harriman offered Jack Lane's son Pete the chance to operate the ski shop in the Challenger Inn. Lane told Harriman he didn't know anything about skiing, but Harriman said, "Neither does anyone else . . . but you know retailing." Lane opened his ski shop in the inn and ran it until the resort closed for World War II. He reopened the store after the war and sold fishing tackle, sportswear, and tennis gear in the summer, with ski instructor Sigi Engl as the tennis pro. In the winter, the shop had a wax room, sold high-fashion ski wear, operated a ski rental, and sold ski gear.[35]

Cost of Building Sun Valley

The Construction Accounting Office at Sun Valley was discontinued in late 1938. Its records were boxed up and sent by company baggage to U.P. headquarters at Omaha.

In late 1938, H.C. Mann, U.P.'s chief engineer and vice president in charge of operations, asked B.H. Prater, U.P. engineer for the Challenger Inn and Village, to provide him the cost of building the lodge and inn to calculate the architect's fee. The lodge's cost for that purpose was $850,000, including everything within the walls of the building except furniture and boiler room equipment. Its furniture, carpets, flooring, draperies, linens, and miscellaneous items cost $88,400. The Challenger Inn's cost was $722,854, including everything within its walls except furnishings and the theater and the cottage (Aspen-Willows). The cost of the two swimming pools was included in the costs of the lodge and inn. The architect's fee was $10,842.81, of which $7,500 had been paid, leaving $3,342.81 owed.

A Sun Valley News Bureau document prepared later gave different totals. Sun Valley Lodge cost $1,174,109.24; Proctor lift $41,000; Dollar lift $30,000; ski huts $8,000; and roads $19,000, for a total of $1,276,109. Challenger Inn cost $1 million, for a two-year total cost over $2.5 million. The cost of building the village and amenities such as tennis courts and golf courses was not given. By 1940, $3.5 million had been invested in Sun Valley.[36]

14

1939

Friedl Pfeifer Takes Over Ski School; Harriman Cup Downhill Is Held on Bald Mountain

Sun Valley and its many attractions continued to be advertised nationally. In fall 1938, Union Pacific advertised its resort through the new Sun Valley ski film *White Magic*, which was shown at Rhodes Department Store in downtown Seattle. Filmed in Sun Valley by Hollywood crews and sponsored by the Union Pacific, the one-hour color film featured a personal appearance by Darroch Crookes, international ski champion from Seattle.

On December 31, 1938, the *Saturday Evening Post* published the article "The Valley of Sun and Snow":

> *It all started with the skiing craze which has swept the country during the last four winters. The Union Pacific energetic chairman, W.A. Harriman, looked upon the New England railroads' profitable ski-train business and found it good. A side glance at American winter travel to Swiss, German and Austrian Alpine sports centers suggested another source of cash customers.*

Sun Valley Lodge offered

> *two hundred members of the carriage trade every comfort and luxury they left behind in New York, Chicago, San Francisco or Hollywood. To the Lodge, Sun Valley welcomes film stars, debutantes, not too tired businessmen and any winter-sports*

> *lover who belongs to the ten-dollars-a-day-and-up class. Hard by the Lodge is a second hotel, for thinner pocketbooks. The Challenger Inn accommodates another four hundred vacationers.*

On January 1, 1939, the *New York Times* told its readers what to expect from Sun Valley the coming ski season:

> *Woolen stockings, Alpine hats and shorts are converting Sun Valley, Idaho, into an American St. Moritz as vacationists descend on this resort set in the Sawtooth Mountains for Winter sports. Scheduled entertainments appear to leave visitors little leisure. What with party sleighs drawn by reindeer, evening high jinks by cow punchers, luncheons on the ice with music, ski-joring, programs whirl along at fast tempo.*

Sun Valley's hold on the country's imagination is illustrated by an exhibit at the New York World's Fair of 1939, "a $500,000 Alpine Village named Sun Valley—a 'Winter Wonderland'—after Idaho's famous Winter resort," according to the *New York Times*, "deriving its inspiration from the Union Pacific's Winter resort in the Sawtooth Mountains." The Alpine Village was one and a half acres, included a toboggan slide 160 feet long and 45 feet high, an ice rink on a turntable that converted into a dance floor, a ski jump, a 40-foot waterfall, a restaurant, stores, and taverns. An expected seven million visitors would attend. Admission was 25¢.

In late January 1939, *Fortune* published a story titled "Sun Valley: If You Ski . . . it is a $3,000,000 monument to your pleasure, if you don't, W. Averell Harriman thinks you probably will." The story was condensed in February 1939 in *Reader's Digest* to reach more readers.

According to the article, Union Pacific saw its patronage change over the years and had no way to serve vacationers who were "out to see the glories of the West." Harriman "needed an exclusive attraction—some big, glamourous name to pull in the customers." He began Sun Valley to take advantage of the ski boom in the country caused by the 1932 Lake Placid Olympics, which grew after 1936, the "year of the great winter games at Garmisch-Partenkirchen," where U.S. skiing "won thousands of converts, and the new converts demanded and got increased ski facilities."

Harriman, the article noted, expected the resort to double or triple its size:

> *At present, his average guest spends about $15 a day with him, but you can get by on as little as $9—or as much as $35. Counting train fare ($235) a couple out of New York could manage a thoroughly adequate two-weeks stay at Sun Valley for about $500.*

It was also reported that Harriman believed winter vacations would increase and foresaw "a trend away from the southern routes in favor of the North, and he believes that many Southerners will come north for winter sports out of a simple curiosity to see and feel snow." Skiing "will become a major U.S. sport. Most other sports are for young people . . . but you can enjoy skiing as long as you can stand up."

For winter 1939, the ski school had eight teachers from Austria: Hans Hauser, Max Hauser, Roland Cossman, Franz Epp, Al Dingl, Joe Schwaighofer, Paul Deschmann, and Peter Radacher. Radacher was "an all around skier of exceptional ability, as well as a skillful yodeler and accordion player," according to the *Seattle Times*. A racing coach was selected who "will be one of Europe's better-known skiers with an international record." Hans Hauser was head ski instructor, Florian Haemmerle ski guide, Felix Schoffgotsch special representative, and Herich Zehentener a ski instructor.

In fall 1938, Alice Kiaer, the godmother and self-appointed patron of the U.S. women's ski team, hired Friedl Pfeifer to coach the women's team at Sun Valley to prepare for the 1940 Olympics. Pfeifer, from St. Anton, Austria, was a top racer who won the downhill and slalom championship at the Arlberg-Kandahar race in 1936, and taught in the Hannes Schneider Ski School at St. Anton. Pfeifer left Austria after Germany took over the country. Harriman hired him for the Sun Valley Ski School and to make personal appearances to promote Sun Valley. He received a monthly salary plus room and board.

Part way through the ski season of 1939, Harriman asked Pfeifer to replace Hans Hauser as head of the Sun Valley Ski School. Otto Lang, Pfeifer's friend who became his second in command, described how that happened. Harriman asked Pfeifer what he thought about the Sun Valley Ski School. Pfeifer's comments to Harriman were diplomatic but negative:

> *Friedl liked Hauser well enough as a man, but he did not think that he was cut out to be, nor that he particularly liked, being director of the ski school. Friedl had a considerably lower appraisal of Hauser's instructors. They were far below the caliber*

> *of instructors he had worked with at St. Anton, who were dedicated to their profession and discreet in their personal lives. This was not true for Hauser's group, some of whom were chronically late for classes, often appearing unkempt and unshaven after a night's debauchery. As teachers, Friedl rated them as inadequate, lacking experience and the traditionally self-imposed discipline of the profession.*

Harriman responded by asking Pfeiffer to take over the ski school.

At age 28, Pfeiffer took over the prestigious Sun Valley Ski School. Sun Valley ski instructors were well known for entertaining their female students. Shortly after taking over, Pfeifer told his instructors they had to show up at the ski school combed, shaved, rested, and ready to teach. "A few days later," he said, he "met a couple of instructors coming out of the Lodge wearing tuxedos from the previous night's dance. That day I announced an 11 p.m. curfew for the instructors. The non-stop party was over."

In fall 1939, Pfeifer hired Fred Iselin from Switzerland to teach the top class in his ski school, a controversial move as Iselin brought a different skiing technique. Iselin won the Grand Prix de Chamonix at Glaciers, the Brévent-Chamonix, and the Lognon Downhill and set the record at the Grand Prix de Aiguille du Midi, a race later discontinued because it was too dangerous. Islen taught at Chamonix from 1930 to 1938, where he trained the French women's ski team. In 1947, Iselin moved to Aspen to work for Pfeifer's ski school there. He was inducted into the U.S. Ski and Snowboard Hall of Fame in 1972.

Dick Durrance moved to Sun Valley after he graduated from Dartmouth. He became editor of the *Sun Valley Ski Club Annual, 1939*, which he enlarged "to present a more comprehensive report of the races . . . and other activities of particular interest to skiers." Articles covered preparing Bald Mountain for new lifts and skiing next season, climbing in the nearby mountains, the Sun Valley Ski School, ski touring around Pioneer Cabin, summer ice skating, and other topics.

Pfeifer's article about the ski school discussed the goals and methods of the school, based on the techniques developed by the Hannes Schneider Ski School in St. Anton, Austria. Sun Valley offered a considered method of teaching skiing at a time when there were few lessons available in the country.

Pfeifer emphasized the importance of providing a proper technical foundation, since lack of solid technique hampered even many racers. The fundamentals of instruction are "not just boring details . . . but acquisitions which [a skier] will be able to use in his whole

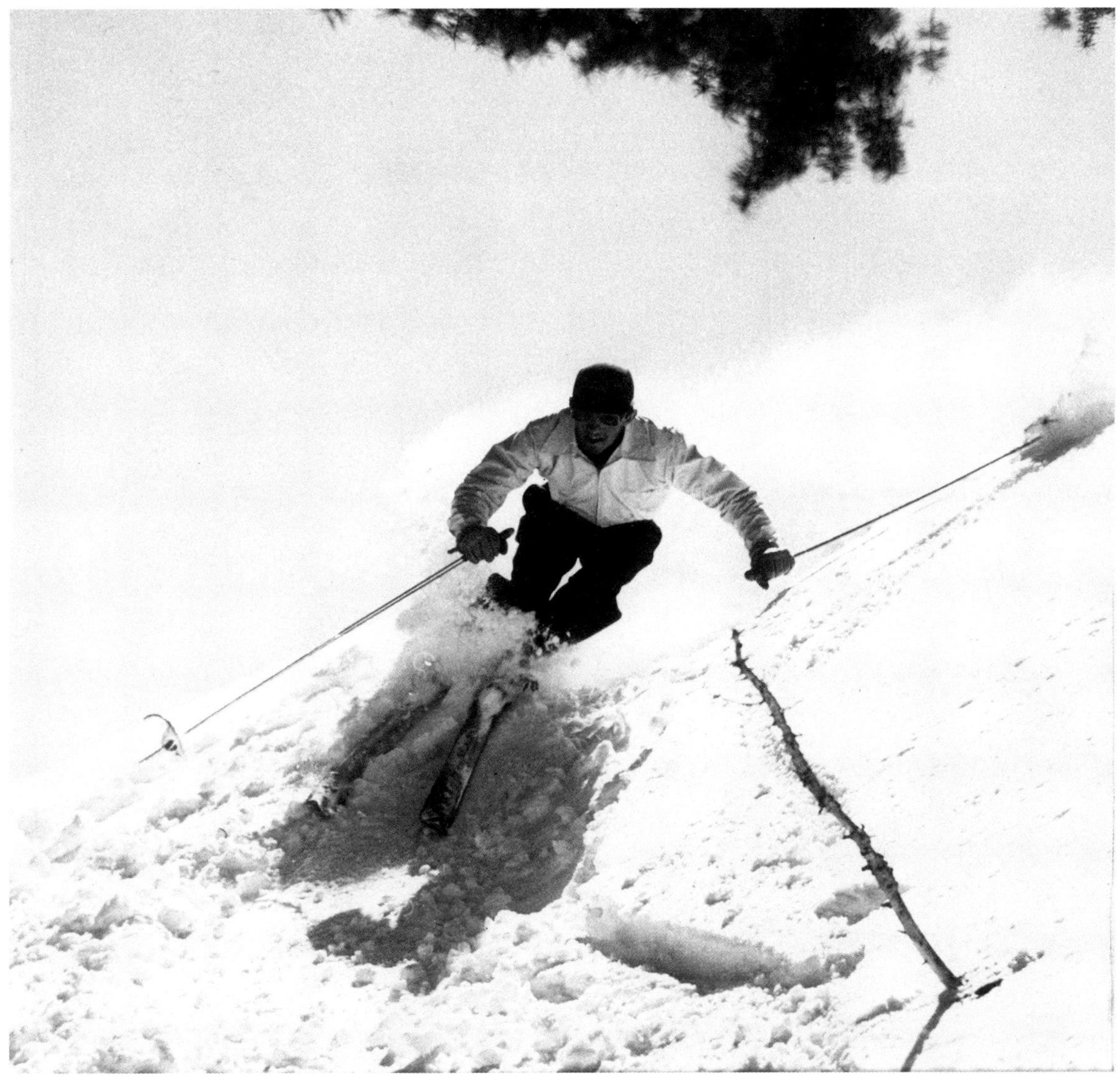

Friedl Pfeifer, from St. Anton, Austria, replaced Hans Hauser as director of the Sun Valley Ski School in 1939.

future career as a skier." Pfeifer made sure each teacher utilized his course of instruction to guarantee uniformity. Beginning ski classes took students from the stem turn to the stem Christiania to the pure Christiania. "The Sun Valley Ski School is organized so that every guest is given the opportunity to learn or to improve his skiing," learning the basic techniques but at the same time providing enjoyment. The school used class instruction, which is more efficient than private lessons limited to a small number of pupils.

RIGHT Students on Dollar Mountain learning to climb hills by poling or using the herringbone technique.

BELOW Learning the snowplow.

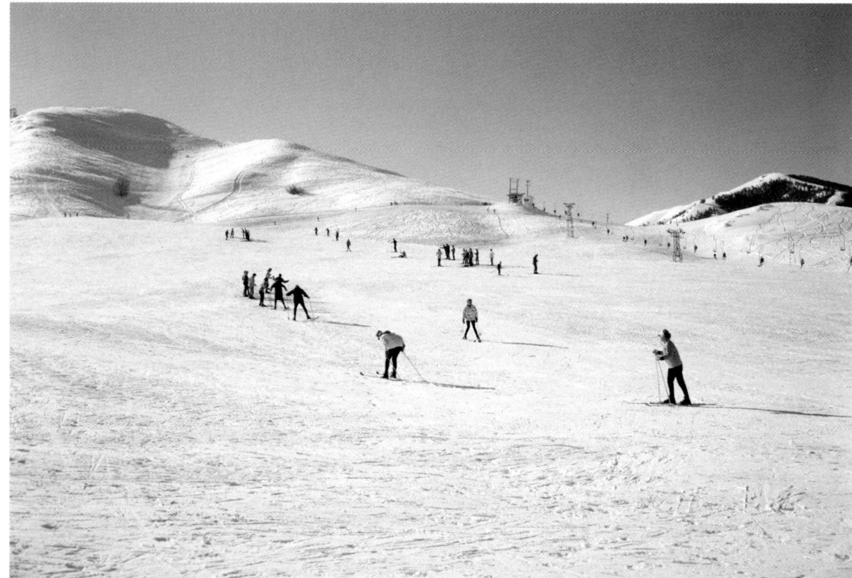

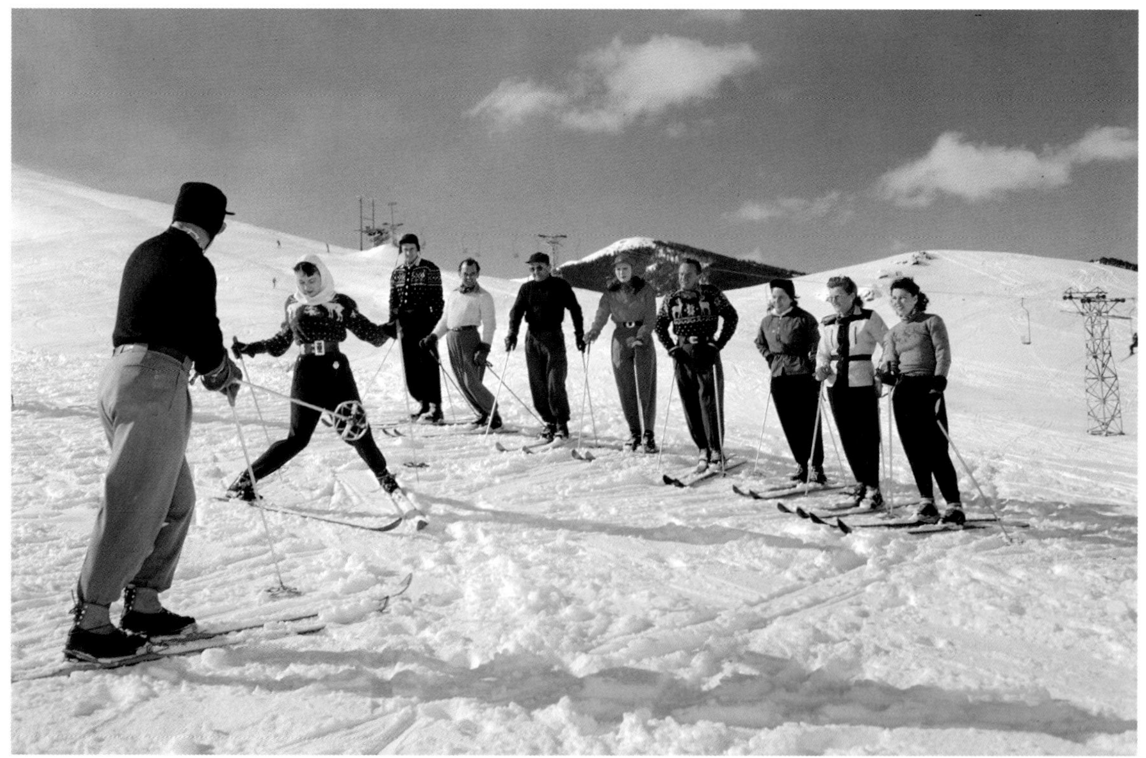

The Austrian technique was very structured. Students learned to fall down and get up, side step, kick turn, and run straight across the hill and down the hill. Pictures from the time show ski lessons on Dollar Mountain using the Austrian method of teaching the fundamentals of skiing.

Once those skills were learned, students graduated into the snowplow and Christiania turns. More pictures of Sun Valley Ski School students learning the classic Austrian technique can be found in the color insert.

After students learned the fundamentals, there were two special classes. The racing class developed good downhill and slalom skiing, where pupils learned to place turns and adapt speed to the run. Turns were practiced in the fall line of steep slopes and in different snow conditions. The touring class offered half- or full day sessions, based on the ability of the pupils, designed to make them familiar with the surrounding ski country.[37]

Harriman Critiques Sun Valley

Harriman spent the Christmas holidays of 1938 in Sun Valley. After Christmas, a Chinook wind melted the little snow Sun Valley had accumulated. The resort had to do something for its guests. Friedl Pfeifer suggested moving skiing north to Baker Creek. Harriman brought buses from Union Pacific's operations at the Grand Canyon to Sun Valley. The buses were equipped with sandwiches and drinks "and everything else," according to Dorice Taylor, and took the guests to an area where there was good skiing. "We got up there and built a fire and had steaks for lunch." A circus tent was set up "to serve hot food on the lodge's fine china, and an accordion player added the entertainment. . . . And, of course, that was a big party. Everything was on the house." Snow finally came on January 16, 1939.

On January 2, 1939, while he was on his way to New York on a Union Pacific train, Harriman wrote a four-page letter to U.P. president Jeffers discussing Sun Valley:

> *Things at Sun Valley have been going remarkably well in spite of the fact that we had no additional snow. The skiing at Baker Creek was excellent and the transportation facilities and lunch so well handled that on the whole the guests enjoyed the experience. The guests' chief disappointment was in not having the use of the ski lifts.*

> *If the sagebrush on Proctor Mountain had been cut, it could have been used for skiing instead of Baker Creek.*
>
> *The snow conditions on Mount Baldy are amazingly good on the direct northern slopes. These slopes, of course, are heavily timbered, and to make full use of these slopes for early and late skiing, additional clearing will have to be done. I believe for the next season we should not only complete the cutting on Proctor Mountain, but also make every effort to induce the Forest Service to develop the north slopes of Baldy for skiing to a greater extent than they have so far been willing to do. From our experience to date, the snow conditions on Mount Baldy are far better than anywhere else in the vicinity for more consistently good snow conditions during the entire season.*

The Forest Service wanted Baker Creek to be developed for early and late season skiing, but Harriman disagreed. Baker Creek had more snow than Sun Valley, but its slopes faced southeast and their snow was subject to crusting. Its slopes could not have been used that year except for the work done tramping down the crust, an expensive and tedious process that does not make the mountain as readily usable as the north slopes of Baldy. "We may find, however, that it is desirable to have Baker Creek as an additional string to our bow in the event we have still different conditions than we found this year," Harriman wrote.

Snow conditions should be studied the upcoming spring, Harriman said, but he believed that would show Proctor and Baldy were their two best bets. "Some day, if the interest in Sun Valley develops as I am still confident it will, there will be a demand for a conveyance to the top of Baldy, which will be an attraction for summer time as well as for winter."

Pat Rogers "has the entire operation well in hand," Harriman wrote, with an organization to deal with emergencies with speed and competence. Some people had transferred from the Challenger Inn to the lodge, having offset the prejudice against the lodge that developed the prior year. There was constant activity on the ice rink, and the orchestra and the Arthur Murray dancers made "the Duchin room popular and in fact people are apt to leave the Ram after dinner and finish their evenings in the Duchin Room." The food "was of good quality and the best I have found at Sun Valley." It would take Rogers a season to deal with the minor problems, but Harriman found his judgment good, with the capacity to follow through.

Harriman said the intercollegiate ski meet held over the holidays "went off very well and the general comment of the contestants was that it was the best run meet they had ever attended." Friedl Pfeifer, Harriman wrote, *is a great success. He is by far the best skier that had ever come from Europe and is an attraction to all of the guests who have an opportunity to see him ski. He is far more intelligent than any of the Austrian boys that we have had so far. The contestants all have a great respect for him, and I heard no grumbling of any kind with regard to the Austrians.*

A party of six went up to the Pioneer Cabin for one night and enjoyed it so much, they spent two nights there "and came home with glowing reports. I believe this hut will be popular this winter." Harriman wanted musical entertainment during the summer.

So many skiers came to Sun Valley in February 1939 the resort could not accommodate any more guests, and it stopped accepting reservations until March. Ticket agents were instructed to cancel all educational trips that month, including booster clubs and old timers' clubs.

In 1939, the women who expected to be on the 1940 U.S. Olympic team trained in Sun Valley, their expenses paid by the resort, where they were coached by Friedl Pfeifer. Gretchen Kunigk, the up-and-coming racer from Tacoma, Washington, was one of those coached by Pfeifer after recovering from a serious injury that kept her off skis for much of 1939. She said Pfeifer was the best slalom skier she had ever seen. According to her biographer,

Gretchen quickly saw the rationale behind some of Pfeiffer's smooth moves and began the difficult process of integrating these into her own technique. Her performance in training was somewhat uneven, but she obviously was the young racer to watch on the 1940 women's team.

In 1939, Sun Valley began offering medals similar to those given at European resorts such as Kitzbuhl to give skiers symbols showing their capability in standard races. Silver, gold, and diamond pins were offered "as an institution to raise and promote the competitive skiing spirit in Sun Valley," according to the Sun Valley Ski Club. The Diamond Sun pin was the "supreme test of speed, skill . . . and intestinal fortitude." The first competition was held in 1939 on Warm Springs, which had been widened "just enough to allow for turning." It had two speed control gates at the entrance of the steilhang, and the terrain determined the course for the skiers. The Diamond Sun was a way to measure average skiers' capabilities against those of the best skiers.[38]

SKI TOURNAMENTS IN 1939

Sun Valley's college ski tournament, held in late December 1938, fielded 50 racers from Washington, Dartmouth, Yale, Washington State, Nevada, Utah, Oregon, Stanford, UCLA, College of Puget Sound, and Idaho, who competed in cross-country, slalom, downhill, and jumping. The fun began two weeks before the tournament as racers arrived for training during the holidays under Friedl Pfeifer, Paul Deschman, and Peter Radacher. Christmas Eve celebrations included round-table exchanges of gifts, a Gluhwein party hosted by Kathleen Harriman, and a tango by Norma Shearer.

Races were held at Baker Creek due to a lack of snow at the resort. Dartmouth's Steve Bradley won the combined title, followed by Washington skiers Carl Neu, Ragnar Qvale, and Otis Lamson. Mary Cates of Stanford won the women's slalom, followed by Yvonne Blossom of Nevada and Kathleen Harriman of Bennington College.

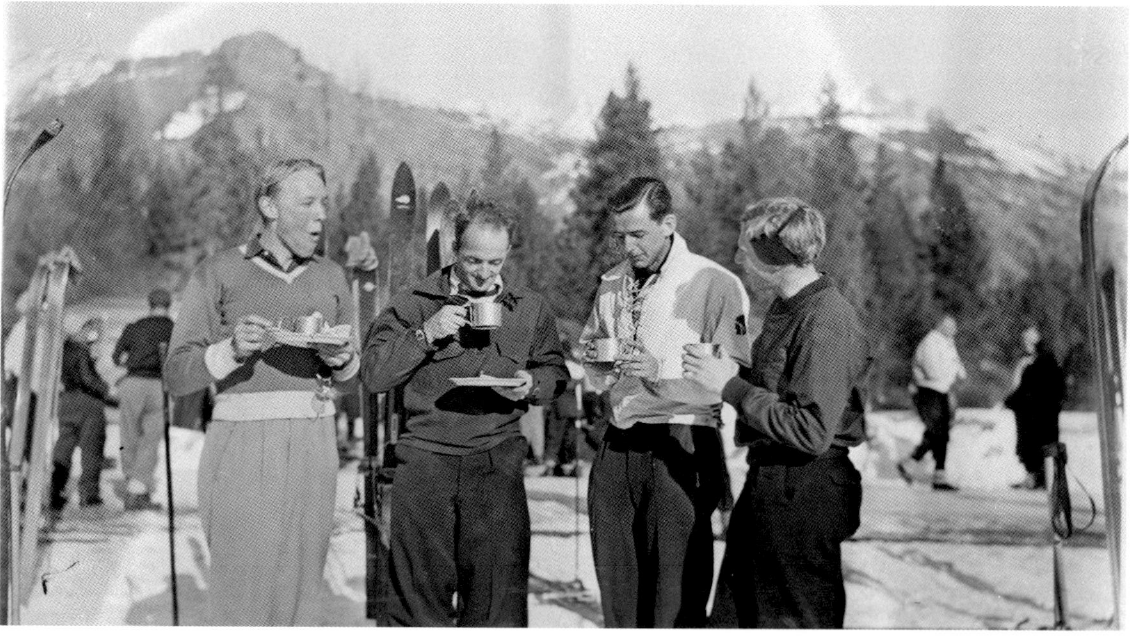

Dartmouth skiers Steve Bradley and Dick Durrance, with Lloyd Davis and Wolfgang Lehrt, enjoy a day at Baker Creek after Christmas 1938, when Sun Valley had little snow and guests were taken to Baker Creek by bus where there was good skiing. A circus tent was set up, hot food was served on fine china, and an accordion player added entertainment. It was a big party, since everything was on the house. Snow arrived January 16, 1939.

Sun Valley hosted one of the major ski meets of the year in late March 1939, the National Four-Way Championships, the third annual Sun Valley Harriman Cup Invitational Open, where entrants competed in downhill, slalom, cross-country, and jumping. Ski instructors competed against amateurs, but separate prizes were awarded. The Harriman Cup was awarded to the best skier in the downhill and slalom. Unseasonably warm weather had the racers "practicing their high-speed turns in bathing suits under a burning sun," reported the *Seattle Times*. Snow conditions remained good in spite of the warm spell.

Al Lindley described the tournament in the *Sun Valley Ski Club Report, 1939*. The race, he said, attracted "the foremost skiers of a half dozen nations." The Swiss women's team "rank among the world's best in downhill and slalom running." Erna Steuri and Nini Arx-Zogg, "two of the best women racers in the world," were fresh from the European race circuit. The best American "girl skiers," including Marian McKean and Betty Woolsey, trained at Sun Valley most of the winter, "and were in top form," so the women's competition took a "performance of F.I.S. caliber to win the event."

Several top professionals raced at Sun Valley for the first time: Toni Matt, the sensational young Austrian; Heinz von Allmen, three-time Arlberg-Kandahar winner; Friedl Pfeifer and Peter Radacher, leading Austrian racers with the Sun Valley Ski School; and Reidar Andersen from Norway, "one of the three leading jumpers of the world, also known as a dangerous downhill competitor," according to Lindley, and one of Norway's most promising cross-country men. A number of Northwest racers were selected to compete based on a tournament at Mount Baker: Don Fraser, Don Amick, Paul Gilbreath, Sigurd Hall, Ragnar Qvale, Henry Seidelhuber, and Olaf Rodegard. Paul Sceva Jr. and Bert Mortensen competed in individual events.

The arduous 18-kilometer cross-country course set by Andy Hennig went up Trail Creek, looped up and over the shoulder of several hills, past Proctor Mountain, came down to the flat just short of the base of Morgan's Ridge, and then down the valley, mostly on the flat. FIS amateur Walter Prager finished first, "with his beautiful, easy technique . . . looking at the finish as if he had just come from a tea party," Lindley wrote. Peter Radacher was second and Heinz von Allmen of Quebec third. They were followed by "true amateurs," Norway's Reidar Andersen (known chiefly for his jumping but at one time one of Norway's most promising cross-country men, who raced at Sun Valley with "no training whatsoever" on borrowed skis), and Dick Durrance of Dartmouth ("thoroughly competent but not overly enthusiastic on cross-country skis"). Reidar Andersen won the amateur cross-country title, and Seattle's Sigurd Hall finished tenth. Sun Valley's Alf Engen "dropped his bruised body into bed early yesterday after he fell through a bridge during the langlauf," finishing fourth among the amateurs.

For the first time, the Harriman Cup downhill was held on Bald Mountain, "under perfect conditions," on the Warm Springs course designed by Dick Durrance. As before, skiers had to climb the mountain before they could race down.

The downhill course, said by Friedl Pfeifer to be "one of the five most difficult downhill courses in the world," was in excellent shape after a week of daily packing by Sun Valley's instructors:

> *It is a timber trail about two miles long, but different from most, for although the average width of the trail itself is probably fifty feet, the undergrowth and small trees for another fifty feet on each side have been cleared out giving a choice of either swinging down in linked turns or cutting it straight through the open timber with only an occasional check in open spots. The top portion . . . was most difficult—considerable sidehilling and very rough and crooked. Eight control gates in this stretch added to the strain on legs but also to the safety. Next came what the German boys called a "Steilhang," or steep pitch, about 300 feet long, 100 wide, and quite reminiscent of the Leavenworth, Washington, jumping apron except that an abrupt turn, enforced by heavy timber, commenced right where the "dip" should have been. From here, the course was a dream of sweeping turns, interrupted just ahead of the finish line by a sharp right curve on the outside of the hill and below a temptingly smooth schuss.*

Lindley said the course was "far more interesting than the old course on Boulder Mountain, requiring considerably more skiing but still a fair test." Control flags slowed skiers down on the steilhang, a steep slope where considerable turning was required. "The rest of the course was left wide open and was certainly skied wide open as the best men were cutting through the trees on almost every corner in the lower half and running it practically without a check." The women's start was just above the steilhang.

The steilhang presented problems for many skiers. Matt, Pfeifer, and Durrance were the smoothest at this point. Hannes Schroll, Alf Engen, and others who did not check their speed "came to grief," and there were many "severe crackups." Schroll caught an edge and went down, "most of it in a series of somersaults in full layout position." Lindley reported that Reidar Andersen "fell near the start, dislocating a shoulder and missing a pair of control gates in the spill."

Toni Matt of the Conway Ski Club won the downhill, with the *New York Times* saying the German ski artist got "his first big American win" on "a difficult 2.3 mile course that left a heavy toll on hurt and disqualified amateurs." Peter Radacher was second, Walter Prager third, Sigi Engl fourth, and Friedl Pfeifer fifth, all FIS amateurs because they were ski instructors. Dick Durrance, "who did not have time to practice, was out of the running for the first time," finishing sixth, but was the highest true amateur. The Swiss women, Erna Steuri and Nina Zogg, finished one and two "on a course only half as long but just as trying. . . . The women—like the men—finished after bad spills that brought bloody noses and gashed faces."

Friedl Pfeifer won the slalom. Otto Lang said, "Pfeifer's first run in the slalom was of such superiority, elegance and ease that he can rightly be called the 'Nijinski on skis,' whereas his second run was a masterpiece of cool-headed judgment." Radacher finished second and Durrance third, followed by Engl and Robert Blatt.

Alf Engen won the jumping event on Ruud Mountain, followed by Gordon Wren of Steamboat Springs. Washington's Ragnar Qvale finished highest of the Seattle skiers, placing sixth. Henry Seidelhuber was ninth, Bert Mortensen was 11th, and Sigurd Hall was 14th.

Two awards were given in 1939. The first was for the Four Event Combined Championships, won by "Little" Pete Radacher, a Sun Valley ski instructor, who received recognition as the best all-around skier in America. Walter Prager was second, Dick Durrance (who won the Amateur Four-Way competition) was third, and Alf Engen was fourth. For the Washington skiers, Ragnar Qvale was ninth, Sigurd Hall 11th, Bert Mortenson 13th, and Henry Seidelhuber 14th.

The second award was for the Sun Valley Open/Harriman Cup, for the downhill and slalom. Durrance yielded his two successive Harriman Cup titles to Peter Radacher. Pfeifer was second, Sigi Engl was third, Durrance fourth, Walter Prager fifth, and Toni Matt sixth. Radacher, Pfeifer, Engl, Prager, and Matt were FIS amateurs. Washington skiers included Robert Blatt, eighth; Don Fraser, 12th; Paul Gilbreath, 15th; Don Amick, 17th; Ragnar Qvale, 18th; Peter Garrett, 26th; Sigurd Hall, 28th; Henry Seidelhuber, 29th; and Bert Mortensen, 30th.

Erni Steuri, "a slender Swiss miss, overshadowed all feminine competition," as reported by Lindley, winning the downhill, slalom, and combined and the women's

Harriman Cup. Grace Lindley of Minneapolis, formerly of Seattle, finished 10th in the downhill, 10th in the slalom, and 10th in the combined. Dorothy Hoyt finished 15th in the downhill, 15th in the slalom, and 14th in the combined. Virginia Bowden finished 24th in the downhill and Gertrude Mann was 26th.

Many racers left for Mount Hood in Oregon for the National Downhill and Slalom championships, the next major race on the circuit, and then went to Mount Rainier for the Silver Skis race.

Filmmaker Warren Miller told a story about Durrance's 1939 race. About halfway down the Warm Springs course, Friedl Pfeifer cut seven turns on a steep hill that were narrow and twisting, requiring racers to make abrupt turns to miss the trees, which served as control gates. Racers tried to straighten the course as much as possible to keep their speed, skiing close to the trees. Durrance, looking for a faster line through the turns, figured if one tree was cut down, he could straighten out all seven turns and gain significant time. The day before the race, Durrance and a friend climbed up Warm Springs and sawed down the tree that opened "Dick's secret shortcut." To hide their handiwork, they cut down a smaller tree and propped it up where the tree had been removed. On the day of the race, they learned Durrance's race order, his friend hid in the trees, and when Durrance's turn came, his partner removed the tree so he could take his shortcut through the trees, replacing it after he got through. Durrance got through the trees in control but was skiing so fast that he missed the last turn at the bottom of the course and skied into Warm Springs Creek, missing the finish line. He climbed out of the water and fell across the line. Miller said Durrance was fined $2 by the Forest Service after the race for chopping down a tree without a permit. In Durrance's oral history, he confirmed the story, saying he did it but that it was legal under the rules. You could choose your own course in the downhill in those days, and he was always looking for shortcuts.

The National Downhill and Slalom Championships were held at Timberline on Mount Hood in early April 1939, back in the Northwest for the third time in four years. CCC workers prepared the courses for the race, clearing trees and snags and extending the rope tow. A mile-long chairlift was installed to take skiers nearly halfway up the race course. Forest Service "snow motors" took racers higher up the mountain.

"The entry list is so crammed with famous skiing names that skiers—and the public—have been kept frantic trying to calculate who has the best chance of winning," wrote the *Seattle Times*. The Pacific Northwestern Ski Association sent 18 skiers, an "unprecedented" number. More than 125 men and women entered, constituting "the greatest field of great skiers the West Coast ever saw. . . . Women's competition will reach the highest plane in history at the tournament."

Because of icy conditions, the men's downhill course was shortened to two and a half miles and the women's to two miles. Friedl Pfeiffer won the slalom, becoming the open national champion, and Toni Matt won the open downhill, barely beating Hannes Schroll, "the unpredictable Austrian from California," in the words of the *Seattle Times*.

Dick Durrance was the star of the tournament, with the *New York Times* of April 4, 1939, reporting, "Feats of Durrance Marked Skiing Meet." Durrance won the top two trophies—the national open and amateur combined downhill and slalom title, by taking second in the slalom and fourth in the downhill. He also won the amateur downhill and amateur slalom. The only title he didn't win was the open slalom, where he was second to Pfeifer. Elizabeth Woolsey won the women's open and amateur downhill titles, delighting "the 5,000 spectators who burned red under a hot sun, by keeping the national downhill championship in this country."

After the tournament, the National Ski Association announced the skiers eligible for the American FIS team to compete in Europe in 1940. "These ski fields are getting too big," said the president, "And yet every man and woman entered in that race had a right to be there."

Seattle had an interest in six of them as past or present residents: Grace Carter Lindley, Dorothy Hoyt, Shirley McDonald, Bob Barto, Peter Garrett, and Bobby Blatt. Unfortunately, the 1940 FIS meet and that year's Olympics were canceled because of the growing conflict in Europe.[39]

Sun Valley in Summer and Fall

The Valley Sun's Special Summer Edition described Sun Valley's summer of 1939. A new 60-by-120-foot outdoor ice-skating rink was opened, overlooked by the dining terrace at the lodge with a "generous dance floor" that could be used in winter or summer. New tennis courts were built. Summer rodeos started in August in "the most modern western sports stadium ever created." Four ski chalets were built behind the Challenger Inn in the same architectural style, for 196 guests. A children's playground opened in June. The resort offered swimming, badminton, paddle tennis, croquet, bicycling, canoeing, horseshoes, archery, golf on a "tricky" new nine-hole course with 18 tees, trail riding, fishing in local streams and at Silver Creek, and pack expeditions into the nearby wilderness area.

On July 29, 1939, Pat Rogers told Harriman that 8,020 people visited Sun Valley in 1937 and 1938, including 3,900 from December 1936 to December 1937 and 4,120 from January 1938 to December 1938. In August, W.A. Jeffers told Harriman that Sun Valley would have more guests the upcoming winter and that it was necessary to provide additional accommodations for both guests and employees. He proposed building north of the Challenger Inn. Ground would be broken for new construction after Labor Day.

In 1939, Dr. John Moritz moved to Sun Valley to become the resort's doctor, receiving $1,000 a month and room and board. His hospital in a wing on the third floor of the lodge was little more than a first aid center for skiers. Dr. Moritz headed the Sun Valley hospital until his retirement in March 1972.

In October 1939, the next season's ski racing schedule was announced by the Pacific Northwestern Ski Association, which included three races at Sun Valley: the Sun Valley Intercollegiate meet on December 30–31, 1939; the Jeffers Cup competition, a four-way tournament for Western states on January 20–21, 1940; and the National Downhill-Slalom Championships on March 21–24, 1940. The National Four-Way Championships would be held at three different ski areas in Washington on March 30–31, 1940, which was the major tournament of the year.

In November, Harriman wrote Steve Hannagan about minimizing "publicity about divorces at Sun Valley." He should, Harriman said, avoid "sending to the press any releases or photographs about divorcees during the winter season." There were "many married women who can get off to Sun Valley without their husbands and who may be afraid to go to Sun Valley alone if gossip columnists comment on this fact as indicating an approaching divorce. As you know, no married women not contemplating divorce would dare go to Reno without her husband."[40]

15

BALD MOUNTAIN IS PREPARED FOR SKIING

Three Chairlifts Are Installed; Otto Lang Joins Ski School

Dick Durrance graduated from Dartmouth in spring 1939 and became a full-time employee at Sun Valley, paid $250 a month plus room and board, "a handsome salary," as he wrote in his book.

> *Sun Valley was coming into its golden age, with a top-notch clientele, much of it from Hollywood. The tireless Steve Hannagan corralled Claudette Colbert, Norma Shearer, Clark Gable, June Allyson, Darryl F. Zanuck, the Gary Coopers, for summer as well as winter recreation—and got the word out to the nation's press. Ernest Hemingway was a regular. Wealthy socialites began to find Sun Valley a congenial place to rid themselves of pestiferous spouses.*

Harriman was "a most enthusiastic skier," a good, strong intermediate, Durrance said.

> *He loved the sport, enjoyed being outdoors, and really wanted to run a good shop at Sun Valley. . . . He did want to put on good competitions . . . and was fascinated by racing, his daughter was very good, became a racer, and made the U.S. team.*

Skiing on Bald Mountain had been anticipated from the beginning. Felix Schaffgotsch, Charles Proctor, and John E.P. Morgan forecast that Bald Mountain would become one of Sun Valley's ski hills but believed it was too challenging for American skiers in 1936.

A snow tank carried expert skiers up Baldy's slopes to access its wide open terrain and runs through the trees in the winters of 1938 and 1939. Harriman was a proponent of developing skiing on Bald Mountain, and the success of the 1939 Harriman Cup downhill there convinced him it should be opened for general skiing. In summer and fall 1939, Harriman had a series of three chairlifts installed to the top of Baldy on the River Run side and new runs cut, significantly expanding Sun Valley's skiing areas.

A special use permit was issued by the U.S. Forest Service on August 1, 1939, to the Union Pacific for a right of way 100 feet wide and 5,500 feet long, for the construction of a chairlift and telephone line. The permit included one acre of land at the middle section of the lift for a rest and lunch cabin, a right of way a quarter mile long from Cold Springs Creek to the rest cabin for a pipeline, and control houses at the middle and top stations of the lift.

The permit cost $15 from August to December 31, 1939, and $35 a year thereafter. Improvements had to be approved by the Forest Service, including "color scheme, design and exact location." Sun Valley agreed to assist in forest fire prevention and suppression, report all fires, and assume responsibility for fires set by employees or guests. Merchantable timber destroyed by construction or operation would be paid for at the regular commercial rate.

Harriman initially considered installing a funicular to the top of Baldy, as was done in Europe. However, he decided to divide the trip up the mountain into smaller segments. With a funicular, a skier would have to go all the way from the bottom to the top and down again. There could be good skiing at the top of the mountain and poor skiing or no snow at the bottom.

Friedl Pfeifer took credit for locating the Roundhouse, ski runs, and the lifts on Bald Mountain in his autobiography. Pfeifer believed there should be skiing on Bald Mountain since he arrived in Sun Valley: "We needed such a mountain. Nowhere in America could you ski long runs on lift-served terrain. . . . It was just a matter of convincing Mr. Harriman to build the lifts there for the next season." Pfeifer spent many hours during winter 1939 exploring Bald Mountain and "became familiar with its contours, how the wind blew and sun exposure. I sketched a design in my mind that combined everything I knew about mountains, about skiing, about trails for skiing, and trails for teaching." Kathleen Harriman told Pfeifer that Bill Jeffers opposed expansion of the resort in light of Sun Valley's financial losses. Pfeifer replied that if Sun Valley did not develop Baldy, it would fall behind its competition. A cable lift was being installed on Mount Hayden in Colorado; Alta, Utah, had plans to install a lift; Hannes Schneider was pushing for lifts at Mount Cranmore; and a chairlift was being built at Mount Hood, Oregon.

In winter 1939, Pfeifer took Averell and Kathleen Harriman to the top of Bald Mountain, going up Cold Springs using skins. He explained how a lift line cut through the trees would be protected from the wind, the lower mountain could be used to teach beginners, and skiers of all abilities would have suitable terrain. Harriman said he would take the idea of skiing on Baldy to the board of directors. U.P. engineers and president Jeffers wanted one lift going up Baldy to save money, and Jeffers wanted the restaurant at the bottom of the mountain. Harriman accepted Pfeifer's suggestion and directed U.P. engineers to start work on the three-lift system.

In 1939, Harriman took Lloyd Castagneto, Al Bannerman from American Steel and Wire (who helped design the original Sun Valley chairlifts), and U.P. bridge engineer Glen Trout up Baldy on horseback. Harriman asked Trout to have a cost estimate of building chairlifts to the top of Bald Mountain prepared by six o'clock that night. Even though they had no survey, no plans, and no idea how many towers would be needed or the concrete necessary for the footings, they came up with a remarkably accurate estimate. Castagneto estimated the concrete and the labor costs, Bannerman the cost of the steel, and Trout the cost of motors and tramlines. That night, they gave Harriman their estimate of $205,000, which he accepted, bringing in a crew to build the lifts. The lifts were built for $185,000, $20,000 below the estimate. They used the remaining $20,000 to build a shelter. Charley Davidson from Boise, who was in charge of landscaping at Sun Valley, got the lumber, and Pat Rogers brought a mason from the Grand Canyon to do the stonework. Together, they created the Roundhouse, an octagonal restaurant with 46 windows and a giant fireplace.

The chairlifts on Dollar and Proctor had wooden towers, but Baldy's had steel towers built by American Steel and Wire. Bill Castagneto and Val McAtee worked on construction crews in 1939. Lloyd Castagneto was the overall supervisor, Ed Seagle managed the work, and Richard Salvadore was the foreman. They started in July 1939, "and it was a rush to get them finished before the snows started," according to Bill Castagneto. The top lift was constructed first, because it would be the first to get snow in the fall.

Lloyd Castagneto had three crews working on Baldy, one at the bottom working up, and two near "Little Baldy" where the Roundhouse was built. The central work depot with a cook shack was about 300 feet from the Roundhouse site on the east side of Little Baldy near a spring. The crew stayed there to eliminate a long daily trip from town. Materials were taken up Cold Springs by trucks to a slide area, where horses or crawler tractors with trailers hauled them to the work depot.

The men mixed concrete for the foundations using materials hauled up the mountain, and the footings and bases for the lift towers were poured on site. Water was hauled in 50-gallon drums on trailers. McAtee was in charge of unloading the partially assembled steel towers and ensuring they were taken to the proper tower bases. There was no direct communication between the construction site and town, no telephone or telegraph lines, so messages had to be carried by men hiking up and down. Clubs in Ketchum raced to see which could send beer up to the camp at night to keep the men happy.

The Roundhouse was built under the supervision of Ted Trowridge, a bridge and building foreman on U.P.'s main line. There were no plans for the Roundhouse, so Lloyd Castagneto and Charlie Davidson sketched the facility, and it was built from the sketch. The trails on Baldy were partly natural and partly cleared. Skiers could go down Cold Springs to the highway or down Warm Springs where a trail had been cut, and buses would pick them up at both locations to take them back to the River Run lift or the lodge. There was very little in Warm Springs Canyon except for a few old buildings close to town.

A crew of ski racers from Washington, Idaho, Utah, Oregon, Colorado, Nevada, and Dartmouth spent two and a half months working on the ski runs with several ski instructors. They cleared Dollar Mountain's runs of sagebrush until they resembled golf greens, along with the gullies on both sides of the lift. On Rudd, the wide runs on both sides of the jump were cleared and smoothed out.

Moving to Bald Mountain, where Freidl Pfeifer had marked trees for removal, the students worked with Forest Service and CCC crews directed by Alf Engen to cut new runs on Baldy. They worked on the Warm Springs downhill course, living in tents near the steilhang with a cook who was supplied by a pack train. They thinned trees above the open traverse and steilhang, and cut a new section on the upper part of the trail leading toward the ski lift. Alf Engen's CCC crew smoothed the surface of the trail from the steilhang down to the finish, cleaning out the stumps so you "could almost ski down on the grass . . . closely resembling a four-lane highway for skiers," according to the *Sun Valley Ski Club Annual* for 1940. Other crews built a horse trail from the steilhang to the summit, and cleared ski runs on the other side of Bald Mountain.

On October 26, 1939, Union Pacific bought 140.23 acres from Frances Venerable for $4,000 in what became the River Run area to use for the base of its chairlifts to the top of Baldy. A series of three single chairlifts were installed on the "Riverside Run" side of Baldy to the top of the mountain. The first lift started at the bottom of Riverside Run, at 5,947 feet, and was 3,792 feet long. The loading area was east of the Big Wood River, so skiers rode over the river on chairs. The second lift began at 6,554 feet, was 3,776 feet long, and went up to the Roundhouse station. The third lift began at the Roundhouse at 7,876 feet and was 3,976 feet long, ending at Bald Mountain summit, elevation 9,200 feet. The Roundhouse had outdoor terraces for sunbathing and eating. The General Electric Company of Salt Lake City provided three big electric motors weighing seven tons apiece that drove the lifts.

The *Hailey Times* of September 28, 1939, said the trip up Baldy took 22 minutes on chairs that had windbreaks and brackets on which skiers could rest their feet and skis. The lifts could carry 426 skiers per hour over 2.5 miles at six miles per hour. Two ski trails were cut. One went down from Little Baldy Cabin through Cold Springs Canyon to the road at the foot of Baldy, "so gradual that an auto can be driven almost to the top." The other trail went from the summit through the same canyon as the lift to Wood River.

The chairlifts greatly expanded the skiable area on Baldy, which, according to Van Gordon Sauter, opened

> *the crown jewel of Sun Valley's winter resort activity and arguably the best ski mountain in the world. . . . Baldy is insistent, with a constant, steep pitch that produces burn from top to bottom. Interminable to some, exhilarating to others, it is a mountain that has hosted the world's skiing royalty.*

A significant amount of work was done on Baldy for the 1940 ski season. "First of all came the 'Chairway to the Stars' extending from Wood River to the summit of Baldy," according to the *Sun Valley Ski Club Report for 1941*. "This was the last word in ski lifts and had proven very popular both in summer and in winter." Then, more ski runs had to be provided for both novice and expert skiers. The Riverside and Sunnyside runs were created, along with Canyon Run, which was "studded with occasional trees and included a tricky traverse." The Roundhouse was built on the summit of Little Baldy "with friendly fireplaces, spacious windows, and delicious food."

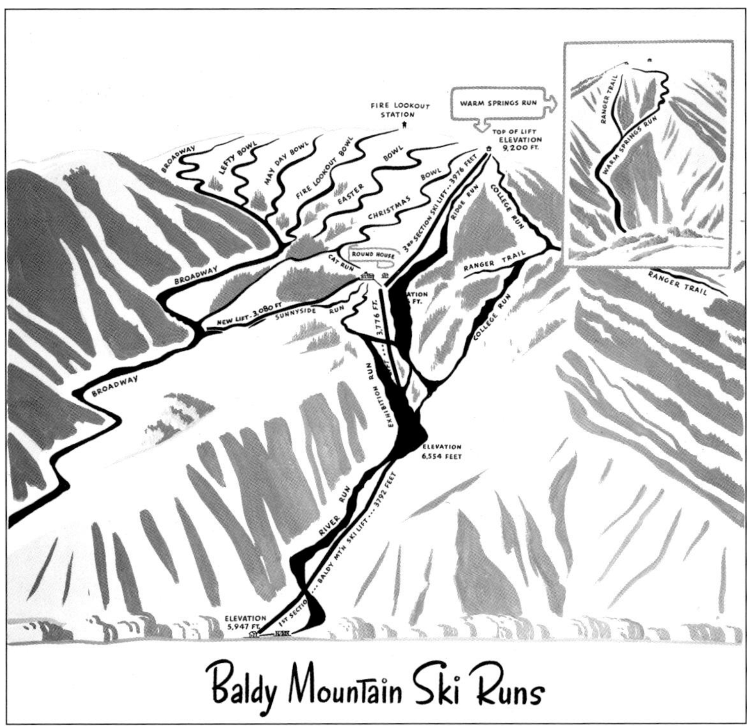

Drawing showing Bald Mountain ski runs, early 1940s.

By 1939, James Curran had designed a new footrest for Sun Valley's chairlifts, and in 1940, a patent application was filed for an improved chair, the Sun Valley Aerial Ski Tramway. The leg rest on the original chair was eliminated and a footrest was added, consisting of a flat surface to support the passenger's feet and skis. It hung from a shaft on one side of the chair and rotated away to permit easy mounting or dismounting, controlled by the passenger using a hand lever that also served as a safety bar across his front.

The resort also developed a first aid stretcher that was in use in 1940, the "Sun Valley Stretcher Chair," for which they applied for a patent.

The work done at Sun Valley was described in *Railway Age* on September 30, 1939. Improvements included a new ski lift on Bald Mountain, a new octagonal "cabin, restaurant and observatory," and four new skiers' chalets to accommodate 196 guests, with rooms equipped with four bunk beds and lavatories with central bathrooms for men and women. An addition was built on Trail Creek Cabin for a dining/dancing room. Pioneer Cabin was doubled in size to accommodate a party of 10 "on those

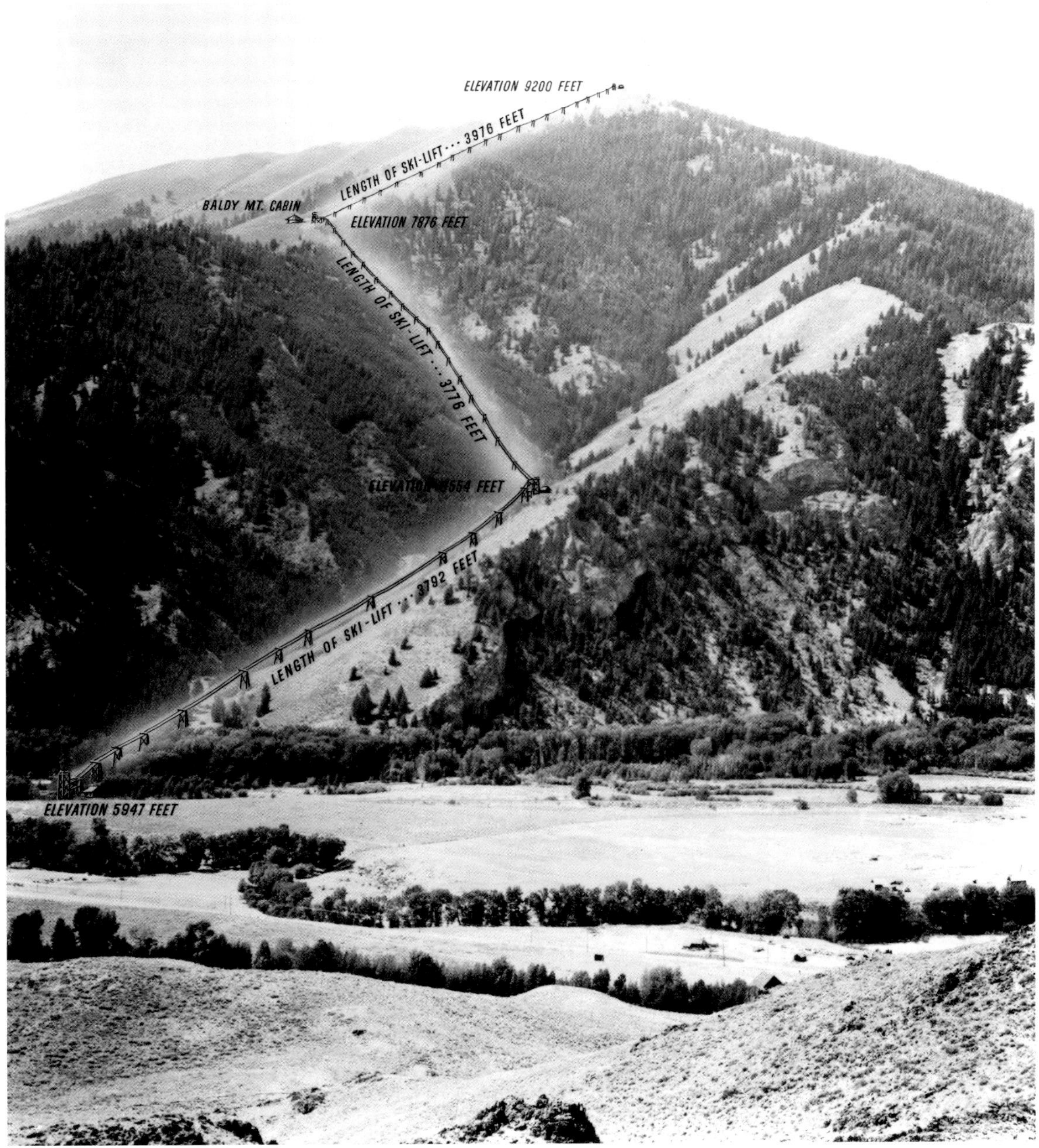

Diagram of chairlift locations on Bald Mountain, 1939.

famous spring skiing tours." The cabin had air-mattress sleeping bags, a new stove, a large stock of nonperishable foods, and a new battery for the radio. A touring class would teach pupils to become familiar with the ski country surrounding Sun Valley. The cabin was for the

> *seasoned touring skiers—ski mountaineers . . . those who have gone to Pioneer cabin for several days and have come back with a new line of experiences which they say are difficult to describe, yet so pleasant that any of the many ski lift fiends who picture heaven as a succession of super ski lifts, Duchin Rooms, etc., will immediately include a Pioneer cabin as a portion of their Valhalla with the many rolling hills and wide canyons to ski-tour in and around.*

Sun Valley was expecting a big season in 1940 because of the opening of Bald Mountain and the war in Europe that made European ski resorts inaccessible, diverting more skiers here. The ski school expanded to 20 carefully chosen instructors. Union Pacific changed its train service between Shoshone and Ketchum. Trains would travel from Ketchum to Shoshone in the evening to pick up passengers from the morning westbound trains, who would be brought back to Ketchum, where the trains would remain during the day.[41]

Otto Lang Becomes Co-Director of Ski School

For the ski season of 1939, Friedl Pfeifer brought Otto Lang to Sun Valley as the co-director of the ski school. Lang and Pfeifer had taught together under Hannes Schneider at St. Anton, Austria. Lang came to America in winter 1935 to teach skiing at Peckett's Inn at Sugar Hill, New Hampshire, where Nelson Rockefeller was his student. After one season, Lang decided to open his own ski school where there were higher mountains and more reliable snow. Lang chose Mount Rainier in Washington to start the first Hannes Schneider ski school in the United States, which opened in December 1936. Paradise became one of the Northwest's premier places to ski, with its huge snowfall and celebrity instructor. In 1937, 20th Century Fox filmed portions of a movie, *Thin Ice*, on Rainier, with Lang directing the ski sequences using his 18-year-old star pupil, Gretchen Kunigk, as a double for Sonja Henie. The following year, Lang opened ski schools on Mount Baker and Mount Hood in Oregon.

Lang came to Sun Valley in the winter of 1938 as the private instructor for Nelson Rockefeller and his family, and fell in love with America's "glamour ski resort." Harriman asked Friedl Pfeifer why Rockefeller did not take lessons from their instructors, and was told, "because Otto is wonderful company and an inspiring teacher." Harriman suggested hiring Lang. Lang had not planned to leave Washington but wanted some place "with a more stable climate, ample snow, and sunshine," and he accepted Pfeifer's offer.

For 1939, Pfeifer hand-picked a staff of instructors who were "balanced in experience," including the first woman ski instructor to work at Sun Valley, Elli Stiller, a member of the 1932 Austrian ski team Pfeifer coached. Instructors included Richard Woerle, Toni Walch, Fred Iselin, Elli Stiller, Percy Rideout, Harold Hillman, Marty Arrouge, Dick Mitchell, Willy Meyer, Hal Fletcher, Ragnar Qvale, Sigi Engl,Victor Gottschaulk, and Hans Teichner. Lang and Pfiefer adapted techniques taught at the Hannes Schneider School to accommodate American skiers who were more impatient than Europeans, shortening and expediting the teaching process to fit the American temperament. Lang wrote:

> *Our students were more interested in reaching a semblance of proficiency than in perfecting certain basic maneuvers. It was all well and good to practice snowplow turns ad infinitum on a gentle slope at the bottom of a hill, but what our students really aspired to was to get to the top of the mountain to ski safely down an appropriate run. That's what the sport of skiing was all about, the freedom and speed felt while soaring down a mountainside.*

Dollar Mountain was the ideal place "to put a streamlined version of the Arlberg technique to a test," where beginner and intermediate skiers "could make remarkably rapid progress." Elli Stiller and Fred Iselin married in 1946 and moved to Aspen in 1948 to work for Pfeifer.

Harriman expected his ski instructors to market Sun Valley around the country in the off-season, including attending indoor ski shows to demonstrate their skills. In fall 1939 and 1940, Friedl Pfeifer participated in indoor ski shows in New York, Boston, and Seattle.

Seattle held an indoor ski tournament at the Civic Ice Arena in November 1939, with a sanctioned ski meet including ski jumping and slalom competitions. A spidery scaffold was erected, rising "to the roof of the enormous building, and from its peak, cascading down toward a canvas-covered window, was the in-run of a ski jump," the *Seattle Times* wrote. Over 11,000 attended the two-day event. The entry list was headed by Friedl Pfeifer, one of the world's greatest, and local Norwegian ski jumpers Olav Ulland and Nordal Kaldahl. Ski vendors exhibited equipment, and skating exhibitions were given.

Friedl Pfeifer "gave a brilliant performance," according to the *Seattle Times*, swinging "through the slalom flags on the 35-foot wide out-run with a flicky-flicky mastery of a difficult flush," and won the slalom. "Olav Ulland performed veritable miracles as he turned somersaults off the high jump in spite of the handicap of a projecting girder eighteen inches above his head, his skis hit the girder every time he looped . . . the steel will shine for weeks." Ulland said, "I'll do a somersault if you'll buy me a new pair of skis every time I break one."

When Pfeifer arrived back in Sun Valley in fall 1939, the resort "proved almost as exciting as the World's Fair," he said. "We were about to open the most advanced ski mountain on the American continent. By the middle of November, rows of lift towers reached to the top of Baldy Mountain and a new set of trails followed the contours of the mountain from top to bottom."[42]

16

SUN VALLEY ATTRACTS THE RICH, FAMOUS, AND TOP SKIERS

Sun Valley was known for attracting Hollywood stars and the rich and famous thanks to Steve Hannagan's efforts. Stories of the "good life" at Sun Valley have been told by many of its well-known visitors.

Kathleen Harriman

Averell Harriman's second daughter, Kathleen, was a fashionable fixture at Sun Valley. Dorice Taylor said Kathleen, Hannah Loche, and Clarita Heath "were among the pretty girls who skied the slopes and posed for the first publicity pictures." Kathleen and Gretchen Kunigk Fraser became best friends through skiing.

Born in 1917, the youngest of two daughters of Averell and his first wife, Kathleen spent her life in luxury and "knew well the whirl of dances, luncheons and teas that were traditional for women of her time and station," according to the *New York Times*. Her father was one of the wealthiest men in America, and she was raised in the 40-bedroom Arden House, her parent's 20,000-acre estate in New York's Hudson Valley. Her obituary in the *New York Times* of February 19, 2011, read:

> *Her life is a window into both Gilded Age America and the changing role of American women in the era between the world wars. . . . For her life—which encompassed*

extraordinary privilege, spirited adventure, associations with the most prominent actors on the world stage and also a measure of heartache—stood squarely on the nexus between 19th-century old money and the 20th-century New Woman.

Kathleen was in school, so she missed the trip to Sun Valley in February 1936 after Count Schaffgotsch discovered Ketchum. The count took her family skiing down the "wrong side" of Dollar, facing town where there wasn't much snow but lots of rocks. He got them down safely, even though they were not experienced skiers. Averell Harriman decided the family should have one ski racer. Kathleen's older sister refused, and "I became the skier," she said, "much to Friedl Pfeifer's horror."

Kathleen was a student at Bennington College in Vermont when Sun Valley opened in December 1936, so she came to the resort during her vacations. She was on Bennington's ski team, won an Eastern championship, and competed in the intercollegiate ski meets at Sun Valley over Christmas. In 1940, her senior year, she "outraced her competitors by a comfortable margin," and was named the best woman skier and the combined winner in the "girls competition," according to the *Sun Valley Ski Club Annual* for 1940. The December 1940 *Ski Illustrated* published a picture of Kathleen with the Idaho women's ski team that won Sun Valley's Interstate Ski Meet, dressed in Tyrolean costumes, presenting "a pretty picture for the cameraman."

In Sun Valley's second summer, during the Idaho potato growers' conference, Kathleen heard a conventioneer's wife say, "This is a lovely place. What do you suppose they do with it in the winter?"

Kathleen knew Ernest Hemingway, who came to the Harriman estate in New York. Taylor Williams, the hunting and fishing guide, was a wonderful man, she said, full of stories: "He'd make the country come alive to you."

Friedl Pfeifer took Kathleen and Averell to the top of Bald Mountain in winter 1939. They went up Cold Springs using skins, traveling at their own speed, using kick turns. It took three hours to get to the top and five minutes to ski down, but it was a good way to get fit.

We climbed on sealskins in the beginning, which were much stiffer than the plush ones made out of cloth. You'd get to the top of Baldy and take those darned things off your skis and they'd be frozen stiff, and you'd wrap them around your waist and ski down, hoping you got down before they melted and you were wet solid to your knees.

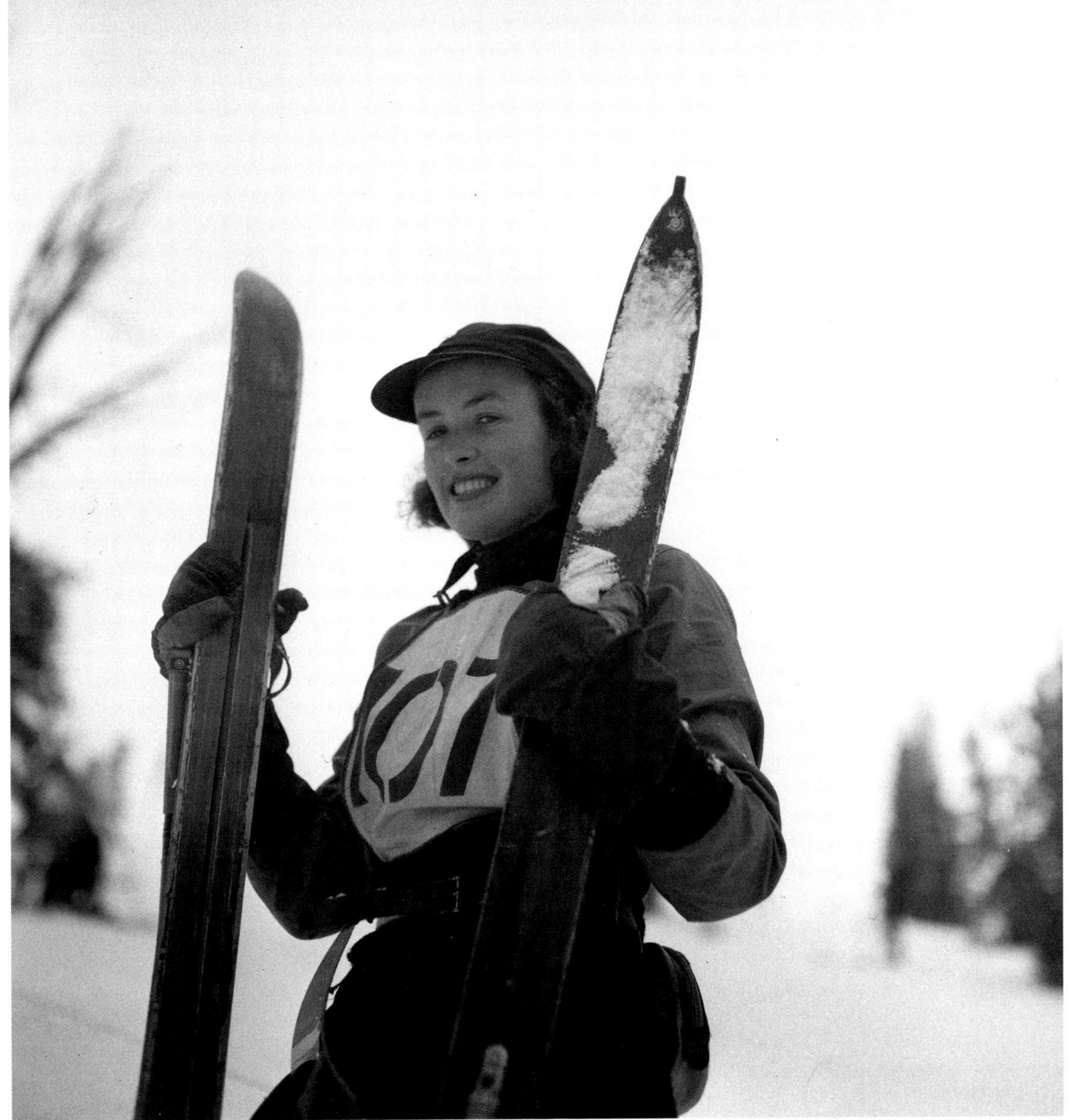

Kathleen Harriman on Bald Mountain in race bib, 1938.

In the early days of Sun Valley, she said, "you knew pretty much everybody that was here." After skiing, everyone would gather in the lodge living room with its huge fireplace and comfortable chairs. You could order tea and sandwiches, and the instructors joined you. On Fridays, they would go to Galena, be taken to the top and ski down in deep powder snow. There were informal parties in the Dollar cabin during full moons, and "famous parties" at the Roundhouse in the evenings with a band, attended by the

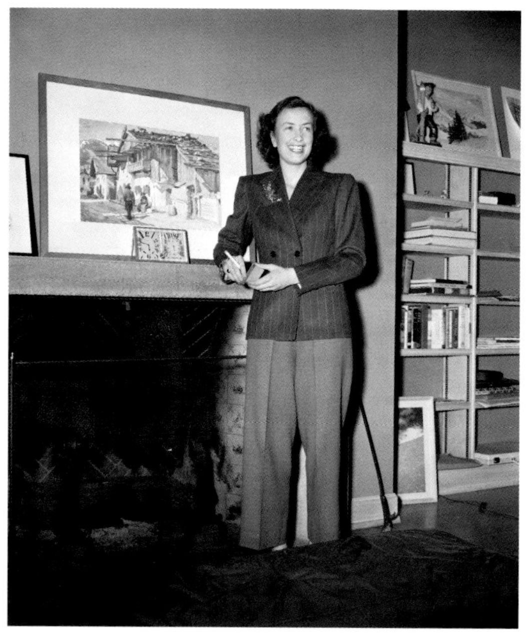

Kathleen Harriman in front of fireplace at Sun Valley.

ski instructors. You could ride the lift or ski down, although you had to "pass muster" to be allowed to ski, i.e., prove you hadn't had too much to drink. There were "gambling joints" in Ketchum, the Alpine Club and Slavey's, where you could get a wonderful steak on a plank for $3.50. The Christiania attracted "the most sophisticated Hollywood gamblers."

After graduating from college, Kathleen worked for Steve Hannagan in New York. Hannagan did public relations and represented people who wanted to stay out of the press. He advised clients such as Barbara Hutton to take taxis instead of her limousine.

Kathleen accompanied her father on his overseas assignments during World War II. She went to London in 1941 while her father oversaw the Lend-Lease Act, where she worked as a reporter for *Newsweek*. In November 2011, *Vanity Fair* published an article about her wartime experiences in London, "To War in Silk Stockings," saying she could "out-ski and out-shoot" Averell and was a "woman from another era who never surrendered her principles." Her roommate was Pamela Digby Churchill—who was married to Randolph Churchill, the prime minister's son—with whom her father had an affair during the war and married years later. Kathleen went with Averell when he was U.S. ambassador to Russia in 1943, where she learned Russian, was the official hostess at her father's diplomatic functions, and accompanied him to the Yalta Conference. She was able to ski in Russia. In February 1944, she placed second in the women's slalom race of the Russian Republic Ski Championships held on the hill where Napoleon watched French troops invade Moscow. The Russian government wouldn't let her accept her prize, a trip to the Caucasus Mountains.

In 1947, Kathleen married Stanley G. Mortimer, an heir to the Standard Oil fortune, after which she largely dropped from public view, although she made periodic trips to Sun Valley. It was later learned that Mortimer suffered from bipolar disorder and had attempted suicide.

Kathleen Harriman Mortimer died in 2011 at the age of 93. The *New York Times* said she was "rich and adventurous . . . a first-rate skier and equestrienne, riding magnificent cavalry horses that were a gift from Stalin. . . . Mrs. Mortimer was quietly accomplished throughout her life." *The Times* of London said she was an "American heiress who won hearts in wartime London as an aide to her father, an envoy to Churchill," and showed a picture of Kathleen with one of the two horses given to her by Stalin.[43]

Clara Spiegel

Clara Spiegel's husband, Frederick, owned a clothing store in Chicago that became a successful mail-order catalog. She first came to Sun Valley in January 1937, traveling on the "very comfortable" Portland Rose from Chicago, taking two and a half days. Spiegel exemplified the wealthy socialites who became regulars at the resort.

In 1937, only the lodge was open and everything happened there, including meals and entertainment. Clara took ski lessons from Austrian instructors who were "of varying degrees of beauty," and were, she said, "all Nazis." Swastikas were in their rooms, and they regularly said "Heil Hitler," which did not go down well with the students. Her ski instructor, Hans's brother Max Hauser, was the biggest Nazi she knew. Clara's first class was not allowed to use the chairlift. They climbed Penny Hill north of the lodge, as instructors had "no idea of equipment replacing skill," before moving to Dollar. At 4:00 in the afternoon, a whistle blew and the instructors schussed down the hill, leaving their classes to fend for themselves. Buses took students to the Ram, where they had hot chocolate, tea, or beer. The best pastries she ever ate were served in the lodge lobby, except for those in Vienna. At night, they danced to the Hal Smith orchestra in the Duchin Room.

During Clara's second year at Sun Valley (1937–1938), there was no snow early in the season so the guests were taken by bus to Baker Creek, where a cat pulled them up the mountain. There was an immense tent where hot food was served and lessons were given, two hours in the morning and two in the afternoon. Everyone had a good time, she said.

In the evenings, guests went to Ketchum in sleds pulled by dogs or reindeer. There was not much there except a couple of saloons, a drugstore, and a post office. The

Tram, Alpine, and Sawtooth Clubs offered drinking and gambling. Poker was played in back and there was roulette, blackjack, and dice in the front. Slot machines were all over the place. Many of the guests and locals played for high stakes. She remembers sheepherders with large stacks of cash and their sidearms on the tables. The St. Georg Hotel was a nice place, she said, but it burned down.

Spiegel came to Sun Valley for four to six weeks to ski while her husband went to Florida to fish. After one of her sons was diagnosed with asthma in 1937, his doctor told them to leave Chicago, and they came to Sun Valley four times a year, falling in love with the area she called a "velvet trap." Spiegel met Averell Harriman her first year there. He was a "marvelous man," one of the most fascinating people she ever met. He was "very masculine, but in a subdued way," brilliant, charming, and delightful.

Pat Rogers, Sun Valley's manager, was a character, she said. He loved baseball, which was a major form of recreation for employees and guests. Rogers was the catcher for his team, and he couldn't stand to lose. During baseball season, everything stopped from 2:00 to 4:00, as everyone was on the ballfield. One summer, Clara's son's team played Rogers's team. Her son hit a home run that broke the game open, and Spiegel and others razzed Rogers. He turned around and said, "Clara Spiegel, I've had enough of you. Pick up your paycheck and get out of here." Clara and her family were staying in a six-room suite in the lodge, a fact Rogers apparently forgot. That night at a party in the lodge, Rogers's wife told Clara that he was hiding from her, saying, "He fired you and realized later you didn't work here, you've been staying here so much." Pat Rogers was notorious for not apologizing to anyone.

Spiegel's husband met Ernest Hemingway in Europe during World War I, where they both drove ambulances, and they met again in Europe during the 1920s. When Hemingway came to Sun Valley in 1939, the Spiegels saw him often—he was a "wonderful man," she said. Clara went hunting with Hemingway and Martha Gellhorn around Richfield, Dietriech, and on Bud Purdy's property near Picabo.

Few people came to Sun Valley in the autumn. The lodge was closed, so guests stayed at the inn. Everyone knew each other and had great fun together. The Hemingways and Gary Cooper and his wife, Rocky, were regulars. There were parties at Trail Creek Cabin and elsewhere. Gary Cooper was, she said, "a peach . . . a modest, unassuming and quiet man with a delightful smile and couldn't have been nicer." They had many birthday parties, which included skits and silly costume parties, and people would have given "their eye teeth" to have been invited.

One winter, Clara got hurt skiing and was out for the season. She decided to "abdicate as the Valley Lush," and held an Abdication Ball at Crony Cove, 11 miles up Warm Springs, sending invitations for "the Ritz Crony Cove, White Tie." Everyone was in costume. Jeanne and Pete Lane came as Lord and Lady Sheepdip. Dr. Moritz wore his Navy uniform and a cape with a red lining. The highlight of the party was a procession to an outhouse where there was a "throne." Clara abdicated, and Jeanne Lane became the new Valley Lush.

Clara bought property in Sun Valley in the late 1930s on Sun Valley Lake but sold it to Bob Guggenheim, who later was U.S. ambassador to Portugal, because it was not private. She and her husband divorced after World War II, and she moved to Ketchum in the early 1950s. She said it was a mistake to close Proctor Mountain. It had everything—meadows, trails, steep places, gentle places, and was comparatively short so you didn't spend much time on the lift.

She met Mary Hemingway after the war. Both Clara and Ernest were boxing fans, and they watched Friday Night Fights on TV together. One day, Clara visited Hemingway in his Ketchum house and saw a large pile of mail on his desk. It was his fan mail, which he told her he did not have time to answer, so Clara volunteered to do it. One letter was from a schoolteacher in Georgia who said Hemingway's newest book had been banned, asking if he could send her a copy so she could discuss it with her students. Clara wrapped a copy of *For Whom the Bell Tolls* in a paper bag, writing "recipes" on the outside because she was afraid the post office would not deliver it. She was shocked by Hemingway's suicide in 1961.[44]

Ernest Hemingway

In fall 1939, a man who became closely associated with Sun Valley came to the resort, fell in love with the area, and became a well-known persona there for over 20 years. Ernest Hemingway's network of Sun Valley friends included both Hollywood stars and local hunting associates. His time in Idaho is described in *Ernest Hemingway & Gary Cooper, An Enduring Friendship*, by Larry E. Morris. Contemporaneous accounts can be found in *High on the Wild with Hemingway* by Lloyd R. Arnold, Sun Valley's original photographer, and *The Idaho Hemingway* by Tillie Arnold, his wife. The Arnolds met Hemingway in 1939 and were close friends until his death.

By 1939, Hemingway was already famous as a novelist, journalist, and adventurer. *The Sun Also Rises* was published in 1926, and *A Farewell to Arms* in 1929, which was partially based on his time as an ambulance driver in Italy during World War I. *A Farewell to Arms* was called "the best American novel to come out of World War I," became Hemingway's first best seller, ensured his stature as a leading American author, and made him financially independent.

Gene Van Guilder was a Sun Valley publicist who knew how much the resort gained from publicity about celebrities who stayed there. In 1938, he learned that Hemingway spent time in Montana in the fall. He sent an employee to Key West, Florida, to offer him free room and board at Sun Valley in exchange for the right to use Hemingway's photographs. Hemingway was too busy covering the Spanish civil war as a journalist to accept the offer.

His coming to Sun Valley in fall 1939 involved his complicated relationships with his four wives, at least indirectly, as Morris describes. Hemingway married Hadley Richardson in 1921, divorcing her in January 1927 after he had an affair with Pauline Pfeifer. Ernest and Pauline married in 1931. They became estranged in 1935 after Ernest met Martha Gellhorn in Key West and they had an affair while covering the Spanish civil war.

In September 1939, Hemingway drove from Florida to Wyoming to hunt and fish with his sons Jack, Patrick, and Gregory. When Ernest met Jack near Cody, Wyoming, he learned that Hadley and her new husband were fishing nearby. They had not seen each other for eight years after their bitter divorce, but they met that summer. Hemingway took Jack to a ranch farther north in Wyoming. After Hemingway's employee Toby Bruce arrived with Patrick and Ernest, Pauline called, saying she was joining them. The visit turned out to be a disaster, "and the final dissolution of their relationship became increasingly evident," according to Morris. Bruce left with Pauline and her kids.

Martha Gellhorn then met Hemingway in Billings, Montana, and they drove to Sun Valley to take up Gene Van Guilder's invitation made the prior year. There was one problem—Hemingway neglected to tell Sun Valley he was coming. When he arrived on September 20, 1939, Sun Valley photographer Lloyd Arnold saw "a big man with an attractive blond girl" who looked familiar, before realizing it was Hemingway. Arnold told Gene Van Guilder that Hemingway had arrived. Gene called Hannagan in New York and was told to "roll out the red carpet but to do so gently because the famous writer 'spooks easily.' " Pat Rogers welcomed them personally and took them to room

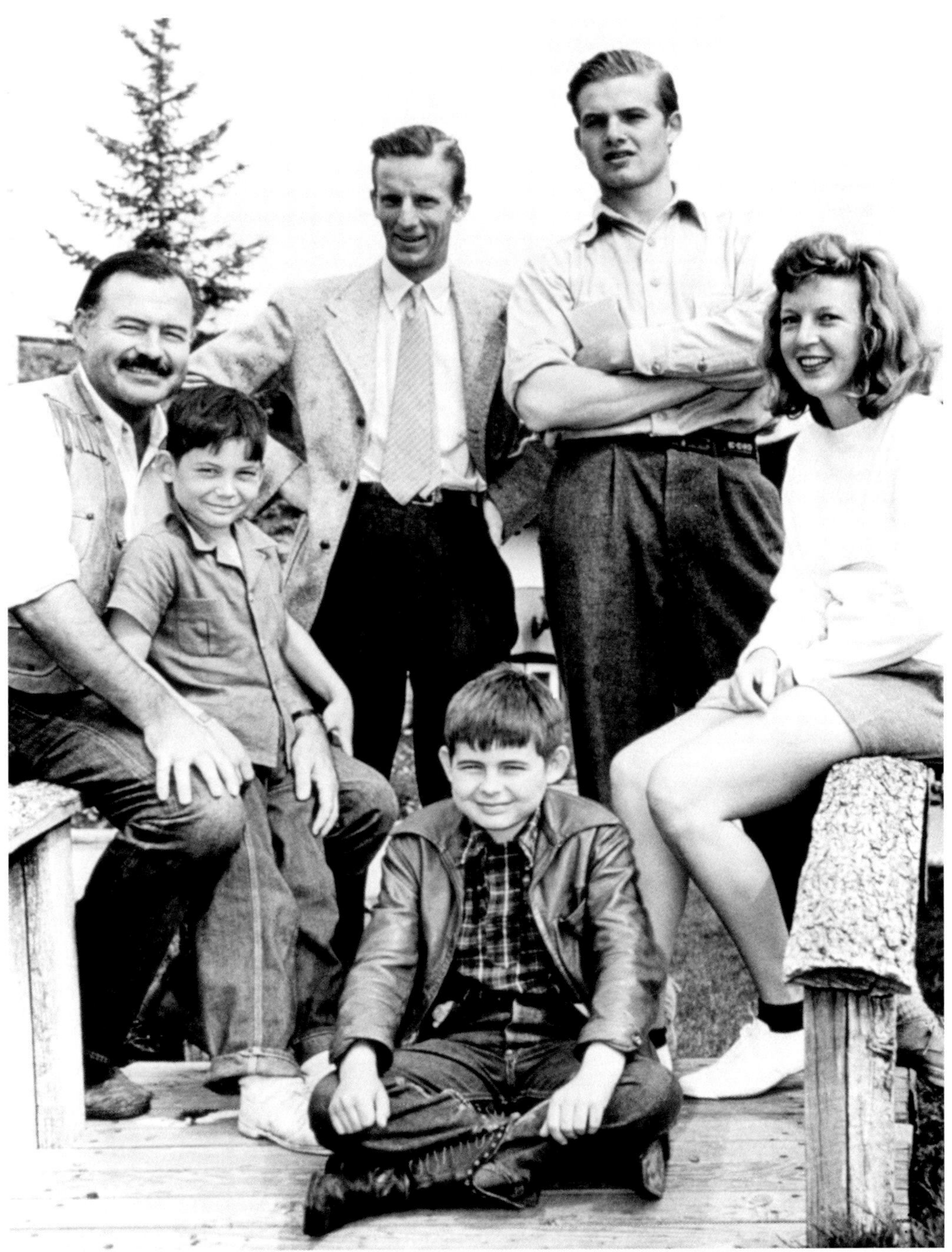

Ernest Hemingway, Martha Gellhorn, three sons from prior marriage (Gregory, Patrick, and Jack) and friend/driver Toby Bruce, Sun Valley, 1940.

206, a suite in the lodge with two bedrooms, each with its own bath and balcony and a living room with a separate balcony. The men knew that the woman, introduced as "Miss Gill," was not his wife. Hemingway was endearing to Arnold and Van Guilder, discussing hunting and fishing, entering into a "laughing, joking, teasing, friendly, lovable relationship." Gene and Lloyd and their wives spent time with Hemingway and became close friends.

The resort's offer of a complimentary stay gave Hemingway a perfect place to work on *For Whom the Bell Tolls*. Hemingway had already written 12 chapters but said it would be "a long book" and "the fall weather in Idaho was invigorating, perfect for writing a book."

He wrote several chapters in suite 206, which he called "the Glamor House," working from dawn to early afternoon. Later in the afternoons, he went horseback riding, played tennis, or explored Silver Creek near the town of Picabo, which became his favorite hunting spot in Idaho. Evenings consisted of group dinners followed by socializing and alcohol at Glamor House. Hemingway "found that drinking sharpened his life for him like nothing else, perhaps even made it meaningful; life without it was flat and dull," according to Morris. Hemingway mentioned Sun Valley in a draft of *For Whom the Bell Tolls*, when the book's hero, Robert Jordan, talks about marrying his young Spanish lover, Maria, saying they might be "Mr. and Mrs. Robert Jordan of Sun Valley, Idaho; Corpus Christi, Texas; or Butte, Montana." Bernice Hicks, a secretary at the lodge, typed most of the first 24 chapters of the book.

For Whom the Bell Tolls was published in 1940, becoming a best seller. Reviews called it "a tremendous piece of work," Hemingway's "finest novel," and "one of the finest and richest novels of the last decade." It was nominated for a Pulitzer Prize, which he eventually won in 1952. The book made Hemingway a lot of money at a time when he needed it. Paramount Pictures paid $100,000, plus 10¢ for every copy of the book sold up to 300,000, for the film rights. Tillie Arnold said Hemingway was broke before the book was published, living on money borrowed from his publisher, Scribner's. His wife Pauline was divorcing him and forcing him to pay support for their two boys, even though she was wealthy and he was supporting his mother. Tillie said Hemingway was relieved he could then live in the independent style he loved.

Hemingway fell in love with the hunting around Sun Valley, going to Silver Creek near Picabo, the area around Shoshone, the Pahsimeroi Valley, and the Middle Fork of the Salmon River. He associated with movie stars and the rich and famous but also appreciated local hunting and fishing guides who shared his love of the outdoors.

"Hem took unique pleasure in long, animated conversations, sometimes telling stories of his own but more often than not asking questions of others, listening, pondering, asking more questions, and showing an extraordinary interest in the experiences and thoughts of his dinner companions," according to Morris. Bud Purdy, owner of a ranch near Picabo through which Silver Creek flows, did a lot of hunting with Hemingway in 1940 and 1941. Purdy said he never acted like a celebrity, was considerate of others, always wanted someone else to take the first shot, never drank while he hunted, and was always polite. For larger hunts, "General Hemingway" would organize parties of more than 20 Hollywood and local friends. Tillie Arnold said Hemingway did not fish much in Idaho, but he loved the hunting, particularly upland birds.

Hemingway made his presence known around Sun Valley—he was a bigger-than -life persona. Tillie Arnold described an evening at Trail Creek Cabin when he got into an argument with a Norwegian who knew ju jutsu, about whether a boxer or a ju jutsu expert would win a fight. They went at it, and Hemingway hit him several times, decking him before the crowd stopped things. They ended up drinking together afterward. Hemingway later showed a friend his bruises where he had been kicked, saying that was why he was never a fighter, and admitted he could have "gotten the shit kicked out of him." Louis Holliday said everybody thinks Hemingway was a macho type, but that it wasn't true. He looked like he might be and was built like a linebacker, "But he was not macho. He was gentle and polite."

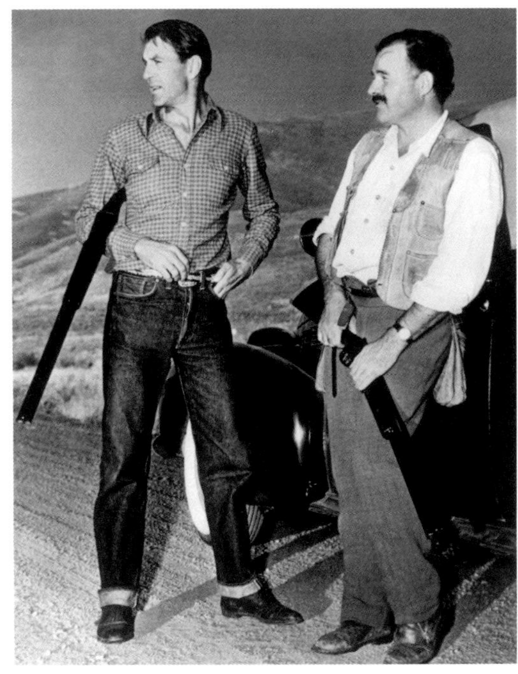

Ernest Hemingway and Gary Cooper on hunting trip near Sun Valley.

Tillie Arnold related an incident in fall 1940, showing a different side of Hemingway. He was throwing clay pigeons for his wife Mary at the gun club so she could test a new shotgun he had given her for her birthday. When Mary took a break, an older man came on to the range and Ernest threw clay pigeons for him. When he was done, the man gave Ernest a shiny silver dollar as a tip. "Ernest accepted it with a straight face. . . . For years we joked about the money Ernest could earn in tips if he ever decided to quit writing."

Sun Valley became Hemingway's primary fall home, with his winter residence in Cuba. He met Gary Cooper at Sun Valley. Cooper starred in the 1932 movie version of *A Farewell to Arms*, which won two Oscars and was nominated for best picture, and also played as Robert Jordan in the film of *For Whom the Bell Tolls*, released in 1943. Hemingway said he had Cooper in mind when he wrote about Jordan. Hemingway met Ingrid Bergman in Sun Valley, who played Jordan's lover Maria in the movie.

In 1940, *Life* sent Robert Capra to Sun Valley to photograph Hemingway for an article that appeared on January 6, 1941. Capra knew Hemingway and Martha Gellhorn from their time in Spain. The article describes *For Whom the Bell Tolls*, his life in Idaho with his new wife, and the war in Spain where the novel takes place. It shows pictures of Ernest writing in his pajamas, dancing at Trail Creek Cabin, and hunting near Shoshone. It has six pages of pictures taken by Capra of the civil war, showing where scenes to be played by Gary Cooper and Ingrid Bergman would take place in the movie. Hemingway was upset about the caption on Capra's picture of him holding a dead pheasant, which said that in 10 days of hunting, he never missed a shot. Hemingway felt that made him look like a phony—hunters, he said, know it is impossible to never miss a shot.

After a tempestuous relationship, Ernest and Martha divorced in December 1945 in Havana. Ernest married his fourth wife, Mary Welsh, in Havana; she came to Sun Valley with him in fall 1946. They spent time in Sun Valley until the late 1940s, and moved there permanently in 1958, buying a house in Ketchum in 1959 where he committed suicide in 1961.[45]

ELIZABETH (BETTY) WOOLSEY

Betty Woolsey was one of the top U.S. racers in the 1930s. She was raised in the outdoors of New Mexico, where her father worked for the U.S. Bureau of Forestry. She described her life in her book *Off the Beaten Track*.

Betty lived in Europe with her family, learning to ski before attending Vassar College, where she learned to rock climb and mountain climb. She became a serious climber after college, scaling peaks in Canada, Europe, and the United States, while working in the Yale Art Gallery. She spent much of 1934 in Switzerland. In 1935, she was in St. Anton, Austria, one of the American women training for the 1936 Olympics, coached by Hannes Schneider and Otto Furrer. At the end of the winter, she returned to the United States to pursue mountaineering and ski racing, saying, "Fortunately, I had the freedom and income to do so."

Betty was a member of the U.S. women's ski team at the 1936 Olympics in Garmisch-Partenkirchen, Germany, She was team captain and its best downhill racer. She described the instructions the team received after arriving in Europe:

> *Eight hours of sleep, a limit of seven cigarettes a day and not more than two glasses of wine or beer. A week later we were asked how we were getting along. Mary Bird said she loved to sleep, was enjoying the wine, but was having trouble with the cigarettes as she had never smoked.*

Betty become lifelong friends with teammates from the 1936 Olympics—Clarita Heath, Marian McKean, and Grace Carter. Carter married Al Lindley, a fellow member of the 1936 Olympic team, who was president of the Sun Valley Ski Club. Another friend was Alex Bright, a member of the 1936 U.S. ski team who was on the board of governors of the Sun Valley Ski Club. Bright later married Clarita Heath. Beginning in 1939, Woolsey trained, raced, and worked at Sun Valley.

Woolsey described the attractions of St. Anton, Austria, where she trained in 1935, which could have been a plan for Sun Valley:

> *There was one place we'd all been . . . where you could settle down for a long stay, ski every day, and the sun would seem as bright and the snow as delightful as it did the day we'd come. . . . St. Anton was actually the skiing center for the Americans . . . who went to Europe before the war. Incidentally, in spite of its simplicity, it attracted in large numbers gilded members of society and minor royalty.*
>
> *Why was St. Anton popular? First of all, of course, it was* [Hannes] *Schneider and his Arlberg school that attracted us, because we wanted to learn how to ski. . . . There was no lift when we first went to Anton. . . . I think that the charm of Anton was this. It was an entire community devoted to skiing in all its forms; teaching, racing, touring, writing, making motion pictures of skiing, and every conceivable related activity. . . . Skiing gave the illusion of being an integral part of the daily life of the people rather than a somewhat superficial sport imported to amuse the foreign visitors.*

Betty wrote an article for the *American Ski Annual, 1937–1938*, "The 1937 Women's Team," discussing priorities for developing an internationally competitive women's ski team. The choice of a trainer was first, and the selection of Friedl Pfeifer to coach the U.S. women's team was key. The choice of a place to train was second, which anticipated Sun Valley's hosting the team:

> *Although there should be . . . some climbing for general physical training and heath, the training center must have a funicular and long runs. The "downhill muscles" are not the same as the climbing muscles. . . . Long runs must be stressed. . . . The greatest handicap for the American girls' team at present is in having to go to Europe in order to get the long downhill runs, funiculars, trainers and competition necessary for developing first-class skiers.*

Sun Valley became the major training area for serious skiers after it opened, with its long runs and chairlifts, and became the training ground for the U.S. women's ski team.

> *It's hard to imagine now that in 1939 there were almost no lifts of any kind. These we felt were essential were we to field a decent team for the 1940 Olympics. An exception was Sun Valley, a resort in the Sawtooth Mountains of Idaho. . . . There, on the modest hills of Proctor, Ruud and Dollar, a U.P. engineer had built the first "chair" lifts, patterned after the lifts used in Central America to transport bananas.*

The architecture of the mountains at Sun Valley was disappointing, but,

> *the works of man were most satisfactory. There was a luxurious lodge, an attractive inn, both with heated swimming pools; a movie theater, all nicely landscaped with plenty of space between the buildings. I was quartered in the Harriman cottage, sharing it with a couple of teammates and Kathleen Harriman who was training with the ski team.*
>
> *I settled down to a pleasant routine of skiing and partying with the emphasis on the latter. . . . The "inmates" as* [a friend] *called them, included many friends from Europe and the East, some of whom may have been rich, but they certainly weren't idle. With them I toured on outlying mountains and found light, dry powder snow of a better consistency than anything I had seen in Europe.*

The Hollywood celebrities at Sun Valley took their skiing seriously and were fairly good, she said, but,

> *The standard of skiing in America was very low. We generally had an audience at our downhill and slalom practice and found ourselves to be celebrities. I overheard one Mainline type say to another, "You know they seem to turn well in both directions."*

After the 1939 Harriman Cup at Sun Valley, Betty went to the National Downhill and Slalom Championships at Mount Hood, which were the tryouts for the 1940 FIS and Olympic teams. The Timberline Lodge, built by the WPA, "was an extraordinary building, high up on the mountain and buried in snow." The teams were assigned beds, and "we slept many to a room." Woolsey won the women's downhill by nearly 10 seconds. They celebrated the race "according to time-honored tradition with appropriate beverages."

Betty made the 1940 FIS team to compete at the championships in Europe and at the 1940 Olympics, although they were canceled because of the war. Averell Harriman invited the women to come to Sun Valley to train under Otto Lang in winter 1939, "our headquarters," which was the focal point of racing in the United States. The women were given "jobs of one sort or another. I became editor of *The Valley Sun,* a weekly publication and got experience that was helpful when I replaced Frank Wrensch . . . as managing editor of *Ski Illustrated.*" Dick Durrance's wife, Miggs, worked two hours a day at the opera house taking tickets while skiing and racing.

In her book published in 1984, Woolsey described changes in ski racing since the 1930s, when she was on the international circuit. These included

> *higher speeds, universally excellent technique and precise control, made possible by modern skis, bindings and boots. It has become a year-around discipline with conditioning exercises and training obligatory for the competitors.*
>
> *Other changes would be the carefully prepared and controlled race courses which we never had as there were no mechanical snowpackers. Some countries were able to call on their soldiers and labor battalions for help in preparing snow surfaces, but it was the racers themselves who did a good deal of the work. So a lot of our racing, especially downhill, took place on soft and rough courses, according to modern standards. Secondly there were many fewer controls in downhill races; the "line" one took was up to the*

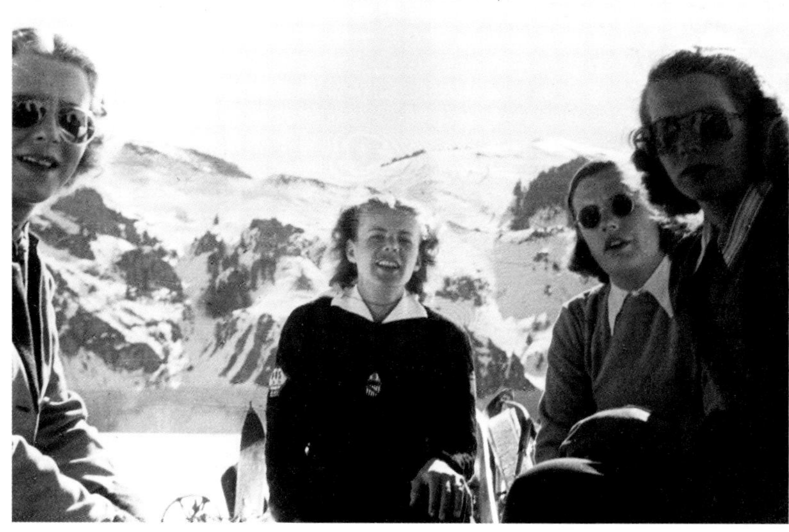

Members of the U.S. women's ski team at Sun Valley, 1939. Betty Woolsey, Grace Carter Lindley, Ann Cook Taylor, and unidentified.

> *individual; also men and women often raced on the same course. The slaloms were more open and resembled skiing rather than the specialized kind of acrobatics that seem to me more like ice skating on an inclined surface that one sees nowadays.*

Woolsey ended up moving to the Jackson Hole area, where she bought a ranch, which she operated for much of the rest of her life. She was known for leading backcountry tours into the wilderness and leading ski expeditions up Teton Pass. She was inducted into the U.S. Ski and Snowboard Hall of Fame in 1969. She died on her ranch in 1997 at age 88.[46]

Don Fraser and Gretchen Kunigk Fraser

In August 1939, two members of the Northwest's ski royalty announced their engagement: Gretchen Kunigk from Tacoma and Don Fraser from Seattle, two prominent and popular skiers. Don was an established ski star and Gretchen an up-and-coming racer. He won the first Silver Skis Race on Mount Rainier in 1934, going from Camp Muir at 10,000 feet down the glaciers and snowfields to near Paradise

Lodge, a race of three and three-quarter miles with 4,800 feet of vertical drop. He was on the 1936 U.S. Olympic team, won the Silver Skis race again in 1938, was on the 1938 FIS team that competed in Chile, and won many races in the Northwest. Gretchen would go on to win gold and silver medals in the 1948 Olympics, the first American to medal in a skiing event at the Olympics.

Don and Gretchen met on the ski racing circuit in the late 1930s, and Sun Valley played a role in their marriage, as Dorice Taylor described:

> *At the competitors' dinner at Trail Creek Cabin before the 1938 race, Averell Harriman announced Gretchen and Don's engagement. The trouble was Don had not yet proposed. They were married before they returned to Sun Valley the following fall—one of the first of the long series of romances for which the resort is famous.*

Don proposed six months after the banquet. The couple would live in Omaha, Nebraska, where Don was the Midwest representative for Sun Valley. In October 1939, they moved to Sun Valley, where he worked in the publicity department. In December 1939, Don became Sun Valley's sports director.

Don directed all sports activities, including skiing and winter sports, golf, tennis, hunting and fishing, and sleigh parties to Trail Creek. He helped start trap shooting and was involved in acquiring the property on Silver Creek that became Sun Valley Ranch. They lived in the lodge above the dining room. In 1940, Don broke his leg in a skiing accident before the Harriman Cup where he was one of the top-ranked favorites. Both he and Gretchen made the U.S. team that would have competed in the 1940 Olympics. Harriman praised the Frasers' contributions to Sun Valley in his oral history:

> *Don Fraser played a very important role. He came to Sun Valley in 1937, the second year of its operation. . . . He had a great deal to do with the development of everything. Both the skiing and the summer time. We owe a great deal to him and his wife, Gretchen. . . . It was the first romance of Sun Valley. . . . I would say that Don Fraser and Pat Rogers were the two men that perhaps did the most. Don Fraser from the standpoint of the outdoors, and Pat Rogers from the standpoint of the operations of the Lodge and Challenger Inn.*

Don and Gretchen both said that in its early days, Sun Valley was primarily Hollywood stars, starlets, tycoons of industry and finance, and socialites from the East who were served by French chefs. Sun Valley was very friendly, and it didn't matter who you were—an employee, a guest, wealthy or of modest means, everyone was welcome and got along. They met stars such as Ernest Hemingway, Gary Cooper, Claudette Colbert, Norma Shearer, and others. Don and Gary Cooper and Gretchen and Kathleen Harriman were good friends. Sun Valley accommodated the wishes of the rich and famous. They could rent the Roundhouse for parties, and food and champagne would be shipped up, which "flowed freely." Coming down on the chairlift, sometimes there would be an empty chair and its passenger would be found sitting in the snow, "happy as can be and didn't care to be disturbed, but they had plain fallen out." Dorice Taylor echoed what the Frasers said about the hazards of riding the chairlift after Roundhouse parties:

> *Another precaution taken was that the numbers of all occupied chairs were phoned down to the bottom. If chair eight came down empty, for instance, and there should have been a body in chair eight, the ski patrol skied under the lift to gently scoop that body from the snow into which it had fallen and deliver it to the bottom of the mountain.*

The Frasers emphasized the help Harriman gave to ski racing. Before coming to Sun Valley, racers would sleep in sleeping bags wherever they could. Once the Challenger Inn opened, racers stayed four to a room for $4 a night with a bathroom down the hall. Harriman saw to it that racers with potential had jobs at Sun Valley, usually as waiters or waitresses so they could work at night and ski during the day. The Sun Valley Ski Club began a program to train junior racers, which was taken over by the Sun Valley Ski Education Foundation.

On October 15, 1940, the *Seattle Times* reported that Don "relinquished his post as sports director at Sun Valley and recently accepted the position of Sun Valley representative out of the Union Pacific's Denver office." John Litchfield, a member of the 1936 U.S. Olympic team and a Sun Valley ski instructor, replaced him as sports director. Don and Gretchen continued their association with Sun Valley. In 1941, *Ski America II*, a movie by Sidney Shurtcliff, featured ski exhibitions at Sun Valley by Don Fraser, Dick Durrance, Friedl Pfeifer, Otto Lang, and others. In February 1941, Gretchen doubled in the ski sequences for Sonja Henie in *Sun Valley Serenade* at Sun

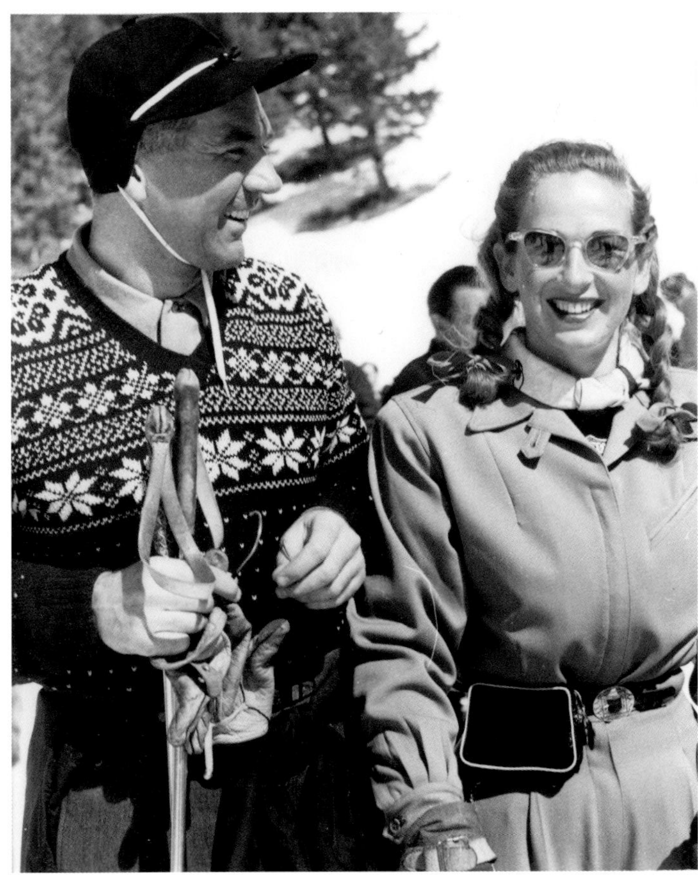

Don and Gretchen Kunigk Fraser on Baldy.

Valley, although this affected her racing. Thanks to her motion picture work, she was now considered a professional, eligible only as an FIS amateur.

In March 1941, Gretchen won the women's downhill in the National Four-Event tournament at Sun Valley, making her America's No. 1 woman skier, having won the combined downhill and slalom events at Aspen. In April 1941, she won the women's giant slalom in the second annual Sun Valley Spring and Snow Sports meet.

Gretchen said that after World War II, both Harriman and Pat Rogers wanted Don to become the manager of Sun Valley. However, the Frasers decided to move to Vancouver, Washington, where Don opened his own business, an oil company. When Gretchen won a gold and silver medal in the 1948 Olympics, Harriman gave her a four-year contract to publicize Sun Valley and a Labrador retriever puppy.[47]

A CRITIQUE OF SUN VALLEY

In May 1940, Harriman received a letter from an acquaintance who stayed at Sun Valley from October 1939 to May 1940. He was the kind of wealthy, worldly outdoorsman the resort attracted. He commented on the resort's operations and included criticisms not often found elsewhere.

"Everyone seemed pleased and impressed by the warmth and attention of the service, its pleasant mixture of Western and American hospitality, even during the most crowded and trying periods," the guest wrote. A number of changes were necessary though, including better radio reception, cheering up the Continental Café, and better room service.

Big game hunting was "well organized,"and guide Taylor Williams was "worth his weight in gold." Duck hunting at Silver Creek was "well organized and excellent," but boats were necessary for hunting on the big reservoirs. Snipe offered "excellent shooting, but should not be offered to anyone unless they are extremely competent and experienced guns." Pheasant hunting was "very good shooting, but ill organized." Sun Valley needed to "acquire sole right to large tracts of farmland near Jerome, Shoshone and Gooding." He thought that $5 should secure 240 acres for a year. Pigeon hunting at Malad Canyon "is a unique sport for America" and Sun Valley should press for a closed season on those unprotected birds. Clay pigeon and target shooting were "well organized, well run."

Guides needed policing, he wrote. "Except for Taylor, all were more or less deficient in the fundamental requirement of 'safety first.'" Properly trained retrievers "are very badly needed." Trained pointers would be useful. Guests learning to shoot should use only "ordinary double-barreled guns of a sort they might later be expected to use in civilized shooting abroad," and never pump guns. Fishing "is absolutely excellent. More dams were needed on Trail Creek for beginners and boats for fishing on beaver dams would be useful."

Skiing was "well done," but changes were needed. Beginners who were not in shape and struggled with the altitude were rushed to advance before they were ready. Instructors didn't realize the condition of their students, and accidents from fatigue and fright were common. Beginners taken down Canyon Run were terrified and discouraged. The message "skiing is fun" should be "beat into the heads of instructors." People ski to have a good time, "not to be barked at or sworn at." Instructors who lose

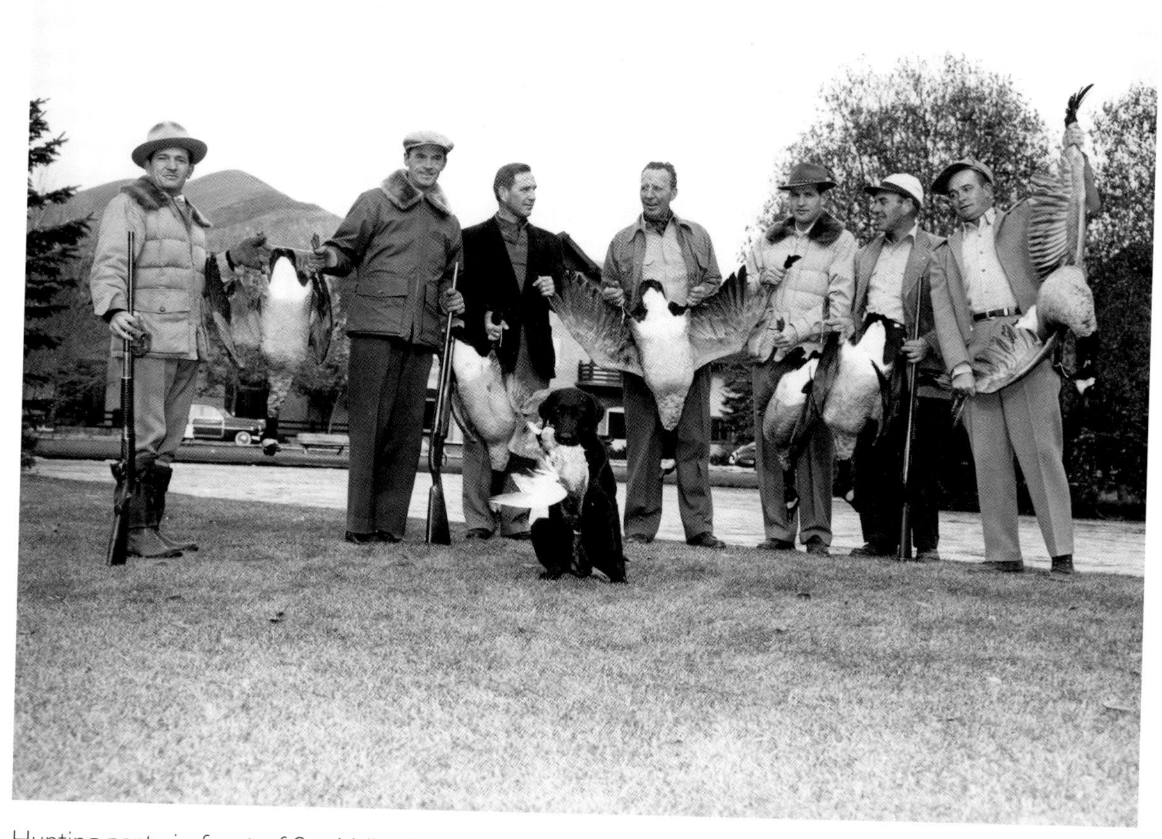

Hunting party in front of Sun Valley Lodge with Labrador retriever and game.

their tempers or patience need to be disciplined. Young, inexperienced instructors who let their classes get out of hand, lost, or left behind "drove pupils nuts." Accidents were common, and there was no excuse for allowing inexperienced people to teach skiing.

More communication was needed between the sports desk and ski school. "No one ever knew anything. For those who, like myself, wanted an afternoon of skiing, it was double bloody hell to find out where classes were being held. . . . The ski school (with certain notable exceptions) never reported to us about our young, nor sent them home, nor policed them; nor were they cooperative as to getting them into classes they could keep up with or were not too far ahead of. Friedel and Otto on this score were totally useless and altogether uninterested."[48]

17

1940

Bald Mountain Opening Begins a New Era in American Skiing; Durrance Wins His Third Harriman Cup

Sun Valley was known for two things in 1940. First, Bald Mountain was opened for general skiing. Second, Dick Durrance daringly (or foolishly) schussed the steilhang in the Harriman Cup downhill on Warm Springs, winning the race for the third time, for which he was awarded permanent possession of the cup, making him a skiing icon.

Bald Mountain was opened for general skiing in winter 1940. A series of three single chairlifts took skiers from the bottom at Riverside run (River Run) to the top of the 9,200 foot mountain, and new ski runs were cut, significantly expanding skiing at the resort. Bald Mountain became famous for its long cruising runs, according to Holland.

> *On Baldy, with good snow, skiers can feel at one with the soul of skiing. Each of its three canyons offers long, consistent vertical descents. The rounded summit leads down to open, undulating terrain with slopes swooping downward through glades and drainage—without long flat shoulders requiring poling, like so many other flagship mountains have.*

Only the River Run side was served by lifts, but Warm Springs was open for skiing down a narrow run through the trees, which was thinned and improved, and a bridge built over Warm Springs Creek. Skiers could ski down from the top of Baldy using three routes: down Warm Springs; down Ridge, Rock Garden, Canyon, and River

Run; and down the bowls, through Cold Springs Canyon to the highway. Buses picked up skiers at the bottom of Cold Springs and Warm Springs and brought them to River Run or the lodge.

Chair No. 1 loaded on the east side of the Big Wood River, so skiers traveled over the river on their way up the mountain. Chair No. 2, the Exhibition lift, took skiers to the Roundhouse where they could eat, warm up, and socialize. Chair No. 3 took skiers from the Roundhouse to the top of the mountain.

The Bald Mountain chairlifts opened up a number of excellent skiing areas, and the Roundhouse was the setting for social activities on Bald Mountain during the day and in the evenings.

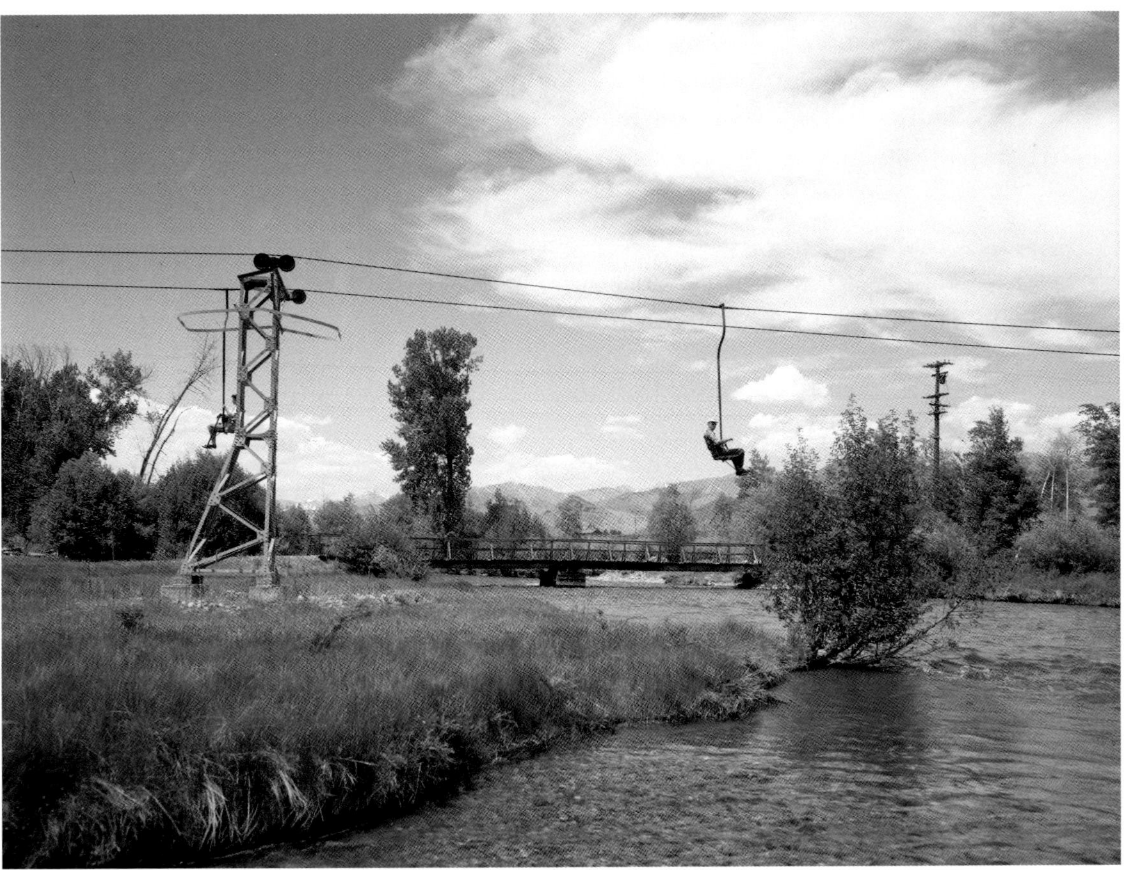

Baldy's Chair No. 1, looking south along the Big Wood River in the summer.

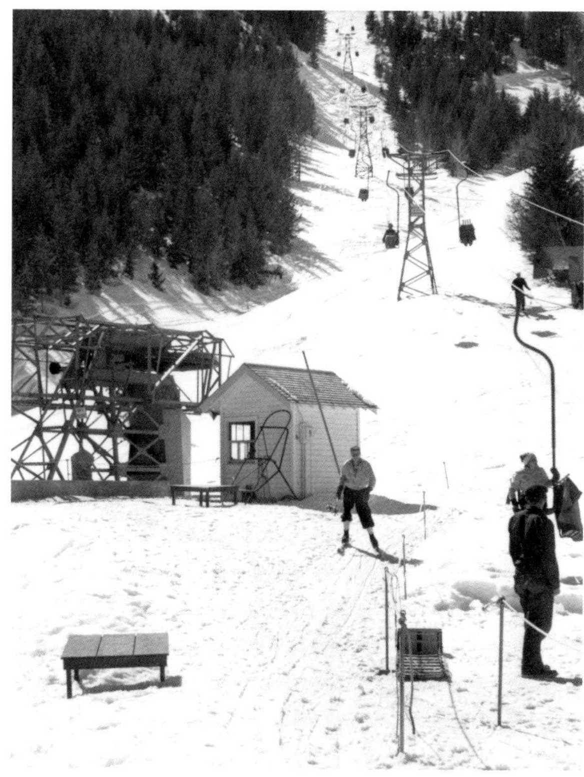

LEFT Baldy's Chair No. 2, Exhibition Lift, leading to the Roundhouse.

BELOW Top of Chair No. 2 and walk to the Roundhouse.

OPPOSITE View to Roundhouse from Chair No. 3, which took skiers to the summit.

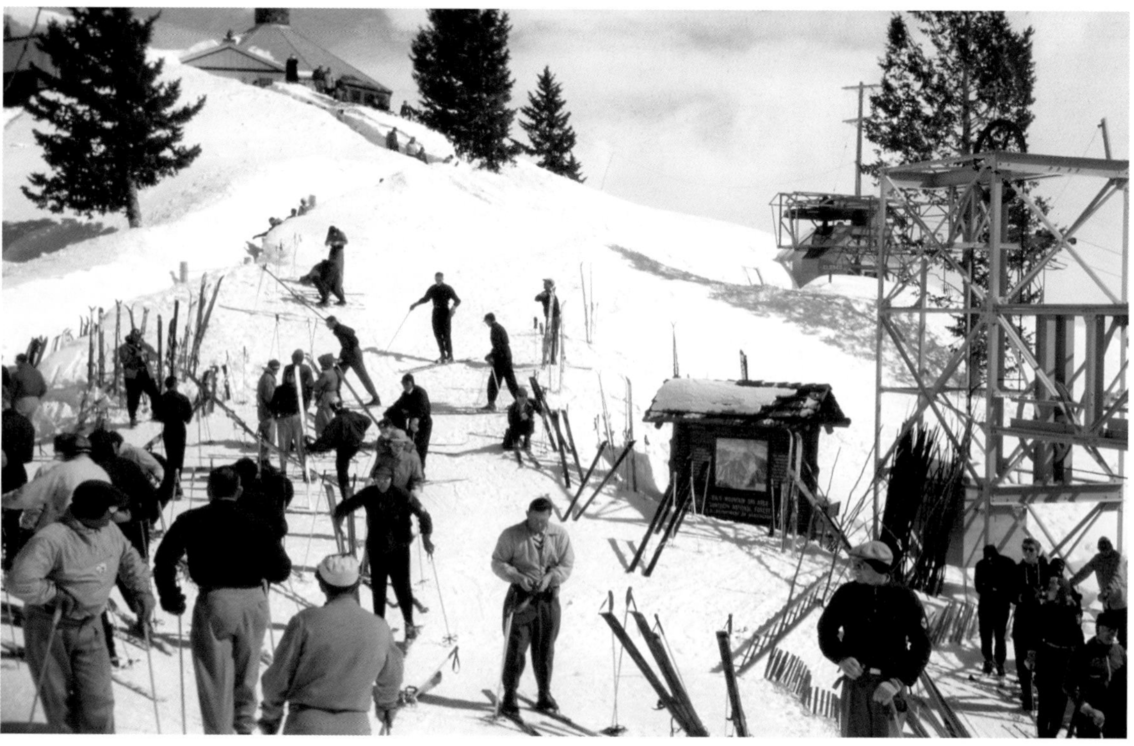

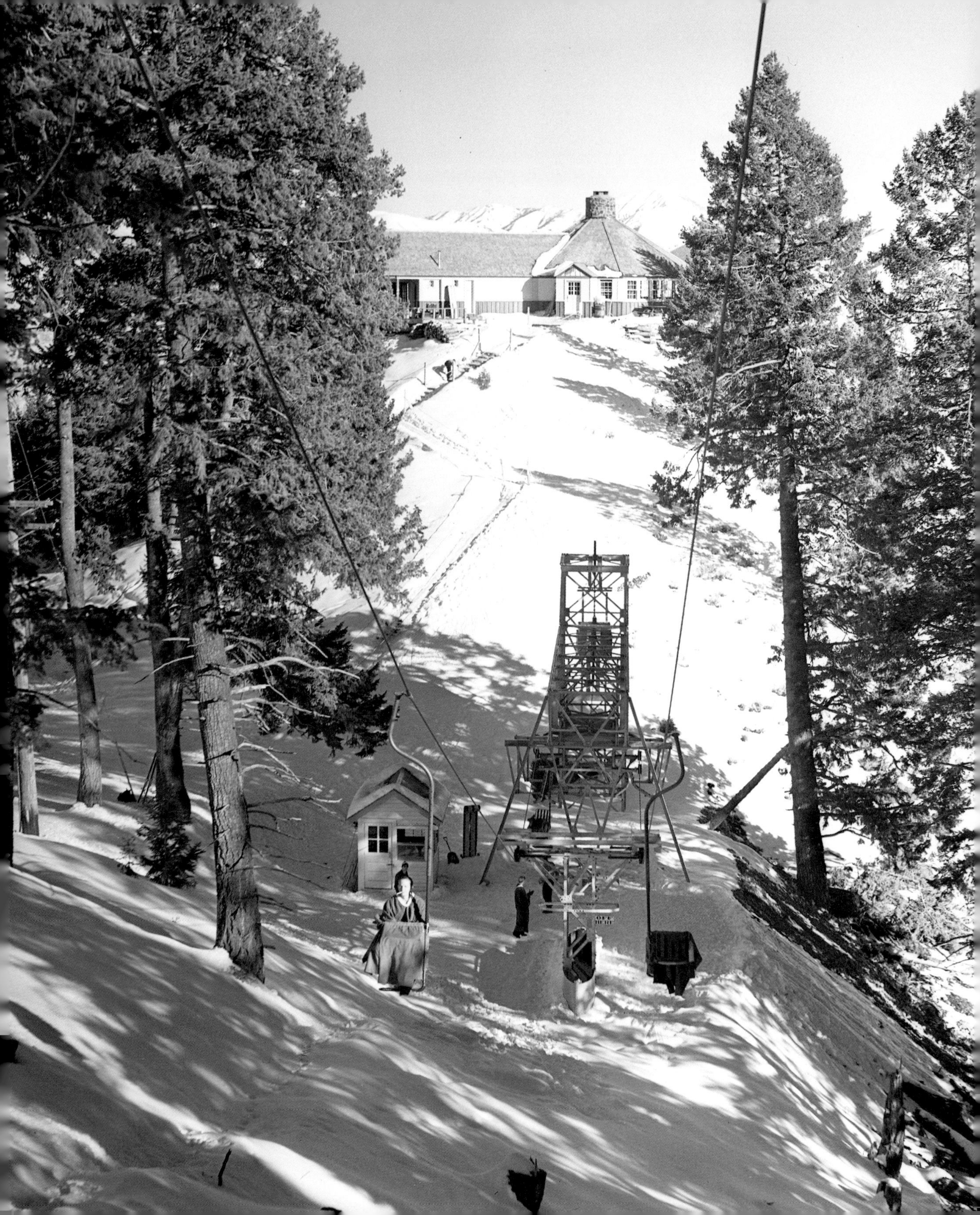

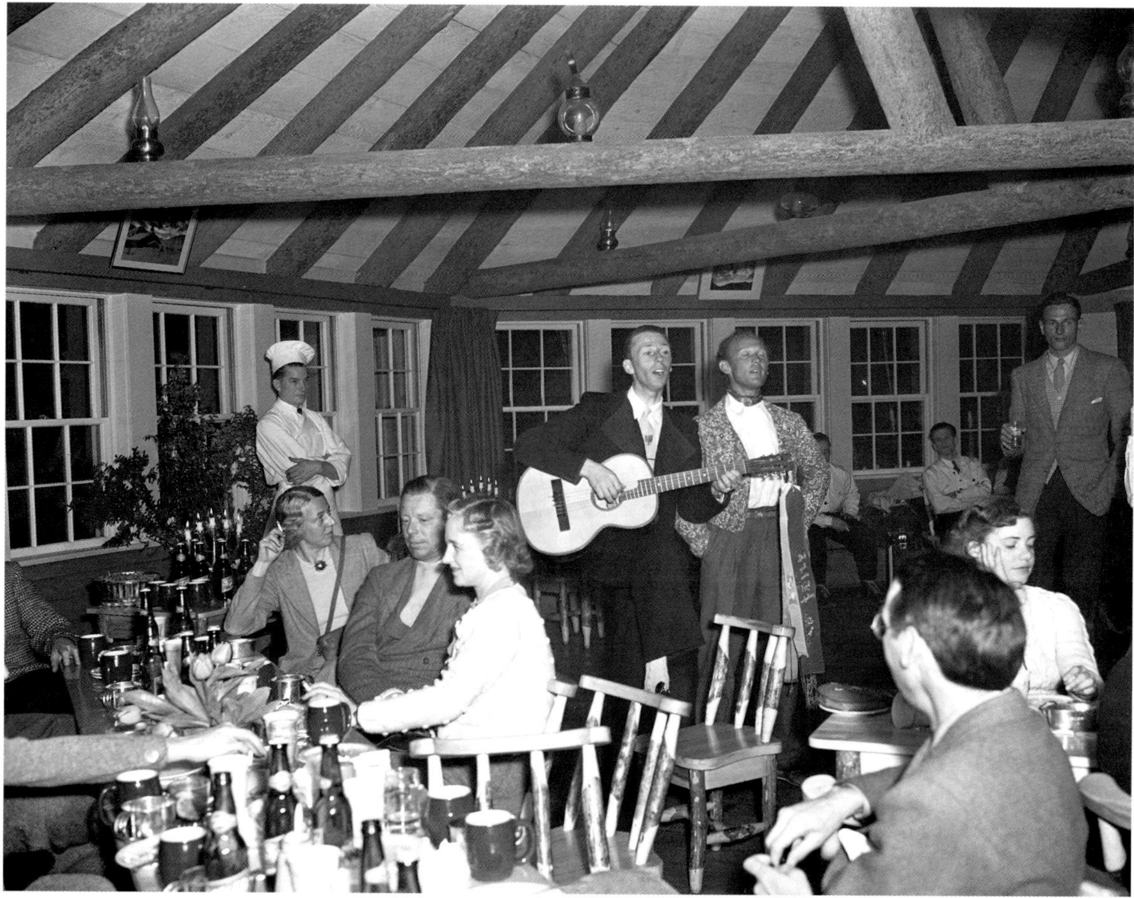

The Roundhouse could be rented for private parties where champagne often flowed freely. Sun Valley had to make sure all the revelers made it safely down the hill on the lift.

On March 10, 1940, the *Seattle Times* called Sun Valley the "ideal center of winter sports":

> *where there are unlimited miles of long, smooth mountain slopes not "obstacled" by timber or rocks, where the snow is always "powder" and never wet and crusted, where ski lifts take all the dirty work out of climbing. . . . All you do is sit down and go merrily to the top of the hill. No need to take off your skis.*

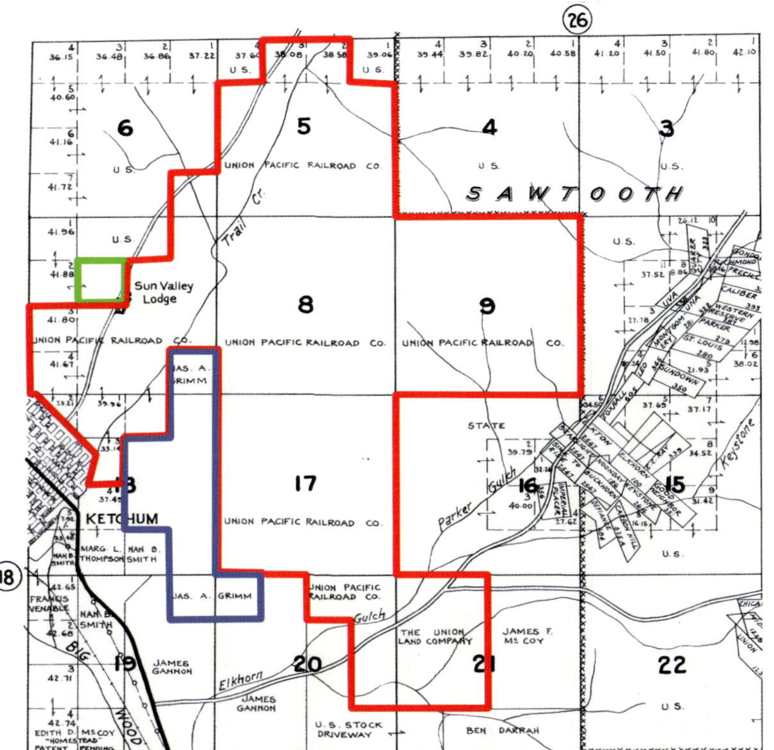

LEFT Union Pacific land purchases for Sun Valley in 1936, outlined in red and green. Grimm family land is outlined in blue, later acquired by Sun Valley.

BELOW Riding the new Dollar Mountain chair installed after World War II.

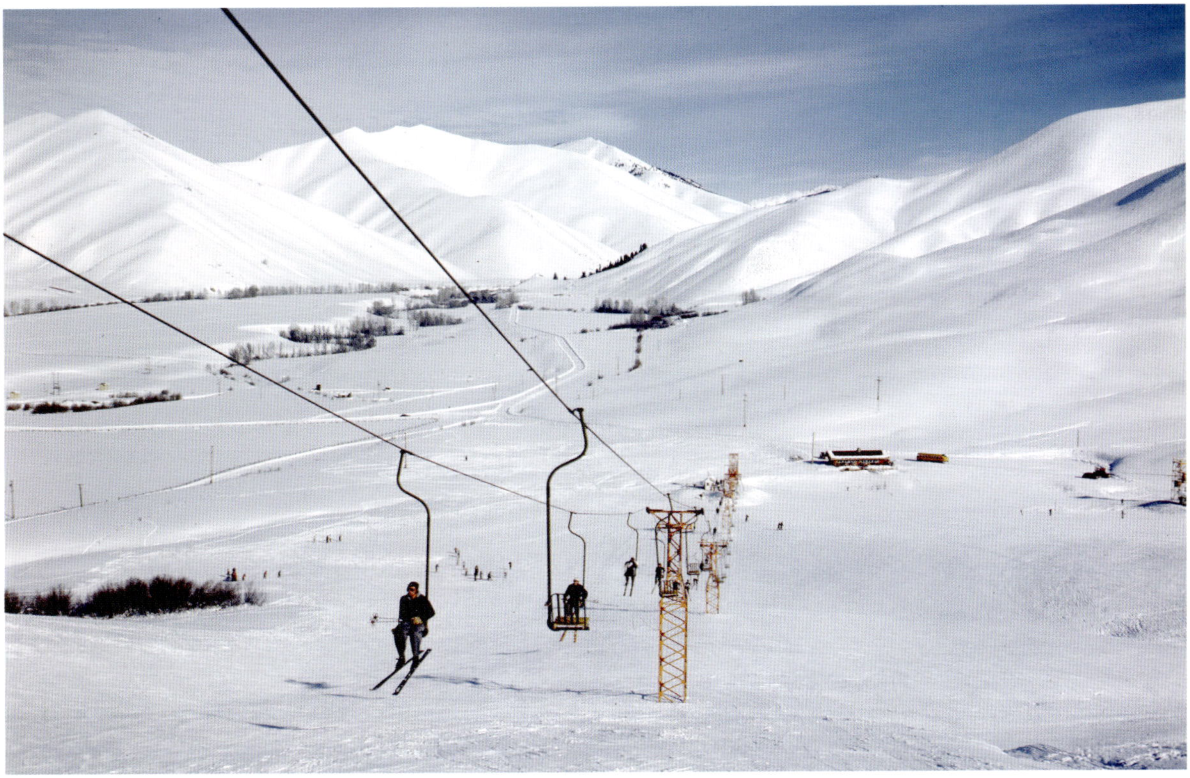

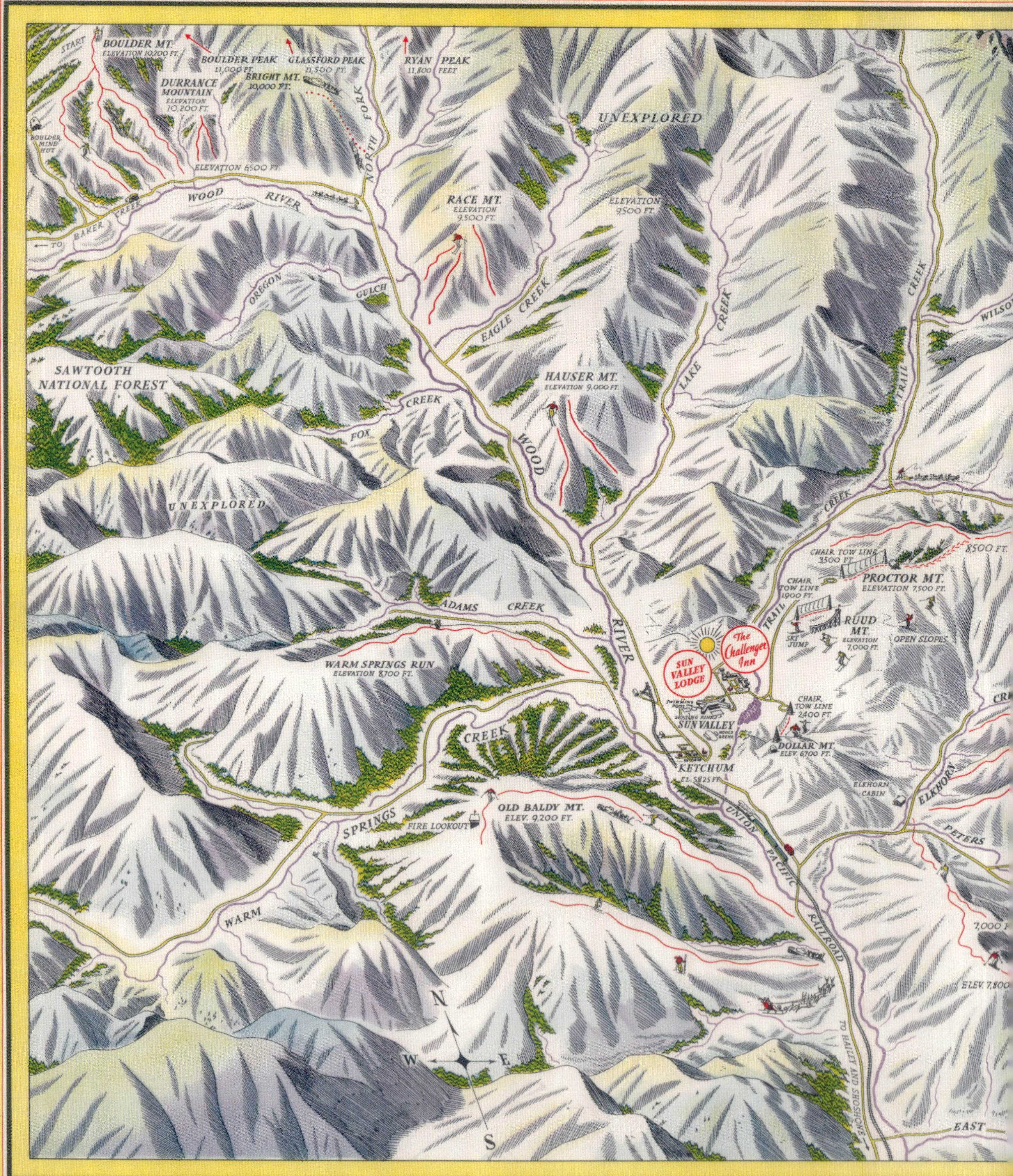

START
BOULDER MT.
ELEVATION 10,200 FT.
BOULDER PEAK
11,000 FT.
GLASSFORD PEAK
11,500 FT.
RYAN PEAK
11,800 FEET
DURRANCE MOUNTAIN
ELEVATION 10,200 FT.
BRIGHT MT.
10,000 FT.
NORTH FORK
UNEXPLORED
BOULDER MIND HUT
ELEVATION 6500 FT.
WOOD RIVER
BAKER CREEK
TO
RACE MT.
ELEVATION 9,500 FT.
ELEVATION 9500 FT.
OREGON GULCH
EAGLE CREEK
LAKE CREEK
TRAIL CREEK
WILSON
SAWTOOTH NATIONAL FOREST
HAUSER MT.
ELEVATION 9,000 FT.
FOX CREEK
WOOD RIVER
UNEXPLORED
CHAIR TOW LINE 3500 FT.
8500 FT.
CHAIR TOW LINE 1900 FT.
PROCTOR MT.
ELEVATION 7,500 FT.
ADAMS CREEK
RUUD MT.
ELEVATION 7,000 FT.
SKI JUMP
OPEN SLOPES
The Challenger Inn
SUN VALLEY LODGE
WARM SPRINGS RUN
ELEVATION 8,700 FT.
CHAIR TOW LINE 2400 FT.
SUN VALLEY
DOLLAR MT.
ELEV. 6,700 FT.
CREEK
KETCHUM
EL. 5825 FT.
ELKHORN CABIN
ELKHORN
OLD BALDY MT.
ELEV. 9,200 FT.
FIRE LOOKOUT
SPRINGS
UNION PACIFIC RAILROAD
PETERS
WARM
7,000 FT.
ELEV. 7,800
N
W
E
S
TO HAILEY AND SHOSHONE
EAST

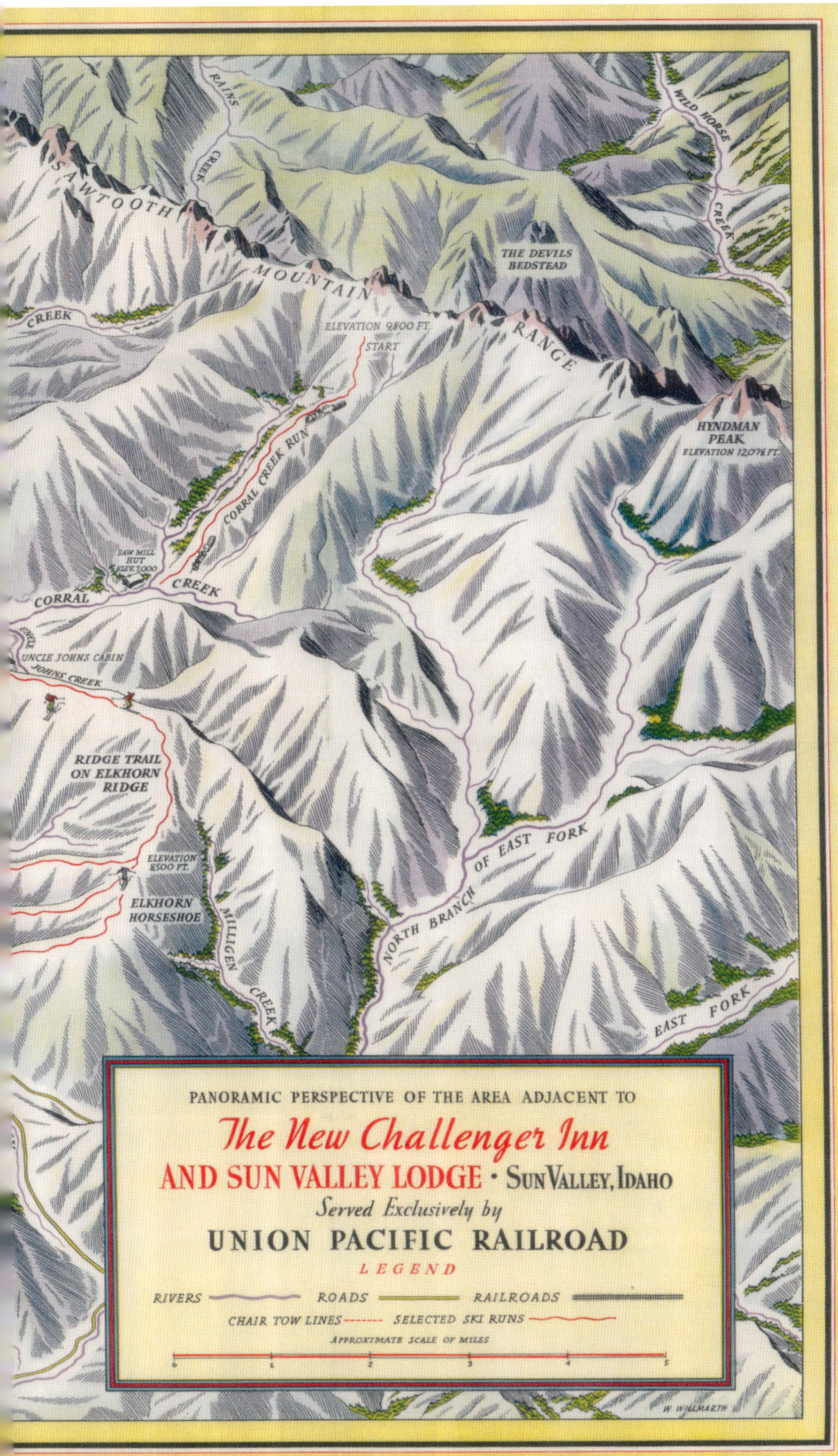

1938 Sun Valley map showing northwest of the resort backcountry skiing locations.

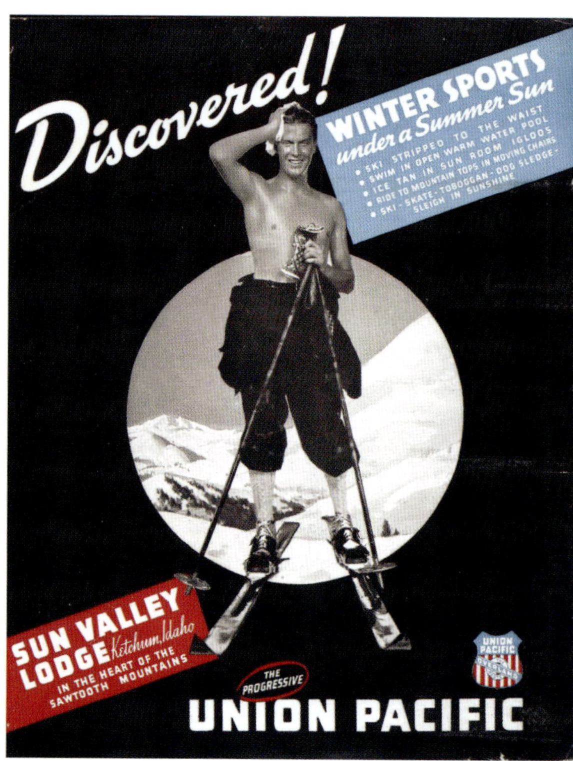

LEFT Poster showing Steve Hannagan's promotional theme, "Winter Sports under a Summer Sun." *Courtesy of Union Pacific Museum.*

BELOW Buses line up in front of the ski school assembly area to take skiers to their lessons.

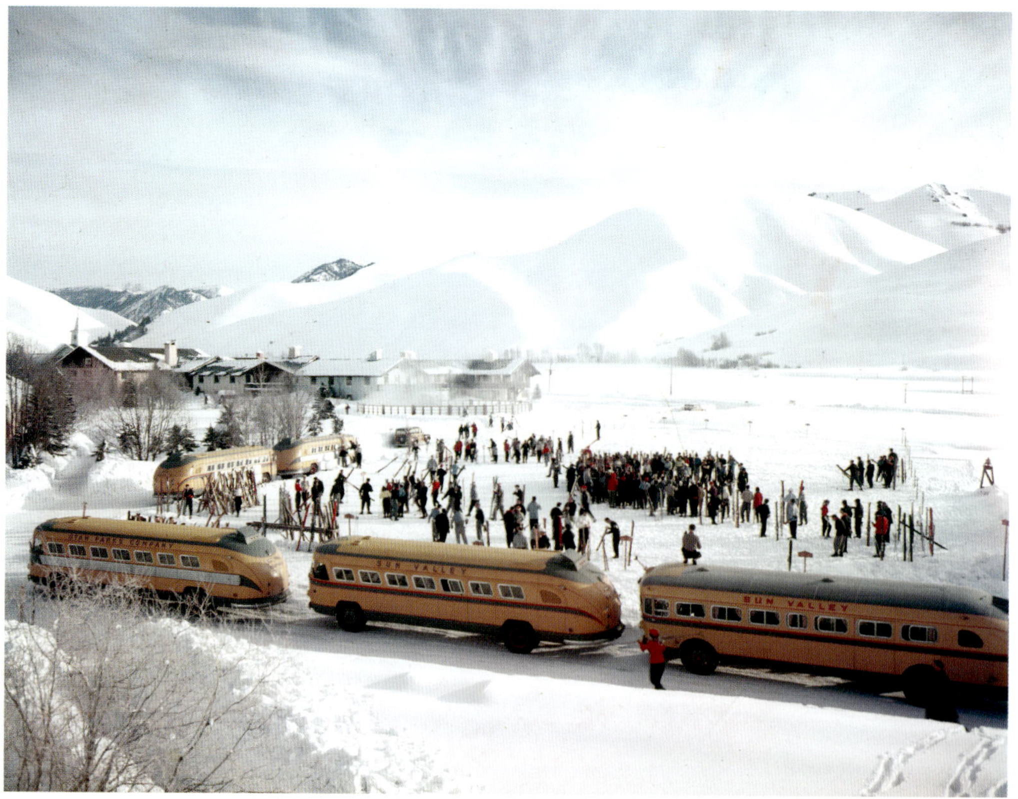

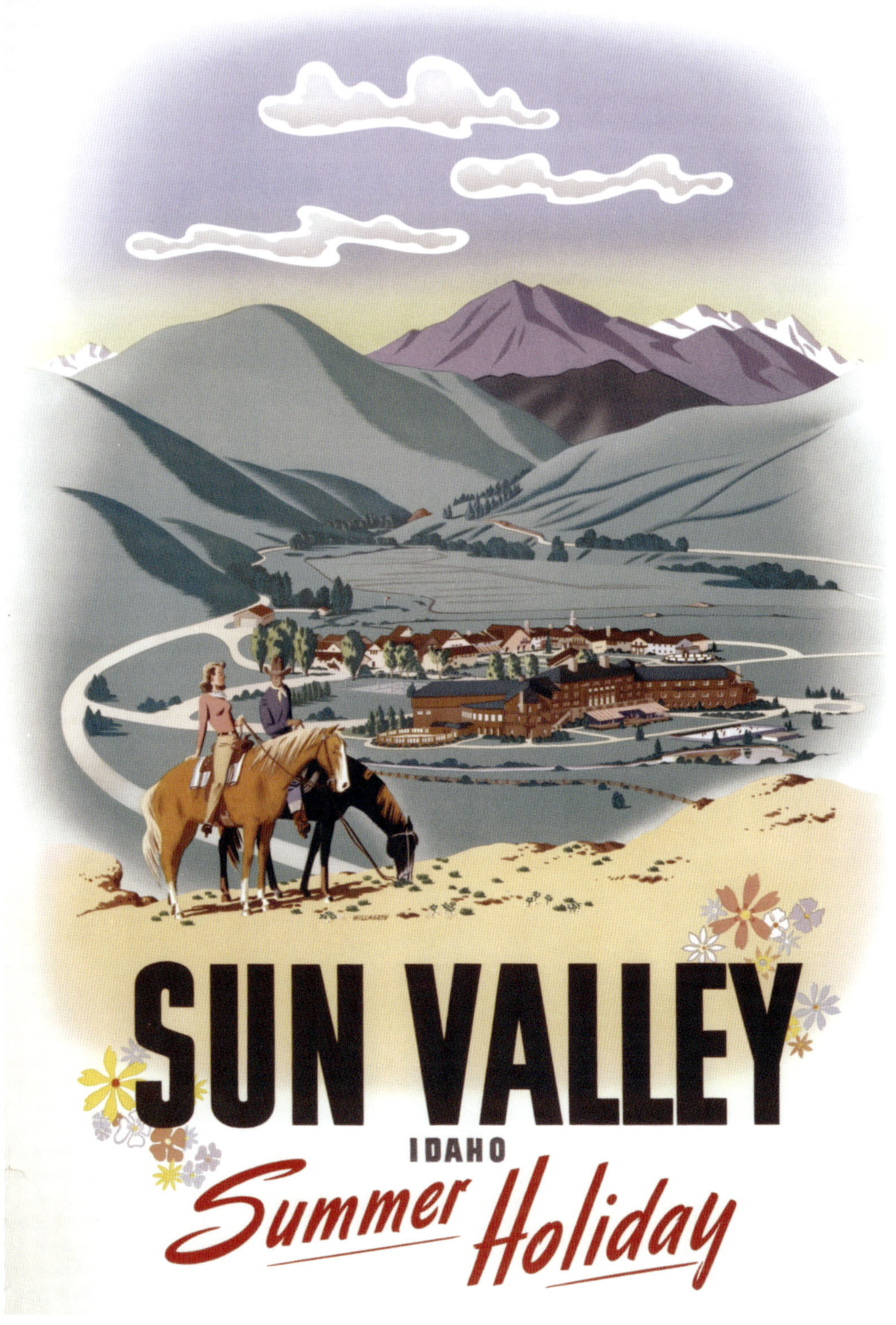

Poster for Sun Valley summer activities. Union Pacific produced many such posters with different themes. *Courtesy of Union Pacific Museum.*

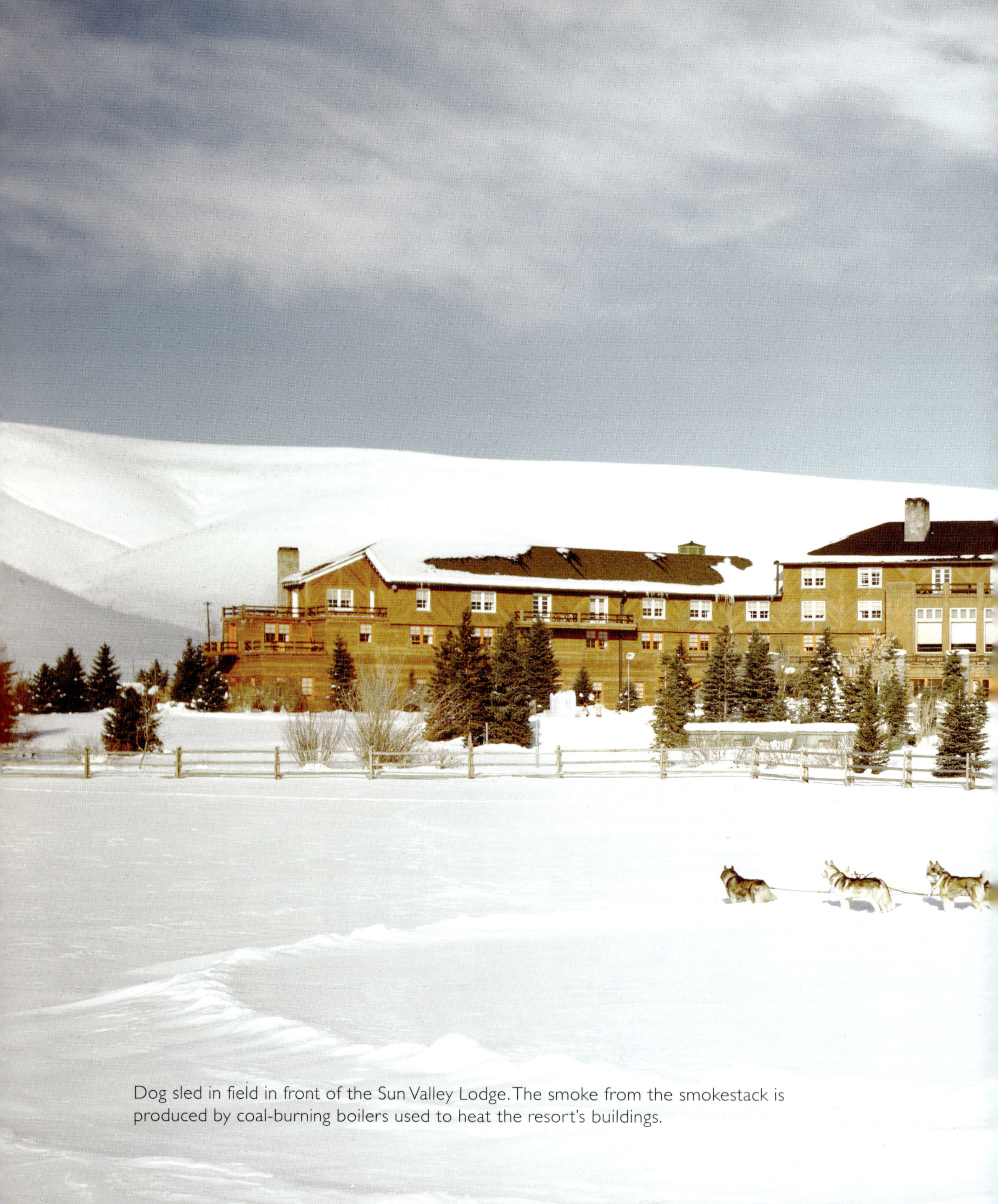

Dog sled in field in front of the Sun Valley Lodge. The smoke from the smokestack is produced by coal-burning boilers used to heat the resort's buildings.

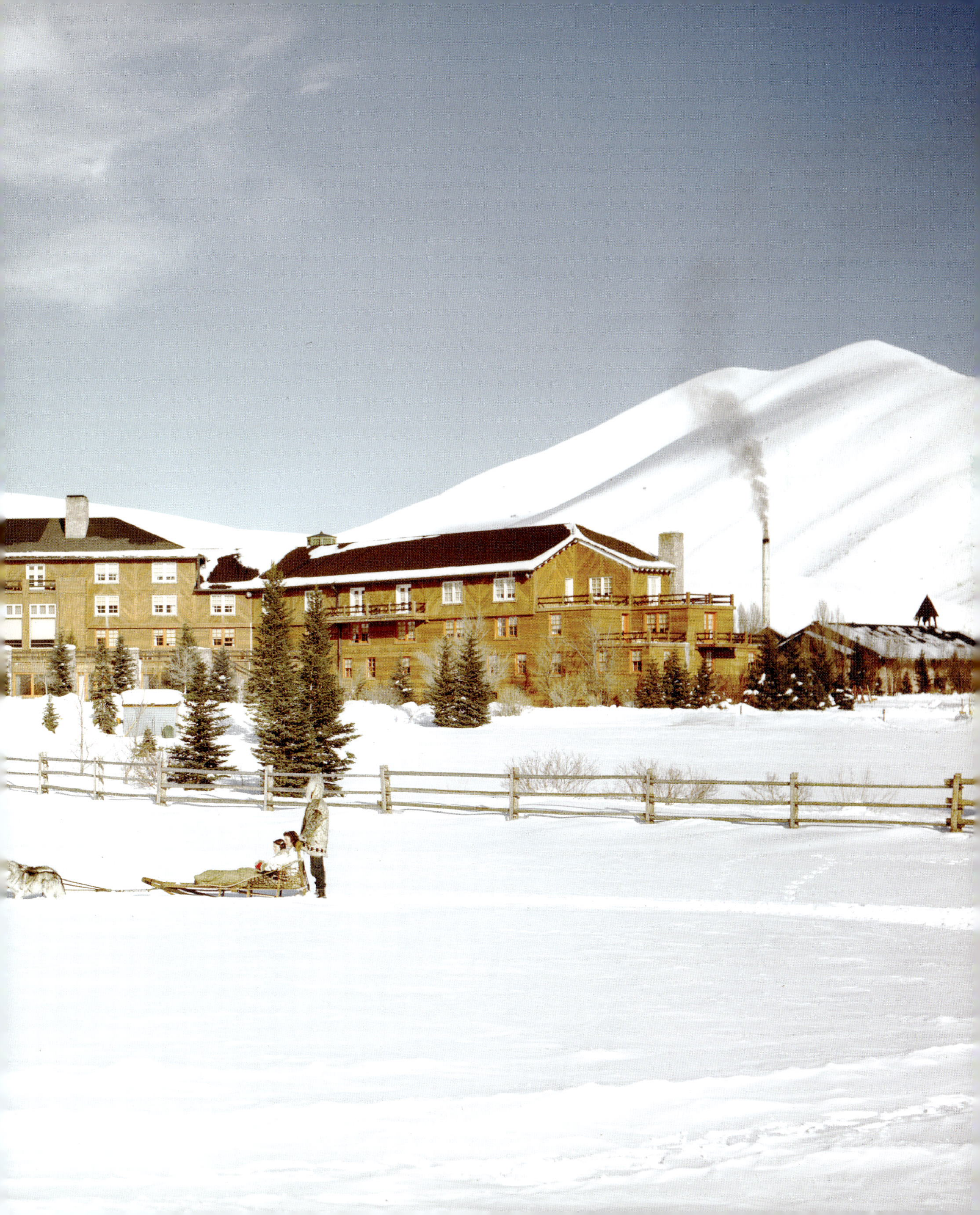

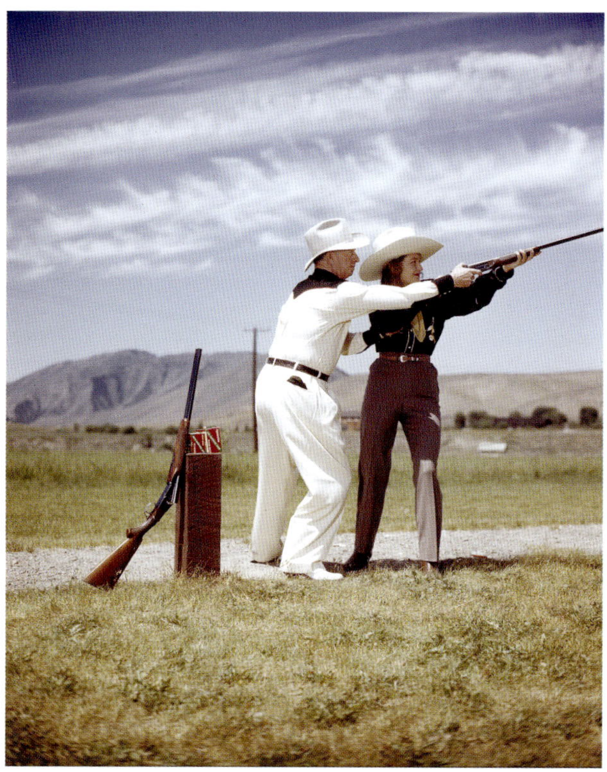

LEFT Shooting lessons at Sun Valley. The shooting range was located in Elkhorn and was directed by Joe Burgy.

BELOW Summer ice skating at Sun Valley.

OPPOSITE, TOP Students learning the kick turn.

OPPOSITE, BOTTOM Learning the Christiania turn. "Bend ze knees."

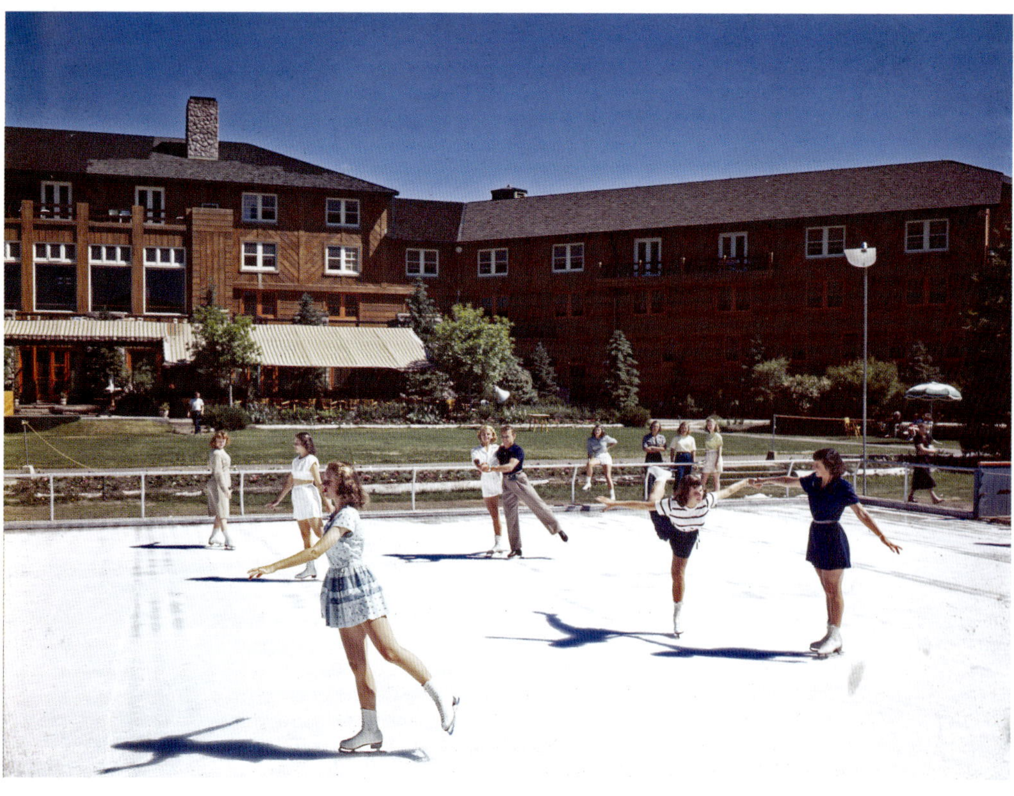

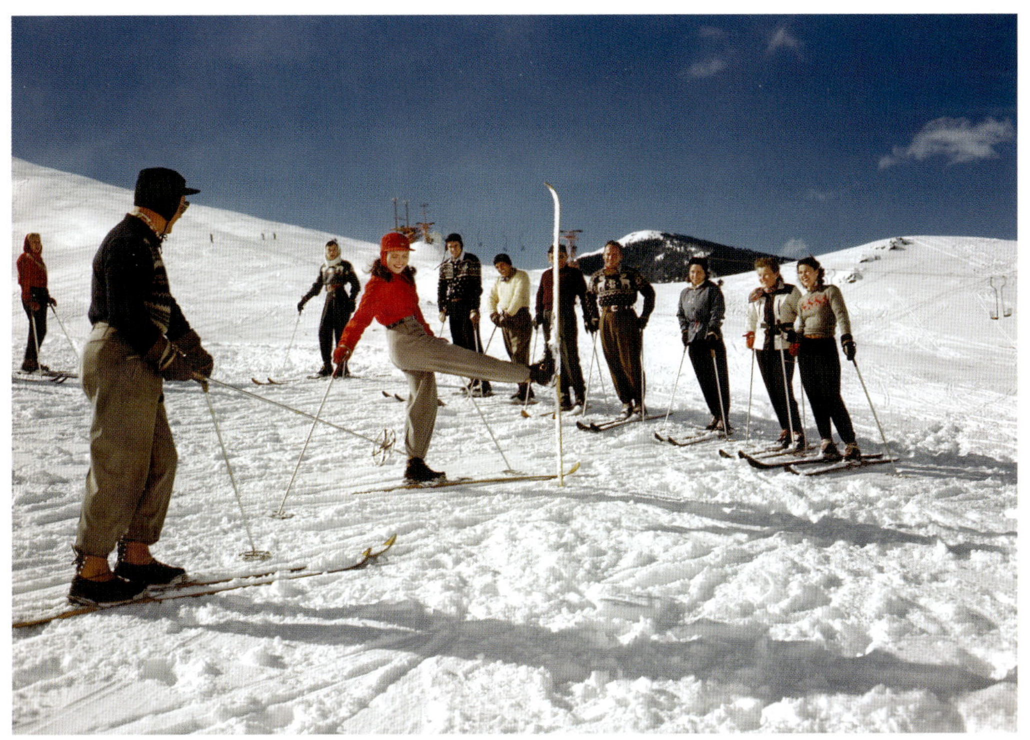

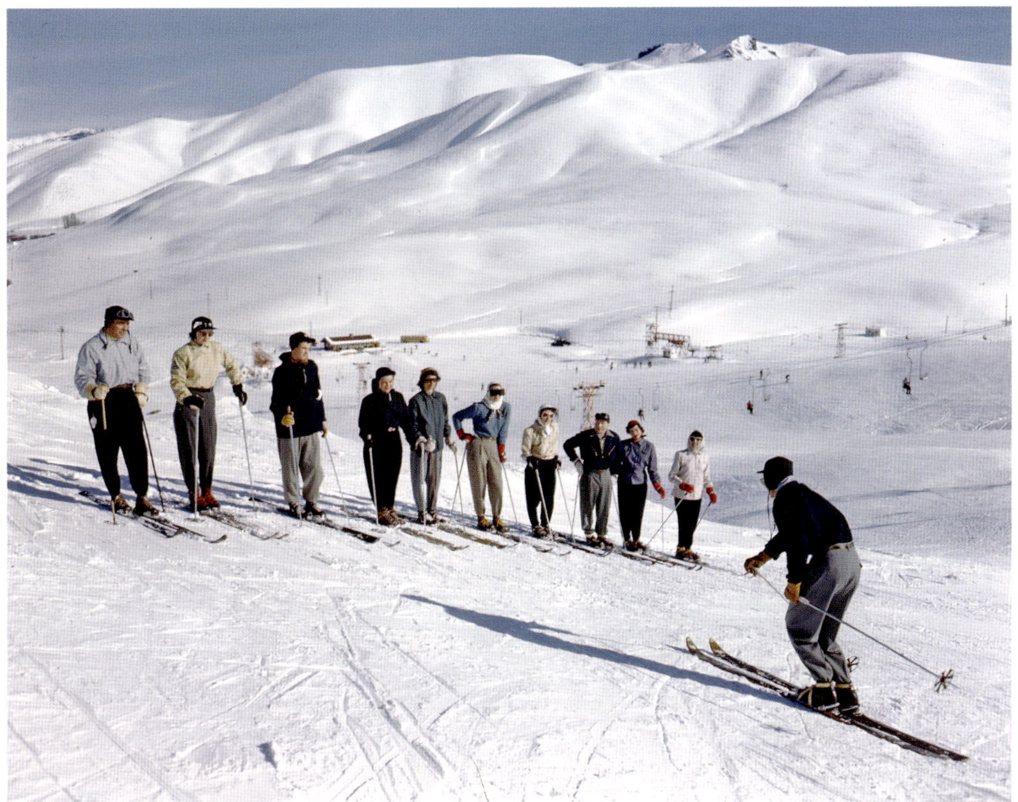

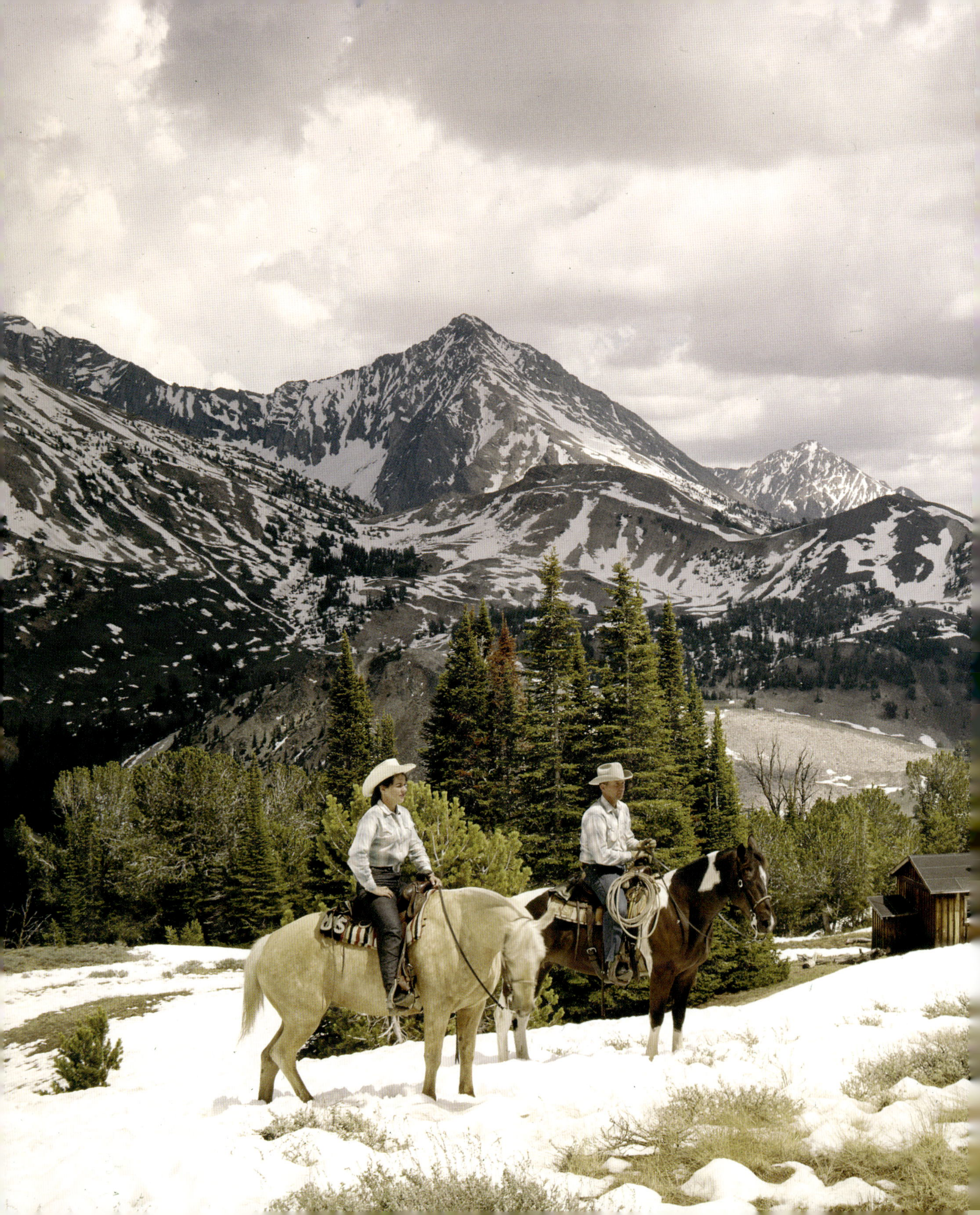

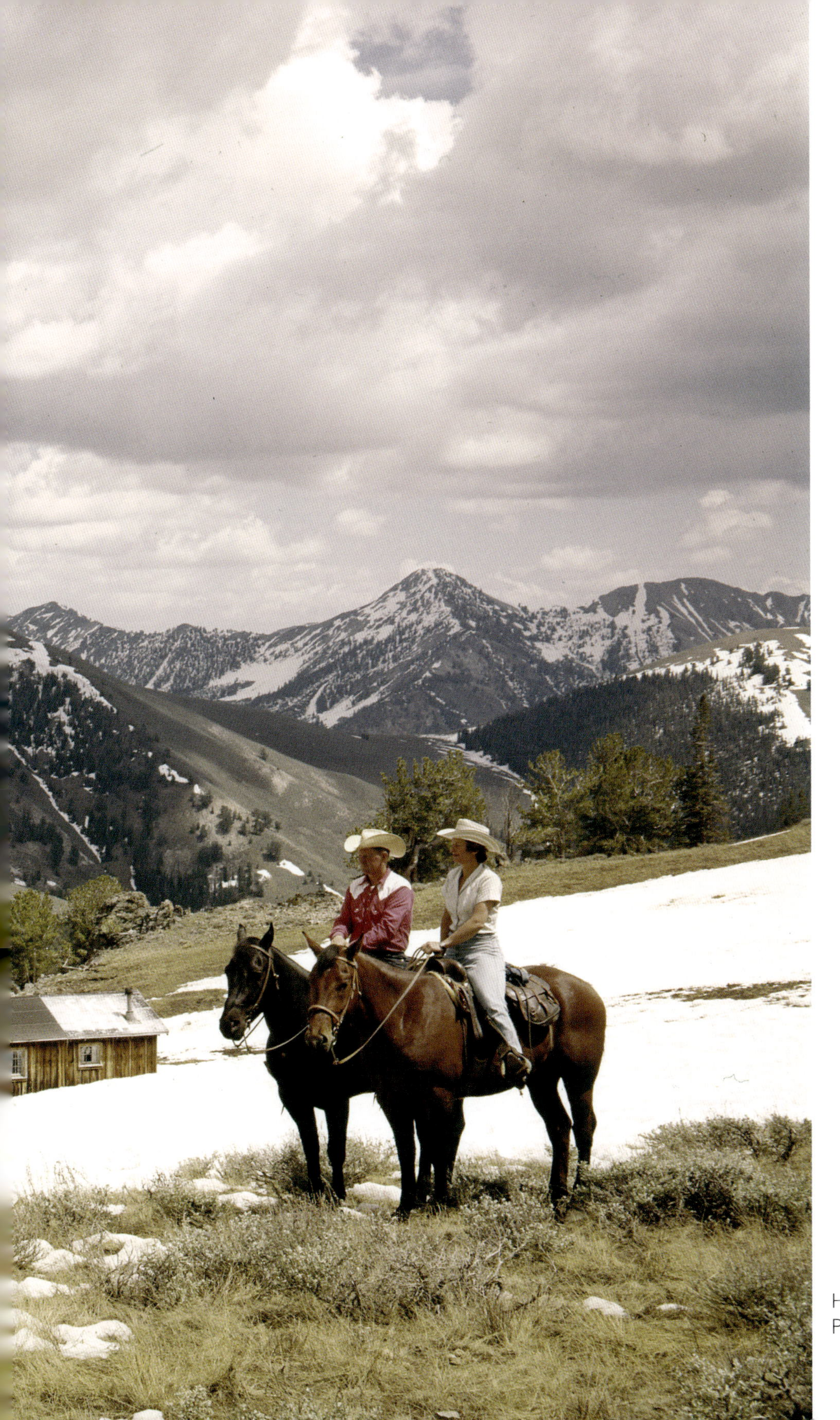

Horseback riding at
Pioneer cabin in the summer.

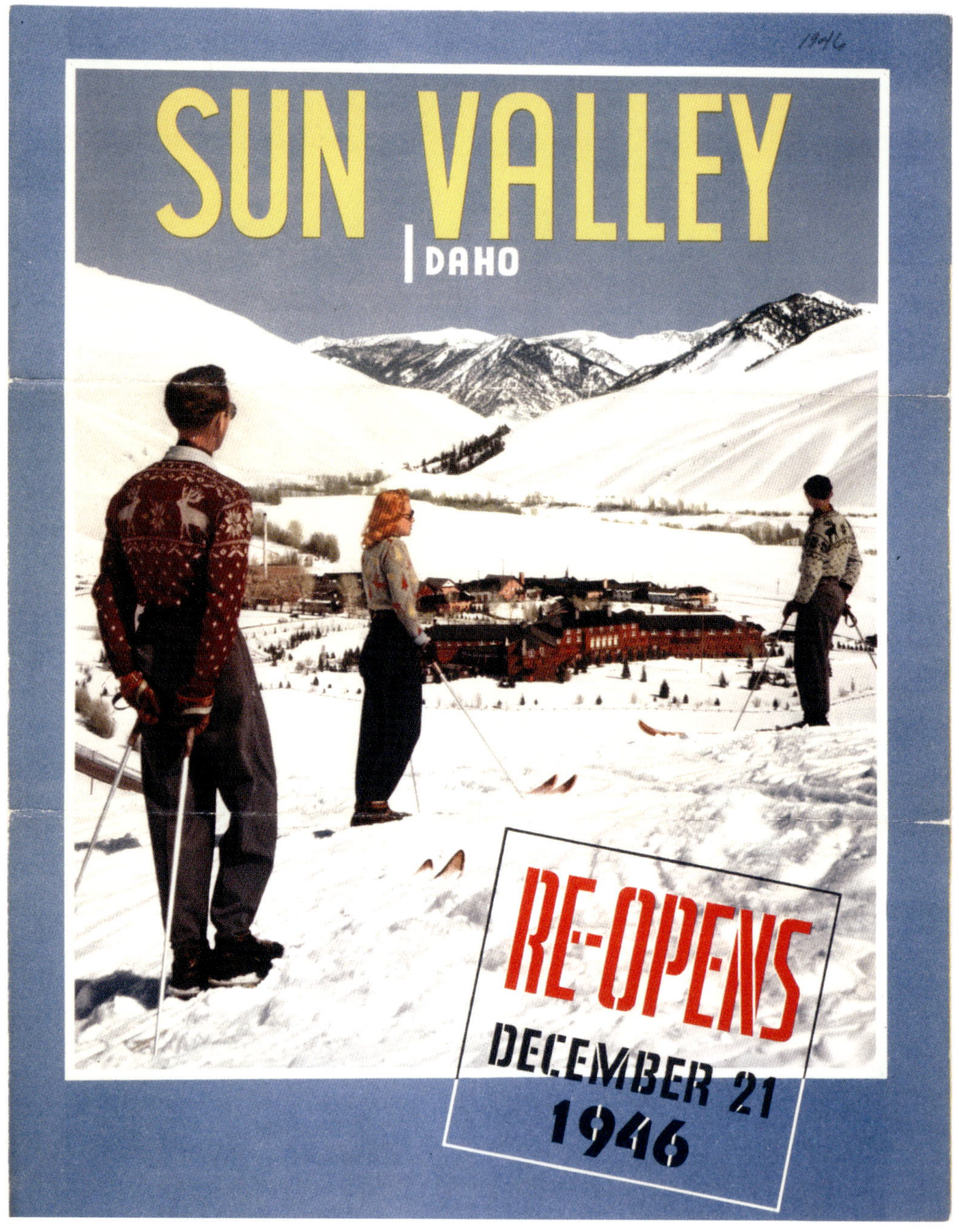

ABOVE Poster announcing Sun Valley's reopening after World War II on December 21, 1946. *Courtesy of Union Pacific Museum.*

OPPOSITE, TOP Aerial view of new Dollar Mountain chairlifts, 1949.

OPPOSITE, BOTTOM New Dollar Cabin at bottom of mountain.

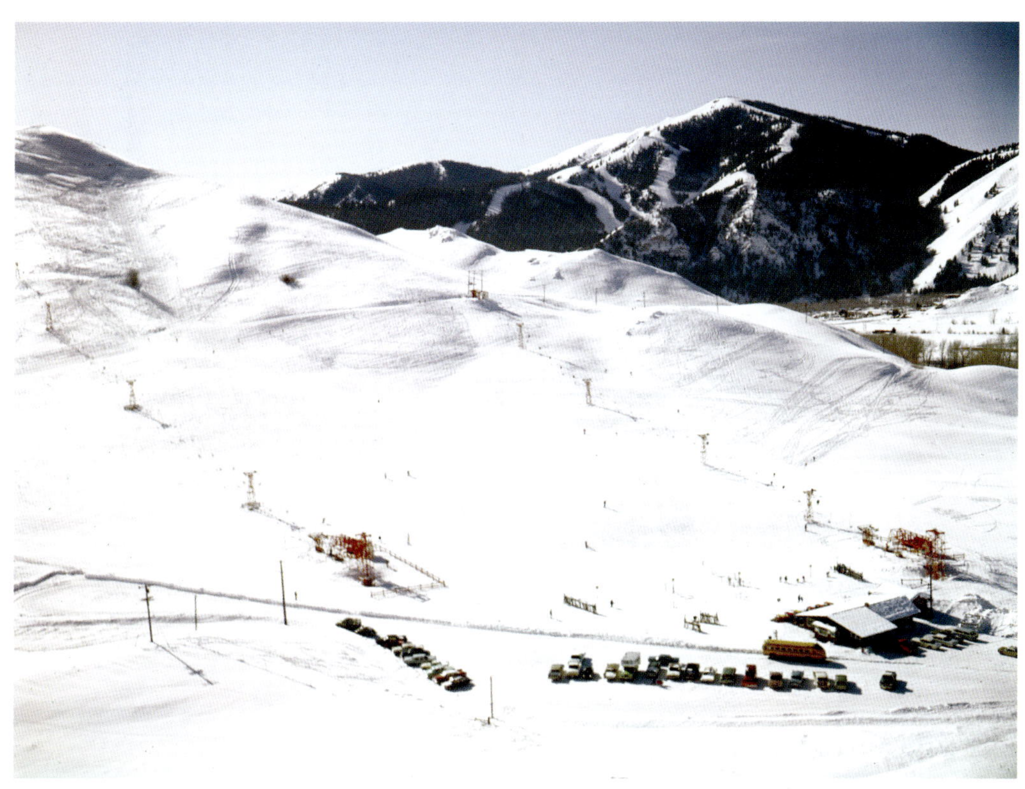

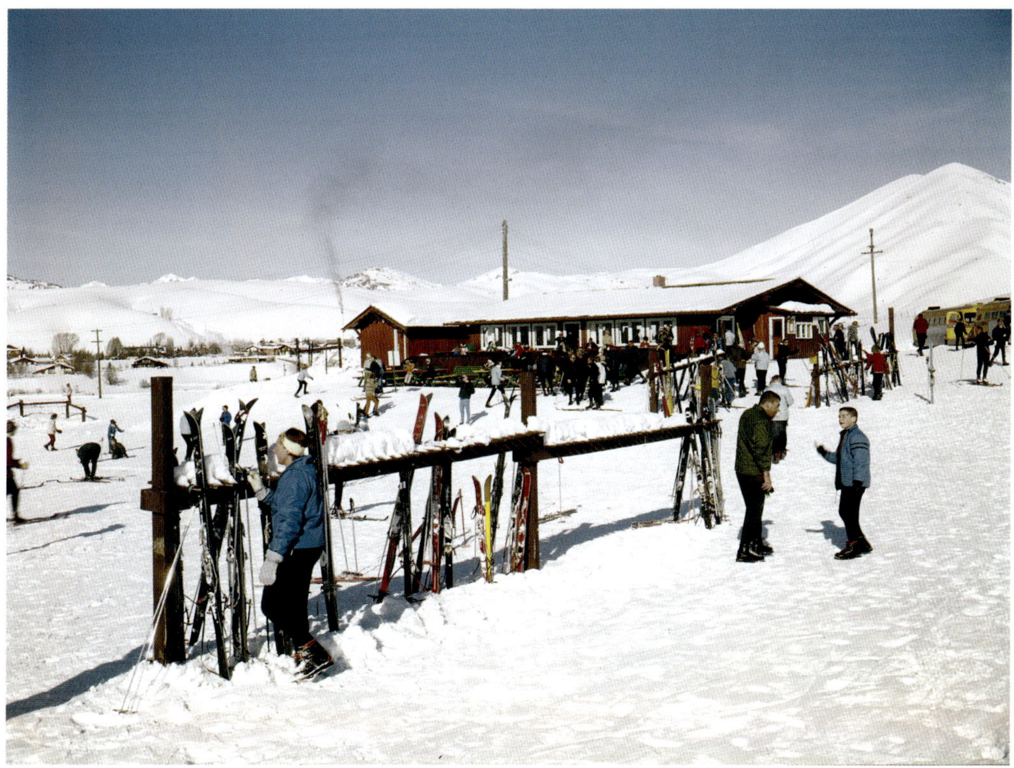

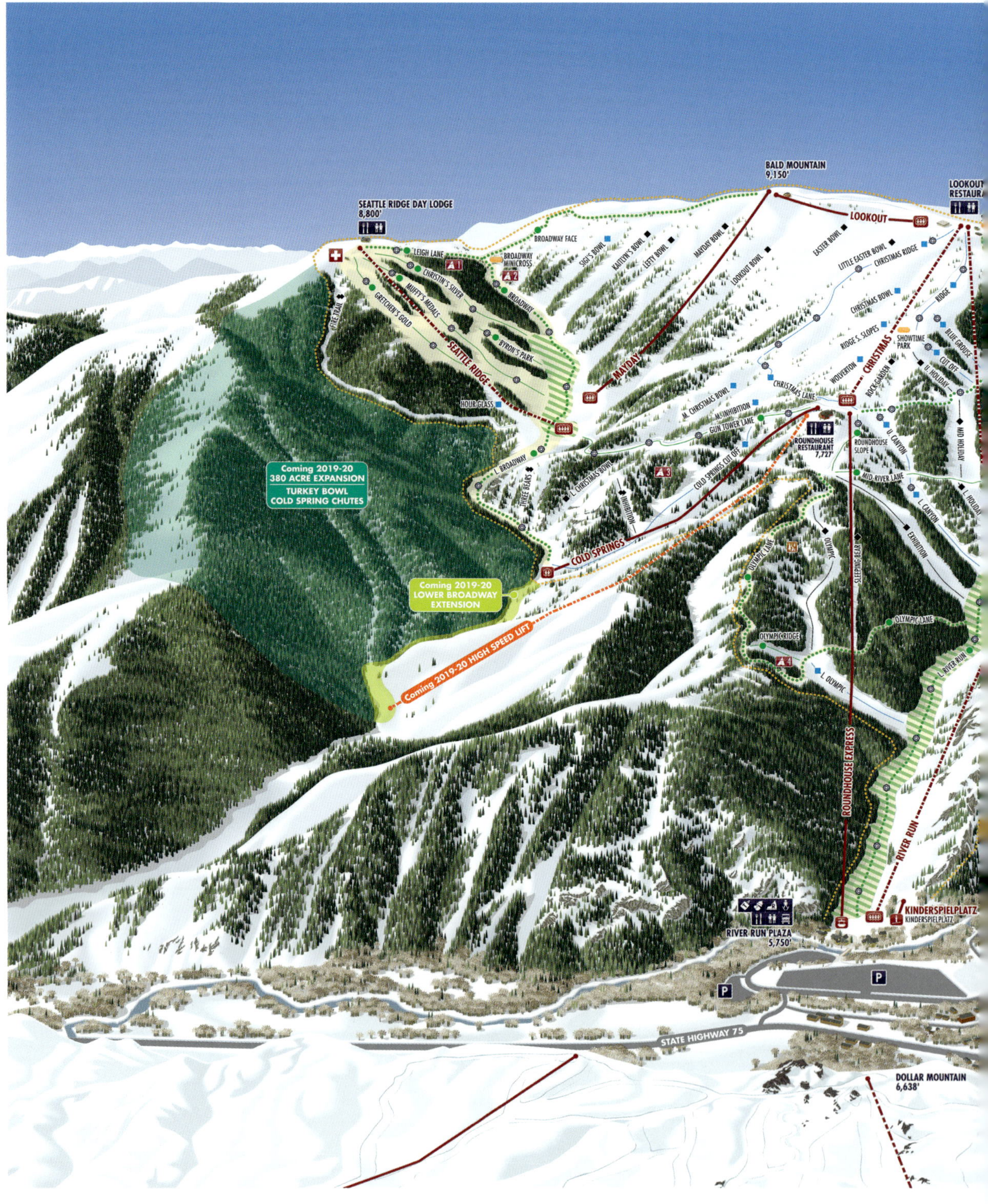

Bald Mountain trail map, 2019. *Courtesy of the Sun Valley Company.*

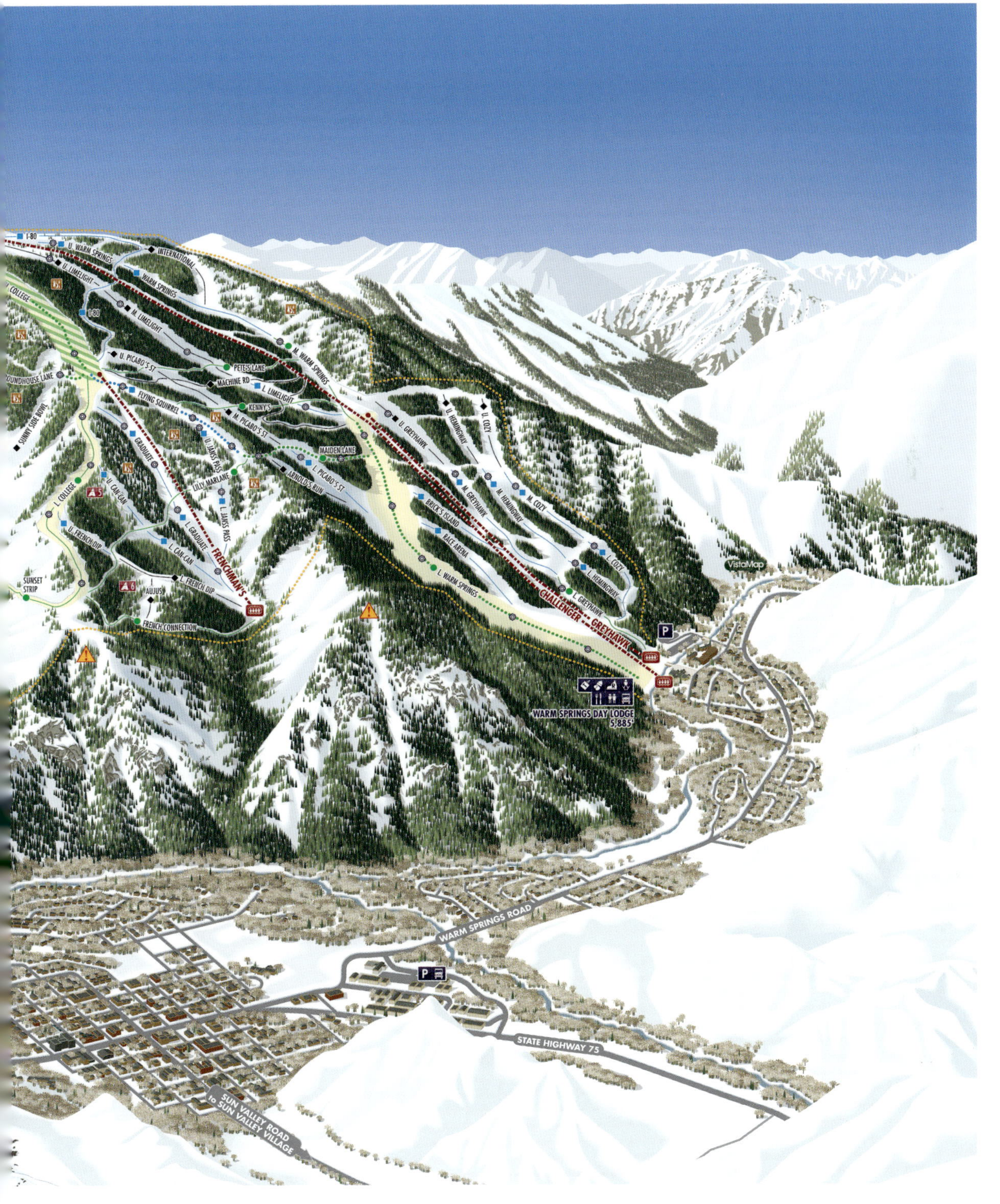

I-80
U. WARM SPRINGS
U. LIMELIGHT
INTERNATIONAL
WARM SPRINGS
COLLEGE
M. LIMELIGHT
M. WARM SPRINGS
U. PICABO'S ST
PETES LANE
ROUNDHOUSE LANE
MACHINE RD
L. LIMELIGHT
FLYING SQUIRREL
KENNY'S
M. PICABO'S ST
SUNNY SIDE BOWL
GRADUATE
U. JANSS PASS
MAIDEN LANE
L. PICABO'S ST
ARNOLD'S RUN
LILLY MARLANE
L. JANSS PASS
U. CAN-CAN
L. COLLEGE
U. FRENCH DIP
L. GRADUATE
L. CAN-CAN
FRENCHMAN'S
SUNSET STRIP
L. FRENCH DIP
AUJUS
FRENCH CONNECTION
U. HEMINGWAY
U. COZY
U. GREYHAWK
M. GREYHAWK
M. HEMINGWAY
M. COZY
BRICK'S ISLAND
RACE ARENA
L. WARM SPRINGS
L. COZY
L. HEMINGWAY
L. GREYHAWK
CHALLENGER
GREYHAWK
VistaMap
P
WARM SPRINGS DAY LODGE
5,885'
WARM SPRINGS ROAD
P
STATE HIGHWAY 75
SUN VALLEY ROAD
to SUN VALLEY VILLAGE

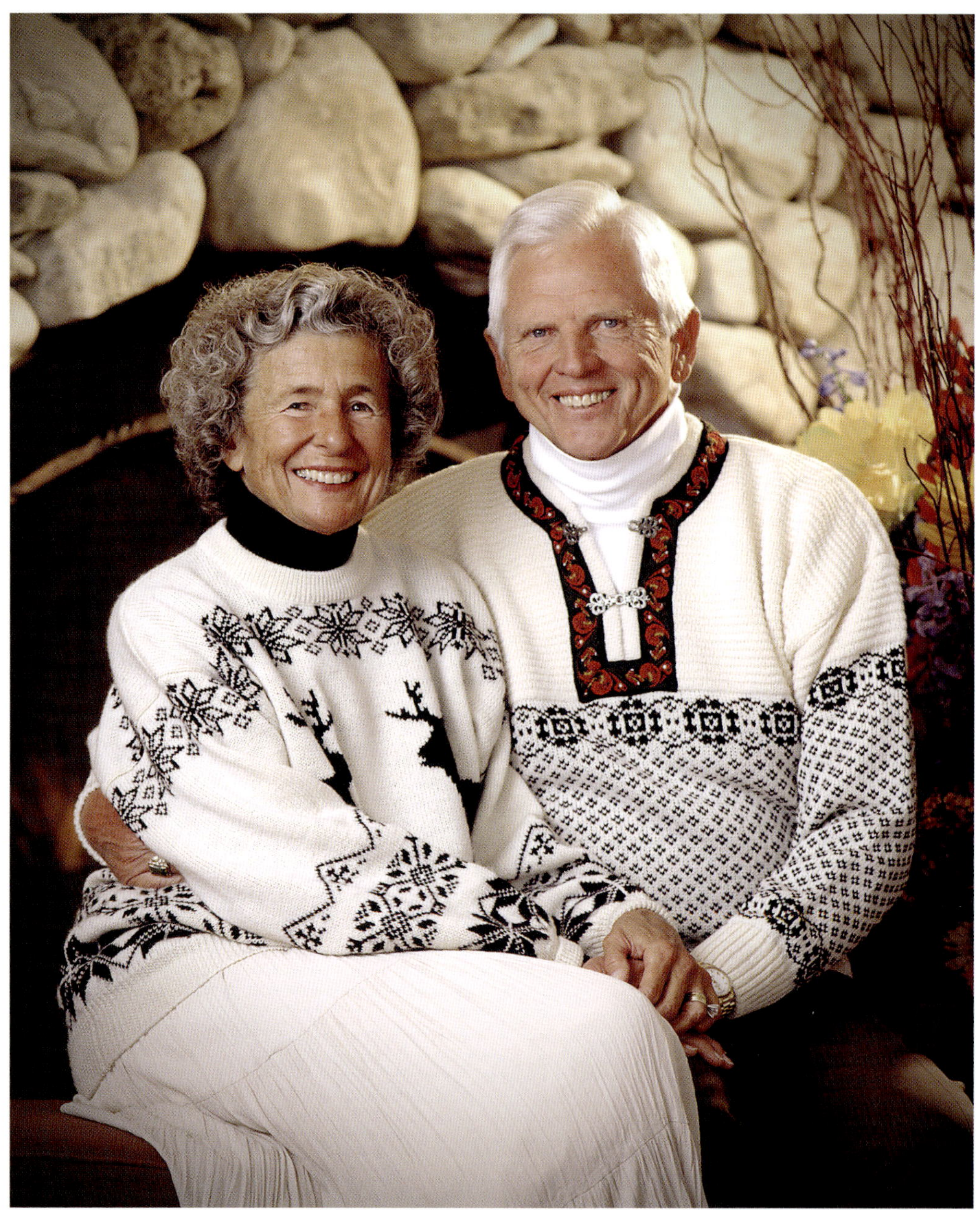

Earl and Carol Holding. *Courtesy of the Sun Valley Company.*

The paper also praised Sun Valley's "usually mild" climate. "Life at Sun Valley is leisurely and comfortable as well as gay and continental," it wrote, with "the choicest of foods from jumbo crabs from Portland; trout from cold mountain streams; and succulent vegetables from the Imperial Valley."

The *New York Times* of March 21, 1940, called Sun Valley a "skiers' paradise" that

> *compares favorably with the best the continent has to offer in trail and slope running. . . . Mile after mile of timberless terrain, four chair-lifts that make skiing all downhill and fields of all degrees of descents and constant sunshine make this mountain resort the only one of its kind in North America. . . . With the completion of the gigantic ski lift on Baldy Mountain . . . an enormous ski area with a wide variety of runs for all skiers has been opened. . . . Besides its tremendous lift, probably the largest in the world, it is the locale of the championship Warm Springs Run, Sunnyside Run, Ridge Trail and unlimited open slopes. One can ski down any side of the mountain.*

Two skiers in powder on Baldy.

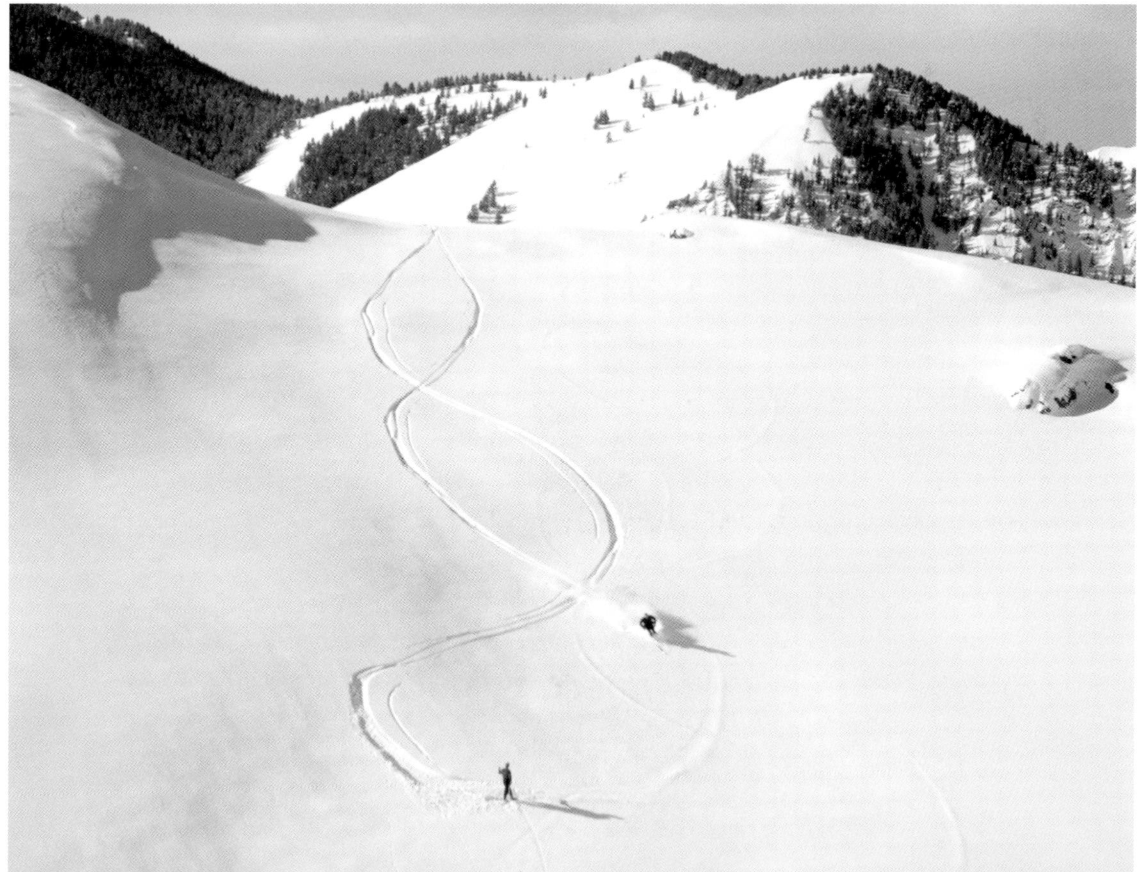

Union Pacific provided train service to Sun Valley from Seattle. Skiers could leave Seattle for Portland at 1:00 p.m., 4:40 p.m., or 11:30 p.m. daily to catch eastbound trains. The 4:40 p.m. connected to the Portland Rose leaving Portland daily at 9:35 a.m., heading east for Chicago (arriving at 8:30 a.m. the third day after leaving). Meals cost 90¢ per day. Passengers were dropped off at Shoshone for a ride on the Wood River Branch to Ketchum, or taken by bus directly to Sun Valley.

A big snowstorm hit Sun Valley on December 23, 1939, so early skiing was possible for the first time, according to Friedl Pfeifer. "Just before Christmas, Baldy Mountain opened to rave reviews in the press and from the public. It was the first world-class resort on the continent and people flocked to see it and ski it." The war in Europe shut down many ski resorts, "so affluent Americans who would have skied the Alps, joined main-stream skiers and skied in Idaho." As a result, the ski school "was put to the test," Pfeifer said. He doubled the number of instructors, with

> *the largest gathering of experienced racers and instructors outside of Europe working for him in his ski school. . . . Ski classes were packed. The resort seemed to be riding a perpetual rising curve. . . . From the day Baldy opened, almost every guest at the resort took ski lessons. The focus of the ski school had changed from how to have a good time to how to ski better, and have a good time. Everyone received equal attention as the on-hill courting of students dissipated. . . . It was part of the magic of the resort and the sport.*

Entire classes came back to ski with the same instructors. Pfeifer arranged for ski weeks, packages including lodging, skis, lift tickets, and lessons at a low set price, bringing in as many skiers in January as were there during Christmas. One-week packages cost $90, which included meals, six days of ski lessons, unlimited use of ski lifts, dancing, and other evening entertainment, or $60 without meals.

In February 1940, Averell Harriman celebrated his 10th wedding anniversary by hosting a surprise dinner dance at the Roundhouse, reported in the *New York Times* of February 22. The guest list read like the New York social register. Harriman took advantage of his wealthy friends to raise money for the Finnish Relief Fund as the war grew in Europe.

> *An all-day sale, at which men and women of prominence, among whom were many who later attended the Harriman party, acted as sales clerks, was held today at the shop*

> *of Frederick A. Picard, Swiss designer, as a benefit for the Finnish Relief Fund. The campaign will be continued tomorrow with a series of "Skiers of Finland" dinners to be held in the dining room of Sun Valley Lodge, at the Ram and the Café Continental in Challenger Room.*

President Al Lindley's message for the Sun Valley Ski Club's 1940 report reflected the impact of the war in Europe:

> *The golden age of downhill skiing probably ended on September 30, 1939. It is doubtful whether the charm of the life in the European skiing resorts and the keenness of the competition among the skiers of the many skiing countries during the preceding decade can ever be recaptured. But America can and must hold on to some of the things that make life worth living, and certainly the wonderful life in the mountains in the winter and the keen thrill of downhill skiing and racing are among the things that one remembers most fondly. The Sun Valley Ski Club has played a preeminent role in this country in continuing on this continent the great traditions of free and easy companionship and wonderful sport that characterized the decade of skiing that has just closed in Europe.*

Sun Valley Serenade, the best known movie filmed in Sun Valley, was made by 20th Century Fox and its studio chief, Sun Valley regular Darryl F. Zanuck, considered one of the most powerful image makers in America. Zanuck got the idea for the movie during a ski vacation when he asked an associate, "wouldn't this be a good setting for a Sonja Henie film?" according to Turner Classic Movies.

Henie was a famous Norwegian ice skater who won gold medals in the 1928, 1932, and 1936 Olympics. In 1936, Zanuck signed her to a long-term contract. Henie made $2 million per year from her shows, touring activities, and marketing deals, making her one of the wealthiest women of her era. By 1940, she had starred in several movies for Zanuck, although he was fed up with her temperamental nature. This was the last movie she did for Fox.

The full-budget musical starred Henie, John Payne, Milton Berle, and the Glenn Miller Orchestra, the top band in the country. Several new songs were introduced, including "Chattanooga Choo-Choo," the first gold record, which sold over one million copies and was nominated for an Oscar as best song of 1941. Its other well-known songs include "In the Mood," "It Happened in Sun Valley," "Moonlight Serenade,"and "I Know Why."

Filming the movie in Sun Valley was difficult and expensive, costing $1.3 million. The equipment had to be shipped there, and terrible weather led to frequent delays. Henie's skiing and skating scenes were filmed at Fox Studios in Hollywood. Otto Lang filmed the skiing scenes using Gretchen Fraser and local skier Jack Simpson (who was five feet, six inches and dressed in women's clothes) as stand-ins for Henie. Simpson could ski powder well, and some of his scenes were filmed on the backside of Warm Springs and on the old Galena toll road. One shot involved him skiing between Hans Hauser's legs (who was doubling for John Paine) as he was doing a snowplow. Simpson was not paid, but received ski clothes for his part, because Friedl Pfeifer wanted to preserve his amateur status. Ski instructor Joe Burgy doubled for Glenn Miller, and Dave Brandt doubled for Milton Berle.

Turner Classic Movies says more than movie-making went on in Sun Valley during filming. Zanuck used the shoot "as an excuse to frolic at Sun Valley with a French girlfriend," and Henie did her own frolicking:

> *The place was overrun with handsome young blond ski instructors from Austria or Germany. All good-looking men, and I'm sure that Sonja knew all of them—intimately. I think she was very good in the sack, she had such enormous enthusiasm . . . she was always hungry for sex.*

The movie was a box office hit, received an Oscar nomination for best director, and reinforced Sun Valley's image as an exciting, romantic destination.

Friedl Pfeifer said the movie was one of several events in 1940 that "would forever change the image of Sun Valley in America. . . . The movie became a big hit and retained its popularity for decades," romanticizing Sun Valley. Another was Lowell Thomas, who broadcast his radio show from Sun Valley, which was followed by 20 million listeners, giving the area great publicity. Hollywood celebrities such as Gary Cooper, Clark Gable, and Claudette Colbert began spending more time at Sun Valley.

Charles Proctor's work in 1936 teaching local kids to ski paid off, as they went on to teach other local kids. This included Jack Simpson, Mary Jane Griffith, and her brother Jim Griffith, all of whom competed at a high level. Mary Jane and Jim starred

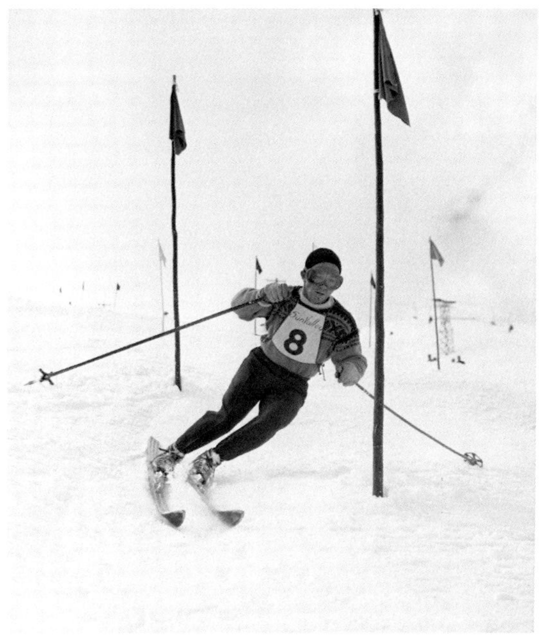

Jack Simpson racing at Sun Valley.

at Denver University, and Jim made the 1952 U.S. Olympic team before he was tragically killed in a ski accident. Simpson said they received a free pass and lunch for packing snow for half a day on Ruud or Proctor Mountain. He skied with the U.S. women's Olympic team training for the 1940 Olympics and Alf Engen. Simpson was the forerunner for annual collegiate races and for a Harriman Cup downhill and raced as a junior in one Harriman Cup. In 1941, he won the combined downhill and slalom titles in the Sun Valley Ski Club championships. In 1942, he won a Diamond Sun pin when he was 16, setting the course record, beating ski instructors Friedl Pfeifer, Fred Iselin, Sepp Benedikter, and Sigi Engl. The following week, Barney McLean ran the course in perfect conditions, beating Jack's time by a few seconds.

In fall 1942, the *Seattle Times* announced that Jack Simpson was "the outstanding junior skier of the United States" and would be the University of Washington ski team's "No. 1 man." When Simpson returned to Ketchum after World War II, he and Monty Skinner coached junior racers using a rope tow near the Ketchum cemetery. Simpson worked for his father, Owen, at the Sawtooth Club and later taught skiing at Squaw Valley in 1951 under Émile Allais, and coached the Sun Valley race team on Penny Mountain where the ski club had a Mitey-Mite tow, assisted by Christian Pravda, where Pete Patterson was one of his students. Patterson was on the U.S. ski team, placed 14th in the downhill at the 1976 Innsbruck Olympics, fifth in the Olympic downhill in 1980 at Lake Placid, and was elected to the U.S. Ski and Snowboard Hall of Fame in 1978.[49]

Major Ski Meets Are Held in the West

The Sun Valley Four-Event Intercollegiate Ski Meet was held from December 30, 1939, to January 1, 1940, involving skiers from Washington, Utah, Colorado, Wisconsin, Wyoming, Washington State, Idaho, Dartmouth, Stanford, Bennington, Yale, and Scripps. According to the *Sun Valley Ski Club Annual* for 1940,

> *A tradition had been started in the first races . . . that called for a balance of good fun, eager training under the friendly coaching of Sun Valley's experts, and hard fought competition with generous laurels for the victors and plenty of laughs over the humorous incidents.*

Fred Iselin, Sigi Engl, and Friedl Pfeifer "directed a concentrated program of downhill and slalom training" for the competitors.

Washington won the meet, winning the slalom and the top three places in the downhill. Washington's Harold (Tass) Gjolmie was second in the slalom behind his brother Reidar, who won the jumping event, and he won the Bradley Plate as the tournament's outstanding overall skier. The Mary Cornelia trophy for the combined winner of the "girl's competition" was won by Kathleen Harriman from Bennington College, who won the downhill and slalom.

The Western Interstate Ski Meet was held the third week in January, featuring men's and women's teams from Idaho, Colorado, Utah, Montana, Wyoming, and California, who competed in downhill, slalom, and jumping. Beer-Fest nights in the Ram broke the pressure of training for the teams. U.P. president W.M. Jeffers donated a trophy to the winning team. Idaho's team was led by two Engen brothers, Alf and Kaare, and their brother Sverre raced for Utah. Colorado was led by Barney McLean and Gordon Wren. California had Bob Blatt, Roy Mikklesen, and Bill Janss. Idaho's women's team featured Gretchen Fraser, Nancy Reynolds, Kathleen Harriman, and Elizabeth Durrance. The downhill was run on the Warm Springs course, where the steilhang presented a challenge. Bill Janss lost two minutes extricating himself from the creek at the bottom. There was excitement in the jumping competition when Bobby Blatt (a Seattleite studying at Stanford), who had only jumped once before, leaped twice for 36 meters, clinching the win for California. Gordon Wren defeated two national champions, Alf Engen and Roy Mikkelsen.

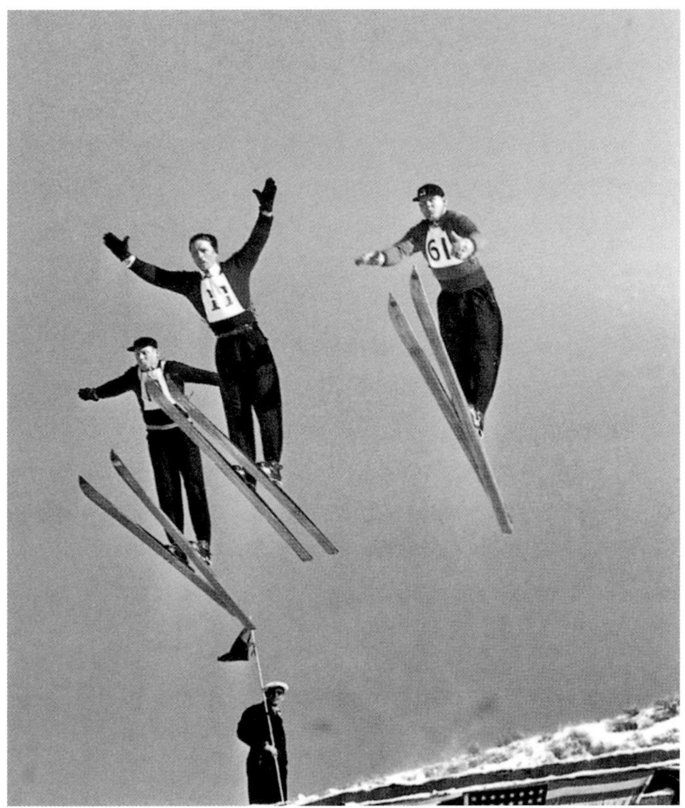

Art Devlin, Alf Engen, and Torger Tokle jumping at Ruud Mountain, 1942.

The National Four-Way Championships held in Washington between March 13 and 17, 1940, featured "the country's foremost all-around skiers," according to the *New York Times*, who would compete "in the most difficult of all national championships." Alf Engen, "the stocky skiman from Sun Valley went off with the works," won the Four-Way Championship after battling Seattle's upcoming ski racer Sigurd Hall in the downhill, slalom, and cross-country, and Torger Tokle in the jumping. Sverre Engen was second, Hall third, and Hjalmar Hvan of Portland fourth.

Hall was a Norwegian immigrant, a well-known Northwest mountaineer who completed the first ascent of Mount Rainier on skis and was making his presence known on the national ski racing circuit. Tragically, he died in April 1940 in the Silver Skis race on Mount Rainier when he hit some rocks while skiing through a fog bank. His was the only death to occur in a sanctioned ski race in this country, and it caused a reevaluation of the rules governing downhill events.

The 1940 National Downhill Championships were held the third week of March at Sun Valley, featuring the first downhill in America on a course of full FIS qualifications served by a ski lift to the top. The tournament was described by Al Lindley:

> *Any skier knows what a tremendous difference a ski lift makes in training the course and in the times made in the race. In the past, racers were limited to one run a day since they had to hike to the top. This year, they could make four or five runs, and the times certainly showed the effects of this training.*

Nearly 90 men and women entered, representing 40 clubs, 16 states, and nine countries. The best skiers in the United States were at the race, but because of the looming war overseas, few came from Europe. Dick Durrance lived in Sun Valley all winter preparing for the race, and the downhill would be run on the Warm Springs course he had designed. Durrance lost the Harriman Cup in 1939, and said, "I realized if I didn't win it this time I probably never would." Gretchen Fraser trained at Sun Valley that winter with Friedl Pfeifer, who "tried to teach her to flow with the course rather than fight it and she spent a lot of time following me through the bumps, rough snow conditions and down steep pitches," according to Pfeifer.

On the Warm Springs downhill course, the top had been cleared the previous summer, allowing racers to ski straight to the top of the steilhang. A decision was made to control the course below the steilhang to eliminate shortcuts and force skiers to stay in the main glade.

The 1940 race will forever be known as the time Dick Durrance schussed the steilhang at great risk, winning the downhill, causing a sensation all over the country. Al Lindley's article about the race said that Durrance made history:

> *From the easy starting point . . . almost everybody went practically straight to the top of the steilhang, but one approached the steilhang with very great speed if one had not checked on the traverse. Very few who did not check could hold their turns on the hang and many severe crackups resulted. Hannes Schroll, Alf Engen, Max Muller of Switzerland, Richard Werle, and many others came to grief on the steilhang.*
>
> *But Dick, with iron nerves and the inspiration of genius, flew into the steilhang with absolute full speed on a forty-foot jump, turned down the slope, shouting to himself, "Too Fast! Too Fast!" Obviously unable to check or turn, he bounded down the slope*

> *in about three jumps, his skis leaving only intermittent tracks, and tried to grind around the corner into the wood run at about seventy miles an hour. Unable to hold on the hard-packed, icy snow at the bottom of the hang, Dick skidded in his turn up near the woodpile on the far side of the gully and actually went over a small pine tree. Dick kept his nerve and his skis pointed downhill and by a supreme effort threw himself forward up onto his feet again without in any way slacking his speed. From there on, eyes popping and feet wide apart, he cut every corner as closely as it could be cut to the finish, which he approached with such terrific speed that he flew off the course on the last turn and wiped out a few spectators. Scrambling to his feet quickly, he lost only about fifteen seconds and finished with a time of 2:56:1 . . . it had not been thought possible to run under three minutes.*

In his book, Durrance said he was determined to go fast until he got to the top of the steilhang, then decide whether to check. "And when I got there I just said to hell with it, I'll go straight into it." He jumped into the steilhang and

> *the moment I hit, I realized I was sinking in a foot deep, and there wasn't going to be any turning, there wouldn't be a turn at all. I was heading straight down. At that point I do remember the fear of God sweeping over me, and I started talking to myself: Whoa, this is too fast. I was cussing in German and English. This is bad, I'm in trouble. But there was no choice, I had to take it straight.*

At the bottom of the course, Durrance had too much speed to make a 90-degree turn into the finish flat. "I slid over into the crowd that were roped off . . . and I know I crashed into a whole mess of people and stuff and really got stuck there." He missed the finish line, went through a roped off area, taking out a hot dog stand and ending up with the spectators. His skis did not come off, so he got up and raced back to the finish line, taking about 15 seconds, but still won the race.

The *Hailey Times* of March 28, 1940, said Durrance shot down the steilhang "like a cannonball and [flew] into the air as he hit a bump," taking it "at express-train speed" and had to turn at the bottom "with one ski in the air. A slip there might have ended the story of Dick Durrance. How he did it no one knows—but he did it." The *New York Times* of March 23 said Durrance sped "down the steep mountainside apparently without regard for life and limb. . . . Veteran followers of the sport said that never in the history of skiing in America or abroad has a man performed so riskily and yet maintained such control."

Durrance won the downhill with his wild schuss of the steilhang and his 60 mile-per-hour run down the two-and-five-eighths-mile course on Warm Springs. Walter Prager was second, and Friedl Pfeifer third. Toni Matt, the prior year's winner, "went tumbling twice, an unheard-of occurrence for him," according to Al Lindley, to place sixth, making it the first ski race in the United States Matt lost. Paul Gilbreath was the highest Northwest finisher in the downhill, placing 11th. Sigurd Hall finished 24th, Hans Grage 25th, Don Amick 30th, and Portland's Hjalmar Hvam 44th.

The women's downhill course was identical to the men's, unlike the prior year when its starting point was lower, and had more vertical drop than any previous women's downhill in the country and probably any FIS course in Europe. According to Lindley, "practically a who's who of girls' racing" cracked up on the steilhang. Grace Lindley won the women's downhill. Second was 15-year-old Marilyn Shaw of Stowe, Vermont, the only racer not to fall. Miggs Jennings Durrance (newly married to Dick), finished fourth. Betty Woolsey said the downhill course was too long, tiring, and difficult for women, since almost all the men fell on the steilhang, as did "every dashing" woman skier.

The slalom was held on the open slope from the top of Baldy, down toward the Round House. The 32-gate course "provided a sheer drop that made control absolutely necessary. Those who were unable to check their speed came to grief many times," Lindley said. Friedl Pfeifer "paced the field with two flawless runs executed in his usual perfect style," beating Durrance, although "there were many casualties and disappointments among the other skiers as bad errors were frequent." In the women's slalom, Nancy Reynolds of Sun Valley won, Gretchen Fraser was 11th, Shirley McDonald was 12th, and Grace Lindley was 13th.

Durrance's first-place finish in the downhill and second in the slalom put him in a tie with Pfeifer for the Harriman Cup. However, race rules said first place went to the winner of the downhill, so Durrance won the combined title and the Harriman Cup. Pfeifer retained his national slalom title. Seattle's Sigurd Hall finished 16th, the highest of the Northwest competitors in the combined, Hans Grage finished 17th, and Don Amick 22nd. Fifteen-year-old Marilyn Shaw won the women's combined title, followed by Gerda Paumgarten from Austria. Miggs Durrance was third, Grace Lindley was fifth, and Gretchen Fraser sixth.

Alf Engen, one of the world's best ski jumpers and the national jumping and four-way champion, made two flawless leaps to win the invitational ski jump event that attracted 18 jumpers from 10 clubs. He turned aside the challenge of 21-year-old Gordon Wren of Steamboat Springs, Colorado. "Following the regular competition the spectators were thrilled by double jumps, particularly the pair leap by Engen and Wren," Lindley wrote.

At the Harriman Cup banquet, Averell Harriman said, "Never ski like that again, Dick, never ski like that." This was Durrance's third Harriman Cup victory and he was given permanent possession of the trophy.

On March 26, the *New York Times* published a postscript to what it called the "best meet in the National Ski Association's history," "Durrance's Daring Talk of Ski World." Racers were still saying,

> *Dick did what nobody else will probably do. . . . Wherever one goes, be it Shoshone, Ketchum or even distant Boise, the conversation still centers on the dynamic performances of Dick Durrance, truly one of the world's outstanding, all-around skiers. . . . Unlike in other meets, the contestants were able to conserve their energy for the national races by using the 11,499 foot chair lift to the top of Baldy Mountain instead of making the usual two and one-half mile climb to the start.*

The FIS National Downhill and Slalom tournament was held in Alta, Utah, at the end of March with "the brilliant cast of sixty top skiers from 21 clubs, eleven states and five countries," according to the *Seattle Times*, headed by Dick Durrance. Despite a 60-mile-per-hour wind that reduced visibility to nearly zero, Bill Klein, a ski instructor from Lake Tahoe, won the downhill, schussing the course from the start. Durrance failed to see a snowdrift and "went soaring through the air fifty feet for a severe spill," although he finished the race.

Durrance won the slalom, but Walter Prager won the combined title. "A 20-year old University of Washington lad, Bill Redlin, who started to ski only two years ago at Mount Rainier, was runner up," reported the *Seattle Times*. However, a recheck of the downhill scores led to Klein's disqualification, so Redlin won the downhill, giving him enough points to win the combined honors and make him the U.S. downhill and slalom champion. Redlin was called the next Dick Durrance.

In April, the first Silver Belt World Cup competition was held at Sugar Bowl Ski Area in California near Lake Tahoe, a ski area started in 1937 by Hannes Schroll with the backing of wealthy investors including Walt Disney. Sun Valley's Friedl Pfeifer and Gretchen Fraser won the Silver Belt races on one of the most challenging courses of the era. In later years, the race was won by Sun Valley's Jannette Burr (the only three-time winner), Alf Engen, Tom Corcoran, Andrea Mead Lawrence, Jack Reddish, and others.

Sun Valley racers were recognized for their performances during the ski year. "Darting" Dick Durrance won the National Open Downhill and Combined, the National Amateur Downhill, Slalom and Combined championships and Harriman Cup, along with the FIS slalom in Alta. Alf Engen won the National Jumping Championship in Berlin, New Hampshire, the National Four Event championship in Washington, and the award for the man who did the most for American skiing in 1940. Friedl Pfeifer won the national slalom championship for the second year in a row, the Sugar Bowl slalom, the Far West Kandahar slalom at Mount Hood, and the Sun Valley giant slalom in the spring ski meet. Grace Lindley won the women's open and amateur national downhill championship and the Sun Valley Club slalom and combined championship. Nancy Reynolds won the national open and amateur slalom and the Far West Kandahar at Mount Hood. Gretchen Fraser "shone brightly,"according to the *Sun Valley Ski Club Annual*, winning the Pacific Northwest Combined Championship, the Jeffers Cup in Sun Valley's Western Interstate Race, Sun Valley's Ski Club downhill championship, and the giant slalom at Sugar Bowl. Kathleen Harriman "showed the most improvement last winter and distinguished herself by winning the Mary Cornelia trophy in Sun Valley's Christmas intercollegiate races." Later in the year, she won the Hochgebirge Invitational Downhill, was second in the slalom, and first in the combined at Franconia, New Hampshire. Marian McKean was the outstanding skier in the western interstate meet, winning the downhill and slalom, leading the East team to victory.

Alf Engen was awarded the American Ski Trophy from the National Ski Association as the "amateur who furthest promotes skiing in the United States through sportsmanship and performance." Dick Durrance, the prior year's winner, received an honorable mention, as did Charles Minot Dole, who started the National Ski Patrol. On December 22, 1940, the *New York Times* named Dick Durrance and Alf Engen skiers of the year, along with Torger Tokle, the young Norwegian jumping star, and 15-year-old Marilyn Shaw of Stowe. Durrance had been "America's No. 1 skier" for years and held every major downhill and slalom title in the country.

After the women's FIS team trained in Sun Valley all winter, Alice Wolfe, the team manager, wrote Harriman, thanking him for his contributions:

> *Like everyone who goes to Sun Valley, I feel somehow completely identified with it. . . . I love no American mountain as much as old Baldy. . . . And I have never been treated so well. In fact I am afraid we were all spoiled by your hospitality. . . . So many thanks for a wonderful winter of skiing.*[50]

Off-Season in Sun Valley

In late March, a 1,200-foot rope tow opened at Baker Creek, operating daily. This was the second local lift outside Sun Valley—a portable lift was operating in the Picabo hills. Because of unusually warm weather, the Gold Star meet scheduled for Bald Mountain had been transferred to the Boulder peaks three miles beyond the Russian John ranger station. A course going from 10,000 feet to 6,500 feet was mapped out, with a three-hour climb to reach the start. Other events would take place on Dollar Mountain, and 25 entrants were expected.

A Spring Sports Meet was held on May 5, 1940, in the glorious days of spring "when we still had wonderful corn on Baldy and sometimes fresh powder up at Galena," as reported in the *Sun Valley Ski Club Annual*. Most of Sun Valley's top skiers participated, except for Dick Durrance, as he was in Twin Falls at a dentist's office getting the teeth fixed he damaged by "the way he ran the steilhang in the nationals six weeks before." Friedl Pfeifer set a course from the fire lookout on top of Baldy, with three open gates. Pfeifer dominated the men, his "fluency, that perfect rhythm that prevents the minute delays of turns, jerked or pulled over so slightly, was the margin of victory." He was followed by Sigi Engl and Steve Bradley. Women competitors included members of the U.S. women's FIS/Olympic team: Nancy Reynolds, Miggs Durrance, Gretchen Fraser, Elli Stiller, and others. Competitions were also held in the "inferior sports" of golf, tennis, and "something you do with a gun," which was won by Don Fraser. Sigi Engl won the tennis final. Pfeifer won the combined, followed by Fred Islin and Sigi Engl. The women's winners were Nancy Reynolds, Gretchen Fraser, and Miggs Durrance.

> *Think of it—skiing in the morning and then tennis after lunch. It makes almost a perfect combination, and where else but Sun Valley could you find it? So that was the first Sun Valley Spring Sports Meeting. Let's hope it becomes a regular annual event.*

Harriman as usual was deeply involved in Sun Valley affairs. In March, he sent W.M. Jeffers a critique of a draft "new Sun Valley book." He commented on placement of photographs, suggested changes to better show the area's attractions, changes to the descriptions of Sun Valley's winter attractions, and alternative words to use. He wanted to counter the impression that Sun Valley was hot during the summer.

In May, Harriman sent letters to Jeffers suggesting changes to the design of an electrotherapy setup in the lodge and commenting on plans to install bowling alleys and a game room. In June, Harriman sent Jeffers suggestions about Union Pacific's acquisition of land from J.A. Grimm on Dollar Mountain. In August, he sent Pat Rogers two letters about improvements at Sun Valley, including installing more toilets at the Roundhouse, plans for the lodge's dining room and lounge, uniforms for waitresses, redecorating the Café Continental, and doors to be used at the lodge. Harriman opposed using a certain ski instructor, as "he doesn't ski well enough," and urged the hiring of "high class American boys" for the ski school in spite of Friedl Pfeifer's dissatisfaction with some of them. He supported Pfeifer's "desire to make the School the best in the world," but said hiring American instructors will "make us more friends in the long-run." Harriman commented on proposed changes to Sun Valley's rates and prices of meals, and suggested starting a "skiers table" at the chalet.

The *New York Times* of August 11, 1940, described the Sun Valley rodeo honoring Idaho's 50th year of statehood in the West's most modern sports stadium:

> *Here will be enacted the drama of cowpunchers atop whirling broncos and bulldoggers wrestling squirming steers against a background of the Sawtooth Mountains raising almost from the arena's stage. Fourteen competitive events will be staged each day. Among them will be bronc riding, calf roping, bulldogging, Brahma bull and steer riding, men's and women's trick riding and relay racing, Pony express racing, trick roping, cowboys' Roman racing, wild-horse racing and bell-calf roping.*

The chairlift to the Roundhouse operated once a week so guests could see the greatest mountain on which to ski in the country.

In September 1940, Harriman told Rogers he opposed bringing hockey teams from the East to play at Sun Valley. "Ice hockey, except as occasionally played by our guests here, does not belong at Sun Valley. The type of spectacle that is proposed belongs in Madison Square Garden." Harriman attended a meeting in mid-September 1940 at Sun Valley with Pat Rogers, architect W.T. Wellman, Ed Seagle, Charles Davidson, and others about construction at the resort. A memo regarding the meeting described changes to be made at the Sun Valley Lodge (including the lower lounge, Duchin Room, and exterior trim), the lodge swimming pool, the lodge sun deck, and the lodge skating rink.

Beginning in 1940, Sun Valley expanded recreational opportunities for its summer and fall visitors on Silver Creek, 25 miles southeast of Sun Valley near Picabo. The area was prime territory for hunting and fishing in one of the West's best spring-fed creek fisheries and the nearby farms, which included two miles of stream front. Don Fraser and Pat Rogers negotiated the purchase of two small ranches: the Gillahan Ranch in 1940 for $8,000, which was the downstream half; and the Sullivan Ranch on the upper section of the river (where Sullivan Lake was located) in July 1941 for $4,285, creating Sun Valley Ranch.

Under Pat Rogers, the major use of Sun Valley Ranch was recreation. The railroad built two cabins and a dog kennel on the west arm of Sullivan's Lake to house guides and entertain clients. Sun Valley guests took the train from Ketchum to the closest rail stop, Hay, near the present Hayspur Fish Hatchery. They were then taken by buckboard or motor vehicle to the Sullivan Lake cabins. The resort's horses were pastured at Sun Valley Ranch in the fall. The site became a popular location for fishing and hunting in the summer and fall for Sun Valley guests.[51]

During summer and fall 1940, new ski runs were cut on Bald Mountain, and existing runs were cleared and widened to make them easier and safer to ski. Those who skied Baldy the prior year "won't recognize the place," predicted *The Valley Sun*. Baldy "has finally come into its own. . . . Many other gentle slopes have been prepared on the very summit of the mountain, so that the neophyte can enjoy his skiing here with the expert, from October until May."

Baldy had a new warming hut for the upcoming season—the Forest Service lookout. From the top of the two-mile-long "Chairway to the Stars," a short hike to the summit brought skiers to a new two-story, three-room combination lookout and ski shelter that replaced the old one-room Forest Service lookout. It was kept open in the winter so

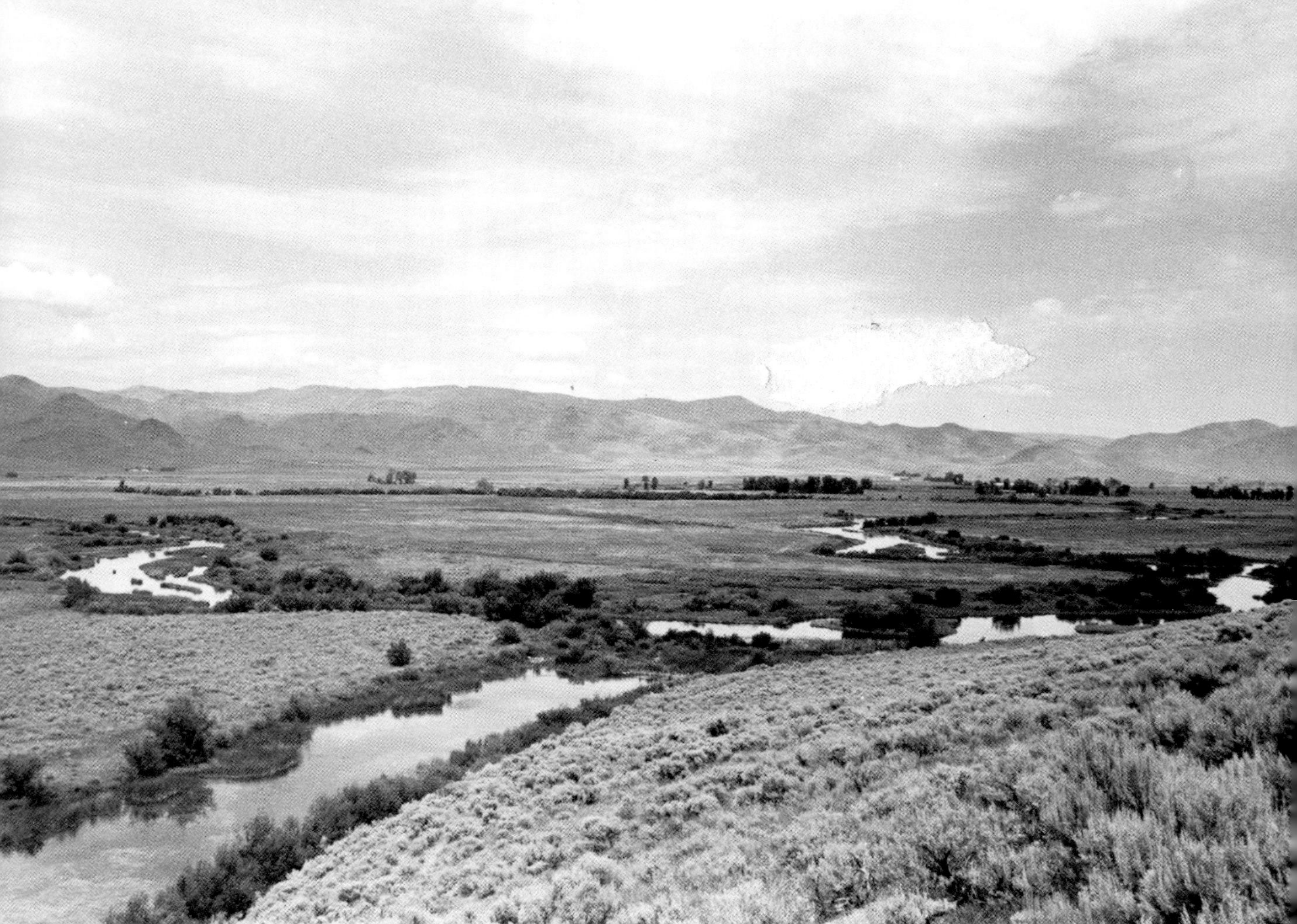

ABOVE Overview of Silver Creek and Sun Valley Ranch.

OPPOSITE, TOP Fishing on Silver Creek at Sun Valley Ranch.

OPPOSITE, BOTTOM Hunting at Silver Creek.

skiers could "rest before a warm stove in comfortable chairs before starting down," said the Sun Valley Ski Club. The number of chairs on Baldy's lifts was increased to 202, allowing 300 skiers an hour to be carried uphill, each chair with a wool-lined, waterproofed cape.

The "standard run," Ridge Run from the summit to the Roundhouse Station, was cleared and rocks were removed from Rock Garden. "Gone are rocks and the troubles. In its stead, is a smooth open run, a pathway of light even to the most mediocre snow fan," wrote *The Valley Sun*.

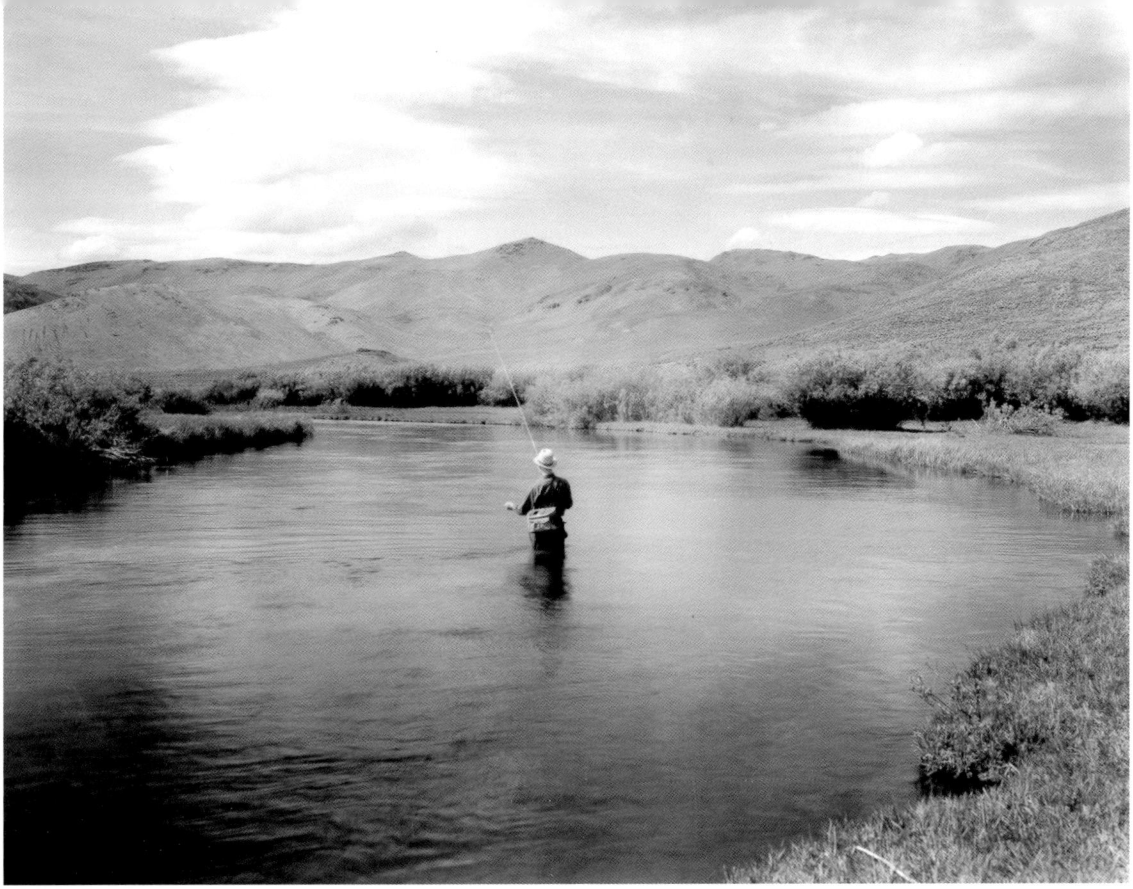

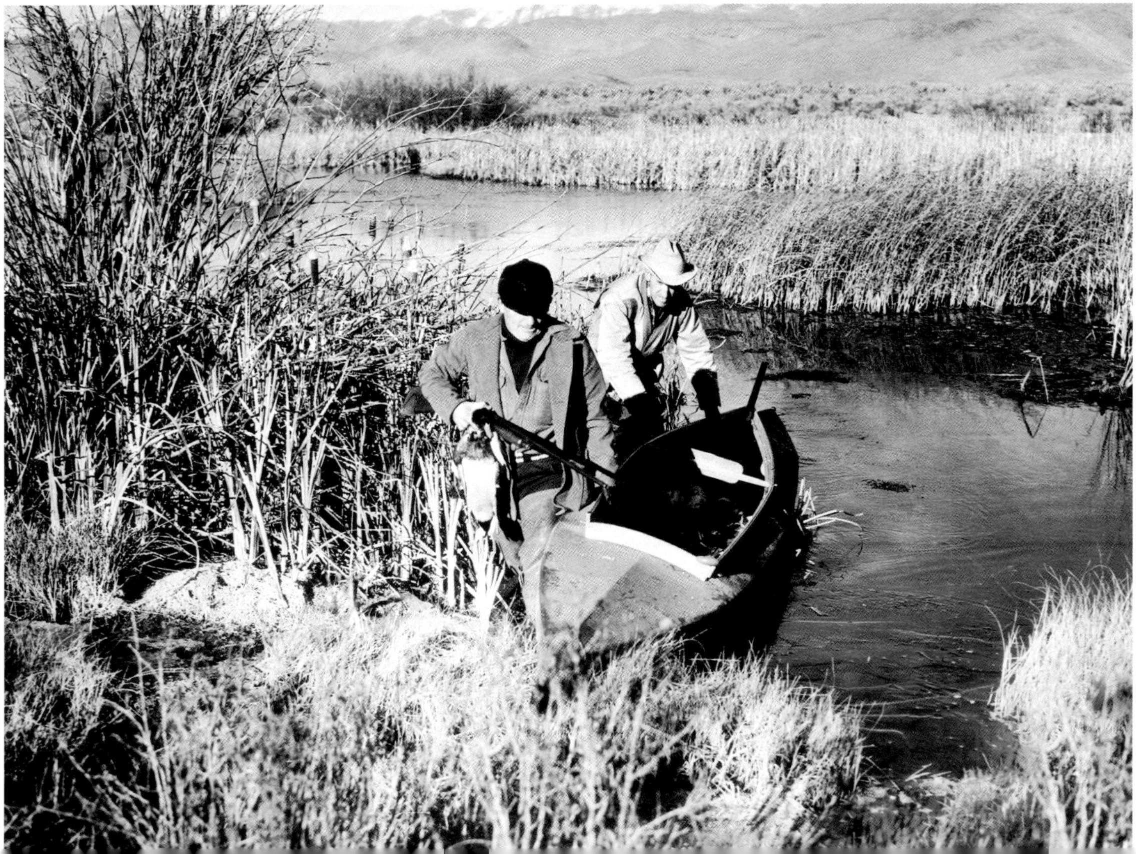

A new three-mile run was created, named Broadway, taking skiers 3,200 feet from Baldy's summit to its base. Broadway started at the new Forest Service tower at the top of the mountain and ran down an open ravine almost to the bottom. South of Ridge Run, there were five timber-free gullies, or bowls, which were connected with the Roundhouse by a new caterpillar road.

New, easier trails were blazed from the summit to the Roundhouse, including College, averaging a 10-percent grade, "providing a slope that can be negotiated by the most unskilled skier," wrote *The Valley Sun*. Skiing College meant a person "graduated" from Dollar Mountain. College "made the top section of Bald Mountain lift usable in the very early winter." A new ranger's trail was cut across College to the Roundhouse, where skiers could catch the lift back to the summit. A run was cut through to the Canyon Station lift.

Canyon had been cleared and widened to more than 100 yards, making it "a broad highway down the mountainside," in the words of *The Valley Sun*. "The skier can maneuver its length in graceful linked turns, with no fear of anything that might retard his progress." Sage brush and aspen trees were removed from the bottom of Canyon so there was ample room for skiers to go past Canyon Station into Riverside Drive, or stop at the lift "with ease and safety." The traverses at the end of the run were eliminated, and the lower section was widened from 50 feet to 200 feet. Rough spots on River Run were graded, "so the course is more even and much finer for running."

A toboggan run was built paralleling River Run from the top of the first chairlift to the base of the mountain, with "plenty of tricky turns," according to *The Valley Sun*. The ski patrol built a skier's bridge at the bottom of Warm Springs Run over the creek, called the Cottonwood Bridge, several hundred yards downstream and east of the present bridge. It was made from a large cottonwood trunk with a narrow deck with railings. A game room was added to the Sun Valley Lodge with six bowling alleys, a bar, pool tables, an electric shooting range, and ping pong tables to provide more entertainment for guests. These new offerings, plus the "old faithful" ski slopes on Baldy, Dollar, Ruud, and Proctor, "make Sun Valley still the seventh heaven for the winter sports fan."

The *Seattle Times* of October 14, 1940, said Sun Valley had a busy summer preparing for "what promises to be a record winter season." The lodge had been completely remodeled, and a new cocktail lounge occupied the southern corner of the room with comfortable overstuffed chairs and couches. There were "physio-rooms" for "those who spend too prolonged periods in positions which only the skiers assume."

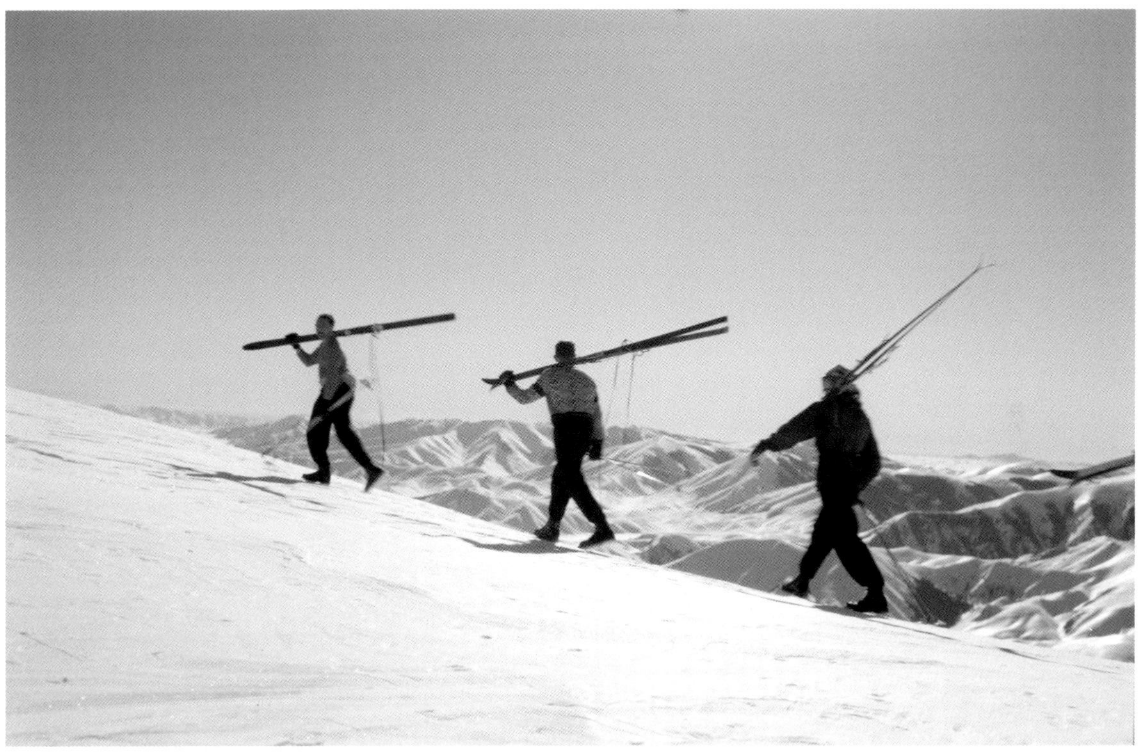

Skiers hiking from top of Baldy's chairlift to the Forest Service lookout that served as a warming hut. The bowls were also reached along the ridge leading to the lookout.

When Dick Durrance worked as a photographer at Sun Valley in 1938, he wanted to include a ski chase scene in a promotional film Averell Harriman considered doing. Durrance got his chance in spring 1940. After the lifts closed, he talked Harriman into letting him make the film, talked Sun Valley instructors into starring in it, and brought in his friend Steve Bradley to help. They selected the locations to shoot, and Durrance would ski, chased by instructors, while Bradley filmed them. The Fairbanks Film Company in California edited the footage. The film, *Sun Valley Holiday*, *Sun Valley Ski Chase*, won first place in the first International Film Festival at Cortina d'Ampezzo in 1949. The U.S. State Department distributed 100 prints of the film to 90 countries "to give foreign peoples a broader knowledge of the American Way of Life."

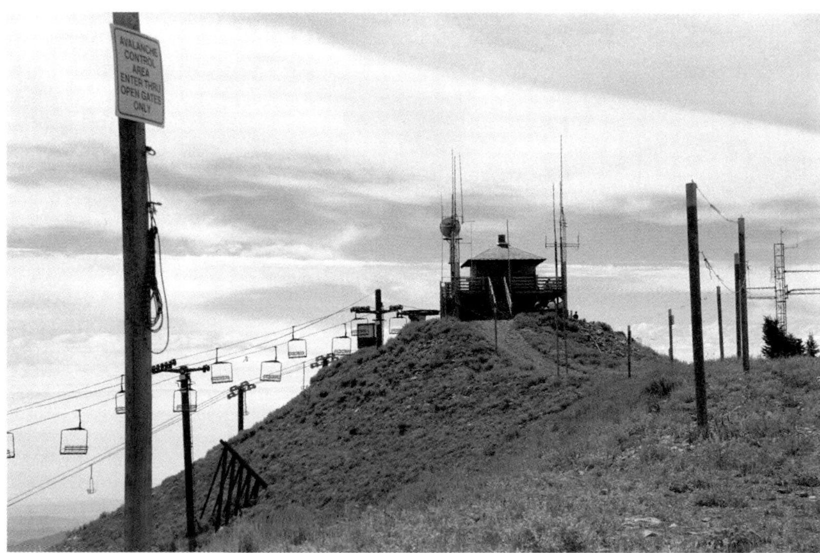

Forest Service fire lookout seen from the top of Baldy. *Courtesy of Karen Bossick.*

In 1940, Durrance left Sun Valley for Alta, Utah, a place he and his wife fell in love with when they raced there earlier in the year. Alta was developed in the late 1930s by the Salt Lake City Winter Sports Association. The Denver & Rio Grande Western Railroad contributed $25,000 for a lodge, which was not enough to finish it, and construction stopped. Alta was "a faltering ski area set in Little Cottonwood Canyon within Utah's Wasatch Mountains . . . [with] a half-finished lodge, a creaky makeshift chairlift and no school," according to a history of the area. Durrance talked the association into letting him take it over, becoming manager of the Alta Ski Area and starting an "American ski school." His friend James Laughlin, heir to a Pittsburgh steel fortune, invested $25,000 to finish construction in return for an interest in the lift and the lodge. Laughlin became Alta Lodge's first owner, which opened November 29, 1940. The ski area struggled to get by. Durrance said, "Tvhere was no profit from the lodge."

The year 1941 started out badly for Durrance. A fire destroyed the old cabin at Alta in which he and his wife were living, burning more than 50 medals and trophies. The damage was $5,000, although what was lost was irreplaceable.[52]

Other Railroads Consider Opening Ski Areas

Union Pacific's bold move to open Sun Valley during the Great Depression was regularly described by the trade publication *Rail Age* and watched by other railroads. Snow trains were a Depression-era innovation to boost passenger ridership that spread throughout the country from California, New England, the Midwest and the Northwest, described in *Trains Magazine*.

The Chicago, Milwaukee, St. Paul & Pacific Railroad (or Milwaukee Road) was completed in 1909, going from Chicago over Snoqualmie Pass to Seattle. In January 1938, the Milwaukee Road opened Washington's first modern ski area at Hyak, the east portal of its tunnel under the pass. It was accessible by train in two hours, had a modern ski lodge and a J-bar. The *Seattle Times* provided free ski lessons to Seattle high school students. Ski trains had reserved seats, a baggage car with waxing tables, and a recreation car for dancing. The Milwaukee Bowl closed in spring of 1950 after a fire destroyed its lodge, a major blow to Washington skiing.

The Northern Pacific Railroad was completed in 1884 from Minnesota to Tacoma, Washington, over Stampede Pass. In the 1920s and 1930s, trains took skiers to Martin, a stop at the east portal of its tunnel under the pass, and provided rail cars where they could spend the night. In 1938, the Northern Pacific announced it was opening a major new ski resort at Martin, with a hotel for 200 to 250 and a ski lift (tram). A small facility was opened in 1939, the Martin Ski Dome, with room for 30 people, dormitories, and a kitchen where skiers cooked their own meals. The Ski Dome operated until World War II, offering six hours of skiing for $2. After the war, the Ski Dome was sold to the University of Washington for its winter sports activities.

In 1940, Al Lindley was a member of the National Park Service Advisory Committee on Winter Sports. He was commissioned by the Great Northern Railroad to find a location for a ski resort along its route to the Northwest. His team concluded the best skiing was "in the vicinity of Flattop Mountain, Heaven's Peak and McDonald Creek," inside Glacier National Park. The area had good terrain and snow, but needed the cooperation and capital of the Park Service and the Great Northern to build a resort, an access road, accommodations, and ski lift for a resort that would be "second to none in the United States."

In 1946, the Great Northern asked Lindley to complete the reconnaissance. After World War II, the National Park Service supported ski touring and mountaineering, including the use of ski huts, but took a more rigid approach to ski lifts, which had to be removed at the end of winter. Lindley concluded that the west side of Glacier Park was perfect for touring and hut skiing, using 10th Mountain Division veterans as guides and "Weasels," snow vehicles used by mountain troops in the war, to shuttle skiers from place to place. Lindley discussed a possible alpine-style resort with a ski tram up Heaven's Peak if the agency's policy changed. The Great Northern built neither facility.[53]

18

SKI SEASON OF 1941 IS BUSY AS WAR LOOMS

Harriman Leaves for War Work

Winter 1941 was the last ski season before World War II started for America. Enthusiasm for skiing continued to grow, but hints of the conflict to come were seen as Army troops were training at Mount Rainier in Washington. Sun Valley provided bus service from Shoshone to supplement its once-a-day passenger train.

Averell Harriman began 1941 in the same manner as prior years, by being involved in all details of Sun Valley's operation. His telegram to W.P. Rogers on January 4, 1941, from the train en route from Sun Valley to New York, raised a number of issues. He was disappointed in the toboggan run—it was an expense without being an asset. It was in excellent shape, but there was no effort to promote its use. A moderate rate should be charged, someone should be available to take people down the run, and there should be a sign advertising it, he said.

One major change in 1941 was the disappearance of Count Schaffgotsch from Sun Valley. The count's Nazi sympathies were well known. When war broke out, he returned to Germany, became an officer in the Waffen SS Florian Geyer Division, and was killed fighting in Russia in 1942. The Waffen SS was an elite paramilitary wing of the Nazi Party that ran concentration camps and carried out assignments from Hitler and Himmler. Its mission in 1942 was to "deal with" Jews, Gypsies, and Slavic populations in Central Europe by burning villages and massacring civilians so Germans could resettle the area.

Actor David Niven was one of the Hollywood celebrities who came to Sun Valley in its early days. He met Schaffgotsch while crossing the Atlantic from Europe in 1937:

> *On the return journey in the Ile de France, I met an Austrian named Felix Schaffcotsch* [sic]. *He was on his way to Sun Valley, Idaho, where, at the request of Averell Harriman, he had designed and built a new ski resort. A handsome and affable "Graf", he was also a died-in-the-wool Nazi. He spent hours extolling the virtues of Hitler, sympathizing with his problems and enthusing over his plans. I listened politely but took none of it seriously. . . . Felix said that he was bringing over a dozen good ski instructors from near his home in Austria—"all Nazis too." I promised to go to Sun Valley after I finished the picture.*

Niven went to Sun Valley in February 1938. "Only two hotels were built, the 'Lodge,' very good and very expensive and 'The Challenger Inn' where I went, very gay and much cheaper." The skiing was perfect, he said, and he had a wonderful six weeks. "Felix had made a huge success of the place. Given half a chance he was still liable to lay down the law about 'Lebensraum,' but he was a most agreeable companion."

After England declared war on Germany, Niven and Schaffgotsch met in Rome. "Felix talked about the new ski lifts he was planning for Sun Valley and I talked of pictures I was going to make," Niven said. At the end of the evening, "Felix headed northeast for the Brenner Pass to join the S.S. . . . Felix was killed in Russia."

Nelson Bennett was hired as a ski patrolman for the 1940–1941 season, and became the resort's second ski patrol director in January 1941, replacing Esuebio (Sebby) Arriaga, who joined the ski school. He graduated from the University of New Hampshire, was on its ski team, and worked at Peckett's Inn on Sugar Hill. His first year at Sun Valley, the ski patrol improved College Run, where fallen trees were left when the run was cut, creating ruts and grooves that had to be skied around, and shovel crews filled in the areas between them. They removed the trees the following summer. The ski patrol's priorities were shoveling and packing snow to prepare courses, maintaining first aid supplies, and evacuating injured skiers. Ski patrollers were stationed on the top of the mountain, where they waited for reports of injuries relayed by lift operators. There were five or six members of the ski patrol when Bennett took over, which doubled for 1942.

During World War II, Bennett served in the predecessor of the 10th Mountain Division, the 87th Infantry Battalion, training at Fort Lewis, Washington, and on Mount

Rainier, and transferred to Camp Hale, Colorado, where he trained troops in skiing and rock climbing. He and his brother Eddie saw significant combat in Italy with the 10th, and he was sent home because of a medical condition. Bennett returned to Sun Valley as superintendent of recreational facilities, later mountain manager, in which role he expanded and created a number of new ski runs on Baldy. Appendix C contains a description of how the runs on Baldy were named. Bennett stayed until 1960, when he left Sun Valley to become general manager of White Pass, Washington. Bennett was an official in a number of international ski races, head of the U.S. alpine ski program in the 1956 Olympics, assistant director of ski events at the 1960 Olympics at Squaw Valley, and chief of course for the men's downhill at the Lake Placid Olympics. He was inducted into the U.S. Ski and Snowboard Hall of Fame in 1986.

New Sun Valley awards were introduced in 1941. The Silver Sun course was an easy six-tenths-mile course down Riverside Run—skiers who negotiated it without a spill and with only one or two checks made the time and received a ski with one tiny star. The Golden Sun course started at the Roundhouse and went 1.3 miles down Canyon and Riverside Runs, dropping 1,929 feet. Men who finished the course in 1:45 and women who finished in 2:00 received a ski with two stars. The secret of success, it was said, was to schuss—and to keep on your feet.

The Diamond Sun was the resort's highest award for the skier who was an all-around expert. Its 2.1-mile course started at the top of Bald Mountain, went down Ridge, into Rock Garden, through Canyon, and ended at the bottom of Riverside Run. In February 1941, Gretchen Fraser won the Diamond Sun in a time of 3:47:4. "Many of Sun Valley's best skiers have tried to earn the award and failed," the Sun Valley Ski Club reported. Only five women won Diamond Sun pins in 1941 and 1942: Nancy Reynolds, Gretchen Fraser, Rettles de Cosson, Catherine Henck, and Clarita Heath.[54]

Sun Valley Remains the Country's Only Major Ski Resort

Ski Illustrated of December 1940 had three articles about Sun Valley and a number of references to the resort in other articles.

The article "Who's Who in Pfeifer's Ski School" said, "At Sun Valley, Idaho, there are American, Austrian, Swiss and German ski teachers but the method of instruction is Friedl's." A number of the instructors were champion racers from Europe, attracted to Sun Valley by its international prominence, much of it based on the ski races it hosted. Of 20 instructors, 13 were from Europe (including one woman) and seven were from the United States (including one woman).

Austrian members of the ski school included Sigi Engl, Hans Hauser, Otto Lang, Andy Hennig, and Richard Werle. German instructors included Florian Haemmerle, Victor Gottschaulk, Hans Teichner, Ali Mauracher, and Elli Stiller. Fred Iselin and Willi Meyer were Swiss. American instructors included a number from Dartmouth College who trained under Walter Prager—John Litchfield, Bob Fletcher, Harold Hillman, and Harold Codding. Marion McLean from Massachusetts was a member of the U.S. women's FIS ski team.

"Skiing Among the Stars" said, "An amazing number of movie stars ski, and many of them ski very well indeed. Most of them learned abroad or at Sun Valley, Idaho." They included Sonja Henie, David Niven, Ray Milland, Robert Young, Gary Cooper, Tyrone Power, Henry Fonda, Claudette Colbert, Madeline Carroll, Norma Shearer, Binnie Barnes, and others. The "ablest skier in Hollywood" was Seattle's Ragnar Qvale, a member of the University of Washington ski team and Sun Valley ski instructor, whom Darryl Zanuck recruited to make movies.

GRETCHEN TRIUMPHS

Boiling down a Sun Valley slope in the women's downhill race of last week's National Four-Event ski races, Mrs. Gretchen Kunigk Fraser shows the form that won the event for her. The former Tacoma girl, wife of Don Fraser, today ranks as America's No. 1 woman skier, having won the recent combined downhill and slalom at Aspen, Colo.

"Gretchen Triumphs," headline after Gretchen Fraser won the women's national championship in Alta, Utah, for the second time. *Seattle Times*, March 24, 1941.

The magazine published a picture of the Idaho women's ski team that won Sun Valley's Interstate Ski Meet, singing at the Sun Valley Lodge, dressed in Tyrolean costumes: Eleanor Steiglitz of Sun Valley, Nancy Reynolds, Kathleen Harriman, Gretchen Fraser, and Elizabeth Durrance. "America's finest skier, Mrs. Fraser, won both the downhill and slalom events to score 200 points which greatly assisted her team in securing the victory."

Even the article "Colorado Winter Sports News" was full of Sun Valley references. Don and Gretchen Fraser were in Denver, where he was the Sun Valley rep. "The two of them should set the Colorado ski world afire with their hotshot scudding." Don won the Silver Skis, and "Gretchen is one of the twelve

'A Class' women skiers in the United States." Sun Valley's Dick Mitchell and Florian Haemmerle were in town. "Barney McLean, No. 1 Colorado skier, has been offered the primrose path to Sun Valley." Gordon Wren, the No. 2 Colorado skier, trained at Sun Valley the prior year "and now has a fast downhill look on his face."

A letter to Steve Hannagan dated January 9, 1941, described movies to be made involving Sun Valley. *Strange Honeymoon* starred William Powell and Myrna Loy. Darrel Zanuck's *Sun Valley* would have a crew in Sun Valley in mid-January. An MGM picture, *A Woman's Face*, had a crew in Sun Valley making location shots, and another, *The Great Canadian*, would star Clark Gable. An independent film by Tay Garnett starring Marlene Dietrich would be released through United Artists. An independent writer, M.H. Doyle, was working on a script with snow sequences shot in Sun Valley.

The *Seattle Times* continued to publish a number of articles about Sun Valley since so many local skiers considered it their second home. On February 4, 1941, the paper said Seattle skiers could "go over to the swanky Sun Valley, which is fast becoming the winter playground of the entire effete United States." On February 15, the *Times* reported on Seattleites at their favorite resort. Don Fraser recently arrived after greeting the Chilean ski team in New York that would race at Yosemite, Sugar Bowl, Mount Rainier, and Sun Valley. Gretchen Fraser was doubling in ski sequences for Sonja Henie in *Sun Valley Serenade*. Grace Lindley was skiing just five months after breaking her back in a fall from a horse. Ralph Bromaghin was in his first year as "part of the gang of Fancy Dans on skis," as a Sun Valley ski instructor, but had been drafted into the Army. "We notice . . . it's our own Seattle 'gang' which is first out in the morning and the last to leave the ski slopes at night."

The *Seattle Times* sent two reporters to Sun Valley to describe its many attractions. Virginia Boren reported on the social aspects of life there on February 4, 1941:

> *This is an entirely different world . . . a world where the unconquerable spirit rides in shining splendor on a pair of skis—even after some bad breaks . . . where, in the pristine glitter of the falling snow, you feel you're on the slate for the "Nutcracker" ballet—the second act, when the Queen goes to the Snow Country. . . . Sun Valley, the St. Moritz of the North American continent, is anything you want it to be.*

Rita Hume of the *Times* visited Sun Valley "for a bit of brushing up on her racing technique." Her February 23 article shows how classes were conducted: "'Ya,' said

Friedl, 'you go in Sepp's class' and I was off to my first day of instruction at Sun Valley." Sigi Engl and Sepp Benedikter instructed the racing class.

Hume's class rode to the top of Baldy, and "the next thing I know Sepp was headed down the deep and untracked snow of Warm Springs trail. 'Follow me,' said he, very blithely swinging fast christies in and out among the trees in snow up to his knees."

> *Skiing in deep snow after a fresh snowfall is daily practice for racing classes on the theory that* [if] *you can ski perfectly on untracked slopes you can do anything on packed snow. Another day found us swinging christies on the chopped-up crust of Ruud Mountain. . . . But if I was worried about not getting some fast skiing, one nonstop run of swinging turns down the canyon or following on the heels of Sepp down Sunnyside Run was all I needed. Keeping five or six pupils from not swinging turns into each other or whipping safely through some of the snowplough classes brought forth a frequent admonition from Sepp, "Look always forward."*

Friedl Pfeifer inspected the class and "frequently leaves one gaping as he schusses down the canyon or comes to an abrupt stop with a trick somersault maneuver."

On March 27, 1941, the *Seattle Times* used Sun Valley's widely admired chairlifts to lobby for such lifts to be built in Washington:

> *Back from an enjoyable visit to Sun Valley we can think of no more appropriate subject than chairlifts. "Appropriate" because in a couple of days at Sun Valley we got in more downhill skiing than we have in any one season at Paradise Valley. . . . Legs rested by a sit-in-a-chair ride up the mountain respond much more quickly to mental dictation and perform their chores more surely than those fatigued by zigzaging uphill traverses, herring-boning and sidestepping.*

Ski Tournaments in 1941

The Sun Valley Four-Event Intercollegiate Ski Meet was held from December 29, 1940, to January 1, 1941. Four feet of new snow made the conditions nearly perfect for racers from Washington, Stanford, Washington State, Utah, Colorado, Bennington, Wyoming, Wisconsin, and Gonzaga.

The downhill was a one-and-three-quarter-mile course on Bald Mountain, starting 200 yards above Roundhouse Station, going down "the newly widened Canyon and Riverside Runs, with a total drop of 2,300 feet," reported the *Seattle Times*. A newcomer, Washington's Bill Redlin, beat the old timers to win the event, followed by Bobby Blatt of Stanford and Carl Neu, Washington's captain. Neu won the cross-country race but Redlin won the slalom with Blatt a close second. The Bradley Cup competition was determined by the jumping event, where Blatt placed fourth, even though he was new to the sport, and nosed out Redlin for the award, with Neu finishing third. "Bill Redlin showed an intensity and speed reminiscent of Dick Durrance. We'll be hearing of him again for he's one of America's most promising young skiers." The University of Washington first team won the team competition, with the school's second team finishing second.

The fourth annual Jeffers Cup Tri-State team competition was held on January 20, 1941. California's team won the team championships. Washington was second, followed by Utah, Oregon, Colorado, and Montana. Individual honors went to Alf Engen and Gretchen Fraser representing Idaho. UW's Bill Redlin took second in the slalom and finished third in individual points after Alf and Kaare Engen. In the downhill run on Warm Springs, Kathleen Harriman "took the race's fanciest 'wingding' and suffered a slight injury," according to the *Sun Valley Ski Club Annual* for 1941.

The year 1941 was perhaps the greatest one in U.S. ski jumping history. The national jumping championship held at the Milwaukee Ski Bowl in Washington in early March 1941 attracted the world's best jumpers. Ski jumping was still more popular than alpine skiing, and there was an intense fascination with the competition for the longest jump. Sun Valley's Alf Engen was engaged in a nationwide battle with Torger Tokle, a young Norwegian living in New York. On February 9, Engen jumped 267 feet at Iron Mountain, Michigan, in front of 25,000 people, setting a new North American distance record by 10 feet, but losing to Walter Bietila on form points. Two hours later, Tokle had a "mighty leap of 273 feet," according to the *Seattle Times*, breaking Engen's record at Leavenworth, Washington. Tokle's new record made him a favorite in the national jumping championships at the Milwaukee Ski Bowl on March 3, 1941, but the prior year's winner, Alf Engen, wanted his revenge. On March 3, Tokle, "the human sky rocket from New York," jumped 288 feet, breaking his own North American record. Engen was second and Arthur Devlin of Lake Placid third. Tokle said if the takeoff was moved back 30 feet, he could jump 325 feet, and he could jump 400 feet "on the proper sort of hill," said the *Times*. He later set another American record at Iron Mountain, Michigan, of 289 feet.

Showing the level of competition at the Washington tournament, six of its competitors were inducted into the U.S. Ski and Snowboard hall of Fame. Tokle had an amazing record in his short career. He competed in the United States from 1939 to 1943, winning 39 of the 44 tournaments he entered, and establishing 22 new hill records.

In March 1941, the national downhill championships were held at Aspen. Toni Matt of North Conway, New Hampshire, "flashed down Roch Run course high in the Rockies," reported the *Seattle Times*, to win the men's championship, beating Dick Durrance from Alta. Bill Redlin, a freshman from the University of Washington, was third and Bill Janss of San Francisco was fourth. Tacoma's Gretchen Fraser, the "blond skier from Sun Valley, Idaho," won the women's downhill with "a brilliant run," finishing 11 seconds ahead of the second-place finisher, becoming the national downhill and slalom champion. "The 22-year old bride had made it all the way to the top spot in the nation."

Fraser said Aspen was very primitive in 1941. There were limited accommodations, so racers stayed in people's homes. She stayed at the Gould house with 13 other racers, sharing one bathroom. There were no lifts and just a little snow. There was a little scow that skiers rode up 200 feet, "a mining company marvel," that took racers straight up a mine shaft. "You got out at Zaugg Point, which was two-thirds the way up the downhill course, so you walked the rest of the way." It took half of the skiers through the mine shaft one day and half up the second day.

An "Ace field" competed at the third annual National Four-Way Championships at Sun Valley in late March 1941, according to the *Seattle Times*. Alf Engen was the favorite, as he won the prior year's Four-Way Championship in Washington. The event was also the Pan-American Tournament, featuring teams from Chile, Canada, and the United States competing in downhill and slalom. The tournament was described by Otto Lang in the *Sun Valley Ski Club Annual* for 1941.

The cross-country race ran in a wide circle around Dollar Mountain in two loops. Lang said it was "obvious that the golden age of cross country running in the United States . . . belongs to the past," because of the commitment it takes for practice and its lack of glamour that downhill and jumping events have. Olav Rodegaard of Portland's Cascade Ski Club won the event, followed by Dave Bradley, formerly of Dartmouth. Alf Engen finished third, "with little training . . . but with a big heart," in the words of the *Seattle Times*.

"In a novel experiment in the history of the Harriman Cup Races," Otto Lang wrote, "the down hill was held on the River Run side of the mountain, following the chairlift line from the top of Baldy, instead of using the traditional Warmsprings course." This received a divided response from the racers but was popular with spectators, whose best vantage point was around the Roundhouse Station, where they could see skiers negotiating the traverse heading into canyon. Sixty-four skiers entered the downhill, where the ski patrol and volunteers eliminated every bump and put the "course in the best possible condition."

> *Warm Springs is a difficult course demanding utmost technical ability and high speed turn control. It is also a longer course, more tiring and exhausting. The Ridge-Canyon-Riverside run is a 100% speed course with hardly a turn in it. From the top of Baldy the course follows the towers of the chair lift with slight deviations, practically pointing down towards the valley in a beeline. The most difficult is the "Steilhang" above the Round House Station and the crucial traverse. The racers entered this traverse with full speed and the problem presented was not to check too much, not to tire the legs out and to keep low and as close as possible to the trees on the left-hand side when rounding the curve at the Round House Station to "schuss" the Canyon. The Canyon was taken straight without the slightest suggestion of a turn by the majority of the field. . . . The contestants drop approximately 3,200 feet in two miles or a little less. The final two-tenths of a mile of the course has been eliminated because of snow conditions and its all "fast business."*

Sigi Engel won the downhill, racing with his trousers bound tightly with string to diminish air resistance, followed by Friedl Pfeifer. Dick Durrance finished 10th, 10 seconds slower than the winner.

The women's downhill started just above the steilhang, and "competition was stiff," Lang wrote. "One of the girls spilled going into the Canyon Run proper Thursday morning and it took her twenty-eight seconds to slither to the bottom of the run. It takes the top-flight racers about twenty seconds to ski it. That's how steep it is." Gretchen Fraser won after taking Canyon "in the rather unorthodox but obviously profitable Durrance manner—a wide snowplow at full speed." Nancy Reynolds, skiing for Sun Valley, was second.

Friedl Pfeifer, "headman in Sun Valley skiing," according to Lang, was again "the superior master of the Slalom," winning the "snaky" slalom race on Christmas Bowl, beating Chris Schwarzenbach of Stanford and Sigi Engl. Washington Ski Club's Hugh Bauer and Don Amick "did themselves proud" by finishing 13th and 14th in the slalom, since last year's Harriman Cup winner, Dick Durrance, placed 18th. Gretchen Fraser was fourth in the slalom behind the winner, Nancy Reynolds of Sun Valley.

In the jumping competition, Alf Engen "displayed his supremacy in the air overwhelmingly," Lang wrote. Gordon Wren of the Durrance Ski School in Alta was second, and Leon Goodman of the Sun Valley Ski Club was third.

The Canadian team won the Pan-American Championships, with the Chilean team placing second. Judges disqualified the U.S. team because "Bill Redlin of the University of Washington . . . broke a ski in a nasty spill on the roundhouse turn and did not finish," according to the *New York Times*.

Pfeifer won the Harriman Cup for the best combined performance. According to Lang, Alf Engen "again demonstrated his all-around skiing proficiency today by soaring to first place in jumping and winning the national four-event combined championship for the second consecutive year." Gretchen Fraser won the women's combined title with Nancy Reynolds second, after winning the slalom. Fraser received the 1941 Harriman Cup from Otto Lang, who taught her to ski on Mount Rainier.

Two weeks later, Dick Durrance won the second annual Alta Snow Cup race, beating Barney McLean of Denver, the defending titleholder. Gretchen Fraser, skiing for the Sun Valley Ski Club, won the women's national championship for the second time.

Showing how the federal government supported the ski industry, the district forest ranger wrote an article for the Sun Valley Ski Club's report in 1941. Before the resort arrived, he said, Bald Mountain was just a fire lookout station in the summer. After Baldy was opened for skiing, the Forest Service replaced the old one-room lookout with a new lookout and ski shelter, and the rangers of the Sawtooth National Forest kept it open for skiers. The CCC camp closed in June 1941, and the Sun Valley trail crew completed several new trails on Baldy in summer 1941—a trail from Baldy's summit to College, a cutoff from Roundhouse to Riverside, and one under the ski lift to the Canyon station. "It is the aim of Sun Valley and the Forest Service to make this area the greatest winter sports area in the world."

In December 1941, the *New York Times* named the year's outstanding skiers. Torger Tokle, the 22-year-old Norwegian ski jumper living in New York, was No. 1. He won 12 of 13 events he entered that year, taking several major championships and setting seven hill records. Toni Matt won the national downhill and combined downhill-slalom

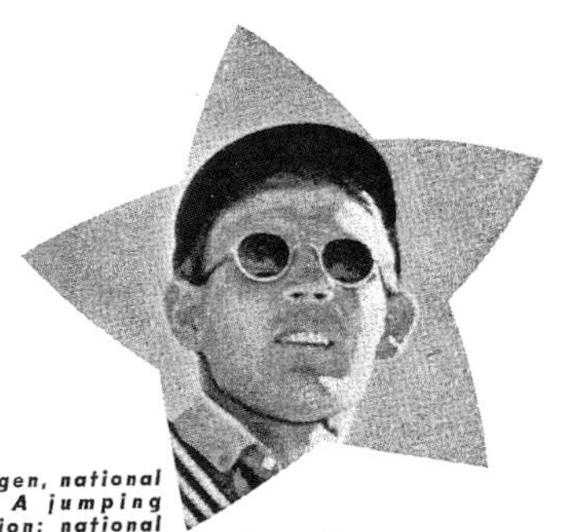

Alf Engen, national class A jumping champion; national four-event combined champion and 1940 winner of the All-American Ski Trophy.

Dick Durrance, national open downhill and combined champion; national amateur downhill, slalom and combined champion and F.I.S. slalom winner for 1940.

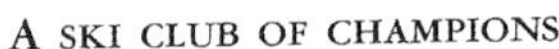

A SKI CLUB OF CHAMPIONS!

That's the reputation achieved by the five-year-old Sun Valley Ski Club whose members are presently the holders of 10 national championships and a host of minor awards offered in various sections of the United States.

Responsible for a good measure of the club's success is the excellent training given to racers in Friedl Pfeifer's Sun Valley Ski School, where special racing classes are held for their benefit. Particularly among the women stars has this been so. Another factor is the varied runs offered by the Sawtooth Mountain region, which more than prepares training contestants for any terrain conditions.

Prospects for the coming year are bright, with new runs offering even finer training facilities, and the club looks forward to maintaining its high position in American ski circles.

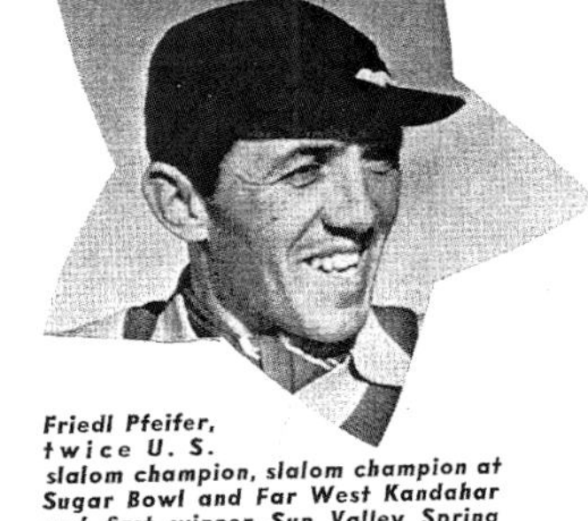

Friedl Pfeifer, twice U. S. slalom champion, slalom champion at Sugar Bowl and Far West Kandahar and first winner Sun Valley Spring and Snow Sports Meet.

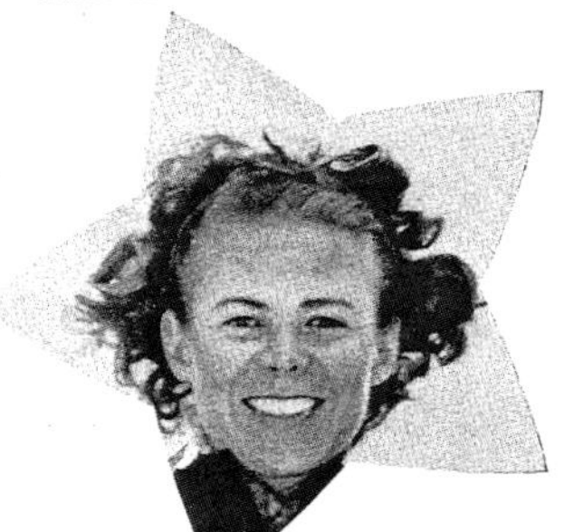

Grace Carter Lindley, national women's open and amateur downhill champion and Sun Valley Ski Club combined champion.

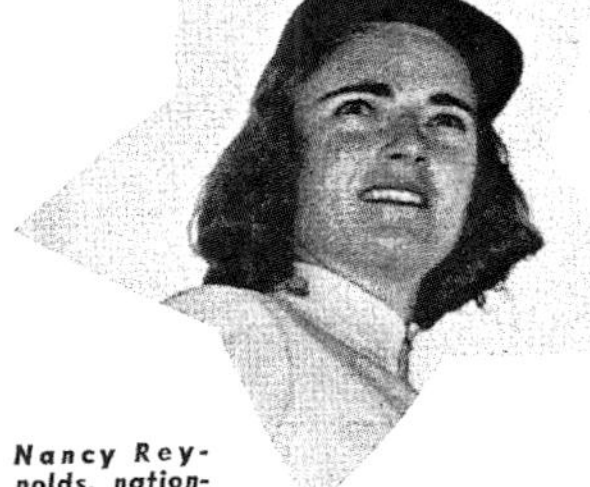

Nancy Reynolds, national women's open and amateur slalom champion; Far West Kandahar and Silver Skis winner for 1940.

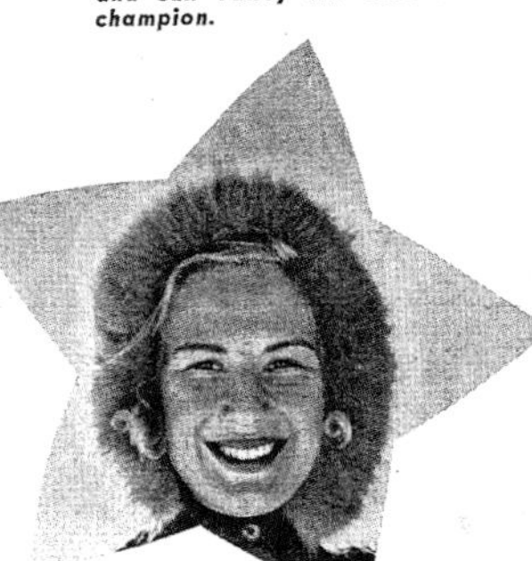

Gretchen Fraser, Pacific Northwest women's combined champion; Jeffers Cup winner in the Sun Valley Interstate Meet; Sun Valley Ski Club downhill champion and women's giant slalom winner at the Sugar Bowl.

Kathleen Harriman, first winner of the Mary Cornelia Trophy in 1939 intercollegiate ski meet for victories in downhill, slalom and combined and combined winner of the Hochgebirge Invitational meet at Franconia, N. H.

Picture from *The Valley Sun* of Sun Valley Ski Club champions, 1941.

titles, beating Dick Durrance, who won the national open slalom title. "Young Bill Redlin of the University of Washington romped off with the amateur laurels in the downhill, slalom and combined events at Aspen" at the national downhill and slalom championships. Gretchen Fraser, skiing for Sun Valley, "dominated the women's championships," winning downhill and combined downhill-slalom titles. Nancy Reynolds, also representing Sun Valley, was the combined restricted amateur champion. Alf Engen, "a Sun Valley color-bearer," won the national four-way championships.

In late 1941, Dick Durrance, Gretchen Fraser, and Alf Engen had their status as amateur skiers revoked. Durrance developed Groswold FIS skis and his name was used to advertise them. Fraser doubled for Sonja Henie in skiing sequences in *Sun Valley Serenade*, and Engen permitted his name and title to be used in an advertisement for Alf Engen skis, where he was called "All-American Champion." In December 1941, the National Ski Association cleared Durrance of violating its rules. A skier could continue to be an amateur even if certified as a ski teacher, the association said, as long as he did not teach for money. Open-class competitors could endorse ski equipment "so long as titles were not thereby exploited." In February 1942, the amateur status of Fraser and Engen was reinstated.[55]

Averell Harriman Becomes Involved in the War Effort, Leaves Sun Valley

Beginning in 1940, Averell Harriman became deeply involved in public service with the U.S. war effort, and later in diplomacy and politics, and his connection with Sun Valley changed. In 1941, Harriman became chief of the materials branch of the production division in the Office of Production Management. Later that year, he was sent by President Roosevelt to Britain to administer the Lend-Lease Act, which provided U.S. aid to allies. Averell's brother Roland took his place on the Union Pacific board because Averell "wanted it to be in the family." Harriman went with Lord Beaverbrook of Britain to Moscow in 1941 to arrange Lend-Lease shipments to the Soviet Union. In August 1942 Harriman returned to Russia, this time with Churchill, to discuss opening a second front in Europe. The work done in England during the war by Harriman, newsman Edward R. Morrow, and U.S. Ambassador

John G. Winant is told in *Citizens of London: The Americans Who Stood With Britain in its Darkest, Finest Hour* by Lynne Olson.

Harriman was joined by his daughter Kathleen in London, and he had Steve Hannagan arrange a job with Hearst's International News Service and had Harry Hopkins get State Department approval for her trip. She found Averell was a significant figure "in the drama that now captivated and alarmed Americans." He knew everyone of note, and "everyone who has a constructive part in the workings of the war, and they all love him," according to Abramson.

Harriman was kept informed about the Union Pacific and Sun Valley while he was overseas. On July 14, 1941, U.P. president Jeffers wrote Harriman at the American embassy in London. The resort, he said, had "a fine spring business, and everything points to a very active summer business." There were some large parties at Sun Valley in the spring, and "Pat Rogers is doing an outstanding job of taking care of them." He reported that $20,000 would be spent to increase the capacity of the Bald Mountain lifts and provide additional ski runs. There would be no expenditures on the Dollar Mountain ski lift except for repairs. Union Pacific business was "heavy," but problems were emerging for the railroad industry from increasing war demands. "Revenues for June were at a peak for that month since 1920, and, with the defense programs developing and expanding as it is daily, we will most assuredly reach the peak of what we can properly handle in the late Fall." Expected heavy business in the coming fall, Jeffers felt, would get railroads into no end of trouble. "All of these Lines, with one or two notable exceptions, of which the Union Pacific is one, have been carrying over the terrific increases in gross revenue into net, instead of pouring this increased revenue back into the property in order to keep the motive power and cars in condition, as well as the track, to take care of the tremendous increase in business."

Harriman was made ambassador to Russia in 1943, a post he held until 1946, and he took Kathleen with him to Moscow. Even in Russia, Harriman kept up with skiing:

> *During the war there were only three ambassadors constantly followed—the English, the Japanese, and myself. When I would go skiing on Lenin Hill* [now the site of the University of Moscow] *the "bodyguard" assigned me could not keep up with me. So one day I was assigned one of the instructors from the Red Army Ski Troops. Then I could go skiing anyplace.*

In November 2011, *Vanity Fair* published an article about Kathleen Harriman's wartime experiences in London, revealing her father's wartime affair with Pamela Digby Churchill. She was Kathleen's friend, 28 years younger than Averell, and married to Winston Churchill's son. Kathleen knew of the affair—"I am not a total fool. . . . I had to either go home and not be a part of it or—but I thought I should protect my father, and the best way to do that was by staying." When Averell's wife, Marie, learned of the affair, she cabled him, "keep your affairs clean and out of the papers or you will be facing the most costly divorce in the history of the republic." When Averell broke off the affair during the war, he had Kathleen break the news to Pamela. Although the *Vanity Fair* article caused a sensation, Abramson's *Spanning the Century*, published in 1992, discussed the affair in detail, saying the war "brought on an epidemic of marriage suspensions."A report in 2013, "The Last Courtesan: The Life of Pamela Digby Churchill Hayward Harriman," provided a salacious description of Pamela's life as a courtesan living off wealthy men. In 1971, at age 79, after Marie died, Averell married Pamela. The Harriman house in Georgetown became a "social and political center for Democratic leaders, aspirants to office, distinguished foreign visitors and Mr. Harriman's many journalist friends." After Averell died, Pamela was named ambassador to France by President Bill Clinton.[56]

Part Five

SUN VALLEY DURING WORLD WAR II

19

SKIING CONTINUES BUT WAR BEGINS TO AFFECT THE COUNTRY; SUN VALLEY CLOSES IN DECEMBER 1942

In late 1940, the U.S. Army began training mountain troops thanks to the efforts of Charles Minot "Minnie" Dole and John E.P. Morgan (who helped lay out Sun Valley in 1936). Dole and Morgan helped organize the National Ski Patrol in 1939, with Dole becoming its president and Morgan its treasurer.

Dole and Morgan were influenced by the performance of Finnish soldiers in the Battle of Suomussalmi, where a lightly armed contingent of 11,000 fast-moving Finnish troops on skis surrounded a heavily armed Russian force of 50,000, supported by tanks, and trapped them on a mountain road. According to Minnie Dole, the ski troops "nimbly kicked and glided through the snow-laden pines, then encircled the hapless Russians, and either shot them or waited for their food and firewood to run out." Over 13,000 Russians were killed and 43 tanks were seized.

Dole and Morgan believed the performance of the Finnish army demonstrated the need for U.S. ski troops trained in mountain and winter warfare. In September 1940, they met with Army chief of staff General George C. Marshall to discuss their ideas. Dole's philosophy was to "make soldiers out of skiers, don't try to make skiers out of soldiers." Marshall was persuaded and directed the Army to develop clothing and equipment for mountain forces, forming six small experimental ski units to lay a foundation for future winter training. In December 1940, five Army division commanders began ski training in different locations. Existing units from Fort Lewis, Washington, were used to test winter equipment on Mount Rainier. The rigorous training the men received on Mount Rainier turned novice skiers into experts, and shaped the techniques of the ones who became ski instructors.

In fall 1941, the Army advanced its plans for a specialized mountain warfare unit. Three regions with different areas of focus were selected: winter and low-altitude mountain training in Wisconsin and Virginia and alpine training at Fort Lewis, Washington. When the country entered the war on December 8, 1941, the 87th Mountain Infantry Battalion was activated at Fort Lewis, becoming the first formal unit of mountain troops. It became a "who's who" of skiing, that included Walter Prager (the ex-Dartmouth ski coach), Friedl Pfeifer (head of the Sun Valley Ski School), Ralph Bromaghin (ski instructor in Washington and Sun Valley), John Woodward (captain of the University of Washington ski team), filmmaker John Jay, and many others.

In December 1940, Averell Harriman offered to let the War Department use Sun Valley to train ski troops, based on advice from ski instructor Fred Iselin, who served with the Swiss alpine troops. In Switzerland, officers were trained at winter resorts such as St. Moritz, where the training period was sped up five-fold when ski lifts were available. Harriman offered to train Army officers at Sun Valley at a reasonable expense rate, under Iselin or Willi Meyer. They could get ski training and be taken into the higher mountains for mountaineering work.

Fred Iselin published an article in the *Sun Valley Ski Club Annual* for 1941, "Why Not Military Skiing at Sun Valley?" Sun Valley, he wrote, was "better than in any other place in the United States" to train ski troops, offering over 10 miles of slopes from easy and gentle to the most difficult rock peaks.

Soldiers must first be trained as first-class skiers, Iselin argued, then trained to be high alpine soldiers. Sun Valley, with its chairlifts, was the best area to train soldiers in a short time. The Proctor lift could be reserved for ski troops. Once trained in proper skiing techniques, soldiers needed to learn skiing and camping in high alpine terrain, and the Pioneer region of the Sawtooth mountain range offered the perfect location, with its rocks, snow, and ice. Advanced training would involve

> *building ski sleds, building bivouacs, fixing meals in snow and ice, handling an avalanche shovel, avalanche rod, avalanche thread, first aid, skiing on the rope, roping down, walking with crampons, and a knowledge of reading maps and compass.*

Although not selected as a training site, Sun Valley played a role in the war. Darryl Zanuck, head of 20th Century Fox Studios, produced *Sun Valley Serenade* using Otto Lang to film ski sequences. In 1942, Colonel Zanuck of the U.S. Signal Corps believed the Army needed a film to teach its ski troops the Arlberg technique that Lang taught at Sun Valley. Zanuck arranged for the Army to make the film, with Lang directing it.

In spring 1941, Lang filmed the first mountain training movie made in America, *The Basic Principles of Skiing*, at Sun Valley. He used a five-man detachment of soldiers from Fort Lewis led by Lieutenant John Woodward, which included Sergeant Walter Prager. John Jay, an Army photographer, was assigned to the project. Lang used Sun Valley ski instructors as soldiers—Sepp Benedikter, Fred Iselin, John Litchfield, and Pepi Teichner. The film demonstrated the Arlberg method of skiing, which was thought to be well suited to military skiing. "Lang's eye for graceful motion together with his passion for detail produced what is arguably the most beautiful military training film ever made," said *Skiing Heritage*. John Jay said the movie was "filmed so beautifully that, for years afterward, recruits into what eventually became the 10th Mountain Division complained bitterly that the ski troops were nothing like the movie." Lang ended up making a series of ski training films at Sun Valley for the Army.[57]

War Buildup Affects Railroads and Sun Valley

In the late 1930s, the Union Pacific began to upgrade its rail system in anticipation of the demands from a possible war. In 1939–1940, it relaid 800 miles of its main line and planned to do an additional 655 miles the next year. Significant investments were made in new power and rolling stock. Bill Jeffers said Union Pacific was going to put its system in "top shape, and he had the authority for whatever was needed," according to Maury Klein.

Union Pacific had to deal with the exodus of a number of its executives for war duty. Averell Harriman's government service escalated to full time in June 1940, and he later was posted to London. In December 1940, Robert Lovett, chairman of the board's executive committee, became an assistant secretary of war. President Bill Jeffers became Roosevelt's "rubber czar" in September 1942, a role he forcefully played, imposing gas and tire rationing and a 35-mile-per-hour speed limit on the country's highways within

10 days of taking office. Union Pacific lost workers as the war took many into military service and war-related jobs (12,000 of its employees served in the military). By 1943, the company was losing employees as fast as it could hire them and faced threatened strikes over wages and other issues.

Railroad business was booming, having picked up since spring 1940 as defense spending triggered an economic boom in the West. California got 10 percent of all federal money spent during the war. The buildup for the war in the Pacific meant an unprecedented amount of traffic used Union Pacific's Los Angeles line, the weak link in its system. By 1943, U.P.'s Wyoming Division handled the heaviest traffic west of the Mississippi, and a third of all transcontinental traffic passed through it. Union Pacific had to "handle the largest traffic in its history with the least experienced work force it had ever had," Kleinn wrote. This placed stress on Union Pacific's operations, rolling stock and track, and personnel, which would affect the railroad's plans following the war's end, including for Sun Valley, according to Klein.

World War II started for the United States on December 7, 1941, when the Japanese bombed Pearl Harbor. The war changed everything in the country, although it took time for its full effects to be felt. Skiing slowed as men went off to war and women had to deal with wartime conditions, including rationing of food, clothing, gasoline, and tires.

In January 1942, Sun Valley manager Pat Rogers assured the public the resort was open and offered a special experience:

> *The greatest resort of its kind in the world, Sun Valley has curtailed none of its entertainment. . . . As in the past, the skiing and the skating, as well as the other winter sports, in the clear mountain air will invigorate and refresh guests, making them fit and prepared for resumption of civilian assignments in the war program.*

Alf Engen would be in Sun Valley giving jumping instructions and competing for the Sun Valley Ski Club. *Sun Valley Serenade* was showing at the opera house. Learn to Ski Weeks in January were so successful that "the Spring Learn to Ski program inaugurated last year will be repeated the end of March and during April," the *New York Times* reported.[58]

SKI TOURNAMENTS

The annual Four-Event Intercollegiate Ski Meet was held at Sun Valley over Christmas 1941. H.C. Bradley wrote:

> *At Christmas, Sun Valley turns collegiate—with all the life and fun and gaiety, the arrogance, the deference, the shy reserve and the boisterous noise that goes naturally with a crowd of boys and girls, away from their books and laboratories—out for a good time—but tempered by the responsibilities and anxieties that come from competition.*

The University of Washington first team won in downhill, slalom, and combined, followed by the UW second team, Washington State, Dartmouth, University of Utah, University of Idaho, Stanford, and UCLA For the second year, UW's Bill Redlin and Stanford's Bill Blatt battled for individual honors. Blatt turned the tables on Redlin, winning the mile-and-a-half downhill race, with Redlin second.

At the Interstate Race in mid-January 1942, which involved downhill, slalom, and jumping events for men, the California team walked off with team trophies. The downhill was run on Warm Springs, where the steilhang presented the greatest challenge. The most popular racer was 15-year-old Jack Reddish from Salt Lake City, who weighed 90 pounds. "No praise is too great for this courageous little skier who, despite the tremendous handicap resulting from his lack of poundage, skied right along with the field and more than held his own," the Sun Valley Ski Club reported. The slalom, held on Christmas Bowl, consisted of two courses, one above the other, each with separate timing and gate keepers. Contestants ran the first course, had a short rest, then ran the lower course, eliminating the need to climb back up the hill between runs. Barney McLean of Colorado won the downhill and slalom races. Washington's Bill Taylor finished second in the slalom. Gretchen Fraser, who won the prior year's combined, was ineligible to compete but opened the downhill with "a very fine run." Roy Mikkelsen from California won the jumping competition. In the men's combined three-event contest, California finished first, followed by Utah, Washington, Colorado, Montana, Idaho, Nevada, and Oregon.

The sixth annual Harriman Cup/International Downhill and Slalom Tournament was held March 28–29, 1942. "Just as it is the dream of every tennis player to compete once at Wimbledon, it is every skier's hope to participate in the famous Harriman

Cup Races at Sun Valley," boasted the *American Ski Annual 1943*. The tournament was described by Otto Lang in the *Sun Valley Ski Club Annual 1942*.

The two-mile downhill with 3,000 feet of vertical drop was set by Fred Iselin on the River Run side of Baldy. The course started at the top of the mountain, went straight down the far ridge of Christmas Bowl, then on to the steep knoll above the Roundhouse and down Canyon, where, according to Otto Lang, a "short but vicious incline . . . definitely elevated the rating and difficulty of the course," finishing at the end of River Run. Barney McLean from Denver won the downhill, setting a record for the course. Alf Engen was second, and Dick Durrance of Alta was fourth ("if Dick had more than only one day to practice on the course he might have fared better"). Washington racers included Don Amick who finished fifth, Hugh Bauer seventh, Paul Gilbreath 10th, Bill Taylor 12th, and Walter Hampton from Wenatchee 20th.

Catherine Henck from the Yosemite Ski Club won the women's downhill, which started on the knoll above the Roundhouse. Gretchen Fraser and Clarita Heath, both skiing for the Sun Valley Ski Club, were second and third. Washington skiers included Bettie Amick (10th) and Betty Rae Norman (11th). "There were a few mean looking falls," Lang wrote.

The slalom was changed at the last minute from Ruud Mountain to Dollar Mountain and was won by Gordon Wren, followed by John Litchfield. Dick Durrance was fifth. Northwest skiers included Don Amick (sixth) and Bill Taylor (15th).

The Harriman Cup was won by Barney McLean after what Lang described as a stiff battle with Alf Engen. Both skiers had 268 points, but under Harriman Cup rules, the winner in case of a tie was the winner of the downhill. Engen placed second and Dick Durrance was third. Seattle's Don Amick was ninth and Bill Taylor was 16th. Sun Valley skiers Clarita Heath, Gretchen Fraser, and Turid Thorsen swept the first three places in the women's Harriman Cup.

At the jumping exhibition on Ruud Mountain, Torger Tokle competed against Alf Engen and Art Devlin of Lake Placid. Tokle lived in New York and competed for the Norway Ski Club. He and Alf Engen had been competing for top honors in jumping tournaments around the country for several years. Their competition continued in 1942, when Tokle jumped 289 feet at Iron Mountain, Michigan, in early March, a new American distance record, breaking the hill record of 267 feet set by Engen the prior year and Tokle's own American distance record of 288 feet set in Washington.

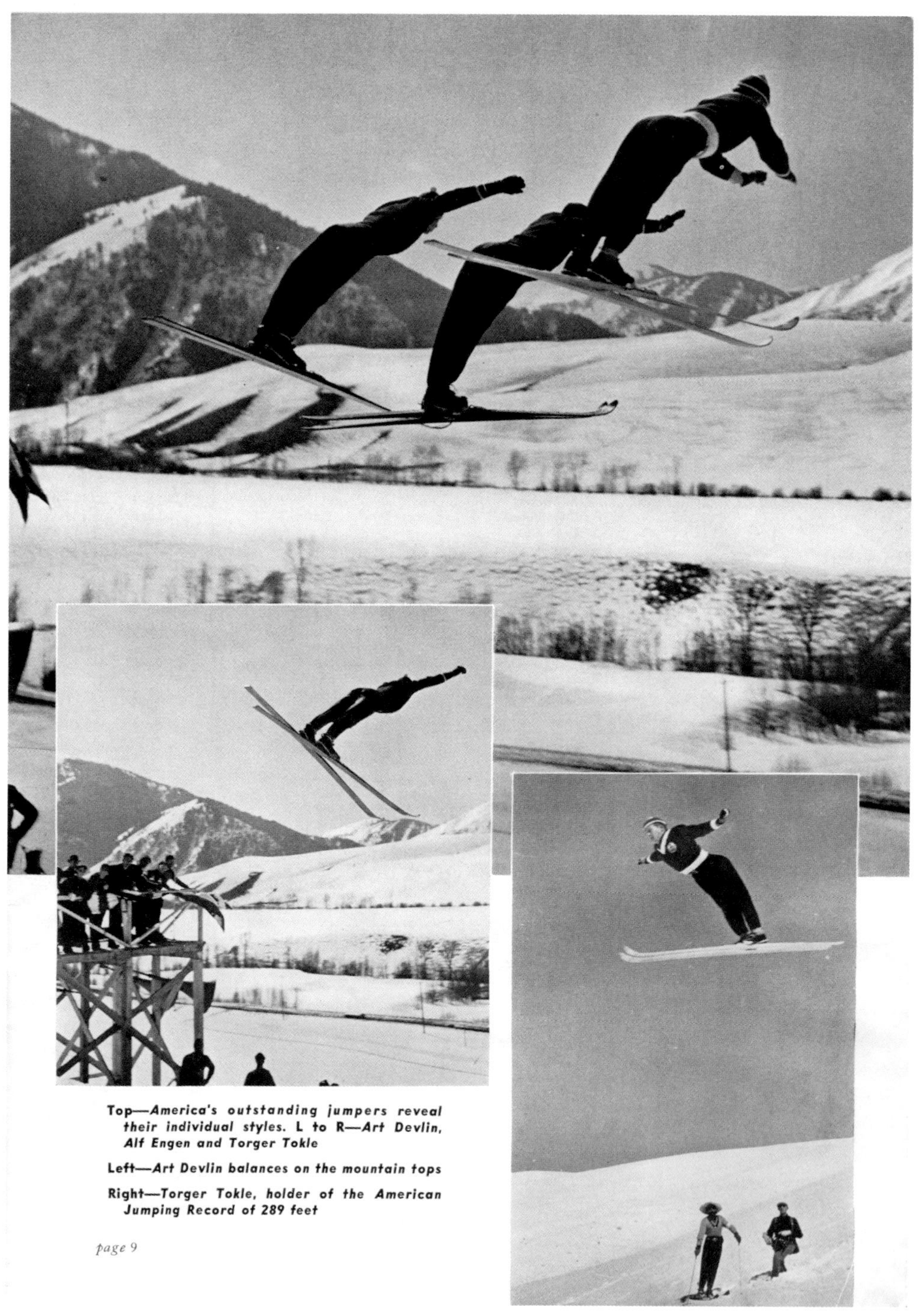

Top—*America's outstanding jumpers reveal their individual styles. L to R—Art Devlin, Alf Engen and Torger Tokle*

Left—*Art Devlin balances on the mountain tops*

Right—*Torger Tokle, holder of the American Jumping Record of 289 feet*

page 9

Pictures of ski jumpers on Ruud Mountain, *Sun Valley Ski Club Report 1942*.

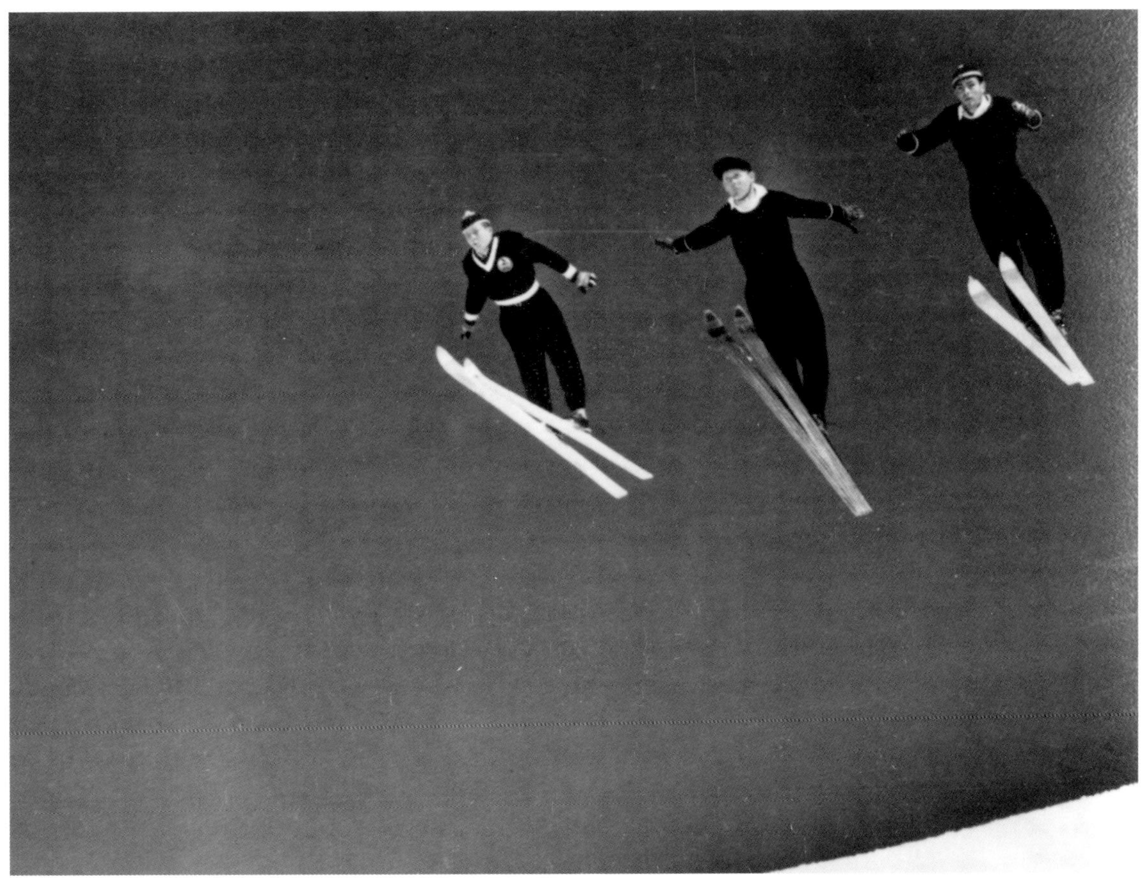

The famous Engen brothers jumping at Ruud Mountain, at the 1940 Western Interstate Ski Meet—Karre, Sverre and Alf. Alf competed for Sun Valley from 1938 to 1948.

The Sun Valley jumping hill had been built for 150-foot jumps, but the takeoff was moved back 25 feet, artificially enlarging the hill. A number of jumpers broke the old record of 166 feet. Tokle's "prodigious drive," according to the Sun Valley Ski Club, set a new hill record of 188 feet, leaving "far behind the mark of 164 feet set by Engen, who reeled off a 175-yard jump." Tokle was "a most powerful jumper and is constantly improving. Undoubtedly he has not yet reached his ultimate peak." After the exhibition, the skiers jumped in group formations, with from two to eight in the air at one time.

War Causes Sun Valley to Close

Not long after the United States entered the war in December 1941, the FBI detained three Austrian Sun Valley ski instructors for being enemy aliens. Friedl Pfeifer and Hans Hauser were taken to a North Dakota detention camp, and Sepp Froehlich was held in a county jail. Pfeifer was the head of the Sun Valley Ski School and married to the daughter of a prominent Salt Lake City banker. Froehlich was married to a daughter of a wealthy Eastern family. After an investigation, Pfeifer and Froehlich were released in mid-February. In March 1942, Pfeifer resigned as head of the ski school and applied for enlistment in the U.S. Army para-ski troops. Otto Lang directed the ski school in Pfeifer's absence. Hauser, who had expressed Nazi sympathies when he taught at Sun Valley, was kept in an internment camp for the duration of the war, and Harriman ignored his pleas to help him get out.

Otto Lang, Florian Haemmerle, and Andy Hennig were already American citizens, but Sigi Engl was not and he immediately enlisted. Pfeifer, Froehlich, and a long list of Sun Valley ski instructors later joined the 10th Mountain Division.

During winter 1941–1942, Sun Valley's ski school taught 12,417 skiers in 37,251 teaching hours, and 160,000 people were taken by ski buses to and from ski lifts. The average stay was 19 days. The war affected Sun Valley more as the year progressed. In October 1942, Pat Rogers wrote W.M. Jeffers in Washington, D.C., informing him that because gasoline and rubber were rationed, the Union Pacific was restricting the use of gas-powered vehicles and converting to other transportation modes. Sun Valley changed from bus service to gas-electric motor cars to bring passengers from Shoshone. Stagecoaches took passengers from the Ketchum depot to Sun Valley to conserve gas and rubber. All cars and buses at Sun Valley and the Utah Parks Company, except for "equipment absolutely needed," were replaced by horse-drawn vehicles. The order regarding rationing of gasoline would go into effect on November 15, 1942, but Sun Valley was able to secure a permit and enough gasoline to operate its required equipment (coal truck, commissary truck, ambulance, and rotary snowplow).

Sun Valley was experiencing an "exceptionally fine fall business," Rogers wrote. Sun Valley Ranch was served by its rail motor car, which stopped within a half mile of the Silver Creek property, where guests continued to the property on a surrey. The best pheasant hunting was around Richfield (north of Shoshone), and Rogers was attempting to make arrangements with a rancher to meet their guests at the depot and take them to the hunting area. Winter reservations were "coming in very rapidly for this time of year." Rogers expected to have sufficient personnel to operate as usual.

Rogers gave acting U.P. president Ashby the inventory of Sun Valley's buses, tires, trucks, and other equipment, and suggested they lease it to the government to transport employees to and from war projects, "at a fair rental basis." The government would furnish fuel and lubricants, and Sun Valley would supply drivers. This would keep the equipment under their supervision and get sufficient revenue to pay the original cost of the equipment. There had been a number of inquiries about purchasing the vehicles, but Sun Valley would take a big loss on any sale, and after the war, would not have any equipment to use in its operation. The resort had a considerable stock of groceries and commissary items.

In fall 1942, Sun Valley's bookings were "the heaviest ever," according to Dorice Taylor. The lodge and inn could hold 800 guests, but there were over 1,000 reservations for Christmas. There was no skiing in Europe, and some East Coast families were planning on spending the entire winter at the resort due to a concern about possible bombings. Don Fraser said, "some meets will be held at Sun Valley, including the Inter-collegiate" event during Christmas 1942, and the University of Washington ski team planned to compete there, "provided adequate means of transportation can be acquired," according to the *Seattle Times*.

In December 1942, the Office of Defense Transportation ordered railroads not to run sports specials for the duration of the war. On December 7, Union Pacific announced that Sun Valley, "winter sports resort of the nation," would close its doors to the public on December 20 "for the duration." Hundreds of people with reservations over Christmas were notified. "Scarcity of help, shortage of food, fuel rationing and rail-traffic conservation are the reasons for closing," the *Seattle Times* reported. The University of Washington ski team had to cancel its trip to Sun Valley, and 500 Seattle-area skiers were forced to change their plans. Three ski meets planned for 1943 were canceled, and 625 Union Pacific employees, a ski-instructing staff of 10 headed by Otto Lang, and 1,000 skiers with reservations for the holiday were affected.[59]

20

1943

Sun Valley Becomes a Naval Rehabilitation Center; Skiers Join Army Mountain Troops

In spring 1943, W.M. Jeffers, realizing the advantages Sun Valley offered due to its ideal climate and excellent facilities, negotiated an agreement with the Navy Department to use Sun Valley as a convalescent hospital. Averell Harriman was delighted: "I think it was a very appropriate thing," he said, "for Sun Valley to be used for that purpose."

On July 1, 1943, Sun Valley was commissioned as a naval special hospital offering facilities for the hospitalization, rehabilitation, and recreation of servicemen, one of 14 naval convalescent facilities in the country. The first was at Harriman, New York, the ancestral home of U.S. ambassador to Russia and Sun Valley founder W. Averell Harriman.

A Navy publication, "Convalescent Hospitals of World War II," described the facilities where "war-battered" sailors and marines received treatment. By 1945, Navy hospitals treated 90,635 patients who did not need general hospitalization but could neither return to service nor be discharged. They needed rest, psychotherapy, physical therapy, a "salubrious climate," and a good diet. The hospitals were havens of rehabilitation where occupation and physical therapists applied "paths to recovery through physical education, hydrotherapy, light and heat therapy, massage, corrective exercises, and recreational services."

Sun Valley's hospital operated between July 1, 1943, and December 1, 1945, and was second in bed capacity but "first in actual load. . . . It was especially equipped to administer physiotherapy to orthopedic convalescents. Neuropsychiatric cases, except psychosis, epilepsy, and 'constitutional psychopaths' were accepted." Along with Asheville, North Carolina, it was the only facility "which accepted all members of the naval service, officers, enlisted men, and WAVES. . . . The maximum complement of staff and patients was reached shortly before V-J Day when 1,603 naval personnel were aboard." An integrated rehabilitation program was started in 1944 to provide orthopedic surgery. The mental and physical wounds of 6,578 Navy, Marine, and Coast Guard patients were treated at Sun Valley through December 1, 1945.

Isolation was Sun Valley's biggest problem, but it had many recreational facilities that mitigated the loneliness of the situation, the Navy publication reported.

> *The facility maintained two glass-enclosed, heated, year long swimming pools. Three of the six ski lifts were kept in operation . . . and . . . advantage was taken of the excellent skiing in the very fine powder snow of the area. Ice skating . . . was amply provided for, although the artificial rink was discontinued. Fishing, hunting, soft ball diamond, a golf course, tennis, badminton, and archery courts were available. . . . A 500-seat theater with excellent equipment and first-run pictures obtained from Salt Lake City provided entertainment. Bowling alleys . . . were on hand as were pool tables, ping pong tables, and ample equipment.*

Pat Rogers and Ed Seagle remained at the resort during the war. Seagle was in charge of maintenance, managing a skeleton crew of 12 who received draft deferments. Sun Valley paid for maintenance, and the Navy had to make up for the wear and tear it caused and put the resort back into the condition it was in when the Navy took over.

On July 1, 1943, the first 90 patients arrived at Sun Valley, sailors suffering from tropical fevers, according to Seagle. Psychiatric cases came later, and the Old Chalet was turned into a psychiatric hospital with six psychiatrists. There was a checkpoint by the Sun Valley garage where everyone had to stop before entering. The ice rink and golf course were kept open, and Dollar Mountain was operated with two lifts, Dollar and Half Dollar.

The first Navy captain in command only lasted 90 days. His successor was careful to coordinate things with the local communities and law enforcement. Soon after he took over, he called in the managers of the bars and gambling facilities in Ketchum and the red light district in Hailey, along with the county sheriff and local police departments.

He said he did not mind Navy personnel drinking and gambling, as long as they did not get drunk and the games were not crooked. If his rules were not followed, he would make their places off-limits to military personnel. They got his message and followed his rules. The Navy had its own police, the shore patrol, and an undercover agent who went to local establishments to make sure the rules were obeyed. The agent knew all the tricks, and made sure the gambling places in Ketchum and Hailey ran straight houses. The state kept the road open between Sun Valley and Ketchum, and buses and taxis carried Navy personnel back and forth. Union Pacific trains came into Ketchum three times a week, and Sun Valley Stages carried people to and from Twin Falls. Seagle built a brig in the lodge basement containing two cells with bars that the Navy used to maintain discipline. Someone was in them most of the time, and they were given only bread and water.

Ketchum gambling was wide open during the war, with sailors who had not been paid for a long time while overseas suddenly having a lot of money to spend. There were no banks in town, but the bars cashed checks for the men. Seagle got unlimited gas coupons and tires, which were rationed during the war, since he was working at a Navy facility and had responsibilities taking him to Hailey. Showing the continuing cooperation between Sun Valley and local merchants, Seagle picked up the daily proceeds from Ketchum's gambling facilities and bars, which he took to the First Security Bank in Hailey for deposit, in effect acting as their bag man.

Val McAtee built an extension to Trail Creek Cabin for a naval officer's club. Seagle's staff poured the footings and foundations on the south end of the cabin in November 1943. McAtee's crew cut dead lodge pole pine trees five miles north of the Galena store after wading through three feet of snow, using a two-man crescent saw. A system of pulleys and cables was used to skid the logs to the road. A sawmill owner sawed them flat on two sides and delivered them to Trail Creek Cabin. A tent was erected over the building site, and carpenters built the extension as fast as the logs were delivered to them. "We finished the new room in three months and the officers had their club and they never did a lick of work," McAtee related.

Andy Hennig said Sun Valley was called a "concentration camp," since there were no girls around. The officers' mess was at Trail Creek, and they were well fed and happy. The sailors didn't take advantage of the skiing. They were worried that if they skied, the doctors would believe they were well enough to be sent back to the war. Dorice Taylor said the lodge "looked as much like a barracks as Sun Valley could be made to look." Local women welcomed the Navy to the Valley. "The number of cookies, cakes, and bowls of potato salad that wives of Ketchum, Hailey, Bellevue and Cary provided would have sunk a battleship."

A Japanese American held at the detainment camp at Minidoka, Idaho, during the war told a moving story about Sun Valley at an Ancient Skiers meeting there. Yosh Nakagawa was a child at Minidoka and was on a baseball team that, near the end of the war, was permitted to leave the camp to play other local teams. On one trip, the Minidoka kids were taken by bus to Easley Hot Springs just north of Sun Valley. As they passed Sun Valley, they were told they could not go near it or they might be shot, presumably because the patients with post-traumatic stress disorder might react strongly upon seeing Japanese. They did not know what Sun Valley was, but this warning stayed with Nakagawa for years. Much later, he worked at Osborn & Ulland Sporting Goods in Seattle, which sold ski equipment. When his customers talked about Sun Valley, he had a difficult time reconciling their dreamy descriptions with his childhood memory.

Although Sun Valley closed at the end of 1942, *The Valley Sun* produced papers in December of each of the war years. A 1943 article, "Sun Valley Joins the Navy," described the Navy's use of the resort. The inn's lobby was the reading room. Its first floor was Ward A, containing offices and doctor's and dentist's offices. The second floor was Ward B, where patients were placed two to a room. The Café Continental was the mess hall, the Ram was the officers' and nurses' mess, and the camera shop was the laboratory. The lodge's front office was used by the officer of the day. The bell-boys' room was the office of the master-at-arms. The Duchin Room was the accounting office. Sun Valley offered everything, the article said, "starting from a horseshoe game to a lift ride to the top of Baldy." Tennis and badminton courts, golf course, bowling alleys, skeet field, ice rinks, and swimming pools were available, and "Trail Creek tested the patients' fishing skills."

The Navy published a newsletter, *The Sun Valley Sage*. Its farewell edition said that medical care fell into three categories: medicine, surgery, and neuro-psychiatry in the milder forms of combat fatigue, which was one of the prevalent types of disorders treated. "Sun Valley was one of the few hospitals which successfully used group therapy for combat fatigue patients." Although remote, "the ladies of Ketchum, Hailey, Bellevue, Shoshone, Carey, and Twin Falls USOs did all they could to brighten the time men spent off the compound." Sun Valley offered a wide variety of recreational activities. In March 1945, a Ski Carnival was held featuring Alf and Cory Engen and

Captain Alfred J. Toulon, (MC), USN, Medical Officer in Command

The Navy Way Back To Health At Sun Valley

To the many enthusiastic patrons of Sun Valley, who by force of circumstances contingent on the present war have been unable to indulge in the health building climate and recreational facilities available at this famous resort, the Navy submits the accompanying pictures to illustrate to you what your temporary loss means to the officers and men of the Navy who are giving their services to their country, that we all may be assured a total victory and a lasting peace.

The Medical Officer in Command of the U. S. Naval Convalescent Hospital at Sun Valley feels sure that when you see these pictures and appreciate the wonderful results that are being obtained in restoring the health and vigor of our fighting men that you will experience a justifiable pride and a feeling that in addition to what ever else you may be doing, at Sun Valley, too, you are doing your bit; for which we congratulate you and extend the Season's Greetings.

Alfred J. Toulon

Captain (MC), U. S. Navy

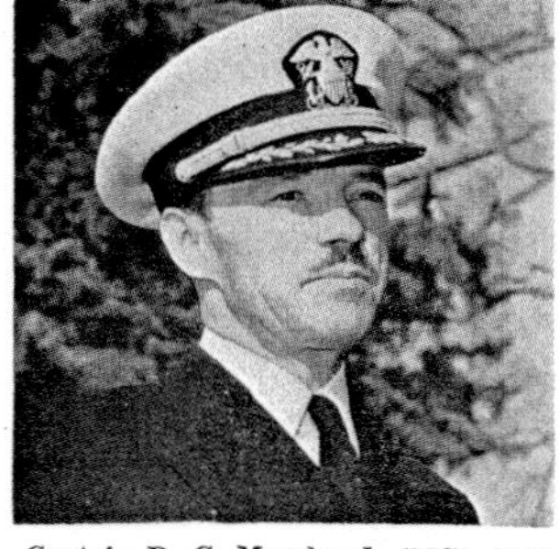

Captain D. C. Marchand, (MC), USN (Ret.) Executive Officer

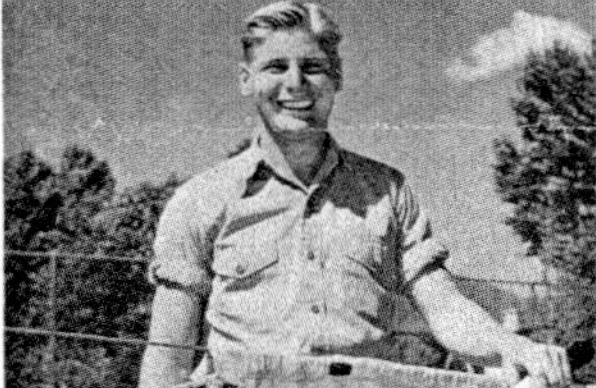

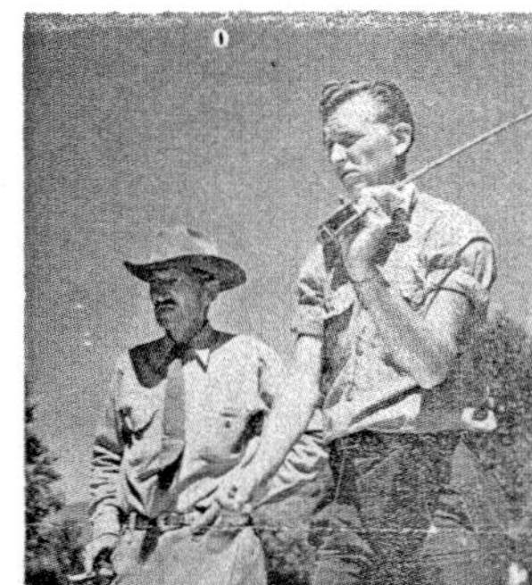

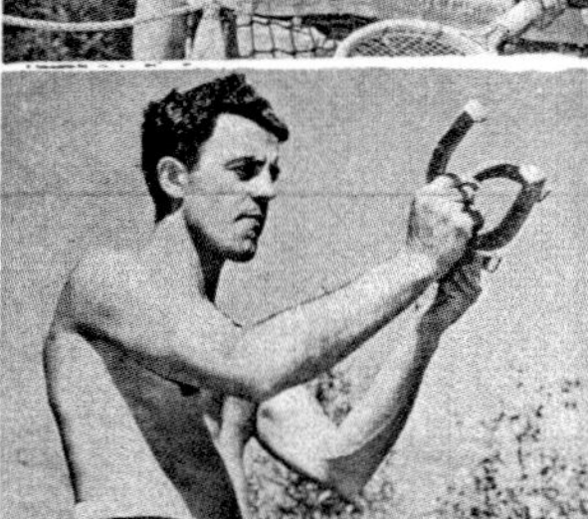

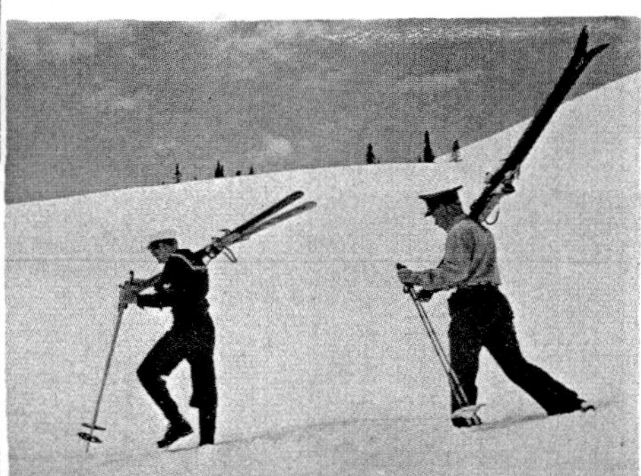

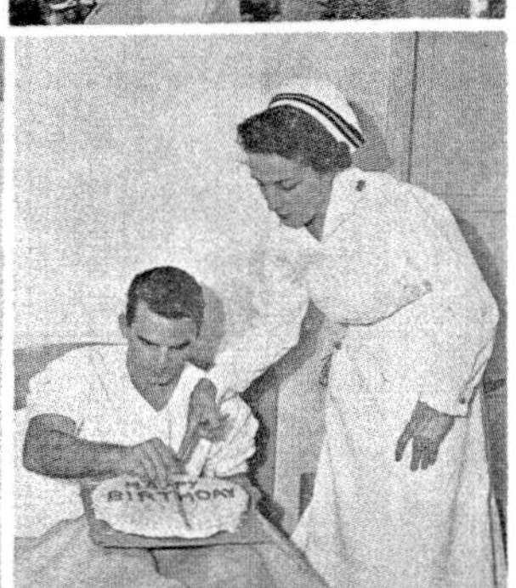

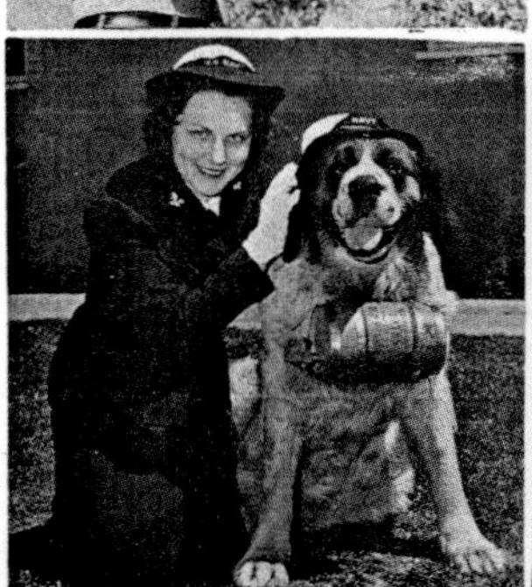

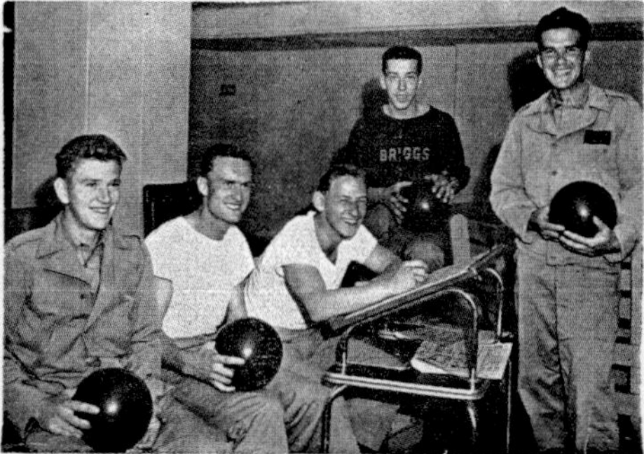

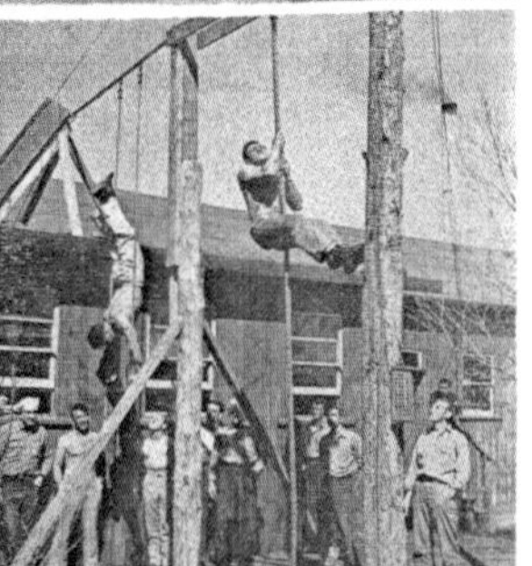

Sepp Benedickter. Bing Crosby came to Sun Valley in June 1945 to fish but took time to entertain the troops.

Steve Hannagan told Harriman what he saw at Sun Valley in April 1945 on one of his frequent visits to keep a close eye on the operation: "The Navy is making very good use of the property as a rehabilitation center, caring for between 600 and 1,200 men at a time." Pat Rogers supervised operations with 40 men, and the property was "very well maintained." The Navy held a ski meet that drew a fine crowd. Snow conditions were excellent all winter and the Dollar lift worked overtime. "An awful lot of sailors are learning to ski who never had any idea they would slide the boards over fluffy powder snow." Officers were quartered in the lodge, the enlisted men at the Challenger Inn, and the civilian personnel in other buildings. There was more activity during the summer.

The Navy began moving out of Sun Valley in January 1946 and turned the resort over to Union Pacific in July. Seagle's crew was responsible for getting Sun Valley back into shape, which took until December.

Virtually all well-known skiers served in the military during World War II, many in the Army mountain troops where their skiing ability could play a role. *The Valley Sun* of December 1942 said, "A large contingent of former ski instructors are of course where they would best fit—in the 87th Mountain Regiment, which is rapidly developing into a crack regiment with all its members almost hand-picked." Al Lindley, Don Fraser, Marti Arrouge, and Dr. John Moritz served in the Navy. Gretchen Fraser moved to Sun Valley and worked as a volunteer at the naval rehabilitation facility with the wounded. She was able to climb and ski for exercise, and she entered the few races that continued during the war.

Two Sun Valley ski instructors fought for Germany, Felix Schaffgotsch and Max Hauser. Several Austrians who taught at Sun Valley served as interrogators of German prisoners for the U.S. Army.

Walter Prager was a famous Swiss racer who won the Arlberg-Kandahar race several times in the 1930s, considered to be the world championship at the time, and became Dartmouth's ski coach in 1937. Prager joined the 87th Infantry in 1941,

OPPOSITE Article about Naval Rehabilitation Center at Sun Valley, *The Valley Sun*, December 1943.

training on Mount Rainier, served with the 10th Mountain Division at Camp Hale, and fought in northern Italy. A story about Prager was related by a Swiss whose father was in the Swiss mountain troops during World War II. During the 10th's campaign in Italy, a U.S. Army vehicle showed up at a Swiss border control facility. The driver said a sergeant in the U.S. Army wanted to visit his mother. The sergeant was Walter Prager. His fame was such that once the border guard learned his identity, he was allowed to enter the country. Civilian clothes were brought to the border since he could not come in wearing a U.S. military uniform, and he was able to visit his mother, whom he had not seen since 1937.

Among the many war-time tragedies, on May 3, 1945, Torger Torkle was killed in Italy fighting with the 10th Mountain Division. After the war, the Norway Ski Club of New York created the Torger Tokle Memorial Trophy, housed at the National Ski Museum. Three Sun Valley ski instructors were killed in Italy fighting for the 10th Mountain Division, and peaks were named for them around Sun Valley after the war: Ted Handwerk Peak, Jonathan Duncan Peak, and Ralph Bromaghin Peak.[60]

21

UNION PACIFIC MUST DECIDE WHETHER TO REOPEN SUN VALLEY AFTER THE WAR

Railroad historian Maury Klein described the changes in conditions faced by the Union Pacific after the war and its internal restructuring, which affected how Sun Valley was treated.

World War II took a toll on Union Pacific's management. Many in its senior ranks were involved in the war effort, including Averell Harriman, who left in June 1940. "Although he remained chairman of the board until 1945 and kept abreast of company affairs, he never again assumed a major role in its management," Klein wrote. When Jeffers and Robert Lovett left for Washington service, senior vice president Frank Robinson took charge. The loss of these experienced men left Union Pacific's board without a strong leader, and "suddenly the board took on a more parochial character than had been typical of the Union Pacific." Roland Harriman went on the board's executive committee.

The war placed a huge strain on Union Pacific as demand for rail services ballooned while the company operated with a skeleton staff. It had to handle the largest volume of traffic in its history with the least experienced workforce it had ever had. The war triggered an economic boom in the West that transformed the region.

At the end of the war, Jeffers was seriously ill. His long-time assistant, George F. Ashby, was appointed president in late 1944, but could never fill the shoes of the dynamic man he replaced. According to Klein, "Ashby dwelled in Jeffers's giant shadow in every sense, haunted by his predecessor." He was quiet, didn't like to give speeches, had difficulty communicating clearly, had a drinking problem, and "his brief reign careened wildly between comedy and tragedy. At its abrupt end he was a ruined man whose downfall was hailed with a mixture of cheers and sighs of relief." Averell blamed his brother Roland for appointing Ashby as president and was unhappy with the choice, but was too far removed to get involved.

Board members were waiting for Averell Harriman's return from the war. Early in 1945, word came from Europe hinting that Harriman would soon be back on the job and planned changes, including to those involved with running the railroad. When Averell returned to the United States in 1946, he was still U.P.'s chairman of the board, but decided he didn't want to interfere with Roland's position and so moved on. According to Klein,

> *Harriman plunged into another government job as Secretary of Commerce, which forced him to sever all ties with the railroad in October 1946. . . . At the dawn of a momentous new era in railroading, the Union Pacific found itself with both a new chairman of the board and a new president. . . . Averell's decision not to return to Union Pacific left a vacuum of leadership on the board and affected the railroad's ability to respond to rapidly changing conditions, which in the long run, spelled the demise of his pride and joy, Sun Valley.*

Roland Harriman became chairman of the board, but was unlike Averell, without the "fierce, unquenchable drive of his father." As a result,

> *The quiet, uncombative brother* [was] *thrust into a leadership role he didn't want, one better suited to his more energetic and aggressive brother. . . . In the 1930s Averell had responded to a major crisis in the rail industry with a bold program that overhauled not only the road's equipment but its public image as well. . . . In 1946 Roland found himself in a similar position. . . . He took charge at a critical time when almost every basic element of the industry seemed on the verge of major change, and intermodal competition resumed in even more virulent form.*

Roland missed the point of his father's triumph, like many stewards—"the key lay not merely in the new methods but in his understanding that changed conditions required new approaches."

After the war, Union Pacific was led by a new president and directed by a board led by a new, cautious board chair, both lacking the experience and vision to confront the new challenges. The Union Pacific could afford to coast because it was a rich company and, like all roads, had more business than it could carry during the war. But it was not getting maximum return from the resources at its disposal. Two Harriman traditions had faded badly: high-level maintenance and large investments in innovations if they promised large future returns.

George Ashby could see what had to be done but he had a "tragic flaw of character," Klein wrote. "He was his own worst enemy. . . . He turned everybody against him. . . . Somewhere in that man . . . was some sort of inferiority complex which resulted in his chief difficulty." These traits raised leadership issues when Union Pacific faced serious challenges:

> *The railroad...was in its worst shape since* [E.H.] *Harriman overhauled it. . . . During the depression maintenance and improvements had dropped sharply because business did not warrant large expenditures. Then came the war, which overwhelmed the roads with business while depriving them of the materials and manpower to get in good shape. The result was that old equipment and an undernourished physical plant were run harder than they had ever been, with little chance to upgrade or replenish them. . . . Union Pacific had lost its lead in maintenance and fallen behind other, less prosperous roads. The source of the trouble was spread across the entire operation.*

At the end of his reign, Jeffers told Ashby that railroads "are confronted with the most serious situation they have ever faced in their history. There is some doubt in my mind that the railroads can survive."Ashby responded by entering the third major construction era of Union Pacific, spending large amounts of money on track and road reconstruction and equipment purchases, mainly diesel locomotives. Between 1946 and 1948, Union Pacific expenditures averaged $44.7 million a year, compared to $15.5 million a year when it was investing in its streamliner fleet in the 1930s. Ashby knew he faced leadership issues. "What is clear is that Ashby sensed their lack of complete faith in him, just as he felt the resentment of those men and officers who scorned him as an unworthy successor to a real railroader like Jeffers," Klein said. This led to greater bouts of drinking.

Union Pacific was a "sleeping giant, rich in assets and slow to maximize it use of them," and passenger service was becoming more of an economic drag, according to Klein:

Thanks to Averell Harriman, the Union Pacific had spent heavily during the depression to revive the passenger trade. It was a bold gamble to sink so much into what was the smallest part of the railroad's business, and it did not pan out. The streamliners and Challenger service had captured headlines but not large profits. World War II soon wiped out whatever gains were made, deranging regular service with its enormous demands and running even the finest equipment into the ground. To revive the service in 1946 meant another large investment in a dubious enterprise with a limited future.

Union Pacific was faced with a major dilemma at the end of the war—what to do with passenger service. The railroad began a retreat from passenger service in 1943, when it sold a large minority share of two subsidiaries that provided bus service to Greyhound: Union Pacific Stages and Interstate Transit. The railroad sold the rest of the companies to Greyhound in 1952. Long-time board member Robert Lovett wanted to get out of the passenger business completely. However, this meant getting out of the resort business, which had been a major focus since the 1920s. Its resorts lost money but represented high-profile advertisement, drawing passengers to the railroad.

The issue of whether to reopen Sun Valley divided Union Pacific's management. Averell Harriman no longer had a formal place on its board, and the issue was complicated by the fact that new president George Ashby was not popular, had strong ideas about the decline of passenger service, and favored cutting Sun Valley's operating budget and subsidy. Harriman was kept informed of the debate and at times made his opinions known, but he no longer had a formal position on the board.

Although not well known at the time, Union Pacific considered not reopening Sun Valley because of the subsidy necessary to cover its operations and the changing nature of railroad operations, according to Klein:

Sun Valley posed a special problem because it was a unique operation with a mood and ambiance perfectly attuned to the prewar era, and because it was Averell Harriman's pet project. . . . In 1946 the question was what to do about reopening it. The world had changed greatly in four years. Not the least of those changes was about a 50 percent rise in the costs of operating Sun Valley, which had never made money under its old setup. To restore the resort would cost a lot of money, as manager Pat Rogers itemized in a full report. Was the outlay worth it?

In fall 1945, Pat Rogers prepared a report discussing the work necessary to bring Sun Valley back to a condition to accommodate guests in its traditional style. His report, dated November 23, 1945, "Proposals and Suggestions for Post-War Purposes covering Construction—Renovating—Decorating and Future Policies," discussed the requirements necessary to handle the increased volume of business that was certain to materialize, in order to improve and maintain the reputation of Sun Valley.

Rogers submitted a budget for needed new equipment and facilities, and a description of the repair and maintenance necessary before reopening. The capital investment needed must have grated on the nerves of the railroad executives, who had little interest in running a ski resort.

Rogers's report listed nearly $1 million for specified work and more for projects that had not been priced. Before Sun Valley closed for the war, its automotive equipment and livestock had been disposed of to transportation companies, and needed to be replaced. It would cost $85,100 to purchase new vehicles, $70,000 to build a heated steel building for auto storage and a carpenter and paint shop, and $35,084 to build stables and acquire 100 horses. A new ski lift and warming hut for Dollar would cost $54,000, upgrading the Bald Mountain lifts would require $6,000, and the Roundhouse needed improvements and new systems including (heating and a water source) costing over $8,000. New guest buildings would cost $200,000, new employee housing $450,000, revamping existing employee housing $16,000, and an undetermined amount to build a new 30-room hospital. A new shop to centralize ski repair and storage would cost $75,000. Substantial amounts were required for a new greenhouse, to excavate and refill Sun Valley Lake, install a new sprinkler system and new water lines, and redo the tennis courts. The Lodge, Inn, theater, and other buildings needed to be rehabilitated and upgraded at an undetermined cost. Sun Valley's accounting system needed upgrading as well, and the resort's recreation and athletic facilities needed substantial improvements.

Rogers's report caused significant controversy. W.M. Jeffers was scheduled to turn over the presidency to Ashby in February 1946. On December 1, 1945, Jeffers sent a copy of Rogers's report to F.W. Charske, chairman of the executive committee, with a copy to Ashby. Jeffers said it was necessary to spend "considerable money" to maintain Sun Valley's reputation as one of the greatest resorts in America. Wages, materials, and supplies would increase by 50 percent. "It will be necessary to start almost from scratch in re-establishing Sun Valley as a resort," he said. The key issue was who would be responsible for the operation. Pat Rogers "has done an amazing job" but was outraged at some of the treatment he received. Harriman, it was felt, would have definite views and should be consulted.

Ashby responded to Charske on January 3, 1946, showing his negative feelings toward Rogers. Ashby met with Rogers to discuss his "so-called budget." The fixed improvements Rogers recommended were "not pressing . . . their importance would depend on future policy with respect to operation of the resort." Harriman would decide whether to operate Sun Valley during summer 1946. With respect to the people of Idaho, it might be advisable to resume both summer and winter operations, even though summer would bring a greater loss. Not opening Sun Valley but re-opening Utah Parks was not inconsistent, since "we are obligated to the Department of Interior to operate Utah Parks, which is largely for the benefit of automobile tourist travelers."

Rogers told Ashby he wanted to continue at Sun Valley but "would like to be eventually relieved of the Sun Valley operations . . . it exposed him to criticism from officers of the company" Ashby told Rogers if he continued working, "I would expect full cooperation and support and he assured I would have it." Rogers replied that, "he has always been loyal to his employers and particularly to Mr. Jeffers and that if it had not been for Mr. Jeffers he would still be running a beanery." Ashby concurred: "That would have been likely."

Steve Hannagan wrote Harriman on April 2, 1946, with his recommendations for Sun Valley. His March 1936 report, he felt, should be used "as guide posts in the post-war rebirth of Sun Valley. . . . Those who are taking a new, intensive interest in the project" should read the report, but it was likely not the news U.P. executives wanted to hear:

> *It seems amazing how accurately we indicated the project which has become history. Sun Valley has become the most famous winter sports resort in the world. It has a good reputation, integrity, drawing power. It is known as a first class resort, but it has a reputation of accommodations for all type purses with the common denominator of affability among all guests. Unquestionably, it has become a hallmark of Union Pacific progressiveness, and has been a vehicle for world-wide acclaim for the railroad.*

If Union Pacific was not willing to continue its subsidy to the resort, Hannagan felt, it should not be reopened.

> *That it has not made money—in tangible dollars and cents—is perhaps less important than the fact that it has brought attention to the Union Pacific at a cost, cheaper than any other known means. If it were conceived or is to be rededicated on the basis of an important money-making project, per se, it seems doomed to failure and should be liquidated immediately.*
>
> *But if it is to be operated with enthusiasm, foresight, affection, attention and intelligence, it can continue to set a pace for Union Pacific service, progress and acclaim—at a cost cheaper than any other vehicle of public presentation.*
>
> *This is a policy decision which must be met firmly and now. If we are not prepared to subsidize the endeavor, as an advertising, good will and business projecting endeavor, to the extent of $350,000 to $500,000 annually, it should be abandoned. . . . However, it must be done with flair, enthusiasm and acknowledgment of the service it performs.*

The necessary expenditures, Hannagan said, could be part of the advertising budget, business entertainment and public relations "along our vast rightaway, which would make it an inexpensive project."

Hannagan suggested changes at Sun Valley to operate it "on a more streamlined basis, at less cost and higher operating profit. . . . Rents and services must be realigned, upwards. Services must be telescoped to compensate for increased service costs." A cafeteria could work, and the lodge's noon lunch service could be changed to a buffet. Evening entertainment could be restricted to one public room, eliminating double service. "I would advise holding hotel rates and meals to the most attractive possible rates, but increase charges" for services such as lifts, buses, etc. "We must have ample service, but guests should pay for it. . . . At the same time, it had to maintain the touch of class that set it apart from other places." Summer operations had the same value as winter ones. The rodeo could be eliminated and Sun Valley could be operated as a deluxe dude ranch. "Certain people" could be encouraged to build homes at Sun Valley, leasing the ground to them, which if properly taxed would "provide for sound expansion of community ventures. . . . We will have to hit as hard as when we opened the resort originally."

Harriman sent a telegram from London on July 24, 1946, saying he had been too busy to study Roger's report carefully and he was "ready to approve whatever is agreed upon by you. . . . I feel Rogers had done first rate job and we will fare better by following his recommendations on details as a result of his experience. . . . After all most resorts are made successful primarily by man on spot and not by absentee direction."

Union Pacific reluctantly reopened Sun Valley in December 1947, with Pat Rogers in charge. However, the annual subsidies continued to be an issue that led to Rogers leaving in 1952, and "the resort never really came all the way back," according to Klein. Passenger service continued to be a losing proposition which, by the 1960s, led railroads to lobby Congress to let them abandon it.

Harriman's focus on passenger service in the 1930s turned out to be a pyrrhic victory. Abramson said, "Impressive though it was, his success in restoring passenger service was ephemeral. The heyday of the passenger train was gone, in spite of the streamliners and the Challengers. Under the circumstances, he and the rest of the Union Pacific management might have made a historic mistake in their decision to save it." Klein agreed:

> *The Union Pacific had the money and never hesitated to spend it, but time would show that it had put too many eggs in the wrong basket. . . . If the financial resources and competitive energy devoted to passenger service between the wars had been funneled instead into a concerted effort to improve freight operations, the postwar history of the railroads might have turned out very differently. Freight made most of the money, after all, and it desperately needed new thinking, new technology, and new techniques. But in the 1930s, the threat to passenger traffic looked far more grave. Few people believed another world was coming, and fewer still grasped what effect it would have on the national transportation system.*[61]

Part Six

SUN VALLEY AFTER WORLD WAR II

22

SUN VALLEY REOPENS IN 1947 TO CHANGED SOCIAL AND ECONOMIC CONDITIONS

Skiing resumed in 1945 in anticipation of the end of the war and expanded as men returned and the country hurried to get back to normal life.

On November 27, 1945, the Navy announced it would close its convalescent hospital at Sun Valley on December 1 and return the property to the Union Pacific. Sun Valley did not open in winter 1946, as the Navy's departure date left insufficient time to get the resort ready for that season. Its re-opening was set for December 21, 1946. Pat Rogers continued as general manager in spite of his growing unhappiness with Union Pacific's approach to running the resort. The Navy's bill for its war-time use of Sun Valley was $6,080, after deductions for restoration, according to Holland.

Not willing to wait for its opening, Gary and Rocky Cooper, Clark Gable, and Ingrid Bergman and her husband Dr. Peter Lindstrom came to Sun Valley in February 1946. Ernest Hemingway's son Jack joined the group after being seriously injured in Europe with the OSS and enrolling in the University of Montana on his return. They stayed at Bald Mountain Hot Springs Lodge. Initially, they climbed Dollar Mountain on skis, but Cooper rented Ruud Mountain so they could use the lift. Sigi Engl was "summoned from Pasadena as an instructor and anyone in the community willing to help pack the mountain was invited to ski," according to Dorice Taylor. Nelson and Bobbi Bennett, Sebbi Arriaga, and others skied with the Hollywood party. This illustrates how well Sun Valley treated its celebrity guests during the glory days of the resort.

Nelson Bennett returned from military service in fall 1945. His wife, Bobby, worked for the Navy, and Nelson and his brother Eddie taught her to ski that year. Nelson was head of Sun Valley's ski patrol when the resort reopened and was later mountain manager, responsible for creating new runs on Bald Mountain.

In October 1946, the National Ski Association announced that tryouts for the downhill and slalom teams for the 1948 Olympics at St. Moritz, Switzerland, would be held at Sun Valley in March 1947, "the peer of all American racing centers." The Seattle Ski Club won the right to host the Olympic jumping trials at the Milwaukee Ski Bowl east of Snoqualmie Pass, after spirited competition with Steamboat Springs, Lake Placid, and Iron Mountain. The national championships would be held at Alta on March 1–2, 1947.

Gary Cooper, ski instructor Sigi Engl, and Clark Gable at Sun Valley, February 1946.

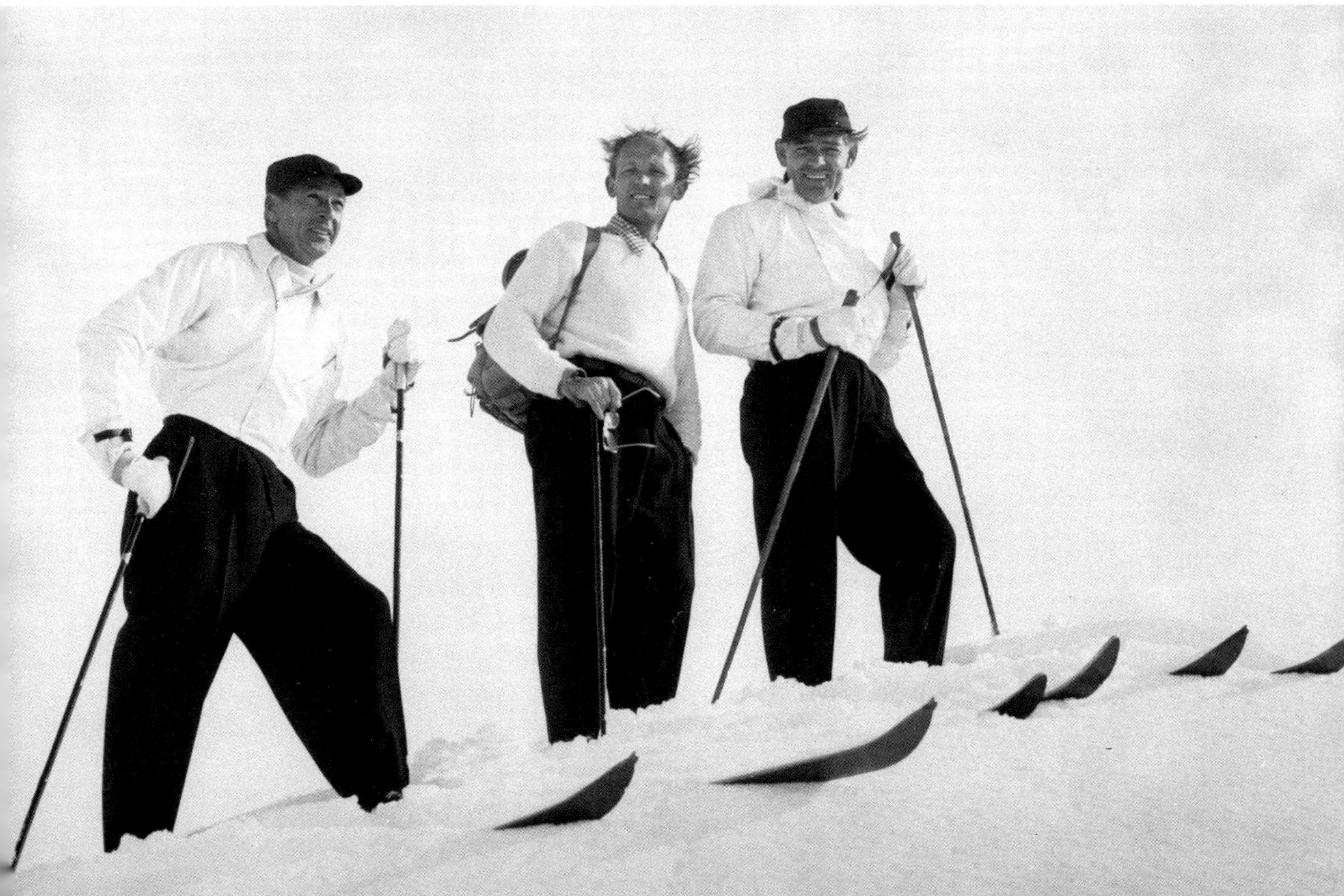

After the Navy left Sun Valley, the resort was a madhouse, with staff working to get it back in shape for its reopening in December 1946. The lodge, inn and all guest amenities had to be remodeled and upgraded after three years of use as a hospital, and major improvements were necessary to the ski hills and ski lifts, as detailed in Pat Rogers's report. The *American Ski Annual* for 1947 described the work.

Trees and brush grown up on the ski runs were removed by a trail crew, and new runs developed. Olympic Run was cut from the Roundhouse to the middle of River Run, a fast one-mile course.

> *For the better skiers, this line of descent will provide some of the most interesting variations found at Sun Valley and promises to be very popular with those who like their skiing somewhat on the rugged side. When used in conjunction with Ridge Run, the Olympic trail would constitute a race course of real championship caliber.*

Six electric ski lifts served Dollar, Ruud, Proctor, and Baldy Mountains. The Bald Mountain lift was the longest in the world, and the area's ski runs were designed by "outstanding ski experts of Europe and America in cooperation with the U.S. Forest Service." Baldy offered long downhill runs and "miles of timber-free slopes with a variety of runs that will please the novice looking for a gentle decline as well as the skiing veteran in serious competition." The three-mile Broadway run started from the top of Baldy and ran down the entire mountain through thinned timber that was like an open road. Six ravines (or canyons) at the top of Broadway offered easily accessible runs for every type of skier, with good snow from early December to late May. Ski touring at the Owl Creek Cabin in the Galena Summit region offered backcountry skiing in "some of the most beautiful mountain country in the country." Non-skiers could find skating, skeet shooting, moonlight bobsled parties, bowling, ping pong, and outdoor swimming.

In fall 1946, Ernest Hemingway arrived in Sun Valley with a new wife, Mary Welsh, whom he had married on March 14, 1946, after divorcing Martha Gellhorn in December 1945. Mary described the resort when they arrived in her book *How It Was*:

> *In every department Sun Valley was industriously primping for the mid-December opening of its first winter since the war. Workmen checked every hook, buckle and hinge on the chairlifts up Dollar Mountain and Baldy. New lamps appeared in the lobby*

of the Lodge and a little hill of four-foot logs grew in a corner by the big, hospitable fireplace. Young helpers around the place turned into bellboys in new uniforms and at the Ram . . . new napery appeared on old oak tables on which hundreds of customers had carved or burnt their initials.

Although Sun Valley was a fashionable resort, Ketchum was still a small western town . . . a sentimentalist's dream of the old West. Aged wooden sidewalks provided footpaths along the two blocks of Main Street. . . . Most of the one-story brick or frame buildings held up innocently pretentious peaked false fronts another story high. . . . There was no bank but all the bars cashed personal checks.

The Alpine Restaurant, where we devoured "sizzling steaks" . . . for $1.25, was the town's refuge for stomach hunger, and its adjoining bar and casino, where silver dollars clanked day and night at the poker and roulette tables, appeased other appetites. Ernest admired the Alpine especially for its rule that drinks were on the house from the morning opening, about six o'clock, until 7 or maybe 8 a.m., thus enabling the town's impecunious drunks to "get a hold on" themselves for the day. But he was also a patron of the Tram, a long dank-smelling bar on one side of the Alpine, and its twin on the Alpine's other flank, the Sawtooth. Across the street was the Casino, also offering booze, games of chance and light conversation. Opposite on one corner was Bud Hegstrom's Drug Store . . . and on another corner was Jack Lane's store and warehouse, essentially a storage place for the requirements of his sheepherders, but anyone could buy denim Levi's or Pendleton pants and shirts there and watch the world go by from a couple of long benches on the store's front porch.

Friedl Pfeifer Moves to Aspen but Remains Head of the Sun Valley Ski School

Before World War II, Aspen was a small local ski area with a "colorful boat-tow built of old mining equipment," in the words of the 1947 *American Ski Annual*, using "a donated motor and spare equipment from the Midnight Mine." Andre Roch, the famous Swiss mountaineer, visited Aspen before the war and marked a trail that was named Roch's Run. In 1941, the tiny town hosted the National Downhill and Slalom Championships, which attracted a number of top racers, including Dick Durrance and Toni Matt, who said it was among the best races in which they participated. Gretchen Fraser said the conditions were primitive.

After World War II, Aspen was slowly transformed into a major ski area that would eventually compete with Sun Valley. Two skiers who were critical to Sun Valley's early days played major roles there—Friedl Pfeifer and Dick Durrance. "The man behind it, and certainly the most directly responsible for turning into fact the dreams that many have had, is Friedl Pfeifer," the *American Ski Annual* for 1947 reported.

Pfeifer described his role at Aspen in his autobiography. He was in the 10th Mountain Division at Camp Hale during the war and fell in love with the Aspen area, deciding to open a ski area there after the war. He met with Aspen City Council to discuss plans for a ski area, and the council began the work of "unraveling old titles and mining claims in order that a right of way for a lift up the mountain could be secured." While Pfeifer was in the hospital recovering from wounds he received in Italy, he recruited Percy Rideout and John Litchfield to work with him. He obtained the financial backing of H.F. Klock, a Denver financier, who formed the Aspen Skiing Corporation. Separately, Walter Paepcke, a Chicago philanthropist who was working to make Aspen a cultural center, formed the Aspen Company to restore the town.

In spring 1946, the Aspen Skiing Corporation began work under Pfeifer's guidance. The boat tow was renovated and repaired, new rope tows and a chairlift were installed, new runs were cleared, a 60-meter ski jump was constructed, and much else was done in time for the 1947 season. Crews prepared more than 15 miles of new trails, old mining roads were restructured, and a race course was prepared, Olympic trail, with a drop of 3,000 feet. Its new chairlift was the longest (8,400 feet) and fastest (275 people per hour) in the world, with the greatest vertical rise (2,200 feet in 8,400 feet). Plans were made for annual Roch Cup races. Pfeifer established the Aspen Ski School with Litchfield and Rideout.

Pfeifer approached Averell Harriman looking for funds to develop Aspen, but Harriman declined, giving him a job offer instead. Pfeifer continued his work at Aspen, but he also served as the director of the Sun Valley Ski School, splitting his time between the two resorts, driving 800 miles each way. He spent one week in Sun Valley, then two weeks in Aspen. "Aspen was my dream, but Sun Valley became my bread and butter," he said. Pfeifer hired Fred Iselin to be his assistant at Sun Valley.[62]

Sun Valley Opens to a Changed Social and Economic Scene

When Sun Valley re-opened in winter 1947, the resort had a different focus, according to Holland, who titled her chapter on the period "Postwar Malaise."

> *Instead of appealing only to the rich and famous, Sun Valley hoped to put its ledgers in the black by attracting a greater number of people from a wider range of social levels. Families and fun-loving recreationists joined the beautiful people. The resort began to attract conventions—and criticism. Some said its glory had faded.*

Oppenheimer and Poole said instead of aiming at the rich and famous, Sun Valley broadened its appeal to get others to "enjoy the unique climate and facilities." Railroad historian Maury Klein described the Union Pacific's approach to Sun Valley after World War II:

> *Although the decision was made to reopen on the basis Hannagan suggested, the resort never really came all the way back. Money was spent for redecorating but without the close attention to detail originally lavished on it by Marjorie Oelrichs Duchin and Mary Harriman. Averell tried to offer advice but was too far away. . . . Every year saw Averell's hand farther removed and the company less patient for a purpose that grew increasingly opaque.*

After the war, Bill Castagneto worked for the Union Pacific in Omaha as a special representative of Sun Valley. He said the pre-war period was a special time for Sun Valley, and Pat Rogers was responsible for much of the atmosphere. The ratio of employees to guests was uncommonly high and gave the guests something special. "You can't do that and make money," he said, but Sun Valley was "fabulously productive" for the railroad.

Harriman was the "driving force," but Bill Jeffers, U.P.'s president, was "a very willing accomplice. Other people . . . were just as willing," and they brought in personnel who "were harmonious to their philosophy. . . . Unfortunately, the war came along and that broke up." When Union Pacific took Sun Valley back from the Navy, there were no longer "the same personnel with the railroad. . . . The emphasis and the driving force just wasn't there." Union Pacific's policy toward Sun Valley was the result of changes in philosophy of the people in charge. They took responsibility out of the hands of Sun Valley employees and gave it to higher-ups, placing the railroad's dining car and hotel department in charge of the resort. "Those people did not have the interest at heart nor the desire, nor the purpose to make it back to what it was. It simply went from pillar to post and ultimately was sold. . . . It was a totally different world."

George Ashby became president in February 1946, replacing William Jeffers, and he was replaced by Arthur Stoddard in March 1949. Harriman was critical of Stoddard—he "was never very keen on Sun Valley. He didn't understand . . . your goodwill value throughout the West, particularly Idaho."

Dorice Taylor described how Ashby differed from Jeffers. Ashby considered himself to be an enthusiastic shooter and donated a trophy to the trapshooting contest held every summer. However, Ashby was "no sportsman" and had several conflicts with Taylor Williams, Sun Valley's popular fishing and hunting guide who was a favorite of many guests, including Ernest Hemingway. One time, Ashby was riding on a car fender shooting doves as the car moved, which was illegal. A game warden, trying to be politic, asked Williams to speak to Ashby, which he did, but Ashby was not pleased. Another time, Williams took Ashby and a group of business executives on a hunting trip. When they left the car and started hunting and shooting in all directions, Taylor returned to the car. Ashby was furious and asked Williams what he was doing. He replied that unless the men allowed him to have them hunt properly, he wasn't going to risk getting in their crossfire. Ashby demoted Taylor and wanted to fire him.

Hemingway was upset by the way Ashby treated Williams and had his own run-in with him. One day when Hemingway met Ashby and Pat Rogers in Sun Valley, he heard Ashby say, "So the great white hunter is still around," a remark Hemingway resented. He began staying in Ketchum and using a Ketchum byline instead of Sun Valley. Sun Valley was changing from the vision that Harriman had for the resort.[63]

Dorice Taylor said Sun Valley reopened just before Christmas 1946 "after a wild scramble to undo all the damage the Navy had done." Nonetheless, "former Sun Valleyites came back as if the reopening was the one moment they had been waiting for during the war-torn years." Taylor was asked to write a gossip column for *The Valley Sun*, perSUNals, which she did without pay. Two years later, she was hired by Steve Hannagan for a full-time job in the news bureau, where she worked until 1971.

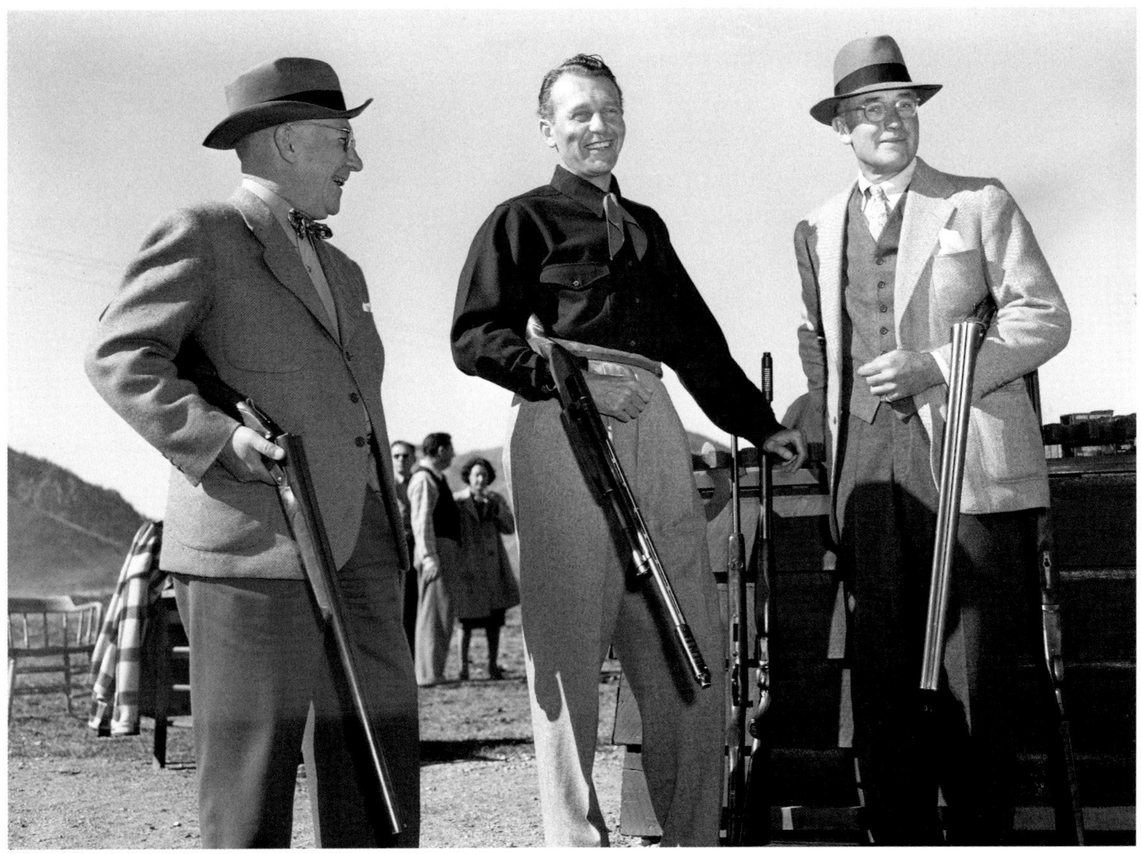

Shooters at Sun Valley: Ralph Bellamy, George Ashby, and Roland Harriman.

In December 1946, *The Valley Sun* reported that, after serving for three years as a Navy rehabilitation center, Sun Valley "proudly reopens its doors on December 21st. Around 80% of its staff returned, and everything will be in its regular place." Friedl Pfeifer's ski school featured "a substantial part of the 1942 School," along with new instructors whose names were familiar in skiing circles. Fred Iselin was assistant director and Sigi Engl would "conduct the top racing class. . . . With previous guests representing more than 50 per cent of advance reservations, this season promises to be a real get-together for Sun Valleyites."

Sun Valley celebrated Christmas in its traditional way, according to Taylor. "Friedl Pfeifer and his ski instructors made their torchlight descent of Dollar Mountain—a beautiful and spectacular event which has never failed to thrill Sun Valley visitors." Hollywood celebrities included the Coopers, Millands, Claudette Colbert and her husband Dr. Pressman, Norma Shearer and her fiancé Marty Arrouge, Merle Oberon, and Virginia and Darryl Zanuck, with the Hemingways coming and going. Van Johnson came later in the year, as did Anne and Henry Ford and their children. Lowell Thomas stayed at Sun Valley for a considerable length of time, making his radio broadcasts twice a day from the Harriman Cottage. A gala dinner was hosted by Mrs. George Ashby, who was shown cutting a huge cake with Gary Cooper watching, to celebrate Sun Valley's 10th anniversary. U.P. president Jeffers had donated a cup for the winner of a Sun Valley ski race. Not to be outdone, George Ashby donated the President's Cup for the winner of the Western Interstate Meet, although he was never enthusiastic about skiing.

Otto Lang described Sun Valley's fifth annual intercollegiate tournament over Christmas in the *Sun Valley Ski Club Annual Report* for 1947. The resort hosted 140 men and women from 25 schools to perform in front of "the cream of the Hollywood film colony, plus a score or more persons representing Europe's and Park Avenue's best drawing rooms along with a smattering of American industrialists."

A record 114 skiers entered the downhill race that began above the Roundhouse. The Narrows at the bottom of Canyon presented the greatest challenge, particularly to skiers not familiar with the course. Although Utah's Bill Beesley won the downhill, "the University of Washington team made a pretty clean sweep of the downhill event," with David "Rabbit" Faires taking second, Gene Moore third, Cliff Schmidtke fourth, Bob Powers fifth, Don French seventh, and Rees Stevenson 10th. Ketchum's Jim Griffith, skiing for the University of Denver, took sixth. Only 12 women competed in the downhill, which was won by Mary Alice Peel of Washington State. Utah won the two top slots in the slalom held on Ruud Mountain, with Dick Movitz first and Jack Reddish second. University of Washington skiers won five of the top 10 places in the cross-country race. "A galaxy of Hollywood stars" saw Gustav Raaum, an exchange student from Norway studying at Washington, win the jumping event on Ruud Mountain.

The *New York Times* reported that the Utah Utes won the team trophy followed by Washington and Stanford. Utah's Jack Reddish won the Bradley Plate for the four-event combined, followed by Dick Movitz, Cliff Schmidtke, and Bob St. Louis, both from Washington. Barbara Kidder of Denver University won the Mary Cornelia Trophy.

Lang concluded that changes had to be made in the tournament's format. The field was too large and overcrowded, with skiers who were not in condition or ready for the demanding competition. Sun Valley had to be more discriminating, basing entry on past performance. The number of team members from each college needed to be reduced and the downhill course controlled with gates to reduce injuries. Lang was concerned about competitors arriving after traveling long distances to "rush over to the start of the race course and hurtle themselves down at breakneck speed, far beyond a possible measure of control."

Al and Grace Lindley donated a pair of permanent trophies for the Sun Valley Ski Club championships for 1947, onto which the names of all prior club champions would be engraved.

Celebrities continued to ski at Sun Valley, maintaining the atmosphere Steve Hannagan desired. In January 1948, Dorice Taylor reported that George Ashby hosted a party for Roland Harriman in the swank Christiania Club. Darryl Zanuck skied with a broken arm and gave a talk on the contributions of the 10th Mountain Division during the war. Kathleen Harriman threw a birthday party for Harry Whitney at the Roundhouse. Averell and Katherine returned to Sun Valley in 1947, both in the winter and summer, mixing with celebrities including Senator William Fulbright and Alice Faye.

On March 7, 1947, the *New York Times* described Sun Valley's many attractions, making Eastern skiers turn green with envy:

> *Sun Valley, in the heart of the Sawtooth Mountain range of south-central Idaho, today is back from the war on a record peacetime playtime basis. Since its formal reopening last Christmas, this skiing paradise has been jammed to capacity, catering to the whims of "snow bunnies" and "kanonen," and today was typical of the type of sport one finds at this mammoth showland.*
>
> *From early morning till the bright sun had cast its lengthening shadows on the many miles of timberless slopes, the skiing facilities were alive with activity. Recreational enthusiasts gathered from all parts of the world mingled with international, Olympic and national champions. Visualize four to thirteen inches of new powder snow on bases ranging from two feet in the valley to more than seven on the top of Baldy Mountain, and a hot sun that sent the temperature soaring to 40 degrees. . . . You can understand why this Idaho resort, in its tenth year, is ranked as America's foremost winterland.*[64]

Hennig Writes *Sun Valley Ski Guide*

In 1947, Averell Harriman asked ski instructor Andy Hennig to write a guide to skiing and alpine touring at Sun Valley. In 1939, Hennig joined the ski-touring ski school run by Florian Haemmerle. That spring, they scouted the best skiing in the peaks surrounding Sun Valley. Otto Lang said Hennig had a reputation as a rock climber and mountaineer in the Alps before he came to the United States, with an enviable collection of first ascents. Hennig wrote *Sun Valley Ski Guide*, published by Union Pacific in 1948. The book described skiing on the lift-served areas (Ruud, Proctor, Dollar, and Bald Mountains), with a large section on spring and summer skiing and ski touring.

Primary access to Sun Valley was by the Union Pacific Railroad via a 70-mile spur from Shoshone to Ketchum. "During the winter months through sleeping cars are operated direct to Ketchum, where modern streamlined motor buses meet guests and transport them to Sun Valley Lodge or Challenger Inn. . . . Buses also meet trains at Shoshone." Sun Valley was also accessible through a commercial airport at Gooding, 78 miles from Sun Valley, and an airfield for private planes at Hailey, where transportation could be arranged in advance.

Proctor Mountain, Hennig wrote, "is an ideal ski mountain, offering every type of terrain and every grade of ski slope." He showed 10 runs on Proctor, although after chairlifts were installed on Bald Mountain for the 1940 ski season, the Proctor lift "only operated on special occasions by posted announcements, usually during the peak season" in February or later in the spring.

Hennig took 24 pages to describe skiing on Bald Mountain, which he said was a "Skier's Paradise."

> *No mountain in the country offers the winter sports enthusiast a greater variety of runs and slopes. Here are found areas to satisfy the desires of every type of skier. There are gentle slopes of "Sunny-Side," the vast terrain of the "Christmas-Bowl," and the precipitous Steilhangs of "Warm Springs," "Exhibition," and "Olympic" runs.*

Baldy chairlifts took skiers to the top in about 30 minutes, although they could get off at the end of any of the three. The Roundhouse was the "noon-hour rendezvous of all Baldy Mountain skiers," where lunches were served.

Hennig showed 30 runs on Bald Mountain, from Cold Springs in the south, extending north to Warm Springs. Skiers could ski from the top of Baldy down Broadway and Cold Springs to the highway, where Sun Valley buses took them to River Run or the lodge. Skiers could also go from the top of Baldy down Warm Springs, where "a trail wide enough to make any kind of turn, has been cleared from the top down to the bottom." There was a bridge over the creek, and buses would pick skiers up there.

Backcountry skiing continued to be an important part of Sun Valley's activities, which Hennig took 32 pages to describe. Trips were available using Sun Valley ski instructors or through the Sun Valley Ski School touring classes. Sun Valley had two backcountry cabins, Pioneer Cabin and Owl Creek Cabin near Galena. Backcountry trips were led by Florian Haemmerle and Hennig, both 10th Mountain veterans, and Victor Gottschalk, who made many first ascents of local mountains. While April is a time when skiing is over for the average skier, "there is excellent skiing through April, May, June, and sometimes into the middle of July." Bald Mountain offered spring skiing in its bowls, ridges, ravines, and upper part of Broadway through April. Proctor Mountain had several runs offering skiing until mid-May.

The Galena area "is a gateway to an immense and most beautiful skiing country. This is still a wild and undeveloped skiing terrain and the only immediate skiing area is in the vicinity of the road." It was accessible from the end of March, when the government cleared snow to the Galena summit. Buses or station wagons took skiers to Baker's Creek and Galena from the resort early in the morning.

Hennig described numerous ski trips around the Galena area and gave detailed directions about the location of the runs and how to follow the landscape. The Galena run went from the summit down to the Galena store, and a variation went from a no-name peak just south of the summit. A ski trip for advanced skiers went to Owl Creek Cabin, six miles from Galena Summit, that took three to four hours. It included a vertical drop down Bromaghin Peak to Owl Creek Cabin, offering a breathtaking view into Stanley Basin. It was four miles from the cabin to the highway, where transportation to Sun Valley was available. An alternative trip started two miles before Galena Store, 18 miles north of Sun Valley, and involved a ski trek through a gradually rising and beautiful mountain valley dominated by Silver Peak. The cabin could be a base camp for extended spring ski trips, accommodating up to 16 guests. "A cook is available to provide skiers with good meals." In late spring, jeep travel was possible to the cabin.

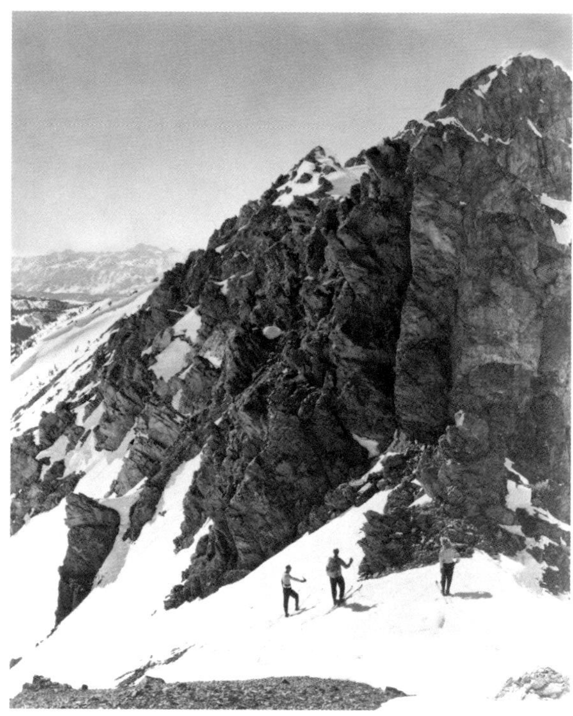

ABOVE Bobbi and Nelson Bennett and Eddie Bennett backcountry skiing near Galena Summit.

OPPOSITE Ski touring in Boulder Basin. The skiers are approaching the old Golden Glow mine site.

The ski tour to Silver Peak was for advanced skiers using a guide from the Sun Valley Ski School. The climb started from Owl Creek Cabin and went up for two and a half miles, taking two to three hours. There were several routes back to the cabin, and transportation arrangements had to be made in advance. Other areas included Galena Peak, the "most outstanding alpine ski trip in the Galena area," which was the only peak in the area offering a continuous drop of nearly 4,000 feet. Transportation could be arranged from the Galena Store back to Sun Valley. Durrance Mountain was another option for advanced skiers.

"The Pioneer Range is ideal spring skiing country. It offers everything for touring—wide-open spaces, inspiring scenery, plentiful sunshine, and a variety of untracked snow slopes." Pioneer Cabin was a "cozy and comfortable cabin, providing space for a maximum of ten people." Ski instructors guided parties into the cabin, arranging transportation and supplies. Motor cars or snowcats took skiers toward Trail Creek Summit, turned off at Corral Creek Valley, and dropped them off at the Saw Mill Cabin at the end of the valley where the five-mile climb started, which gained 2,400 feet of vertical in a two-and-a-half- to four-hour trip. There were a number of routes from the cabin for intermediate skiers and seasoned ski mountaineers, including Duncan Peak, Hyndman Basin, Salzburger Spitzl, Handwerk Peak, Goat Mountain, Duncan Peak, and others.

In spring 1947, Andy Hennig discovered an old mining settlement in Boulder Basin north of Ketchum, with good snow into spring and summer. In summer 1947, Harriman toured Boulder Basin and directed that spring and summer skiing be promoted there.

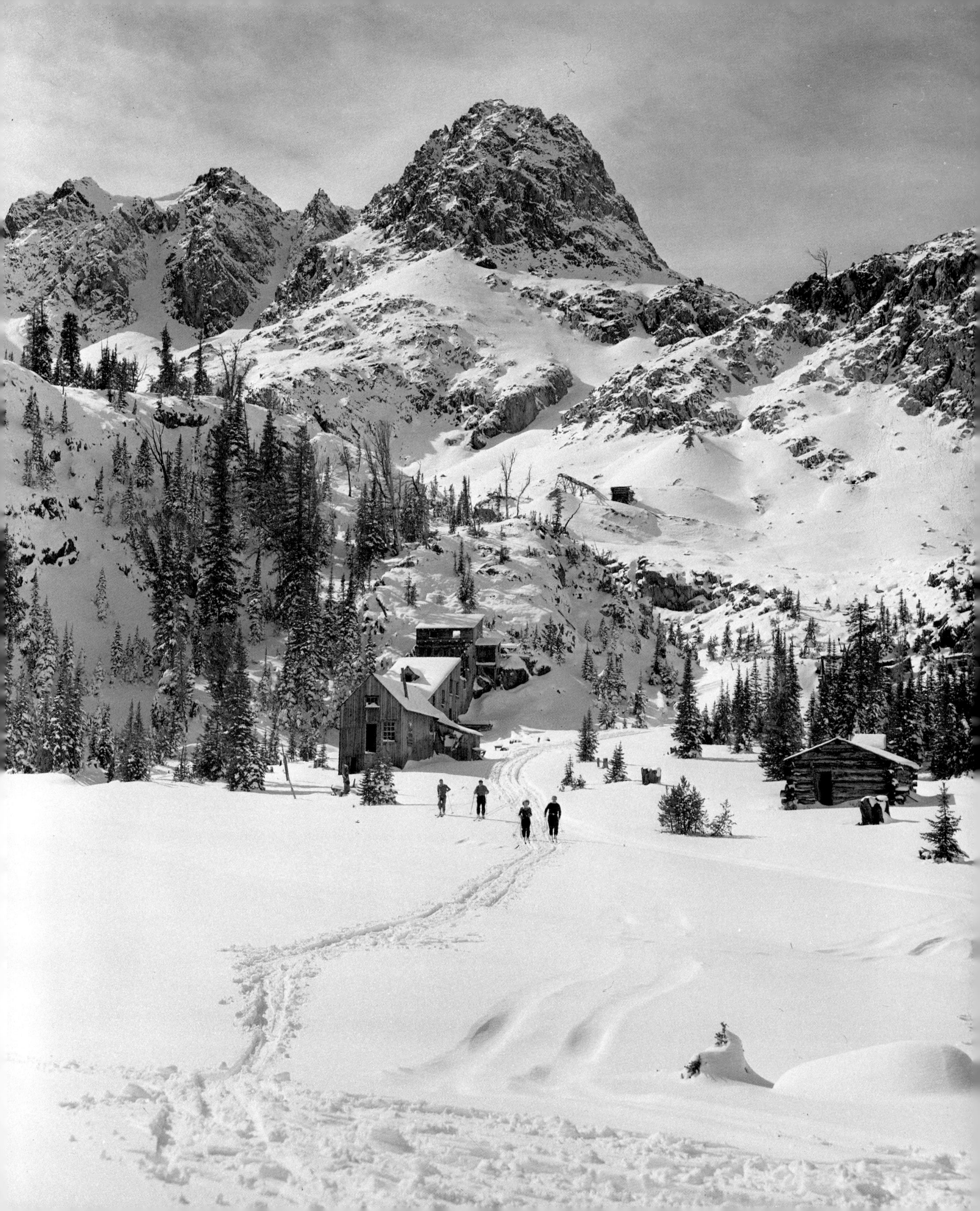

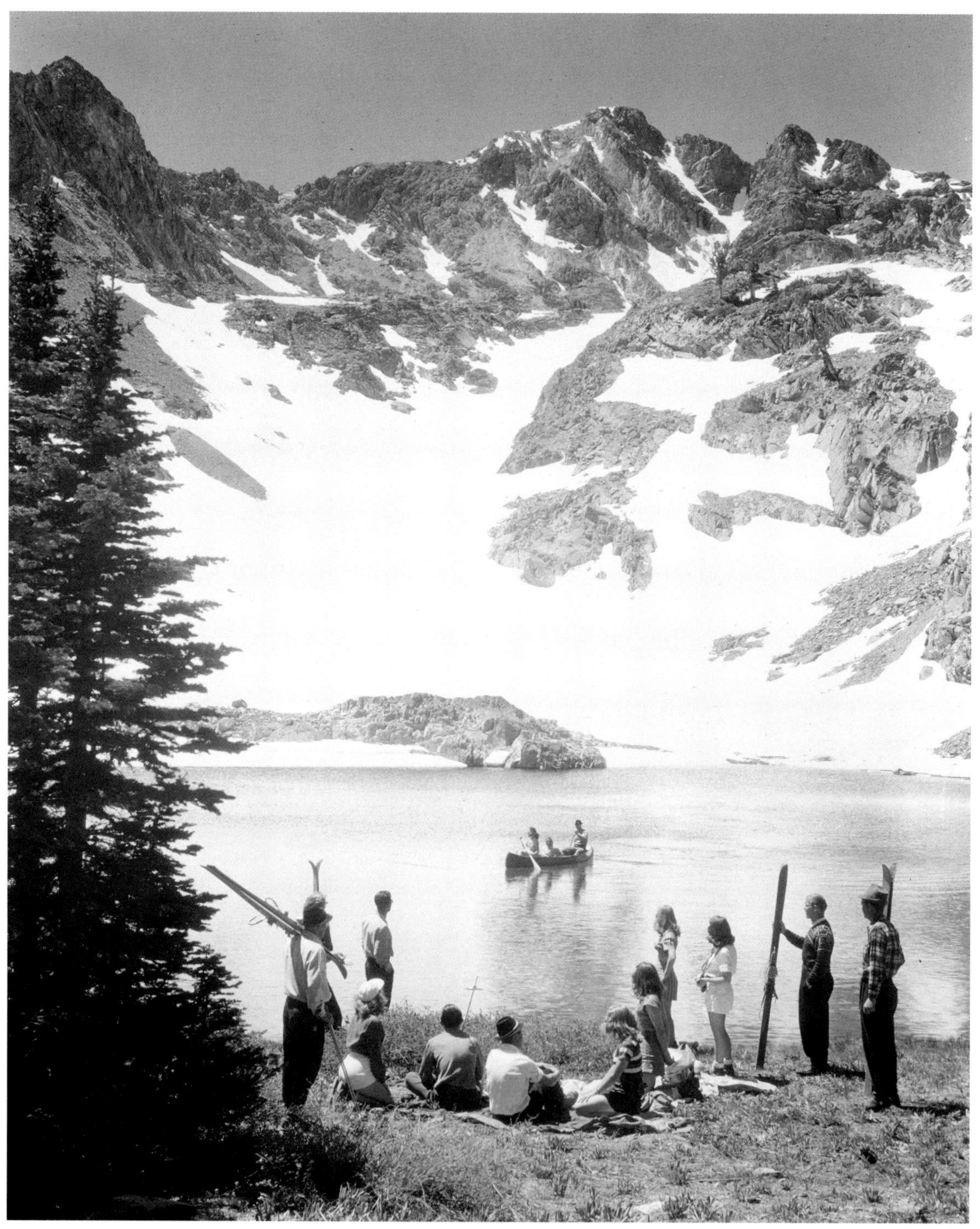

Summer outing at Boulder lake: Alf Engen, Dorothy Thomas, Bobbie Bennett, and others.

Two jeeps were available to transport skiers to the basin, which was used for slalom races on the Fourth of July in 1948.

Boulder Basin was "Sun Valley's newly discovered spring skiing area . . . only 18 miles and 45 minutes by Jeep from Sun Valley by a wagon trail used by the abandoned Golden Glow Mine." The snow was too deep there during the winter, but spring season started at the end of March. Snow in the basin lasted longer than anywhere else around Sun Valley, as it was a natural snow basin surrounded by high peaks and ridges. During April, ski classes for beginners were held on the gentle slopes of Baker's Creek, 15 miles north of Sun Valley, and advanced classes were on "the vast snow-fields of Galena." When snow in the lower areas receded, "ski-classes move up to Boulder Basin, where skiing is good until July." There were ski slopes for novices and intermediate skiers and five huge bowls for experts. Expert ski-mountaineers with guides from the ski school could climb the 10,966-foot Boulder Peak. Boulder Basin placed Sun Valley in the

> *unique position of being able to offer the skiing enthusiast an opportunity to pursue his favorite sport not only throughout the spring but into summer, as well. Just imagine skiing in the morning, and in the afternoon, playing tennis or golf or going swimming or horseback riding.*

The basin's mountain lake could be used for summer sports, and the area became popular for picnics, hiking, and rock climbing. Expansion of skiing into other areas around Sun Valley was planned, "so that even wider fields of activities will be open to skiers in the years to come," wrote *The Valley Sun*.

Dorice Taylor said Sun Valley sent a camera crew to make a newsreel to publicize Boulder Basin. The script called for Nelson Bennett and Faith Whitney, a guest from New York, to ride a canoe down the ski slope and slide into the lake. Two dry runs worked well, but when the cameras were running, the "canoe rocketed into the lake, overturned and dumped Nelson and Faith into the icy water. 'There I was,' Faith told me, 'flailing around in heavy ski boots in that Bering Sea with everyone yelling, 'Get the picture.' Finally, someone said, 'Now get Faith.'"

An avalanche destroyed Owl Creek Cabin in 1952. It was not rebuilt, and the alpine touring school dissolved, except for occasional trips. The backcountry part of the Sun Valley Ski School ended, and Hennig and Haemmerle joined the alpine ski school.[65]

23

1947

U.S. Olympic Alpine Team Is Selected and Trains at Sun Valley for the 1948 Games

Sun Valley's winter of 1946–1947 had "more than its share of gaiety, tension and downright brilliant racing." Otto Lang said 1947 was "one of the most exciting in Sun Valley's history," and the country's collegiate skiers were "our mainstays in competitive skiing." Sixteen of the 30 skiers selected for the 1948 Olympic team were college students, and others had only recently graduated.

The selection of the U.S. Olympic alpine team began in 1947, with regional tournaments where skiers competed for a chance to enter the Olympic tryouts held in March at Sun Valley. These included the Pacific Northwestern Ski Association's Annual Amateur Downhill and Slalom Championships at Stevens Pass in early February. The National Downhill and Slalom Championships were scheduled for Ogden, Utah, in late February. The action-packed year ended with the Olympic team tryouts at Sun Valley on March 8–9, followed by the Harriman Cup competition, after which the alpine team would be announced.

The U.S. Olympic jumping team would be selected at trials at the Milwaukee Ski Bowl in Washington on March 22–23, 1947, preceded by the Leavenworth jumping tournament in January and a pre-Olympic meet (the Northwest Jumping Championships) at the Ski Bowl on February 16. The events brought the country's best jumpers to the Northwest to compete where the "jumping trials become little Olympics," as the *Seattle Times* reported.

Alf Engen left Sun Valley in 1942 to help develop the Snowbasin ski area and to work with the army. He returned after the war to work, and he and his family lived in the lodge in an apartment next to Gary Cooper's. Alf's son Alan remembers how big and how nice Cooper was, allowing Alan to tag along with him. Alf taught skiing at Sun Valley and helped to develop young racers. He left Sun Valley after the 1948 season, taking over the ski school at Alta.[66]

In winter 1947, Alf Engen, "skiing's iron man and winner of every national ski title . . . who still skis and jumps with great elegance and plenty of speed," in the words of the Sun Valley Ski Club, used Sun Valley's steep slopes to coach six men and five women from the Sun Valley Ski Club for possible Olympic team places. They included Don and Leon Goodman of Idaho, Gene Gillis of Oregon, Dave Faires of Washington, Jack Reddish and Dick Movits of Utah, Gretchen Fraser of Washington, Doris Post of Nevada, Rebecca Fraser of Vermont, Ellen Ulery of California, and Alma Hansen of Oregon. Gretchen Fraser described Engen's coaching in her article, "Women's Racing Comes of Age" in the *Sun Valley Ski Club Annual Report* for 1947:

> *And the old master is throwing everything in the book at these skiers as the rugged training schedule progresses. . . . Alf has outlined a schedule of conditioning and practice which would make the most ardent skier wonder if it is worth it. But all of the team members are working hard in maintaining the program. In the mornings the team skis Mount Baldy non-stop with many turns three or four times and afternoons are spent practicing slalom and jumping on Ruud Mount. Alf leads the pack throughout the training, and his ability has served as a great incentive to the team.*

Friedl Pfeifer emphasized the need to bring the country's best skiers together and "scientifically put them through the proper conditioning program," to train them to compete at the international level. "We must work as a unit, as the French, Swiss and Austrians do, in order to give our boys a chance." Racers should get tough downhill practice on steep long slopes at Sun Valley, Alta or Aspen, he said, and ski "until their legs burn, as that is the only way to condition for the long downhill runs in Europe."

On March 3–4, 1947, the national championship races at Ogden brought the top skiers from all over the United States. The first 50 men and 20 women finishers would be eligible to compete in the Olympic tryouts at Sun Valley. The Pacific Northwest Ski Association sent 16 skiers, including Jack Nagel, Rees Stevenson, Don Amick, Paul

Gilbreath, Gretchen Fraser, Rebecca Fraser, Alma Hansen, Dodie Post, Mary Alice Peal, and Ann Volkmann. Karl Molitor from Switzerland won the national combined championships, sweeping the events. Alf Engen was second, followed by another Swiss, Paul Valear, Dick Movitz of Salt Lake City, and John Litchfield of Aspen. Rhoda Wurtele of Montreal won the women's combined title. Alma Hansen of Sun Valley placed ninth. However, the races were a disappointment since continuous snowfall before the meet closed the road to Alta, and the event was relocated to Mount Ogden, which was too easy for such high-class competition. The racers "came up to Sun Valley itching to show what they could really do," reported the *American Ski Annual* for 1948.

The Olympic tryouts and Harriman Cup at Sun Valley were described by Kathleen Harriman in the *Sun Valley Ski Club Annual Report* for 1947. The tryouts were held on March 8–9, 1947:

> *Seventy-five of the foremost downhill slalom racers in this country, male and female, were out on Baldy Mountain and Ruud Mountain practicing for the Olympic tryouts. . . . Pat Rogers . . . is to be complimented for work this Union Pacific development had been doing for the development of junior skiing in the country and its contribution to the Olympic fund-raising project.*

This was the year Jack Reddish, a young Navy veteran skiing for the Alta Ski Club, became known on the national circuit. Reddish first made his mark at Sun Valley in 1942 as a 90-pound 15-year-old. He was coached at Alta by Dick Durrance and Alf Engen and came into his own after the war. In 1947, Reddish "led the field with some of the finest skiing ever seen in a Harriman race," Kathleen Harriman wrote.

Reddish won the men's downhill on Warm Springs, finishing in 2:35.2, beating the course record set by Dick Durrance by 20 seconds, traveling between 60 and 65 miles per hour down a trail, not an open slope. Seventeen of the 38 racers "smashed the 7-year old Warm Springs standard," wrote the *New York Times*. Even Durrance was surprised, since in his time there were no control or direction flags as there were in this "thrill-packed test."

> *Reddish's feat demonstrated the advances that skiing has made in this country. . . .* [He] *bounded out at the most feared point, the ever-dangerous 'steilhang'—a 3,100 foot pitch of more than 40 degrees about one-half mile after the start—and took the 'fall-line' high, not even bothering to throw in a quick check!*

> *Seattle's David Faires, skiing for the Sun Valley Ski Club, was 2nd in the downhill, George Macomber of the Alta Ski Club was 3rd and Bobby Blatt from Stanford was fourth. Seattle's Don Amick, skiing for the Sun Valley Ski Club, was 5th.*

In the women's downhill, Sun Valley Ski Club president Al Lindley was the forerunner. Shortly after he began his run, Harriman reported,

> *an over-zealous female, dressed in a plaid skirt and rumored to be Olivia Pratt from "down under," started out behind him. As "she" was apparently out of control, a great shout went up from the audience on the "Steilhang" and was carried on down the mountain. Al thought they were cheering for him. It was later learned the "ardent Miss" was none other than Kris Berg, Norwegian champ.*

Gretchen Fraser "displayed her superiority by topping the field with a margin of better than five seconds," according to *High Times at the Harriman*, while 14-year-old Andrea Mead of Pico Peak, Vermont, was second ("but give that Mead girl time to finish school and college and brother, watch out!"), followed by Paula Kann of New Hampshire and Rebecca Fraser.

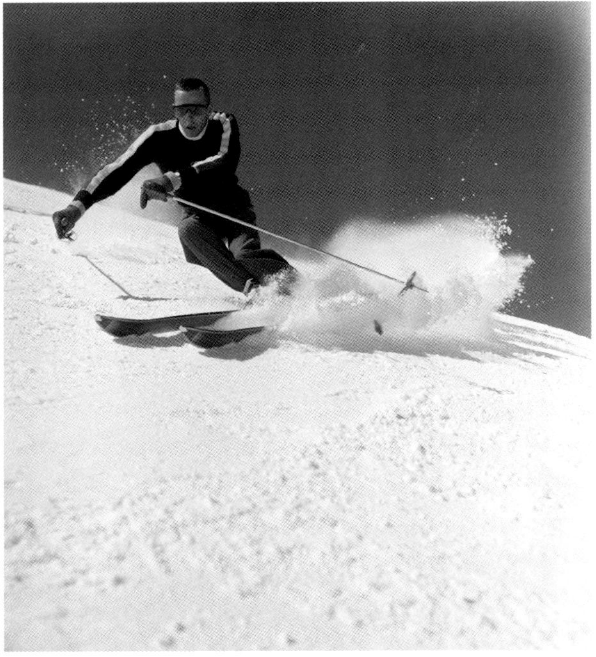

Jack Reddish skiing on Bald Mountain.

Friedl Pfeifer's slalom on Ruud Mountain was typical of those in European competitions. The men's slalom was won by Gordon Wren, and Bob Blatt was second. "Dave Faires, who had done so well in the Downhill, got off on the wrong foot at the beginning of his second run and was unable to recover his composure," Harriman wrote, and finished 30th.

In the women's slalom, Andrea Mead won by a huge margin, followed by Gretchen Fraser and Paula Kann. Mead was still only a child, but "she is a sensible, self-possessed young lady who skis like a dream," Harriman wrote. "When she stops growing she will be a big girl, but she carries it very gracefully and has a lovely style."

Bob Blatt from Stanford won the combined title, followed by Jack Reddish of Salt Lake City and George Macomber of West Newton, Massachusetts. The top Washington skiers were Don Amick in sixth, Leon Goodman eighth, and Karl Stingl 11th. Gretchen Fraser won the women's combined title, followed by Andrea Mead and Paula Kann.

Walter Prager and Alf Engen were named coaches of the 1948 U.S. Olympic ski team. Prager, from Switzerland, was a holder of world and Arlberg-Kandahar championships, was with the 10th Mountain Division during the war, coached the Dartmouth Ski Team from 1936 through 1946, and later became head of the ski school at Jackson Hole. He would coach the women's and men's downhill and slalom squads. Engen was from Norway, held 12 national championships, and was "universally regarded as the finest skier in the country," according to the *New York Times*. He would coach the U.S. cross-country and jumping skiers.

The 20 men and 10 women "who sparkled in the Olympic trials . . . over the weekend," according to Harriman, were invited to race in the International Open Downhill and Slalom Tournament and Harriman Cup against visiting skiers from Norway, Switzerland, Canada, and France. After the race, 12 men and eight women would be selected to the 1948 Olympic team. Seattle skiers included Don Amick, Jack Nagel, Dave Faires, Paul Gilbreath, and Gretchen Fraser. The Swiss skiers who swept the American speed skiing championship in Utah, Karl Molitor and Olivia Ausoni Villars, were favorites to win the event.

The seventh annual Harriman Cup and International Open Downhill and Slalom took place on March 15, with a field of top American skiers plus competitors from Switzerland, Norway, France, and Canada.

The downhill was revived, and moved back to Warm Springs from the River Run side of the mountain, where it had been held before the war. Kathleen Harriman wrote that the course was "fast and treacherous. . . . Melting snow due to a hot sun ran into shady areas to form ice which tripped up many skiers racing down the slope and preventing them from finishing the run." Edi Rominger of Switzerland won the downhill in a time of 2:22.3, beating Jack Reddish's record set a week before. Toni Matt of New Hampshire was a second behind. Nine racers beat the record for the course set by Jack Reddish, including Reddish himself, who beat his own record by two seconds. Don Amick took the day's most spectacular spill, hurtling into a ditch but popping out unhurt and finishing in 32nd place. France's Georgette Thiollière won the women's downhill. Ruth Marie Stewart of New Hampshire was second, Gretchen Fraser of Sun Valley was third, and Andrea Mead fourth.

The fast 45-gate slalom course on Ruud Mountain was set by Friedl Pfeifer. The men's slalom was won by Barney McLean, beating Edi Rominger and Toni Matt. In the women's slalom, Gretchen Fraser finished third. Andrea Mead ran first, wearing her favorite blue jeans for luck and finishing seventh.

Edi Rominger won the men's combined title, with Toni Matt close behind. Georgette Thiollière won the women's combined title, followed by Gretchen Fraser. The U.S. women won the team slalom event, beating the second-place Swiss team by 11 points, to the "complete surprise" of the Americans, according to the *New York Times*.

After the meet, a ski jumping exhibition was held on Ruud Mountain with visiting Norwegian skiers Arnold Kongsgaard, Fagnar Raklid, Harold Hauge, and the University of Washington's Gustav Raaum, who jumped against Alf Engen, Dick Durrance, and Gordon Wren.

Averell Harriman and his daughter Kathleen attended the events, along with Lowell Thomas and a number of other celebrities. The Sun Valley Ski Club banquet celebrating the Harriman Cup served as a fundraiser for the Olympic Ski Fund. It cost $10 to attend. Attendance was so large that, according to Dorice Taylor, "the Ski Club went mad trying to find tickets for all the handsome young hopes of the nation who wanted to go to the dinner." Kathleen Harriman presented the Bradley Plate to Jack Reddish and the Mary Cornelia Trophy (which she herself had won in 1941) to Barbara Kidder, winners of the intercollegiate ski meet. Averell presented awards for the club championships.

An auction was held under the direction of "that soft persuasive Irish tongue of Joe Burgy," as described by the *Sun Valley Sun*, who ran the shooting range. Burgy "had the guests bidding up in the hundreds for skiing lessons. Top price, of $250, went for the old master himself, Friedl Pfeifer." Other high bids were received for "glamour ski lessons" with Georgette Thiollière and Marty Arrouge, dates in the Duchin Room with Dolly Pike "of the golden hair," and pictures with Bebe de Roces, "the prettiest Eskimo we've ever seen," in a mink parka. The General Store donated skis and equipment and there was a Picard Shop grab bag. A special toast was given to Averell Harriman.

The U.S. ski team for the 1948 Olympics was announced on March 18, 1947, by the chairman of the Olympic Ski Committee.

The *Seattle Times* of March 24, 1947, reprted that 11 out of the 19 berths went to Western skiers. Two Washington skiers made the team, Gretchen Fraser and Dave Faires as an alternate. The men's downhill and slalom team consisted of three Salt Lake skiers, George Macomber, Jack Reddish, and Dick Movits; plus Colin Stewart of New Hampshire. Other berths went to Robert Blatt of Palo Alto, California, and three Colorado skiers, Steve Knowlton, Barney McLean, and Gordon Wren. A separate combined team included Ralph Townsend of Durham, New Hampshire; Don Johnsen of Salt Lake City; and Corey Engen of Ogden, Utah (Alf's brother). Wendall Broomhall of Rumford, Maine, would represent the United States in cross-country. Five alternates were chosen: Dave Faires of Seattle, Gene Gillis of Sun Valley, John Blatt of California (brother of Robert), William Distin of Vermont, and Dev Jennings of Colorado.

The women's downhill and slalom team was led by Gretchen Fraser and Andrea Mead. Other members included Paula Kann of New Hampshire, Brynhild Grasmoen of California, Ruth Marie Steward of New Hampshire, Dodie Post of Nevada, and Rebecca Fraser of Vermont. Anne Winn of Salt Lake City was an alternate.

The teams remained in Sun Valley for two weeks of spring skiing. According to Prager and Engen in the *Sun Valley Ski Club Annual Report* for 1947, the coaches

> *will mold a downhill and slalom team capable of giving the European teams a battle all the way. . . . Intense Sun Valley workouts should make the team ski faster, and the coaches "will attempt to smooth the skiers" styles so the United States runners will be able to clip vital tenths of seconds off their times when they compete at St. Moritz next February.*

Although not originally selected, in October 1947, Don Amick, "the veteran Washington Ski Club speedster," was named to the U.S. Olympic downhill and slalom team, according to the *Seattle Times*. Darroch Crooks, in an article for the 1947 *Sun Valley Ski Club Report*, described the "amazing skiing" of veteran racer Amick, "whose trick of coaching himself aloud as he raced down the courses, not only proved highly effective but was also a warning signal for unwary spectators."

On March 22–23, 1947, the final 1948 Olympic ski-jumping team tryouts were held at the Milwaukee Ski Bowl. Six jumpers were selected for the team, the first five finishers plus Art Devlin from Lake Placid, who injured his knee at the Leavenworth tournament earlier that year but who earned his berth in other

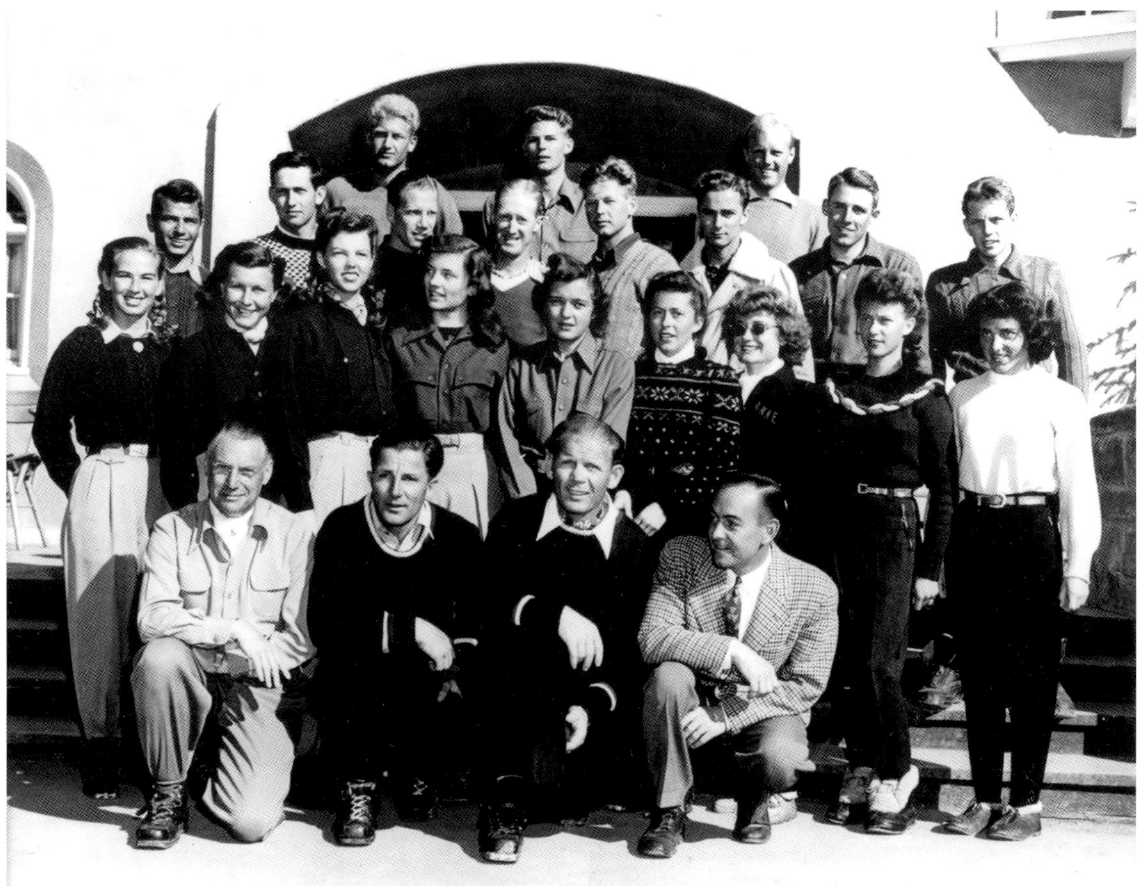

Men's and women's U.S. Olympic ski teams at Sun Valley, 1947.

events. Joe Perrault from Ispeming, Michigan, finished first. Two veterans from the 1936 U.S. Olympic team finished in the next two places—Walter Bietila from Iron Mountain, Michigan, and Sverre Fredheim from St. Paul, Minnesota. The others included Gordon Wren from Colorado and Ralph Bietila from Iron Mountain. After the competition, they left for Sun Valley for two weeks of intensive training on Ruud Mountain. Alf Engen, the co-coach of the jumping team, strapped on his jumping skis to try the hill for the first time since the war, and "the old master" flew 260 feet, according to the *Seattle Times*.

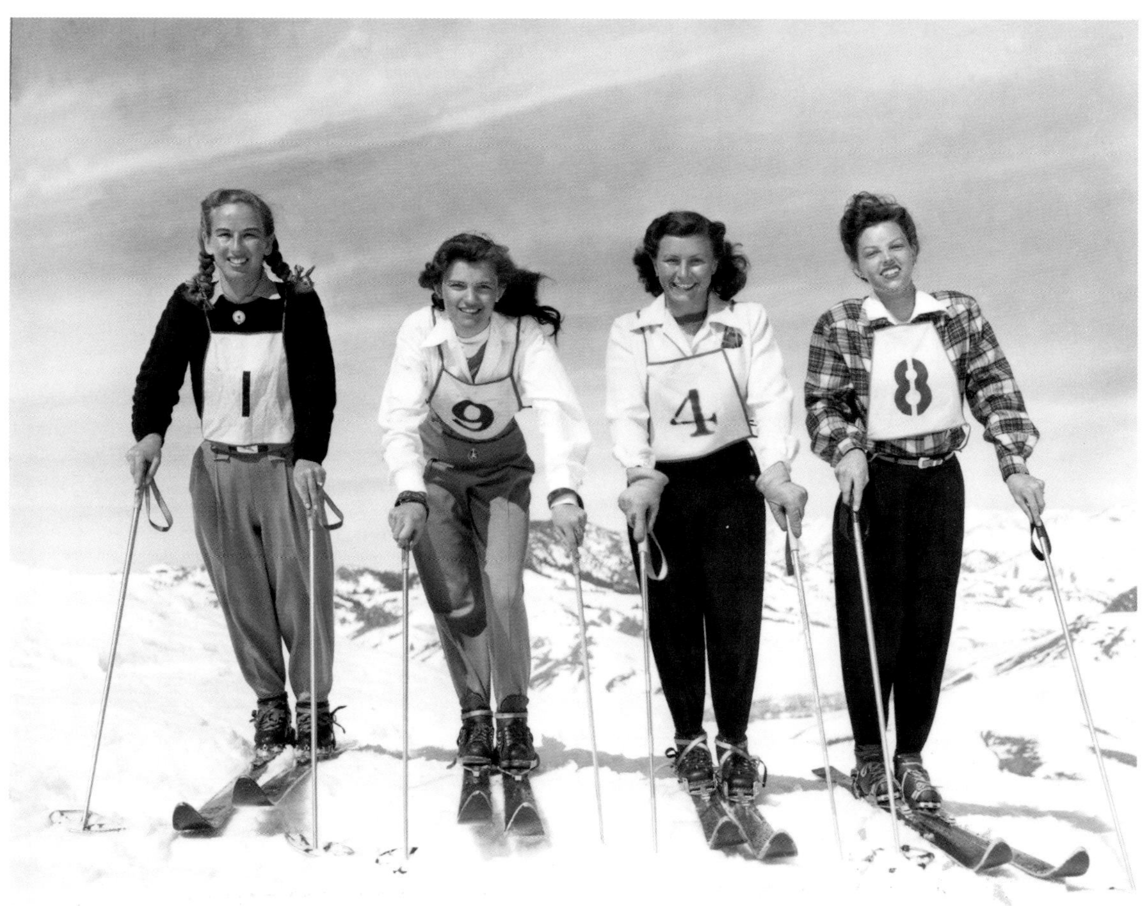

U.S. women's Olympic ski team at Sun Valley: Gretchen Fraser, Andrea Mead, Paula Kann, and Brynhild Grasmoen.

James Laughlin described the 1948 U.S. Olympic team and Gretchen Fraser, "master of the snow-plow schuss and infallibly the steady in slalom," in the *American Ski Annual* for 1948:

> *Of the veterans, the standout was Gretchen Fraser. Who could have guessed that this dignified married lady would stage a comeback and outski Hannes Schneider's Conway protegee, Paula Kann? . . . How will our teams do in St. Moritz? I'm afraid we should not place our hopes too high. We saw this winter how much better—on the average—the Swiss were than our best, and it is to be remembered that the French have been beating the Swiss consistently.*

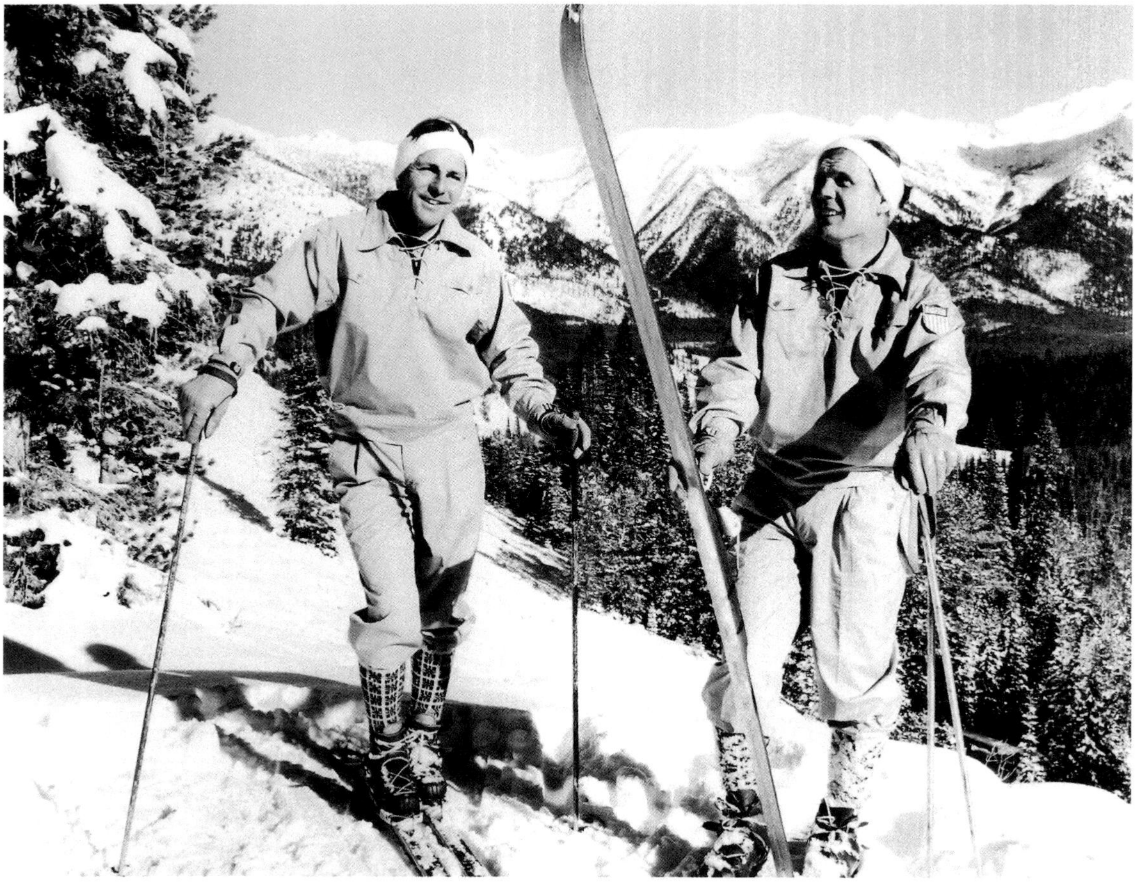

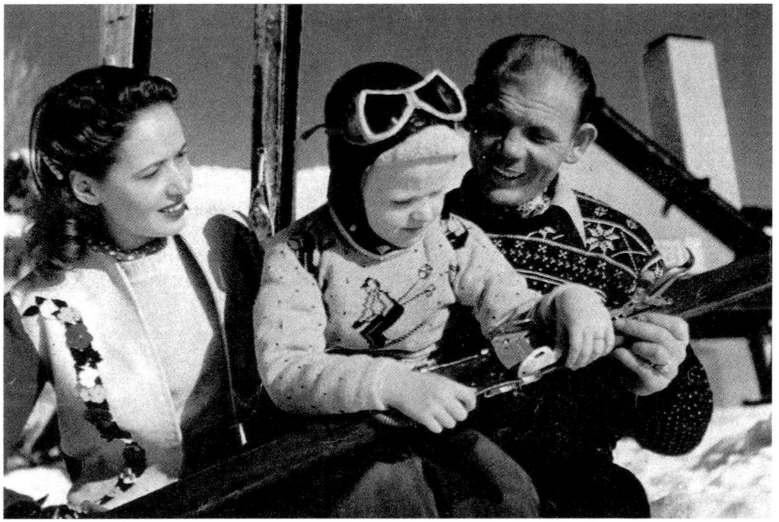

ABOVE Walter Prager from Switzerland and Alf Engen from Norway were co-coaches of the 1948 U.S. Olympic teams for the St. Moritz Games. Engen trained prospective Olympians at Sun Valley before the selection process, and both trained team members at Sun Valley before the Olympics.

LEFT Alf, Evelyn, and Alan Engen, Sun Valley, around 1947. *Courtesy of Alan Engen.*

Sun Valley played a critical role in preparing American skiers to compete at the 1948 Olympics. The team received no support from the government, unlike European teams, and depended on private contributions to cover training and travel expenses. In cooperation with the National Ski Association, Sun Valley held a number of fundraising events throughout 1947 and 1948, and raised more than $9,000. Sun Valley provided lodging for the teams, its ski instructors coached prospective members of the teams, and the alpine and jumping teams trained at Sun Valley in 1947 and 1948.

Summer at Sun Valley

Over the Fourth of July holiday, the Idaho state trapshoot competition took place at Sun Valley, where many of the best shooters in the United States competed for seven trophies, including the George F. Ashby trophy and a $3,000 purse.

Sun Valley opened a climbing school directed by Walter Prager, who taught Army mountain troops climbing and skiing during the war. Students spent their first day climbing rocks "about three or four men high," according to *The Valley Sun*, where elementary skills were learned. The second day was spent learning to rappel down steep rocks using ropes. Using pitons came next. Finally, students were taken on a two-day trip into the high country around Sun Valley.

Sun Valley's three tennis courts were resurfaced, and plans made to hold several tournaments, directed by Sigi Engl, the resort's tennis pro. Sun Valley's drive-yourself service offered station wagons that could be rented for trips or hired with a driver. A recommended one-day trip went over Galena Summit and included Alturas, Pettit, Redfish, and Stanley Lakes and the towns of Stanley and Challis. Carl Bradsher, the shooting instructor, taught pistol, rifle, and shotgun skills, but his speciality was skeet, derived from the Scandinavian word for "shoot."

24

1948

Gretchen Fraser Wins Two Olympic Medals at St. Moritz and Becomes an American Heroine

The *Valley Sun* of December 1947 described the work done at Sun Valley for winter 1948. On Baldy, a new 3,080-foot double chairlift was installed from the bottom of Spring House Canyon [Broadway] up to the Roundhouse, the first double chairlift on the mountain, with 1,072 of vertical lift and an hourly capacity of 300 riders. It was known as lift No. 4 or the Broadway lift and is now the Cold Springs lift. It opened up a "virtually limitless skiing area below Christmas Bowl," and "literally doubles the skiing possibilities of this already highly developed mountain," the *Sun* said. Louis Holliday said everyone wanted the new chairlift to go up Easter Ridge to the top of the mountain, so they could ski the bowls. However, Ed Seagle, a non-skier, insisted it be built to the Roundhouse. Andy Hennig said, "The Broadway lift opens up an immense skiing area that includes the wide open slopes of Firelookout, Mayday, Easter and Lefty Bowls, and the lower portion of Christmas Bowl. These runs end at the lower terminal of the lift."

Previously, skiers going down the bowls had to go down Broadway/Cold Springs to the highway, where buses took them to River Run or the lodge. Now they could ride the lift back to the Roundhouse and continue to the top of the mountain. The new lift had steel towers and would eliminate practically all waiting, making more downhill skiing possible for everyone.

A new 16-by-24-foot log warming hut was built next to the top lift station on Baldy, replacing the Forest Service lookout station a short hike away. The "Cabin," according to *The Valley Sun*, offered "a pleasant meeting space at a spot representing the starting point of a number of Sun Valley's very finest runs." It was maintained by the ski patrol and later became the ski patrol cabin.

Dollar Mountain had a new short lift for beginners, "the nursery lift," serving a gentle and varied slope. It took beginners off the existing lift and eliminated the halfway station, leaving the chair for skiers who wanted to go to the top. There was a new 20-by-50-foot cabin at the bottom, designed in Swiss style, with one large multi-windowed room and a 33-foot terrace for soaking up the sun. It was a place for beginners not experienced enough to go to the cabin on top of the mountain. Light refreshments were served, and food was no longer available at the mountaintop cabin, which remained a warming hut.

In summer 1947, Friedl Pfeifer resigned as head of the Sun Valley Ski School to work full time developing the Aspen Ski Area. Otto Lang was made executive director of the ski school. Lang had been working with Darryl Zanuck making movies, and he needed someone to manage the school's daily operations. He hired Toni Matt as head instructor, a world-class ski racer from St. Anton, Austria, who was teaching for Hannes Schneider at North Conway, New Hampshire. This allowed Lang to go to San Moritz to cover the Olympics for the *Seattle Post-Intelligencer*, where his star pupil, Gretchen Fraser, led the women's team. Lang planned to "garner some international publicity for Sun Valley, with me acting as the resort's official goodwill ambassador."

Lang described the instructors for 1948. Toni Matt from St. Anton, Austria, was the head instructor. "Just wait until you see Toni churn up a slalom course, or hurl himself down such runs as 'Exhibition Run' and the 'Steilhang' on Warm Springs," Lang said. John Litchfield, who skied at Dartmouth with Dick Durrance, returned after teaching at Aspen under Friedl Pfeifer. Sigi Engl was back, "one of the finest technicians operating on boards," according to Lang. Florian Haemmerle and Andy Hennig were returning to oversee backcountry skiing, as were Victor Gottschalk, Sepp Froehlich, Aldolph Roubicek, Floyd Dupuis, and Les Outzs. Don and Leon Goodman were new.

On January 8, 1948, Steve Hannagan wrote G.F. Ashby about MGM's plans to include Sun Valley in an upcoming movie, *Duchess of Idaho*. Eighty percent of the movie would be filmed at Sun Valley by a staff of 150 in summer 1948, and there would be winter scenes as well. They were to film part of the movie on a private car on a Union Pacific streamliner. Hannagan tried to get the studio to change the name

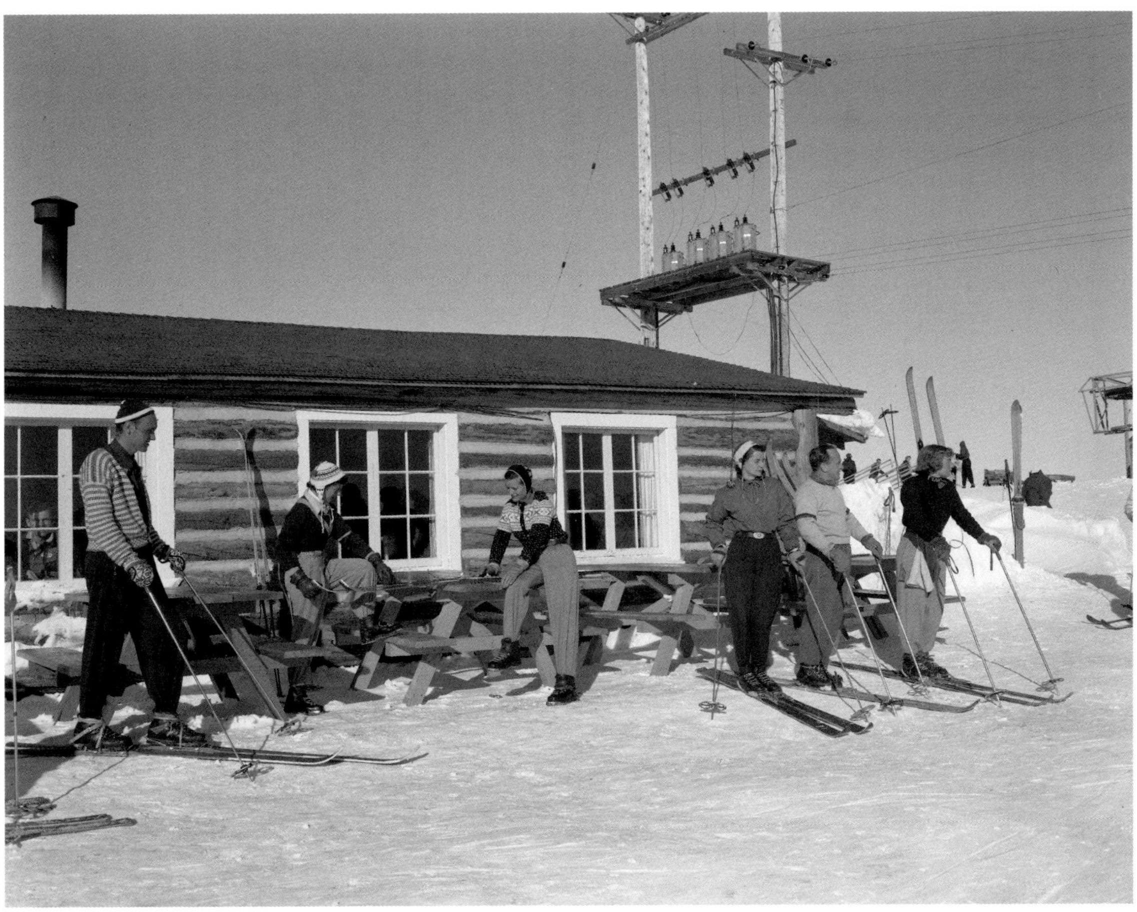

New warming hut on top of Baldy built for winter 1948, replacing the old Forest Service fire lookout. This is now the ski patrol cabin.

to *Duchess of Sun Valley*. They declined, but there would be plenty of publicity for both the Union Pacific and Sun Valley.

The *New York Times* published an article about Sun Valley on February 15, 1948, "Wide-Open Idaho, Ketchum Near Sun Valley Revives the Old Wild West." While Sun Valley was modern and glitzy, next-door Ketchum was an old-timey Western town where sheepherders and cattlemen mixed with the celebrities and Hollywood stars the resort attracted in its bars, restaurants, and gambling dens.

> *This is the one town in the nation where winter-sports enthusiasts can step nonchalantly from a dog-sled, imbibe such tasty Basque dishes as arroz con pollo, chorizos or patatas en salsa verde, and then, well fortified against the Idaho climate,*

listen to the clanking of silver dollars in a slot machine, watch a spinning roulette wheel or follow the antics of expertly rolled dice.

The dog sled is a licensed taxi. Basque shepherds come into town when snow sets in and the gaming tables put this tiny town . . . in a class with Reno. Herders and cowmen mix with resplendent skiers in town. Ketchum is a magnet for well-healed vacationists at Sun Valley's Lodge and Challenger Inn, and the 93-Club attracts many a connoisseur.

A score of high spots offer warming beverages of a rather different vintage. The town's emporiums seek to capture the spirit of rough, tough frontier days with fair success, catering to hardy New York and Los Angeles pioneers. The Christiania Club is currently the last word in snow country décor. . . . Western dance music is presented by a bevy of Hollywood girls at the Alpine Club.

Sun Valley visitors who make the mile-long pilgrimage via dogsled to Ketchum often find themselves dining or dancing beside the strikingly familiar outdoor enthusiasts customarily glimpsed only on the silver screen. Ralph Bellamy, Jane Russell, Ingrid Bergman, Gary Cooper, Daryl Zanuck, Ernest Hemingway, Dorothy Lamour and Phil Harris have all lent a cosmopolitan touch to such way stations along the ski trail as the Sawtooth Club and the Tram, where a former trainer of Jack Dempsey adds to the atmosphere.[67]

GRETCHEN FRASER IS THE HEROINE OF THE WINTER OLYMPICS

The year's big story was the winter Olympic Games in St. Moritz, Switzerland, the first since 1936, and the first to feature a full array of alpine events, three men's and three women's races. The *Seattle Times* announced that three Northwest skiers were set to compete—Gretchen Fraser, Don Amick, and Dave Faires. Fraser was the captain of the women's team and its No. 1 skier, and Faires was an alternate. Dr. Edmund H. Smith of Seattle was the surgeon for the Olympic teams.

The U.S. men's and women's teams, coached by Walter Prager and Alf Engen, trained at Sun Valley, receiving free room and board and coaching. Europeans were expected to win the skiing events, but the training the team received on Sun Valley's long runs prepared them to compete on equal terms. According to Luanne Pfeifer, Fraser's biographer, the women's team were "told to get physically fit on their own over the summer and admonished . . . not to wear high heels . . . so our Achilles tendons wouldn't get short." Ski team members were given six pairs of skis for the Olympics, American made, but they were not specifically designed for them. Kathleen Harriman Mortimer was in charge of the women's uniforms. She had a wardrobe designed for the team by Picard's of Sun Valley, which included a grey worsted ski suit, a poplin parka with fur trim, hand-knit sweater by Marjorie Benedicker, alpaca coats, and long, black après-ski skirts.

Otto Lang, who was Fraser's coach at Mount Rainier in the late 1930s, covered the 1948 Olympics as a special correspondent for the *Seattle Post-Intelligencer*. He described her in his autobiography:

> *Gretchen Kunigk then about sixteen years old. . . . She was petite and muscular, well proportioned, and blond, and radiated charm. She enrolled in the school, and in only a short time I could tell that this young lady had the determination to go far in the skiing world. She grasped important technical points quickly and improved rapidly. . . .*
>
> [In 1948], *Gretchen was touted by the American press as a dark horse and potential threat to the elite European women skiers in downhill and slalom, as was the up-and-coming Andrea Mead, the youngest member of the Olympic squad.*

The team left New York by ship in early December 1947 and spent three weeks training in Davos, Switzerland. Fraser described problems faced by the women's team in the *Sun Valley Ski Club Report* for 1948. The women were the team's "stepchildren," since the coaches spent most of their time with the men. Fraser's biographer Luanne Pfeifer said the women's team received coaching from a rotation of coaches from the men's team, including eight different men in eight days. "Every day, we were sitting around waiting for one of the boys to come along. And we became very discouraged and mixed up with so many coaches, each pushing a different technique."

Alice Kiaer, the women's team manager, saw their training was not going well "and took drastic measures on her own." An American at the Olympics donated money to hire Walter Haensli, "the young Swiss star," to coach the women, and he pulled the team together. Haensli said the women had been training too long and hard. He established a different training schedule and worked on waxing issues and improving equipment. There was not enough time to change their skiing techniques, so he "tried to show them little things which would add speed, and, above all, to get them into a frame of mind where they would not be cowed of the competition." He recognized Fraser's potential and took special pains with her.

The Games opened on January 30. The first women's skiing event was the downhill, where the U.S. team did not fare well. The highest U.S. finisher was 12th, with Fraser 13th.

In the women's alpine combined, Fraser finished fifth in the downhill. In the slalom, racing against "sure winners" from France and Austria, she finished second, winning a silver medal, narrowly losing the gold to Trude Beiser of Austria by 37/100 of a point. "Europeans were stunned," said Luanne Pfeifer. "Americans were not supposed to win medals in alpine skiing." Fifteen-year-old Andrea Mead was three seconds ahead of the field at mid-course in the downhill but fell and did not finish, although she came back to win gold medals in slalom and giant slalom in the 1952 Olympics at age 19.

In the special slalom held the next day, Fraser faced a series of difficulties. She drew the difficult first start position. Alf Engen escorted her to the starting line, but the crowd was so large they were unable to make their way to the front of the line. Time was running out, and she was in danger of being disqualified. Engen got help from members of the St. Moritz ski patrol, who got her directly to the lift. The day was freezing cold and the course icy. Fraser won the first run and had to start in first position again on the second run. The electric timing system, which was being used for the first time, malfunctioned, and she had to wait 17 minutes for it to be fixed. She spent most of the time in the starting gate, which was "terribly nerve wracking," she said, putting her at a significant disadvantage. After 10 minutes, Fraser got out of the starting gate and took some turns. After the timing issue was resolved, Luanne Pfeifer said, "Gretchen plunged off with that relaxed smoothness and awesome power that was her trademark, holding her speed down just slightly—going fast enough to preserve her lead but without undue risk, a beautifully thought-out run." Gretchen Fraser won the race and an Olympic gold medal, the first for an American skier.

The Tacoma native became the unexpected heroine of the games. Otto Lang said, "Gretchen Fraser is the Toast of American Skiers and cheered by them whenever they gather in St. Moritz tonight. . . . It was a turning point in American skiing—an historic achievement, considering the field of international competitors." Fraser's victory was immensely popular at St. Moritz. She was flooded with congratulatory telegrams and "her room resembles nothing less than a florist's showroom—simply a mass of flowers," Otto Lang wrote. She was "in a veritable whirl of excitement and the thrill of becoming an Olympic champion was almost overpowering."

Gold medals were also won by 18-year-old Dick Button in figure skating and the U.S. men's four-man bobsleigh team. Lang said the U.S. men's ski team failed to live up to the country's hopes and did not win a medal. Henri Oreiller, "the daredevil French ski ace," won the men's alpine championship. Jack Reddish, the highest finishing American, was 12th in the alpine combined; Steve Knowlton was 25th, Barney McLean 26th, and Robert Blatt 29th.

Fraser was a natural with the press, even though there was no training given to athletes as is done today. She told an Associated Press reporter, "I trained at Sun Valley," and was thereafter associated with Sun Valley, according to Luanne Pfeifer.

> *The next day, around the world Sun Valley had more publicity than dynamo Steve Hannagan could have ever dreamed up. The resort was on the ski destination maps forevermore. As far as Hannagan & Associates were concerned she was to be referred to as Gretchen Fraser of Sun Valley, Idaho, regardless of the fact that she lived and continued to live in Vancouver, Washington. She raced for the Sun Valley Ski Club, and, after all, had trained in Sun Valley before the war when she lived there.*

Otto Lang sent a telegram to Sun Valley saying Fraser's performance "was nothing short of sensational. Displaying perfect composure and flawless style, she swept through both runs of an intricate 45-gate pattern without the slightest flutter to top a field comprising the finest women skiers in the entire world." Her accomplishment, he said, was "one of the greatest in the history of American skiing."

After the Olympics, Fraser traveled to Norway to meet her mother's relatives. Crown Prince Olav, with whom she skied on Mount Rainier in 1939, had her to lunch at the royal palace. Her Norwegian relatives took exception to her being described as a "girl with pigtails." They insisted she had braided hair, which had no connection with pigtails.

Gretchen Fraser and Dick Button were given a welcome parade in New York and a reception at Mayor LaGuardia's office. She also was given parades in San Francisco, Portland, Vancouver, and Eugene. She and her teammate Brynhild Grasmoen (the top American in the downhill) were taken in a horse-drawn sleigh in a parade at Sun Valley as Nelson Bennett's ski patrol welcomed the Olympic heroines by marching in formation with their skis on their shoulders.

Fraser's performance under the agonizing pressure of Olympic competition was "one of the classic feats of ski history," according to the *American Ski Annual* of 1949,

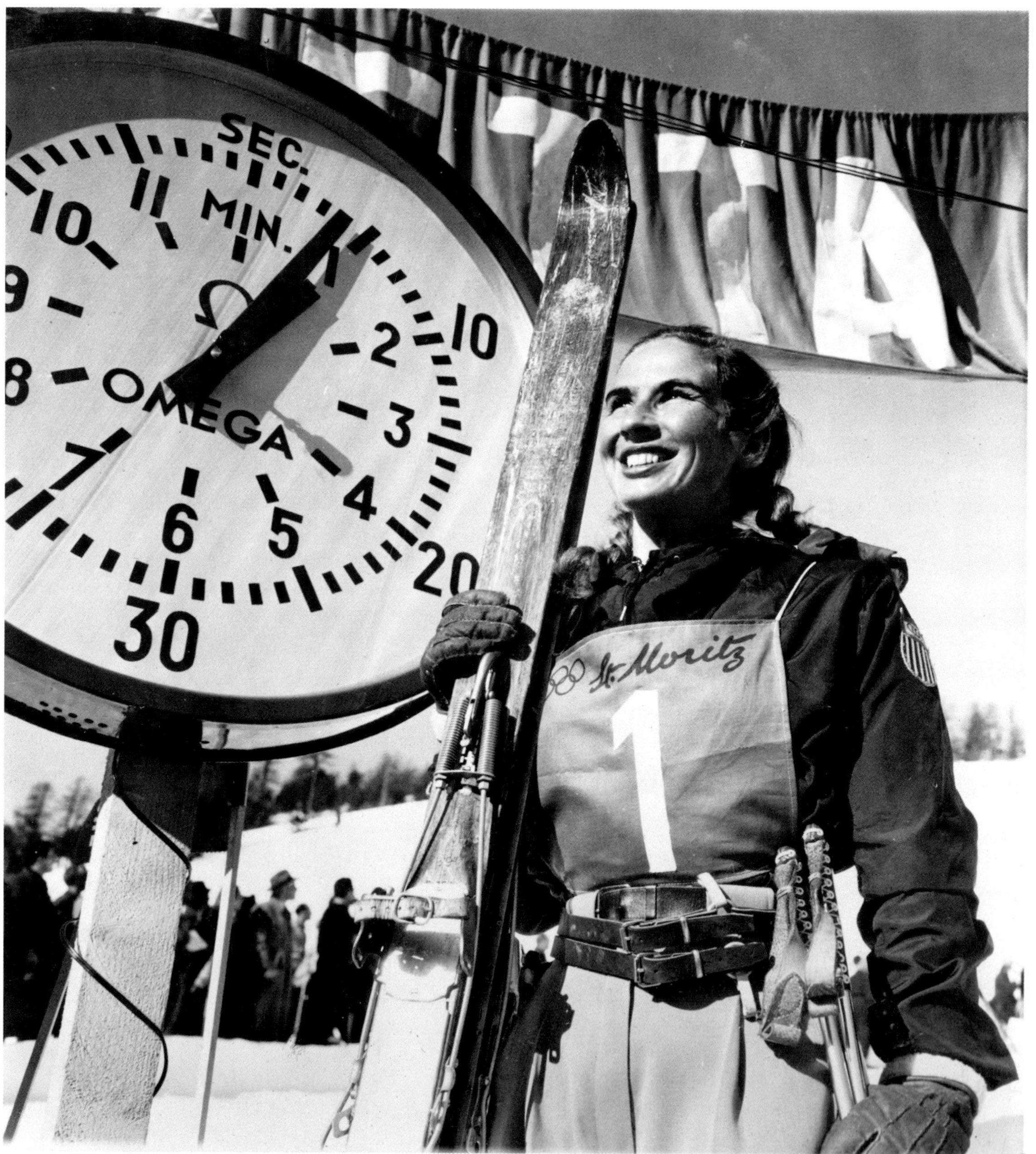

Gretchen Fraser at St. Moritz.

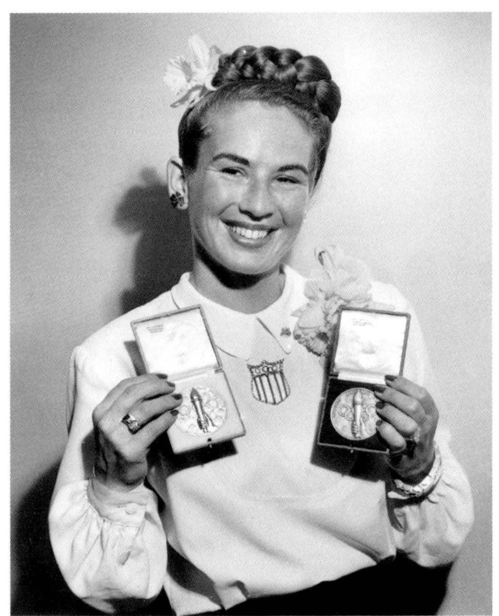

Gretchen Fraser with her two medals from the 1948 Olympics. *Courtesy of Tacoma Public Library.*

making her "the sensation of the Games" as "she licked the tar out of a half a dozen girls whose experience and records far eclipsed her own." In his president's message in 1948, Al Lindley said the extraordinary triumph of Gretchen Fraser "is a product of her many visits and training at Sun Valley. The Club can be justly proud in having America's most distinguished skier as a long-time and devoted member."

Fraser thanked Sun Valley for its contributions to the Olympic Ski Fund, as the resort "did more than its share and was largely responsible for the success of the program, without which no more than a handful of our team members would have been able to make the trip to Europe." The U.S. Ski Team had its way paid to the Olympics in 1948, an improvement over the 1936 Games, when her husband, Don, had to pay his own way. Don Fraser said in 1936, the U.S. team was "given the privilege of getting themselves to Europe." He traveled to Europe working on a Norwegian fruit boat, taking 35 days from Seattle and earning $1 a day chipping paint. As an Olympic team member, he got an overcoat, sweater, and cap as a uniform, along with $50.

Sun Valley's assistance to the U.S. Olympic squad was lavishly praised, backed "by the resources of the Union Pacific Railroad and the manpower of Pat Rogers's Sun Valley staffs" that went well beyond the money raised there to support the team, reported the *American Ski Annual* of 1948:

> *Not only was free accommodation provided for forty men and twenty girls for a week . . . not only was every conceivable technical preparation planned out without thought or expense (there was even a special man at the top of the Downhill to dust the snow off the competitors' skis as they stood in the gate) . . . but for months before the Trials promising young runners were given easy jobs at the Valley so that they could train daily for the squad under Alf Engen, and after the Trials, the squad that had been chosen was*

invited to stay on at Sun Valley for a further two week's intensive training with Olympic coaches Alf and Walt Prager.

Too many take Sun Valley's contributions for granted and don't see the work done by the ski school's Friedl Pfeifer and Fred Iselin, Nelson Bennett's Ski Patrol, and others.

Pat Rogers runs the whole Sun Valley plant in such perfect style that skiers imagine the Valley makes a million a year and can afford to be generous to the racers. Actually, it isn't so. Sun Valley only thrives for a few brief months in winter and summer; in between come the slack seasons, with overhead mounting up just the same. From the accountant's point of view, Sun Valley is still a losing venture, so that these huge contributions of manpower and accommodations are out-and-out philanthropy.

The Olympics made Gretchen Fraser a celebrity. She announced her retirement from competition in April 1948, after winning 17 championships for the Sun Valley Ski Club and two Olympic medals. Her success helped break barriers against women in the ski world, including at Sun Valley, where women were not readily hired as ski instructors. Jannette Burr Johnson was one of the beneficiaries. She was hired as a ski instructor, but Sigi Engl assigned her to Dollar Mountain to teach beginners even though she was on the 1952 Olympic team. Fraser signed a three-year contract with Union Pacific to be a public relations assistant to market Sun Valley, capitalizing on her signature look with her hair in pigtails. She got $500 plus expenses and a railroad pass, and also a $1,000 contract from Jantzen sweaters plus all the Jantzen pants and sweaters she wanted. She appeared in motion picture shorts and advertisements but would not teach skiing. Averell Harriman gave her one of his prize Labrador retriever puppies, who was "the perfect pup," she said. "He likes to sleep until ten in the morning."

Gretchen Fraser was the unanimous winner of the American Ski Trophy for 1948, one of the most coveted of all ski honors.

In 1952, she was manager of the U.S. women's Olympic team for the Oslo Games, which was the first year the team flew to Europe instead of traveling by steamship. In 1968, she and Don made Sun Valley their permanent home, remaining there until their deaths. Gretchen Fraser is honored at Sun Valley with a ski run (Gretchen's Gold), a restaurant in the lodge named after her, and a bronze statue in a field between Ketchum and Sun Valley. Her picture adorns the lodge hallways and a replica of her gold medal is on display. She is also honored at the large Olympian display at the Washington State Ski and Snowboard Museum, which has a replica of her gold medal and other memorabilia.[68]

Ski Tournaments at Sun Valley

The national intercollegiate meet was held over the Christmas holidays in December 1947, "which are always an exceptionally gay and colorful interlude at Sun Valley," according to the *Sun Valley Ski Club Annual* for 1948. Eleven colleges sent "the most brilliant field of collegiate skiers ever to have gathered at the Valley," consisting of nine men's teams and five women's teams. The men competed in four events, including cross-country and jumping. The races took place at "scenic Galena Ski Area." Racers had to climb to the start of the mile-long downhill that had a vertical drop of 1,200 feet, a "genuine test of racing ability." The slalom, which took place adjacent to Galena Summit, was open and long, with 25 gates. The cross-country race was a five-mile course that led up the draw past the "weather-beaten Galena Store."

Middlebury College was the winner, followed by Washington, Dartmouth, Utah, British Columbia, Colorado, Portland, and Washington State. U.W.'s Gustav Raaum, an exchange student from Norway, won the jumping competition, with the commentators saying "it was immediately evident that this lad was something of a jumper. He possessed superior style and his jumps of 126 and 129 feet cinched first place."

The eighth annual Harriman Cup Races/National Downhill, Slalom and Combined Championships were held March 27–28, 1948, and described by Otto Lang in the *Sun Valley Ski Club Annual* for 1948. There were 65 male entrants, although the women's field was "disturbingly small and lacked the star-studded appearance of the men's roster." This was the first appearance of Jannette Burr from Seattle.

Lang set the downhill course on Warm Springs, which required two turns on the steilhang, "two of the most pleasant and exciting high-speed turns ever to test a racer's skill." Jack Reddish of Alta Ski Club, who led the 1948 U.S. Olympic team, dominated the event "with incomparable assurance, elegance and skill." In the downhill, he beat second-place Yves Latreille from Quebec, skiing for Sun Valley, by five seconds. In the slalom, a challenging course set above the Roundhouse, Reddish "outshone the entire field," in spite of breaking a pole at the start of his second run, and Barney McLean was second.

Gretchen Fraser fore-ran the ladies' downhill course, "and with her elegant and most efficient way of negotiating a lay-out of the gates, provided a great welcome for all her fans on the sidelines." Jannette Burr, the "unheralded co-ed" from the University of Washington, won the downhill in an "astounding time," beating the record from the prior year's winner, France's Georgette Thiollière. Grace Carter Lindley "long retired and mother of one, made a most remarkable comeback in placing second." Anne Winn of Gannett, Idaho, won the women's slalom.

Two Salt Lake skiers, Jack Reddish and Suzie Harris (skiing for the Sun Valley Ski Club), won the combined titles and the Harriman Cup trophies, becoming the 1948 national downhill and slalom champions. Grace Carter Lindley was second and Jannette Burr third in the combined.

SPRING AND SUMMER

Skiing at Boulder Basin was promoted in 1948, where seven feet of snow ensured the season would last well into summer. Guests could leave Sun Valley after breakfast, ski and lunch at Boulder, and be back in time for tennis or golf. "At Boulder, the skier may drive right up to the area and literally step out onto a ski run. . . . Boulder Basin provides the sportsman with some of the grandest scenic beauty in all the West," the *Valley Sun* wrote. Over the Fourth of July, the Firecracker Slalom Derby was held in Boulder Basin. The second Sun Valley handicap shooting competition in July was won for a second time by Maynard B. Henry of Los Angeles, who won the coveted George F. Ashby Trophy for having the highest score over the 800-target route.

President Harry Truman visited Sun Valley in July 1948, bringing his wife, Bess, daughter Margaret, and an entourage of officials. The Trumans stayed at Harriman Cottage. The president went fly fishing in the lake, shot skeet, saw the resort's hunting dogs go through their paces, and inspected the stables. Sun Valley publicists wanted Truman to ride the Baldy lift, but his Secret Service detail vetoed the idea. He rode the Dollar chair instead, and photographers laid on their backs so one could not tell if he was on Dollar or Baldy. Margaret rode the Baldy lift to the top of the mountain, expressing delight.

General George Marshall, secretary of state and architect of the Marshall Plan to rebuild Europe after World War II, came with the president. His picture was taken on the baseball diamond batting at home plate with Pat Rogers behind him in a catcher's outfit.

The Baltimore Colts professional football team trained at Sun Valley for a month in summer 1948, following the lead of the Brooklyn Dodgers baseball team the prior summer. They worked out daily at the rodeo grounds. The Colts played an inter-squad game, led by quarterback Y.A. Tittle, offering a chance to see some of the top players in the league. The game was part of a gala Sunday affair that included rides up Bald Mountain on the ski lift in the morning, an ice carnival in the evening, and a parade featuring the Idaho Falls High School Band.

Dorice Taylor said 1948 "was one of Sun Valley's most exuberant times. Among the guests were Hollywood celebrities, business tycoons, glamour girls, and playboy millionaires." Jane Russell came in the fall and was photographed skiing on Galena Summit with ski instructor Toni Matt and shooting pheasants with Ernest Hemingway, although she had never tried either sport before. "The Henry Fords, the Gary Coopers, the Darryl Zanucks, and the Henry Hathaways joined forces to give the New Year's Eve party at Trail Creek Cabin," attended by Hemingway, Ingrid Bergman, Claudette Colbert, Celeste Holm, and Merle Oberon. Bergman was the center of attention, in spite of wearing no lipstick and having a simple hairdo, enthralling Hemingway and Cooper, with the other glamorous women pretending not to notice.

Taylor said, "Two of the worst movies ever flashed on the screen" were filmed at the resort that year—*Duchess of Idaho* with Esther Williams and Van Johnson, and *That Wonderful Urge*, starring Gene Tierney and Tyrone Power, with Otto Lang filming the ski scenes. The movies showed Sun Valley in all its glory, pleasing management, and a number of employees were in them in crowd scenes, but they "sagged sadly in the hodgepodge plot."

Sun Valley "broke its own record again this season," reported the *American Ski Annual* for 1949. "The resort hosted 2,000 more skiers than in any previous year. More celebrities flocked to the lodge, the resort could have sold out four times because of the demand in reservations, skiing never was better as the season wore on, and the Ski Club produced the first champion in the history of Olympic ski competition, Gretchen Fraser."[69]

25

1949

Upgrades Are Made to the Ski School, Mountain, and Village; French Ski Team Races in Sun Valley

Major changes were made at Sun Valley for 1949, described in the *American Ski Annual* for 1949. The original Dollar Mountain chairlift was replaced after having served for 10 years and logging nearly three million skier trips, "an achievement equal to that of transporting the entire population of the city of Philadelphia from the valley floor to the top of the mountain." The lift "performed heroically under the heaviest of loads and was never out of commission for more than ten or fifteen minutes at a time." Losing the old Dollar lift created a touch of sadness. It was the first chairlift in the world and had helped "more people learn to ski well than any other mechanical device ever built."

The new lift was 2,470 feet long, rising 628 feet and carrying 340 skiers per hour, compared with 300 before. The head tower of the new lift was in the same position as the old one, but the tower line followed the ridge line rather than going down the bowl, ending at a point 250 feet above the Dollar cabin, opening up a "fine skiing area." The lower tower was 600 feet west of the old one, eliminating the long hike from the bus turnaround to the loading point. It provided beginners with a lift of their own and relieved much of the traffic from the old lift, which had its halfway station removed. The new lift served a gentle and timber-free area, longer than the practice slope previously used, giving Dollar "three perfect runs for early-stage and intermediate skiers."

On Baldy, a new run was cut by Nelson Bennett's trail crew, branching off Ridge, 70 yards above Rock Garden, dropping down to meet the cat track from College to the

Roundhouse. Bennett's crew removed trees along the ridge north of Christmas Bowl to allow skiing from Ridge to the Bowl and reaching the Roundhouse by way of a cat track. Exhibition was widened to three times its original size, averaging 150 feet across. Olympic was opened up, making it faster and safer.

Learn to Ski Weeks, begun in 1940, were set for January 2, January 9, January 16, and January 23, 1949. For $75, skiers got accommodations in chalets, meals in the Skier's Café, six days of ski lessons, and use of all lifts and ice-skating facilities. Challenger Inn rooms with shared showers cost $96 a week for a single and $90 per person for a double. The Sun Valley Ski Club started Guest Slalom Races on Dollar Mountain on easy, wide open courses.

Otto Lang said the ski school functioned well under Toni Matt, his head instructor in 1948. However, Matt became involved in an affair with a married woman that became public, and a scandal resulted. Matt left, and Lang appointed John Litchfield head instructor. Litchfield was a Dartmouth teammate of Dick Durrance, the national collegiate jumping champion in 1936 and 1937, and the top jumping qualifier for the 1940 U.S. Olympic team. Litchfield taught in Sun Valley before the war, was in the 10th Mountain Division, and taught at Aspen with Friedl Pfeifer after the war.

In his autobiography, Lang said it was time to revitalize the ski school to renew its former preeminence and glamour, and it needed "a celebrity with the charisma of a superior ski racer who could also teach." With the approval of Kathleen Harriman ("who was her father's alter ego concerning Sun Valley since he was immersed in the political problems of the Democrats"), Lang hired Émile Allais, a French ski star he met at the 1948 Olympics. Allais used the "French technique," a major departure from the Arlberg technique that had been the mainstay of the Sun Valley Ski School. Hannes Schneider, godfather of the Arlberg technique, encouraged Lang to hire Allais, since "only time will tell which of the techniques deserved to last." Allais brought "the two feuding factions together under one roof," and the ski school taught a modified Alberg technique in 1949. Allais taught the "ruade," which Lang said was "a christiania with the skis held parallel, and in order to initiate the change of direction, one lifted the tailends of both skis off the snow and started the turn in midair to head the skis in the opposite direction." Lang participated in Allais's seminars but was not overly impressed. "I found it to be a physically taxing maneuver, but very useful under certain conditions, such as a crusted or deeply rutted snow surface. The sight of a bunch of skiers doing the ruade reminded me of a flock of bunny rabbits hopping around and frolicking in the snow."

Allais taught racing, and top-class skiers were "right down his alley since he has been twice world's champion in Downhill and Slalom." Sigi Engl was supervisor on Dollar Mountain. In spite of the differences in skiing philosophy, Allais worked out well and was a popular ski instructor. He left Sun Valley after 1949 to direct the ski school at Squaw Valley, California, where Warren Miller worked for him in 1950. Allais left Squaw Valley after two years over "artistic differences" with the owner, and returned to France, where he had a successful career. When Lang saw Allais years later, he asked, "what about the ruade?" Allais replied, "extinct as the dodo bird."[70]

Sun Valley opened its winter season on December 18, 1948, "ready for the yearly influx of Hollywood's 'names' and ski enthusiasts from all over the Western Hemisphere," according to *The Valley Sun*. The resort was booked through the Christmas holidays, most of January, all of February, and the first two weeks of March. To the regret of college racers all over the country, no intercollegiate ski meet was held over the Christmas holidays as had been the tradition since the resort opened. A jumping exhibition was held on Ruud Mountain in late December.

Otto Lang's ski school had a staff of 27 experienced instructors and three supervisors, including crack personnel such as Yves Latreille, who won the U.S. downhill championship, and Leon Goodman, who was a member of the American FIS downhill and slalom squads. The ski school averaged 200 pupils a day for the four-month season.

The proposed budget for Sun Valley from January 12, 1949, shows Union Pacific was planning to make significant investments. The company planned to enlarge the hospital in the lodge's northwest wing, but Pat Rogers needed to provide additional information to determine a budget.

New dormitory for men employees	$77,000
New dormitory for women employees	$77,000
Convert Barracks to Employee dormitories	$103,000
Convert Administration building into dormitory for married couples	$22,000
New commissary and administration building	$217,000
Addition to employee's cafeteria—kitchen	$11,000
Addition to employee's cafeteria—recreation room	$24,000
Addition and alteration to garage	$19,000
Install employee laundry in basement of Lodge	$5,900
TOTAL	$555,900

In January 1949, Union Pacific budgeted $22,000 to purchase 260 acres of land from Eleanor K. Grimm, to "enlarge and enhance skiing terrain and to complete acquisition of lands beneficial to the Sun Valley operations." The Grimm property was next to the Dollar Mountain ski lift. In 1936, Union Pacific had to obtain an easement from the Grimms for the Dollar chairlift to go over their land.

On January 3, 1949, the U.S. Forest Service notified Union Pacific that fees for the special use permits for Sun Valley had been adjusted. The fees had increased, as they were based on a percentage of the gross revenue from their use. Sun Valley did not keep a separate record of revenue from individual ski lifts and provided a single figure for all the ski lifts, principally Dollar and Baldy. The Forest Service allocated the income equally between the two mountains. Sun Valley's ski lift revenue for 1948 was $129,800, of which $64,900 was allocated to Bald Mountain. The total length of the Bald Mountain lifts was 14,600 feet, of which 7,300 feet were on Forest Service land, so revenue of $32,450 was apportioned to that use of Forest Service land. This led to a fee of $636.

Proctor Mountain lift and cabin had "not been in use for some time," so the permit fee continued at $15 a year. The fees for Pioneer Creek and Owl Creek Cabins were reduced from $25 to $5 per year. There was no reason to continue the permit for the Warm Springs ski run since that run had the same status as dozens of other runs on Bald Mountain used in connection with Sun Valley's operation, for which no permits were necessary.[71]

Nelson and Edward Bennett Develop a New Toboggan

Beginning in 1946, Nelson Bennett and his brother Edward, working with the Sun Valley Ski Patrol and engineering department, designed a new ski patrol rescue toboggan that is used all over the country today. Previously, the ski patrol used a regular toboggan with pads and a rope in the front and back.

In his oral history, Nelson Bennett described problems they had with the old-style toboggans and mistakes they faced developing the new one. He realized they needed a new toboggan when he rescued a girl with a sprained ankle in one of Sun Valley's bowls. He loaded her in the toboggan and started to take her down the hill, but they began to speed up. He was at the front end of the toboggan and it caught up with him, pushing him into a snow drift. The toboggan flipped upside down and he was knocked over. When he got the girl upright, she was a good sport about the event, saying her ankle was OK, but she had wet her pants.

The brothers initially used wooden shafts or handles for their toboggan. However, in a test run with a ski patrolman strapped in simulating a victim, one of the shafts broke when they were going down Christmas Ridge. The toboggan got loose and disappeared into the fog. Nelson chased it into the bowl, where it hit a mogul, went up in the air, flipped over, and stopped. The "victim" was yelling "get me out of here." If the toboggan had not stopped, it could have gone all the way down the bowl and killed the patrolman aboard. The Bennetts redesigned the shafts using thin wall conduit welded on, added fins to the bottom for directional stability so the toboggan would follow the patrolman, and added a rope on the back to use as a brake.

The test of the new model down Roundhouse Slope resulted in a well-known Sun Valley story. Nelson was in front and the toboggan was performing nicely going down Exhibition, so he decided to go faster. He turned around and yelled, "Let's go." The patrolman in back thought he said, "Let go," which he did. The toboggan pushed Nelson and the victim, who was strapped into the toboggan, and they started going faster and faster. Nelson decided, "When in doubt, schuss." They did not stop until reaching the bridge at River Run. Thereafter, they used hand signals to avoid confusion and added a chain under the toboggan as a brake. When the front patrolman wanted to increase speed, he pushed down on the handles to raise the rear of the toboggan, which released the pressure on the chain. They developed a flexible wooden toboggan, but most patrols now use a stiff fiberglass version, which Nelson does not believe works as well.

The rescue toboggan was put into use at Sun Valley in winter 1949, which Nelson described in an article for the *Sun Valley Ski Club Annual* for 1949. "It was safe, light and easily maneuverable. The toboggan had three removable components (the rescue litter basket, a tail rope and chain, and the transport handle and rails) that allowed them to be transported on a single chairlift by one ski patroller. When the toboggan reached a lift or the bottom of the mountain, its detachable shafts could be removed and the unit used as a stretcher, eliminating the need to move the injured skier from when he was picked up until he reached the hospital. Two patrolmen covered all accidents, one in front and one in back. The second one skied behind the toboggan using a rope to maneuver and brake, which could be looped under the unit and used as a rough-lock. Two fins on the bottom give control to the toboggan. Each toboggan has a two-inch foam pad that insulates and cushions the patient, a tarpaulin and two wool blankets, and a first-aid kit, which all together only weighed 70 pounds.

The Bennetts decided not to patent the device so it could be cheaply replicated for use by other ski patrols. They gave the design to the National Ski Patrol in 1950. The features of their toboggan are still used in virtually every rescue toboggan around the world.[72]

Ski Tournaments

Sun Valley's retreat from its premier position as the center of ski racing began in 1949, although the Harriman Cup continued to attract the world's best skiers.

First, the traditional intercollegiate tournament over the Christmas holiday was not held. This tournament had marked the beginning of the ski season since 1937. It had given the best college racers the opportunity to experience a fashionable ski resort that was beyond their financial means, train under Sun Valley's racing instructors, and race against colleagues from all over the country. This was a great loss for college ski racing. Second, the interstate ski tournament, which pitted the best racers from Eastern and Western states against each other, was held for the last time. The tournament, also dating from 1937, was another important training ground for racers. Sun Valley subsidized both events, and Union Pacific's interest in economizing after the war played into these decisions.

Sun Valley held a jumping exhibition on Ruud Mountain during the Christmas holidays, which included Gustav Raaum, who attended the University of Washington. A classic picture was taken of Raaum going off the jump on Ruud Mountain with Olav Ulland from Seattle, Alf Engen from Sun Valley, and Kjell Stordlallen, a teammate at the University of Washington. Raaum told the author they had a couple of close calls during practice, but the takeoff structure was wide, so the four of them had no problem going off side by side. The picture is displayed at the Nordic Museum in Seattle and in the basement of the Nordic Center in Sun Valley.

On January 21, the eighth annual Western Interstate Ski Meet for the President's Cup and Rogers Trophy attracted six teams, with many of the finest all-round skiers in the West. The tournament included a new type of competition, involving cross-country, giant slalom and jumping for men, and a giant slalom for women.

Nelson Bennett's cross-country course taxed the competitors, especially the alpine specialists who were not used to the rigorous training necessary for the event. The event was won by Don Johnson of Idaho. Otto Lang's giant slalom course on Bald Mountain was a 45-gate maze that started at the top of the Roundhouse slope and went down to the bottom of Exhibition, a vertical drop of 1,200 feet. Jack Reddish of Utah, the 1948 national downhill and slalom champion, "rode every inch of the route with amazing speed and in perfect control" to beat his teammate Dick Movitz by four seconds, according to the *Sun Valley Ski Club Annual* for 1949. Washington's Karl Stingle was third. Utah's Suzie Harris won the women's giant slalom. Colorado jumpers Perry-Smith, Wren, Griffith, and Jones took four of the first five places on Ruud Mountain. The President's Cup went to Colorado, this time for good, since the state won it three years in a row. The men's individual combined competition ended in a tie between Corey Engen and Gordon Wren, with Perry-Smith a close third. Sun Valley announced it would suspend the tournament the following year based on difficulties in arranging a balanced schedule and housing the competitors.

The big race of the year was the Harriman Cup, where "all eyes were on the visiting French with their inimitable dash and style," reported the *Annual*. The Harriman Cup was like "a return visit to the Winter Olympics: International rivalry, spine tingling tension, and the greatest field of runners ever to visit Sun Valley stormed down Baldy Mountain and swung through the flags on Dollar." The French team was the "most hard-bitten and thoroughly-trained opposition the American skiers ever had faced at home" . . . representing "a higher uniform standard of competition than we have heretofore seen on this side of the water."

John Litchfield set a different downhill to better challenge the racers, moving it back to the River Run side of the mountain, to the Olympic course. Litchfield's course was 2.3 miles long, with 3,000 feet of vertical drop, and was "one of the toughest and most exacting on this continent . . . a real test by any standard," according to the *Annual*. The Warm Springs course was suitable in its time, but the Olympics changed things. "Sun Valley's answer was the Olympic course," going down Ridge, Rock Garden (where Litchfield placed control gates), into Roundhouse Slope, and a schuss onto Olympic.

Racers were sent onto the "Meadows," a bumpy, open slope that took them to the steilhang, an "ugly-looking pitch, longer and steeper than its counterpart on Warm Springs," through gullies into the bottom funnel of Olympic, where

> *the Ski Patrol had engineered a fantastic series of bumps, designed to throw the least unbalanced runner on his ear. It was impossible to recover between them; you simply had to ride them out. . . . The finish, after a long right turn, was a short distance down River Run.*

Henri Oreiller, "a natural clown," in the words of the *Annual*, set the standard for spectacular running. "He was fast and sure, and he was willing to shave the corners . . . and he races with a nonchalance that is unnerving to our more serious Americans." Oreiller was challenged by Toni Matt, skiing for the Whitefish Lake Ski Club, who used "more technique than most racers. He never gives an impression of speed; and, during the Downhill, his turns were so flawless that they looked almost like the 'school figures' he might teach on a slope." However, he finished second. France's George Panisset tied for third with Ketchum's Jim Griffith. Dave Faires was the top Washington finisher, at 19th. Spectators watched the race at the Roundhouse for its view of Rock Garden. The largest crowd of 500 watched from the junction of Olympic and River Run, 150 yards above the finish line, giving a good view of the out-run from Olympic where the course was "diabolically entrapped with bumps," providing plenty of wild action.

The women's downhill started at the top of Rock Garden, where the sun melted the ice before the race started. France's Lucienne Schmidt-Couttet was first, Paula Kann from the Eastern Slope Ski Club was second, and Jannette Burr of the Sun Valley Ski Club was third. Andrea Mead lost a pole and fell, but came in fourth.

Litchfield set two 39-gate slalom courses on Dollar. The women's was on the face to the left of the new lift and the men's in the bowl to the right. Oreiller won the slalom, coming "through the finish gate on one ski, an exaggerated skating step, and a broad grin on his face," according to the *Annual*. France's George Panisset was second, and Matt was third. Lucienne Schmidt-Couttet won the women's slalom, followed by Kathy Rodolph of the Sun Valley Ski Club. Andrea Mead finished fourth.

The Valley Sun reported that the French made a clean sweep of the races, with

> *a willingness to take chances, a complete disregard for technique, and an appallingly intimate knowledge of just how far and fast it was safe to go. They were interested in*

> *getting to the bottom in a hurry; how they looked was of no concern, and bore only a fleeting resemblance to the method of skiing taught in France, as opposed to Arlberg, Swiss, or other systems.*

One commentator asked, why didn't Americans do better against the French? "Their equipment was more modern—skis which are streamlined beyond the classic Telemark design, with plastic soles, wax-impregnated. A good many of our runners seem to have forgotten the fine points of waxing," the *American Ski Annual* lamented. The French were not cowed by technique and weren't concerned with how they looked, teaching the Americans that they should be less stylish and more willing to violate the rules. Except in an Olympic year, it was difficult to get Americans together as a team. The French subsidized their team, enabling them to keep their best racers together as a group. Also, this country was short of young racers at the time and the French had a better attitude toward training.

OTHER SUN VALLEY EVENTS

On September 14, 1949, Steve Hannagan wrote Arthur E. Stoddard, who became U.P.'s president in March, about "the Sun Valley situation," after visiting the resort. Hannagan sent Stoddard his two previous reports so he could see his thinking when Sun Valley was created and reopened in 1946, to better understand his present thinking. Presumably he was referring to his belief that "if we are not prepared to subsidize the endeavor, as an advertising, good will and business projecting endeavor, to the extent of $350,000 to $500,000 annually, it should be abandoned." Hannagan said, "as a result, you may want to shift some of the policies, and advise me and others in that regard." He had already discussed his opinion about Union Pacific's decision to not actively participate in a 1950 publicity campaign, the start of Stoddard's cutbacks.

Sun Valley was "in fine shape," Hannagan said, and Pat Rogers did not talk about retiring. "His current gripe with life is the amount of entertaining of guests that he feels he must do," when 90 percent "is not only unnecessary, but unwarranted." It was the same group of "celebs" that come for entertainment, and the problem could be simplified if Rogers sent them flowers or fruit or a personal phone call. "I think Pat has the feeling that when Union Pacific makes a special request for special attention to be paid to a guest, all stops must be pulled on the entertainment panel." He believed, Hannagan felt, that U.P. wanted those special guests to get "all courtesies and attention, but not to be carried around on an expensive entertainment platter."

Sun Valley was overstaffed. Rogers was "easy prey" to anyone who wanted to stay there. "On the whole, he does a masterful job, though, and I don't see anyone around who could do as well even if he were to retire." He understood the Western outdoors, both winter and summer, and was well liked and respected by guests and personnel. The ski school "wags the dog," and, while important, "it should be the Sun Valley Ski School, instead of being built around a personality." Sun Valley's food was "undistinguished." Service was generally good, but "we could do better." The rodeo grounds could be used in the winter for kid's activities and a sled dog race course. There would never be an appreciable "between-season," but it was less expensive to stay open than to close and reopen.

The next ski season looked positive. Resort operators hoped the upcoming FIS world championships at Aspen and Lake Placid would bring a better winter than the prior year, when snow was short. A large contingent of Europeans was expected. Railroads were improving their rolling stock for 1950, and there would be "many new coaches and sleeping cars in service for the winter resort trade," according to the *New York Times*. Sun Valley could be reached by one-night-out service from Chicago via the Union Pacific's City of Portland to Shoshone. New York–Sun Valley fares would be $137.31 by coach and $248.49 by lower berth. Round trip tickets were extended from three to six months.

The Sun Valley Ski Club's president's message for 1949 said the club helped bring the French ski team to the resort

> *and the reports they have given on their return to France have been most glowing about competition and life at Sun Valley. Sun Valley continues to be known as one of the most internationally minded ski clubs in the States. Next year we will have the opportunity to be host to many of the foreign teams who will be coming over for the World Championships at Aspen and Lake Placid. They all want to come to Sun Valley for the Harriman Cup and again we will give them top racing and a very pleasant time.*

Bob Blakslee's "Sun Valley Review" said the winter of 1948–1949 would go down in Sun Valley's history as the season of "big crowds, of big snows, and of big races."[73]

26

COUNTER-CULTURE AT SUN VALLEY

Warren Miller's Life as a Ski Bum, 1946–1949

Filmmaker, author, and storyteller Warren Miller has been closely associated with Sun Valley since the end of World War II, through his ski movies and his life as a ski bum at the resort, living in an unheated trailer, supporting himself through innovative means.

Miller died in January 2018 at age 93, leaving a lasting legacy to the skiing world. Through his 500 films, he became the voice of skiing for several generations. He said, "I don't think I've worked a day in my life," but that must be viewed in light of his schedule. He spent 30 years on the road, traveling up to 175 days a year, showing his films all over the country, doing back-to-back shows in different cities in the winter, battling impossible travel conditions and struggling to get from one show to the next. His films embodied his philosophy of life: "I won't ruin a good story with the absolute truth." According to his obituary in the *Seattle Times*, he asked people to ski their favorite ski run when they heard of his death. His was Christmas Ridge at Sun Valley.

After serving in the Navy during World War II, Miller decided to go on a life-long adventure in search of freedom, which turned into a 30-year nonstop motion picture filming and producing trip around the world. Miller described his experiences as a ski bum in Sun Valley in *Wine, Women, Warren and Skis; Are My Skis on Straight?*; *Lurching from One Near Disaster to the Next* and his brutally honest 2016 autobiography, *Freedom Found, My Life Story*.

After leaving the Navy, Miller spent a month learning to ski at Badger Pass in Yosemite in winter 1946. He rented a bed from a lift operator for $1 a night and figured out how to avoid paying for rope tow tickets that cost $2.50 a day, using methods he refused to discuss. During lunch hours, Miller drew cartoons of skiers that he sold for $1. The ski area was managed by Charles N. Proctor, who helped Averell Harriman lay out Sun Valley. Proctor hired Austrian ski instructors, including Sigi Engl, who soon left Badger Pass to teach at Sun Valley, and Hannes Schroll, who beat Dick Durrance in 1935 on Mount Rainier at the National Downhill and Slalom Championships. Miller met Bill Janss, a college racer at Stanford and member of the 1940 FIS team, at Badger Pass. Janss taught Miller how to ski using the Austrian Arlberg technique, and his company bought Sun Valley from Union Pacific in 1964.

In fall 1946, Miller bought two pairs of Army surplus white 10th Mountain Division skis, seven feet, six inches long, scraped off the paint, varnished them, and sold one pair for $25. He spent $20 on Army surplus poles, ski boots, a parka, goggles, hat, sweater, gloves, and a pair of pants. He bought his first motion picture camera, a Bell & Howell Sportster, for $77, using his $100 Navy mustering-out pay, and four Army surplus down-filled mummy sleeping bags (two apiece for him and fellow adventurer Ward Baker). For $200, Miller bought what would be his home, an unheated trailer eight feet long, four feet wide, and five feet high, with a double bed in it, which could be hauled by his 1937 Buick. It had a "homebuilt, aerodynamic, 'teardrop' design," with a flip-up back door giving the built-in kitchen a roof, making it possible to cook outdoors and have tailgate parties. "It was possible to live and ski out of this rig," although no one warned him how cold it would be sleeping in an unheated trailer in the parking lot of a ski resort.

Miller and Ward Baker spent the early part of the winter of 1946–1947 skiing in Colorado and Utah, living in the trailer, selling copies of Miller's first cartoon book, *Are My Skis on Straight?*, for $2 and eating game they shot. At Alta, they met two girls just back from Sun Valley who told them about hot water swimming pools, the ski runs, nice restaurants, après-ski dancing, and free buses. "After the cold, cold skiing at Alta, just thinking about soaking ourselves in the hot water of the Sun Valley swimming pool made up our minds," Miller said. They headed to Ketchum and ended up living in the trailer in a parking lot where the Sun Valley garage is now, with the approval of Pat Rogers, Sun Valley's manager, who felt they offered "local color."

Miller's 1957 book, *Wine, Women, Warren, & Skis*, describes his first year in Sun Valley. It is dedicated to the inventor of the oyster cracker, since "without her foresight in offering vitamin-enriched oyster crackers to the Union Pacific Railroad for their Sun Valley, Idaho, operation, I might never have survived the cold winter of 1946/1947." Their stay lasted from November 13 to April 16, 154 days, and cost $268.

It was so cold in their trailer their breath would freeze and fall as snow. In the mornings, they struggled out of their sleeping bags and fought their way into their frozen clothing, which was "like playing a trombone in a deep freeze." Miller's boots froze so solid one night the tongue broke off. He and Baker went to the skiers chalet in the mornings to thaw their boots and get milk for their oatmeal. They sneaked on lifts without paying, hunted rabbits and ducks near Shoshone for food, and ate oyster crackers smothered in ketchup for lunch. Forty-eight tea bags cost 50¢, which they brewed with free hot water at the Roundhouse, using each tea bag 11 times. They shaved, washed, and cleaned the game they shot in the bathrooms at the skiers' chalet. Guests thought they were employees and employees thought they were guests, allowing them to get employee discounts with guest privileges. Life couldn't get any better.

> *In the Sun Valley parking lot, I liked the smell of rabbit frying above the totally silent evening. At the same time, I could look up and see the constellation of Orion high in the black canopy of winter nights. No one ever had it as good as I did then, except Ward Baker, who was cooking the rabbit at the time.*

Miller did all of this "to glide effortlessly down steep mountains, carving graceful arcs of ecstasy in the deep powder snow." He got his first national publicity when *Look* did an article on Sun Valley in winter 1947, which included a picture of the two men outside their trailer, "strangely because our trailer life was the exact opposite of the Sun Valley image, the Steve Hannagan world," he said. Miller skied every day, learned to race, and returned to Sun Valley the next three years. He sold his book, sold cartoons of skiers, and decorated the casts of hospital patients. "My financial endeavors proved to be a success in Idaho," he said.

In winter 1948, Miller returned to Sun Valley with a new car, a 1946 Ford, and a new teardrop Kit Kamper trailer on loan from a distributor who Miller had convinced that the picture in *Look* would lead to publicity for his version. He had made $1,000 selling 1,000 copies of his book, *Are My Skis on Straight?*, and showing a ski movie to a group in Malibu, where he received $8.35.

Miller had more success that year, earning a living while skiing every day and entering ski races with Baker as the Sun Valley Parking Lot Team. Miller convinced Pappy Rogers to hire him to paint murals on the employees' cafeteria at the Challenger Inn in exchange for a season pass worth $250 and three meals a day for as long as it took him to finish. Not surprisingly, it took him all season. He took cafeteria food back for Baker to supplement the rabbits. Pete Lane traded ski equipment for a mural for his store, and the owner of a ski shop in Ketchum sold a dozen copies of his cartoon book and paid Warren $200 to paint murals on the walls of his shop. At one ski race at Donner Summit, Miller and Baker were hired to pack the hill, making two round trips down the course for three days in a row, each earning $120.

The shah of Iran was one of the high-profile visitors to Sun Valley after World War II. Warren Miller, Nelson Bennett, Dorice Taylor, and Wendolyn Holland described the shah's visits to the resort. They tell somewhat different stories, but they show how Sun Valley accommodated well-known guests in those years. Miller said the shah loved Hollywood films and believed *Sun Valley Serenade* was the best movie of all time. The shah knew Otto Lang, head of Sun Valley's ski school, had directed the ski scenes, inspiring the shah to ski there.

Nelson Bennett said the shah's first visit was initiated by the U.S. State Department, which Holland said was in December 1947, before the resort reopened after the war. Arthur Stoddard, president of Union Pacific, and Pat Rogers wanted to accommodate the State Department and realized how valuable the publicity would be.

Sun Valley typically does not have enough snow in early December to ski. Bennett was sent to check on the snow in Boulder Basin, north of Sun Valley, where there was an abandoned mining community with cabins still standing. He found there was sufficient snow to ski in the surrounding couloirs. Bennett and a crew fixed up one of the cabins, hauling in supplies on a Tucker SnoCat including a wine-colored carpet and a wood burning stove, creating a luxurious and comfortable site. Two new outhouses were built behind the cabin. The shah was accompanied by Otto Lang and "Sun Valley Dicks." Bennett took the shah up the hills in a SnoCat, and said he spoke good English and was a good skier. Hot food was brought from Sun Valley in big Thermos containers. The shah had such a good time that on his next trip he brought an entourage of around 50.

The shah's next trip to Sun Valley was in December 1949. He was "a man of absolutely outstanding energy" and engaged in most that Sun Valley had to offer, according to Dorice Taylor. He shot skeet at the Gun Club, went skating and

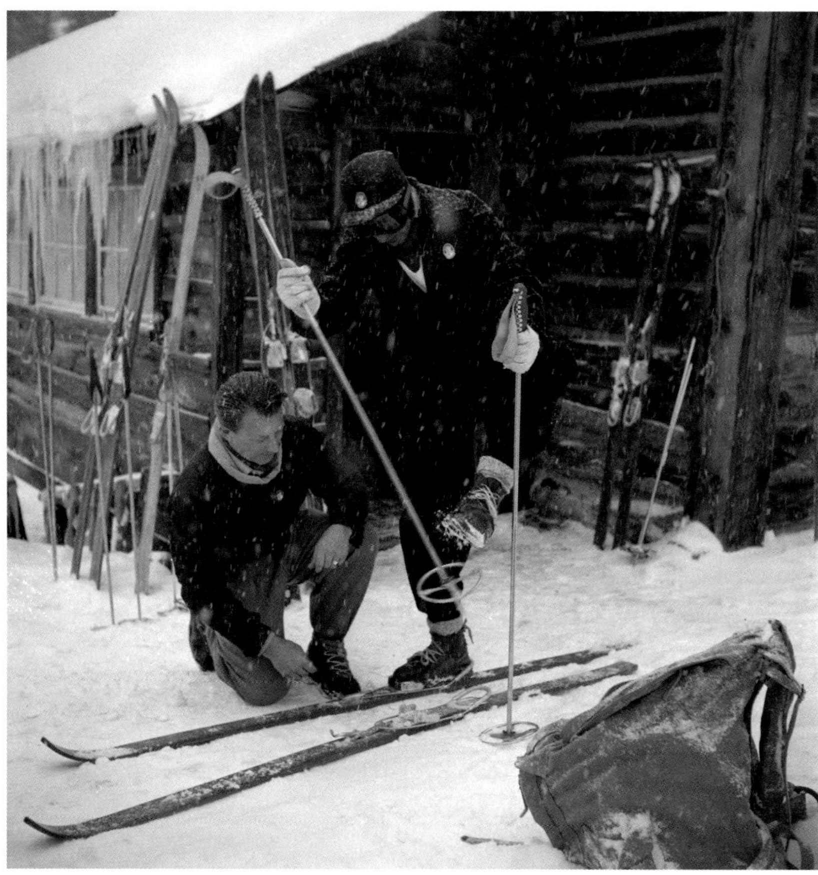

Shah of Iran at Boulder Basin being helped by Otto Lang.

swimming, went bowling (where the pro was ordered to let him win), shot pool, and enjoyed the ambiance of the resort.

In *Lurching from One Near Disaster to the Next*, Warren Miller says the shah was in Sun Valley with 16 bodyguards, but none could ski. The head of the ski patrol asked for volunteers who could handle a .45 caliber pistol to help with security, and four ski patrolmen with service in the 10th Mountain Division were selected. They took target practice out at Warm Springs and showed up to protect the shah the next day. After several days of skiing, with two patrolmen in front and two in back and Sigi Engl skiing with the shah, the guards began to relax. The next day, the shah had lunch at the Roundhouse and the patrolmen hung their weapons on the clothes rack, covered by their ski patrol parkas. Miller and a friend went to the clothes rack, switched their parkas for ski patrol parkas, and each took a pistol. After skiing to the bottom, they left the guns and parkas on a fence. Not knowing his firepower had been cut in half, the shah skied the rest of the afternoon. At the end of the day, "one of the ski-patrol-guards-without-guns skied over and was very embarrassed when he was handed the two guns and parka we had 'borrowed' at lunch," Miller said. The shah never learned of the incident. Beatrice Haemmerle, wife of ski instructor Florian Haemmerle, said that one of the ski instructors with a gun fell, and his gun went off.

The shah held a nighttime party at the Roundhouse on a beautiful evening lit by a full moon, arranged by Pat Rogers, where champagne flowed. Rogers gave strict orders that only one person could ride in each one-person chair at a time. Victor Gottschalk, a ski instructor, let his girlfriend load for the ride down, then he jumped on her chair, fell off, and ran back yelling, although he was unhurt. It was so entertaining the guests wanted him to do it again.

After the party, where much caviar and champagne was consumed, the shah wanted to ski down rather than ride the lift. Sigi Engl arranged for ski patrol members to hold lighted torches for him on one side of Canyon, but the shah skied down the other side. The run was so enjoyable, the shah said, "Now . . . we'll do it again," according to Taylor. The ski patrol followed the shah down the mountain a second time, with a toboggan in case of an emergency, which was used to retrieve a ski patrolman out of a snowbank, according to Bennett. Miller said when several of the non-skiing members of the party rode the lift to the bottom, one partygoer threw a bottle of champagne to another in the chair behind him, and the person trying to catch the bottle fell out of the chair. He was stuck in the snow and had to be dug out by the ski patrol.

Miller contrasted the shah's Sun Valley ski vacations with one taken by President Clinton's family in 1998 at Deer Valley, Utah, that cost taxpayers $3.7 million.

> *I couldn't help but wonder what today's ever-present media would have had to say if a drunk had fallen off a chairlift or a prank with guns had been played during the Clintons' learn-to-ski vacation. Somehow, I think that our journalists would have raised these incidents to the level of a national crisis, and Janet Reno would have ordered a multi-million dollar investigation.*

"Because of the genius of Steve Hannagan," Miller said, "Sun Valley pulled Americans into the age of high-mountain, luxury resort living," attracting "everyone from ski bums such as ourselves to the top end of the celebrity chain." Miller had lunch at the Roundhouse most days, eating "tomato soup" made from free hot water, ketchup, and oyster crackers, sharing the facility with "people such as the Shah, Otto Lang, Gary Cooper, Cooper's wife Rocky, and Ernest Hemingway—a celebrity network only Sun Valley could knit together." At the end of a typical lunch, Hemingway had gone through a bottle of wine and rode the lift down, while the shah and his group rode to the top of the mountain to ski. Miller and Baker tagged along behind the group on the mountain, "where everyone was equal," and talked to celebrities on equal terms. Gary Cooper was always friendly, eager to talk about waxing, and invited Miller to visit him when he was in Hollywood.

Dorice Taylor said the shah returned to Sun Valley in 1955 with his second wife. Sigi Engl, head of the ski school, was supposed to teach the shah how to ski but the shah would have none of it. Engl skied in front at a speed he thought the shah could handle, but the shah would ski past him. One time Dorice was skiing on Ridge when she saw the shah go by in "his wide, sturdy snowplow," with no sign of Engl. She looked at the Warming Hut and saw Engl struggling to put on his skis, trying to catch the shah. Engl told the shah he was concerned he was skiing beyond his ability and might get hurt. The shah replied he "would be a hero in his country if he was hurt skiing." Engl thought, "and I'll be a bum in mine if you're hurt."

The life led by Miller and Baker was in contrast to that of the celebrities who stayed at Sun Valley. The men shot ducks and rabbits near Shoshone, cooking them outdoors in the back of their trailer. "Productive Shoshone hunting trips lasted us two weeks, at a rabbit a day on the Coleman stove," Miller said. "We had rabbits fixed every way possible on the outdoor stove: fried, stewed, boiled, and singed close to burnt."

One time they were planning a rabbit roast party at their trailer. They took 20 newly killed rabbits to the skiers' chalet late at night to clean them in the bathrooms, figuring everyone would be in bed. They were skinning the rabbits when a drunk guest came in, saw the blood all over, and ran to bring the house detectives, thinking a murder had taken place. The men quickly cleaned up the mess and left, leaving the "crime scene" relatively free of evidence, so the detectives thought the drunk guest was lying. In spite of their financial state, life at the resort had many attractions.

> *The attractions of Sun Valley did not end with good skiing, but included a large population of good-looking girls and guys, either guests or employees, and especially the*

confident young ladies in the lift line who came from all over America. I managed to meet lots of ladies.

One evening, Miller watched East Coast ski filmmaker John Jay narrate his fourth-annual ski lecture film at the lodge, and thought, "Hey, I can do that." At the end of that season, "it was hard to leave Sun Valley, a place that had begun to feel like home."

When Miller returned to Sun Valley for his third season in winter 1948–1949, he rented a 15-by-30-foot garage with a dirt floor in Ketchum for $5 a month, which he turned into a paying proposition.

The garage was so cold that the pot of water on the oil stove never melted all winter. I rented floor space to Edward Scott for his sleeping bag for fifty cents a night. Scotty was a real pioneer: he invented lightweight ski poles by making smaller baskets and finding a source for lightweight tapered aluminum shafts. I even had another renter part-time, Bob Brandt, who married actress Janet Leigh; he also paid me fifty cents a night, so I was parlaying my five dollars a month rent into more than thirty dollars a month. The additional income helped me buy my first 16mm rolls of film, to jump-start my own motion picture career.

Nelson Bennett convinced Miller to apply to teach skiing for the Sun Valley Ski School. Miller bought new equipment from Pete Lane on credit. He didn't think he stood a chance of getting hired. It was only his fourth year of skiing, no one had ever taught him to teach skiing, and he had to convince the famous Sun Valley instructors that he was qualified using the techniques he was taught by Bill Janss at Yosemite.

They were all there: The Gods of Ski Instruction, the leaders of the Sun Valley Ski School, men you read about and watched from afar: Ski School Director Otto Lang, Assistant Director Johnny Litchfield, and Supervisors Sigi Engl and Sepp Froehlich. I really wanted the job. Sun Valley treated its instructors well. Becoming an instructor meant being given a warm room in the instructors' chalet, three square meals a day at the Challenger Inn Dining Room, and a monthly check for $125, plus a percentage of all the private lessons.

Life was instantly better when Otto Lang came over to me at the end of day three, saying "OK, Warren, you can teach beginners, but you have to take a shower and get a

> *haircut before you do." I was on the gravy train! Free food and $125 a month in pay! It would be easy to live on that paycheck. And I was really lucky to have Franz Klamer as my roommate.*

Miller taught group ski lessons on Dollar Mountain to beginners and "never-evers" as one of 34 instructors. In addition to teaching, instructors were expected to be at the lodge and Challenger Inn for after-ski cocktails and show up in the bars after dinner, duties to which the young, single Warren Miller did not object.

He had a new plan to make money that year, fabricating boot laces out of nylon parachute shrouds that were far better than the factory supplied ones, calling them "The Ski Bootlace of the Future." His attempts to be a capitalist were filled with misadventures that only Warren Miller could experience. He showed his first ski movie at the Sun Valley Opera House, his first venture into the "money-making" portion of his life. Thirty-seven people bought tickets; the theater held 300. When he got his share at the casino later that night, Miller's 40 percent of the $37 proceeds was $14.80.

In winter 1949, Miller met two men in Sun Valley who changed his life, Chuck Percy and Hal Geneen, president and comptroller of Bell & Howell. After the three bonded over skiing and discussing Miller's attempts to make ski movies, they agreed to provide him with a high-end Model 70 DA Bell & Howell that cost $256. He could repay them from his earnings. "After closing the door on Sun Valley, it was all over for that era of my life, and I never looked back. . . . I was now committed to a different goal: making films."

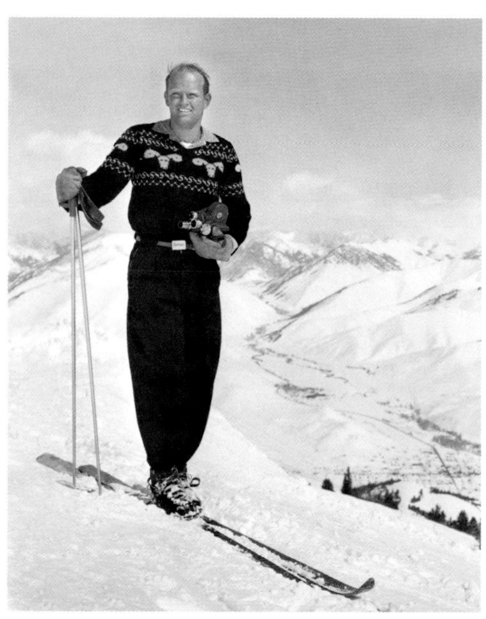

Warren Miller standing on Baldy. *Courtesy of the Warren Miller estate.*

Miller spent the next few winters at the newly opened Squaw Valley, teaching skiing for French racer Émile Allais, working construction in the off-season, and promoting his ski films. At one of his first movie presentations made to a southern California ski club, he had no script, so he ad-libbed stories about his life as a ski bum living in a trailer in Sun Valley, spending $18 total for lift tickets for four months of skiing, shooting rabbits

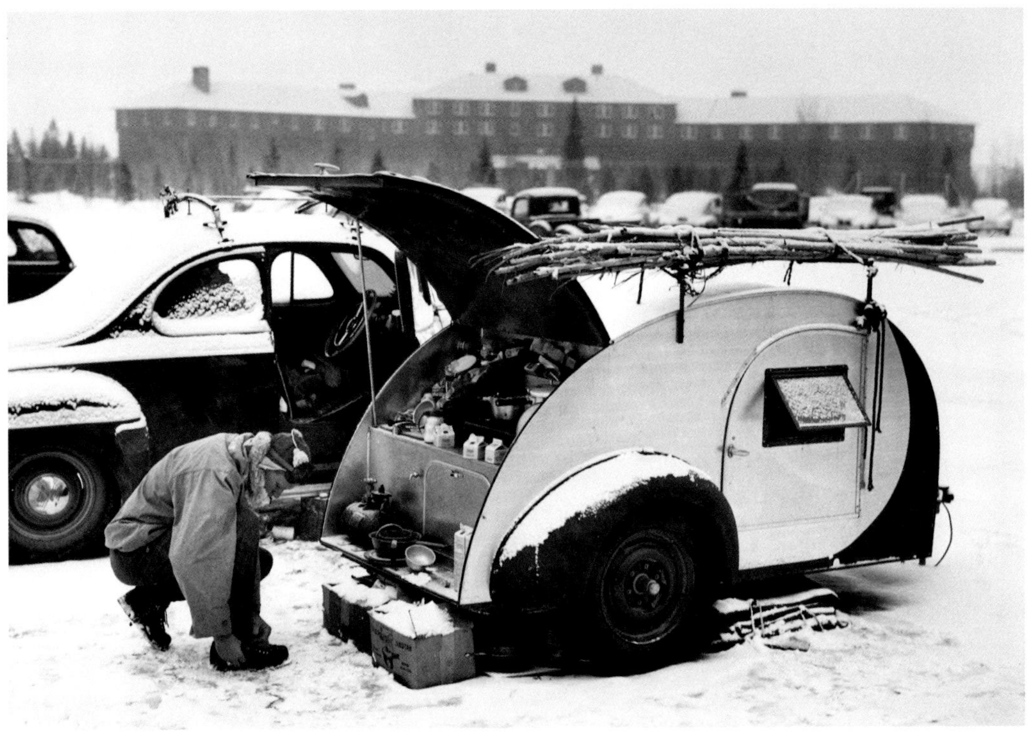

Warren Miller's trailer parked in a Sun Valley parking lot, 1947. *Courtesy of the Warren Miller estate.*

near Shoshone for dinner, and "the intricate dance routine involved in getting undressed outside in the freezing night air in order to get into bed in the freezing teardrop trailer after a dinner date." The audience responded so positively that Miller realized he could make a living entertaining skiers.

He returned to Sun Valley virtually every year to show his movies and film new ski scenes—he considered the area to be one of the best in the world. He filmed Stein Eriksen teaching Christian Pravda and Jack Reddish how to do a forward somersault on skis. Later, he took his family to Sun Valley for Christmas vacations and developed land near Dollar Mountain after his old ski teacher, Bill Janss, bought the resort and hired him to do marketing films. Janss used one of Miller's films, *A Place for All Seasons,* showing the resort's year-round attractions to convince the John Mannsville Corporation to buy land that became Elkhorn for $4.5 million, the amount Janss had originally paid for the entire Sun Valley Resort.[74]

Pictures of Warren Miller's life in Sun Valley can be found in the Ketchum Starbucks, reminding patrons of the resort's early days.

27

1950

FIS World Championships Bring Europe's Best Skiers to Aspen and Sun Valley

Substantial work was done at Sun Valley to prepare for the winter, as described in the *Sun Valley Ski Annual, 1950*. Its slopes, the publication said,

> *received a summer workover that brought them to the best shape in the resort's history. On Baldy, the trail crew had widened College Run to more than double its prior breadth, the approach from the summit was cleared, an island of trees was removed, and the cat track leading to the Roundhouse was widened. Exhibition and Cold Springs trails were widened, and on Canyon, the narrow tunnel at its bottom was widened. The warming hut on the summit of Baldy had been enlarged to three times its previous size, and sandwiches and hot soup would be available for skiers. Otto Lang had 23 instructors in the Sun Valley Ski School.*

The warming hut at the top of Baldy, called the Sun Valley Ski Club Hut, had two tables reserved for the exclusive use of club members. "Those indefatigable all-day skiers will find this a great convenience since they will now be able to restore their energy on the run," the *Annual* said. Lower College run was opened for 1950, extending College to the bottom of the Exhibition chairlift.

Sun Valley's celebrity season "got off to a whooping start with the arrival of His Excellency, the Shah of Iran. Persia's youthful ruler took the Valley over lock, stock and barrel and his athletics left many a winded subject in his whirlwind wake." Hollywood was there too, according to the *Annual*. Ann Sheridan, the Ray Millands, and Ann Sothern, Betty Hutton, and Darryl Zanuck were there over Christmas, while Lex Barker (Tarzan) came later. Arturo Toscanini, "dean of the symphonic conductors," came in May with the NBC Symphony Orchestra.

International events showed how the world had changed and the effect Sun Valley had on skiing everywhere. When Sun Valley opened in 1936, it was described as America's St. Moritz, a resort that brought European skiing ambiance to this country. In 1950, a Vienna newspaper published a story about its Arlberg region becoming "Austria's Sun Valley," a concept promoted by Averell Harriman, President Truman's top Marshall Plan representative in Europe. The article praised Sun Valley as the "center of a beautiful, gigantic skiing carousel." With the help of the Marshall Plan, the Arlberg resorts of Lech, Zurs, and St. Anton "now had the chance to become a ski carousel as spectacular as Sun Valley."[75]

FIS Races Put Aspen on the International Map, Racers Come to Sun Valley

In 1950, a major event in U.S. ski racing history took place when the FIS world ski championships were held in this country for the first time. The nordic world championships were held in Lake Placid, New York, from January 3 to February 5, 1950. The men's and women's slalom and downhill world championships were held in Aspen February 13–18. The events brought the world's best skiers to this country to compete.

Two people with a strong Sun Valley connection played critical roles in Aspen's FIS races: Dick Durrance, Aspen's general manager, and Friedl Pfeifer, head of the Aspen Ski School. Durrance made a film of the races that is still shown in Aspen and remained Aspen's general manager until 1952.

In his book, Durrance takes credit for bringing the tournament to Aspen. He got Aspen's proposal to host the races approved by the U.S. Ski Association, and in Europe, "rather surprisingly," it was approved. His finance committee raised $72,000, and he, Pfeifer, and Fred Iselin laid out the race courses, including Ruthie's Run and others, which remain some of Aspen's most popular trails. Pfeifer coached the U.S. women's team, which included Andrea Mead from Vermont. Six Sun Valley skiers were on the U.S. team: Jimmy Griffith, Dean Perkins, Leon Goodman, Katy Rodolph, Jannette Burr, and Brynhild Grasmoen.

Fifteen hundred competitors, coaches, officials, and spectators came for the tournament. There was not enough space in Aspen's hotels, so many were housed in private homes. Stein Eriksen was one of the young competitors. Giant slalom races were run for the first time in a major international competition. The first Olympic giant slalom was in 1952 in Oslo, and the race has been run in every world championship and Olympic competition since. It began as a one-run race, with a second run added in the 1966 world championships and the 1968 Olympics. A second run for women was added in the 1978 world championships and the 1980 Olympics. The giant slalom displaced the combined event in 1950, but combined events returned in the 1954 world championships in Åre, Sweden. Austria's Hans Nogler won the slalom, beating Zeno Colò—the Italian who was considered a "wild man" on skis—by four tenths of a second, but Colò won the giant slalom and downhill and the combined title. Europeans dominated the races and Americans had a difficult time, although Jannette Burr finished seventh, bringing some pride to the home crowd. Sun Valley's Jimmy Griffith had an unfortunate fall that was the only thing that kept him out of the top three. Jack Reddish, Katy Rodolph, and Andrea Mead proved that Americans could place among the elite.

The FIS championships were a major event for the United States and put Aspen on the international map. Friedl Pfeifer said they "were a turning point, not only for Aspen, but for the ski racers," cementing "Aspen's reputation as a mecca for international skiing and racing." Durrance said the international press raved about "the quality of the skiing and the race courses. . . . The skiing establishment felt it was a real milestone, a turning point in the development of skiing in Aspen and in the U.S. . . . After that Aspen began to prosper and grow." The *New York Times* of February 26, 1950, said that Aspen's facilities were praised by the visiting skiers and thousands of spectators. Competitors said the skiing conditions were the finest they ever encountered and that "areas in Switzerland and Chamonix in France do not compare with Aspen."

This began Aspen's rise to international prominence, challenging Sun Valley's dominance as the country's primary ski resort.

After the FIS tournament, most of the racers went to Sun Valley for two major races, the Harriman Cup on March 4–5, 1950, and the National Downhill and Slalom

Championships on March 25–26, which were described by Otto Lang in the *Sun Valley Ski Annual, 1950*. Gretchen Fraser, the new president of the Sun Valley Ski Club, said in that year's report,

> *Never has the Harriman Cup field seen so many superb International skiers, 11 nations represented in all. . . . The courses were magnificent and they were raced by the brilliant field in a flawless manner. Both slalom and downhill were witnessed by more spectators than had ever before crowded in to watch a race at Sun Valley.*

Otto Lang said, "the world's finest skiers of ten nations" provided Sun Valley with "a rare treat." Lang wanted a downhill course giving

> *every competitor the opportunity of displaying his formidable prowess in competition. . . . The Warm Springs course, once a severe test and highly respected racing trail, had become somewhat obsolete in its present shape. It is fearfully fast, but does not offer any particular problems from a technical point of view, as most racers take it plumb straight.*

Olympic run, "a superior run in many ways," according to Lang, had a flat spot after the Roundhouse slope "which is frowned upon by the international racing community." He wanted a new downhill course to "offer a supreme test of speed, stamina and technical chicaneries."

Lang designed the course to go down Exhibition to "provide the piece de resistance," also offering excellent spectator opportunities, which became the classic route used in later years. Both the downhill and slalom courses were foot-packed by the ski patrol, instructors, and employees. Exhibition presented a major challenge, as described by Dick Dorworth in "Sun Valley's Ski Racing Roots":

> *Sun Valley's precipitous Exhibition, bristling like a hedgehog with jagged bumps, got its name because skiers coming down it can exhibit their skill and daring to riders on the chair going up. . . . Exhibition's unrelenting steepness over a distance makes it America's most formidable mogul run today. . . . You may gasp at the idea of someone schussing straight down it, but world champion Émile Allais did so, and America's daredevil Mad Dog Buek once did it ten times in succession, cartwheeling in spectacular crashes more often than not.*

The downhill was 1.8 miles long with a vertical drop of 3,000 feet. It started on top of Baldy, followed the upper section of the lift line, then went straight over the hump to the Roundhouse corner, which required two exacting highspeed turns in the narrow passage. Skiers then went under the chair at the Roundhouse, onto a traverse leading to Exhibition. There were four control gates on Exhibition, one at the end of the traverse as a speed-checking device, and the others to guide racers onto a prescribed line down the treacherous clope. At the bottom of Exhibition, the course joined River Run. The women's course started above Rock Garden and went down Canyon, finishing on River Run.

Lang set two separate slalom courses on Ruud Mountain alongside each other as an experiment. Ruud Mountain, he said, "lends itself ideally for slalom event," and with the improvements planned for the upcoming summer, it would, he said, become "the premier site of the United States."

One of the highlights of the Harriman Cup races over the years came when Austrian's Hans Nogler ("the Clown Prince of Skis") won the event, beating the greats of the day, including Zeno Colò, Jean Pazzi, Georges Schneiger, Olle Dalman, François Baud, Toni Matt, and Christian Pravda. "When Zeno Colò cut a magnificent schuss down exhibition for the fastest time, the crowd went wild," Bob Reilly wrote in the *Sun Valley Ski Annual, 1950*. Nogler "shaded the Italian avalanche to snatch the downhill crown, and on the following day ran two superb slaloms to capture the combined." Nogler beat Colò to win the Harriman Cup, and later became an instructor at Sun Valley.

Eighteen-year-old Andrea Mead became the youngest racer ever to win the women's Harriman Cup, sweeping the downhill and the slalom. She had "a spectacular, calculated and well nigh perfect run" in the downhill, according to Friedl Pfeifer. Mead's slalom run was "an outstanding display of first-rate skiing and competitive spirit. She had no peer that day in sheer determination. . . . Andy, fairly burned up the course with her locks flying in the wind—like a possessed creature." France's Jacqueline Martel was second in the combined and Jannette Burr 14th. Lang said women's competitive skiing had come a long way since the 1948 Olympics: "The technical skill and daring displayed by the representatives of the various nations were quite impressive. . . . America's hopes for a more permanent place in the sun are brighter than ever," with Gretchen Fraser's successor "approaching peak performance," and Katy Rodolph, Jannette Burr, and others just beginning to gain experience and confidence.

Europeans dominated the men's Harriman Cup, finishing in the top eight places. Ketchum's Jim Griffith was the highest U.S. finisher in the downhill at 20th, placing 19th in the combined.

A crew from *Life* was at Sun Valley for the race, "clambering over every mountain in the Valley to get their shots," A. Royalle Lane wrote. Later in the year, Sun Valley photographers "rang up some laurels by garnering footage" of the shah of Iran, who vacationed there with his family.

The National Downhill and Slalom Championships were held on March 25–26. The downhill was on the same course as the Harriman Cup, going down Exhibition. Ketchum's Jimmy Griffith won the national downhill championship. Jannette Burr won her second national downhill title. "With Jannette, it was simply a case of having too much of everything for the rest of the girls," Lang wrote. Jack Reddish won the men's slalom on Rudd Mountain, getting enough points to win the amateur combined title, with Griffith second. Ernie McCulloch of the Sun Valley Ski Club won the open combined title and was the outstanding skier of the tournament. Reddish was second, and Sun Valley's Yvan Tache was third. Lois Woodworth won the women's combined, followed by Sun Valley's Jeanette Johnson.

The United States sent an FIS team to compete in Chile in 1951, a continuation of the Pan American Championships that began in the summer of 1937 when much of the Dartmouth ski team and Seattle's Don Fraser competed in the tournament. A South American team competed at Sun Valley in 1941. Ketchum's Jim Griffith, a ski star at Denver University, was a member of the 1951 FIS team, along with Brookes Dodge, and they won every race they entered. Griffith become South American champion.

In the summer, several new runs were opened on Baldy. Lower College was cut, extending College to the bottom of lift No. 2, which took skiers up to the Roundhouse. Cutoff run was created going from Ridge to College, bypassing Rock Garden and providing an easy route off Ridge for intermediate skiers, according to the *American Ski Annual and Skiing Journal* for 1950.

> *Sun Valley scored the greatest competitive year in its history and the most successful winter season on the books. The numerous ski greats who were in and out of the Valley during the year and the great championship meets combined with celebrity-laden lists of regular guests and the pleasurable routine of resort activities to make Winter, 1950, a golden season.*[76]

28

U.S. OLYMPIC TEAM IS SELECTED AT SUN VALLEY

SVSC Skiers Dominate; Ski Club President Al Lindley is Killed

Sun Valley was blessed with near perfect conditions in 1951. Dorice Taylor's article, "More People Had More Fun," in the *Sun Valley Ski Club Annual* for 1951 said the year was Sun Valley's best winter since Averell Harriman began building his retreat:

> *If all skiers' prayers were laid amen to amen, Sun Valley had the answer to them all in the made-to-order winter of 1951. An early assurance of snow, Baldy Mountain* [was] *little short of perfect on opening day, and from then on fresh powder snow whenever the skiers needed it.*

The year started on New Year's Eve with 36 instructors and 25 patrolmen performing in a torchlight procession on Dollar "that serpentined down its slope like a line of gnomes from a Disney fairy tale" to entertain the gathered celebrities. Four hundred skiers joined the Sun Valley Ski Club. The year included one of the best racing seasons the resort had ever seen.

Ski Tournaments

In a break with tradition, Sun Valley hosted the Olympic tryouts in downhill and slalom for the 1952 Olympics in Oslo, Norway, a year before the Games instead of the same year—"the physical requirements of skiing are such that it is necessary to select the squads a full year ahead of time," said the *Sun Valley Ski Club Annual* for 1951. This led to

> *one of the most exciting weeks in Sun Valley's history. . . . All during the week the nation's foremost skiers had been working out on Baldy's famed terrain, threading their way down slalom courses and executing practice runs for the Downhill. The tenseness which pervaded the contestants was beyond description, for it is a well-accepted fact that a place on the Olympic Team is the dream of every American racer. . . . The eyes of the entire skiing community were focused upon Sun Valley and upon the 40 men and 20 women readying themselves for the big test.*

Five days of snowfall before the downhill made for "exceptionally rough going in the practice sessions," according to the *Annual*. The snow led to injuries to two "of the West's brightest lights—Seattle's Jack Nagel, who the week before captured the National Combined at Whitefish, Montana; and Ketchum's Jimmy Griffith, generally regarded as one of the greatest downhiller men of all time. The sidelining of these two favorites was keenly felt by the local fans."

Race day was perfect and attracted 1,200 spectators. The women's one-mile downhill course, with a vertical drop of 1,600 feet, "started at the top of the National Slalom Slope where it entered Rock Garden, crossed under the lift at the top of the No. 2 lift, swept down Roundhouse Slope and went over the cut-off into Canyon, down through the Narrows, through the 'Chute' and into River, to a finish 100 yards below the Silver Star start." It had 12 control gates, with six on Rock Garden and four in Canyon. Sun Valley Ski Club women won the first four places: Sally Neidlinger, Betty Weir, Katy Rodolph, and Imogene Opton.

The men's downhill started at Baldy's summit and went down Roundhouse and Exhibition. The 1.6-mile course dropped 3,000 vertical feet with 11 control gates, including six on Exhibition, permitting a line that was "fast and fluid but commensurate to the racers' over-all ability." The SVSC's Jack Reddish "cut a perfect line down through the gates and roared into the flats at close to 50 miles per hour," winning the downhill, followed by Dick Buek, also of the SVSC, both of whom had "the best understanding of Exhibition's exacting requirements."

The highlight was Darrell Robison from the University of Utah, who finished seventh after he "almost lost his pants on Rock Garden." Dick Dorworth said Robison finished the downhill

> *despite breaking the belt on his pants coming off Exhibition and finishing the toughest downhill in America in his underwear with his pants piled around his boot tops. . . . The crowd loved it. . . . How high he might have placed had he worn a belt is a matter of conjecture, although many observers maintained that his near calamity may actually have saved him a second or two since it served to keep him hunched forward over his skis.*

There were side-by-side slalom courses on Ruud Mountain for men and women. The women had 32 gates and the men 40, and the lines of descent were "sufficiently tricky to require plenty of judgment and all-round ability," the *Annual* reported. The men's race was a tight duel between Darrell Robison of Utah, who won the event, and Jack Reddish. Seattle's Dave Faires took third. Sally Neidlinger won the downhill and slalom, beating Suzy Harris Rytting of the Alta Ski Club. SVSC racers took the next four spots.

The 1951 Harriman Cup came one week after the Olympic tryouts. According to the *Sun Valley Ski Club Annual* for 1951, the race

> *enjoyed the advantage of having the very best skiers in America already assembled at Sun Valley. Virtually the entire group which had participated in the Tryouts remained over for this traditional meet, generally regarded as the top Alpine competition held in the Americas. . . . The meet has always attracted the finest skiers in the world, for to have one's name inscribed on the big bowl is the goal of every top-notch racer.*

Jack Nagel and Jimmy Griffith competed, bolstering "the strength of the American boys." Canada's Ernie McCulloch and Norway's Guttorm Berge could not compete in the Olympic tryouts but raced in the Harriman Cup. McCulloch, a Sun Valley ski instructor, had won the North American and national downhill championships and the national giant slalom. Berge, an exchange student at Whitman College in Washington, was a brilliant competitor. In the women's division, "Sun Valley's formidable quintet of Sally Neidlinger, Betty Weir, Imogene Opton, Katy Rodolph and Sandra Tomlinson" were driving forces, the *Annual* said.

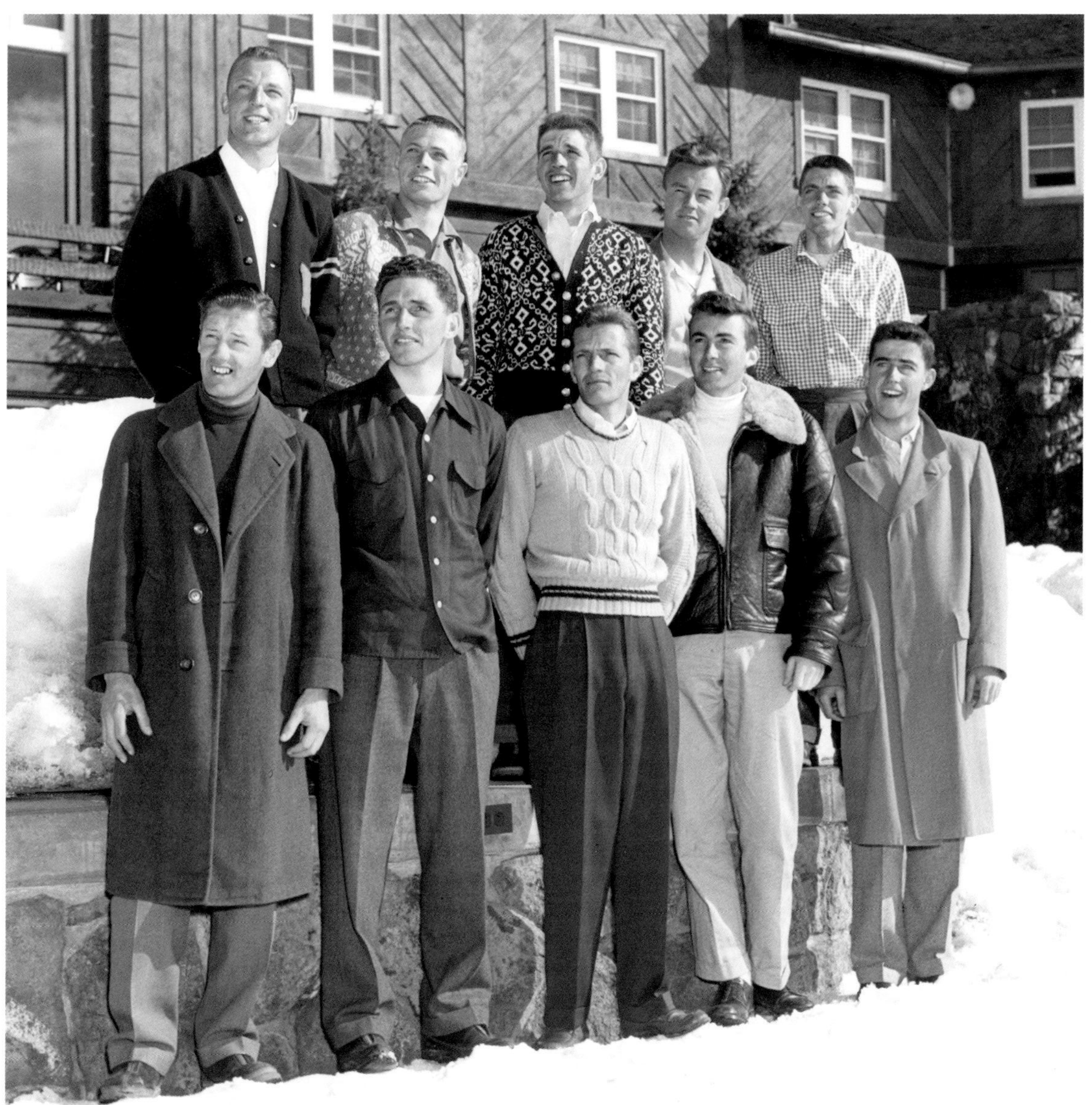

1952 U.S. men's Olympic ski team in Sun Valley. Front, Dick Buek, Bill Beck, Jack Reddish, Brooks Dodge, and Jimmy Griffith. Back, Alan Fischer, Jim Murphy, Verne Goodwin, Jack Nagel, and Darrell Robison. *Courtesy of the Griffith family.*

Toni Matt set the men's two-mile downhill course with a 3,000-foot vertical drop. The Olympic tryout downhill went down Exhibition, but the Harriman Cup course went down Olympic because of snow conditions. Verne Goodwin of Middlebury Ski Club edged out Ernie McCulloch by six-tenths of a second. Some of the top-ranked favorites, including Guttorm Berge, Jack Reddish, and Toni Matt, "ran the course straight as a string, but seemed hampered by slow wax."

The women's 1.2-mile downhill had a 1,200 vertical foot drop and nine control gates. Canadian Rhoda Wurtele Eaves won, running away from a high-caliber field. Sally Neidlinger, the Olympic tryout winner and pre-race favorite, caught an edge below the steilhang and hit a tree. SVSC racers Weir, Rodolph, Springer-Miller, Sandra Tomlinson, and Imogene Opton finished second through sixth.

The slalom was held on Ruud Mountain on two adjacent courses. Jack Reddish won, followed by Darrell Robinson and Toni Matt. SVSC's Sandra Tomlinson won the women's slalom, followed by Skeeter Werner of Steamboat Springs. The combined titles were both won by Canadians, "who came into their own in 1951," the *Annual* said. Ernie McCulloch won the men's combined, followed by Verne Goodwin, Dick Buek, and Jack Reddish. Rhoda Eaves won the women's combined, followed by Betty Weir and five other Sun Valley Ski Club racers.

A jumping exhibition took place on Ruud Mountain featuring two University of Washington students from Norway, Chris Mohn and Gunnar Sunde, who both jumped over 150 feet.

The eighth annual Western States American Legion Junior Championships took place at Sun Valley on March 31 and April 1, 1951. Stars of the event were Bud and Skeeter Werner from Steamboat Springs, who battled another brother-sister combination, Dick and Teresa Schwaegler from Washington. This was Bud Werner's first appearance at Sun Valley, at age 15, but he returned on multiple occasions. Dick Schwaegler won the boy's downhill, with Werner finishing second. The results flipped in the slalom, where Werner won and Schwaegler finished second. Werner finished second in the jumping event and Schwaegler finished eighth. Werner won the boys' three-way combined, edging out Schwaegler. In the girl's events, Skeeter Werner beat Teresa Schwaegler in both the slalom and downhill. Colorado won the team event with Washington finishing second.

Sun Valley skiers dominated the 1952 U.S. Olympic teams. Five of the 10 men belonged to the Sun Valley Ski Club: Richard Buek, James Griffith of Ketchum, Jack

Nagel of Seattle, Jack Reddish, and George Hovland. Five of the eight women were Sun Valley Ski Club members: Jannette Burr of Seattle, Sally Neidlinger, Katy Rodolph, Sandra Tomlinson, and Sally Weir. Gretchen Fraser and Corlandt Hill, a member of the Sun Valley Ski Club board of governors, were the managers of the 1952 U.S. Olympic teams. Hjalmar Hvam of Portland was the manager of the men's nordic squad. Émile Allais of Lake Tahoe coached the men's downhill and slalom team.

Jim Griffith was the first Ketchum native to make an Olympic team. He was a descendent of Albert Griffith, who settled in Ketchum in 1880. He never had a formal lesson but began skiing with the Sun Valley Ski Patrol and watching the area's best skiers. He was one of six locals who were extras in the 1943 movie *Northern Pursuit* starring Errol Flynn, produced in Canada but with skiing scenes filmed north of Ketchum in the Owl Creek and Boulder Mountains. Griffith entered the University of Colorado in 1945 at age 15, joining his sister Mary Jane, also a successful ski racer. She wrote:

> *Colorado news articles bragged that Mary Jane and Jimmy were two of the best skiers the university had ever produced. And Jimmy was declared to be one of the best athletes to ever attend the Boulder school, rising to become captain and co-coach of the ski team by his graduation.*

Griffith was high-point man at Colorado for three years and rapidly climbed the international ranks. In 1948, he placed seventh in the national amateur combined. In 1949, he was third in the national open downhill, third in the national slalom, and third in the Harriman Cup downhill behind Toni Matt. He won the U.S. men's downhill amateur and open championship in 1950. Griffith joined the U.S. Air Force in 1951 after graduating from college, receiving a deferment to train for the 1952 Olympics. He suffered a horrific accident while training at Alta when he hit breakable crust near a cat track and skidded into a tree. He died two days later on December 6, 1951, in a Salt Lake City hospital at age 22.

The Griffith Memorial Award was established to go to the Sun Valley Ski Club male racer who best exemplifies the qualities of sportsmanship and excellence of performance characteristic of Jim Griffith's short racing career. The award was hung in the Sun Valley Lodge. Griffith was inducted into the U.S. Ski and Snowboard Hall of Fame in 1971.[77]

Changes at Sun Valley

In summer 1951, the Proctor Mountain single chairlift was removed and installed on Baldy, running parallel to lift No. 3 from the Roundhouse to the summit. Proctor Mountain had been used infrequently after Bald Mountain opened in 1940. Known as lift No. 5 on Baldy, it carried 300 skiers per hour and nearly doubled the capacity to the summit. The top section of Baldy was one of the most popular ski runs, with all-day solar exposure and "exceptionally fine terrain," according to Harvey Diederich.

> *This second chairlift should eliminate all waiting, and will be a natural approach to the Christmas and Easter bowls. Skiers intending to ski Ridge and College would now ride the old Number 3 lift. Many of Baldy's ski runs were cleared of brush, and bumps were smoothed out the prior summer to provide more and better skiing for everyone.*

In his oral history, Andy Hennig said a new chairlift was going to be installed from the Roundhouse to the top of Baldy. Union Pacific's president didn't want to spend the money for a new lift, so the Proctor chair was disassembled and used instead. The Proctor single chair received a more powerful motor in 1954, and remained on Bald Mountain until 1958, when it was replaced by a double chair. Other work included removing an island of trees from Rock Garden and taking down cabins on the top of Proctor and Dollar Mountains, which were remodeled to make a clubhouse at the shooting range. Seven electrically operated traps and a skeet layout were added.

Tragedy hit the Sun Valley community in February 1951 when long-time SVSC president Al Lindley died in the crash of a private plane en route to Aspen piloted by his friend from Minneapolis, Edmund Pillsbury. He was 47 years old and was survived by his wife, Grace Carter Lindley, and two children. Lindley was president of the Sun Valley Ski Club from 1936 to 1949, and its 1951 report was dedicated to his memory.

The American Alpine Club, of which Lindley had been a member since 1932, published his obituary. Lindley, it said, was one of the country's most outstanding amateur athletes. He was born in Minneapolis to a wealthy family. "By inheritance he might have led a life of comparative ease and devoted his time to his great interest in the field of sports, in which he was so proficient; but desire to be of public service was inherent in his character." Lindley graduated from Yale in 1925 and was a member of the Yale crew that won a gold medal in the 1924 Olympics. Lindley was also a well-known mountaineer who pioneered mountain skiing.

He and his wife, Grace, from Seattle, were on the 1936 U.S. Olympic team. They married in 1937 and lived in Minneapolis, where they continued competitive skiing. At the time of his death, Lindley was chairman of the Skiing Committee of the U.S. Olympic Committee. Lindley Hut was built in Colorado in the Castle Creek Valley south of Aspen in 1953 as a memorial to him. The routes to the hut are unmarked and are only for experienced backcountry travelers.

In winter 1951, John Litchfield became the first American-born head of the Sun Valley Ski School. Litchfield first visited Sun Valley in 1937 with Dartmouth teammate Dick Durrance, taught there before World War II, and was a 10th Mountain Division veteran. He returned to the valley in 1948 after teaching at Aspen with Friedl Pfeifer, becoming Otto Lang's head instructor.[78]

29

1952

Olympic Games Held in Oslo; Killer Avalanche at Lookout Bowl; Pat Rogers Leaves

The winter Olympics were held in Oslo, Norway, in 1952, where the giant slalom made its Olympic debut, replacing the combined event. The U.S. cross-country and alpine squads trained at Sun Valley. Émile Allais and Herbert Jochum worked with the women's team at Grindelwald, Switzerland. The nordic team went to Kongsberg, Norway, where jumpers trained under Birger Ruud, and Leif Odmark trained the cross-country team.

The big story was Andrea Mead Lawrence, who at age 14 was on the U.S. Olympic ski team in 1948, with Gretchen Fraser, placing eighth in the slalom. In 1952, she married David Lawrence, a former U.S. ski champion. She became captain of the women's team at age 19 and replaced Fraser as the top American skier by winning gold medals in the slalom and giant slalom in 1952, "an unprecedented feat for an American skier," according to the *New York Herald Tribune*. Her dual victory "epitomizes the United States coming of age in international skiing competition." She was also on the 1956 U.S. Olympic team, after having three children, where she placed fourth in the giant slalom. Andrea Mead Lawrence was inducted into the U.S. Ski and Snowboard Hall of Fame in 1958.

American men failed to win a medal in the alpine events. The highest finisher was William Beck, who placed fifth in the downhill. Italian Zeno Colò won gold, Austrian Othmar Schneider silver, and Austrian Christian Pravda bronze. Norway's Stein Erikson won gold in the giant slalom, Pravda silver, and Toni Spis of Austria bronze. In the slalom, Othmar Schneider won gold, Eriksen silver, and Norway's Guttorm Berge bronze. Austria won seven Olympic medals, the most of any country. "All in all, more American names appear in the upper brackets of the results lists for the Alpine events than ever before," reported the *American Ski Annual and Skiing Journal* for 1953. About 130,000 spectators watched the events at the Holmenkollen jumping hill.

John Litchfield was the Sun Valley Ski School director in 1952, assisted by Barney McLean, Sepp Froehlich, Les Outzs and Sigi Engl. In spite of the economizing imposed by Union Pacific, Sun Valley's ski school was expanded to 37 instructors. After the 1952 Olympics, Averell Harriman invited "three of the biggest names in international skiing—Stein Eriksen, Christian Pravda and our own Jack Reddish" to be Sun Valley instructors, "to inject new blood" into the ski school. Other top instructors included Corey Engen from Norway, Yves Latreille from France, and Ernie McCullough from Canada. When Litchfield was recalled to the Army for the Korean War in 1952, Sigi Engl became head of the Sun Valley Ski School, a post he held until 1975.

Stein Eriksen won a bronze medal in the 1950 FIS championships in Aspen; the Lauberhorn Slalom in Wengen, Switzerland, in 1951; and a gold medal in giant slalom at the 1952 Oslo Olympics. Eriksen taught at Sun Valley in 1952 and 1953 as a guest instructor, trained junior racers, and raced for Sun Valley at the North American Championships in Stowe, the Roch Cup in Aspen, races in Utah, and the Harriman Cup. He had been a gymnast in Norway, was a leader in aerial gymnastics on skis, and "could do things on skis that amazed the best athletes in the world," according to Alf Engen's son Alan. Eriksen performed somersaults every Sunday at Sun Valley on Ridge Run on the flat area before reaching Rock Garden. He later won gold medals in the 1954 world championships in Åre, Sweden, in slalom, giant slalom, and downhill. He returned to the United States as a pro, teaching at a number of ski resorts before ending up at Deer Valley, Utah, where he was director of skiing and built the Stein Eriksen Lodge.

Stein Eriksen said he considered Sun Valley "one of the most desirable resorts in the country." It is, he said, a beautiful mountain, "the whole development is extremely attractive. . . . It has a certain romance." Sun Valley influenced what Eriksen did at Deer Valley. Leon Goodman, who taught at Sun Valley, said nobody skied better on ice than Stein Eriksen, and Christian Pravda could "go down a hill of extreme bumps and make it look as smooth as a floor."

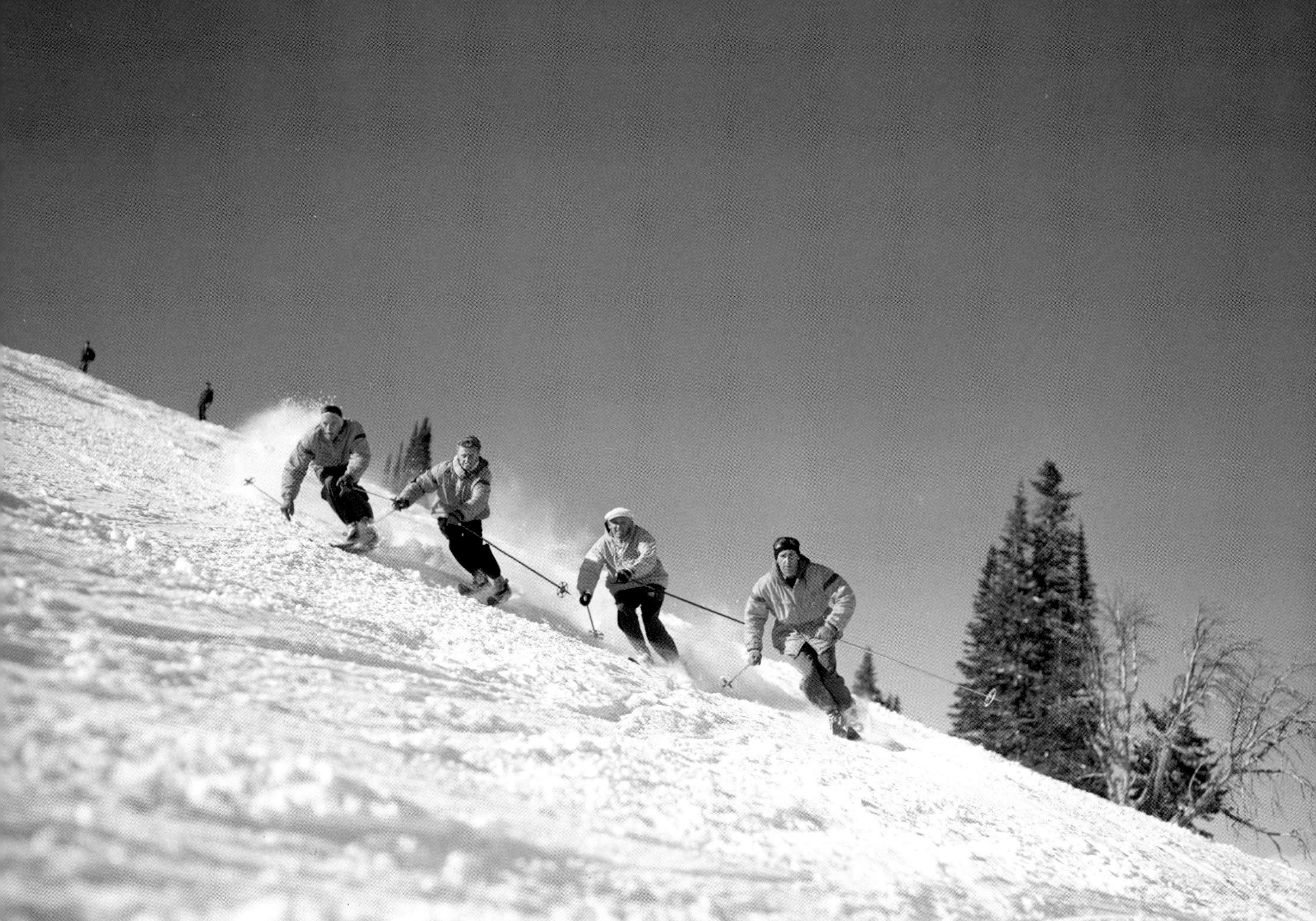

Sun Valley ski instructors Jack Reddish, Stein Eriksen, Sigi Engl, and Christian Pravda on Bald Mountain.

Canadian skiers dominated the Harriman Cup in 1951 and 1952. In 1952, the number of competitors was reduced from prior years since many of the top amateurs stayed in Europe after the Olympics.

In 1951, the downhill was moved from Exhibition to Olympic. In 1952, men skied down Exhibition on a course set by Barney McLean, "to challenge the best of them." The bottom two-thirds of Exhibition was "one long, whistling schuss," according to Dorice Taylor. The women raced down Canyon. Ernie McCullough from Mont Tremblant, skiing for the Sun Valley Ski Club, had the greatest run of his career as he won the downhill by six seconds, the largest spread since the war. McCullough won the Harriman Cup for the second year in a row, followed by Otto Von Ailman and Guttorm Berge. Lois

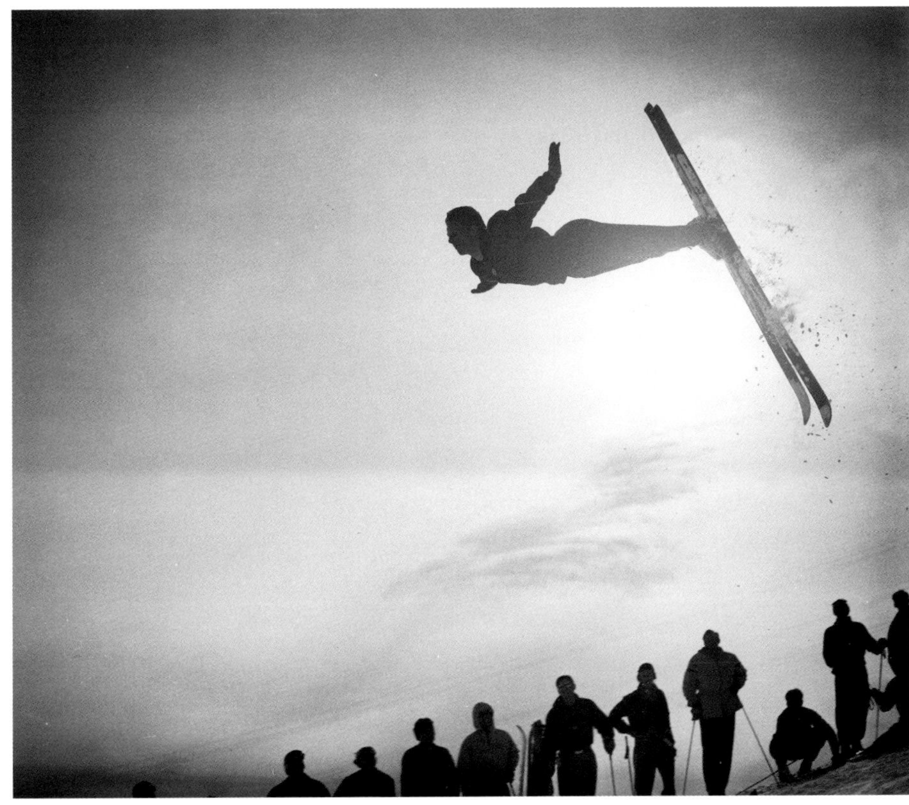

Norway's Stein Eriksen taught at Sun Valley in 1952 and 1953. He performed somersaults every Sunday on Ridge Run above Rock Garden.

Woodworth from Banff won the women's Harriman Cup, followed by Elaine Holmstad and Rhona Gillis. At the 1952 Harriman Cup banquet, the first Jim Griffith Award was presented to Jack Reddish by Jim's sister Mary Jane Griffith Martin. Dorice Taylor said 1952 was the "last of the truly great Harriman Cup races."[79]

1952 Avalanche on Lookout Bowl Kills Four

In winter 1952, there was a huge amount of snowfall at Sun Valley and avalanches in nearby mountains. An avalanche on Bromaghin Peak destroyed Owl Creek Cabin, ending formal backcountry skiing at the resort. Its timbers were taken to Baldy to build a new warming hut. Leon Goodman said it snowed for 12 days in a row. He lived in

Warm Springs Canyon, which got snowbound, and a rotary snowplow had to be sent to rescue the area.

A major tragedy occurred at Sun Valley in 1952 when an avalanche on Lookout Bowl on Baldy killed four skiers. The episode is described in "The Great Sun Valley Avalanche" by David Butterfield.

A large amount of snow fell in January, and the top cornice and ridges between the bowls on Bald Mountain were loaded with snow. Nelson Bennett, the mountain director, left for a meeting and told his number two in command that he did not "want to see any tracks in the bowls when he returned." However, the allure of powder skiing caused skiers to pressure management to open them. On January 19, Bennett's order was countermanded on the authority of Sigi Engl, and the bowls were opened. Ski instructor Victor Gottschalk, Stuart Fraser of Mexico, Arthur Gardner of New York City, and Rudolf Mandl of Washington were skiing on Broadway below the lower bowl meadows, when high in Lookout Bowl,

> *with multiple layers of snow under tons of pressure, a large section of snowpack settled, cracked away and released. . . . The main slab rumbled off the upper northeastern aspect of the ridge, on the skiers' right. Gaining speed and mass by the second, it roared into the gully, on down the bowl, through the meadows and down into the narrows. Some say a good portion skipped the bend in the narrows, blew up and over the facing hill, then rejoined the main slide below. The deluge then ran the remaining quarter mile to the Cold Springs lift where the shack and a few chairs were partially buried. The cable popped off the first roller and the lift stalled. Finally, the beast came to a halt. There was a complete whiteout as a fine mist of snow hung over the mile-long slide, and one has to imagine, a few minutes of dreadful silence.*

Sun Valley employees were mobilized into a search party with Sigi Engl in charge. There was no chairlift to the bowls, so Little Easter and Easter Bowl had to be traversed to reach Lookout. Bob Albrecht, an employee on the search party, told Engl the snow in Easter Bowl looked unstable and could slide at any time. Engl did not respond, but "only stared off into space, seeming to be in some kind of trance," according to Butterfield. Eventually, 150 employees and guests searched for the victims using 20-foot bamboo probes, but the snow was 30 feet deep, and parallel trenches were dug 15 feet deep so the probes could reach ground. Victor Gottschalk was located one and a half

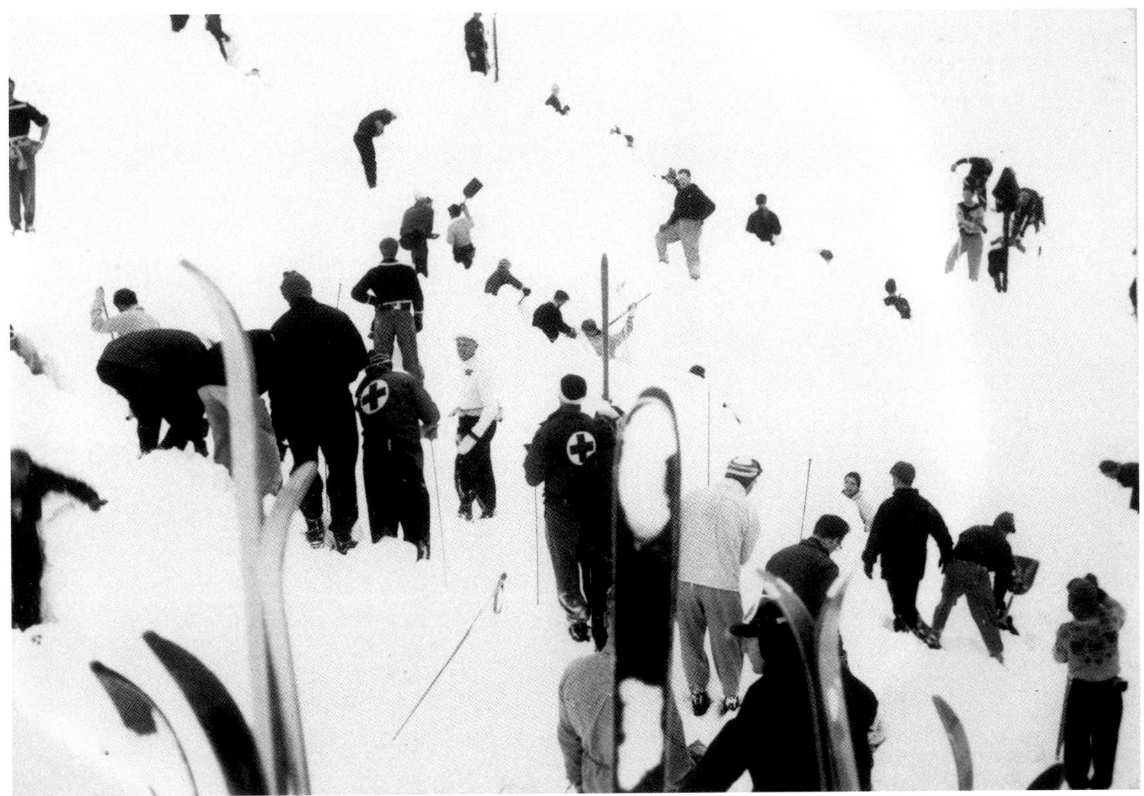

A search party of 150 looked for bodies in Lookout Bowl using 20-foot bamboo probes.

hours after the slide but could not be revived. Searching continued into the night using Coleman lanterns. The lift crew got the Cold Springs chair working, and at 8:00 p.m., nine hours after the slide, Engl called off the search. The crew rode the Cold Springs lift up to the Roundhouse, then downloaded onto the Exhibition chair holding ski equipment in their laps. The lift was so full it "accelerated to almost breakaway speed," as the searchers rode down through the dark. The search continued the next day, and two more bodies were recovered, leaving one buried.

Val McAtee worked with Victor Gottschalk in the summers. Gottschalk had told McAtee that when he was growing up in Austria, he and his friends would purposely trigger snowslides and ride them to the bottom of the hills. According to McAtee, Gottschalk rode the Sun Valley avalanche for quite a way down the hill "and almost made it out but he was buried at the foot of the Cold Springs lift." The man from New York, Arthur Gardner, had been hired to work at Sun Valley and this was his first day in the area. He got his ski pass and went up Baldy, where "he saw Victor and his party takeoff across the bowls and followed them; they found his body next spring when the bowls thawed out."

Holland reported that a lawsuit filed by one of the victim's families was settled before trial. This remains one of Sun Valley's greatest tragedies. Pat Rogers was "torn up" by the avalanche, according to Ed Seagle, and left Sun Valley shortly thereafter.

The year 1952 saw some of the heaviest snowfalls of all time, and it was known as "the year of the big snow." By mid-January, there was six feet of snow on the valley floor and almost 10 feet on Baldy. It will also be remembered for other records. More people visited in winter, more rode the lifts, and more enrolled in the ski school than ever before. Nearly 10,000 people stayed at Sun Valley, and the ski school taught 2,500 students, averaging nearly 300 a day. More than three quarters of a million passenger trips were made on the resort's eight chairlifts.[80]

CONTINUED DECLINE IN PASSENGER REVENUE—PAT ROGERS LEAVES

Arthur Stoddard became president of Union Pacific in 1949, remaining until 1965, leaving after the sale of Sun Valley to the Janss Company. Harriman was critical of the way Stoddard ran Union Pacific, saying that after the war, the railroad "was no longer interested in [Sun Valley]. . . . I would never have approved him as president, because I didn't think he had . . . the breadth or vision which I thought the Union Pacific president should have in being part of the whole West and the development of the West."

Railroad passenger business continued to decline after the war, dropping 33 percent in 1946 with the loss of military traffic, and another 61 percent by 1949 due to increased use of highways and air travel. This made Union Pacific's subsidy of Sun Valley increasingly hard to swallow, leading to significant cuts in services. Stoddard adopted an austerity program with a goal of cutting Sun Valley's $500,000 yearly loss.

Averell Harriman pursued a full-time career in government and politics after World War II, removing him from the resort. Harriman's lack of involvement "undoubtedly contributed to the demise of its reputation . . . and deflated employee morale," according to Holland. Jack Hemingway said, "Harriman's departure from active participation in the Union Pacific for his spectacular diplomatic and political career had left the Railroad, and the resort, in far more prosaic and less imaginative hands." Maury Klein said there was a gradual decline in Union Pacific's interest in Sun Valley after it reopened in 1947. With Harriman removed from any management responsibility since 1940, the money the resort lost every year increasingly became a source of aggravation to the railroad. Since passenger traffic was less important after World War II, and Sun Valley had existed principally as an advertising expense to encourage passenger traffic, the resort began to be seen as a white elephant.

Although many celebrities returned to Sun Valley after its reopening, its status was never the same. New ski areas were developed in Colorado, Utah, California, and New England, challenging Sun Valley's status as the country's primary destination ski resort. According to Oppenheimer and Poore, it was said before the war that Union Pacific "didn't care what Sun Valley lost as long as it wasn't 'more than a million dollars a year,'" but by the 1950s, the economic losses from the resort were less acceptable to the railroad. "What Union Pacific saw was a ski resort where rooms were given away to special guests, dinner tabs were picked up and the company suffered as a result." By 1952, the Union Pacific wanted a different approach, one more resembling a traditional business.

Sun Valley was dealt a significant blow in 1952 when long-time manager Pat Rogers left the resort. In a memo dated March 28, 1952, U.P. president Stoddard announced the change:

> *Mr. W.P. Rogers has asked to be relieved of his duties at Sun Valley, and, effective April 1, 1952, will be appointed Manager, Utah Parks Company. Mr. Winston McCrea is appointed Manager, Sun Valley operations, effective April 1st, and will be in charge of all operations at Sun Valley. The Managers, both at Sun Valley and Utah Parks, will report to Mr. H.I. Norris, Manager, Dining Car & Hotel Department, Omaha.*

Louis Holliday, who worked at Sun Valley since 1936, said Rogers was "the greatest man that ever lived. In my opinion, he is the reason that Sun Valley got the name it did." He was responsible for 90 percent of the glamour, and "made Sun Valley.

He was the greatest public relations man" that ever walked the earth. When a bus arrived, whether it was 6:00 a.m. or 1:00 p.m., Rogers was there to greet everyone, and was there to say goodbye when they left. Seventy-five percent of Sun Valley's guests were repeat customers and usually knew employees by their first names. Rogers served soup to guests at the Roundhouse at lunch. Practically everyone who worked for him was fired two or three times but rehired with no hard feelings. He was a father or friend to most employees. Union Pacific used traditional methods of accounting developed for railroad operations, which was incompatible with the way Sun Valley operated:

> *Rogers was often at odds with the accountants who ran Union Pacific. To them, the flowers and gifts Rogers gave to his guests were reckoned in dollars lost. Sun Valley had been a money-loser from the start, and although Rogers was doing exactly what Harriman told him to do, he increasingly had to contend with railroad executives who preferred freight to passengers.*

Louie Stur, the night accountant at Sun Valley, described the way Rogers operated the resort:

> *He was a real hotelman in the old sense of the word, and I say this because perhaps this would express somewhat that he didn't care much about profit-and-loss statements or money. He would just give away the whole place, and of course, he was loved by everyone, guests and employees; he was just very generous and very understanding. . . .*
>
> *Of course we lost our shirts while under his reign, which I am sure no business organization would tolerate too long. So when people talk about the good old times, it is an historical thing. I am always realistic and I say, well, there is no way that an organization could go on that way year after year, losing that kind of money, and have somebody up there liking it. Sure, it is nice for everybody who is here. . . . Somebody up there, specifically the Union Pacific hierarchy, didn't like the way Rogers threw money around, gave out free rooms, and in general ran Sun Valley as if it was his own private inn.*

Rogers's management philosophy was one Harriman supported. Without Harriman's participation, his model was not supported by Union Pacific, which began to watch finances more carefully, and Rogers was the one who felt the pressure, according to Klein:

> *Every year saw Averell's hand further removed and the company less patient over deficits that grew increasingly opaque. Pat Rogers, whose geniality held the Sun Valley style together, had grumbled for years at the abuse heaped on him by railway officers. As the deficits climbed, no one realized more than Rogers that he was the wrong man to impose economy on the operation. In 1952 he begged Stoddard to let him go back to managing the Utah Parks.*

"Pat's departure marked the end of an era," wrote Oppenheimer and Poole. Rogers was remembered as "a big bear of a man who brought the resort a profit that couldn't be measured in dollars and cents." Sun Valley was never the same. The new manager, they said,

> *like most Union Pacific board members . . . cared for neither skiing nor snow. . . . With a decline in operating support, Sun Valley lost some of its glamour and appeal to elites from both coasts. . . . Winston McCrea . . . proved to be a better administrator but less of the jovial innkeeper. And McCrea was hampered by the fact that the railroad simply didn't seem to be able to spend the dollars needed to improve Sun Valley enough.*

According to Klein, "The next decade saw a very different tone at the resort. McCrea economized at every turn." Tillie Arnold said Pat Rogers was "the heart and soul of Sun Valley," and when he left, the "family spirit of Sun Valley began to decline." Andy Hennig said Union Pacific did not want to spend the money necessary to keep it going. It refused to spend money to groom its trails and cat tracks at a time when Aspen was doing it and Ed Seagle was dying to do it. Kathleen Harriman Mortimer said her father was the only member of the Union Pacific board "who really cared about Sun Valley as a ski place."

One of the first communications between Stoddard and McCrea discussed how to handle bodies still buried by the 1952 avalanche, emphasizing the public relations aspects of the issue. On April 2, 1952, Stoddard asked McCrea to work with Ed Seagle on a plan to recover the bodies so they could be excavated on the same day to "close this accident from a publicity point of view with one more announcement, thereby avoiding attracting any more comment than absolutely necessary." This would "help considerably on the publicity angle, which, as you know, is very important to Sun Valley."

McCrea began working at the front desk of the Sun Valley Lodge in summer 1937, becoming Pat Rogers's assistant and manager of the lodge in 1938. In his oral history, McCrea said that during the last years under Rogers, Sun Valley lost $750,000, and he was critical of him. "He picked up too many checks," McCrea said. He didn't want anyone to have a complaint about anything, and guests "made a sucker out of him" and laughed about it. Ed Seagle said that when McCrea took over in 1952, Union Pacific's president told him it was all right if Sun Valley stayed within a $200,000 yearly loss. Union Pacific continued to write off expenses to Sun Valley's account, and railroad personnel still stayed for free at the resort's expense.

McCrea was under pressure to economize. He couldn't spend money on anything and there were many things that needed to be done. Sun Valley was beginning to be rundown. Only 20 of the Challenger Inn's rooms had private baths, and the rest shared bathrooms. McCrea promoted conventions at Sun Valley, with many coming by private train. Learn-to-ski weeks continued, costing $100 for a week including train fare. Skiers stayed four to a room and were happy. Although Stoddard insisted on cutting many things, he wanted ski trains kept, and they did very well. McCrea installed a cafeteria at the inn. Guests liked not having to eat a sit-down breakfast and lunch every day with waiters, who were eliminated. McCrea said Union Pacific did not plan to make a lot of money at Sun Valley, but after four or five years under his management, they almost broke even.

Passenger Revenue Continues to Decline and Conditions Worsen

Sun Valley was still a major destination resort, but Union Pacific did not invest the money necessary to provide the level of ambiance that made it famous before the war. McCrea had to implement Union Pacific's austerity program to cut Sun Valley's yearly $500,000 loss, according to Dorice Taylor. "No more did returning guests find flowers in their rooms; the lavish gardens were cut back and the ice sculpture melted into the past. Elegance began to go. . . . Times were changing." The Union Pacific could never make Sun Valley a paying proposition, Taylor said, which led to the decision to sell it in 1964:

> *By the late 1950s Sun Valley was running down. . . . A cafeteria was installed at the Challenger Inn, and other services were reduced. . . . At the Challenger Inn . . . they were still sleeping on the same mattresses that they put in the building when they built it. The more passenger traffic dwindled, the less sense Sun Valley made for the Union Pacific as a national billboard or anything else. Stoddard liked Sun Valley but didn't want to spend money on it; he couldn't go there without being besieged with requests for improvements. . . . By the early 1960s the place was . . . "patches on patches."*

In the 1950s and 1960s, passenger train service declined even further due to competition from private cars and airlines, made worse by the railroads' lack of investment in facilities and rolling stock. Between 1953 and 1961, passenger revenue fell an average of four percent a year. For many years, Union Pacific considered getting out of the passenger business. Dorice Taylor said she knew the writing was on the wall for Sun Valley when Union Pacific published a map of the United States from Chicago west with all its lines in vivid colors and "Sun Valley was not included." When Taylor toured Union Pacific facilities at Omaha, she saw the railroad making significant investments in modernizing ways to move freight. "I began to understand at last what the Union Pacific was," she said. "Forget its passenger service, forget Sun Valley. It was a freight railroad and the concern of the men involved was to keep that freight rolling."[81]

30

WARM SPRINGS CANYON IS DEVELOPED

In the early 1950s, Warm Springs Canyon was largely undeveloped. It contained several farms and the historic Guyer Hot Springs site west of the present Warm Springs lift.

In the early 1880s, the Philadelphia Smelter was built on a 160-acre bench on the west side of the Big Wood River at its confluence with Warm Springs Creek at the head of Warm Springs Canyon, which was expanded to several hundred acres. The smelter company owned nearly 1,000 acres east of the river where the Oregon Short Line depot was located. In 1884, the Rhodes Addition to the Ketchum Townsite annexed the Philadelphia Smelter site and the area east of the river owned by the company. The Rhodes Addition was divided into streets, alleys, and lots that were never developed. Much of the land contained holding pens for sheep waiting to be shipped out by train.

West of the smelter site, there was a 300–400-acre farm homesteaded by Horatio Stewart, which was acquired by August Farnlund. The smelter closed in the 1890s as the international silver depression shut down mining in the valley. In 1928, the smelter site was sold for $1,000 to Alonzo Price, who then sold the property to a California farmer, Earl Weatherhead. Descendants of two pioneering families, Lewis and Lloyd, owned much of the land where Warm Springs Village was later built.

In 1966, the portion of Warm Springs Canyon not included in the Rhodes Addition was annexed into Ketchum, and a zoning map was adopted for the canyon. In 1970,

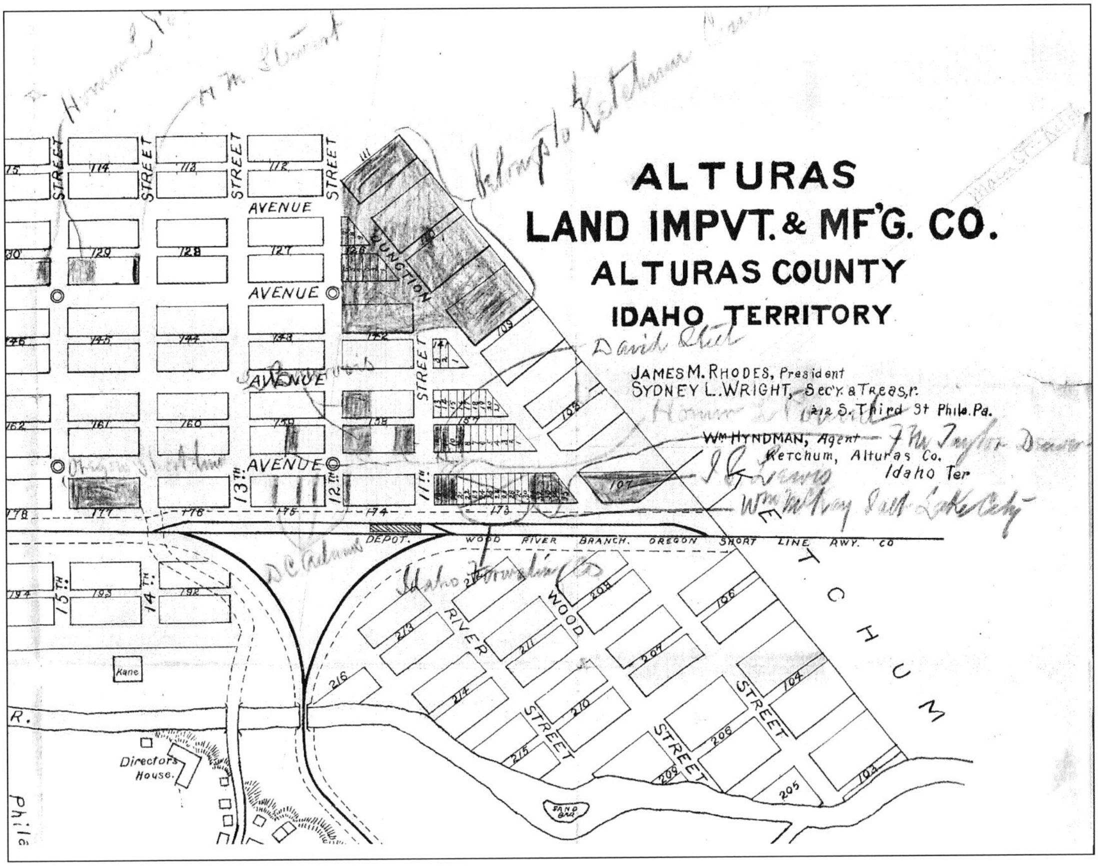

ALTURAS LAND IMPVT. & MF'G. CO.
ALTURAS COUNTY
IDAHO TERRITORY

JAMES M. RHODES, President
SYDNEY L. WRIGHT, Sec'y. & Treas'r.
212 S. Third St Phila. Pa.
Wm HYNDMAN, Agent
Ketchum, Alturas Co.
Idaho Ter.

STREET
AVENUE
JUNCTION
13th
12th
11th
15th
14th
DEPOT.
WOOD RIVER BRANCH. OREGON SHORT LINE RWY. CO.
KETCHUM
RIVER
WOOD
STREET
Kane
Directors House.
SAND BAR

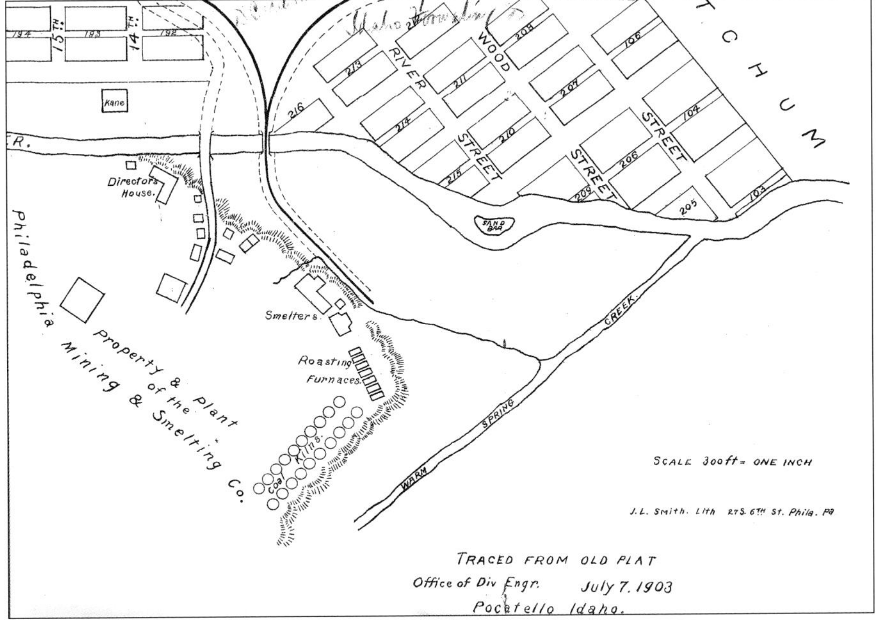

THIS PAGE Map of 1884 Rhodes Addition that brought the Philadelphia Smelter and its nearby property into Ketchum.

the streets and alleys in the Rhodes Addition were vacated, and parts of the land were rezoned to light industrial and residential.

Development in Warm Springs Canyon began after World War II. In 1948, Shelly Ivey, an executive with Crown Zellerbach, bought 87 acres of the Smith/Farnlund farm for $46,000. He sold ski instructor Leon Goodman one acre of the property for $300. Goodman built his house into the south-facing hill to take advantage of the solar energy, on Huffman Drive. It was the only house there for 10 or 15 years, except for the Brandt house at Guyer Hot Springs.

Subdivisions were approved in three parts of the canyon beginning in 1948. First in the east end of the canyon containing the smelter site and nearby land, second midway up the canyon near Heidelberg Gulch, Wanderer Way and Four Seasons Way, where the Fields Development is located, and third for Warm Springs Village, even though there was no lift there until 1965.

Idaho's gambling laws played a role in the development of Warm Springs Canyon. After World War II, Owen Simpson, who owned the Sawtooth Club, one of Ketchum's popular gambling establishments, formed the Sun Valley Realty Corporation along with a group of Ketchum and New York investors to develop land in Warm Springs Canyon. The company included Owen and Josephine Simpson, Shelley and Florence Ivy Jr., George Reynolds, Raymond E. Marquis, and Lawrence McKeon. The company purchased the Farnlund and Weatherhead ranches, acquiring land on both sides of Warm Springs Road from the head of the canyon west to near where the Cimino property is now. There were no buildings on the property except the Farnlund potato cellar.

In his oral history, Owen Simpson's son Jack described his work after returning from the war teaching skiing for Sun Valley, dealing cards at the Sawtooth Club, and later working at the Warm Springs Ranch. There is a rumor that Owen Simpson had won the property that became Warm Springs Ranch in a poker game. However, he won $12,000 from a New York gambler, which he used as his investment in the company that bought the land, according to Simpson family members.

Idaho's constitution said there could be "no lottery or gift enterprise" in the state, but there was no law saying gambling was illegal, so it was tolerated. Ketchum had gambling clubs and Hailey had prostitution. Casino-type gambling was popular in the 1930s and 1940s, and the clubs offered blackjack, craps, and wheel games. Clubs did not have regular poker games, but poker was played. Jack Simpson said Ketchum was wide open when he returned in 1946, and there were five or six bars offering gambling that were open all night:

> *In fact, things didn't really pick up in Ketchum until about 11:30 PM or 12:00 a.m. when things shut down in Sun Valley. All the guests and employees at Sun Valley would come to town at Ketchum and stay there until nearly daylight. It was a tough sort of group but also involved movie stars. . . . Ketchum was full of movie stars, movie producers and other various assorted important people. At that time, no body paid attention to the movie crowd and they were treated just like everyone else.*

A local, Pappy Haines, was known for riding his horse into the Alpine Club, circling around before he left. Nobody thought much about that kind of behavior in those days. Jack Simpson said every nightclub on Ketchum's Main Street had to take care of its own problems, especially when the Rodeo Cowboys Association (RCA) rodeo came to town. After rodeoing during the day, the cowboys partied at night. When they weren't riding bucking horses or bulldogging, they fought. One night, Simpson witnessed a big fight involving RCA cowboys at the casino, which to him "looked like a real movie fight scene but better."

Owen Simpson was concerned gambling might not be allowed to continue in Ketchum, so he planned to build a casino complex in Warm Springs Canyon with an adjoining airport. In 1946 or 1947, Simpson's group built the Devil's Bedstead as a gambling facility on the north side of Warm Springs Road between what is now East and West Canyon Boulevards. It had 50 rooms and looked like the Challenger Inn, but was never finished. When one of the investors died, the corporation was dissolved. Jack Simpson said the land was divided between the remaining owners, with his father getting property between Warm Springs Road and Warm Springs Creek that became Warm Springs Ranch, and other investors getting property north of the road. Walsworth, in her report, said ownership of all the land reverted to Owen Simpson and his wife.

In 1947, Idaho law changed to permit the sale of liquor by the drink, but on-site gambling was outlawed. In August 1947, the Blaine County sheriff raided the Sawtooth Club and arrested Owen Simpson for allowing illegal gambling and selling liquor without state stamps. Simpson continued offering gambling at the Sawtooth and sponsored poker games at Guyer Hot Springs, and Jack said they "were in court and jail a lot" between 1948 and 1950.

Devil's Bedstead was never finished after gambling was outlawed, and approval for the airport was denied because of dangerous crosswinds. Owen Simpson became one of the first developers in Warm Springs Canyon and subdivided land around what became Warm Springs Ranch. He was involved in the Sun Valley Subdivision, the Sun Valley First Subdivision, the Owen Simpson Subdivision, and the Canyon Run and Sunny Bend Subdivision, according to Walsworth. After sitting unfinished for around 20 years, Devil's Bedstead was purchased by Clyde Hawkes, who moved the building onto Ketchum's Main Street, where it operated as a restaurant and office/business complex until being torn down in 2004.

As gambling ended, slot machines appeared. "From 1947 to 1953, one-armed bandits could be found on the outskirts of Idaho Falls, Pocatello and Garden City," according to the *Coeur d'Alene Press*. There were slot machines in the clubs, at Sun Valley, even in grocery and drugstores. The Cities of Sun Valley and Ketchum incorporated in 1947 when Idaho law gave incorporated areas local option for the sale of liquor by the drink. The City of Sun Valley's board consisted of all Sun Valley employees, with Ed Seagle, assistant to the manager and chief engineer, serving as chairman. There were no local taxes, and expenses were paid with slot machine taxes and revenue.

Seagle said there were slot machines in the lobbies of the Sun Valley Lodge, the Challenger Inn had 14, and there were small portable slot machines guests could take to their rooms. The resort paid a license fee of $125 per machine to the state, and $25 to the county. Sun Valley had a Games Department that collected revenue from the bowling alley, pool tables, and slot machines, which often totaled around $41,000 a month. The accounting department in Omaha did not know about the gambling and asked how it was possible to earn that much money from bowling and pool. Pat Rogers would only reply, "It's possible."

The Idaho legislature made slot machines illegal in 1953, and owners faced the option of "destroying them or shipping them to Nevada," according to Jack Simpson. Many club employees went to Las Vegas. The Christiania closed, and George Kneeland, Don Siegle, and Chuck Atkinson bought the property, opening Atkinsons grocery store.

In the early 1950s, Owen Simpson developed the 78-acre Warm Springs Ranch south of Warm Springs Road, building a restaurant, rodeo grounds, a golf course, and tennis courts. The restaurant was built in 1951, and the Warm Springs Ranch Inn opened in August 1953 with fish ponds surrounding its deck. It was run by Owen and his wife, Josephine, until 1960, and by Jack and Mary Lou Simpson until 1975. The restaurant, a favorite place to eat for decades, operated until 2004. Owen built rodeo grounds on the ranch, getting equipment such as chutes and gates from Sun Valley. Rodeos were held there every weekend for several years beginning in 1952, big events bringing crowds from all over. Jack Simpson participated as the "Sun Valley Cowboy." He raised horses on the ranch that could be rented and had a landing strip in Warm Springs Canyon north of the road that he used for his outfitting and guiding business.

The restaurant initially did not have a liquor license. However, Idaho law changed to authorize liquor licenses outside city limits if a facility was associated with a golf course or on a lake. Simpson's fish ponds did not qualify as a lake, so he took a bulldozer and graded the farmland on his property, creating the Warm Springs golf course, and got his liquor license. The course opened in 1960. The ranch later became a game reserve and an elk feeding station. The Warm Springs Tennis Club opened in 1973 on the former rodeo grounds.

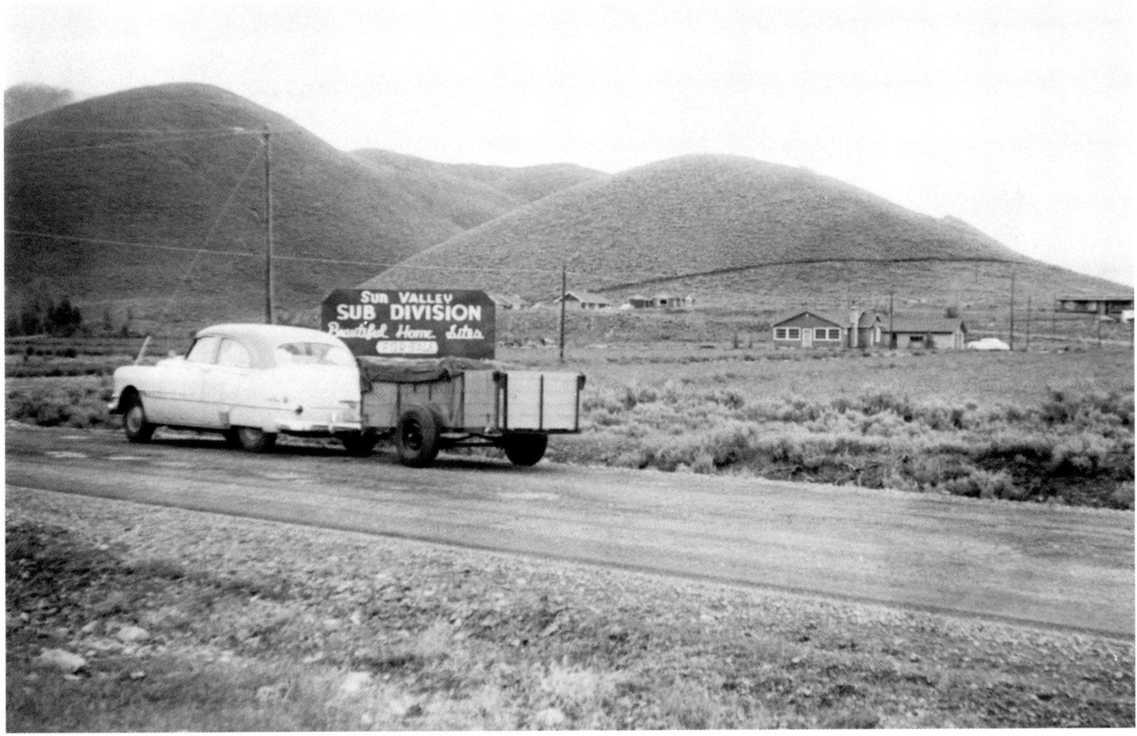

Sales sign for Sun Valley Subdivision in Warm Springs Canyon, late 1940s.

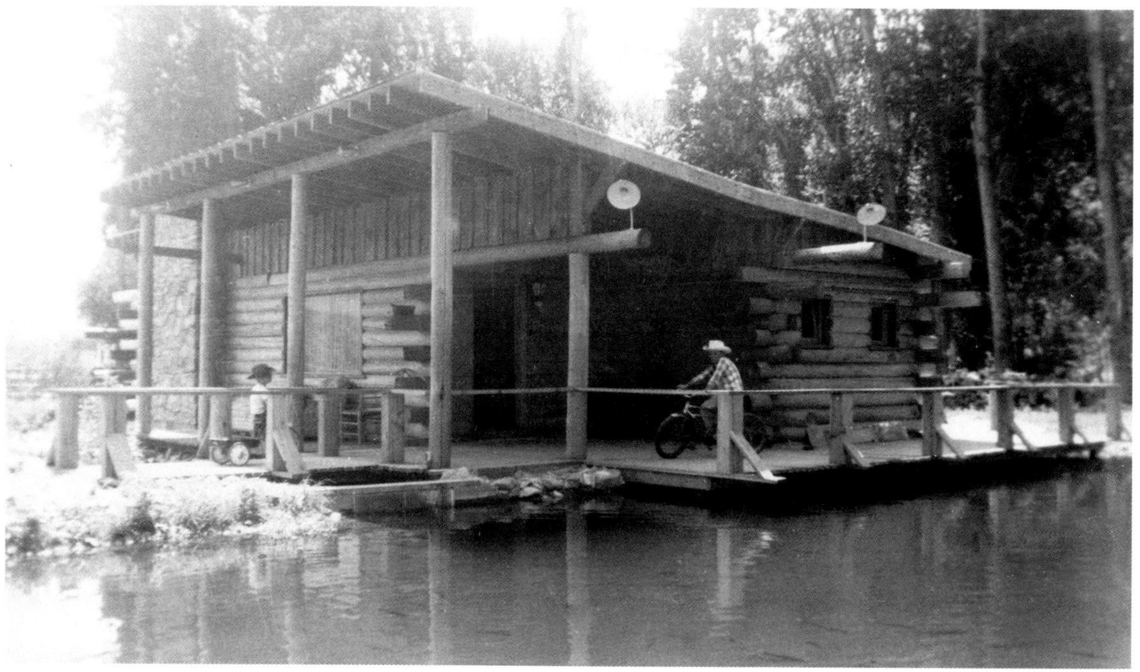

The Warm Springs restaurant surrounded by fish ponds, opened in 1953.

The Simpson Family Trust sold the ranch in 2000 to Sun Valley Ventures LLC, which planned a major development. Since then, the property has changed hands several times and has been the subject of multiple lawsuits. A major redevelopment of the site was halted by the recession of 2008, and the property remains undeveloped, used as the popular Warm Springs dog park. Extensive residential development took place elsewhere in Warm Springs after 1980.[82]

31

1953–1964

Harriman Cup Attracts Top Racers; Hemingway Commits Suicide

During the 1950s and 1960s, Union Pacific cut its subsidy to Sun Valley, and its physical plant deteriorated. However, the Harriman Cup continued to attract many of the world's best racers, some of whom were hired by its ski school, helping to keep Sun Valley's international reputation alive. The race continued until 1965, one year after the Janss Company bought the resort. Details of the races appear in annual Sun Valley Ski Club reports and in Dick Dorworth's book *High Times at the Harriman*. Improvements made at the resort are discussed in *History of Sun Valley* by Ken Longe.

1953–1956

Dick Dorworth arrived in Sun Valley in 1954 to race in the American Legion Western States Championships and described the unique culture of the resort in "Sun Valley's Ski Racing Roots":

> *Baldy was the finest ski mountain I'd ever seen and immediately became (and remains) my favorite place to ride lifts up and ski back down. But, for a 14-year-old boy whose passion was skiing, there was nothing—nothing—to match the sight of Stein Eriksen*

> *skiing a run called Canyon. In 1953, few people could beat him in slalom or giant slalom, and only then on some days. But no one has ever skied quite like Stein. . . . Some of the other skiers we studied, emulated, idolized and made friends with included Christian Pravda, Jack Reddish and Dick Buek, all of them working as instructors or patrolmen for Sun Valley in 1953. Can anyone today even imagine Lindsey Vonn, Ted Ligety, Bode Miller, Mikaela Shiffrin or Marcel Hirscher working for Sun Valley, living in the dorms, eating in the employee cafeteria, training and racing on the side and being a normal part of the working culture of Sun Valley?*

Averell Harriman attended the 1953 Harriman Cup for the first time in several years. "The tournament's founder displayed a keen interest in all phases of competition, and his presence did much to make the meet one of the finest in our history." Dorworth said the 1953 race was

> *a race of superlatives. The fastest. The most dangerous. The worst weather. The most injuries. The toughest field. The downhill was run in a driving blizzard with fewer gates than usual on Exhibition. . . . There were many falls and serious injuries. It might have been worse. According to Nelson Bennett, gates were placed on Rock Garden for the first time because Pravda was seen practicing a line through some trees that was very fast. Says Bennett, "We felt Pravda could have made it, but we were concerned about some of the others, so we put gates in to slow the racers."*

The men's downhill was

> *an exacting Ridge-Rock Garden-Exhibition course . . . probably the fastest course of any Harriman Cup downhill. The racers put on one of the most spectacular performances ever seen on our slopes, many of the runners literally flying into space as they roared out of the big schuss on Exhibition and bounced over the bumps in the transition above the "bottleneck" into River Run.*

The run down Exhibition produced "devastating crashes, including a leg-breaking, career-ender for Toni Matt." Austria's Christian Pravda was the fastest, taking "an absolutely perfect line down Exhibition's awesome face." Dick Buek was second, almost catching Pravda. Dartmouth's Ralph Miller, North American and national downhill champion, finished third, and Othmar Schneider, Olympic slalom gold medalist, was fourth. Andrea Mead Lawrence won the women's downhill, "running in her own inimitable style," narrowly beating Jannette Burr down a mile-long route through Canyon and lower Exhibition, according to the *Sun Valley Ski Club Annual*.

At the slalom races on Ruud Mountain, Sally Neidlinger, the national downhill champion, won the women's event, with Lawrence finishing second. Lawrence won the combined, becoming the first woman to win the Harriman Cup twice. Stein Eriksen, with two perfect runs, took the men's slalom after Pravda fell, followed by Schneider and Jack Reddish. Christian Pravda won the combined and the Harriman Cup.

For 1954, additional chairs were added and more powerful motors installed on Baldy's single chairlifts, increasing their capacity. Lift No. 1 received 27 new chairs, increasing its capacity from 300 to 400 people per hour. On lift No. 2, a new 125-horsepower motor replaced the old 50-horsepower motor and 53 chairs were added, increasing its capacity from 300 to 580 riders per hour. Lift No. 5, the old Proctor chair running from the Roundhouse to the summit, received a 50-horsepower motor. Waiting in lines would be "virtually eliminated," according to Longe, meaning "more skiing for everyone." A new run was added on Baldy called Question Mark. It began at the top of Rock Garden, went across the cat track leading to the Roundhouse, and entered Canyon, "adding one more race course of Olympic caliber to the network of runs." A new bridge was constructed over Warm Springs Creek, straightening and extending the run.

In the 1954 Harriman Cup, Jack Reddish won the downhill and many expected him to win the combined as he had in 1948. However, he had bad luck in the slalom, which was won by Dartmouth's Tom Corcoran, who won the Harriman Cup. Jannette Burr swept the women's events and won the women's Harriman Cup. Burr won a bronze medal at the 1954 world championships in giant slalom and finished second in the combined at the Alberg-Kandahar and Garmish Classic tournaments. She was inducted into the U.S. Ski and Snowboard Hall of Fame in 1970.

Sun Valley's long-time publicist Steve Hannagan died in 1953, and the relationship between the resort and his New York firm was lost, according to Dorice Taylor. For a long time, Union Pacific's publicity department lobbied the board of directors to take over Sun Valley's publicity, and they won the battle in 1955. Taylor became the director of the Sun Valley publicity office that year, reporting to her railroad bosses in Omaha.

One of Taylor's first accomplishments was to secure the filming of *Bus Stop* at Sun Valley, produced by 20th Century Fox and starring Marilyn Monroe. The North Fork

Store, five miles north of Ketchum, was used as Gracie's Diner, where key scenes took place when a bus was marooned in a snowstorm. Monroe disrupted filming by being perennially late. Wanting to capitalize on the movie, Taylor had pictures taken of Monroe and the "little adopted Navajo Indian son" of the owners of the store. The photographs became a hit all over the world, but except for the dateline, did not mention Sun Valley, "and it turned out to be costly non-publicity" for her employer.

Taylor said changes to Sun Valley's operations imposed by Union Pacific were becoming apparent, including a widespread hotel practice of "overbooking." To keep a hotel at a desired occupancy rate to operate profitably, more rooms than were available were booked on the assumption that a certain number of guests would cancel their reservations. Union Pacific was pressuring Winston McCrea to make the resort's hotels pay their own way, "and he was ready to gamble," Taylor said. The practice upset long-time guests and backfired. It would never have happened under Pat Rogers, Taylor said, "who was more concerned that every guest found the exact room he wanted ready and waiting on arrival than that a few extra dollars went into the coffers."

European skiers dominated the 1955 Harriman Cup, with Martin Strelz and Madeleine Berthod winning the downhill events. The slalom races were won by Martin Julen and Thea Hochleitner. Austria's Anderl Molterer won the men's combined, and Switzerland's Madeleine Berthod the women's.

Sigi Engl's Sun Valley Ski School had 50 instructors in 1956, who gave over 30,000 lessons to beginners on Dollar and experts on Baldy. In fall 1955, the ice rink was enlarged to 16,200 square feet, making it Olympic size and the largest year-round outdoor ice rink in the world.

The 1956 Harriman Cup was described in lyrical terms in the *Sun Valley Ski Club Annual* for 1956. The event's prestige was such that racers "regard a Harriman invitation as the ultimate honor in skiing. And to win the big cup—well, that is to take a place in the sun."

> *The Harriman stands for even more than tops in ski racing. There is something almost magical about this famed classic—some intangible quality which sets it above, and apart from, all other ski competitions. . . . It is possible the answer lies in the fact that the Harriman brings to skiing a touch of grace and elegance not generally associated with sports events. In these days when top-level athletics are subject to so much turmoil, the Harriman goes serenely along, expressing a quiet but unmistakable dignity.*

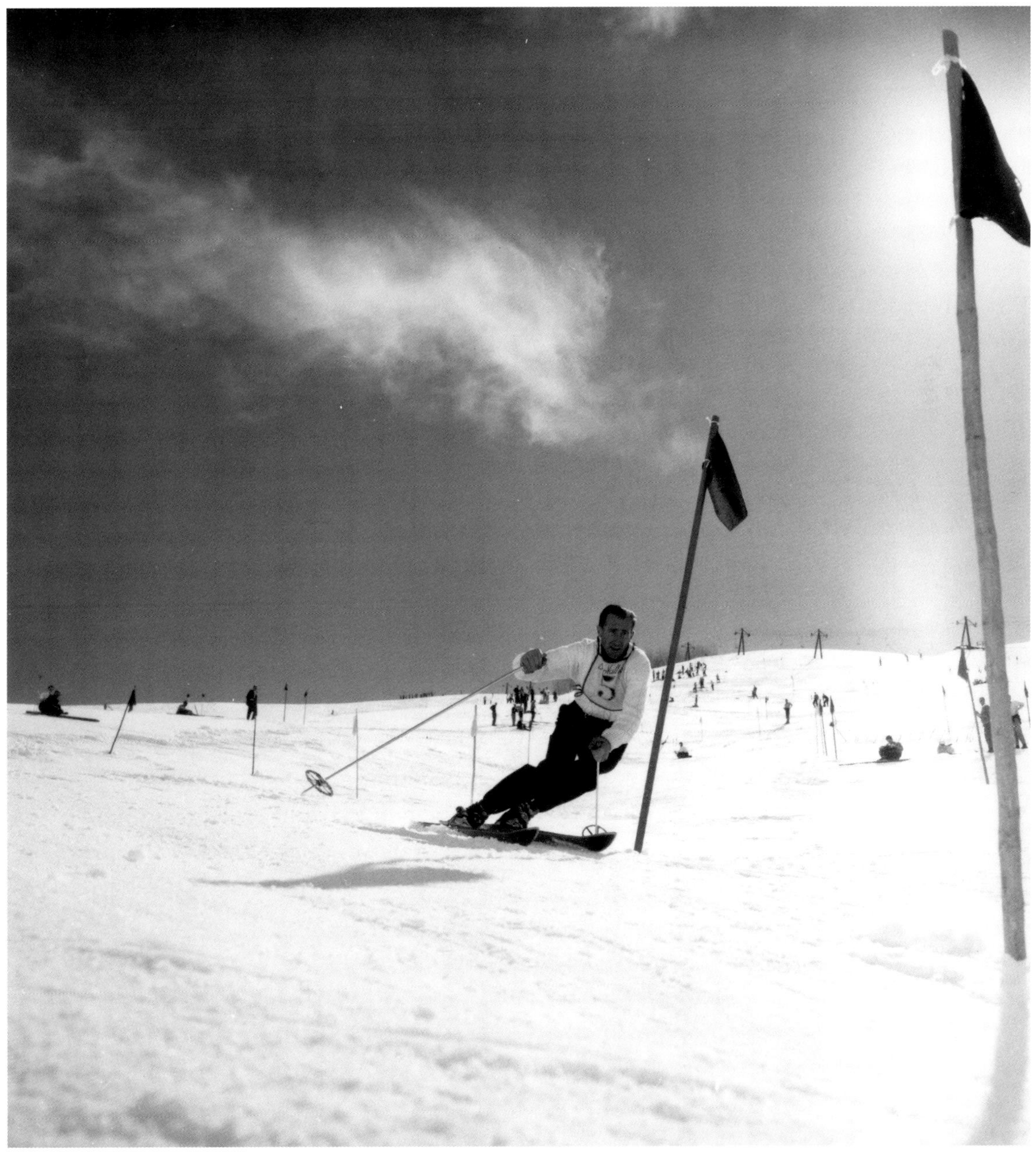

Christian Pravda taught at Sun Valley for many years and was the only person to win three Harriman Cups besides Dick Durrance.

A problem emerged over conflicts during the Olympic and FIS championship years when top U.S. skiers traveled to Europe and Europeans stayed home. This led to a decision to hold the Harriman Cup on alternating years, skipping the years of the Olympic and FIS competitions.

The 1956 Harriman Cup lacked balance, since Christian Pravda was the prohibitive favorite. Pravda was the world's downhill champion and one of the finest alpine skiers of the day. He was expected to be challenged by Tom Corcoran, who made a clean sweep at Aspen's Roch Cup, and Jack Reddish, member of the 1956 Olympic team, both former Harriman Cup winners. However, 1956 was the Pravda show.

The downhill saw 18 men start but only 11 finish. Pravda won, beating Corcoran by seven seconds, and Jack Reddish, skiing for the Sun Valley Ski Club, was third, according to the *Sun Valley Ski Club Annual* for 1956.

> *Christian ran the entire course in masterful fashion, whizzing down the schusses as if guided by a plumb line and setting himself up to reach the control gate so as to reduce drift to an absolute minimum. . . . So perfect was the skier's line that it seemed he, too, was unaware of these obstacles and was simply racing down the slope in a track of his own choosing. Here was downhill skiing in its ultimate form, serving once more to confirm the fact that Christian Pravda is one of the truly great stars of all time.*

The women's downhill started at the Roundhouse, went down Olympic, and ended at the men's finish, a mile in length with a vertical drop of 1,500 feet. Sally Deaver of the Aspen Ski Club won by nearly five seconds, beating Sun Valley's Jannette Burr.

The men's slalom course on Ruud had 48 gates and the women's 35. Pravda, "whose slalom running ranks only a hairbreadth behind his downhill ability," won by seven seconds, followed by Corcoran and Reddish. Sally Deaver won the women's slalom. Pravda won the men's combined, and "plucky" Sally Deaver won the women's combined after sweeping all the races, just as she had in Aspen's Roch Cup. Jack Reddish came out of retirement to finish third in the slalom, "joining Burr in earning his fifth top-three Harriman placings and a diamond Harriman pin," according to Dorworth.[83]

1957–1964

For 1957, Nelson Bennett's trail crew "widened into a boulevard" the transition from Rock Garden onto the Roundhouse slope that had "sent many racers . . . into the tules," according to the *Annual*. The dip in the first part of the cat walk from College to the Roundhouse was eliminated. The 1957 Harriman Cup "had one of the most exciting fields of foreign racers in the history of the race," with the best alpine competitors in the world from Austria, Switzerland, Italy, and France competing along with the American Buddy Werner. According to the *Annual*, two words describe the event: "Toni Sailer."

> *Ever since his triple win in the '56 Olympics the famed Austrian had become the Ben Hogan, the Lew Hoad and the Mickey Mantle of skiing, all rolled into one. . . . Even among the hard core of super skiers this personable young man from Kitzbuhel constituted the color, the glamour, the focal point which set this tournament apart.*

The two-mile downhill course, with 2,500 feet of vertical drop, had 11 control gates, six in Rock Garden and five on Exhibition. Buddy Werner took a spectacular fall on Exhibition after running the top portion in beautiful style. "A big bump tossed him into a violent egg-beater, thrashing him around for another 40 yards or so." He finished but was out of contention. Sailer won the downhill in

> *characteristic style, seemingly relaxed and out for a little fun skiing . . . he had every foot of the course firmly photographed in his mind. . . . His descent of Exhibition was one that will always be remembered at Sun Valley—not simply because of the precise nature of his line but even more because of the masterful control displayed throughout. . . . He had the mogles* [sic] *working for him, floating over them rather than fighting the way through. . . . I doubt if I shall ever see a finer downhill run than that displayed by this great champion.*

Christian Pravda was eight seconds behind. "That a skier—even a Sailer—could pick up eight seconds on Christian Pravda in a two-and-one-half-minute downhill is something no one could ever believe if he had not actually seen it accomplished," the *Annual* wrote. Switzerland's Roger Staub was second.

"Toni Sailer took all events in the men's race and made history by his superb form and speed." In the slalom, Sailer had "two magnificent runs. . . . Toni's slalom is truly something to watch—powerful and driving." Pravda and Kitzbuhel's Anderl Molterer tied for second, and Buddy Werner was fourth, finishing "more than ten seconds behind the leaders." Switzerland's Freida Dancer won the women's downhill, Inger Bjørnbakken won the slalom, and Thérèse Le Duc from France won the women's combined.

For winter 1958, a Riblet-designed double chairlift was installed on Bald Mountain from the Roundhouse to the summit, replacing lift No. 5 (the original Proctor single chairlift). It was 4,300 feet long with a vertical gain of 1,350 feet, with 125 chairs spaced 75 feet apart moving at 500 feet per minute and providing a capacity of 800 passengers per hour. It was "the last word in skier transportation. . . . Another advantage from the new line will be that of having company while in transit up the hill—a circumstance which cannot help but find favor with practically everyone," predicted the *Annual.* Lift No. 1 on River Run had a capacity of 320 skiers per hour, No. 2 up Exhibition and No. 3 to the summit carried 580 per hour, and No. 4 (Cold Springs) carried 300 per hour. Central Park was joined to the Canyon run to provide a new route down the mountain. A cat walk was built at the top of Baldy, giving easier access to the bowls.

There was no Harriman Cup in 1958, but Sun Valley sponsored a veterans' downhill and slalom championship that attracted 29 "seasoned campaigners ranging from 32 years of age to well into the 40s," according to the *Annual*, virtually all of whom had competed at Sun Valley before. Corey Engen won the veterans open after a battle with Seattle's Jack Nagel. Betty Amick from Seattle won the women's.

In 1958, Lucille Ball and Desi Arnaz came to Sun Valley, where they filmed an episode of *I Love Lucy* titled "Lucy Goes to Sun Valley." It includes a skiing scene showing Lucy and Fernando Lamas skiing on Baldy. Leif Odmark doubled for Lamas, and Jannette Burr Johnson doubled for Lucy.

Also in 1958, Ed Scott, an engineer and ski racer, designed the first tapered aluminum ski pole to replace traditional bamboo or steel poles and began producing them in Ketchum. His business became Scott Sports, a worldwide company that produces and sells a variety of sporting goods. In 1965, Bob Smith developed the first double-lens ski goggle to prevent fogging and founded Smith Sports Optics in Ketchum, which became one of the leading producers of ski goggles.

In 1959, a fabric canopy was installed over the skating rink that cut the sun's rays by 75 percent, making all-day use of the rink possible. A new 18-bed Sun Valley Municipal

Hospital opened behind the Challenger Inn, funded by a bond issue and contributions from local residents, matched by federal funds. A new ski hut for the top of Baldy was approved to replace the old hut. The Elkhorn run on Dollar Mountain was constructed.

The 1959 Harriman Cup was a contest between Christian Pravda and Bud Werner. Werner's bad luck continued when he took a line onto the top of Exhibition he couldn't hold and fell. Austria's Putzi Frandl won the women's downhill and Linda Meyers won the slalom, with Frandl winning the combined. Pravda became the second man to retire the Harriman Cup by sweeping all the races and winning his third combined title.

Dorice Taylor said Pravda was one of the "greatest skiers the world ever had." However, he thought he should be head of the Sun Valley Ski School, where he had been a long-time instructor, but "he didn't have enough brains."

In 1960, there was a special running of the Harriman Cup after the Olympics at Squaw Valley, and Olympic skiers made it "the most brilliant field to compete in a Harriman Cup," according to the *Annual*.

The 73-gate slalom race on Ruud Mountain was held first, where soft, wet snow presented problems and limited racers to one run. Twelve racers fell or were disqualified. Austrian racers finished first, second, and third. Mathias Leitner won, and only four seconds separated the first 12 finishers. The women's course had a shorter and easier descent, but only 11 of 24 starters finished. Austrians 16-year-old Traudl Hecher and Marianne Jahn finished first and second.

The downhill course on Baldy was in excellent shape after the ski patrol and ski school "worked feverishly to pack out the new snow." Sigi Engl "set another magnificent course embracing Ridge, Rock Garden, and Exhibition," with 12 gates, six on Rock Garden, one on Roundhouse Slope, and five on Exhibition, "permitting plenty of speed within the limits of safety." The course was shortened to eliminate a flat area on River Run, with the finish 100 yards up the hill opposite the outrun of Olympic. Switzerland's Willy Forrer won the men's downhill, edging France's Guy Périllat and Italy's Bruno Alberti. The surprise was that the highest Austrian finisher, Egon Zimmerman, was 16th. The women's downhill had 17 control gates and took "the time-tested Olympic route with the start at the Roundhouse and the finish line in the regular spot some 100 yards below the junction of Olympic and River." Austrian Putzi Frandl won the women's downhill for the second year in a row, followed by teammate Herlinda Beutlhauser.

Adrien Duvillard of France and Marianne Jahn of Austria won the men's and women's combined titles, and "for the first time in the history of the tournament neither champion could claim victory in at least one of the individual events." The highest U.S. racers finished 12th in the men's combined (Jim Barrier) and third in the women's (Beverly Anderson). Gretchen Fraser presented the awards at the banquet, attended by notables such as Lowell Thomas, Bill Janss, Kathleen Harriman Mortimer, and Dick Durrance.

Dorworth said the 1961 Harriman Cup was a "portent of things to come" for American skiing:

> *The 1961 Harriman cup will go down in history as the tournament in which youth manifested its right to compete on even terms with the elite of ski racing, as young American racers dominated the events. University of Colorado's Buddy Werner won the downhill running in his inimitable, wide-open style.*

However, Werner fell in the slalom on Ruud Mountain, which was won by 17-year-old Billy Kidd from Stowe. "The New England youngster is truly one of the coolest competitors ever seen on the local slopes," the *Annual* said. Seventeen-year-old Jimmie Heuga of the Lake Tahoe Ski Club won the combined, Kidd was second, and Werner was third. "The .35 FIS separating the top four finishers was far and away the tightest Harriman competition ever staged and attested to the balance of strength existing among the top-seeded entrants." Sixteen-year-old Barbara Ferries from Michigan, skiing for the Aspen Ski Club, won all the women's events.

In summer 1962, nine holes were added to the Sun Valley Golf Course, making a 6,227-yard par-71 course. Two Tucker snow-cats were purchased to groom the slopes and eliminate many of the moguls that had become a hazard to skiing.

No Harriman Cup was held in 1962. The 1963 event "not only attracted an outstanding field but was significant in that it represented only the third time in 21 tournaments that both the men's and women's winners managed clean sweeps," the *Annual* reported. Giant slalom competition was included for the first time. For Buddy Werner, the event was the culmination of a long and trying road where "perseverance finally triumphed." He first raced in Sun Valley in 1953. In 1959, he made his fourth appearance but fell twice in the downhill after a second place in the slalom. In 1961, he won the downhill but fell in the slalom and finished third in the combined.

Werner swept the downhill and slalom, winning the Harriman Cup after five tries, his last big win, according to Dorworth. Werner beat Switzerland's "sensational" Jos

Minsch in the downhill. According to the *Annual*, Werner was so far ahead after the first run of the slalom that his supporters told him to take an easy second run. He ignored them and took the title after another very fast run,

> *winning the cup the way he wanted to win it. . . . And so, after ten long years, Bud had his Harriman Cup. It would be difficult to conceive of a more deserved or more popular victory, since everyone had known for some time that Bud Werner's name rightfully belonged on the big bowl.*

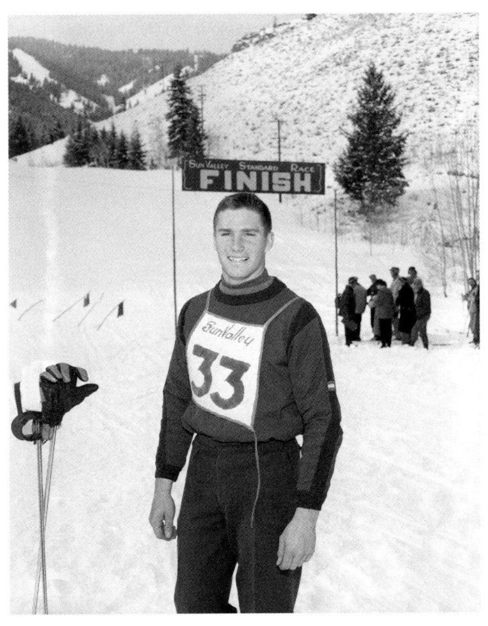

In 1963, Bud Werner finally won the Harriman Cup, sweeping the events, after racing in Sun Valley since 1953.

In the women's races, "it was a furious battle between Jean Saubert from Mammoth Mountain and Barbi Henneberger from Germany," but Saubert won all three races and was the combined champion. Eleanor Bennett from Mammoth Mountain was second, and Canada's Nancy Greene was third.

In 1964, the Saunderson Pro-Am was the featured race, since there was no Harriman Cup. Dorworth said the 1965 race was the last of the

> *true Harriman Cups competitions. Austrian superstar Karl Schranz and the French phenom Marielle Goitschel won that year. Schranz, among the best Austrian downhill racers in history, proclaimed the Harriman "the most difficult downhill in the U.S." That would be a fitting epitaph for one of America's great ski race traditions.*

Sadly, those traditions, like the Roch Cup, Snow Cup, Silver Dollar Derby, Silver Belt, and other races have all been abandoned, all casualties of the demands and schedules and requirements of the newer World Cup circuit, which has so far maintained its own traditions.[84]

THE COMMUNITY LIBRARY IS FORMED

In fall 1954, three Ketchum women, Elorna Seagle, Clara Spiegel, and Mary Ellen Moritz decided the area needed an organization to keep women occupied. Seagle was the wife of Ed Seagle, chief engineer of Sun Valley operations. Spiegel had been a regular visitor since January 1937 and lived in Ketchum since the early 1950s. Moritz was married to Dr. John Moritz, who came to Sun Valley in 1938.

The women decided to open a thrift shop using donated goods. They organized a group of 17 women, who famously contributed $1 apiece. They opened a thrift shop in an old miner's cabin rented for $5 a month, west of Main Street across from the old fire station on Washington Avenue near Fourth Street, which they fixed up themselves. They named it the Gold Mine. George Kneeland, a local lawyer whose wife was one of the 17, drew up documents forming the organization. Jay and Helen Fassett contributed $100.

The group then decided to build a Community Library for Ketchum, Sun Valley, and the Triumph Mine area in East Fork and formed the Community Library Association. They considered setting up a library district to fund a public library, and Idaho senator Frank Church offered to get money from Congress. They decided against it so they could remain in complete control without a lot of red tape and government interference, according to Elorna Seagle.

The group believed it would take five years to raise money to build the library. The community donated goods to the Gold Mine and others donated money and labor. Seagle said, "People cleaned out their attics. They cleaned out all sorts of things they had been saving for years . . . and donated it to us." To their surprise, they made $1,500 the first year.

The following year, the group determined they needed $25,000 to build a library. When library representatives met with Roland Harriman at Railroad Ranch, he said if the group could raise two thirds of the sum needed, he would donate the remaining third. When they raised their two thirds, they wrote Harriman and received a check for more than the remaining one third from the Marie Harriman Foundation.

Union Pacific donated a lot in Block 44 to the Library Association, a huge donation at a time when they did not have a lot of funds. The lot is where the Gold Mine is presently located on East Street. Ed Seagle arranged for a Union Pacific architect in Omaha to draw plans for the library building and had his workers construct it on their off time, along with other volunteer labor. One of Seagle's workers supervised the work and "everyone who knew how to do anything at all worked on it," according to Elorna Seagle. Florian Haemmerle did the painting with donated paint. The stove for the library and the grass seed for the landscaping were donated.

The library was built for $24,000, since very little was spent on labor. It received a tremendous number of books from the community, with some families donating their entire collections. A visitor from Michigan, Dr. Richard Light, was a friend of the Yale University librarian James Babcock, who donated 500 duplicate books from his library that formed the initial basis for the collection. The Mormon church let the library store books in its basement. Starting a children's library was one of the group's top priorities.

Jean Burr was the first Gold Mine manager, and funds from the store paid for library operations. The association has always been conservatively run. At one point, Mrs. John Scott gave the association IBM stock, but Elorna Seagle said in 1983, "We haven't had to use the IBM stock for anything and we haven't had to borrow money. We've never built a thing that wasn't paid for. We had the money to do it before we ever began it."

The Community Library quickly became the community's intellectual and cultural center. It outgrew the old building, and in 1976, a new one was built across the street on a city block between East Avenue and Walnut Avenue that was purchased for $85,000. The building has been improved and expanded over the years and has become one of the country's premier private libraries. In 2017, the library set out to raise $12 million to renovate the building and "reinvent" itself. This major project was completed in 2020 and will allow the library to expand its many services to the Wood River Valley.[85]

Ernest Hemingway Commits Suicide

Hemingway continued his writing in the 1950s, although he lived primarily in Cuba and did not return to the Wood River Valley until 1958. In 1950, he published *Across the River and into the Trees*. In 1952, he published *The Old Man and the Sea,* winning the Pulitzer Prize in 1953 and the Nobel Prize for literature in 1954. He also saw several of his works made into movies in this decade: *The Snows of Kilimanjaro* in 1952 with

Gregory Peck and Susan Hayward, *A Farewell to Arms* in 1957 with Rock Hudson and Jennifer Jones, *The Sun Also Rises* in 1957 with Tyrone Power and Ava Gardner, and *The Old Man and the Sea* in 1958 with Spencer Tracy. Hemingway continued to work on material that would be published after his death, *A Moveable Feast*, *True at First Light*, *The Garden of Eden*, and *Islands in the Stream*.

After being away for most of the decade, Ernest and Mary returned to Idaho in 1958 as the Castro regime consolidated its hold on Cuba, while Ernest struggled to continue writing and battled depression. The Cuban government seized Hemingway's house and its contents, including 5,000 books. In October 1959, Ernest bought a house in Ketchum from Bob Topping. The house was built using the same cement forms used on the Sun Valley Lodge, making the concrete house appear to be wood. It is on a bluff in the Warm Springs area on the west side of the Big Wood River, with views east over the river to the Pioneer and Boulder Mountains.

Journalist and writer Hunter S. Thompson captured the attraction of the Wood River Valley for Hemingway in his book *The Great Shark Hunt*:

> *In the end he came back to Ketchum, never ceasing to wonder why he hadn't been killed years earlier in the midst of violent action on some other part of the globe. Here, at least, he had mountains and a good river below his house; he could live among rugged, non political men and visit, when he chose to, with a few of his famous friends who still came up to Sun Valley. He could sit in The Tram or The Alpine or The Sawtooth Club and talk with men who felt the same way he did about life, even if they were not so articulate. In this congenial atmosphere he felt he could get away from the pressures of a world gone mad and "write truly" about life as he had in the past.*

Ernest Hemingway's suicide at age 61 in his house in Ketchum on July 2, 1961, has become part of Sun Valley's history. His death was front-page news in many countries. President Kennedy said Hemingway was one of America's greatest authors and "one of the great citizens of the world." According to his obituary in the *New York Times* of July 3, 1961, his wife, Mary, said he killed himself accidently while cleaning a shotgun. The Blaine County sheriff said the death "looks like an accident," and there "was no evidence of foul play," but said his head wound was "self-inflicted. . . . I couldn't say if it was accidental and I couldn't say it was suicide." Dr. Scott Earle, who responded to Hemingway's death, said there was a conflict between Mary and the coroner. Mary

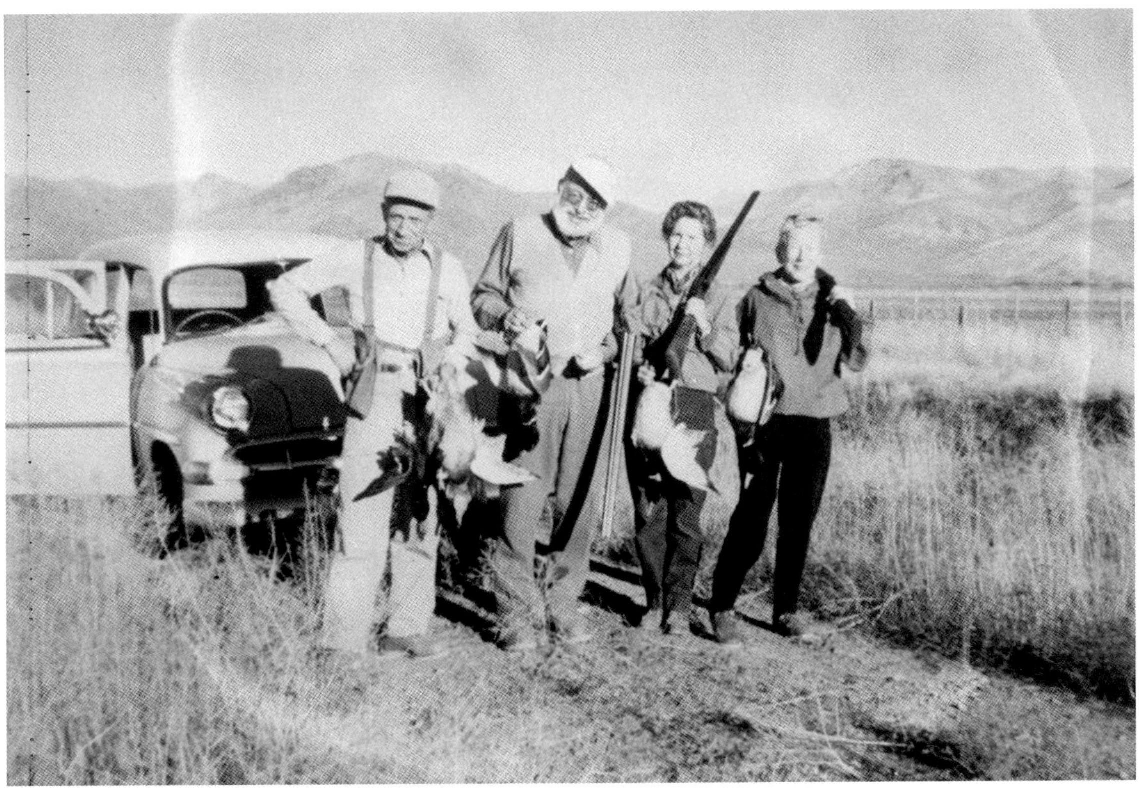

Ernest and Mary Hemingway with friends Lloyd and Tilly Arnold at Silver Creek. Lloyd Arnold was Sun Valley's photographer.

insisted it wasn't suicide. She wanted it called an accidental death and put pressure on the coroner to do so.

Hemingway's Ketchum friends saw him decline and fight depression for years before his death. He was taken to the Mayo Clinic several times, where he was treated for depression using electroshock therapy, and was sedated by his Ketchum doctor to keep him stable. Gary Cooper had died of cancer shortly before, although there is some question of whether Hemingway knew of his good friend's death. His long-time friend Tillie Arnold said before his last trip to the Mayo Clinic, Hemingway had complained about "the incurable disease he had." In 1939, Hemingway had told Arnold there were three circumstances when a person was justified in taking his own life—one was an incurable disease. He said, "There is no other way out for me. I am not going back to Rochester [Minnesota] where they will lock me up. I can't live like that. I am not going." Hemingway's Ketchum physician, Dr. George Saviers, said Hemingway told him when he couldn't write, his life didn't mean anything. He said, "It won't come anymore," with tears streaming down his face. Saviers took him to the Mayo Clinic one more time when Hemingway seemed to be looking for ways to kill himself.

Several friends described how Hemingway acted shortly before his death. Chuck Atkinson was with him the day before his death, and he "seemed to be in good spirits." Atkinson had the shotgun used by Hemingway to kill himself cut into pieces, which he buried in a secret place, not wanting it to become a macabre collector's piece. It was an English-made Boss 12-gauge shotgun he had bought at Abercrombie & Fitch to shoot pheasants. Clara Spiegel was a friend of Hemingway's for many years, and his death was a shock to her. She frequently socialized with him, and they watched Friday Night Fights on TV together since they both loved boxing. Shortly before Hemingway's death, he asked Clara to dinner at his house the following Sunday. He had recently returned from the Mayo Clinic, bringing his trainer with him, and said they were starting a training program on Monday. He would not have any social activities until he was finished, when he was going back to work, so he wanted to see her on Sunday. He killed himself on Saturday.

Ernest's son Patrick and Tillie Arnold were upset at Mary Hemingway, who left Ernest's guns unlocked at their house knowing he had tried to kill himself before with his shotgun. Tillie was not angry at Ernest:

> *I truly felt that for Papa it was a relief. He could not be the man he wanted to be, and he did not want to be a mental cripple. In his mind he had a disease that was incurable and he had no other way out. As I told him to his face, I did not blame him for doing what he did.*

Others watched Hemingway battle depression, ill health, and an inability to write for a long time. For years, heavy drinking combined with multiple head injuries caused him to suffer headaches, weight problems, and diabetes. He complained about his inability to write and became paranoid, saying the FBI was monitoring his movements. His father, brother, and sister all killed themselves, and his daughter Margaux later committed suicide. Some believe Hemingway's depression was the result of multiple head traumas, similar to football players suffering from concussions.

One forensic psychiatrist believes "Hemingway's depression and psychosis were a textbook case of chronic traumatic encephalopathy (CTE), the brain disease caused by repeated blows to the head."

A.E. Hotchner, Hemingway's long-time collaborator, suggested another contributing factor that he previously dismissed as a paranoid delusion. Hemingway was aware the FBI had him under surveillance for a long time, as directed by J. Edgar Hoover, who was suspicious of his links with Cuba. Writing in the *New York Times* on the 50th anniversary of Hemingway's death, July 1, 2011, Hotchner said he believed FBI surveillance "substantially contributed to his anguish and his suicide," and he "regretfully misjudged" his friend's fear of them. Hotchner described a visit with

Hemingway house in Ketchum, purchased in 1959, where he lived until his death in 1961.

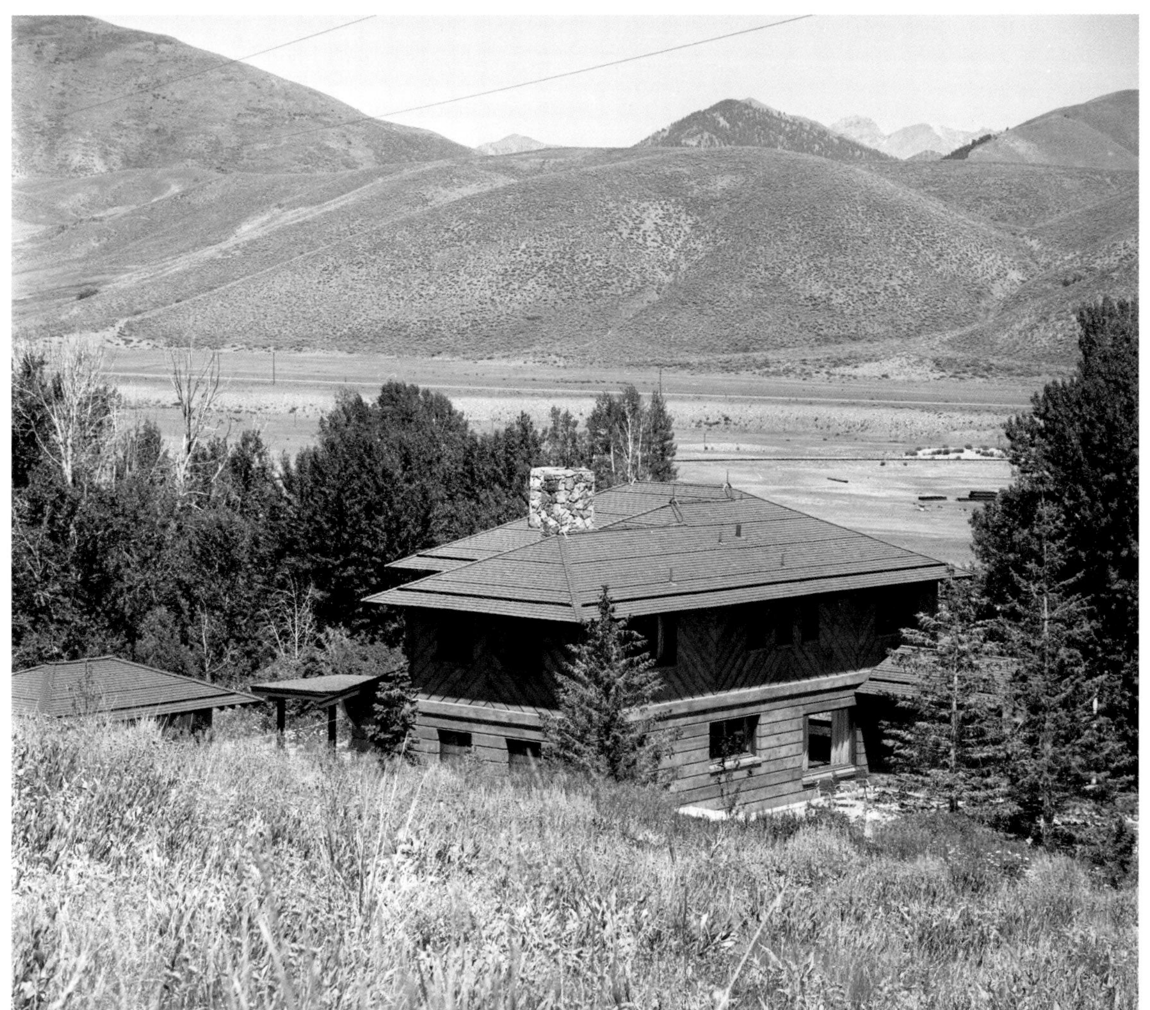

Hemingway in Idaho in November 1961. Hemingway and his friend Duke MacMullen picked Hotchner up in Shoshone in Duke's car, hurrying to leave. When asked why the hurry, Hemingway said, "The Feds. . . . They tailed us all the way." When asked why the FBI was pursuing him, he said, "It's the worst hell. . . . They've bugged everything. That's why we're using Duke's car. Mine's bugged. Everything's bugged. Can't use the phone. Mail intercepted." When they got to Ketchum, Hemingway told Duke to pull over and cut his lights. He pointed to two men working in a bank, saying they were "Auditors. The FBI's got them going over my account."

In the 1980s, Hemingway's FBI file was made public, showing the agency's long-term interest in him, which continued until he entered the Mayo Clinic in 1960. The file convinced Hotchner that he should have taken Hemingway's complaints more seriously, and he failed to consider the impact such surveillance could have had on a man entering a period of mental illness.

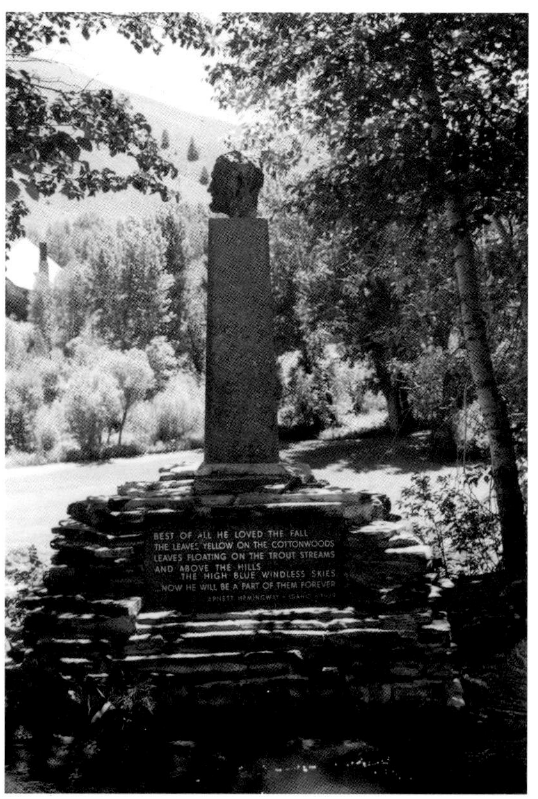

Hemingway memorial on Trail Creek, east of Sun Valley.

At the end of her book, Tillie Arnold relates a discussion she had with Dr. George Saviers, Hemingway's physician, after Ernest was dead. When he was in Idaho, Hemingway was a "kind, humble, generous, playful, mischievous, loyal, polite gentleman." His friend and hunting companion, Bud Purdy, said Hemingway wasn't a macho guy. "He was shy, kind of. He wouldn't do anything that he felt offended anyone." Yet after his death, he was portrayed as a "liar, braggart, back-stabber, immodest philanderer." Saviers said Hemingway was a complex man who never let people get close enough to really know him. However, they concluded his drinking was likely the source of the Hemingway they did not know. His long-time friend Forest "Duke" MacMullen said, "I think booze is the only way to account for Papa's bad behavior." He was relaxed in Idaho, made friends and did not want to jeopardize those friendships. They concluded there was an Idaho Hemingway and another Hemingway who was not like him, inspiring the title of Arnold's book *The Idaho Hemingway*.

Hemingway's legacy lives on in Sun Valley. He is buried in a simple grave in the Ketchum cemetery with a view of the surrounding mountains. The Community Library administers the Hemingway house and holds an annual Hemingway festival in the fall, bringing in academics to discuss his work. There is a simple Hemingway memorial in a grove of trees above Trail Creek east of Sun Valley. It contains part of a eulogy Hemingway wrote for his friend Gene Van Guilder, who was killed in a hunting accident in 1940, which expressed Hemingway's feelings for the area:

> *Best of all he loved the fall.*
> *The leaves yellow on the cottonwoods,*
> *Leaves floating on the trout streams,*
> *And above the hills*
> *The high blue windless skies.*
> *Now he will be a part of them forever.*

In 2015, a portion of the Sawtooth National Recreation Area north of Ketchum was designated a wilderness area and named the Hemingway-Boulders Wilderness Area as a tribute to the man who is so identified with Sun Valley.[86]

Part Seven

SUN VALLEY AFTER UNION PACIFIC

32

1964

Continued Decline of Passenger Travel Leads to Sun Valley's Sale to Janss Company

Trains were the lifeblood of the Wood River Valley from its earliest development to Sun Valley's opening in 1936. However, by 1951, train service from Shoshone to Ketchum was reduced to three days a week, providing mixed freight and passenger service partially to service Sun Valley's needs. Sun Valley was heated by coal-fired boilers with coal brought in by train, and the resort did not have its own laundry service, so its dirty laundry was sent by train to Ogden or Omaha, requiring three trains a week. By 1959, the number of train stops between Shoshone and Ketchum had been reduced from 12 to six, as the area's economy changed.

Ever since the end of World War II, passenger traffic had been on a steep downward slide. In 1946, passenger income dropped 33 percent due to the loss of military traffic. By 1949, it dropped another 61 percent. Between 1953 and 1961, it fell an average of 4 percent a year and took a 9 percent drop in 1963. According to Maury Klein, as rail passenger traffic continued to decline, "the less sense Sun Valley made for Union Pacific." Union Pacific no longer needed heavily subsidized destination resorts since the high profile they gave was no longer justified. U.P. president Stoddard "didn't give a damn about passenger service." He liked Sun Valley, but didn't want to spend money on it.

> *Stoddard's zeal to cut the service wherever possible had gained ground. Increasingly, passenger earnings were being sustained by mail and express income. . . . The passenger business was dead and only awaited a decent burial.*[87]

Janss Company Buys Sun Valley

In 1963, Union Pacific hired the Janss Company to analyze Sun Valley to determine its potential and calculate the cost to make it competitive. The Janss Company was a family-owned real estate development firm that had done large developments in Southern California, including Westwood and Thousand Oaks. One of the owners, Bill Janss, had a long-time association with Sun Valley. He competed in Harriman Cup races in 1940 and 1942, and was selected for the 1940 U.S. Olympic ski team before the games were cancelled.

The Janss Company's report, "The World of Sun Valley—A Development Program," contained the outlines of a physical and economic program and discussed the concept of the overall environment of Sun Valley:

> *Sun Valley today combines a unique heritage and a unique potential. Its identification with Union Pacific Railroad provides a natural theme for the development program—a theme that carries the romance and excitement of the railroad into the setting of a great resort area.*

The company proposed upgrading and increasing the Sun Valley Center and Village, hospital, and Bald Mountain and Dollar lifts, adding 18 holes to the golf course, and developing areas around Sun Valley owned by the railroad. This would cost at least $5 million, although there was significant potential revenue from developing land around the resort. However, according to Van Gordon Sauter, "the Janss group found Sun Valley a muddle. The railroad had no concept for enhancing the resort or mountain; developing condos; expanding recreational opportunities, instituting cost accounting and controls."

Union Pacific initially considered forming a joint venture to develop Sun Valley land, the Sun Valley Development Company, with the Janss Company owning 51 percent and Union Pacific 49 percent. Victor Palmieri, president of the Janss Company, described the proposal to A.E. Stoddard on December 27, 1963:

> *In the first phase, Sun Valley Development Company would undertake a series of development activities for which there appears to be an immediate need. These would include construction and operation of a new hotel of 200 to 300 rooms, development of a custom lot subdivision and development of a cooperative condominium cottage*

> *project. In addition, the new company would have responsibility for formulating (1) a master plan of development for the Valley, including all commercial and residential features, and (2) an operations program for all the resort elements built around a unified merchandising concept and a streamlined method of operations.*

In the second phase, the new company would purchase Sun Valley from Union Pacific and assume responsibility for all aspects of the operation. Union Pacific would provide sufficient working capital to begin the first phase, "assuming that the lands to be developed and sold could be bought from Union Pacific on favorable terms."

In a letter to Stoddard dated January 6, 1964, Union Pacific lawyers identified several problems with the proposed joint venture. Union Pacific considered its ownership and operation of Sun Valley to fall within its general corporate powers of railroad purposes, "on the theory that it encouraged passenger traffic," and there was a question whether the railroad had the corporate power to engage in the new venture. In addition, the U.S. government owned mineral rights in many of Sun Valley's lands. The railroad only owned surface rights, and those lands remained subject to general prospecting and mineral development by the public. They would not be suitable for residential or commercial development "particularly in the area of the Lodge and along Trail Creek Road, where such commercial or residential development would be most likely to be located."

Union Pacific decided it did not want to invest the money required to restore Sun Valley, did not want to get into land development, and decided to sell the resort to the Janss Company.

Roland Harriman wrote Averell on August 6, 1964, discussing Union Pacific's plans to sell Sun Valley. Sun Valley's physical plant, he said, had not been well maintained:

> *It will obviously take a lot of money and the direction of a lot of top management to put Sun Valley on a break-even basis in the future—money and management which probably can be more profitably diverted in another direction. Under all these circumstances, we believe it is wise to dispose of Sun Valley if our prospective purchaser is prepared to pay us in cash which he has indicated he is willing to do.*

Roland asked what Averell wanted to do with his cottage at Sun Valley. Averell decided to keep the cottage as family property and purchased Harriman Cottage on November 30, 1964.

According to Holland, Union Pacific's cost basis for Sun Valley was $4,986,929, depreciated to a book value of $745,765. Union Pacific accepted the Janss Company's offer of $3 million. Dorice Taylor said the price sounded outrageously cheap, but Union Pacific had written the property off as a tax loss, and "any additional profits would have been treated as capital gains." After the sale, a Union Pacific shareholder asked why the railroad sold Sun Valley when land values were rising so fast. Stoddard said while the resort had met its founders' dreams and increased passenger traffic, "with the increased use of highways and airlines as a means of getting to and from Sun Valley, our passenger revenues declined sharply. It was only natural that the Railroad would want to divest itself of a losing enterprise."

On October 6, 1964, Sun Valley general manager Winston McCrea informed the resort's employees the Janss Company would take over on December 1. At a press conference on October 7, 1964, the Janss Company announced its purchase of the Sun Valley Resort and its plans for the future. Janss was "programming a major development effort . . . to create a modern year-round resort which will retain the charm of the area." Preliminary plans called for improving existing facilities; building new accommodations, recreation, and restaurant facilities; and expanding the ski slopes and ski lifts. Existing Sun Valley staff would be retained and Winston McCrea would continue as general manager. Arthur Stoddard said, "The operation of Sun Valley has been rather remote from our business of running a railroad, but under Union Pacific ownership, it has become a world-famous resort. I am glad that it now can pass into hands which will continue to provide the development it deserves." Idaho governor Robert Smylie was gratified to learn of the substantial investment to be made by the Janss Company, which would "add substantially to the recreational potential of the entire area on a year-round basis." Sun Valley's sale was reported around the country.

Averell Harriman was surprised to hear of the Sun Valley sale, said he would never have done it, and was unhappy it was sold, but his brother had approved it. Harriman was critical of the decision and of the president of Union Pacific at the time, Stoddard. Harriman had not been actively involved with the railroad since 1940 and was not in a position to influence the decision.

> *Sun Valley was a nuisance to him, and there* [were] *a lot of demands. . . . I never would have approved that sale if I had stayed on the Board. . . . From the standpoint of the railroad financially, it might have been wise. But I thought it was very important for*

> *the goodwill of Union Pacific to keep Sun Valley. . . . I couldn't have taken an interest in it. I kept my house there, my family went there and skied, but I took no part in the management. I've had no connections with any business activity since then, except as a limited partner in my banking firm.*

Dorice Taylor said, "Until 1964, we were kind of a private club for wealthy people." However, Sun Valley had always been a headache to Stoddard, so "with the full approval of the board of directors—to put it bluntly—he dumped us."

In his oral history, Bill Janss said Union Pacific wanted out of Sun Valley so badly "they'd been hawking it on the streets." However, no one could put together the land use side, the development side, and the skiing side. Union Pacific asked Janss "if you think it's so good, why don't you buy it?" George Eccles, a U.P. director, wanted to get rid of the resort so badly he offered to loan the Janss Company money to buy it. Janss's company knew the necessary management elements and were experts in land use and development; they knew what needed to be done from their plan, and could hire people to help in areas where they did not have expertise, like running the hotel. Janss said buying Sun Valley was like buying a national park. "We jumped in because we knew that it was a tremendous opportunity and you'll forever hate yourself for not taking a shot at it." They got over 4,200 acres of land in the sale. One incentive was the chance to operate the mountain with the village. Janss said Aspen had horrible experiences separating the two. Access to Sun Valley was tough, and transportation was needed from the village to the mountain, but those issues "could be solved in time." Janss was involved in developing Snowmass at the time and his brother would handle Sun Valley.

The deed transferring Sun Valley to the Janss Company was signed on December 1, 1964. This gave them one month to learn how to "run a hotel and a bar and restaurant, which we had never done before in our life." They decided not to keep the Sun Valley employees. Janss said they were not professional, everyone was stealing from Union Pacific, and no one worked hard. They moved everyone out, even the top manager. Union Pacific had not been running Sun Valley like a business. It never kept a ledger or balance sheet to track Sun Valley's operations, and the resort's accounting transactions were "commingled with the railroad accounts."

Things did not work out well for Winston McCrea, Sun Valley's general manager from 1952 to 1964, and other Sun Valley employees, who received letters dismissing them effective December 10, 1964, "out of a clear blue sky." McCrea was particularly

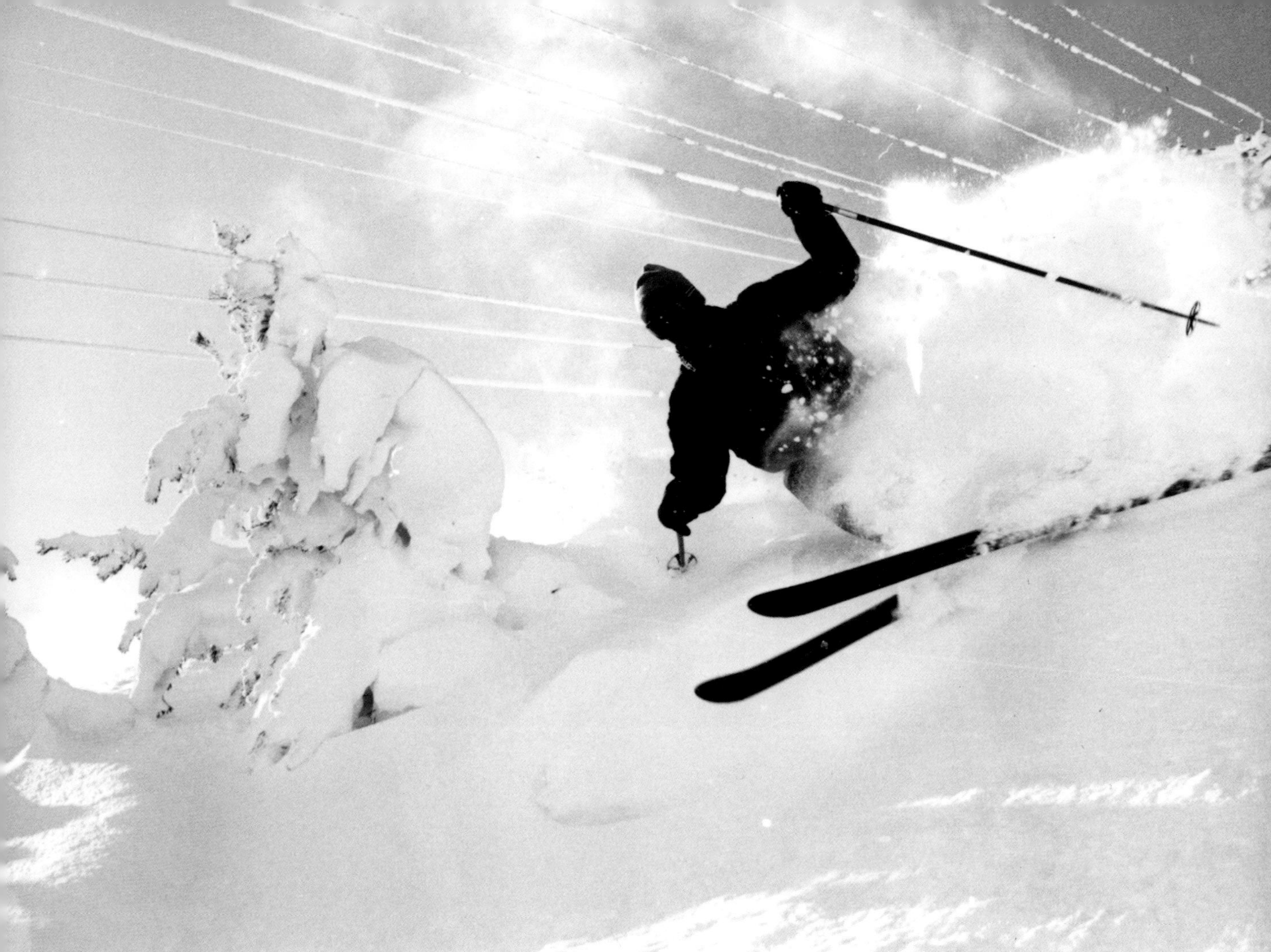

Ex-racer Bill Janss skiing on Baldy, 1965.

upset, since before he was let go, the Janss Company convinced him to sell his property at the foot of Warm Springs for $600, land he bought 14 years before for $300 and had paid taxes on. McCrea was asked to stay on at Sun Valley for a couple of weeks to "break in the new General Manager," Harry Holmes, the former manager at the Santa Barbara Biltmore and Cliff House in San Francisco.

The sale of Sun Valley in 1964 coincided with another change in leadership. Stoddard retired several months after its sale, in April 1966, and Ed Bailey became president of the Union Pacific, which "no longer had room for Sun Valley," according to Dorice Taylor.

Janss Purchase Results in a Cultural Change

There was a major cultural change when the Janss Company took over Sun Valley. When Sun Valley opened in 1936, there were virtually no places for employees to live in the area, so most senior staff lived in the lodge and ate in the lodge's dining room, and other employees lived in employee housing and ate in facilities provided by the railroad, a tradition that was followed for years. Sun Valley employees received many benefits, typically including room and board, and U.P. supported local activities and contributed to the community. The Janss people believed these activities were wasteful and the resort badly managed, with employees and townspeople taking advantage of the railroad's slack management style. Sun Valley employees saw a short-sighted money-grubbing outfit arrive to throw out the people and the approach to running the resort that made Sun Valley attractive, rushing to build unattractive units not designed for a mountain environment.

Dr. Scott Earle came to Sun Valley in 1959, becoming one of three doctors at the resort's hospital. Dr. Earle and his wife, Barbara, who was a nurse at the hospital, got free train passes, use of the ski tows, free ski lessons, free ski passes, "and we all ate at the Challenger Inn, and that was all free, which was really amazing, and then discounts at all of the Sun Valley shops . . . a lot of perks that represented considerable money if we had to pay for them." Scott said when Janss purchased Sun Valley, the whole tenor of the place changed dramatically. Janss, he said, "put all the tenements in." People came from California, many to get away from their problems, and "they brought their problems into our community. People never locked their doors, people never took their keys out of their cars. I realized that the first summer, I went out to get my car and it was gone." Drugs appeared for the first time, and cases of psychosis appeared in the hospital.

Dorice Taylor said the inexpensive condos built by the Janss Company were so small, "they will sleep two comfortably, four adequately, six in a pinch. Eight is an orgy." Prefabricated condos "filled a meadow like so many barracks and was quickly called Camp Janss." Louis Holiday said three years after the Janss company took over the resort, it was "an instant ghetto" with too many condos done without much taste. They wanted to get in, sell property, and get out.

Ed Seagle said Union Pacific felt an obligation to the local communities around Sun Valley that contributed to its success and wanted to be a good neighbor. After World

War II, many of the resort's employees lived in Ketchum, their kids went to its schools, and Seagle used his work crew to fix people's homes. His workers maintained the boilers at Ketchum and Hailey schools. When the Community Library was established in the 1950s, Union Pacific played a major role, from donating the land to having an architect in Omaha work on the plans. "We were part of the community," Seagle said.

Val McAtee said with the Janss Company, the resort "underwent a sudden change. . . . That was the end of an era." Union Pacific maintained a family atmosphere with its employees and the town. Kids got a free ski pass and ski clubs got free professional training. This all went away. The first five condominium buildings Janss built were designed by a California architect who had no idea what was required in a cold climate. They put the plumbing in the outside walls, which was a disaster the first winter. Pipes froze and cold air poured into the residences, making it so cold that cases of Coke froze and broke. Janss's contractors didn't build the roofs correctly, so ice dams built up, windows wouldn't open, and doors jammed shut. McAtee was told to fix the problems in the cheapest way, "half-way jobs." He and his crew had "been trained ever since Sun Valley was built, to do everything the quickest, easiest we can to keep the guest happy and comfortable. . . . All the guys left, they didn't like it. . . . And so our old Sun Valley family was stopped." McAtee quit too—"it was just hard for an old dog to learn new tricks."

When the Janss Company purchased Sun Valley, it formed the Sun Valley Company as a subsidiary to operate the facilities. Harry Holmes became its president and general manager. In his oral history, Holmes said he was asked on December 1, 1964, to come to Sun Valley since the sale would close by year's end.

Holmes said the resort never made a profit under Union Pacific, it was run down physically, had not been operated in a profitable way, there were a lot of problems, and it needed lots of work and money. Union Pacific was a big operation, and Sun Valley was such a small part of it, they couldn't keep track of what was going on. Union Pacific's operating loss was larger than it knew because of its inadequate accounting system. Coal for Sun Valley's boilers was brought by train from Wyoming, but the resort was not charged for the coal or transportation. Since Janss could not buy coal as cheaply as Union Pacific, they converted its boilers to gas, reducing the need to bring trains into the valley.

Holmes said they inherited a half-dozen labor unions with whom they had problems. Union Pacific ran buses to Shoshone four times a day to meet its passenger trains, which often only had a few people. He stopped the practice and had the buses run only when justified by need. A union representative threatened to shut down the railroad unless the old system continued, which might have worked under Union Pacific. Holmes said he couldn't care less and continued the shortened schedule. There were several votes on union membership, resulting in the decertification of many of them.

Holmes had problems with Sun Valley employees. Some kitchen employees drank too much. Employees were "on the dole," eating at the cafeteria with their families. Some employees ordered groceries at Atkinson's store that were charged to Sun Valley.

Sun Valley faced competition from other ski areas being developed. Aspen had been operating since after World War II, and new areas like Vail were starting. Sun Valley did not have enough beds to operate profitably, so Janss went into real estate development.

Holmes provided surprising insight into the Janss Company. He said Bill Janss was originally opposed to the acquisition of Sun Valley. Bill took his lawyer to a board meeting to oppose the purchase and threatened to sue if it proceeded. The company owned land near Aspen that later became Snowmass, along with skiing rights for the mountain, with which Bill was involved, and he wanted the company to continue there. Bill said Sun Valley was old and it didn't get enough snow. He liked Aspen and thought the company should put its emphasis there.

However, the company made a profit at Sun Valley by the second year and did well its first four years, making such good profits that other ski resorts visited to see what they were doing. This may have helped to change Bill's mind. Bill Janss and his mother ending up buying Sun Valley from the Janss Company in 1968 by trading assets in the company, and the resort was sold to Bill for what the company had paid for it plus what they had invested, between $4 and $4.5 million. Holmes left Sun Valley in 1973. He said Bill Janss did not have deep enough pockets to keep it all going, so he sold Elkhorn and later sold Sun Valley to Earl Holding.

Bill Janss made no mention of his initial objection to the Janss Company's buying Sun Valley in his oral history but expressed enthusiasm for the resort, although he was critical of the way Union Pacific had run it. Union Pacific "really did not like Sun Valley," he said, and had not done anything there since the war years. Sun Valley lost $750,000 a year, spending badly, but his company saw where it could be changed. The railroad could have muscled it through but they would have run a bad resort. Janss saw inefficiencies arising from Sun Valley being part of a company headquartered far away. Everything had to be ordered through Omaha, using Union Pacific forms, including Sun Valley lift tickets.[88]

Janss Company Remakes Sun Valley—Bill Janss Buys Resort

The Janss Company invested heavily in Sun Valley, installing lifts and developing the Warm Springs and Seattle Ridge portions of Bald Mountain, remodeling the lodge and improving golf and tennis facilities. The company revitalized a flagging ski resort by making Sun Valley into an all-season facility.

The company remodeled the lodge and inn, expanding the size of rooms and modernizing them with new bathrooms and amenities. It closed the lodge dining room and built the Boiler Room in the inn, creating a new nightclub with a boiler that many believed came from the lodge's basement, but actually came from the Board Sawmill west of Ketchum. They expanded and improved the resort's summer attractions, including its tennis, golf, horseback riding, and skeet shooting, according to Holland.

The company believed developing land was the key to Sun Valley's financial success. In 1966, they convinced the Idaho legislature to pass a law permitting condominiums in the state. This allowed the company to develop apartments and condominiums on its extensive real estate holdings to provide alternative housing arrangements. The company took advantage of the new law, using its own philosophy of controlled growth. Condos were becoming very popular, "forever changing the landscape of ski resorts" according to Holland, and large numbers of new residents were able to buy condos and homes at Sun Valley to take advantage of its year-round activities. Unlike other ski resorts that sold large blocks of land to developers, the Janss Company kept the land and controlled the development, although some land was sold to builders who would adhere to its standards. According to Holland, there were 800 hotel beds in the Wood River Valley in 1964, and by 1976 there were 8,000, and Janss built 865 condominiums.

The company emphasized the development of Bald Mountain with new lifts, lodges, and snowmaking to deal with the lack of reliable natural snow. Janss said Sun Valley's slopes "are more demanding than . . . Colorado's. They are steeper, and seem to attract the best skiers," and grooming was critical.

In 1964, there were five ski lifts at Sun Valley, with three on Baldy on the River Run side. The company's first focus was Warm Springs, which was a single narrow run down the north face of the mountain. Janss saw potential for "tremendously long runs on that side. The development of Warm Springs has made Baldy a mountain that had the greatest variety in the country." In 1965, two Riblett double chairlifts were installed on the Warm Springs side of Bald Mountain. The highest one, Limelight, had a 2,200-foot vertical rise, the largest in the country at the time. These lifts enabled skiers to begin and end their day at Warm Springs, instead of being bused to the lodge or River Run. Sunnyside lift (No. 7) was built in 1967, going from the top of chair No. 1 on River Run to the bottom of College, allowing skiers to go from one side of the mountain to the other (this lift was taken out under the Holdings). These chairlifts opened the Warm Springs area to development, where there was substantial privately owned property. Warm Springs village was built along with nearby residential units, a vibrant après-ski environment evolved, and Warm Springs became a popular way to begin and end the day on Baldy.

In his oral history, Bill Janss said that in 1968 he decided to focus on Sun Valley. Janss started racing in Sun Valley in 1937 but drifted away in 1950 as "Aspen started to take off with the new lifts and a whole new spirit. A town that was dedicated to skiing. Sun Valley was just everything and not done well. And then I felt [Aspen] was really a much better place." He changed his mind after becoming frustrated developing Snowmass. According to Oppenheimer and Poore, by the 1960s, Janss believed Sun Valley was better located than Aspen and had a greater year-round potential:

> *Colorado is very pretty and lovely, but it's not as fine as this country is for summer, because it rains every afternoon. There really aren't as many lakes and streams when you look at Colorado. Here, it's trees and lakes and streams and good snow, and we knew the advantages of being here, because we knew it had to be an all-season resort.*
>
> *The area which was just starting, a new modern village, a tremendous variety of skiing and a success story. . . . Much more opportunity, although it would be smaller. . . . It has the advantage of the big alpine slopes and the bowls, a very fine combination of all types of slopes and snow conditions. . . . So I gave up on Snowmass, which had become a great success . . . but I lost heart when our corporation decided to allow the Aspen Ski Corporation to run the skiing side of it. . . . And I felt that then there would be problems in the town.*

Janss said he had a horrible experience at Aspen because the mountain and village were separated—the city was pitted against the mountain. "I wanted a town that was built for these guests to come here," Janss said. He could see that Sun Valley was one of the best resorts in the country, "so it was easy to step in and start making corrections immediately." His interest in Snowmass was bought out by a partner, American Cement, and he liquidated his interest in the Janss Corporation. In 1968, an announcement was made that the ownership and management of Sun Valley was transferred from the Janss Company to the Sun Valley Company Inc. Bill Janss was the chairman of the board, and he and his wife and their three children were the sole owners. Janss Company was a land developer that developed real estate until maturity, then moved on to other projects. By removing Sun Valley from the Janss Corporation, "continuity of ownership will be assured." Bill Janss's major interest was to develop the summer potential of Sun Valley, and he would devote all his time to Sun Valley.

> *The ideal summer climate of the Idaho mountains and Sun Valley's complete complex of sports facilities has been overshadowed too long by its reputation as one of the country's finest ski resorts. Our ambition is to make this a resort where families can enjoy all the advantages of Idaho's great outdoors and where their children can be taught sports in the most specialized manner.*

Since the Janss Company took over Sun Valley in 1964, an Olympic-sized swimming pool had been built and a tennis school under a well-known pro would be started in summer 1968. The company obtained 4,200 acres of land in the valley and nearly 500 acres on Silver Creek, and had sold 25 acres for residences. Houses ranging in price from $25,000 to $200,000 had been built, along with condominiums priced from $12,750 to $58,000.

A deed was signed on March 20, 1968, transferring Sun Valley land from the Janss Company to Sun Valley Company Inc.

Janss asked Harry Holmes to remain as general manager of Sun Valley. In his oral history, Holmes said that he would agree to stay if there was a corporate structure, which included a board of directors that would adjudicate disagreements over management issues between Janss and himself. Holmes disagreed with the way that Janss wanted to spent money—"he was wild to have advertising." Holmes wanted to invest in more beds for the resort, but he didn't want to spend money Janss did not have. Janss lacked the personal wealth or access to the capital to allow Sun Valley to make the big investments necessary to remain a major player in an increasingly competitive environment. Holmes said he saved half a million dollars for Janss before he left Sun Valley in 1973 and was proud he helped take a business that had never made a nickel and turn it into a profitable company. The year after his departure, Janss spent $1 million on advertising and lost $1 million.

Dorice Taylor stayed on after the Janss Corporation bought Sun Valley in 1964, as did Sigi Engl. In spring 1972, after being head of the ski school since 1952, Engl was promoted to director of skiing, a new position responsible for long-range programs to maintain Sun Valley's reputation as a ski area of the highest quality. Paul Ramlow, a native of Germany who taught at Sun Valley since 1951, became the new head of the ski school, assisted by Sepp Froehlich, Bill Butterfield, and two new supervisors, Don Thurber and Harold Ogelsbee. Konrad Staudinger later became director of the Sun Valley Ski School.

Bill Janss continued to improve Sun Valley's mountains. In 1969, a chairlift was built connecting Elkhorn Valley with Dollar Mountain. In 1970, the Cold Springs double chairlift was installed on Baldy from the bottom of Broadway Run to the Roundhouse, replacing the single chair that had been there since after the war. Also in 1970, the Sun Valley Nordic Ski School and Touring Center was established on the Sun Valley golf course, directed by Leif Oldmark, a member of Sweden's cross-country and jumping teams who came to the area after seeing *Sun Valley Serenade*. Janss invested in snowmaking beginning in 1975, and Sun Valley became the first resort in the West to have an extensive series of snowmaking machines. Janss said they buried big pumps 20 feet down in Warm Springs Creek to draw water from the underground aquifer for snowmaking, a fact few people know now. The company expanded the number of skiers every year by at least 15 percent, starting from 900 a day in 1964.

In 1972, two lifts were built on Baldy. The Plaza lift connected skiers from a boarding point 100 yards below Upper Warm Springs lift to mid-College, allowing skiers to go from one side of the mountain to the other (this lift was taken out under the Holdings). The Lookout Lift was installed, running from the new Lookout restaurant to the old fire lookout, giving access to the southern bowls, called by some "the chair to nowhere." It cost $250,000, which Dorice Taylor said was "undoubtedly the most expensive lift in the country per foot of elevation." The Lookout restaurant was built in 1973. Originally planned as a three-story lodge, only one story was built, which would have been the ground floor of the facility. It replaced a shack that is now the center section of the ski patrol building on top of Baldy, which originally was a warming hut for skiers.

In 1972, the Sun Valley Company sold 1,900 acres to the Johns-Manville Corporation and began developing Elkhorn Valley. The first condos were finished for the 1972–1973 season, Elkhorn Village opened the next summer, the Elkhorn golf course opened in 1975, and the Elkhorn Hotel opened in 1976. Warren Miller produced a promotional video for Janss that was used to sell the land that became Elkhorn. He complained about his fee for the video, since the sale brought Janss more money than the company had paid for all of Sun Valley in 1964.

Beginning in 1976, the Seattle Ridge portion of Bald Mountain was developed. According to Dorice Taylor,

> *Seattle Ridge is named for the rugged skiers of that city who ski their own Cascades in raincoats. In the spring when they come to Sun Valley they didn't mind at all following a long and difficult catwalk out to the Ridge. They would wait there for the snow to soften. Then they would ski down a great open slope that led to the highway well below Ketchum. From this point they walked or hitchhiked back to town.*

Janss installed the Seattle Ridge double chair, which opened in December 1976, developing an intermediate skiing area. Seattle Ridge runs were named for Sun Valley skiers who won Olympic medals. Gretchen's Gold was named for Gretchen Fraser, who won gold and silver medals in the 1948 St. Moritz Games, the first American to win an Olympic medal in skiing. Christin's Silver (originally named Silver Fox for Bill Janss) was renamed for Christin Cooper, the former Sun Valley Ski Team racer who won a silver medal in giant slalom in the 1984 Olympics in Sarajevo. Seattle Ridge's middle run was initially called Southern Comfort, and was renamed Muffy's Medals for former Sun Valley Ski Team racer Muffy Davis, who won three gold medals in the 2002 Paralympics and a silver in the 1998 Paralympics. Sigi's bowl was named for Sigi Engl, Sun Valley's long time ski school director, and Kaitlin's Bowl was named for Kaitlin Fairington, who won gold in snowboarding in the women's half-pipe at the 2014 Olympics in Sochi, Russia. The May Day lift, a triple chair, was installed from the bottom of Easter Bowl to the top of the ridge where the Lookout chair ended, making it possible to ski the bowls multiple times or return across the mountain top. By the time Janss sold Sun Valley to Earl Holding in 1977, he had installed seven chairlifts on Baldy and increased the number of ski trails there from 33 to 62, according to Holland.

In his oral history, Janss said he didn't sponsor more international races as a matter of economics. It cost half a million dollars to hold such races. It was hard to raise enough corporate money to pay the costs, and it had to be done for publicity. Konrad

Staudinger, Janss's ski school director, said when races were held in Kitzbuhel, local hotels put up racers for free to support the events. That was not possible in America. In 1973, Sun Valley did sponsor the first U.S. freestyle championships, giving recognition to this new form of the sport. Freestyle had its debut in the 1968 Calgary Olympics as a demonstration sport. It became an Olympic event in 1972, with aerial competitions added in 1974, and was recognized by the FIS in 1979.

Not only did skiing facilities greatly improve during Janss's ownership, but institutions also grew to support the community.

In February 1965, Dr. John Moritz was honored. He started the Sun Valley Village Hospital at the resort in 1939. He was the only doctor in Sun Valley, and there were two nurses and three beds in the wing of the Sun Valley Lodge that served as the hospital, which lacked modern medical equipment. By 1965, the hospital had its own building. There were four doctors (Moritz, Saviers, Earle, and Ball), 15 full-time nurses, 19 beds, an operating room, and a delivery room. The hospital was equipped with modern equipment and did 400 major operations a year, sometimes as many as six a day.

In 1971, the Sun Valley Creative Arts Center (which became the Sun Valley Center for the Arts and Humanities in 1976) was started by Glenn Cooper on seven acres of land on Trail Creek where kennels for the resort's sled dogs were originally located. Glenn married Bill Janss after his wife was killed by an avalanche in 1973 while skiing. This organization became an important educational and cultural institution in the Wood River Valley, hosting drama and music events and conducting workshops in the arts, literature, dance photography, ceramics, and glassblowing.

The initial edition of *Powder* magazine was published in Ketchum in 1972 by brothers Jake and Dave Moe, designed to document "the other ski experience," which included powerhounds, ski bums, and hot-doggers. Local skier Bobbie Burns was on the cover of the first issue.[89]

1976–Sun Valley Ranch becomes the Silver Creek Preserve

The Janss Company purchase of Sun Valley included Sun Valley Ranch on Silver Creek, consisting of two ranches totaling 479 acres purchased in 1940 and 1941 for $8,000.

Under the railroad, Sun Valley Ranch was used for recreation, a center for bird hunting and trout fishing. Silver Creek is a slow-moving, spring-fed creek fed by underground aquifers bringing water from the Big Lost and Big Wood Rivers. It contains a rich variety of food for a healthy population of rainbow and brown trout, which are famously elusive and hard to catch. The railroad built two cabins and a dog kennel on the west arm of Sullivan's Lake to house guides and entertain clients, and its horses were pastured there in the fall. The ranch was not used for agriculture until after Pat Rogers left Sun Valley in 1952, and Union Pacific cut back its subsidy to the resort. Aerial photographs from 1957 show all arable land on Sun Valley Ranch was under cultivation, and cattle were kept there later. Janss was advised by a Sun Valley guide to end overgrazing on the ranch, and barley was grown.

After Bill Janss bought Sun Valley in 1968, he needed more capital and decided to sell Sun Valley Ranch. Local conservationists, fishermen, and hunters were concerned about losing access to Silver Creek, so they banded together, got the Nature Conservancy interested, and engaged in what Holland called "by far its largest fundraising project in the Northwest. In April 1975, the Union Pacific gave the Conservancy $30,000 to help preserve the 479 acres that, ironically, had been purchased for just that purpose 35 years before." The Nature Conservancy acquired the 479-acre Sun Valley Ranch from the Sun Valley Company, and the Silver Creek Reserve was established in 1976.

The Nature Conservancy significantly expanded the reserve, and by 2017, it owned 851 acres along Silver Creek and protected 12,600 acres through conservation easements acquired from neighboring farm owners and ranchers, "making this one of the most successful private stream conservation efforts ever undertaken for public benefit," Holland wrote. Silver Creek remains a treasure for the Sun Valley area and is a heavily used fishing and outdoor resource for the community.[90]

Ski Races at Sun Valley after 1964

In 1966, two major races were held at Sun Valley: the American International Team Races and the Challenge Cup, attracting many of racing's greats, including France's Jean-Claude Killy, Guy Perillat, and Leo Lacroix; Austria's Karl Schranz, Egon Zimmermann, and Heini Messner; and Canada's Nancy Greene. The American

International Team Race was the only major race featuring team competition except for the Olympics. The tournament featured a battle between Austria and France, resulting in "the fall of the Austrian Empire," as the *Sun Valley Ski Club 1966 Annual* put it. Bill Janss was the chief of race. Team totals determined the final standings, and a separate Sun Valley Challenge Cup was run for individual honors. The women's results were mixed with the men's, and the "overwhelming superiority" of the French women gave the French victory.

The downhill was on Warm Springs, the men starting from the top and the women from just below the steilhang. "The ferocious bumps on lower Warm Springs took their toll, more than making up for any supposed lack of challenge in the length of the course," the *Report* noted. The men's and women's giant slalom courses were on Holiday, although the women's course started lower on the hill. Both slalom races were held on the lower portion of Holiday.

"Austrians Sweep Downhill," reported the *Seattle Times* on March 19, 1966, with Heini Messner winning the event, Karl Schranz second, and Egon Zimmermann third. Schranz was lucky to finish, as he came "over a jump and was in the air for 40 years before he landed on one ski at 60 miles an hour." Killy "came out of his bindings as he made his violent attack on the course." Jim Barrows from the United States was fourth. In the men's giant slalom, Austria's Karl Schranz was first, Killy was second, and Périllat third. In the men's slalom, Killy was first, Schranz second, and Hugo Nindl of Austria third.

In the women's downhill, Austria's Erika Schinneger was first, Canada's Nancy Greene second, and France's Marielle Goitschel third. Cathy Nagel from Enumclaw, Washington, was disqualified when she missed a gate. In the women's giant slalom, Goitschel won, Greene was second, and Annie Famose from France was third. In the women's slalom, Goitschel was first, Famose was second, and Austria's Brigitte Seiwald was third.

France won the team races, followed by Austria, Switzerland, Canada, and the United States.

In the Sun Valley Challenge Cup, Karl Schranz won the men's giant slalom, beating France's Leo Lacroix. Killy finished fifth. "U.S. Women Skiers Beat Europeans in Giant Slalom," reported the *Seattle Times.* U.S. skier Wendy Allen won, followed by Austria's Traudl Hecher and Heidi Zimmermann. Americans Joan Hannah and Jean Saugert were fourth and fifth.

Another big event in 1966 was the Sun Valley Ski Club's Old-Timers Reunion, for those "who skied in the days when skis were hickory and sportsmen had to be tougher than that to survive the unpacked slopes and the unheated huts and farmhouses where they frequently stayed." Invitations went to all prewar members of the ski club. Two hundred and fifty skiers came, 99 of whom had been at Sun Valley during its first three years of existence, and 58 who started skiing in the 1920s. One conclusion was reached—"either skiing keeps people young or that the type of people who take up skiing wouldn't get old anyway," opined the *Sun Valley Ski Club 1966 Annual.*

Seven contestants who competed in the first Harriman Cup were there (Dick Durrance, Alf Engen, Don Fraser, Alex Bright, Hjalmar Hvam, Bob Livermore, and Dave Quinney), along with seven winners of the Harriman Cup (Durrance, Grace Carter Lindley McKnight, Friedl Pfeifer, Gretchen Fraser, Barney McLean, Clarita Heath, and Ernie McCulloch). Four members of the first FIS women's team attended, along with members of the 1936 U.S. Olympic team, the 1938 FIS team, and the 1940 Olympic team. The great regret was that Averell Harriman could not attend. An East-West Reunion Race was held, where the "West trounced the East with Sally Neidlinger Hudson and Dick Durrance as individual winners," according to the *Annual.*

Sun Valley Ski Club reunions were held in other years, including 1970, which was attended by Averell Harriman and Lowell Thomas.

In 1975 and 1977, Sun Valley hosted World Cup ski races, with slalom and giant slalom events for both men and women on the Greyhawk run on the Warm Springs side of the mountain. Sweden's Ingemar Stenmark won the giant slalom both years. The 1975 slalom was won by Italy's Gustavo Thöeni. Hanni Wenzel from Liechtenstein won the women's title in 1975, and Lise Marie Morerod from Switzerland won in 1977. Nineteen-year-old Phil Mahre of White Pass, Washington, won the slalom in 1977, beating Stenmark, and his twin brother Steve placed third. Dick Dorworth called the races in 1975 and 1977 "faux Harriman Cups," since traditional Harriman Cups consisted of downhill and slalom races. "But the true Harriman cup had died 12 years earlier and the most difficult downhill in the U.S. has not been run since."

No World Cup races were held at Sun Valley after 1977, partly because of the disruption to the resort caused by closing off the runs on which the races were held for a significant time.[91]

33

AMTRAK ENDS PASSENGER SERVICE NATIONALLY; RAIL SERVICE INTO THE WOOD RIVER VALLEY IS CANCELED

Decline in passenger traffic nationally led to an organized effort by railroads to convince Congress to allow them to drop the service. After a decade of lobbying, the Rail Passenger Service Act of 1971 was passed, establishing the National Railroad Passenger Corporation and Amtrak to operate limited intercity passenger service, which would allow railroads to drop passenger service. Amtrak began on May 1, 1972, with 21 routes in 43 states. Union Pacific stopped its passenger service in 1971 after losing $27 million the prior year, and regular passenger service into the Wood River Valley ended that year. From 1977 to 1997, Amtrak operated from Seattle to Denver with stops at Boise, Shoshone, and Pocatello, but that route was abandoned as part of a cutback in 1997. Amtrak service has long been criticized.

Ski trains were an important part of Sun Valley's history. They operated from Los Angeles, New York, Chicago, and a few other cities, coming directly to Ketchum. Ski trains from Los Angeles were the best known. They had orchestras and boxcars so skiers could party the whole trip. The LA ski train's motto was "Lock up your women, lock up your beer, the LA ski train just got here." Trains had to slow down and blow their whistles when they crossed the road leading to River Run, and often, excited skiers jumped off with their equipment to go skiing. Their baggage continued to the Ketchum depot, where bellboys took it to their rooms.

The Snowball Express ran from LA from 1958 to 1972, continuing the romance and excitement of the golden years of rail travel, carrying a total of 12,957 skiers directly

Sun Valley railroad line to close

By VERN ANDERSON
Associated Press

SUN VALLEY — Time runs out today for the historic Union Pacific Railroad branch line that once whisked celebrities and other wealthy patrons to the ski slopes at this mountain resort.

The 54.2-mile section of track — the first branch line in Idaho — was built 98 years ago to serve silver mines in the scenic Wood River Valley. For a time later it made nearby Ketchum the sheep-shipping capital of the world.

But mines played out, federal grazing restrictions curtailed sheep ranching, and passenger traffic ended in 1971. The last train to Ketchum was a single carload of insulation in November 1980.

"We have been considering abandonment for the past 10 years," said Dick Tincher, Union Pacific spokesman in Salt Lake City.

He said railroad officials had waited in vain for mining to pick up and revive traffic on the line, which costs the railroad $772,000 a year to operate.

The Interstate Commerce Commission decided June 28 to allow Union Pacific to abandon the line, but said it must continue service on a demand basis until today. Actual cutting of the line won't occur until later this month.

"They'll probably just take out a short piece of the track and put up a barricade," U.P. spokesman John Bromley said.

The branch line runs some 70 miles from Ketchum south to Shoshone, where it connects with the main line, but only the 54-mile section from Richmond to Ketchum is being abandoned.

The branch line hummed with passenger trains after W. Averell Harriman, then U.P. board chairman and later governor of New York, developed Sun Valley resort in 1936, in part to boost passenger traffic along the railroad's main line from Chicago to the West Coast.

"Up until 1964, we were a kind of private club for wealthy people," recalls Dorice Taylor, former resort publicity director.

Gary Cooper, Clark Gable, Ingrid Bergman and the shah of Iran were among dozens of celebrities who made frequent rail trips to the base of towering Bald Mountain. Novelist Ernest Hemingway made Ketchum his home.

In 1964, Union Pacific sold the resort and the surrounding area soon underwent a development and population boom. The valley still attracted the rich and famous, but they came by car and plane, no longer by rail.

Earlier this year, Ketchum hotel owner Norm Fuller made a tentative offer of $775,000 to purchase the branch line and develop it as a tourist attraction. However, the deal died last month after Union Pacific asked $27 million for the track and right of way.

The ICC order set forth a 180-day period in which Union Pacific must bargain "in good faith" with public-use bodies interested in acquiring parts of the right of way.

Several have expressed interest. The Blaine County Recreation District wants part of the right of way for a bicycle path, the state Fish and Game Department wants land for game-bird habitat, and the state Highway Department needs room for expansion of Idaho 75.

Eighty-two percent of the right of way, if it hasn't been sold to a public body, eventually will revert to adjoining property owners.

However, the remaining 18 percent of the right of way — some of it prime property along the Wood River near Ketchum — is not reversionary and can be sold by the railroad to individuals or private developers, Tincher said.

Announcement that Union Pacific's rail line to Sun Valley would close. *Idaho Statesman*, August 21, 1982.

to Sun Valley. Reservations for the train had to be made a year in advance. Etiquette said that skiers would conduct themselves in the spirit of good fellowship, but should never be seen drinking to excess, waxing their skis in the aisles, playing a portable radio too loudly, boasting of their prowess, pushing their way to the best seat, or lolling in the diner when others were waiting.

After the Janss Company bought Sun Valley in 1964, it converted its coal-burning boilers to gas and installed laundry facilities. This eliminated the need to bring trains into Ketchum, so the three-times-a-week train service was cut back. Until November 1980, a weekly freight train still operated into the Wood River Valley, servicing Wood River mines and businesses, particularly its lumber companies.

Regular rail passenger service into the Wood River Valley ended in 1971. The last passenger train to come to Ketchum was the Preamble Express, a 14-car special bringing 130 Union Pacific executives to Sun Valley for a board meeting in August 1975. Union Pacific donated the Ketchum depot to the city in May 1975. The depot was moved from its original site to Kiwanis Park in Warm Springs, with plans to have it

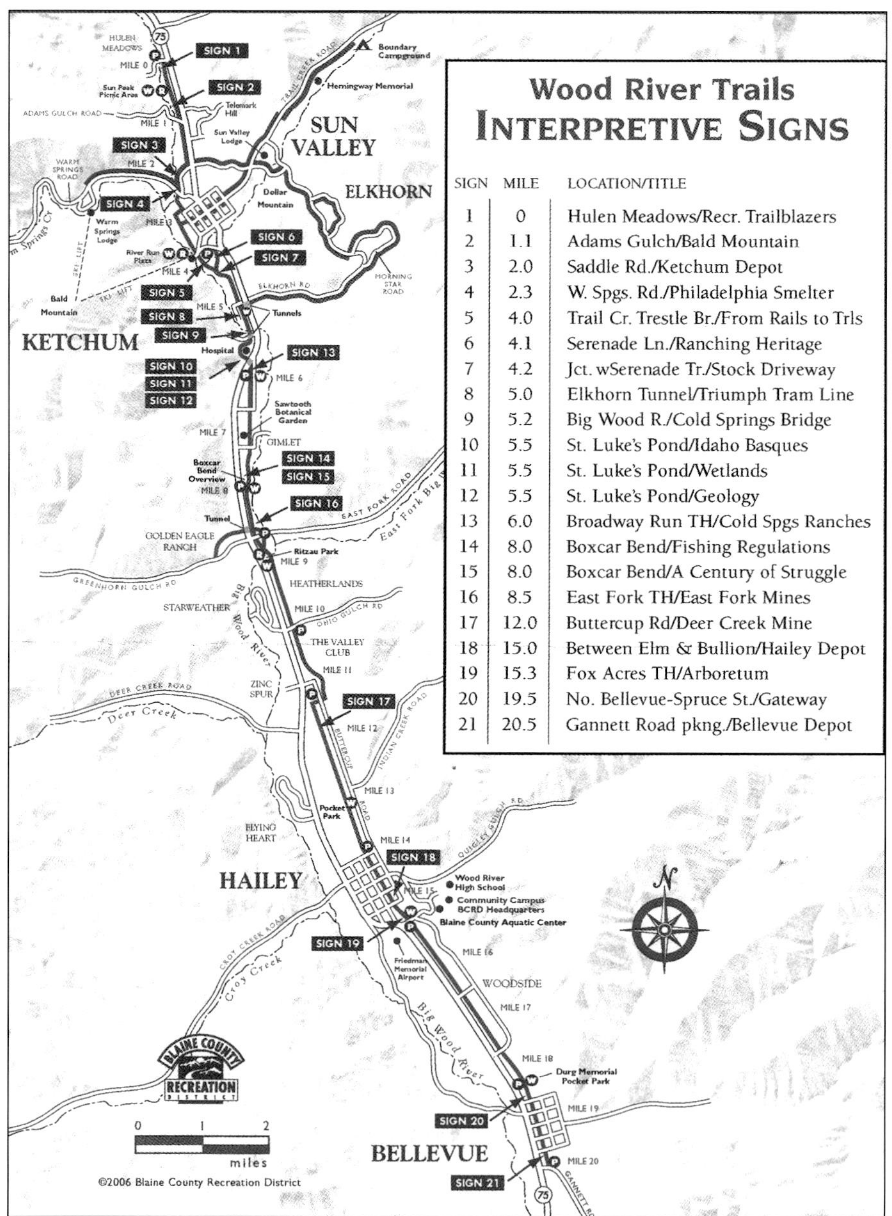

Map of Wood River Trails interpretive signs from Blaine County Recreation District. *Courtesy of Evelyn Phillips.*

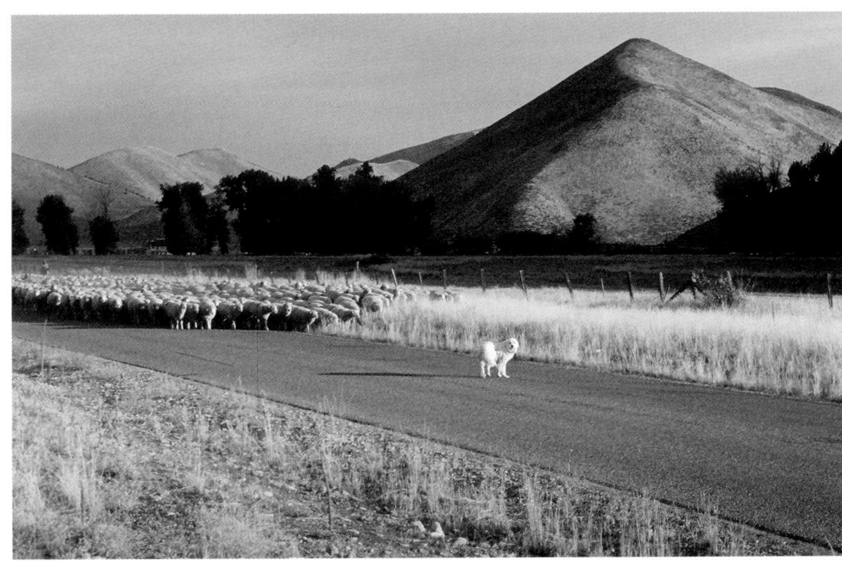

Sheep on Wood River Trail during the Fall Trailing of the Sheep Festival. *Courtesy of Mary Anne Crofts.*

house the ore wagons used in the Wagon Days parade over Labor Day. The depot collapsed the following winter during a heavy snowstorm, but insurance funds were used to build the Ore Wagon Museum in downtown Ketchum.

In June 1982, the Interstate Commerce Commission approved Union Pacific's petition to abandon the Wood River Branch from Richfield to Ketchum, which cost $772,000 a year to operate. A Wood River Valley businessman offered Union Pacific $775,000 for the line, but the railroad wanted $27 million, so the line was abandoned. In 1983, Union Pacific abandoned its Hill City Branch, which ran from Shoshone to Richfield through Camas Prairie to Fairfield and Hill City. In 1987, Union Pacific removed the rails from the Wood River roadbed, the Idaho Department of Transportation obtained the right-of-way under the Rails to Trails program, and the Blaine County Recreation District built a trail using proceeds from a $1.7 million bond issue. The Wood River Trail was finished in 1992, costing $4 million, and has become a heavily used recreational facility for cross-country skiing in the winter and bike riding, running, and other sports the rest of the year.[92]

34

HOLDING FAMILY BUYS SUN VALLEY IN 1977, RESTORES THE RESORT TO INTERNATIONAL STATUS

Bill Janss spent 10 years operating Sun Valley, during which time the resort experienced two hotel fires, three recessions, and a United Airlines strike. Janss said, "I can't ever recall having a year that was just a lot of fun," although he built seven chairlifts, increased the number of ski trails from 33 to 62, and Sun Valley expanded and enjoyed new success as a year-round community. During his tenure, Sun Valley faced increasing competition from other ski resorts in Colorado, Utah, Wyoming, California, Montana, Canada, and elsewhere. Sun Valley no longer had a monopoly as the country's only high-end destination ski resort.

Operating a ski resort is capital intensive, and Janss did not have sufficient capital to continue improving Sun Valley. He sold Elkhorn to Johns-Mannsville and reinvested the proceeds into the resort, building a convention hall and improving the inn. Janss decided to sell the resort and looked for an investor with the resources to expand Sun Valley properly, including the Walt Disney Company (which nearly bought the resort), United Airlines, Marriott Hotels, and others. Disney backed away, deciding it should begin its own resort, "with its own identity, rather than assume ownership of an already existing brand and style," according to Sauter. In his oral history, Janss said it was time to let a guy with dough come in and take advantage of it.

In 1977, Janss sold Sun Valley to the Holding family's Little America Corporation for $12 million. He believed the Holdings, a multimillionaire family that owned Sinclair Oil and the Little America chain of hotels, had the resources to continue developing Sun Valley. Holding was "a savvy Utah businessman with the vision to return Sun Valley to its glorious days and the substantial assets to do so," according to Holland. After the sale, Janss often said "it was good for Sun Valley that it was now owned by a man who could afford it," according to Sauter.

Van Gordon Sauter praised Janss's stewardship of Sun Valley, how he changed the mountain and gave skiers runs and lifts, but noted his financial struggles:

> *The Janss years were good for the resort and the Valley. The Sun Valley customer base was broadened. Condos helped create a new community of visitors. People soon began to view Sun Valley as a rewarding place to live an engaging lifestyle, not just a place to visit. That was the beginning of a large second-home community, which has become a significant economic and cultural asset to the Valley. But for all Janss accomplished, financial success was elusive. . . .*
>
> *Bill Janss loved Baldy. He knew how to manage and enhance it, and did so with a great authority that has benefitted skiers to this day. But by the end of his ownership tenure he was exhausted, personally and financially, by the flatlands—the elusiveness of profits in the Lodge, restaurants, and retail endeavors. He never made a dime from the ongoing operations of the resort. But its flag flew high under his stewardship.*

Once again, the change in ownership was a time of turmoil, and the new management style was disliked by those who had been at the resort under Janss, as Sauter described:

> *But the arrival of the Holdings as the new owners of the Sun Valley Resort was hardly greeted with enthusiasm by the community. Bill Janss had been a very popular owner. His personal charm and casual management style endeared him to the community. On the other hand, Janss's management and the presence of railroad unions had created an overstaffed lackadaisical work force. And a money-losing company. Things changed.*
>
> *As part of the Holdings' purchase agreement, every employee of the Sun Valley Company was dismissed. The unions were scuttled. Everyone who wanted to continue working was obligated to apply for a job. Freebies for employees were abolished. Pilfering was suppressed. The community was outraged. There were "Earl is a four Letter Word" bumper stickers*

> *in town. Those who feared that Disney might have purchased the resort suddenly began to second-guess their opposition to the Magic Kingdom. Less publically stated, but certainly present, was an arch disdain for Mormonism in liberal Blaine County.*

Earl Holding said, "I think the town thought I was the devil himself." Wally Huffman, Sun Valley's general manager from 1977 to 2009, said working there after Holding bought the resort was "the hardest two years you could possibly have in a small town."

However, the Holdings began making significant investments into the resort, its mountain facilities, and equipment, and over the years brought it back to international stature. The attitude of the community changed as Sun Valley improved, described by both Holland and Sauter.

The Holdings began by planting 2,000 trees around Sun Valley Village and later planted 1,000 more trees around the golf course, for a total of 7,000 in all, changing the resort's look. Earl and Carol made themselves popular in the community by working with the nursery crews. Robert Trent Jones Jr. redesigned the golf course, and over $1 million was spent on improvements. The Holdings invested many millions into the lodge and inn. They built an outdoor pavilion for summer entertainment and a new White Clouds golf course. Earl Holding became known for waiting on tables at his resort, and when the remodeled Sun Valley Lodge opened, Carol Holding was seen vacuuming floors and arranging furniture.

Sun Valley was said to be worth $300 million in 1996, as a result of the Holdings' vision and investments into the resort. Sun Valley's ski racing program, through the Ski Education Foundation, continued the resort's tradition of turning out successful racers. Olympic medal winners with a Sun Valley affiliation include Gretchen Fraser, Christin Cooper, Picabo Street, snowboarder Kaitlyn Farrington, and Muffy Davis. All have runs named after them on Bald Mountain. Hollywood stars continued to be attracted to Sun Valley's lifestyle, with Clint Eastwood, Steve McQueen, Bruce Willis, Jamie Lee Curtis, Arnold Schwarzenegger, Tom Hanks, and others buying houses there. Clint Eastwood filmed the movie *Pale Rider* near Sun Valley in 1985.

The Holdings installed seven high-speed chairlifts and invested in state-of-the-art snowmaking. Their first new lift was installed in 1978, a triple chair replacing the old single chair over Baldy's Exhibition run, when a daily lift ticket cost $13. Three high-speed quad lifts were installed in the summer of 1988: Christmas chair going from the Roundhouse to the top of the mountain, Challenger chair, and Greyhawk chair at the bottom of Warm Springs, which goes part way up the hill. In 1992, a high-speed quad replaced an older chair on River Run. In 1993, a high-speed quad replaced the Seattle Ridge chair, and the Lookout Express was installed on the River Run side of the mountain on a new route cut through the trees, leading from the top of the first River Run chair to the top of the mountain. The Frenchman's high-speed quad was installed in 1994, opening Frenchman's Gulch to skiers. In 2009, the Roundhouse Express gondola was opened going from the base of River Run to the Roundhouse, and the Exhibition triple chairlift was taken out. The gondola carries skiers and sightseers to the Roundhouse for lunch and weekend dinners. Baldy's 13 chairlifts have a capacity of 23,000 skiers per hour, keeping lift lines at Sun Valley to a minimum and providing the maximum skiing possible.

The Holdings built a series of new lodges at Sun Valley, "ultimate on-hill facilities," designed by Ketchum architect Jim Ruscitto, who created a "Sun Valley style that elevated the resort's status," according to Sauter. "The designs meld rustic mountain elements with Old World class, and serve as functional ski facilities while luxuriously accommodating guests." The Warm Springs Lodge, built in the fall of 1992, used peeled logs and local riverstone, replacing the old Northface Hut. Similar lodges were built on Seattle Ridge in 1993 and at the base of River Run in 1994. The 18,000-square-foot Seattle Ridge Lodge was built on a mountain top at 8,800 feet, requiring helicopters to carry materials to the site, providing stunning views of the surrounding mountains. Ruscitto won the Best Day Lodge award from *Snow Country* magazine for the facility. The 30,000-square-foot River Run Lodge has a day lodge, a shop maintenance building, and a retail building. At the insistence of Carol Holding, the new 26,000-square-foot Dollar Mountain Lodge was built in 2004, replacing the old Dollar Cabin. A new golf course was opened in 2008, the White Cloud Nine, along with a new Sun Valley Club used as a nordic center in the winter and for golf in the summer.

In 2002, Sun Valley was a training site for many alpine and nordic ski teams for the in Salt Lake City Olympics. The alpine speed events were held at Snowbasin outside of Ogden, Utah, also owned by the Holdings.

In 2008, the Holdings built the Sun Valley Pavilion, a summer performing arts center that seats 1,561 people under a translucent fabric roof, which according to Sauter, is

> *a remarkable architectural and structural achievement. . . . Soaring, compatible and consistent with the mountains that surround Sun Valley, the Pavilion has been host to*

> *some of the world's great musicians. . . . It is a contemporary, cultural landmark at home in its extraordinary setting.*

In 2015, the historic Sun Valley Lodge was remodeled, and a world-class 30,000-square-foot spa and fitness center was built. "It's a complete rebirth—not just a remodel," *Eye on Sun Valley* reported. "The design of the re-imagined lodge respects the history of this iconic building, while bringing it up to today's standards and beyond." The spa has 15 private treatment rooms, large locker rooms with steam and sauna facilities, relaxation lounges, a yoga studio, and a 2,300-square-foot fitness center. The outdoor lodge pool and spa were redone but retain their size, looks, and location. The lodge has 94 spacious guest rooms that replaced the 148 rooms it used to have, 65 with fireplaces and all with bathrooms that are four times larger than those at the old lodge. There are suites named after local celebrities—Clint Eastwood, Ernest Hemingway, Marilyn Monroe, Sonja Henie, and Gary Cooper. The cost of the remodel was not released, but it was substantial, according to *Eye on Sun Valley*.

Sun Valley has regained national prominence as a result of the Holding family's management. Events such as the Allen Company's annual summer conferences, held there since the 1980s, give the resort a high profile. Herbert A. Allen's investment banking firm specializes in mergers, acquisitions, and financial advisory work and brings many of the best-known names in finance, commerce, banking, politics, and news to Sun Valley to meet and exchange ideas. People such as Bill Gates and Warren Buffett are regular attendees. The week is known for filling the small airport in Hailey with so many private jets they hire a firm that specializes in parking large airplanes, and many have to be kept at Twin Falls.

The Holding family also owns the Snowbasin resort in Utah. According to Sauter, Sun Valley's ownership under Holding "was radically different from the first two. Earl and Carol Holding successfully managed the property for profit and growth."[93]

When Earl Holding died in 2013 at age 86, *Forbes* said he was "one of America's most successful entrepreneurs . . . considered to be among the largest landowners in America," including "the world-renowned Sun Valley ski resort," worth $3.2 billion. "Sun Valley is one of the nation's poshest ski resorts," it said. In 2018, *The Land Report* said the Holding family was tied with Jeff Bezos, the owner of Amazon, for having the 28th largest private land holdings in the country, with 400,000 acres in Utah and Idaho

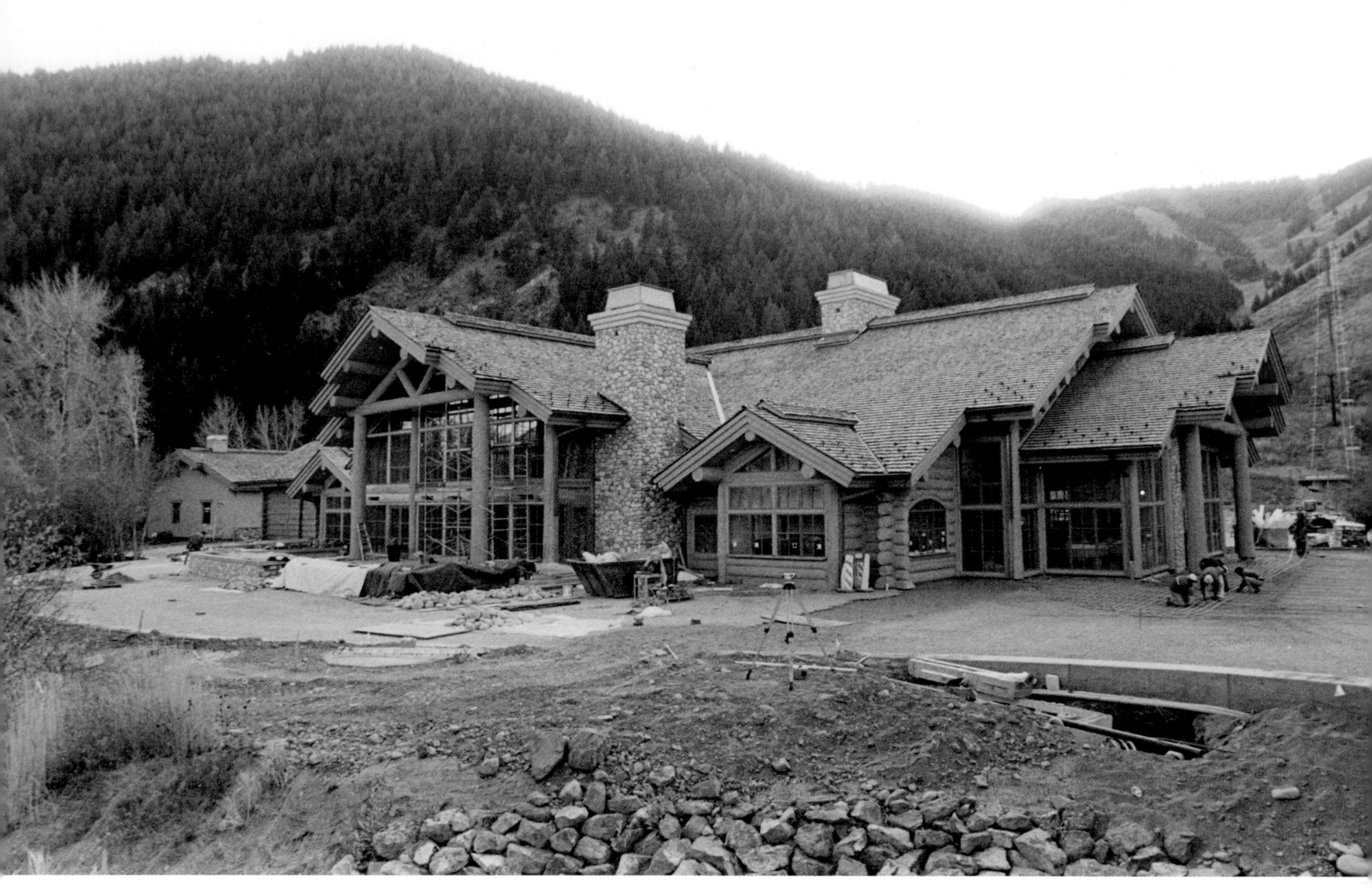

In the 1990s, the Holdings built several new lodges, "ultimate on-hill facilities," designed by Ketchum architect Jim Ruscitto, who created a Sun Valley style melding rustic mountain elements with Old World class, that are functional ski facilities providing luxurious guest accommodations. The River Run complex has a 30,000-square-foot day lodge, shown here, a shop maintenance building, and a retail building.

and an "immense" cattle ranch in southern Montana and northern Wyoming. The Simplot family, fellow Idahoans, were 25th.

In 2016, *Travel and Leisure* named the Sun Valley Lodge the best hotel in Idaho. Other winners included Little Nell in Aspen, the Hay-Adams Hotel in Washington, D.C., and the Four Seasons in Las Vegas. In 2018, two restaurants at Sun Valley, the Ram and the Roundhouse, won *Wine Spectator's* Award of Excellence, which recognizes restaurants with wine offerings from quality producers that match their menu in both style and price.

In 2017, for the second year in a row, Sun Valley was rated the No. 2 ski resort in America in *Ski* magazine's reader's poll. Its ranking reflects the area's excellent grooming, superior guest experiences, unique and historic charm, and virtually no lift lines. It ranked No. 1 in lifts, No. 2 in grooming, No. 2 in character, No. 2 in service, No. 3 in lodging, and No. 4 in après-ski and dining:

> *Sun Valley attracts real skiers. They work hard. Ski just about every (decent) day. Raise ripping kids. And then ski some more. They don't view it as a big deal because that's the natural rhythm of skiing's Shangri-La: lots and lots of turns and very little attitude, which is surprising considering the celebrity lure of this place . . . you've arrived at, well, an alpine Shangri-La. . . . Combine the snow with what many readers tout as "the best natural slopes in North America," and you've got yourself a real vacation—or a home away from home. . . .*
>
> *Forget the history. Forget the movie stars and the Gulfstream gazillionaires. Forget even . . . the über-iconic Sun Valley Lodge, with its recent spare-no-expense makeover. . . . Strip away all the clichés and it's still a place that leaves a lasting impression on visitors and locals alike. It's that Idaho keep-it-realness. It's strolling the streets of Ketchum, a ski town with an unmistakable sense of place, at sunset—or carousing in its lively bars at night. It's the vibe of the folks who live here (and can barely hide their pity for you because you don't). It's the spectacular scenery and wildlife.*

In 2016 and 2018, Sun Valley hosted the U.S. alpine championships sponsored by the U.S. Ski and Snowboard Association, alternating with Sugarloaf, Maine, where they were held in 2015 and 2017. Men's and women's events included a super giant slalom, giant slalom, and slalom held on the Warm Springs side of the mountain, finishing on Greyhawk. This was part of a long-term plan to move the annual celebration of American ski racing to top resorts around the United States.

In 2016, Mikaela Shiffrin "dazzled in Sun Valley at U.S. Alpine Championships," dominating the women's events, with *Sun Valley Magazine* calling it a "Return To Glory."

> *In addition to her dominating win in the slalom championship, Shiffrin went on to win the giant slalom (GS) title as well, dusting her competitors by nearly three-quarters of a second, despite a near fall merely three gates into her run. The GS victory contributed to her standing as America's alpine skiing darling and added to her already impressive list*

> *of accomplishments. The 2016 U.S. National Alpine Championships held in Sun Valley were a return of big-time racing to the slopes of Sun Valley's famed Bald Mountain.*

In summer 2018, the U.S. Forest Service announced that the Pioneer Cabin would get a facelift, after being allowed to deteriorate over the years, according to *Eye on Sun Valley*:

> *The 81-year-old Pioneer Cabin was built by Sun Valley Company as a mountain hostel in 1937 for those who preferred alpine touring to lift-assisted skiing. It is a popular destination for hikers willing to ascend 2,400 feet elevation to its 9,440-foot perch in a partial cirque of jagged mountain peaks.*

A volunteer crew installed thermopane windows designed to maintain the historic look of the cabin and put in a new wood stove with a double or triple firewall.

In spring 2018, the Warm Springs Lodge, which opened in 1993, caught fire, sustaining $1 million in damage. The fire did not damage the old-growth timbers used to build the lodge, and it was redesigned and modernized for the 2018–2019 ski season. The dining area has 100 seats, an expanded bar area with 18 seats, and the lodge has a capacity of 280 instead of 164. New windows let in more light, the Konditerei Warm Springs offers an espresso bar and pastries, and the famous warm chocolate chip cookies are still sold with the old bell announcing their arrival as before (with a new rope).

The next project for Sun Valley is Cold Springs Canyon. A new Cold Springs chair will be installed for the 2020– 2021 season, a detachable quad that will take skiers from the bottom of Broadway 1,525 feet to the Roundhouse in six minutes. Its lower base will be two thirds of a mile farther downhill than the present chairlift, making Lower Broadway 2.5 miles long. The lift replaces a double chair installed in 1970, which replaced the first double chair on Baldy installed for winter 1948. Skiing will then be expanded into Turkey Bowl and Cold Springs chutes, adding 380 acres of terrain, including open bowls, gladed tree skiing, and deep chutes, for a total of 2,434 acres.[94]

Sun Valley's place in the skiing community over the years can be seen by the number of skiers with a connection to the resort who have been inducted into the U.S. Ski and Snowboard Hall of Fame, starting with Averell Harriman in 1969, and the men who helped plan the resort, Charles N. Proctor in 1959 and John E.P. Morgan in 1972. They are listed in Appendix B.

EPILOGUE

Sun Valley has had a history like no other ski resort, since Averell Harriman started it in 1936 as a tool to restore passenger revenue for the Union Pacific Railroad in the middle of the Great Depression, saying, "We didn't run it to make money; we ran it to be a perfect place." Sun Valley had a monopoly on skiing grandeur for several decades, and it influenced areas that were developed later. In its over 80 years of existence, the resort has had only three owners, each showering it with love, support, and money, and each taking it to a higher level.

During its Union Pacific years, Sun Valley created high-end skiing in the United States, attracting skiers from all over the world. The resort made skiing sexy and attractive, its chairlifts opened the sport to a broad array of people, and its ski school provided a model that was followed elsewhere. Sun Valley became a cultural icon, and major newspapers and magazines kept it in the nation's eye for decades. Sun Valley was called America's St. Moritz and brought European skiing ambiance to this country. Its international influence was illustrated in 1950, when an Austrian newspaper said that with the help of the Marshall Plan, its Arlberg region could become "Austria's Sun Valley."

Harriman's departure from Union Pacific during World War II, together with a continued reduction in passenger travel after the war, led to a reduction in the subsidy the railroad paid to keep Sun Valley operating, resulting in the sale of Sun Valley to the Janss Company in 1964. Bill Janss said, "buying Sun Valley was like buying a national park." Janss and his company made significant investments in Sun Valley, creating a year-round community, bringing back much of the resort's appeal. When Janss realized he did not have sufficient capital to continue developing Sun Valley, he sold it to Earl and Carol Holding in 1977. The Holdings remade Sun Valley and its skiing facilities, expanded its athletic and cultural attractions to appeal to younger generations, and restored its status as one of the world's great ski resorts.

At the same time, the Wood River Valley has expanded into an affluent and sophisticated community. In recent years, the community funded a $12.5 million "reinvention" of the Community Library (including $2 million to restore the Hemingway house), the Argyros Performing Arts Center ($15.5 million plus $2 million for performing arts), and a $16 million animal shelter (the Mountain Humane Animal Welfare Center). Private investments followed. The Limelight Hotel, a LEED silver certified facility, opened in 2017. However, as is true in most resort areas, it has become difficult for those who work in the valley to make a living wage and afford housing there.

Winters in the Wood River Valley now consist of a wide array of alpine and cross-country events for adults and the younger generation. The Sun Valley Ski Education Foundation, Sun Valley Ski Academy at Community School, and the Ski Club Masters offer high level instruction and competitive tournaments and are training the next generation of skiers. The area is known as "Nordic Town USA," with over 40 km of groomed trails, including those around Galena Lodge, the Harriman Trail from Galena Lodge to the Sawtooth National Recreational Area headquarters, and the Sun Valley Nordic Center. The Wood River Trail System, the old railroad right-of-way, runs from north of Ketchum to Bellevue in the south valley. The Sun Valley Nordic Festival, Nordic Town USA Sports Sprint, and the Boulder Mountain Tour are big attractions.

The Wood River Valley is also known for its mountain and road biking, claiming the title "Two Wheeled Nirvana." Over 400 miles of single-track riding, hundreds of miles of scenic roads, and over 30 miles of paved, car-free bike paths adds up to "bike Mecca." Lift-accessed mountain biking on Bald Mountain, with 3,400 feet of vertical drop, provides "a hair-on-fire big mountain experience on two wheels." Events such as Rebecca's Private Idaho attract many hundreds of riders. Road bike riders utilize Highway 75 going north from Ketchum to Galena Pass and into the Stanley Basin, and south to farm country.

The Sun Valley area's fly fishing attracts anglers from all over the country, with a wide array of waters available, including the Big Wood River, Warm Springs Creek, Big Lost, Silver Creek, the Salmon, and South Fork of the Boise. Henry's Fork of the Snake, rated as one of the best trout streams in America, is a short distance away.

Cultural events attract thousands to the Wood River Valley every year. These include Hailey Days of the Old West on July 4; the Big Hitch Parade over Labor Day, featuring ore wagons used to haul ore from mines to smelters in the late 1800s; the Trailing of the Sheep Festival, celebrating the history of sheep ranching (named one of the world's 10 best fall festivals); and the Jazz Festival. The Sun Valley Film Festival, Family of Women Festival, Wellness Festival, Wine Auction, Symphony, Writers Conference, and the Arts and Crafts Festivals are just some of the area's other popular events. The Visit Sun Valley website for 2019 listed 16 signature summer events, nine music events, nine running events, five bicycling events, and nine arts and cultural events.

The major issue facing the Sun Valley community now is how long the Holding family will continue to own the resort following Earl's death. Every year, there is a new rumor about another suitor seeking to acquire Sun Valley, raising concerns in this era of large corporate ownership of multiple ski resorts.

Statistics about ski resorts show how different Sun Valley is from other areas. At a recent meeting of Sun Valley Economic Development, information was presented from DestiMetrics, which followed 19 mountain ski resort communities for years. Sun Valley generates less than $5 million from lodging in a fiscal year. By contrast, Aspen/ Snowmass generates $31 million, Jackson Hole $28 million, Mammoth $20 million, and Steamboat Springs $10 million. Crested Butte, the next lowest to Sun Valley, generates $8.5 million. Sun Valley gets 54 percent of its revenue in summer and 46 percent in winter, while Jackson is split 32 summer - 68 winter, Crested Butte 45-55, Telluride 40-60, Mammoth 37-63, and Aspen-Snowmass 32-68.

Sun Valley, like all ski areas, faces severe challenges from global climate change. In the last few decades, 272 ski areas have closed in the United States, more than a third of the country's total, because they could no longer count on sufficient snow. Snow conditions that currently exist at 6,000 feet will rise to 7,000 feet by 2025. A two-degree Celsius temperature change means ski resorts will have 32 fewer days each season for snowmaking at 7,400 feet. "Ski resorts are going to have to reconfigure their operations to get skiers and boarders higher than they currently go," according to one environmental planner. "Then they are going to have to figure out a way to get them back to the bottom—a bottom that may be more mud than snow in another 30 years. Some resorts may have to go to plastic grass that can be skied on year round."

No matter what happens in the future, Sun Valley will remain one of the world's great ski areas and a lasting memorial to the vision of Averell Harriman, as enhanced by Bill Janss and the Holding family.[95]

POSTSCRIPT

Averell Harriman died on July 26, 1986, at age 94. He was lauded by world leaders and U.S. presidents and his obituary appeared in newspapers around the world. The *New York Times* of July 27, 1986, said he was born in privilege, "a patrician heir to a railroad fortune," and raised on his family's "baronial" 20,000-acre estate in New York's Hudson Valley, where he was buried in a family plot.

Harriman served four U.S. presidents in key diplomatic roles: Roosevelt, Truman, Kennedy, and Johnson, "decade after decade, with a striking degree of success." The U.S. State Department called him "one of the most distinguished statesmen of the 20th Century." He was an expert in Russian affairs, played a major part in the development of Soviet-American relations, and dealt with Russian and Soviet leaders from Trotsky and Stalin to Kruschchev and Andropov. He was state chairman of the National Recovery Administration in 1934 while serving as chairman of the Union Pacific board and was chairman of the Business Advisory Council of the U.S. Department of Commerce in 1938. During World War II, Harriman was Roosevelt's lend-lease chief in Britain, ambassador to the Soviet Union from 1943 to 1946, and ambassador to Britain in 1946. After the war, he was Truman's advisor on foreign policy and secretary of commerce. In 1948, he became coordinator of the Marshall Plan in Europe and later a special assistant on foreign policy and head of the Mutual Security Administration. He entered politics in 1952, seeking the Democratic nomination for president, losing to Adlai

Stevenson. He was elected governor of New York, serving from 1954 to 1959, losing to Nelson Rockefeller in 1958.

In the 1960s, President Kennedy made Harriman ambassador at large, and he negotiated the Geneva Accords, ending the civil war in Laos. In 1963, he became undersecretary of state for political affairs and negotiated a treaty with the Soviet Union banning above-ground nuclear tests. President Johnson sent him to Paris to begin negotiations to end the Vietnam War. He remained active in foreign affairs late in his life, meeting with Soviet leaders in the 1980s. He donated $10 million to the Russian Institute at Columbia University, together with $1.5 million from the Harriman Foundation, to promote American studies of the Soviet Union. It was renamed the W. Averell Harriman Institute for the Advanced Study of the Soviet Union. Harriman never achieved the two posts he desired—secretary of state and president of the United States.

His record of public service was so significant that Union Pacific got only a minor reference in his obituaries and Sun Valley almost none. Sun Valley was not mentioned by the *New York Times*, and the *Washington Post* said only, "In the late 1930s, he developed Sun Valley, Idaho, as a world-class ski resort as a means of expanding his railroad's business."

The Union Pacific is no better at keeping Sun Valley's memories alive. Its website has only two minor references to the resort: "Sun Valley Club Lounge Car—Stabled at Council Bluffs" and "Shoshone Business Car—Stabled at Council Bluffs." There is no entry for Sun Valley.

Appendix A

UNION PACIFIC LAND PURCHASES FOR SUN VALLEY

Blaine County property records show the following land acquisitions were made by the Union Land Company (ULC) or the Union Pacific Railroad Company (UPRC). KLA is the Ketchum Livestock Association.

Date	Grantor/Seller	Purchaser	Deed or Page No.	Use/location
May 7, 1936	Ernest Brass, et. al.	ULC	No. 73503	Brass Ranch
May 7, 1936	Ernest Brass, et. al.	ULC	No. 73504	Brass Ranch
May 9, 1936	Ernest Brass, et. al.		No. 73514	Lots in Ketchum
Jul. 16, 1936	Estate of Fred Howe	ULC	No. 73954	Lots in Ketchum
Aug. 5, 1936	KLA	ULC	No. 74014	40 acres for lodge
Aug. 5, 1936	KLA	ULC	No. 74012	Right of Way for water lines
Aug. 5, 1936	KLA	ULC	No. 74013	Right of Way for balloon track
Oct. 8, 1936	Oregon Short Line	UPRC	No. 74388	Near Picabo
Dec. 28, 1936	ULC	UPRC	No. 74724	Transfer of Brass & KLA land to UPRC

Date	Grantor/Seller	Purchaser	Deed or Page No.	Use/location
Dec. 28, 1936	ULC	UPRC	No. 74725	Transfer Right of Ways to UPRC
Nov. 10, 1938	Gertrude Lewis Gates	ULC	No. 77966	Road easement in Warm Springs
Oct. 26, 1939	Frances Venable	UPRC	No. 79926	Property for River Run lift
Feb. 15, 1940	John Brown	ULC	143-279	Unknown
Feb. 15, 1940	John Werry	ULC	143-280	Unknown
Jul. 1940	James & Eleanor Grimm	UPRC	No. 87300	Land on Dollar Mountain
1940	Gillahan			Sun Valley Ranch
1941	Sullivan			Sun Valley Ranch
Jun. 1944	Eleanor K. Grimm	UPRC	No. 87301	Land on Dollar Mountain
Feb. 1948	Eleanor K. Grimm	UPRC	No. 98546	Land on Dollar Mountain
Jul. 26, 1950	Everett & Dorice Taylor	UPRC	No. 97650	Lot in Sun Valley
Jan. 25, 1951	Eleanor K. Grimm	UPRC	162- 21	Land on Dollar Mountain

In December 1936, the Union Land Company transferred property purchased in its name to the Union Pacific Railroad Company in two separate transactions. Deed No. 74724, on December 24, included the lots in Ketchum it acquired from the Brass and Howe families; the two deeds covered 908 acres and 2,480 acres from the Brass family and 40 acres from the Ketchum Livestock Association. Deed No. 74725, on December 28, included the easements from the Ketchum Livestock Association for a right of way for a water pipeline and for a balloon track.

Land Sales

Between 1946 and 1964, Union Pacific sold some of its property, including lots in Ketchum and Sun Valley, for private residences and churches. They are listed as "encumbrances" in the deed transferring Sun Valley to the Janss Corporation on December 1, 1964.

The Church of Jesus Christ of Latter-day Saints bought several tracts in Ketchum: in 1953, lots 1, 2, and 3 in block 101 for $2,300; in 1955, lots 1, 2, 3, and 4 in block 101 (33,000 square feet for $2,300) and lots 1 and 3 in section 18 (9,060 square feet for $634); and in 1959, lot 1 in block 100 and land in Sun Valley for $1,218. In 1953, the Episcopal Church bought lot 4 in block 102 and property in Sun Valley for $577, and more land in Sun Valley in 1959. On November 21, 1955, Union Pacific gave the Community Library Association lot 6 in block 87 for use as a library. In 1958 and 1959, Union Pacific donated 36,882 square feet of land to the City of Sun Valley (incorporated in 1948) and to the Wood River Historical Society in 1963.

Sale to Janss Company, 1964

The deed transferring Sun Valley to the Janss Company was signed on December 1, 1964.

Appendix B

SUN VALLEY SKIERS INDUCTED INTO THE U.S. SKI AND SNOWBOARD HALL OF FAME

The place Sun Valley holds in the U.S. skiing community is illustrated by the people associated with the resort who were inducted into the U.S. Ski and Snowboard Hall of Fame.

Name	Year
Gordon Wren	1958
Andrea Mead Lawrence	1958
Dick Durrance	1958
Torger Tokle	1959
Alf Engen	1959*
Charles N. Proctor	1959
Gretchen Kunigk Fraser	1960
Buddy Werner	1964
Lowell Thomas	1966
Grace Carter Lindley	1966
Marian McKean Wigglesworth	1966
Hannes Schroll	1966
Hjalmar Hvam	1967
Toni Matt	1967
Clarita Heath Bright	1968
Roland Palmedo	1968
Averell Harriman	1969
Betty Woolsey	1969
Jack Reddish	1969
Ernie McCullough	1969
Alice Wolfe Kiaer	1969
Dick Movitz	1970
Sigmund Ruud	1970
Birger Ruud	1970
Jannette Burr Johnson	1970
James Griffith	1971
Sigi Engl	1971
Sverre Engen	1971
Sally Neilinger Hudson	1971
Reidar Andersen	1971
Don Fraser	1972
John E.P. Morgan	1972

Fred Iselin	1972
Hannah Locke Carter	1973
Corey Engen	1973
Billy Kidd	1976
Jimmy Heuga	1976
Susan Corrock Libby	1976
Barbara Cochran	1976
Walter Prager	1977
Sepp Bendikter	1977
Pete Patterson	1978
Warren Miller	1978
Otto Lang	1978
Bill Janss	1979
Friedl Pfeifer	1980
Gus Raaum	1980
Olav Ulland	1981
Stein Eriksen	1982
Christin Cooper	1984
Nelson Bennett	1986
Chuck Ferries	1989
John Woodward	1998
Émile Allais	1999
Edward Scott	1999
James Curran	2001
John Litchfield	2002
Picabo Street	2004
Toni Sailer	2005
Earl Holding	2010
Muffy Davis	2010
Dick Dorworth	2011
Bob Smith	2014

* Also member U.S. Ski Jumping Hall of Fame

Appendix C

BALD MOUNTAIN SKI RUN NAMES

Information herein came from *Sun Valley Ski Club Reports* and *American Ski Annuals* published by the National Ski Association, along with an article by Greg Moore in the *Mountain Express* of November 23, 2018. Moore got information about the names of Bald Mountain ski runs from Nelson Bennett, Sun Valley ski patrol director and mountain manager from 1940 to 1960, whose crews cut most of the runs on Baldy, and Walter Hofstetter, a ski patroller, mountain manager, and ski instructor from 1949 to 1965.

When Sun Valley opened in December 1936, there were chairlifts on Dollar and Proctor Mountains. Bald Mountain was originally for backcountry skiing only but opened for general skiing in winter 1940 after a series of three chairlifts were installed on the River Run side of the mountain.

Harriman Cup Downhill Course on Warm Springs

In 1937 and 1938, because neither Proctor nor Dollar Mountain had sufficient vertical drop to qualify as an official downhill course, Harriman Cup downhill races were held on an unnamed peak near the present headquarters of the Sawtooth National Recreation Area. Averell Harriman named the site Durrance Mountain after Darmouth College's famous ski racer Dick Durrance won the 1937 Harriman Cup.

In summer 1938, Durrance laid out a downhill course on the Warm Springs side of Baldy. Durrance's "tough race course," as he described it, started at the top of the mountain, went down a very steep ridge (now called **International**), and dove into a steep area named the **Steilhang** (German for "steep pitch").

BALD MOUNTAIN OPENS FOR GENERAL SKIING IN WINTER 1939–1940

In summer and fall 1939, a series of three single chairlifts were installed on Bald Mountain from the bottom of **Riverside Run** (later renamed **River Run**) to the top of the 9,200-foot mountain. New ski runs named for geographic features were cut by CCC employees under the direction of Alf Engen, U.S. Forest Service employees, and college students employed by Sun Valley—**Canyon**, **Sunnyside**, and **Riverside**—and the crews removed trees on **Ridge**, widening the run. Sunnyside was a south-facing slope going from the Roundhouse down into Cold Springs Canyon, taking skiers to the highway. **Rock Garden** had a southeast exposure where the snow melted fast, exposing rocks, and was the name of a section of the original Harriman Cup downhill course on Durrance Mountain. **Exhibition**, the run under Exhibition chairlift (the second lift on the mountain leading to the Roundhouse), became famous as a showcase for expert skiers to "exhibit" their skills to those riding the lift above.

42nd Street, the lower segment of River Run, funnels most of the skiers on that side of the mountain and is named for the crowds often seen there late in the day, which reminded Hofstetter of the street he had once stayed on in New York.

In 1940, there were three routes down Bald Mountain. The "standard run" went from the summit down Ridge, Rock Garden, Canyon, and Riverside. The **Cold Springs** run, named after the springs that are now contained in a small building under the Cold Springs lift, started at the Roundhouse, went on a trail cut down to Cold Springs Canyon, then to the highway at the foot of Baldy. Durrance's race course down **Warm Springs** run (named for the creek) was widened and cleared, so one could ski straight from the top of the mountain to the top of the Steilhang, down to Warm Springs Canyon, then down the canyon that Alf Engen's CCC crew had smoothed to the finish.

For winter 1941, the standard run to the Roundhouse Station was cleared and rocks were removed from Rock Garden. **Broadway**, a new three-mile run, was created, starting at the new Forest Service tower at the top of the mountain, running down Cold Springs ravine almost to the highway. The run was named for the famous New York City boulevard, since it was a major artery for skiers exiting the bowls. South of Ridge, there were five timber-free gullies (bowls) from the top of Broadway, offering easily accessible runs for every type of skier, with good snow assured from early December to late May. The bowls were connected with the Roundhouse by a new caterpillar road. **College**, an easier run, was blazed from the summit to the Roundhouse, averaging a 10-percent grade. Skiing College meant a person had "graduated" from Dollar Mountain. A new ranger's trail named **Roundhouse Lane** was cut across College to the Roundhouse, where skiers could catch the lift back to the summit. Another run was cut through to the Canyon Station lift, **Sunnyside**. Canyon was cleared and widened to more than 100 yards, and sagebrush and aspen trees were removed from the bottom so there was ample room for skiers to go past Canyon Station to Riverside Drive, or safely stop at the lift. The traverses at the end of Canyon were eliminated, and the lower section was widened from 50 feet to 200 feet. Rough spots on River Run were graded.

Sun Valley Reopens after World War II in December 1946

Bald Mountain's ski runs were revamped for its post-war opening in December 1946 using a new approach of thinning trees for runs instead of cutting an open swath down the face of the mountain. "All the ski runs at Sun Valley have been designed after careful study by outstanding ski experts of Europe and America in cooperation with the Forest Service," wrote the *American Ski Annual, 1947*, resulting in "longer downhill runs and miles of timber-free slopes with a variety of runs that will please the novice looking for a gentle decline as well as the skiing veteran in serious competition." The three-mile Broadway illustrated this new approach.

For winter 1948, a new 3,080-foot-long double chairlift was installed from the bottom of Spring House Canyon (Cold Springs) up to the Roundhouse, the first double chairlift on the mountain, with 1,072 of vertical lift and an hourly capacity of 300 riders, which greatly increased skiing in the bowls. Nelson Bennett's trail crew developed **Olympic** run, named in honor of the 1948 Winter Olympics in St. Moritz, Switzerland, running from the Roundhouse to the middle of River Run, a fast one-mile course for better skiers. The crew also removed trees along the ridge to allow skiers to go from Ridge to the bowl and reach the Roundhouse on a cat track.

For winter 1949, a new run was cut by Nelson Bennett's trail crew, named **Cutoff**, branching off Ridge 70 yards above Rock Garden, dropping down to meet the cat track from College to the Roundhouse, bypassing Rock Garden and providing an easy route for intermediates. Two other routes were cut later from Ridge to the cat track from College to the Roundhouse—**Blue Grouse**, named after the large, dark ground bird that is common on Baldy and throughout the Sawtooth National Forest, and **Holiday**, the winner in a trail-naming contest held among employees when the run was cut in 1956. Holiday was extended past the cat track all the way to Mid-River Run. Exhibition was widened to three times its original size, averaging 150 feet across. Olympic was opened up, making it faster and safer.

Substantial work was done to prepare Bald Mountain for the winter of 1950. **Lower College** run was opened, extending College to the beginning of Lift No. 2, the Exhibition chair.

Flying Squirrel was cut in 1950, and named by Walter Hofstetter, who said flying squirrels that looked like huge bats came out of the tops of the trees. College was doubled in width and the cat track to the Roundhouse was widened. In 1953, a new temporary run was added called **Question Mark**, since it did not have a permanent name. It began at the top of Rock Garden, went across the cat track leading to the Roundhouse, and entered Canyon, adding one more race course of Olympic caliber. It was later renamed Holiday. For 1957, Nelson Bennett's trail crew widened the transition from Rock Garden onto the Roundhouse slope and the dip in the first part of the cat track from College to the Roundhouse was eliminated. In 1958, **Central Park** was joined to Canyon to provide a new route down the mountain. In 1960, Walter Hofstetter's crew reconfigured the upper Warm Springs run that was part of Dick Durrance's downhill course leading to the Steilhang, and he named it **International** to honor international-level downhill races held there. A cat track was built at the top of Baldy, giving easier access to the bowls.

Baldy's Bowls

Mayday Bowl was named by longtime ski instructor Florian Haemmerle after he organized a slalom race on the bowl on May 4, 1938—St. Florian's Day—for instructors who had decided not to return to Austria for the summer. According to Haemmerle's widow, Bebe, when Florian won the race, "He stuck his pole in the snow and said, 'I proclaim that this is Mayday!'" **Christmas Bowl** and **Easter Bowl** were named by other instructors following Haemmerle's lead in the holiday theme.

Lookout Bowl (originally **Fire Lookout Bowl**) was named for the Forest Service fire lookout built on the top of Bald Mountain in 1941, which also served as Bald Mountain's first warming hut. The building is still there, used as a radio repeater station.

Lefty Bowl was originally the farthest bowl to the left (looking up from the bottom) that could be skied without getting into thick trees. Trees near the bottom of the bowls farther to the left have since been cleared.

Farout Bowl, originally named because it was pretty "far out," was renamed **Kaitlyn's Bowl** after Ketchum's Kaitlyn Farrington won a gold medal in the women's halfpipe at the 2014 Olympics in Sochi, Russia.

Sigi's Bowl was named after former Sun Valley Ski School director Sigi Engl. Originally from Austria, Engl served as ski school director from 1952 to 1975.

Runs Developed after 1964

When the Janss Company purchased Sun Valley from Union Pacific in 1964, there were five ski lifts, with three on Baldy on the River Run side. The company's first focus was on Warm Springs, a narrow run down the north face of the mountain. In 1965, two double chairlifts were installed on Warm Springs. The highest lift, Limelight, had a 2,200-foot vertical rise, the largest in the United States at the time. The run under the chair was called **Limelight**, since skiers were "in the limelight" as they descended the steep and narrow bump run. The run was widened after the current lift line was cut in 1988 for the Challenger high-speed quad. Sunnyside lift was built in 1967, going from the top of chair No. 1 on River Run to the bottom of College, allowing skiers to go from one side of the mountain to the other (this lift was taken out of use under the Holdings).

Plaza run was developed after the Plaza lift was built in 1982. The run received its name because it was the widest on the mountain. It was renamed **Picabo's Street** for former Sun Valley Ski Team racer and Olympic gold medalist Picabo Street. **Flying Maid**, a run going down from the cat track between Flying Squirrel and Picabo's Street, was named by Walter Hofstetter in honor of two young women from Seattle who worked as maids at Sun Valley, who often hiked on Baldy and stopped to visit with the men cutting the run. One day when they were late for work, crew members watched the maids bounding downhill to get back to work on time. It was renamed **Arnold's Run** in 2001 for frequent Sun Valley skier Arnold Schwarzenegger, ex-governor of California.

Seattle Ridge

Seattle Ridge was named for the rugged skiers of Seattle, accustomed to skiing in raincoats back home in the Cascade Mountains. When they visited Sun Valley, they reportedly did not mind making the long, difficult hike out to the ridge. The area's three primary runs were named for Sun Valley skiers who won Olympic medals. **Gretchen's Gold** was named for Gretchen Fraser, who won a gold and silver medal in the 1948 St. Moritz Olympics, becoming the first American to win an Olympic medal in skiing. **Christin's Silver**, originally named **Silver Fox** after Bill Janss, whose company owned Sun Valley from 1964 to 1977, was named for Christin Cooper, former Sun Valley Ski Team racer who won a silver medal in giant slalom in the 1984 Olympics in Sarajevo. The middle run was named **Southern Comfort** and was renamed **Muffy's Medals** for former Sun Valley Ski Team racer Muffy Davis, who won three gold medals in the 2002 Paralympics and a silver medal in the 1998 Paralympics. Davis had been named to the U.S. Ski Team's development squad when she broke her back during a training run on Bald Mountain in 1989, leaving her without the use of her legs. **Byron's Park** was named for Byron Cady, a Sun Valley ski instructor who disappeared while rafting the Salmon River, presumably falling in the river while scouting at high water. **Leigh Lane**, the cat track across Seattle Ridge to Broadway, was named for actress Janet Leigh after she died in 2004 at age 77. She was a frequent visitor and part-time resident of Sun Valley since 1963 who wrote a historical novel about the resort's early years called *House of Destiny*.

Greyhawk Lift

In 1988, the Holdings installed the Greyhawk chair at the bottom of Warm Springs, which goes partway up the hill, and three runs were cut west of the chairlift. **Greyhawk** was named after trail crew members saw a gray hawk fly out of the trees when the run was being cut, similar to what happened at Flying Squirrel.

Hemingway was named for the writer Ernest Hemingway, who made frequent visits to the area beginning in 1939, staying at the Lodge compliments of Sun Valley, falling in love with the local hunting, and writing parts of *For Whom the Bell Tolls* and other works here. He bought a home in Ketchum in 1959, where he lived until he committed suicide there in 1961.

Cozy was named when Sun Valley owner Earl Holding told mountain manager Max McKinnon that he wanted a run cut there that gave him the same "cozy" feeling he got skiing on Seattle Ridge.

Brick's Island was named after a Sun Valley Sno-Cat driver named Gary Grant, nicknamed "Brick," who was killed working on a machine doing summer trail construction at another ski area.

Frenchman's

The Frenchman's Mine was just downhill from where the lower terminal of the Frenchman's chairlift now stands. The shaft was filled in when the lift was built in 1995. Runs here include **Graduate**, which comes after College, and **Janss Pass**, named for Bill Janss, whose company owned Sun Valley from 1964 to 1977. Several of the area's other runs follow a French theme—**Au Jus**, **Can Can**, and **French Dip**.

NOTES

1. Abramson, *Spanning the Century*, 209, 232; OH Averell Harriman, HAR 0058, 18; Pfeiffer, *Sun Valley's Salad Days*.
2. Lund, *Timeline of Important Ski History Dates*, www.skiinghistory.org; Holland, *Sun Valley*, 184; Miller, "All About Chairlifts," www.onthesnow.com; Brinkley, *Rightful Heritage*, 403, 472, 526, 527, 582; Abramson, *Spanning the Century*, 225–229; Jonas, *Ski Magazine's Total Skiing*, 25; *Seattle Times*, January 18, 1933 and July 24, 1938; Durrance, *The Man on the Medal*, 36; OH, Harriman, 0058, 26, 30.
3. Klein, *Union Pacific*, 404, 434, 440, 441, 490–491; Taylor, *Sun Valley*, 329, 245; Holland, *Sun Valley*, 365; OH Harriman, HAR0058, 16–18.
4. Klein, *The Life & Legend of E.H. Harriman*, frontpiece, 111–123, 131, 160, 162, 255–257, 293, 307, 311, 445, 446; Kennan, *Railroad Tycoon*, 192–224, 324–326, 502, 523; Athearn, *Union Pacific Country*, 371–375; Klein, *Union Pacific*, 85, 89–92, 107, 166; Haeg, *Harriman vs. Hill*, 5, 6; "The Most Beautiful Place, Harriman State Park Was Railroad Family's Private Retreat for Decades," *Spokesman-Review*, June 1, 1997; "Idaho's Henry's Fork Rebound"; Peterson and Reed, *Harriman State Park of Idaho and The Railroad Ranch: A History*.
5. Abramson, *Spanning the Century*, 91, 107, 108, 186–208, 209–214, 221, 232–234; "From Rockefeller to Ford, *Forbes*' 1918 Ranking of the Richest People in America"; "The American Heritage, A Ranking of the Forty Wealthiest Americans of All Time," *American Heritage*, October 1998; Klein, *Union Pacific, The Rebirth 1894–1969*, 262, 283, 291–294, 295, 300, 301, 305, 308; Pfeiffer, *Sun Valley's Salad Days*; Taylor, *Sun Valley*, 10.

6. 11/27/35 Letter Harriman to Gray; Abramson, *Spanning the Century*, 222; 9/25/35; Klein note, Klein Collection.
7. *Union Pacific Bulletin*, January 1936, RHD, RM-36 No. 149; Klein, *Union Pacific: The Rebirth*, 308–310; Abramson, *Spanning the Century*, 222, 223; Holland, *Sun Valley*, 165–169; OH, Engen, 8, 9; Taylor, "Sun Valley Opens With a Bang," 3–5, Taylor Papers, MS-343 No. 17.
8. Lundin, "1883–1884: The Oregon Short Line Railroad Is Built and Transforms Idaho," 92, 126, 127, 205–208, 352–355, 357–362.
9. Klein, *Union Pacific: The Rebirth*, 308–310; OH, Brass Garrettson, 15, 27; Telegrams, 1/18/36, 1/21/36, 1/21/36 and 1/28/36, Schaffgotsch to Harriman, Klein Collection; Abramson, *Spanning the Century*, 222–226; Taylor, "Sun Valley Opens With A Bang," Taylor collection, MS-343 No. 17; Memo, RHD Manuscript MS-372l; OH, Roberta Brass Garrettsson, GAR0285, 36–37; OH, Val McAtee, MCA0405 (supplement), 1; OH, Harriman, 0058, 4.
10. Palmedo, *Roland Palmedo*, 27; Abramson, *Spanning the Century*, 225, 226; Klein, *Union Pacific*, 311; Letter 3/2/36 Harriman to Proctor, Letter to Peggy Dean from Charles H. Proctor, Proctor Family Collection, Community Library, MS 0657; Holland, *Sun Valley*, 186.; Ancinas, "Heading West," *Skiing History*, March–April 2011, 18, 19.
11. Longe, *History of Sun Valley*, 1; Taylor, *Sun Valley*, 31, 32; Snoddy papers from U.P. Museum, MS 0694, No. 9, 13, 48, 71.
12. SteveHannagan.com, blog by Michael Townsley; Taylor, *Sun Valley*, 27, 28; Memo, Hannagan to Harriman, March 28, 1935, RHD MS 0365.
13. "Railroads and Southern Utah's National Parks," National Park Foundation; Zaitlin, "Gilbert Stanley Underwood," 29–52, 83, 84, 149–160; "Gilbert Stanley Underwood, Architect," Living Places, National Park Service; Gilbert Stanley Underwood (1890–1969); 4/13/36 letter Harriman to Mann, "Klein Collection;" Snoddy papers from U.P. Museum, MS 0694.
14. Klein, *Union Pacific*, 310; Abramson, *Spanning the Century*, 222–226; Griffith, *Early History of Ketchum and Sun Valley*, 66; 2/20/37 Telegram Harriman to Sawyer, 3/30/36 Proctor to Harriman, 4/11/36 Jeffers to Harriman, 4/11/36 Telegram Jeffers to Harriman, 4/13/36 letter Harriman to Mann, 4/15/36 Telegram Harriman to Mann, 4/15/36 Harriman to Proctor, 4/26 and 27/1936 Proctor to Morgan, 4/30/36 Morgan to Harriman, Klein Collection; OH, Brass Garrettson, 28, 36, 37, Conger, *Jimmy Griffith*, 60.
15. Union Pacific Board Resolution May 5, 1936, Klein Collection.
16. *Railroad Age*, September 5, 12, and October 28, 1936, Klein Collection; OH, Seagle, SEA0123A, 120, SEA0086, 25; OH, Castegnato, CAS, 14; 10/19/36 and 10/28/36 letters Morgan to E.G. Smith, 10/30/36 Telegram Harriman to Gray, 10/11/36 Telegram Smith to Schaffgotsch, 11/14/36 Telegram Harriman

to Gray, 12/1/36 Telegram Harriman to Gray, 12/2/36 letter Selznick to Harriman,12/5/36 Telegram to Stevens and K.C.Schmidt, 12/6/36 Telegram E.C.S. to Hannagen and Morgan, 12/18/36 Telegram H.W.P to W.M.J, 12/29/36 Telegram Harriman to Schaffgotsch, 12/29/36 Telegram Harriman to Stevens, Schaffgotsch and Morgan, 12/29/36 Telegram Schaffgotsch and Morgan to Harriman, Klein Collection; Abramson, *Spanning the Century*, 228; OH, McAtee, OHMCA0405 (supplement), 6; OH, Holliday, HOL0278, 1–3; Taylor, "Guests at the Opening of Sun Valley," and "Sun Valley Opens With a Bang," Taylor Collection, MS-343 No. 16 and 17.

17. 9/21/36 Telegram Harriman to Gray, Klein Collection; OH, Haemmerle, HAE0166, 11; OH, Seagle, SEA0087, 20, and SEA0123, 72; OH, Dorice Taylor, TAY0101, 6, 10.
18. Lang, *A Bird of Passage*, 145, 146; Pfeifer, *Nice Goin'*, 68; OH, Bill Castegneto, CAS0300, 14; OH, Seagle, SEA0333, 120; Snoddy papers from U.P. Museum, MS 0694 No. 42; Klein, *Union Pacific*, 311–313; Abramson, *Spanning the Century*, 227–229; "Significance of Sun Valley Lodge," *Railway Age*, January 23, 1937, "Swim When it Snows And Ski When the Sun Shines," *The Power Specialist*, January 6, 1938, *Railway Age*, July 31, 1937, Klein Collection; OH, Holliday, HOL0278, 4, 5.
19. "Sun Valley, Winter Sports Capital," *Idaho Statesman*, December 19, 1936, RHD RM-36, No. 117; *Railway Age*, January 23, 1937, Klein Collection; Lund and Gilbert, "A History of North American Lifts," *Skiing Heritage Journal*, September 2003; Hennig, *Sun Valley Ski Guide*, 18–28; "The Skiing," Proctor Family Collection.
20. 3/25/74 letter Fegte to Janss, Dorice Taylor Collection.
21. Durrance, *The Man on the Medal*, 36; OH, Harriman, HAE0058, 26, 30; "American Skiers at the Olympics," *American Ski Annual, 1936*; Abramson, *Spanning the Century*, 226; OH, Harriman HAR0058, 26, 30; Constitution and By-Laws of The Sun Valley Ski Club Inc., Taylor Collection, MS-348; Taylor, *Sun Valley*, 101.
22. Lucas, *Ancient Skiers*, 5; "History of the Harriman Cup," *Sun Valley Magazine*, May 1977; Griffith, *Early History of Ketchum and Sun Valley*, 67; Taylor, *Sun Valley*, 111; Durrance, *Durrance, the Man on the Medal*, 37, 38, 55; OH, Durrance DUR0149, 21–27; *Seattle Times*, December 9, 1937.
23. Abramson, *Spanning the Century*, 229.
24. Longe, "History of Sun Valley," 3, 4; March 22, 1937 letter Harriman to Mann, March 24, 1937 letter Prater to Mann, March 27, 1937 letter Harriman to Biddle, U.P. Board Resolutions of April 6 and May 25, 1937, Harriman letters and telegrams of May 3, 1937, May 4, 1937, May 15, 1937, September 23, 1937, August 30, 1937 letter Prater to Singer, and September 23, 1937 letter Wellman to Harriman, Klein Collection; *Idaho Statesman*, James Knipe Sun Valley Scrapbook, The Community Library.

25. Anson, *Jumping Through Time*, 22, 27, 28, 33; "Sun Valley Jumping." *Sun Valley Ski Club 1937–1938*; Hennig, *Sun Valley Ski Guide, 14;* OH, McAtee, MCA0405 (supplement) 15; OH, Castagneto, CAS0300, 38; OH, Seagle SEA0019, 13, 14; Miller, *Jim Curran's Union Pacific Chairlift.*
26. *Idaho Statesman*, James Knipe Sun Valley Scrapbook, The Community Library; Doris Taylor collection, RM 036, No. 062; Holland, *Sun Valley*, 233.
27. OH, Goodman, GOO0180, 24; Taylor, *Sun Valley*, 98; OH, Seagle, SEA0086, 42, 43; OH, McAtee, MCA 0405, 13; OH, Haemmerle, HAE0166, 33; 9/29/37 letter Harriman to Gray, 1/28/38 letter Harriman's Secretary to Schmidt, *The Valley Sun*, December 21, 1937, 11/21/38 letter Crary to Prater, Klein Collection.
28. Taylor, *Sun Valley*, 56, 57, 98; OH, Everett Taylor TAY0163, 2; OH, Taylor, TAY0101, 7, 35 40, 44, 50; Taylor, *Sun Valley*, 56, 57; Sauter, *The Sun Valley Story*, 58.
29. Klein, *United Pacific*, 315, 322, 323; Palmedo, *Roland Palmedo*, 25, 26; Abramson, *Spanning the Century*, 186–194; 9/20/1936 letter from W.A. Harriman to Carl E. Gray, 1/28/38 letter from Secretary to W.A. Harriman to E.C. Schmidt, 11/21/38 letter from Harold Crary to B.H. Prater, United Airlines Schedule, Klein Collection; OH, Seagle, SEA0123A, 38.
30. Abramson, *Spanning the Century*, 230; 1/17/38 letter Harriman to Singer, 3/11/38 letter Harriman to Hannagan, 11/23/38 letter Prater to various addressees, 6/28/38 Telegram Harriman to Schmidt, Council Meeting minutes March 30, 1936, 4/2/38 Telegram Meikle to Singer, Klein Collection; Klein, *The Life and Legend of E.H. Harriman*, 372.
31. OH, Fraser FRA 55, 14; Pfeifer, *Gretchen's Gold*, 28, 33; Pfeifer, *Gretchen's Gold*, 38; OH, Engen, 0185m 18, 19; Engen, *For the Love of Skiing*, 93; Lundin, *Early Skiing on Snoqualmie Pass*, 120–121.
32. Longe, "History of Sun Valley," 5; OH, Durrance, DUR0149, 12, 14, 18, 25, 26; Durrance, *Dick Durrance, the Man on the Medal*, 54–59; U.P. Promotion for Employees, 1/2/38 letter from W.P.R. To W.A. Harriman, Klein Collection; OH, Engen ENG185, 21, 22; OH Joswig, JOS,0340, 2–7.
33. 8/3/37 letter Harriman to Singer, 1/17/38 letter Harriman to Singer, Special Use Permit for Pioneer Cabin, Klein Collection; "The Skiing," Proctor Family Collection; Pfeiffer, "The Passion of Florian Haemmerle," *Skiing Heritage*, March 2001; Taylor, *Sun Valley*, 70–73.
34. OH, McAtee MCA0405 (supplement), 5, 6.
35. OH, Ed Seagle, SEA0123A, 56,–59, 108, 113–117, SEA0086, 19, 49, SEA0019, 18, 19; OH, McCrea, MCC0164, 29; Klein, *Union Pacific*, 315, 316; Taylor, *Sun Valley*, 81; OH, Harriman, 8, 33, 35, 36; 11/29/38 Telegram W.M.J to WPR, 11/29/38 letter Jeffers to H.C. Mann and F.W. Robinson, Klein Collection; Abramson, *Spanning the Century*, 230.

36. 12/8/38 letter Prater to Criswell, 10/24/38 letter Prater to Mann, Klein Collection; Snoddy papers from U.P. Museum, MS 0694, No. 50; Dorice Taylor Collection, MS-0368.
37. *Fortune Magazine*, January 1939, Klein Collection; "Sun Valley—The American St. Moritz," *The Reader's Digest*, February 1939, RHD Rm 36, No. 202; Lang, *A Bird of Passage*, 158, 159; Pfeifer, *Nice Goin'*, 69, 70.
38. Dorice Taylor collection, RM 036, No. 069; 1/2/39 letter Harriman to Jeffers, 2/8/39 Rush Telegram from GJA, Klein Collection; Snoddy papers from U.P. Museum, MS 0694, No. 56,55; Pfeifer, "The One and Only," *Skiing Heritage*, 9.
39. Lang, *A Bird of Passage*, 185; Miller, *Lurching from One Near Disaster to the Next*, 20–23; OH, Durrance, DUR0149, 25, 26; Woolsey, *Off the Beaten Track*, 110–116.
40. 7/29/39 letter Harriman to Hannagan, 8/13/39 Telegram Jeffers to Harriman, 11/10/39 letter Harriman to Hannagan, Klein Collection; Longe, "History of Sun Valley," 6.
41. Durrance, The *Man on the Medal*, 59; Snoddy papers from U.P. Museum, MS 0694 No. 58; OH, Harriman, 13, 14; OH Castagneto, CAS0300, 2, 4, 5, 22; OH McAtee, MCA0405 (supplement), 2; Sauter, *Sun Valley Story*, 110.
42. Lang, *A Bird of Passage*, 134–138, 192, 193, 206, 207; Pfeifer, *Nice Goin'*, 74, 78.
43. Taylor, *Sun Valley*, 100; OH, Katherine Harriman Mortimer, MOR0148, 2–23, 27, 31, 32.
44. OH, Spiegel, SPI0253, tape one, 10–19, 31–34; tape two, 2, 5,6, 8, 11–16, 20–23; Cathy Reinheimer, interview *Eye on Sun Valley*, October 10, 2018.
45. Morris, *Ernest Hemingway & Gary Cooper*, 9–19, 36, 50, 51; Arnold, Tilly, *The Idaho Hemingway*, 47, 50, 75, 85, 86, 90, 95, 96, 96–99.
46. Woolsey *Off the Beaten Track*, 63, 65, 109, 100, 110, 118.
47. *Gretchen's Gold*, 36; Taylor, *Sun Valley*, 100–103; OH, Harriman, HAR0058, 33, and HAR-107, 8, 33, 35, 36. OH, Gretchen and Don Fraser, FRA0262, 4, 5, FRA0232, 5, 15, 17, and FRA 55, 7, 9, 10, 11, 15, 17, 18.
48. 5/15/40 letter to Averell Harriman, Klein Collection.
49. Holland, *Sun Valley*, 249; OH, Pfeifer, PFE, 11,12; Pfeifer, *Nice Goin'*, 74, 75, 83–86, 88–90, 96; *Sun Valley Serenade*, Turner Classic Movies, TCM.com; "Sonja Henie," Wikipedia; OH, Simpson, SIM 0347, 10–12, 17, 18 Jack and Mary Lou Simpson, SIM 289, 18, 20, 22, 23.
50. Lindley, Al, "National Downhill Championships & Fourth Annual Harriman Cup Races," *Sun Valley Ski Club Annual Season 1940*; Durrance, *The Man on the Medal*, 61, 62, 70; OH, Durrance, DUR0149, 15; Taylor, "History of the Harriman Cup," *Sun Valley Magazine*, May 1977; "Sugar Bowl Ski Area," Wikipedia; 4/10/39 letter Wolfe to Harriman, Klein Collection.
51. Letters from Harriman to Jeffers, 3/7/40, 5/6/40, 5/21/40, 5/22/40; 6/7/40, letters Harriman to Rogers 8/16/40, 9/8/40, Memorandum re Sun Valley

Construction, 9/14/40, Klein Collection; Sauter, *The Sun Valley Story*, 142; Hemingway, *Misadventures of a Fly Fisherman*, 44, 45; OH, Fraser, FRA0262, 4, 5.

52. "Alta Lodge; the Ultimate Ski Lodge"; Durrance, *The Man on the Medal*, 72–77; *The Valley Sun*, Vol. XII, No. 22, August 18, 1949.

53. Lundin, *Early Skiing on Snoqualmie Pass*, 130–146; Meyer, "*Alpine Experiments: The National Parks and the Development of Skiing in the American West*," 9, 114, 125, 133–136.

54. Niven, *The Moon's a Balloon, Reminiscences*, 188–190, 196–198; November 25, 1940 Harriman memo, "Sun Valley Improvements for 1940/41 Season"; January 4, 1941 Telegram Harriman to Rogers, January 9, 1941 letter Schmidt letter to Hannagan, Klein Collection; "Ski Patrol Pioneer, Nelson Bennett, Dies at 102," ski-patrol.net; OH, Bennett, BEN 0182 No. 1, 11–20. Hennig, "Ski Touring at Sun Valley," *Sun Valley Ski Club Annual, Season 1941*; Hennig, *Sun Valley Ski Guide*, 58.

55. OH, Gretchen Fraser, FRA0114, 33, 34; Pfeifer, *Gretchen's Gold*, 41, 42; Lundin, *Early Skiing on Snoqualmie Pass*, 165–169; "Alta Lodge; the Ultimate Ski Lodge"; Durrance, *The Man on the Medal*, 72–77; *The Valley Sun*, Vol. XII, No. 22, August 18, 1949.

56. "Ex. Gov, Averell Harriman, Advisors to 4 Presidents, Dies," *New York Times*, July 27, 1986; Pfeifer, Luanne, "Sun Valley's Salad Days."; OH, Harriman, HAR0058, 28; Abramson, *Spanning the Century*, 305–307; 10/8/42 letter Rogers to Jeffers and Union Pacific Telegram, Klein Collection.

57. Denfeld, "First U.S. Army Mountain Ski Unit is Formed at Fort Lewis on November 15, 1941"; Lundin, "Military Personnel Learn to Ski at Snoqualmie Pass During WW II; 12/10/40 letter Harriman to Lindley, Klein Collection; Holland, *Sun Valley*, 308, 309.

58. Klein, *Union Pacific*, 400–401, 404, 413–418, 422, 427; 7/14/41 letter Jeffers to Harriman,1/2/42 Rogers telegram, Klein Collection.

59. Holland, *Sun Valley*, 306–310; *Valley Sun*, Holiday Issue, December 1945; Taylor, *Sun Valley*, 125; 12/7/42 to Hannagan, Klein Collection.

60. OH, Harriman, 28, 29; U.S. Navy, "Convalescent Hospitals of World War II"; Longe, *History of Sun Valley*, 7; OH, Seagle, SEA0019, 9, SEA0086, 27, 33, 36–41, SEA0108, 2–9; OH, McAtee, 14 and supplement, 5, 6; OH, Hennig, 9; *The Sun Valley Sage, Farewell Edition*, 3, 4, 24; Taylor, *Sun Valley*, 131; 4/6/45 letter Hannagan to Harriman, Klein Collection.

61. Klein, *Union Pacific*, 378, 404, 405, 434–447, 486–493; Taylor, *Sun Valley*, 239; OH, Harriman, HAR 0058, 16–18; 11/23/45 Rogers Report, "Proposals and Suggestions for Post-War Purposes covering Construction-Renovating-Decorating and Future Policies," 12/1/45 letter Jeffers to Charske, 1/3/46 letter Ashby to Charske, 4/2/46 letter Hannagan to Harriman, 7/24/46 Harriman telegram to Shipley, Klein Collection; Abramson, *Spanning the Century*, 234.

62. Taylor, 131–133; Pfeifer, *Nice Goin'*, 129–149; Hemingway, Mary, *How It Was*, 219, 220.

63. Holland, *Sun Valley*, 321; Oppenheimer and Poole, *Sun Valley*, 168; Klein, *Union Pacific, The Rebirth*, 439, 490. 491; OH, Castagneto, 11, 16, 20, 39, 52, 53; Taylor, *Sun Valley*, 139.
64. Taylor, *Sun Valley*, 149–152; "Decade of Sunshine," *The Valley Sun*, Vol. X, No. 2, 1947.
65. Hennig, *The Sun Valley Ski Guide*, 3–6, 12, 18, 30, 48, 50, 61–94; Taylor, *Sun Valley*, 168.
66. Engen, Alan, *For the Love of Skiing*, 93.
67. 1/8/48 letter Hannagan to Ashby, Klein Collection; Lang, *A Bird of Passage*, 267–269.
68. Lang, *A Bird of Passage*, 128, 269–273; Pfeifer, Luanne, "The One and Only Gretchen," *Skiing Heritage*, Fall 1994; Pfeifer, Luanne, *Gretchen's Gold*, 56, 72; Engen, Alan, *For the Love of Skiing*, 76, 77; Lundin, *Norway's Crown Prince Olav Skis at Mount Rainier on May 24, 1939*; Lundin, *Early Skiing on Snoqualmie Pass*, 95; OH, Gretchen and Don Fraser, FRA55, 5, 6, 19–22.
69. Taylor, *Sun Valley*, 177, 182.
70. Lang, *A Bird of Passage*, 276, 278–283.
71. Longe, 8; Snoddy papers from U.P. Museum, MS 694, No. 72, 66, 73.
72. OH, Nelson and Edmund Bennett, BEN 0182 No. 1, 24–30, No. 2, 2; Bennett, "The Sun Valley Toboggan," *Sun Valley Ski Club Report for 1949*.
73. Longe, "Union Pacific Papers," 9; Snoddy Papers from U.P. Museum, MS 694, No. 72, 66, 73; 9/14/49 letter Hannagan to Stoddard, Klein Collection.
74. "Pioneering, Inspiring snow-sports filmmaker Warren Miller, 93, dies at Orcas Island home," *Seattle Times*, January 25, 2018; Miller, *Wine, Women, Warren & Skis*, 30, 55, 57, 59, 63, 81, 83, 112, 113; Miller, *Lurching from One Near Disaster to the Next*, iii, vi, 13–16, 93–96; Miller, *Freedom Found*, 112–120, 133, 135, 140–145, 155–159, 166–175, 178–181, 184, 231, 291–293; OH, Nelson and Edward Nelson, NEL 0182 No. 2, 25–27; OH, Haemmerle, HAE276; Taylor, *Sun Valley*, 187–192.
75. Longe, "History of Sun Valley," 8; Bischof, "American Bucks and Austrian Buccaneers: Sun Valley—The Making of America's First Winter Resort,"143, 144, 3rd F.I.S. Annual Ski History Conference, *Leisure Cultures and the Making of a Modern Ski Resort*, Phillipp Strobl editor.
76. Durrance, *The Man on the Medal*, 96–101; Pfeifer, Friedl, *Nice Goin'*, 163–167; OH, Durrance, 37, 38; "Giant Slalom," Wikipedia.
77. Dorworth, High Times at the Harriman, 25; Conger, *Early History of Ketchum and Sun Valley*, 69, *Jimmy Griffith,* 7, 9, 10, 40, 45–47, 59, 71.
78. Longe, *History of Sun Valley*, 8, 9; OH, Hennig, HEN0122, 7*; Alfred D. Lindley, 1904–1951*, http://publications.Americanalpineclub.org; Lindley Hut AspenColorado-Rocky Mountain Adventures.

79. OH, Litchfield, LIT0191, 26; OH, Eriksen, ERI0193, 4–7, 11; OH, Goodman, GOO0180, 20; Engen, *For the Love of Skiing*, 43; Taylor, "History of the Harriman Cup."
80. Butterfield, "The Great Sun Valley Avalanche," *Skiing History* magazine, fall 2016; OH McAtee 0405, supplement 3; OH Seagle 0123A, 26.
81. OH Holliday, HOL09263, 10, OR0278, 3; OH Seagle, SEA0123, 36; OH, McCrea, MCC0164, 14, 15, 37–39, 41, 42, 51; Taylor, *Sun Valley*, 243; Klein, *Union Pacific*, 490; Arnold, *The Idaho Hemingway*, 85.
82. Information about annexations and subdivision approvals comes from Brittany Skelton at the Ketchum Planning and Building Department; Holland, *Sun Valley*, 357; OH, Leon and Evelyn Goodman, OHGOO 018; OH, Simpson SIM289A, 5–9, SIM0347, 21, 23, 25, 26, 30; "A History of Gambling in Idaho," *Coeur d'Alene Press*, March 16, 2015; OH, Seagle, SEA0086, 43, and 0123A, 38; "Sun Valley Incorporation," Dorice Taylor Papers, MS-0368, MS-343 No. 14; Walsworth, *Warm Springs Ranch, A Historic Context Narrative, 1880 to 2000*, 1, 4, 15, 18, 21, 37–52.
83. Dorworth, "High Times at the Harriman"; Taylor, *Sun Valley*, 236, 238; Longe, *History of Sun Valley*, 9.
84. OH, Dorice and Everett Taylor, TAY0101, 57; Sauter, *Sun Valley Story*, 118; Dorworth, "High Times at the Harriman, 27, 28; Longe, *History of Sun Valley*,10, 11.
85. OH, Elora and Ed Seagle, SEA0087, 2–12, 21; OH, Spiegel, SPE0083, 2–15 SPE0253, 21–26; Holland, *Sun Valley*, 357–359.
86. "Ernest Hemingway, An American Writer"; Sauter, *Sun Valley Story*, 30; OH, Scott and Barbara Earle, 2010, 21; OH, Spiegel, SPI0253, 20; Arnold, Tillie, *The Idaho Hemingway*, 226–230, 232–237; "Ernest Hemingway, www.britannica.com/biography/Ernest-Hemingway; Farah, "Behind Ernest Hemingway's suicide, nine concussions that incapacitated his brain, forensic psychiatrist concludes," *National Post*; Hemingway-Boulders Wilderness, Sawtooth National Forest, USDA Forest Service.
87. Klein, *Union Pacific*, 486–492.
88. OH, Scott and Barbara Earle, EAR214, 19, OH2010, 24, 25; OH, Seagle, SEA0123A, 123, and SEA0087, 10–12; Taylor, *Sun Valley*, 248, 249; OH, Holmes, HOL0469, 6–18; OH, McAtee, MCA0405, 18; OH, Holliday, HOL0263, 8; Oppenheimer and Poole, *Sun Valley, a Biography*, 176–179, 182, 183; OH, Janss, JAN0348, 4–6, 8.
89. Holland, *Sun Valley*, 366–369, 371–374, 377; Taylor, *Sun Valley*, 253; OH, Holmes, HO 0469, 18–21, 35, 39, 42; OH, Janss, JA 0348, 4–6, 8, JA 0100, 44–51; OH, Janss and Staudinger, OH 363, 364, 21, 26–28; "Baldy Paces Valley Growth," and "Engl Promoted," *Sun Valley Sun*, Vol. 11, No. 1, May 1972; News Release, March 22, 1968, MS-343, No. 5; Carl Gray Talk at Sun Valley Village Hospital, February 21, 1965,

Taylor Papers, MS 0368, No. 085 and No. 356; Oppenheimer and Poore, *Sun Valley, a Biography*, 178, 182; Sauter, *Sun Valley Story*, 118, 119.

90. Sauter, *The Sun Valley Story*, 142, 143; Hemingway, Jack, *Misadventures of a Fly Fisherman*, 44, 45; Nature Conservancy report (vegetation survey) by Gordon Beebe, The Nature Conservancy, U.S., www.nature.org/; Holland, *Sun Valley*, 382–384.

91. Dorworth, "High Times at the Harriman," 28.

92. OH, McAtee, MCA0405, 15–17; OH, Holliday, HOL 0263, 8; Lundin, "1883–1884: The Oregon Short Line Railroad Is Built and Transforms Idaho"; Mountain Express August 22, 1975; *Idaho Statesman*, August 21, 1982.

93. OH, Janss, JA0100, 40; OH, Janss and Stauginger, OH363, 364, 24; Sauter, *Sun Valley Story*, 132, 134, 154–158, 162. 168; Holland, *Sun Valley*, 384, 390–395.

94. *Forbes,* April 12, 2013; Taylor, *Sun Valley*, 257, 258, 260; "Crown Jewels of the Mountains," *Mountain Express*, January 25, 2006; *Eye on Sun Valley*, "Open and Elegant: Public Tours of re-born lodge start today," June 15, 2015, "Sun Valley Lodge—If You're There, You're at the Right Place," December 25, 2016, "Warm Springs Lodge, a 233 Day Miracle, December 23, 2018, Sun Valley Delays Building New Cold Springs Lift to Give Skiers a Better Experience," March 10, 2019; "Return to Glory," *Sun Valley Magazine*, Winter 2017–2018 edition.

95. "State of the Arts in the Wood River Valley," "Johnny Hagenbuch Makes More History with U.S. Ski Team," and "Sun Valley's Task at Hand-Playing Catch Up," Hill, Jae, "Does the Future of Skiing Look Like Plastic?" Eye On Sun Valley, 1/29/19, 4/11/19 and 4/12/19, 12/3/16.

BIBLIOGRAPHY

Abramson, Rudy. *Spanning the Century: The Life of W. Averell Harriman 1891–1986*. Chapel Hill, NC: William Morrow and Co. Inc., 1992.

"Alta Lodge: The Ultimate Ski Lodge." www.forbes.com. Accessed March 31, 2019.

"American International Team Races at Sun Valley." *Sun Valley Ski Club 1966 Annual Report.*

"American Legion Junior Championships." *Sun Valley Ski Club Annual for 1951.*

"The American Ski Championships." *American Ski Annual 1943.*

Ancinas, Eddy. "Heading West." *Skiing History*, March–April 2011.

Arnold, Lloyd R. *High on the Wild with Hemingway*. Caldwell, ID: Caxton Printers, 1969.

Arnold, Tillie. *The Idaho Hemingway*. Buhl, ID: Beacon Books, 1999.

Barth, Arthur J. "Olympic Tryouts in Ski Jumping." *American Ski Annual 1948.*

Bennett, Nelson. "The Sun Valley Toboggan." *Sun Valley Ski Club Annual for 1949.*

Berfield, Susan. *The Hour of Fate: Theodore Roosevelt, J.P. Morgan, and the Battle to Transform Capitalism*. New York, NY: Bloomsbury Publishing, 2020.

Binns, Ken. "Ecker Hill and Sun Valley." *American Ski Annual 1937–1938.*

Bischof, Gunter. "American Bucks and Austrian Buccaneers: Sun Valley—The Making of America's First Winter Resort." *Leisure Cultures and the Making of a Modern Ski Resort.* Philipp Strobl editor, 2014.

Blakslee, Bob. "The FIS Races." *Sun Valley Ski Club Annual for 1950.*

———. "The Harriman Cup." *Sun Valley Ski Club Annual for 1951.*

———. "The Harriman Cup." *Sun Valley Ski Club Annual for 1953.*

———. "The Harriman Cup." *Sun Valley Ski Club Annual for 1954.*

———. "The Harriman Cup." *Sun Valley Ski Club 1957 Annual Report.*

———. "The Harriman Cup." *Sun Valley Ski Club 1960 Annual Report.*

———. "Sun Valley Report." *American Ski Annual and Skiing Journal 1950.*

———. "Sun Valley Review." *American Ski Annual and Skiing Journal 1950.*

———. "Sun Valley Review." *American Ski Annual and Skiing Journal 1953*.

———. "Western Interstate Ski Meet and Competition for the Jeffers Cup." *Sun Valley Ski Club Annual 1942*.

Bossick, Karen. "Best Hike in Town for Now." *Eye on Sun Valley*. June 16, 2015. www.eyeonsunvalley.com. Accessed March 31, 2019.

———. "Does the Future of Skiing Look Like Plastic?" *Eye on Sun Valley*. December 3, 2016. www.eyeonsunvalley.com. Accessed April 18, 2018.

———. "Johnny Hagenbuch Makes More History with U.S. Ski Team." *Eye on Sun Valley*. April 11, 2019. www.eyeonsunvalley.com. Accessed April 11, 2019.

———. "Sun Valley Delays Building New Cold Springs Lift to Give Skiers a Better Experience." *Eye on Sun Valley*. March 10, 2019. www.eyeonsunvalley.com. Accessed March 10, 2019.

———. "Sun Valley Lodge—If You're There, You're at the Right Place." *Eye on Sun Valley*. December 25, 2016. www.eyeonsunvalley.com. Accessed March 31, 2019.

———. "Sun Valley's Task at Hand—Playing Catch Up." *Eye on Sun Valley*. April 12, 2019. www.eyeonsunvalley.com. Accessed April 12, 2019.

———. "Warm Springs Lodge a 233-Day Miracle." *Eye on Sun Valley*. December 23, 2018. www.eyeonsunvalley.com. Accessed March 31, 2019.

Bradley, H.C. "Sun Valley Four-Event Intercollegiate Ski Meet and Competition for Bradley Plate and Mary Cornelia Trophy." *Sun Valley Ski Club Annual 1942*.

Brado, G.E. "Baldy Mountain—Before and After Sun Valley." *Sun Valley Ski Club Annual—Season 1941*.

Brenner, Marie. "To War in Stockings." *Vanity Fair*, November 2011. www.vanityfair.com. Accessed March 31, 2019.

Bright, Alex. "The Races." *Sun Valley Ski Club Season 1936–1937*.

Brinkley, Douglas. *Rightful Heritage: Franklin D. Roosevelt and the Land of America*. New York: HarperCollins, 2016.

Brumder, William. "Ski Touring at Sun Valley." *Sun Valley Ski Club 1947 Annual Report*.

Burgy, Joe. Oral history. The Community Library, BUR0005.

Burton, Hal. "The Harriman Cup." *Sun Valley Ski Club Annual for 1949*.

Butterfield, David. "The Great Sun Valley Avalanche." *Skiing History*, Fall 2016.

Castagneto, Bill. Oral history. The Community Library, CAS0300.

Conger, Mary Jane Griffith. *Jimmy Griffith, Ketchum and Sun Valley's First Native Born Skier Named to a U.S. Olympic Team: A Young Man's Journey on the Way to Becoming a U.S. Olympian*. Self-published, 2014.

Crookes, Darroch. "The Intercollegiates." *Sun Valley Ski Club Annual for 1948*.

———. "Ski Round Up." *Sun Valley Ski Club 1947 Annual Report*.

Dawson, Louis. "Chronology of North American Ski Mountaineering and Backcountry Skiing." *Skiing History Magazine*.

Denfeld, Duane Colt. "First U.S. Army Mountain Ski Unit Is Formed at Fort Lewis on November 15, 1941." Historylink.org essay No. 20483. historylink.org. Accessed March 31, 2019.

Diederich, Harvey. "Sun Valley's Season." *American Ski Annual and Skiing Journal 1951.*

———. "Sun Valley's Season." *American Ski Annual and Skiing Journal 1953.*

Dole, Charles Minot. *Adventures in Skiing*. New York, NY: Franklin Watts Inc., 1965.

Dorworth, Dick. "High Times at the Harriman: Once Famous for America's Most Difficult Downhill, Sun Valley's Harriman Cup Inspired with Drama, Skill and Character." *Skiing Heritage*, March 2005.

———. "Sun Valley's Ski Racing Roots: How a Community of the World's Fastest Skiers Built a Culture to Last." *Sun Valley Magazine*, Winter 2015–2016.

Dunford, Joe. "Baldy Mountain: Sun Valley's New Skiing World." *Sun Valley Ski Club Annual—1939.*

———. "Christmas Week College Competitions." *Sun Valley Ski Club Annual—1939.*

———. "Sun Valley Four-Event Intercollegiate Ski Meet." *Sun Valley Ski Club Annual—Season 1940.*

Durrance, Dick. Oral history. The Community Library, DUR0419.

Durrance, Dick (as told to John Jerome). *Dick Durrance, the Man on the Medal*. Aspen, CO: Durrance Enterprises, 1995.

"East-West Intercollegiate Meet." *Sun Valley Ski Club Report, 1937–1938.*

Eldridge, Jim, and Ed Martin. Oral history. The Community Library, MAR0210.

Engen, Alan. *For the Love of Skiing*. Salt Lake City, UT: Gibbs-Smith, 1998.

Engen, Alf. Oral history. The Community Library, ENG0342.

Eriksen, Stein. Oral history. The Community Library, ERI0193.

"Ernest Hemingway, An American Writer." www.britannica.com. Accessed May 1, 2019.

Farah, Andrew. "Behind Ernest Hemingway's Suicide, Nine Concussions that Incapacitated His Brain, Forensic Psychiatrist Concludes." *National Post*. www.nationalpost.com. Accessed March 23, 2019.

Fraser, Gretchen. "Operation St. Moritz." *Sun Valley Ski Club Annual for 1948.*

———. Oral history. The Community Library, FRA0144, 0232, 0262.

———. "Women's Racing Comes of Age." *Sun Valley Ski Club 1947 Annual Report.*

Fraser, Gretchen, and Don Fraser. Oral history. The Community Library, FRA00033.

Gale, Richard. "Touring at Sun Valley." *Sun Valley Ski Club Annual 1937–1938.*

Garrettson, Roberta Brass. Oral history. The Community Library, GAR0285.

"Giant Slalom." Wikipedia. www.wikipedia.org. Accessed March 30, 2019.

"Gilbert Stanley Underwood (1890-1960)." www.noehill.com. Accessed March 30, 2019.

Gmuender, Mary Purdy. "Sun Valley Singles: History Made." *Ski Area Management,* May 1999.

Goodman, Leon, and Evelyn Goodman. Oral history. The Community Library, GOO 018.

Griffith, Mary Jane. *Early History of Ketchum and Sun Valle: The Legacy of Al Griffith, A Pioneer and Lifelong Resident*. Ketchum, ID: Mary Jane Griffith Conger, 2018.

———. *Jimmie Griffith*. Ketchum, ID: Mary Jane Griffith Conger, 2015.

Gruber, John. "Snow Train Parade." *Trains Magazine*, December 19, 2011.

Haeg, Larry. *Harriman vs. Hill: Wall Street's Great Railroad War*. Minneapolis, MN: University of Minnesota Press, 2003.

Haemmerle, Beatrice. Oral history. The Community Library, HAM0166.

Hailey Times. Historical archives.

"The Harriman." *Sun Valley Ski Club 1963 Annual Report*.

Harriman, Averell. Oral history. The Community Library, HAR0058.

Harriman, Kathleen. "The Seventh Annual Harriman Cup Races and International Open Downhill and Slalom." *Sun Valley Ski Club 1947 Annual Report*.

———. "Sun Valley Four-Event Intercollegiate Ski Meet and Competition for Bradley Plate and Mary Cornelia Trophy." *Sun Valley Ski Club Annual—Season 1941*.

"Hemingway-Boulders Wilderness." www.fs.usda.gov. Accessed April 14, 2019.

Hemingway, Jack. *Misadventures of a Fly Fisherman: My Life with and without Papa*. New York: Taylor Publishing, 1986.

Hemingway, Mary Welsh. *How It Was*. New York: Alfred A. Knopf, 1976.

Hennig, Andreas. Oral history. The Community Library, HEN0122.

Hennig, Andy. "Ski Touring at Sun Valley." *Sun Valley Ski Club Annual—Season 1941*.

———. *Sun Valley Ski Guide*. Union Pacific Railroad, 1948.

Herbert, John M. "1952 Olympic Ski Teams." *American Ski Annual and Skiing Journal 1953*.

———. "Who's Who on the 1952 Olympic Ski Squad." *American Ski Annual and Skiing Journal 1953*.

Hill, Cortland T. "Olympic Sidelights." *Sun Valley Ski Club 1947 Annual Report*.

———. "Olympic Tryouts." *Sun Valley Ski Club 1947 Annual Report*.

"Historic Trails You Can Ski." *Skiing History Magazine*, October 2013.

"A History of Gambling in Idaho." *Coeur d'Alene Press*, March 16, 2015. www.cdapress.com. Accessed March 23, 2019.

"History of the Harriman Cup." *Sun Valley Magazine*, May 1977.

Holland, Wendolyn Spence. *Sun Valley: An Extraordinary History*. Ketchum, ID: The Idaho Press, 1998.

Holliday, Louis. Oral history. The Community Library, HO0278 & 0263.

Holmes, Gayle, and Harry Holmes. Oral history. The Community Library, HOL0469.

Howard, Frank. "National Downhill Championships and Fourth Annual Harriman Cup Races." *Sun Valley Ski Club Annual—Season 1940*.

———. "Western Interstate Ski Meet and Competition for the Jeffers Cup." *Sun Valley Ski Club Annual—Season 1940*.

Huidekoper, Virginia. "Elizabeth Woolsey, 1908–1997." American Alpine Club. americanalpineclub.org. Accessed March 30, 2019.
Hume, Rita. "Four-Event National Championships." *American Ski Annual 1940–1941*.
Janss, Bill. Oral history. The Community Library, JA0348, 0100.
Janss, Bill, and Konrad Staudinger. Oral history. The Community Library, JAN363, JAN364.
Janss Company. "The World of Sun Valley—A Development Program." 1964. Sun Valley, ID.
Jonas, Bob, and Seth Masia. *Ski Magazine's Total Skiing*. New York: G.P. Putnam's Sons, 1987.
Kennan, George. *Railroad Tycoon: E.H. Harriman: A Biography*. Bellevue, WA: Big Byte Books, 2014.
Kingman, Henry S. "Alfred D. Lindley, 1904–1951." American Alpine Club. americanalpineclub.org. Accessed March 30, 2019.
Klein, Maury. *The Life and Legend of E.H. Harriman*. Chapel Hill: University of North Carolina Press, 2000.
———. Sun Valley Files Collection. John W. Barriger III National Railroad Library at University of Missouri–St. Lewis.
———. *Union Pacific. The Birth of a Railroad 1862–1893*. New York: Doubleday & Co., 1987.
———. *Union Pacific: The Rebirth 1894–1969*. New York: Doubleday & Co., 1989.
Labounty, Patricia. "Railroads and Southern Utah's National Parks." National Park Foundation. www.nationalparks.org. Accessed March 30, 2019.
Lane, A. Royalle. "The Nationals." *Sun Valley Ski Club Annual for1950*.
———. "The Olympic Tryouts." *Sun Valley Ski Club Annual for1951*.
Lang, Otto. *A Bird of Passage: The Story of My Life*. Helena, MT: Skyhouse Publishers, 1994.
———. "Fifth Annual Harriman Cup Races and National Four-Event Combined Championships." *Sun Valley Ski Club Annual—Season 1941*.
———. "The Harriman Cup." *Sun Valley Ski Club Annual for 1950*.
———. "The Harriman Cup and Nationals at Sun Valley." *Sun Valley Ski Club Annual for 1948*.
———. "Jumping Exhibition on Ruud Mountain." *Sun Valley Ski Club Annual 1942*.
———. Oral history. The Community Library, LAN00186.
———. "The Sixth Annual Harriman Cup Races and Official International Downhill and Slalom Tournament." *Sun Valley Ski Club Annual 1942*.
———. "Standard Races." *Sun Valley Ski Club Annual—Season 1940*.
———. "Sun Valley, Idaho Winter Sports Capital of the Nation Closes to Help Win the War." *Sun Valley Ski Club Annual 1942*.

———. "Sun Valley Ski Club Championships." *Sun Valley Ski Club 1947 Annual Report.*

"The Last Courtesan: The Life of Pamela Digby Churchill Hayward Harriman." Manolo Blahnik's World 2013. www.vegasmike433.wordpress.com. Accessed April 7, 2019.

Laughlin, James. "Downhill and Slalom Olympic Trials at Sun Valley." *American Ski Annual 1948.*

———. "International Open Downhill and Slalom." *Sun Valley Ski Club 1947 Annual Report.*

———. "Skiing in the Winter Olympics." *American Ski Annual 1949.*

———. "Spring Sports in the Valley." *Sun Valley Ski Club Annual—Season 1940.*

Lawson, Mike. "Idaho's Henry's Fork Rebound." *Fly Fisherman.* www.flyfisherman.com. Accessed March 23, 2019.

Lindley, Al. "A Message from the President." *Sun Valley Ski Club Annual—Season 1940.*

———. "National Downhill Championships and Fourth Annual Harriman Cup Races." *Sun Valley Ski Club Annual—Season 1940.*

———. "The National Four Event Combined Championship and the Harriman Challenge Cup Race." *Sun Valley Ski Club Annual—1939.*

———. "President's Report." *Sun Valley Ski Club Season 1936–1937.*

———. "Sun Valley International Open." *Sun Valley Ski Club Annual 1937–1938.*

Lindley, Grace Carter. "Women's Events." *Sun Valley Ski Club Annual 1937–1938.*

"Lindley Hut." Rocky Mountain Adventure Rentals. rmar1.com. Accessed March 30, 2019.

Longe, Ken. "History of Sun Valley." Omaha, NE: Union Pacific Railroad.

Lucas, Joy. *Ancient Skiers of the Northwest.* Seattle, WA: Ancient Skiers, 2006.

Lund, Mort. *Timeline of Important Ski History Dates.* International Skiing History Association. www.skiinghistory.org. Accessed April 1, 2019.

Lund, Mort, and Kirby Gilbert. "A History of North American Lifts." *Skiing Heritage Journal*, September 2003.

Lundin, John. *Early Skiing on Snoqualmie Pass.* Charleston SC: The History Press, 2017.

———. "1883–1884: The Oregon Short Line Railroad Is Built and Transforms Idaho; Branch Railroads Are Built." The Community Library, Center for Regional History. Ketchum, Idaho.

———. "Military Personnel Learn to Ski at Snoqualmie Pass During WW II." Sahalie Ski Club. www.sahalie.org. Accessed March 30, 2019.

———. "Norway's Crown Prince Olav Skis at Mount Rainier on May 24, 1939." Historylink.org essay No. 10974. historylink.org. Accessed April 6, 2019.

———. "Sigurd Hall: 1910–1940 Ski Racer and Mountaineer, A Life Tragically Ended Too Soon in the Silver Skis Race on Mount Rainier in 1940." www.alpenglow.org. Accessed March 31, 2019.

Masia, Seth. "Pete Lane's of Sun Valley." *Ski Heritage Journal*, December 2006.
McAtee, Val. Oral history. The Community Library, MCA0405.
McCrea, Winston. Oral history. The Community Library, MCC0164.
McNeil, Fred H. "The Death of Sigurd Hall." *American Ski Annual 1940–1941*.
Meyer, Jeffrey T. "Alpine Experiments: The National Park and the Development of Skiing in the American West." University of Montana dissertation. scholarworks.umt.edu. Accessed March 29, 2019.
Miller, Warren. "Jim Curran's Union Pacific Chairlift." *Idaho Mountain Express*, February 22, 2013.
———. *Lurching from One Near Disaster to the Next*. Deer Harbor, WA: Pole Pass Publishing Co., 1998.
———. Oral history. The Community Library, MIL0507.
———. *Wine, Women, Warren, & Skis*. Vail, CO: Goldfinkle, Masowitch, Kloppenboig, & O'Brien, 1958.
Miller, Warren, and Ray Atkeson. *Ski & Snow Country: The Golden Years of Skiing in the West, 1930s–1950s*. Portland, OR: Graphic Arts Center, 2000.
Miller, Warren, and Andy Bigford. *Freedom Found: My Life Story*. Deer Harbor, WA: Warren Miller Co., 2016.
Mishkov, Aleksandar. "Ernest Hemingway: The Mystery behind his Suicide." www.documentarytube.com. Accessed March 31, 2019.
Moore, Greg. "What's a Flying Squirrel Got to Do with It?" *Idaho Mountain Express*, November 23, 2018. www.mtexpress.com. Accessed April 23, 2019.
Morris, Larry E. *Ernest Hemingway & Gary Cooper in Idaho: An Enduring Friendship*. Charleston, SC: The History Press, 2017.
Mortimer, Kathleen Harriman. Oral history. The Community Library, MOR0148.
"National Four-Event Championships." *American Ski Annual 1939–1940*.
"National Veterans Downhill and Slalom Championships." *Sun Valley Ski Club 1958 Annual Report*.
"Navy Convalescent Hospitals of World War II." U.S. Navy Bureau of Medicine and Surgery. www.militarymuseum.org. Accessed March 30, 2019.
"New Cabin Haven for Ski-Tourists." *Sun Valley Sun* winter pictorial issue.
New York Times. Historical archives.
"1940 U.S. Ski Team Squad." *American Ski Annual 1939–1940*.
Niven, David. *The Moon's a Balloon*. London, UK: Hamish Hamilton, 1971.
Olson, Lynne. *Citizens of London: The Americans Who Stood with Britain in Its Darkest and Finest Hour*. New York: Random House, 2010.
Oppenheimer, Doug, and Jim Poore. *Sun Valley: A Biography*. Boise, ID: Beatty Books, 1976.
"Pacific Northwestern Ski Association, Sun Valley, 1938." *American Ski Annual 1939–1940*.

Palmedo, Philip F. *Roland Palmedo: A Life of Adventure and Enterprise*. Portsmouth, NH: Peter A. Randall, 2017.

Peterson, Keith, and Mary E. Reed. *Harriman State Park of Idaho and the Railroad Ranch: A History*. January 1984. parksandrecreation.idaho.gov. Accessed March 31, 2019.

Peterson-Withorn, Chase. "From Rockefeller to Ford, See Forbes' 1918 Ranking of the Richest People in America." September 19, 2017. www.forbes.com. Accessed March 11, 2011.

Pfeifer, Friedl. *Nice Goin': My Life on Skis*. Missoula, MT: Pictorial Histories Publishing Company Inc., 1993.

———. Oral history. The Community Library, PFE0238.

———. "Standard Races." *Sun Valley Ski Club Annual—1939*.

———. "The Sun Valley Ski School." *Sun Valley Ski Club Annual—1939*.

Pfeifer, Luanne. *Gretchen's Gold: The Story of Gretchen Fraser, America's First Gold Medalist in Olympic Skiing*. Missoula, MT: Pictorial Histories Publishing Company Inc., 1996.

———. "The One and Only." *Skiing Heritage*, Fall 1994.

———. "The Passion of Florian Haemmerle." *Skiing Heritage*, March 2001.

———. "Sun Valley's Salad Days." *Los Angeles Times West Magazine*, December 7, 1969.

Potter, Everett. "Alta Lodge: The Ultimate Ski Lodge." www.forbes.com. Accessed March 29, 2019.

Prager, Walter, and Alf Engen. "Much Depends on Us." *Sun Valley Ski Club 1947 Annual Report*.

Proctor, Charles N. "Sun Valley." *American Ski Annual 1936–1937*.

Proctor, Charles, and Mary Proctor. Oral history. The Community Library, PRO0169.

Proctor family collection. Peggy Proctor Dean, Ketchum, Idaho.

"A Ranking of the Forty Wealthiest Americans of All Time." *American Heritage*, October 1998. Americanheritage.com. Accessed March 11, 2019.

Regan, Neil. "Baldy Mountain Comes of Age." *Sun Valley Ski Club Annual—Season 1940*.

———. "Silver Cups among the Gold." *Sun Valley Ski Club Annual—Season 1940*.

Reilly, Bob. "Having a Wonderful Winter." *Sun Valley Ski Club Annual for 1950*.

"Return to Glory." March 10, 2019. *Sun Valley Magazine*, Winter 2017–2018.

Sauter, Van Gordon. *The Sun Valley Story*. Hailey, ID: Mandala Media LLC, 2011.

Scanlin, Jim. "Skiing in Sun Valley." *American Ski Annual 1949*.

Schwantes, Carlos A. *Railroad Signatures Across the Pacific Northwest*. Seattle: University of Washington Press, 1993.

———. *The Depression Arrives Early* from *Idaho: A Century of Pioneers*. Boise, ID: *Idaho Statesman* centennial edition, July 1, 1990.

Seagle, Edward. Oral history. The Community Library, SEA0086, 0108, 01213, 0119.

Seagle, Elorna. Oral history. The Community Library, SEA0124.

Seattle Times. Historical archives.

Simpson, Jack. Oral history. The Community Library, SIM0347
Simpson, Jack, and Mary Lou Simpson. Oral history. The Community Library, SIM289
"Sixth Annual Harriman Cup Races and Official International Downhill and Slalom Tournament." *American Ski Annual 1943*.
"Skiing Activities in the Pacific Northwest." *American Ski Annual and Skiing Journal 1950*.
Snoddy, Donald. Papers from U.P. Museum, MS 0696. The Community Library, Center for Regional History, Ketchum, Idaho.
"Sonja Henie." Wikipedia. www.wikipedia.org. Accessed March 29, 2019.
Spence, Clark C. *For Wood River or Bust: Idaho's Silver Boom of the 1880s*. Moscow: University of Idaho Press, 1999.
Spiegel, Clara. Oral history. The Community Library, SPI0083, 0253.
"Sugar Bowl Ski Area." Wikipedia. www.wikipedia.org. Accessed March 8, 2019.
"Sun Valley: If You Ski . . . It Is a $3,000,000 Monument to Your Pleasure. If You Don't, W. Averell Harriman Thinks You Probably Will." *Fortune Magazine*, January 1939.
"Sun Valley International Open." *Sun Valley Ski Club Annual 1937–1938*.
"Sun Valley Jumping." *Sun Valley Ski Club Annual 1937-1938*.
"Sun Valley Lodge Born: The Nine Months of '36." *Idaho Mountain Express,* December 23, 1981.
"Sun Valley Plans." *American Ski Annual 1947*.
"Sun Valley Serenade." Turner Classic Movies. www.tcm.com. Accessed March 29, 2019.
"Sun Valley Ski Club Championships." *Sun Valley Ski Club 1947 Annual Report*.
"Sun Valley Ski Club in Other Meets." *Sun Valley Ski Club Annual 1937–1938*.
"Sun Valley Ski Club 1966 Old-Timers' Reunion." *Sun Valley Ski Club 1966 Annual Report*.
Taylor, Dorice. "Harriman Cup Winners—Sun Valley, Idaho." The Community Library, RHD MS-343, #11.
———. "The History of the Harriman Cup." The Community Library, RHD MS-343, #11.
———. "More People Had More Fun." *Sun Valley Ski Club Annual for 1951*.
———. "Painting on the Pioneer Range." *Sun Valley Ski Club Annual for 1949*.
———. "Sun Valley Grooms for 20th Season." *American Ski Annual and Skiing Journal, 1957*.
———. *Sun Valley*. Sun Valley, ID: Ex Librus, 1980.
———. "The Toastmaster Was." *Sun Valley Ski Club 1947 Annual Report*."
Taylor, Dorice, and Everett Taylor. Oral history. The Community Library, TAY0101, 0163.
———. Sun Valley Opens with a Bang. MS-343, No.17.Taylor papers, articles, and press releases. The Community Library, Ketchum, Idaho, MS - 0343.

Thompson, Hunter S. *The Great Shark Hunt: Strange Tales from a Strange Time*. The Gonzo Papers, Volume 1. New York: Summit Books, 1979.

Townsley, Michael K. *Steve Hannagan: Prince of the Press Agents and Titan of Modern Public Relations*. Indianapolis, IN: Dog Ear Publishing, 2018.

———. "Steve Hannagan's Blog." stevehannagan.com. Accessed March 31, 2019.

Underwood, Gilbert Stanley. "Sun Valley Ketchum Idaho." *Architectural Record*, 1938.

The Valley Sun. Historical archives.

Walsworth, Claudia Taylor. *Warm Springs Ranch: A Historic Context Narrative 1880 to 2000*.

Webb, Bob. "Western Interstate Ski Meet and Competition for the Jeffers Cup." *Sun Valley Ski Club Annual—Season 1941*.

"The Western Interstate." *Sun Valley Ski Club Annual for 1949*.

Wheaton, Rodd L. "Gilbert Stanley Underwood." *National Park Service: The First 75 Years*. www.nps.gov. Accessed March 30, 2019.

White, Thornton H. "The Wood River Branch in Idaho." *Streamliner* magazine, volume 4, issue 4.

"Who's Who on the 1952 Olympic Ski Squad." *American Ski Annual and Skiing Journal 1952*.

Wild, Cathryn. "'The Most Beautiful Place' Harriman State Park Was Railroad Family's Private Retreat for Decades." *The Spokesman-Review*, June 1, 1997.

William R. Meiners and E.G. Crosthwaite Resource Planning & Management Associates. "Management Implications for the Stalker Creek Ranch Properties and Adjacent Silver Creek Preserve, Idaho." www.savesilvercreek.org. Accessed March 31, 2019.

"Wintersport Parade." *Ski Illustrated 1937–1938*.

"Women's Events." *Sun Valley Ski Club Annual 1937–1938*.

Woods, Leonard. "Aspen Now." *American Ski Annual 1947*.

Woolsey, Elizabeth D. *Off the Beaten Track*. Wilson, WY: Wilson Bench Press, 1984.

———. "The 1937 Women's Team." *American Ski Annual 1937–1938*.

Zaitlin, Joyce. *Gilbert Stanley Underwood: His Rustic, Art Deco, and Federal Architecture*. Malibu, CA: Pangloss Press, 1989.

Zoeliner, Tom. *Train: Riding the Rails that Created the Modern World, From the Trans-Siberian to the Southwest Chief*. New York: Penguin Books, 2014.

INDEX

D

E

F

G

H

J

K

L

M

N

O

P

R

S

T

U

V

W

Z

ABOUT THE AUTHOR

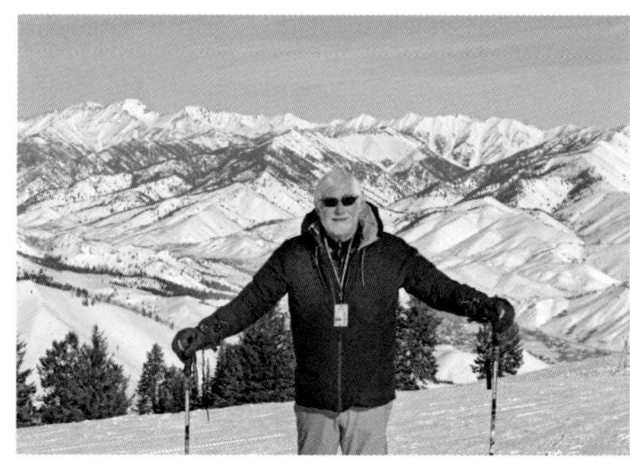

John W. Lundin is an attorney, historian, and author who has written extensively about Washington and Idaho history and has homes in Seattle and Sun Valley. His great-grandparents moved to Bellevue, Idaho, in 1881, drawn by the silver strike, and were early pioneers in the Wood River Valley. His papers about Wood River Valley history can be found at the Community Library. His essays on Washington history are published on HistoryLink.org, the online encyclopedia of Washington history, and on Central Washington University's website. In 2018, his book *Early Skiing on Snoqualmie Pass* received an award as outstanding regional ski history book from the International Ski History Association. John learned to ski using wooden skis, cable bindings, leather boots, and rope tows. He first skied in Sun Valley in 1960 after a 24-hour train ride from Seattle, when a one-week pass cost $39. He is a founder of the Washington State Ski & Snowboard Museum and serves on its board. His website is www.johnwlundin.com.

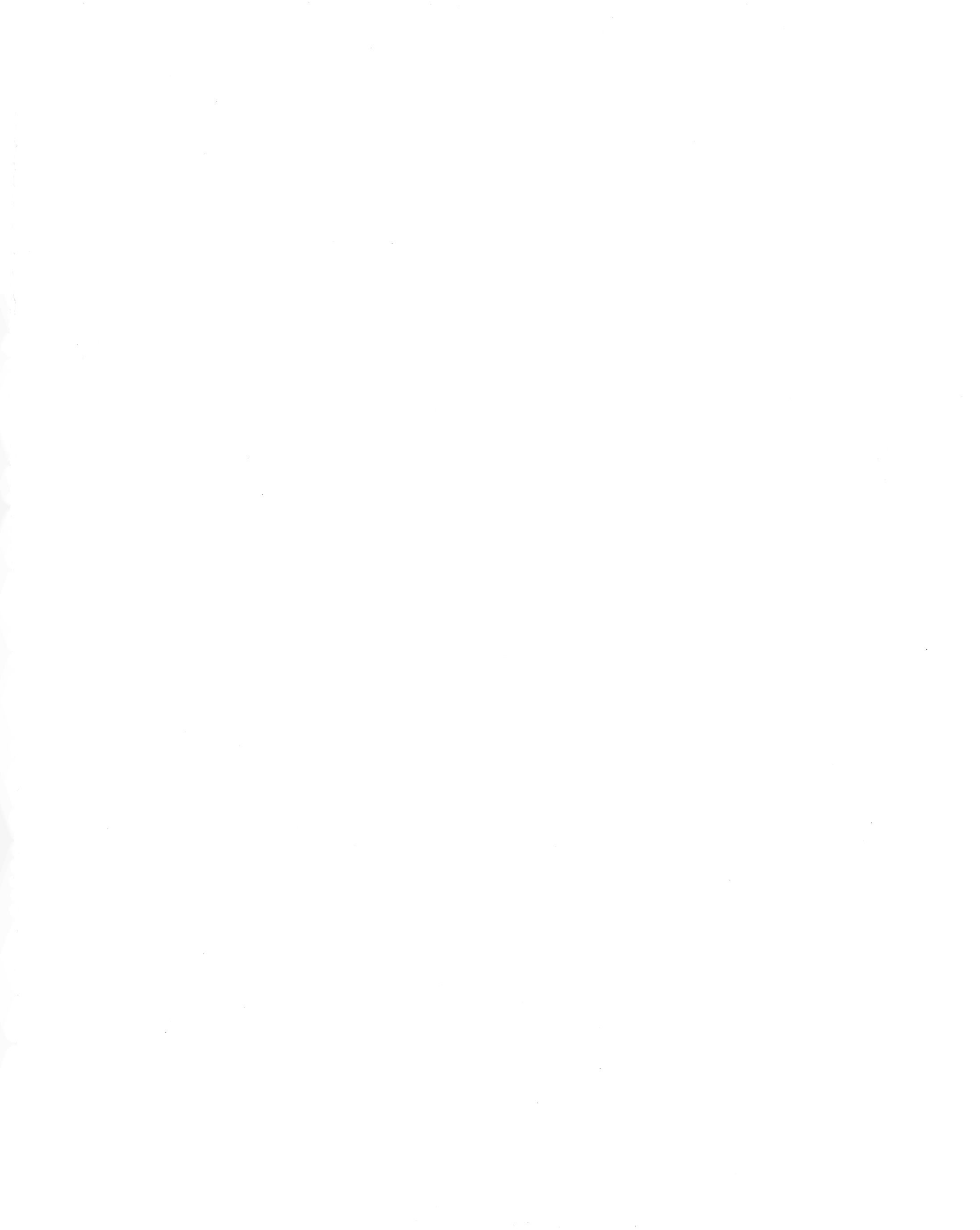